COMPLETE DIGITAL PHOTOGRAPHY

FOURTH EDITION

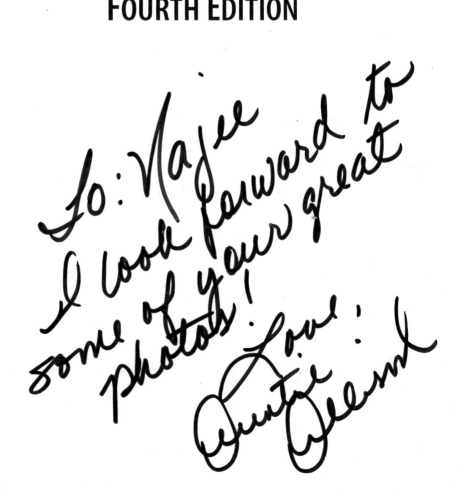

To: Najee
I look forward to
some of your great
photos!
Love:
Auntie ___

COMPLETE DIGITAL PHOTOGRAPHY

FOURTH EDITION

BEN LONG

Charles River Media

A part of Course Technology, Cengage Learning

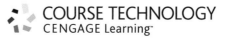

COURSE TECHNOLOGY
CENGAGE Learning™

Australia • Brazil • Japan • Korea • Mexico • Singapore • Spain • United Kingdom • United States

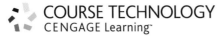

COURSE TECHNOLOGY
CENGAGE Learning™

Complete Digital Photography
Fourth Edition
Ben Long

Cover Designer: Tyler Creative Services

Cover Image: Ben Long

For product information and technology assistance, contact us at
Cengage Learning Customer & Sales Support, 1-800-354-9706

For permission to use material from this text or product,
submit all requests online at **cengage.com/permissions**
Further permissions questions can be emailed to
permissionrequest@cengage.com

Library of Congress Control Number: 2007018885
ISBN-13: 978-1-58450-520-4
ISBN-10: 1-58450-520-6

Course Technology
25 Thomson Place
Boston, MA 02210
USA

Cengage Learning is a leading provider of customized learning solutions with office locations around the globe, including Singapore, the United Kingdom, Australia, Mexico, Brazil, and Japan. Locate your local office at:
international.cengage.com/region

Cengage Learning products are represented in Canada by Nelson Education, Ltd.

For your lifelong learning solutions, visit **courseptr.com**
Visit our corporate website at **cengage.com**

Printed in Canada
2 3 4 5 6 7 11 10 09 08

CONTENTS

CHAPTER 15   SPECIAL EFFECTS   469

CHAPTER 16   OUTPUT   491

1

INTRODUCTION

In This Chapter

- Is This the Right Book for You?
- How This Book Is Organized
- What Counts as Digital Photography?
- The Best-Laid Plans
- What Software Do You Need?
- Digital 101: A Few Basic Ideas

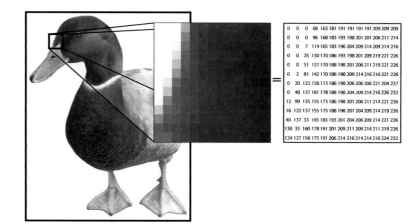

It is something of a cliché now to write about the rapid advancement of digital technology—about how amazing it is to look back just a few years and see computers and digital cameras that had a fraction of the power, at a much higher price. I know this, because I employ this cliché a lot. It's an easy hook to start an article or book, and I used a variation of it in the introduction to the last edition of this book.

And so, it is with some satisfaction that I find myself now able to write that, in the two-and-a-half years since I wrote the last edition, there has *not* been a huge leap in camera technology. Oh sure, there've been some important advancements since then: point-and-shoot cameras now routinely offer 8- or 10-megapixel sensors (the cameras I covered in the third edition topped out around 5 or 6); digital SLRs are cheaper than ever and offer more resolution; Canon now sells a full-frame SLR for under $3000; new focusing technology makes it easier to get good shots from a small camera; while affordable, quality SLR lens options are prevalent and plentiful. These advancements, though, are decidedly evolutionary, and the jump from an 8- to 10-megapixel camera is not nearly as significant as the jump from 4 to 6 megapixels was. Similarly, though the low-end price of a digital SLR has dropped from $800 to $600, this is not as dramatic as the change that happened between the second and third editions of this book, when bottom-end SLR prices dropped from $2000 to $900.

Nevertheless, despite the lack of dramatic technological advancement since the last edition, I feel I can say with confidence that there has been more change between the third and fourth editions of this book, than with any other update. While other editions saw a greater leap in camera technology, this edition sees *huge* changes in post-production and workflow.

Those changes have made it easier to manage image glut, and have greatly simplified the workflow of raw-format photography, opening up raw shooting to more shooters, at more skill levels. As such, a new chapter devoted exclusively to raw processing has been added, while I've also made extensive changes to all workflow discussions, and now provide coverage of new workflow applications like Apple's Aperture™ and Adobe® Photoshop® Lightroom™.

But something else has happened over the last few years: as more and more people have gotten digital cameras, the average skill level has improved. In addition to improvements in camera technology, digital photography forums have facilitated discussions and learning, and photo sharing sites have made it possible for people to show their work, and view the work of other shooters. This combination of technologies appears to be leading to a general improvement in the level of photographic skill many people have.

I've noticed a change over the last few years of teaching photography. For years, people were only interested in the technical craft. They wanted to know what buttons to push, how to use the various features of their camera, and how to perform fancy edits in an image editor. While that desire is still there, many students are now comfortable with the basic craft and are hungry to know more about what makes a good picture. As such, this edition is the first one to spend time covering the "artistic" side of photography, with full discussions of composition, seeing, and shooting process.

As with previous editions, you'll still find discussions of all the technical ins and outs of shooting digital—from choosing a camera to exposing an image to processing and printing. If you're new to photography, you'll learn the basic theory photographers have studied for decades, and the latest tools and techniques made possible by the shift to digital. If you're an experienced film photographer, you'll see how you might need to change your photographic process to adapt to digital shooting. From white balancing to exposing, you'll learn how to translate the knowledge you already have into the digital realm.

IS THIS THE RIGHT BOOK FOR YOU?

This book is for photographers of all skill levels. Whether you're new to photography or simply new to *digital* photography, this book provides the explanations and answers you need to get the best images possible,

Using a film camera is a two-step process. First, you shoot your pictures—with the goal of getting as much color, contrast, and tone into your image as you can manage. Then, you develop and print the images in a way that takes maximum advantage of that information. Shooting digital photographs is no different. As with a film camera, you shoot your subject—after you, or your camera, first calculate the proper exposure. Then, you digitally process and print your image.

Although cameras might change, the physics of light remains the same (fortunately!). Consequently, digital and film photographers share all the same concerns over apertures, shutter speeds, and metering techniques.

This book is divided into four broad sections. Chapters 1 through 4 provide the basic technical information you'll need to understand all the topics covered later in the book. Chapters 5 and 6 help you select the camera, computer, and software that are right for you. Chapters 7 through 9 cover shooting, while the remaining chapters discuss post-production workflow, digital editing, and output.

Because *Complete Digital Photography* is intended for users with a variety of experience levels, many terms have been defined in the *Glossary* rather than within the main text.

No matter what your skill level is, you should find something of use in this book, as I have tried, within reason, to make it "complete." In many cases, there has not been enough room to go into detail on some of the more obscure topics. In those instances, I have tried to at least let you know what the relevant questions and issues are, so you can more quickly track down answers on your own.

HOW THIS BOOK IS ORGANIZED

Chapter 2, "How a Digital Camera Works," gets things rolling with a discussion of how a digital camera works. Even if you're not interested in all the nerdy details of your chosen gear, this chapter is important for all shooters because of its discussion of the technical differences between shooting JPEG images, and shooting raw. These issues are unique to digital photography, so if you're coming from the film world, you'll want to learn more about this important consideration.

As mentioned earlier, whether you shoot digital or film, the process of exposing an image remains the same. If you're new to photography, you'll have an easier time understanding the material in the book if you give a close read to Chapter 3, "Basic Photography: A Quick Primer." Even if you've been shooting for a while, if you have an automatic camera, there might be some basic exposure theory you haven't had to learn, simply because the camera has taken care of those issues for you. Learning the ins and outs of exposure, though, will provide you with more artistic flexibility and choice, and our later shooting discussions assume an understanding of the basic photographic theory presented in Chapter 3.

Chapter 4, "Evaluating an Image," walks you through the basics of "reading" the technical quality of the images you've shot. Learning to recognize the technical differences between one image and another is handy for evaluating a camera when you're ready to buy, and an essential skill when using image-editing software to correct and improve an image. This chapter has been re-written for clarity, and includes new discussions of noise, detail, and sharpness.

As with each previous edition, Chapter 5, "Choosing a Digital Camera," has seen many changes. In addition to the usual updating to make the chapter relevant to the current camera market, the chapter has been restructured to provide more clearly delineated discussions of SLR and point-and-shoot cameras. Many entirely new sections have been added, including a discussion of external flashes, sensor cleaning, choosing a tripod, and much more.

As in the previous edition, the book's image-editing examples and tutorials are built largely around Adobe Photoshop. Although Photoshop is the premiere image-editing application, there are plenty of other good editors out there, and in Chapter 6, "Building a Workstation," you'll learn how to pick a package that provides the tools typically used by digital photographers. Fortunately, most image-editing programs provide the same basic tools and interfaces, so you should have no trouble adapting the lessons described here to other editing packages. Since the last edition, the software landscape has changed dramatically due to the arrival of Apple's Aperture and Adobe Photoshop Lightroom. Both of those products are discussed in Chapter 6, and additional coverage is provided throughout the rest of the book.

As in previous editions, Chapter 6 will help you choose a computer system and monitor, and the new version includes a revised, simpler color management section.

Chapter 7, "Shooting," will get you started with your camera by showing you the basics of shooting. This chapter has been completely rewritten, and now includes in-depth discussions on seeing, composition, how to warm up, and much more. You'll find plenty of technical information as well. In addition to learning how to configure your camera's settings for particular situations, you'll learn the basic details of framing and focusing and simple flash photography. Finally, you'll learn the rudiments of light metering.

Chapter 8, "Metering and Exposure," builds on Chapter 7's basic concepts but delves into the creative possibilities provided by your camera's manual exposure features. You'll learn about motion control, depth of field, contrast, detail, and all the other imaging choices that are possible when you take control of your camera's manual features. Chapter 8 has also been completely restructured and rewritten and now includes an extensive *Shooting for Raw* section that details the exposure approach you'll want to take when shooting raw.

Knowing the basics doesn't do you any good if you tend to shoot in unusual environments or like shooting particularly tricky subjects. Chapter 9, "Special Shooting," helps you with all of the more specialized forms of shooting you might engage in, from macro photography to black and white. Also restructured and rewritten, Chapter 9 includes many new sections such as dedicated coverage of landscape shooting, high dynamic range imaging, sensor cleaning, backcountry shooting, external flash shooting, and more.

Once you have a camera full of images, you're ready to start editing. Chapter 10, "Workflow," covers everything you need to know about your post-production workflow process. An entirely new chapter, you'll learn how to outline a basic workflow, what the considerations are for the way you shoot and what you need to deliver, how to use metadata to improve your workflow, and how to use the latest workflow software to ease your post-production life.

A digital image editor is capable of extraordinary retouching and special effects. However, 90 percent of the chores you'll perform with your editing program are color and tone corrections. In Chapter 11, "Correcting Tone and Color," you'll learn about the basic color correction steps you'll take on most of your images. Covering multiple image-editing applications, by the end of the chapter, you will know how to perform the bulk of the corrections you'll need to make, and have a solid foundation for the more advanced correction techniques discussed later in the book. Readers of previous editions will find many new discussions and tutorials in this chapter, and several new technique examples.

If you've opted to shoot raw (and if you're not sure if you should, don't worry, Chapters 2 and 8 will help you make up your mind), then Chapter 12, "Raw Conversion," will help you through all the raw processing you'll need to perform once you're back from your shoot. You'll learn how to get the most out of your raw converter of choice, how to best approach raw editing, and how to easily work raw processing into your workflow.

With basic correction skills under your belt, you're ready to move on to Chapter 13, "Building Your Editing Arsenal," where you will expand your repertoire with a study of masking, cloning, making complex selections, and some basic layering techniques. Chapter 13 includes many new masking and selecting techniques, and several new examples of blending and compositing tricks.

Chapter 14, "Imaging Tactics," kicks up your image-editing skills several notches with discussions of many advanced masking techniques. Many new sections have been added in this edition, including grayscale conversion, retouching, adaptive shadow/highlight adjustment, distortion correction, and more.

Chapter 15, "Special Effects," rounds out your post-production knowledge with detailed descriptions of how to simulate shallow depth of field, stitch panoramas, process high dynamic range images, add texture and grain, and more. Finally, with your images edited and corrected, you're ready to output. Chapter 16, "Output," covers everything you need to know to get your images *out* of your computer, whether through a printer, web page, or email. Resizing, sharpening, color management, and printer selection are all covered in detail in this heavily rewritten chapter.

ON THE CD

In addition to the tutorials from the first edition, four video tutorials are included on the CD-ROM that accompanies this book. In these QuickTime® movies, you can watch "over my shoulder" as I perform a number of imaging and adjustment techniques. Because many image correction processes are "interactive" rather than strictly procedural, these movies give you the opportunity to learn techniques that cannot be explained in a written, step-by-step form.

ON THE CD

The tutorial movies are included in the Tutorials folder on the companion CD-ROM. You can watch them in any order, but it would be best to view them when they are called out in the text, since some of the techniques assume you have already learned certain concepts.

WHAT COUNTS AS DIGITAL PHOTOGRAPHY?

Many people use the term *digital photography* to cover any photographic process that involves correcting and editing a photograph digitally. By this definition, shooting with your film camera, scanning your film or prints, editing them on your computer, and then printing them on a desktop printer counts as digital photography.

In this book, digital photographs are photographs taken with a digital camera. This is an important distinction because shooting with a film camera and shooting with a digital camera involve different concerns and practices, and scanning is a science unto itself. The simple fact is that there are many things you must do differently with a digital camera. But don't worry—this book covers them all!

THE BEST-LAID PLANS

Although much effort has gone into ensuring accuracy in this book, mistakes do sometimes happen. An updated list of errata and corrections can be found at *www.completedigitalphotography.com/errata*. A quick check of this page will fill you in on any problems that have been found in the book since its publication. You can report any mistakes by sending an email to *oops@completedigitalphotography.com*.

WHAT SOFTWARE DO YOU NEED?

In Chapter 6, we'll cover a number of guidelines for selecting various kinds of photography-related software, from image editors to image catalogers, and more. There are many choices when it comes to digital imaging programs, and which applications you use will affect certain aspects of your post-production workflow, and your editing options.

Overall, this book attempts to be software agnostic. This is not too difficult these days, as most image editing interfaces have been standardized, so it's very easy to translate a discussion built around one application to many other applications. Nevertheless, Adobe Photoshop still rules the roost when it comes to image editing, and the bulk of this book's tutorials and discussions have been built around Photoshop. However, many of these sections also include additional information with guidelines for performing the same tasks in Apple's Aperture, Adobe Photoshop Lightroom, and Nikon™'s Capture NX™. Where possible, I've tried to separate out each discussion, so you only need to deal with the relevant information. The practical upshot is that, no matter what software you're using, you should be able to easily follow along with the examples, theories, and discussions provided herein.

DIGITAL 101: A FEW BASIC IDEAS

In the old days, photographers made their own photographic papers, films, and *emulsions*. Whether it was to achieve a particular style or texture or to gain more control over their printing processes, photographers such as Ansel Adams, Alfred Stieglitz, and Eduard Steichen had to know a good deal about chemistry to create their prints. Similarly, to really understand how to get the most out of your digital camera, it's important to understand some of the technology behind it. Chapter 2 covers the details of how a digital camera works, but before you dive into that, you need to have a basic understanding of the *digitizing process*.

The "real" world in which we live is an *analog* world. Light and sound come to us as continuous analog waves our senses interpret. Unfortunately, it's very difficult to invent a technology that can accurately record a continuous analog wave. For example, you can cut a continuous wave into a vinyl record, but because of the limitations of this storage process, the resulting recording is often noisy and scratchy and unable to capture a full range of sound.

Storing a series of numbers, on the other hand, is much simpler. You can carve them in stone, write them on paper, burn them to a CD-ROM, or, in the case of digital cameras, record them to small electronic memory chips. Moreover, no matter how you store them, as long as you don't make any mistakes when recording them, you'll suffer no loss of data or quality as you move those numbers from place to place. Therefore, if you can find a way to represent something in the real world as a series of numbers, you can very easily store those numbers using your chosen recording medium.

The process of converting something into numbers (or digits) is called *digitizing*. The first step in digitizing is to divide your subject into distinct units. In the case of an image, this is a simple process of dividing your image into a grid of *picture elements* or *pixels*. How fine your grid is (that is, what *resolution* it has) varies depending on the sophistication of your equipment.

Next, each pixel in the grid is analyzed to determine its content, a process called *sampling*. Each sample is measured to determine how "full" it is; that is, a corresponding numeric value is assigned that represents that pixel's contents, a process called *quantizing*. Finally, these numeric values are stored on some type of storage medium.

Figure 1.1 is a simple image composed entirely of black and white pixels. As you can see, it's very easy to assign a 1 or a 0 to each pixel to represent the image. Because it takes only a single *bit* to represent each pixel, this image is called a *1-bit image*.

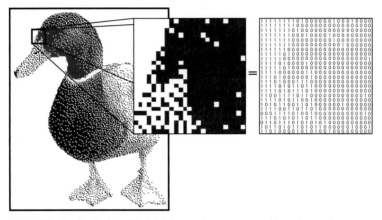

FIGURE 1.1   Each pixel in this 1-bit image is represented by a 1 or a 0.

In the example shown in Figure 1.1, our individual samples can be only 0 or 1 (that is, they have a very small *dynamic range*) because we are storing only one bit of information per pixel. If we want to record more than simple black and white images, we need to be able to specify more colors—that is, we need to have more choices than just 0 or 1. By going to a higher *color depth* (sometimes called *bit depth)*—let's say 8 bits, which allows for 256 different values—we can record more information, as seen in Figure 1.2.

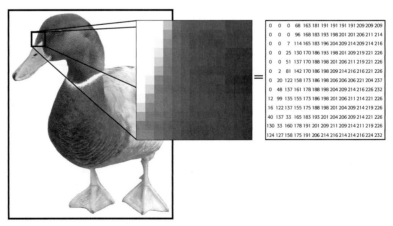

FIGURE 1.2   By storing bigger numbers for each pixel, we can store much more than simple black and white dots. With the ability to use gray pixels, the image looks much more realistic.

With 256 shades from which to choose, we can represent a finer degree of detail than we could with only two color choices. To store full-color images, we must go to an even higher bit depth and store 24 bits of information per pixel. With 24 bits, we can represent roughly 16 million colors, allowing us to store photo-quality images. Note that because we're storing 8 bits per pixel as opposed to 1, our second image requires more storage space.

To sum up, two of the factors that determine the quality of a digitizing process are resolution (the size and number of your individual pixels) and dynamic range (how big a range of color choices you have for each pixel).

Many other factors affect the quality of a digitized image, from your camera's lens to its compression software. Before exploring these questions, though, let's look at how your camera manages all of this sampling, quantizing, and storage. Understanding how your camera perceives, captures, and stores color information will make certain types of editing operations easier later on.

2

HOW A DIGITAL CAMERA WORKS

In This Chapter

- Something Old, Something New
- A Little Color Theory
- How an Image Sensor Works
- How Your Camera Makes an Image
- How JPEG Compression Works
- Meanwhile, Back in the Real World

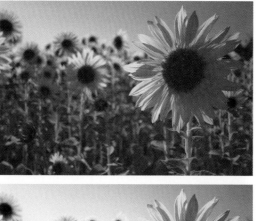

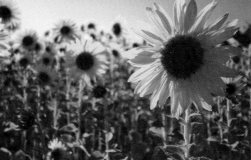

While it doesn't take a lot of know-how to operate a fully automatic camera, serious photography—whether at the hobbyist or professional level—has always required a tremendous amount of craftsmanship and technical understanding. In "wet darkroom" work, everything from paper type to chemical mixtures to the amount of agitation applied to a particular chemical has a bearing on the quality of your final print. As such, skilled film photographers have to have an in-depth understanding of the nature of their papers, chemicals, and equipment.

Digital photography is no different. To fully exploit your camera's capabilities—and to be able to effectively edit and improve your images—you must understand some of the fundamental principles and technologies behind digital imaging.

As mentioned in Chapter 1, "Introduction," the only real difference between a digital camera and a film camera is that a digital camera does not use film to record an image. However, this one fundamental difference affects all of the other systems on the camera, from the lens to the light meter. Consequently, knowing some of the technical details of how a digital camera works will help you select the right camera and help you better understand how to make certain decisions when shooting.

SOMETHING OLD, SOMETHING NEW

Just like a film camera, your digital camera records an image by using a lens to focus light through an *aperture* and a *shutter* and then onto a *focal plane*. By opening or closing the aperture and by changing the amount of time the shutter is open, the photographer can control how the focal plane is exposed. As we'll see later, exposure control allows the photographer to change the degree to which the camera "freezes" motion, how well the film records contrast and color saturation, and which parts of the image are in focus.

While a film camera has a piece of film sitting on the focal plane, in a digital camera, an *image sensor* is mounted on the focal plane. An image sensor is a special type of silicon chip that is light sensitive. Currently, there are two major types of image sensors available: the *charge-coupled device (CCD)*, and the *Complementary Metal Oxide Semiconductor (CMOS)*. CCDs are more popular than CMOS chips, but the role of both is the same. When you take a picture, the light falling on the image sensor is *sampled,* converted into electrical signals. After the image sensor is exposed, these signals are boosted by an amplifier and sent to an analog-to-digital converter that turns the signals into digits. These digits are then sent to an onboard computer for processing. Once the computer has calculated the final image, the new image data is stored on a memory card. (See Figure 2.1.)

Foveon

There's a third type of image sensor made by a company called Foveon. We'll discuss it in Chapter 5, "Choosing a Digital Camera." CMOS and CCDs remain the dominant image sensor technology.

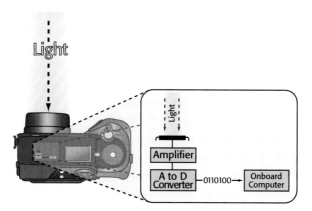

FIGURE 2.1   Light passes into a digital camera, just as it would in a film camera. However, instead of hitting a piece of film, it is digitized by a computer chip and passed to an onboard computer to create an image.

Although the mechanics are simple to explain, to really understand how a digital camera functions, you must know a little color theory.

A LITTLE COLOR THEORY

In 1869, James Clerk Maxwell asked photographer Thomas Sutton (the inventor of the SLR camera) to take three black-and-white photographs of a tartan ribbon. Maxwell wanted to test a theory he had about a possible method for creating color photographs. He asked Sutton to place a different filter over the camera for each shot: first, a red filter, then green, and then blue. After the film was developed, Maxwell projected all three black-and-white pictures onto a screen using three projectors fitted with the same filters that were used to shoot the photos. When the images were projected directly on top of each other, the images combined and Maxell had the world's first color photo.

This process was hardly convenient. Unfortunately, it took another 30 years to turn Maxwell's discovery into a commercially viable product. This happened in 1903, when the Lumière brothers used red, green, and blue dyes to color grains of starch that could be applied to glass plates to create color images. They called their process Autochrome, and it was the first successful color printing process.

In grammar school, you probably learned that you could mix primary colors together to create other colors. Painters have used this technique for centuries, of course, but what Maxwell demonstrated is that, although you can mix paints together to create darker colors, light mixes together to create lighter colors. Or, to use some jargon, paint mixes in a *subtractive* process (as you mix, you subtract color to create black), whereas light mixes in an *additive* process (as you mix, you add color to create white). Note that Maxwell did not discover light's additive properties—Newton had done similar experiments long before—but Maxwell was the first to apply the properties to photography.

Figure 2.2 shows a simple example of how the three additive primary colors of light can be combined to create other colors.

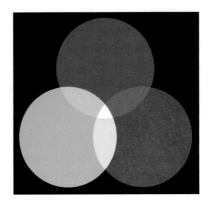

FIGURE 2.2   Red, green, and blue—the three additive primary colors of light—can be mixed together to create other colors. As you combine them, the resulting color gets lighter, eventually becoming white. Note also that where the colors overlap they create the secondary primary colors—cyan, magenta, and yellow. These are the primary colors of ink.

Your digital camera makes color images using pretty much the same process Maxwell used in 1860: it combines three different black-and-white images to create a full-color final image.

The image shown in Figure 2.3 is called an *RGB* image because it uses red, green, and blue *channels* to create a color image.

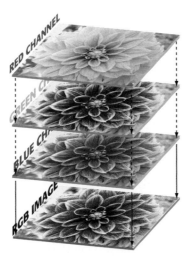

FIGURE 2.3   In a digital image, three separate red, green, and blue channels are combined to create a final, full-color picture.

This color theory is not just a trivial history lesson. Understanding that your full color images are composed of separate channels will come in very handy later, when you start editing. Very often, you'll correct color casts and adjust your images by viewing and manipulating individual color channels.

You Say "Black and White," I Say "Grayscale"

Although film photographers use the term black-and-white to denote an image that lacks color, in the digital world it's better to use the term grayscale. As we saw in Figure 1.1, your computer can create an image that is composed of only black and white pixels. Consequently, it's sometimes important to distinguish between an image that is made up of black and white pixels, and one that is made up of pixels of varying shades of gray.

In the century and a half since Maxwell's discovery, many other ways of representing color have been discovered. For example, another model called *L*A*B color* (also known as Lab color) uses one channel for lightness information, another channel for greenness or redness, and a third channel for blueness or yellowness. In addition, there is the cyan, magenta, yellow, and black (*CMYK*) model that printers use.

Each of these approaches is called a *color model,* and each model has a particular *gamut,* or range, of colors it can display. Some gamuts are more appropriate to certain tasks than others are, and all are smaller than the range of colors your eye can perceive.

We'll deal more with gamuts and color models in later chapters. For now, it's important to understand that digital photos are made up of separate red, green, and blue channels that combine to create a color image.

HOW AN IMAGE SENSOR WORKS

George Smith and Willard Boyle were two engineers employed by Bell Labs. The story goes that one day in late October, the two men spent about an hour sketching out an idea for a new type of semiconductor that could be used for computer memory and for the creation of a solid-state, tubeless video camera. The year was 1969, and in that hour, the two men invented the CCD.

Roughly a year later, Bell Labs created a solid-state video camera using Smith and Boyle's new chip. Although their original intention was to build a simple camera that could be used in a video-telephone device, they soon built a camera that was good enough for broadcast television.

Since then, CCDs have been used in everything from cameras to fax machines. Because video cameras don't require a lot of resolution (only half a million pixels or so), the CCD worked great for creating video-quality images. For printing pictures, though, you need much higher resolution—millions and millions of pixels. Consequently, it wasn't until recently that CCDs could be manufactured with enough resolution to compete with photographic film.

CCD vs. CMOS

Ninety to 95 percent of the digital cameras you'll look at will use CCD image sensors. The rest will use a CMOS chip of some kind. What's the difference? Because much more research has been put into CCD technology, it's more prevalent. CMOS chips, though, are actually much cheaper to produce than the difficult-to-make CCDs found in most cameras. CMOS chips also consume much less power than does a typical CCD, making for longer camera battery life and fewer overheating problems. CMOS also offers the promise of integrating more functions onto one chip, thereby enabling manufacturers to reduce the number of chips in their cameras. For example, image capture and processing could both be performed on one CMOS chip, further reducing the price of a camera.

Although CMOS used to have a reputation for producing rough images with inferior color, Canon®'s excellent EOS series of digital SLRs have shown that CMOS can be a viable alternative to CCDs.

Both chips register light in the same way, and for the sake of this discussion, the two technologies are interchangeable. In the end, image sensor choice is irrelevant as long as the camera delivers an image quality you like.

Counting Electrons

Photographic film is covered with an emulsion of light-sensitive, silver-laden crystals. When light hits the film, the silver atoms clump together. The more light there is, the bigger the clumps. In this way, a piece of film records the varying amounts of light that strike each part of its surface. A piece of color film is actually a stack of three separate layers—one sensitive to red, one to green, and one to blue.

To a degree, you have Albert Einstein to thank for your digital camera, because he was the first to explore the *photoelectric effect*. It is because of the photoelectric effect that some metals release electrons when exposed to light. (Einstein actually won the 1921 Nobel Prize in physics for his work on the photoelectric effect, not for his work on relativity or gravity, as one might expect.)

The image sensor in your digital camera is a silicon chip that is covered with a grid of small electrodes called *photosites*, one for each pixel. (See Figure 2.4.)

Before you can shoot a picture, your camera charges the surface of the CCD with electrons. Thanks to the photoelectric effect, when light strikes a particular photosite, the metal in that site releases some of its electrons. Because each photosite is bounded by nonconducting metal, the electrons remain trapped. In this way, each photosite is like a very shallow well, storing up more and more electrons as more and more photons hit. After exposing the CCD to light, your camera simply has to measure the voltage at each site to determine how many electrons are there and, thus, how much light hits that particular site. (As was discussed in Chapter 1, this process is called *sampling*.) This measurement is then converted into a number by an analog-to-digital converter.

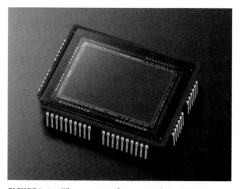

FIGURE 2.4   The sensor from a Nikon D70 has an imaging area of 23.7 mm by 15.6 mm.

Most cameras use either a 12-bit or 14-bit analog-to-digital converter. That is, the electrical charge from each photosite is converted into a 12- or 14-bit number. In the case of a 12-bit converter, this produces a number between 0 and 4,096; with a 14-bit converter, you get a number between 0 and 16,384. Note that an analog-to-digital converter with a higher bit depth doesn't give your CCD a bigger dynamic range. The brightest and darkest colors it can represent remain the same, but the extra bit depth does mean that the camera will produce finer gradations *within* that dynamic range. As you'll see later, how many bits get used in your final image depends on the format in which you save the image.

The term *charge-coupled device (CCD)* is derived from the way the camera reads the charges of the individual photosites. After exposing the CCD, the charges on the first row of photosites are transferred to a *read-out register* where they are amplified and then sent to an analog-to-digital converter. Each row of charges is electrically coupled to the next row so that, after one row has been read and deleted, all of the other rows move down to fill the now empty space. (See Figure 2.5.)

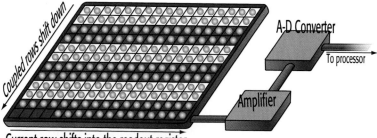

FIGURE 2.5   Rows of photosites on a CCD are coupled together. As the bottom row of photosites is read off the bottom of the CCD, all of the rows above it shift down. This is the *coupled* in *charge-coupled device.*

After all the rows of photosites have been read, the CCD is recharged with electrons and is ready to shoot another image.

Photosites are sensitive only to how much light they receive; they know nothing about color. As you've probably already guessed, to see color your camera needs to perform some type of RGB filtering similar to what James Maxwell did. There are a number of ways to perform this filtering, but the most common is through a *single array* system, sometimes referred to as a *striped array.*

Arrays

Consider the images in Figure 2.6.

If asked to fill in any "missing" pixels in Figure 2.6a, you'd probably say, "What are you talking about?" If asked to fill in any "missing" pixels in Figure 2.6b, though, you probably would have no trouble creating the image in Figure 2.7.

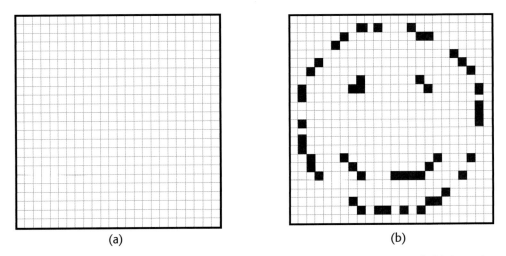

(a)   (b)

FIGURE 2.6   Although you have no idea what pixels belong in Figure 2.6a, you can probably hazard a guess as to what the missing pixels are in Figure 2.6b.

You would know which pixels you needed to fill in based on the other pixels that were already in the image. In other words, you would have *interpolated* the new pixels based on the existing information. You might have encountered interpolation if you've ever resized a photograph using an image-editing program such as Photoshop. To resize an image from 2,048 × 1,536 pixels to 4,096 × 3,072 pixels, your image editor has to perform many calculations to determine what color all of those new pixels should be. (Obviously, in this example, your ability to interpolate is based on your ability to recognize a familiar icon—the happy face. An image editor knows nothing about the content of an image, of course, and must interpolate by carefully examining each of the pixels in an image to determine what the colors of any new additional pixels should be.)

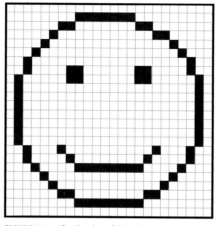

FIGURE 2.7   If asked to fill in the "missing" pixels in Figure 2.6b, you would probably come up with an image something like this.

A typical digital camera uses a form of interpolation to create a color image. As we saw in the previous section, the image sensor in your camera is able to create a grayscale image of your subject by measuring the amount of light that strikes each part of the image sensor. To shoot color, your camera performs a variation of the same type of RGB filtering Maxwell used in 1869. Each photosite on your camera's image sensor is covered by a filter—red, green, or blue. This combination of filters is called a *color filter array*, and most image sensors use a filter pattern like the one shown in Figure 2.8, called the *Bayer Pattern*.

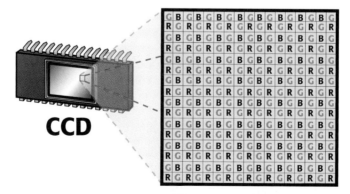

FIGURE 2.8   To see color, alternating pixels on an image sensor are covered with a different colored filter. The color filter array shown here is called the Bayer Pattern.

With these filters, the image sensor can produce separate, incomplete red, green, and blue images. The images are incomplete because the red image, for example, is missing all of the pixels that were covered with a blue filter, whereas the blue filter is missing all of the pixels that were covered with a red filter. Both the red and blue images are missing the vast number of green-filtered pixels.

A sophisticated interpolation method is used to create a complete color image. Just as you used the partial pixel information in Figure 2.6b to calculate the missing pixels, your digital camera can calculate the color of any given pixel by analyzing all of the adjacent pixels. For example, if you look at a particular pixel and see that the pixel to the immediate left of it is a bright red pixel, the pixel to the right is a bright blue pixel, and the pixels above and below are bright green, then the pixel in question is probably white. Why? As Maxwell showed, if you mix red, green, and blue light together, you get white light. (By the way, if you're wondering why there are so many more green pixels than red or blue pixels, it's because the eye is most sensitive to green. Consequently, it's better to have as much green information as possible.)

This process of interpolating is called *demosaicing*, and different vendors employ different approaches to the demosaicing process. For example, many cameras look at only immediately adjacent pixels, but Hewlett-Packard cameras analyze a region up to 9 × 9 pixels. The Fuji® SuperCCD eschews the grid pattern of square photosites in favor of octagonal photosites arranged in a honeycomb pattern. Such a scheme requires even more demosaicing to produce rectangular image pixels, but Fuji claims this process yields a higher resolution. Differences in demosaicing algorithms are one factor that makes some cameras yield better color than others.

Some cameras use a different type of color filter array. Canon, for example, often uses cyan, yellow, green, and magenta filters on the photosites of their image sensors. Because it takes fewer layers of dye to create cyan, yellow, green, and magenta filters than it does to create red, green, and blue filters, more light gets through the CYGM filter to the sensor. (Cyan, yellow, and magenta are the primary colors of ink, and therefore don't need to be mixed to create the color filters; hence, they aren't as thick.) More light means a better signal-to-noise ratio, which produces images with less noise.

As another example, Sony sometimes uses red, green, blue, and emerald filters. They claim these filters give a wider color gamut, yielding images with more accurate color. Dissenters argue that this approach results in bright areas of the image having a cyan color cast.

Image sensors are often very small, sometimes as small as 1/4 or 1/2 inch (6 or 12 mm, respectively). By comparison, a single frame of 35 mm film is 36 × 23.3 mm. (See Figure 2.9.) The fact that image sensors can be so small is the main reason why digital cameras can be so tiny.

By packing more and more photosites onto an image sensor, chipmakers can increase the sensor's resolution. However, there is a price to pay for this. To pack more photosites onto the surface of the chip, the individual sites have to be made much smaller. As each site gets smaller, its capability to collect light is compromised because it simply doesn't have as much physical space to catch passing photons. This limitation results in a chip with a poor *signal-to-noise ratio*; that is, the amount of

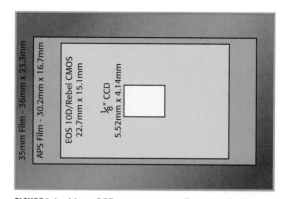

FIGURE 2.9   Most CCDs are very small, particularly when compared to the size of 35 mm film.

good data the chip is collecting—the signal—is muddied by the amount of noise—noise from the camera's electronics, noise from other nearby electrical sources, noise from cosmic rays raining down from space—the chip is collecting.

In your final image, this signal-to-noise confusion can manifest as grainy patterns in your image—visible noise like what you see on a staticky TV channel—or other annoying artifacts. (See the noise example in Figure 4.2.)

To improve the light-collecting capability of tiny photosites, some chipmakers position tiny microlenses over each photosite. These lenses focus the light more tightly into the photosite in an effort to improve the signal-to-noise ratio. However, these lenses can cause problems of their own in the form of artifacts in your final image.

Image sensors suffer from another problem that film lacks. If too much light hits a particular photosite, it can spill over into adjacent photosites. If the camera's software isn't smart enough to recognize that this has happened, you will see a *blooming* artifact—smearing colors or flared highlights—in your final image. Blooming is more prevalent in a physically smaller image sensor with higher resolution because the photosites are packed more tightly together. This problem is not insurmountable, and even if your image does suffer from blooming problems from time to time, these artifacts won't necessarily be visible in your final prints.

As you might expect, interpolating the color in a camera with millions of pixels on its image sensor requires a lot of processing power. Such power (and the memory needed to support it) is one reason why digital cameras have stayed so pricey—lots of fancy chips are necessary to make a digital camera.

Extra Pixels

Not all of the photosites in an image sensor are used for recording your image. Some are used to assess the black levels in your image; others are used for determining white balance. Finally, some pixels are masked away altogether. For example, if the sensor has a square array of pixels but your camera manufacturer wants to create a camera that shoots rectangular images, they will mask out some of the pixels on the edge of the sensor to get the picture shape they want.

HOW YOUR CAMERA MAKES AN IMAGE

The preceding description might sound complicated. In reality, though, the process an imaging chip employs to capture an image is even more complex.

First, the light coming through the lens is passed through several filters. These include an infrared filter (some cameras use a very slight infrared filter, making them ideal for infrared photography, as we'll see in Chapter 7, "Shooting") and a low pass filter, both of which help ensure better color and fewer artifacts. The image is also blurred ever so slightly.

This last fact often causes some photographers to turn pale, particularly those who have just spent lots of money on very sharp lenses. The blurring is there to help in the demosaicing process. Even though an individual pixel is *extremely* small, it is theoretically possible for a single pixel, or line of pixels, to be a separate color from its surrounding pixels. This could confuse a demosaicing algorithm, so a slight blur is applied so the colors of individual pixels are smeared ever so slightly into their neighbors.

After you take a picture, the data is read off the image sensor, amplified, passed through an analog-to-digital converter (Figure 2.5), and then passed to your camera's on-board processor. There, it is demosaiced to produce a color image. However, straight demosaicing does not produce an accurate, attractive color image. A little more calculation is required.

Colorimetric Adjustment

First, the image goes through a "colorimetric adjustment." During demosaicing, the camera's processor knows that a particular pixel was red or green or blue (or whatever colors are used in the color filter array), but it doesn't know which precise shades of those primary colors were used in the filters. So, the color in the image is skewed slightly to compensate for the specific color qualities of the color filter array.

Your camera now has a more accurate idea of the colors of each pixel in your image. For example, it might know that one particular pixel is 100 percent of a particular shade of chartreuse. But what exactly does 100 percent mean? For this number to be meaningful, some boundaries need to be defined, and so your image is mapped into a *color space*.

Color Space Conversion

A color space is simply a mathematical model that can be used to represent colors. Some color spaces are larger than others, and some might allow for more variation in a particular color—reds, for example. Without a color space, your image would be a fairly meaningless array of numbers. Your camera probably provides a choice of two different color spaces, sRGB and Adobe RGB. You'll learn much more about color spaces choices in Chapter 7.

Gamma Correction

In an imaging chip, when twice as much light hits a single pixel, twice as much voltage is produced. In other words, the response of the pixels to light is *linear*—increase the light and you get a linear increase in voltage. Your eyes don't work this way. When you increase brightness, your eyes register a logarithmic increase, rather than a linear increase. So, a doubling of light does not make you perceive a scene as being twice as bright.

The practical upshot of all of this is that your eyes are able to see a lot of really fine detail in shadow and highlight areas. As an example, consider the upper image in Figure 2.10. This grayscale ramp goes from black to white in a linear fashion. This is how your camera sees a change in brightness.

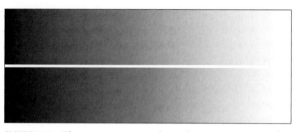

FIGURE 2.10   The upper ramp makes a linear progression from black to white—this is how your digital camera's sensor sees the world. The lower ramp makes a nonlinear progression. This is the type of light response your eyes have.

The lower image goes from black to white in a nonlinear fashion. Notice that there is much more variation in the lower fourth and upper fourth of the nonlinear ramp. In other words, the shadows and highlights have been expanded to show more variation.

Because of their nonlinear nature, your eyes tend to expand the shadow and highlight areas, registering more subtle changes, and allowing you to see more detail. As we'll discover in many places in this book, your eyes are extremely sensitive to subtle changes in contrast—much more than they are to changes in color. This is because the light-sensitive portion of your eye is composed mostly of luminance-sensitive rods, while only a tiny part is composed of color-sensitive cones.

So, to get accurate brightness values—that is, to expand the highlights and shadows so they appear more like what your eye is used to—your camera applies a mathematical curve to all its brightness values. This is called a *gamma curve*, sometimes called *gamma correction* (Figure 2.11).

White Balance and Image Processing

Next, the camera adjusts your image according to your white balance setting. Your camera might also allow you to select several other adjustments, from contrast to brightness to color saturation. These adjustments are just like the ones you might

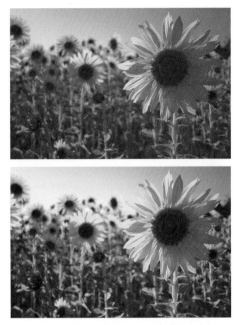

FIGURE 2.11 The upper image shows this picture before gamma correction. Note the difference in overall contrast. As with the gray ramp in Figure 2.10, the lower, gamma-corrected image has darker shadows and more varied highlights.

apply in an image editor and are usually applied after white balancing. We'll discuss white balance and in-camera adjustments in Chapter 7.

Sharpening and Noise Reduction

Finally, many cameras perform some type of noise reduction algorithm to reduce unwanted noise in your image, and almost all cameras perform some type of *sharpening*. We'll discuss noise more in Chapter 4, "Evaluating an Image," and you can see examples of noisy images in Figures 4.2 and 4.3.

JPEG Compression and Saving

Your image is now processed and ready to save. At this point, JPEG compression will be applied, and then your finished, compressed image will be written to your camera's media card.

All this processing takes place as soon as your image has been shot, and as you might imagine, it can take a while to perform all these calculations. I mean "take a while" in computer terms, of course, but even though your camera's processor is very speedy, it can still be overwhelmed with image processing. To counter this, most cameras include an extra memory buffer that allows them to cache a few images for processing, freeing up the camera for immediate shooting.

The procedure described here is what is required to turn the image data your camera captures into a final image. When you shoot in JPEG mode, all of that processing happens in your camera's on-board computer. However, your camera may offer an additional option.

Raw Images

If your camera provides a raw mode, you have the option of deferring all the steps described in the previous section. In raw mode, your camera reads the data off the camera sensor, and writes it to your camera's storage card. No processing is performed—not even demosaicing. Because these files are larger than JPEG files, they'll consume more space on your card and take longer to write (potentially slowing down your burst shooting).

To turn a raw file into a usable image, you must run it through a *raw converter*, a program you run on your desktop computer, which performs all the same steps your camera would have taken if you had shot the image in JPEG mode. However, raw shooting offers several advantages over JPEG shooting:

- Because you're running the conversion process on your computer, you can take control of many of the conversion steps. This extra control will often let you produce better images.
- Your computer is not rushing to try to prepare to take a picture, so it can use some more complex algorithms for its raw conversions. These algorithms can often yield better results.
- When you shoot in raw mode, you can set the white balance of your image after-the-fact. For shooting in tricky lighting situations, and for certain types of color corrections, this feature affords you a level of flexibility you can't get any other way.
- While your camera may capture 10–14 bits of color per pixel, JPEG images only allow 8 bits of color per pixel. So, when your camera converts to JPEG mode, it throws out a lot of the color information it captured. The resulting image will have less "room" for editing. In other words, dramatic edits will more quickly yield artifacts. With a raw file, you can choose to output your image as a 16-bit file. Your raw converter won't add any additional data, but it will be able to preserve *all* the color information it captured, allowing you more editing latitude.
- As discussed earlier, your camera probably lets you dial in certain adjustments— contrast, tone, saturation, sharpening. Once these adjustments are applied, it's very difficult to remove them. So, if your camera is a little too aggressive with its adjustments, you may face some difficult editing. What's more, these adjustments "use up" some of your editing latitude. In raw mode, since you're in control of all processing, you won't ever face an "already over-edited" image.
- Raw processing algorithms are constantly improving. As new raw processors come out, you can return to your old raw files and reprocess them. If you have a particularly difficult image that you've never been able to get quite right, a new raw processor might one day allow you to get the image you want.

- Because raw images aren't compressed, they never suffer from the JPEG artifacts that can plague compressed images.

We'll have much more to say about raw files in Chapters 8, "Metering and Exposure" and Chapter 12, "Raw Conversion."

How JPEG Compression Works

After your image has been processed, it's ready to be stored on whatever storage medium is provided by your camera. While there are many different storage options for camera makers to choose from, they all have one thing in common: they're finite. Consequently, to make the most of the available storage, cameras compress their images, usually using a type of compression called *JPEG*.

Created by the *Joint Photographic Experts Group*, JPEG is a powerful algorithm that can greatly reduce the size of a photo but at the cost of image quality. Consequently, JPEG is referred to as a *lossy* compression format.

When saving in JPEG mode, the camera first converts the image data from its original 12- or 14-bit format down to an 8-bit format, reducing the range of brightness levels from 4,096 or 16,384 all the way down to 256. Once the data is in 8-bit mode, the camera is ready to start compressing.

Most cameras offer two forms of JPEG compression: a low-quality option that visibly degrades an image but offers compression ratios of 10 or 20:1, and a high-quality option that performs a good amount of compression—usually around 4:1—but without severely degrading your image. Some cameras offer an even finer JPEG compression that cuts file sizes while producing images that are indistinguishable from uncompressed originals. In most cases, you'll probably find that any artifacts introduced by higher-quality JPEG compression are not visible in your final prints.

JPEG compression works by exploiting the fact that human vision is more sensitive to changes in brightness than to changes in color. To JPEG-compress an image, your camera first converts the image into a color space where each pixel is expressed using a *chrominance* (color) value and a *luminance* (brightness) value.

Next, the chrominance values are analyzed in blocks of 8×8 pixels. The color in each 64-pixel area is averaged so that any slight (and hopefully imperceptible) change in color is removed, a process known as *quantization*. Note that because the averaging is being performed only on the chrominance channel, all the luminance information in the image—the information your eye is most sensitive to—is preserved.

After quantization, a nonlossy compression algorithm is applied to the entire image. In the *very* simplest terms, a nonlossy compression scheme works something like this: rather than encoding AAAAAABBBBBCCC, you simply encode 6A5B3C. After quantization, the chrominance information in your image will be more uniform, so larger chunks of similar data will be available, meaning that this final compression step will be more effective.

What does all this mean to your image? Figure 2.12 shows an image that has been overcompressed. As you can see, areas of flat color or smooth gradations have turned into rectangular chunks, whereas contrast in areas of high detail has been boosted too high. Fortunately, most digital cameras offer much better compression quality than what you see here.

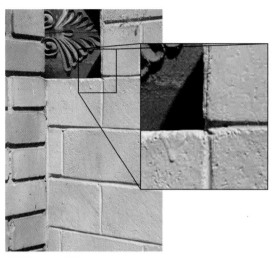

FIGURE 2.12   This image has been compressed far too much, as can be seen from the nasty JPEG artifacting.

MEANWHILE, BACK IN THE REAL WORLD

If the information in this chapter seems unnecessary, it's probably because when you buy a film camera you don't have to worry about imaging technology—it's included in the film you use. However, if you're serious about photography, you probably do spend some time considering the merits of different films. And, just as you need a little knowledge of film chemistry to assess the quality of a particular film stock, the topics covered in this chapter will help you better test a particular camera.

Your camera is more than just an image sensor, of course, so in Chapter 5, you'll learn about the other components and concerns you'll need to weigh when choosing a camera.

3

BASIC PHOTOGRAPHY: A QUICK PRIMER

In This Chapter

- Lenses
- Exposures: Apertures, Shutter Speeds, and ISO
- Mostly the Same

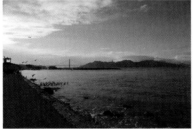

18 mm (28 mm equivalence)

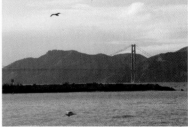

85 mm (136 mm equivalence)

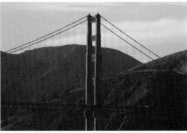

300 mm (480 mm equivalence)

As you saw in the last chapter, there are some big differences between a film camera and a digital camera. While a piece of film can both record and store images, a digital camera needs a complex combination of an imaging chip, on-board computer, and storage device to be able to capture and store images. Fortunately, no matter what type of camera you use, the physics of light work the same way. Consequently, whether you're exposing a piece of film or a silicon image sensor, all of the mechanisms a camera uses to measure and control light follow the same rules. What's more, whether you're shooting film or digital, there are many optical properties that will affect the appearance of your scene.

In this chapter, therefore, we're going to take a quick trip through the basics of optics, apertures, and exposures. Simply put: to understand the rest of this book, you need an understanding of a few photographic principles.

In its most basic form, a camera is really a simple apparatus. A lens focuses the light from an image onto a focal plane where it is recorded by a piece of film or an image sensor. An aperture and shutter, placed between the lens and the focal plane, allow the photographer to control how much light reaches the focal plane and how long the focal plane will be exposed to that light.

An understanding of lenses, apertures, and shutters is not necessary to take simple snapshots using a modern, fully automatic camera. However, if you want more creative control over your image, knowing how these systems work together is essential.

LENSES

If the name Willebrord Snell doesn't sound familiar, don't worry; most people aren't too familiar with Snell. Nevertheless, he got things started for digital cameras in 1621, when he performed the first experiments with refraction.

As Snell discovered, light travels through space in straight lines. However, when it passes through a transparent object such as water or glass, it gets slowed down and bent, a process called *refraction*. This process is why objects look strange when viewed through a glass of water, and it's what makes it possible for a lens to magnify or reduce an image. A lens is simply a piece of transparent material (usually glass or plastic) shaped to bend light in a particular way. A convex lens focuses light inward, whereas a concave lens spreads light rays apart. (See Figure 3.1.)

Unfortunately, making a perfect piece of glass or plastic for a lens is impossible. Consequently, the surface of a lens might have defects and irregularities that can produce a number of different types of problems, or *artifacts*, in your final image. Further complicating lens-building matters is the fact that not all frequencies (colors) of light bend the same amount as they pass through a lens. For example, a lens might bend red light more than yellow light, resulting in color aberrations (or *chromatic aberrations*) in your final image.

When we speak of lenses for a camera, we're not really talking about a single piece of glass, because a camera lens—whether a built-in lens or a detachable one—is actually an array of separate concave and convex lenses, called *elements*, which are engineered to work together to produce a specific magnification. (See Figure 3.2.)

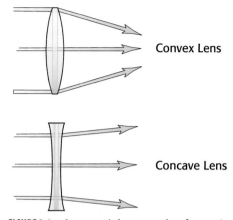

FIGURE 3.1   As you might remember from science class, *convex* lenses bend light inward, whereas *concave* lenses bend light outward.

When designing a lens, engineers add elements to correct for aberrations in other elements until they eliminate as many problems as they can. Multiple elements are cemented together to form *groups*—you'll sometimes see a particular lens listed as having a certain number of elements in a certain number of groups. Although you might think that more elements and groups are inherently better because they will remove more aberrations, be aware that each new element increases the chance of reflections within the lens. These reflections will make the lens more likely to create *lens flares* in your final image. (See Figure 5.23.)

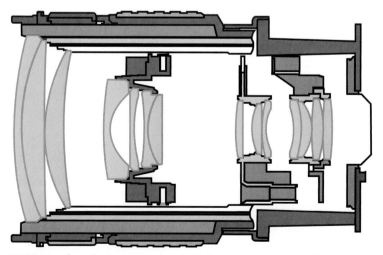

FIGURE 3.2   If you look at a cross section of a camera lens, you will see that it is not a single "lens" at all, but a complex series of multiple lenses.

In Chapter 5, "Choosing a Digital Camera," you'll learn how to test and examine a lens to determine its quality and how to recognize different types of aberrations.

Focal Length

Focal length is a measurement of the magnifying power of a lens. Technically, focal length is the distance (usually measured in millimeters) between the lens and the focal plane, the area upon which the lens is focusing. The longer the focal length, the more magnification a lens will provide. However, as magnification increases, *field of view* decreases. (See Figure 3.3.)

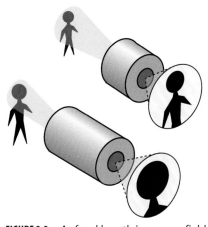

FIGURE 3.3   As focal length increases, field of view decreases. Therefore, a long lens has a very narrow field of view.

If you've ever used a 35 mm SLR camera, you're probably familiar with a 50 mm lens, a lens that provides a level of magnification—and corresponding field of view—that is roughly equivalent to the human eye (50–55°). A lens with a smaller focal length—28 mm, for example—produces a *wide-angle* image; "long" lenses—say, 200 mm—are considered *telephoto* lenses. That is, they provide a lot of magnification and a very narrow field of view. (See Figure 3.4.)

As you'll see in Chapter 5, when you're selecting a camera (or a lens, if your camera supports interchangeable lenses), the range of focal lengths provided will be of critical concern. In Chapter 7, "Shooting," you'll learn how focal length choice can alter the sense of space in your image.

Zooms and Primes

Zoom lenses, as you might already know, are lenses whose focal length can be varied. When you "zoom in" on a subject, you are increasing the focal length of the lens, which serves to produce more magnification and a narrower field of view. A typical

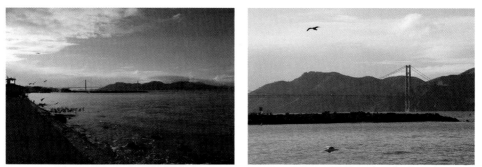

18 mm (28 mm equivalence)   **85 mm (136 mm equivalence)**

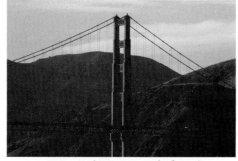

300 mm (480 mm equivalence)

FIGURE 3.4   These three images were shot from the same location. The only thing that changed was the focal length of the lens. As you can see, as focal length increases, so does magnification, while field of view decreases.

point-and-shoot 35 mm camera will have a zoom lens with a range of around 35 to 110 mm—that is, from wider than normal to fairly telephoto.

If you have a camera with interchangeable lenses, you might also be looking at some *prime lenses*—lenses with fixed focal lengths. Until eight or nine years ago, it was pretty safe to say that prime lenses were always higher quality than zoom lenses. Today, advances in design and manufacturing techniques have so improved the quality of zoom lenses that they are often indistinguishable from prime lenses.

However, if you're shopping around at the high end of the lens market, you will see a difference in quality between zooms and primes. In general, quality prime lenses offer better sharpness and the capability to gather light more quickly. A lens that is faster at gathering light offers more creative flexibility, and can be used in more lighting situations. Zoom lenses offer greater flexibility in terms of framing and camera position.

Exposures: Apertures, Shutter Speeds, and ISO

As you saw in the last chapter, an image sensor—like a piece of film—is sensitive to light. Although not as sophisticated as the human eye, your camera's image sensor needs to be exposed to only a tiny bit of light to create an image. The proper amount of light is calculated by your camera's light meter (although, as you'll see later, you'll often want to deviate from your light meter's suggestion).

You can also think of a piece of film or a digital image sensor as a mechanism that "gathers" light. As it gathers more and more light, there's more and more brightness in your final image. If you gather enough light, you'll have an image that is completely white.

In an *overexposed* image, too much light is gathered, resulting in a final image that is too light, and possibly washed out. Conversely, if you *underexpose* an image (that is, if you don't gather enough light), your final image will be dark and muddy. Underexpose it enough, and you'll have an image that is completely black.

Your camera provides two mechanical mechanisms for controlling the amount of light that strikes the image sensor: the shutter and the aperture.

The shutter is actually like a little door that opens and closes very quickly to control how much light passes through to the image sensor. Shutter speed is a measure of how long the shutter stays open, as measured in seconds. You'll usually use shutter speeds of 1/60th of a second or faster. (Once you get below 1/30th of a second, it becomes difficult to hold the camera steady enough to get a sharp image, unless you're using a tripod.) By varying the shutter speed, you can intentionally blur or freeze moving objects. Obviously, a slower shutter speed allows more light to pass through to the image sensor.

In addition to a shutter, your camera has an aperture. The aperture is an expandable opening that provides another mechanism for controlling the amount of light that strikes the focal plane. By choosing a larger or smaller aperture, you can control which parts of an image are in focus. For example, you can choose to have the entire image in sharp focus, or you can elect to blur out the background behind your subject, as shown in Figure 7.29.

The aperture in your camera is usually an *iris* composed of thin, sliding, interlocking metal plates. As you close the iris down to a smaller aperture, it stops more light from passing through to the image sensor. The size of the aperture is measured in *stops* or *f-stops*. The higher the f-stop rating, the more light your aperture is stopping. For example, a lens set on f8 has a smaller aperture than a lens set on f4. (See Figure 3.5.) In other words, f8 stops more light than f4. Smaller apertures—those with higher numbers—yield images with more depth of field.

Aperture and shutter speed are interrelated, and you'll often change one to afford you more flexibility with the other. For example, if you're shooting a moving object and want to use a fast shutter speed to ensure the object is frozen in the frame, you might need to use a wider aperture. Why? Because the fast shutter speed will reduce the amount of light striking the focal plane, necessitating the wider aperture, which will allow more light to pass through to the focal plane to compensate.

F-Stop Defined

In case you're wondering where those f-numbers come from, f-stop values are simply the ratio of the focal length of the lens to the diameter of the opening in the aperture.

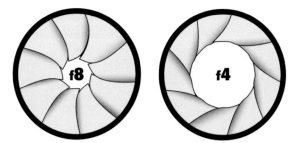

FIGURE 3.5   The iris on the left is stopping more light than the iris on the right; consequently, it has a higher f-stop value.

Reciprocity

Modern digital and film cameras offer a vast selection of aperture and shutter speed settings. For the sake of easing the following example, let's assume for a minute that you're using a more "conventional," all-manual film camera. Traditionally, on such a camera, each aperture setting on a lens stopped twice as much light as the previous setting. Therefore, a lens typically had a range of f-stop settings that went something like f2, f2.8, f4, f5.6, f8, f11, and f16. (The presence of fractional numbers has to do with the fact that apertures are circular, and halving the area of a circle involves some fractional numbers.)

Like apertures, shutter speeds typically double with each setting. Therefore, a list of possible shutter speeds on a camera will often progress as follows (from faster to slower): 1/500th, 1/250th, 1/125th, 1/60th, 1/30th, 1/15th, 1/8th, 1/4th, 1/2, 1, 2, 4, 8, and so on. (All times are in seconds.)

Because aperture size and shutter speed always increase by 2, it's easy to calculate different, equivalent exposures. For example, let's say you are shooting a picture of a very fast-moving race car, and your light meter has told you that the "correct" exposure for the image is f16 at 1/60th of a second (that is, your light meter says you should set your aperture to f16 and your shutter speed to 1/60th). However, because your subject is moving so fast, you have decided that you want to use a higher shutter speed to guarantee your subject won't be blurry.

If you increase your shutter speed to the next setting—1/125th—the shutter will be open for only half as long and the amount of light hitting the focal plane will be cut in half. If your light meter was correct, your new setting will result in an image that is underexposed. To correct this, you simply open your aperture from f16 to f11. (See Figure 3.6.) Your aperture is now twice as wide, which lets in twice as much light, and compensates for the fact that the shutter is open only half as long. Note that *the total amount of light that's striking the focal plane is the same as in your original exposure setting.* This relationship between apertures and shutter speeds is called *reciprocity* because of the reciprocal relationship between the two values.

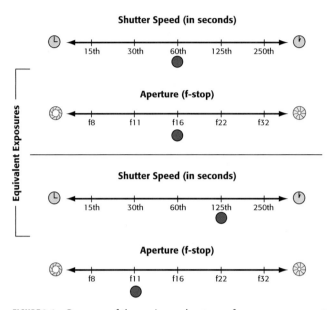

FIGURE 3.6 Because of the reciprocal nature of exposure parameters, if you change one parameter in one direction, you can move the other parameter in the opposite direction and still yield the same overall exposure.

Reciprocity is a powerful function because it means that many different shutter speed/aperture combinations all yield the same exposure. For example, Figure 3.7 shows four different images of the same subject. Each image was shot using a different reciprocal shutter speed/aperture combination. Because they're reciprocal, the *exposure* for each image—the total amount of light hitting the image sensor—turns out to be the same. Because these are all the same exposure, no one image is too bright or two dark. However, there are differences.

The first image (A) is a straight snapshot with everything in the image—both foreground and background—in focus. In the second image (B), a wider aperture was used (and, therefore, a corresponding, reciprocally faster shutter speed) to cause the background to be rendered out of focus, bringing the viewer's attention to the foreground. In the third image (C), an exposure was chosen that blurred the motion in the subject's hand. Finally, in the fourth image (D), an exposure was chosen that would more accurately capture the darker, more saturated tones in the image. Later, you'll see which exposure controls on your camera produce these different effects.

Digital cameras and many new film cameras expand on this traditional approach by allowing aperture settings that progress in increments of one-half or one-third of a stop. Moreover, with the electronic, computer-controlled shutters on modern cameras, you can have odd shutter speeds; for example, 1/252nd. We'll cover the uses and implications of these new settings in Chapter 7.

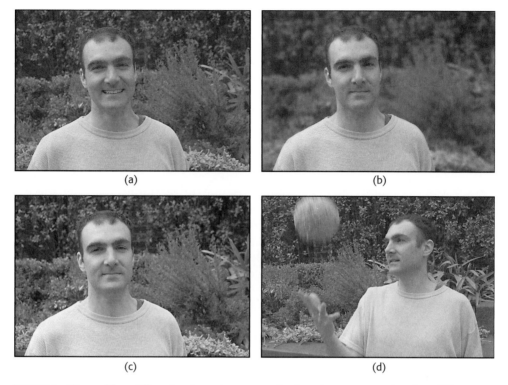

(a)   (b)

(c)   (d)

FIGURE 3.7   We used four different reciprocal exposures for these images, to produce four different results. Moving clockwise from upper-left: in the first image, we shot as the camera's automatic metering suggested and got a well-exposed image with deep depth of field. In the second image, we shot with a wider aperture to reduce depth of field. In the third image, we under-exposed to darken the black tones, while in the fourth image, we shot with a slower shutter speed to introduce blur.

Lens Speed

The quality of your lens will determine how quickly your image sensor can gather light. Simply put, it's going to take more time for the same amount of light to shine through a lens made of murky glass than it will to shine through very clear glass.

The speed of a lens is measured in terms of its widest aperture. Therefore, a lens that can be opened to f1.8 is a faster lens than one that can be opened only to f4. Faster lenses enable you to shoot in less light and provide a greater range of apertures and, therefore, more creative freedom. A faster lens is also more difficult to build and, as a result, more expensive, and often much larger. However, they also offer much better sharpness and improved image quality overall.

Zoom lenses usually have different speeds at different focal lengths. That is, at full telephoto, your lens might have a maximum aperture of f5.6, but at full wide, it might have a faster aperture of f4. Engineering a lens in this way allows lens designers to reduce the size of the front element of the lens, making for a physically lighter, smaller lens.

If your camera supports removable lenses, you'll probably find that prime lenses are available in much faster speeds than zoom lenses.

ISO

Different types of films have different sensitivities to light as measured by their *ISO* rating. (ASA is another measure of film speed, but most photographers now use the more common ISO system.) The higher the ISO rating, the more sensitive the film is to light. Because it is more sensitive, a film with a higher ISO rating doesn't need as long of an exposure to make an image. Consequently, films with high ISO ratings are often referred to as "faster" films. Because faster films need less light to make an image, they facilitate shooting in low-light situations and offer the capability to shoot in bright daylight with faster shutter speeds and smaller apertures.

The downside to a faster film is that it produces images with far more grain. Although grain can be stylish and attractive, it can also be problematic if you want to enlarge your image or blow up just a part of it.

The sensitivity of an image sensor is also measured and rated using the ISO system. As with film, an image sensor with a higher ISO rating is more sensitive to light, and so can capture an image in less time. However, higher ISOs will produce images with more noise. Because the ISO rating on your digital camera can be changed on a shot-by-shot basis (unlike film, where ISO is fixed for the whole roll), ISO is a third factor you can control when choosing an exposure. This is a tremendous advantage digital cameras have over their film counterparts.

Confused by "Speed"

The word speed comes up a lot when speaking of photography because it can be used to describe three different things: the quickness with which the shutter opens and closes, the maximum aperture of a lens, and the sensitivity of a piece of film or image sensor. As you become more comfortable with these concepts, you should have no trouble determining which meaning is being used at any given time.

Summing Up

The relationship between shutter speed, aperture, and ISO setting can be confusing to new photographers. Hopefully, the chart in Figure 3.8 will clarify some of the information presented here.

Remember, if you move any one of these parameters in one direction, you must move one of the others in the opposite direction to maintain equivalent exposure, because all three parameters are reciprocally related. Of course, you can choose to move one parameter or another without moving any others to create an intentional over- or underexposure. In Chapter 7, "Shooting" and Chapter 8, "Metering and Exposure" you'll learn more about why you would choose to do this.

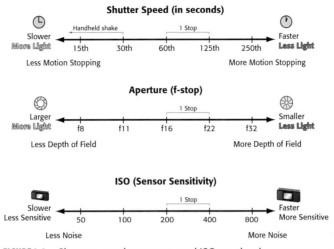

FIGURE 3.8   Shutter speed, aperture, and ISO are the three exposure parameters over which you have control. Each provides a different way of controlling the amount of light that strikes the focal plane. Each adjustment, in turn, affects your image in different ways.

In Chapters 7 and 8, we'll be spending much more time on exposure settings and will cover in more detail what you might use these settings for and how you might change them on your camera.

MOSTLY THE SAME

For the most part, all of the terms and topics we discussed here apply directly to digital cameras. However, because of differences between film and digital image sensors, and because of features made possible by new digital technology, some of the systems and functions we discussed in this chapter work a little differently in the digital world.

CHAPTER

4

EVALUATING AN IMAGE

In This Chapter

- How Things Look On-screen Doesn't Always Matter
- The Top Nine Imaging Problems You're Likely to Encounter
- Good or Bad, Who Can Tell Why?

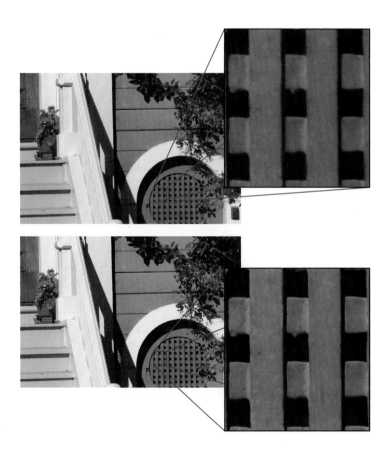

"If it ain't broke, don't fix it" is often a valuable maxim to follow when trying to decide how to improve an image. However, when reviewing images you've shot, there will be numerous times when you'll think, "Well it *is* broke, but I don't know *how* to fix it." The first step in solving a problem is, of course, to identify and understand the problem. Oftentimes, an image may look strange, but you won't know exactly what is wrong with it.

In this chapter, we're going to look at the types of problems that are particular to digital photography, both the symptoms and the causes. In addition to providing you with a vocabulary for discussing these issues, studying these problems will help you train your eye to be more discerning, making it easier to select a camera, avoid problems when shooting, and correct your images later.

As you may have already discovered, a digital image editor lets you make an almost infinite number of edits, changes, and alterations to an image. Sometimes, the number of options can be overwhelming, leaving you paralyzed with indecision. What edits should you make? When should you stop? Which version—of all the ones you can create—is the right one? Learning to evaluate an image will often help you decide which edits to make. When you learn to recognize that an edit has been pushed too far, you'll have some boundaries to work within, which will make it easier to decide on which edits you want to make.

HOW THINGS LOOK ON-SCREEN DOESN'T ALWAYS MATTER

When evaluating an image on-screen, it's easy to get obsessed with problems that are visible at the individual pixel level. Once you zoom in with an image-editing program and start digging around, you can almost always find flaws, artifacts, and trouble spots. (This is also true with high-end scans from film.)

Consider, though, that if you're looking at the full-resolution output of a 4" × 6" image from a 6-megapixel camera, a single pixel is less than 1/512 of an inch! When printed on even the best photo printer, that individual—possibly troublesome—pixel is not going to be visible.

This isn't to say that a high-resolution camera inherently hides bad image data. A *group* of troublesome pixels can definitely show up in a print. The point is that if your images are ultimately destined for printing, then when evaluating an image, you should be evaluating that image as printed on your printer of choice. If your images are going to be viewed at full resolution on a computer screen, then individual pixels do matter. But if not, don't get obsessed over minute artifacts that may not be visible on your target output device. (See Figure 4.1.)

Evaluating prints using a printer lets you see which artifacts are visible and how the colors on your screen will translate into print. We'll have much more to say about printing accurate color in Chapter 16, "Output," and the tips in that chapter should help you get better printed results.

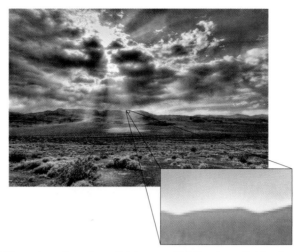

FIGURE 4.1   When viewed up close, this image exhibits some slight color artifacts. When viewed at the target print size, though, the artifacts are completely invisible. Consequently, we don't really need to expend any effort trying to eliminate them.

THE TOP NINE IMAGING PROBLEMS YOU'RE LIKELY TO ENCOUNTER

With all this talk about identifying image problems, you may be thinking, "Do I really want a digital camera?" Fortunately, things aren't nearly as bad as the last few pages may have made it seem. The fact is, even a less-expensive digital camera will produce much better images than a typical point-and-shoot 35 mm camera. (If you're curious about why, or if you don't believe this claim, check out the PDF file "Digital vs. Film" located in the Tutorials > Chapter 4 directory of the *Complete Digital Photography* CD-ROM.)

ON THE CD

The current generation of quality digital cameras may differ in the way they choose to reproduce color, and some may have better or worse lenses than others, but in general, there are only a few image-wrecking problems you're likely to encounter. We're going to look at the top nine in this section.

The problems discussed here are problems you might find in your image file itself. Problems that occur in the printing stage are another issue, and will be covered in Chapter 16.

Noise

One of the easiest problems to identify in any digital image is *noise*. Noise is analogous to *grain* in a film image, and many cameras produce noise that looks very much like film grain. Noise is not necessarily a bad thing; it can add texture and atmosphere to an image, and photographers cultivate grain or noise in their images to produce more evocative results. Unfortunately, you would ideally like to *choose* if you want noise in an image. If your camera has a serious noise problem, therefore, you may become frustrated that *all* of your images have "texture and atmosphere."

Moreover, not all cameras produce noise that looks like film grain. Some produce noise that looks more like static on a TV set, whereas others produce blotchy patterns with lots of red and blue dots scattered about the image.

Digital cameras generate two different kinds of noise, *luminance noise* and *chrominance noise*. Not all cameras produce both, and not all produce both at the same time. Luminance noise is simply noisy patterns of changing luminance—bright speckles that appear in your image, usually in the shadow tones. (See Figure 4.2.)

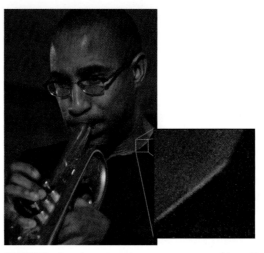

FIGURE 4.2 Luminance noise appears as speckly patterns of varied luminance. If you have to have noise, this is the preferable type, as it looks more like a film texture-type grain.

Chrominance noise appears as splotchy patterns of color, also usually in the shadow tones. Usually, chrominance noise appears as red or magenta splotches, but the color, splotch size, and density varies from camera to camera. (See Figure 4.3.)

Of the two, luminance noise is the less egregious, partly because it looks the most like film grain or texture. Color noise looks very "digital" somehow, and is extremely difficult to remove. Different cameras produce different amounts of noise, and some digital cameras produce "prettier" noise than others. Noise will always get worse as you increase ISO, and usually get worse as light levels lower.

Noise is also the problem that is most exaggerated when viewing an image at 100% on your screen. If your final destination is print, then you need to make a test print before you worry too much about the noise in your image. If you're printing at smaller sizes such as 4" × 6" or 5" × 7" (or even 8" × 10" if you're using a high-resolution camera), then some of the noise in your image might be sampled away when the image size is reduced.

Noise might also be mitigated by the printer you're using and the paper you choose. If you're using a somewhat coarse, "noisy" printing process—such as what you might get when printing on watercolor paper—then the printer might produce enough artifacts of its own that the noise in your image will be obscured.

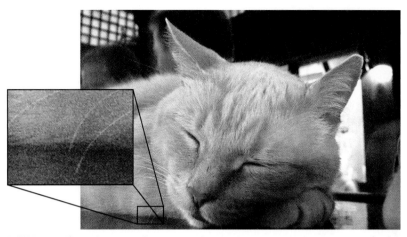

FIGURE 4.3   Chrominance noise appears in your image as varying patterns of color. Chrominance noise has no film counterpart, and so looks very "digital." It's extremely difficult to remove.

Conversely, if you plan on enlarging your images for large printing, noise will become particularly annoying. As you enlarge the image, the noise will be enlarged right along with the good parts of your picture.

Although you can reduce noise with some simple editing tricks, it's difficult or impossible to get rid of it all. Moreover, because certain editing operations can actually make noise more pronounced, it's a good idea to learn about your camera's noise characteristics, so you can try to manage them.

Color Troubles

Many different types of color problems can occur in any image, whether digital or film, but digital cameras have a few problems all their own. Learning to spot them will give you a better idea of where and how to start making corrections.

Downright Incorrect Color

Color reproduction is very subjective, and although some cameras might be more accurate in terms of the colors they capture, they might not produce an image you find as attractive as another model, which does not yield perfectly accurate hues. Some cameras consistently shoot warmer, some shoot cooler, and some shoot more or less saturated. None of these characteristics are "wrong" in any absolute sense, but they might be wrong for your particular taste. Of course, some cameras are so bad that they produce colors that just about everyone would consider bad.

With a film camera, your color concerns are a factor of the type of film you use, and you can change your film choice at any time. With a digital camera, you have to consider image quality when you choose a camera, and you can't change it later! Fortunately, many of today's digital cameras are capable of excellent color reproduction.

Color Casts

Some cameras have a tendency to produce images with particular color casts—overall color tones that make the image appear as if it were shot through a colored filter of some kind. Sometimes, a camera will have a tendency to cast only the colors in a particular range. For example, shadows might appear too blue or yellow but the midtones and highlights are fine.

Although color casts aren't attractive, they're usually not too hard to remove, because they typically present themselves in just one range of colors in an image. You'll learn more about removing color casts in Chapter 14, "Imaging Tactics."

Bad White Balance

As you'll see, before you shoot with a digital camera, you need to calibrate it to your current light source, a process called *white balancing*. If improperly white balanced, the camera will not be able to accurately reproduce colors.

Images with bad white balance are similar to images with color casts, except that white balance color damage usually affects more areas of the image. Figure 7.30 shows the same scene shot with a variety of white balance settings. Notice the shift from red to blue throughout the image as the white balance changes.

Fortunately, most cameras include auto white balance features that do a very good job of calculating white balance for you. We'll learn more about white balance later.

Chromatic Aberration

All cameras—including film cameras—are subject to a type of color artifact called *chromatic aberration*. Sometimes referred to as "purple fringing," chromatic aberration occurs when a lens focuses different wavelengths of light by different amounts.

If some wavelengths are not focused onto the same focal plane as other wavelengths, color halos can form. Chromatic aberration will be most prevalent around the edges of an image, and you'll see them most often when using wide-angle lenses. At the edges of the frame, a wide-angle lens must bend the light a lot to focus it, and it's hard for some lenses to do this accurately. (See Figure 4.4.)

Chromatic aberration typically occurs only on high-contrast lines in your image—black telephone wires against a black sky, for example. You'll find less chromatic aberration on lower resolution cameras (3 megapixels or lower) because there's simply not enough resolution to register the trouble.

Sensor Blooming

When an individual photosite in your camera's sensor "fills up" with too many electrons, they can overflow into adjacent photosites to create a "sensor bloom." Sensor blooming looks very similar to chromatic aberration—colored fringes around high-contrast lines. However, sensor blooming isn't always purple, it's often red or magenta, and it doesn't necessarily just happen on the edges of the frame, or with wide-angle lenses.

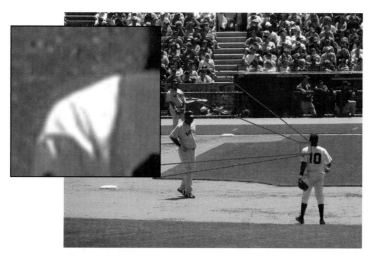

FIGURE 4.4   The purple fringing shown in this crop is an example of chromatic aberration, a color artifact that often appears in high-contrast areas, when shooting with a wide-angle lens.

Many image sensor manufacturers try to eliminate this problem by placing a tiny lens over each photosite to more accurately focus light directly into that photosite.

One of the reasons sensor blooming happens is that, on a small sensor, pixels are packed very closely together, so it's easy for electrons to spill. Consequently, you might assume that this problem gets worse as resolution increases. Remember, though, that it's not the number of pixels that causes the problem, it's how closely they're packed together. Higher resolution cameras sometimes have physically larger image sensors, which can make them less susceptible to sensor blooming.

Detail and Sharpness

After bad or weird color, lack of sharpness or detail in an image is one of the most easily recognized problems faced by any type of camera. The amount of detail visible in an image is the result of several factors:

> **The pixel count of your camera's sensor.** A camera with more pixels can resolve finer details.
>
> **How good your lens is.** A better lens can focus more sharply and produce better image detail.
>
> **How good the sharpening algorithms in your camera are.** As we'll see later, all digital cameras employ sharpening algorithms that help improve apparent sharpness.

Unfortunately, assessing detail can sometimes be tricky because you may not know that there is detail missing. In other words, you might look at an image and think it looks fine because you're simply not aware of what's not there.

Figure 4.5 shows two images shot with the same camera, a Canon EOS 10D, but using two different lenses at the same focal length. As you can see, although there's nothing terribly wrong with the image on top, the image on bottom simply shows more detail. (Note, too, that difference in lens quality can affect color reproduction.)

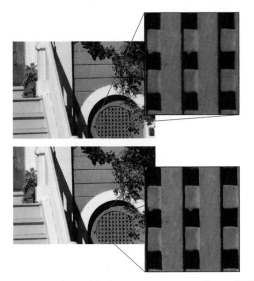

FIGURE 4.5   These two images were shot with the same camera, a Canon EOS 10D, using the same exposure but with different lenses, each set to roughly the same focal length. As you can see, even though both images are acceptable, there is a difference in overall sharpness and color.

Learning to assess image detail is largely a matter of experience and practice. As you spend more time shooting with different cameras and lenses, and spend more time intelligently looking at images, you'll gradually learn how much detail to expect in an image. This will make it easier to recognize low-detail images.

With an inferior lens, sharpness can drop off toward the edges of the frame, so when you're evaluating detail in an image, check to see if the edges of the frame are as sharp and detailed as the middle.

The amount of detail is related to the sharpness of the image. Sharpness is a function of the quality of your lens, and the quality of the sharpening algorithm used both in your camera and in your editing workflow. All digital cameras employ sharpening algorithms, but some are better than others. Believe it or not, too much sharpness is not always a good thing.

Figure 4.6 shows three frames: one with no additional sharpening, one with a reasonable level of additional sharpening, and one with too much sharpening.

How can you tell if an image is appropriately sharp? Lack of sharpness becomes easier to spot with experience. A softer image is similar to a low-detail image in that you don't always know how much sharper it can look until you sharpen it. Over time, though, you'll begin to recognize certain high-contrast transitions in an image as needing some sharpening.

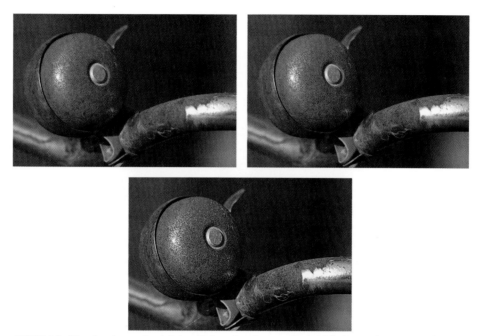

FIGURE 4.6   The first image is plainly a little soft, whereas the middle image has a nice, sharp clarity. You may think that more sharpness is inherently better, but the last image shows that if you sharpen an image too far, you end up with an image that is strangely "overcontrasty."

Oversharpening is easier to spot. First, the image will have a slightly "harsh" look. As we'll see later, sharpening algorithms work by adding white and black halos around areas of high contrast in an image. Figure 4.7 shows what an oversharpened area looks like up close.

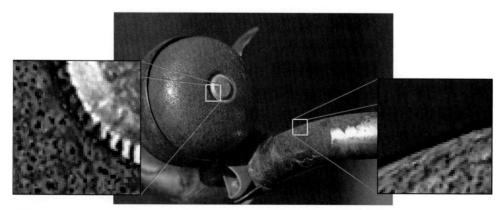

FIGURE 4.7   To make this image look sharper, the computer has greatly increased the contrast along any line where there appears to be an edge. So, the dark side of edges have a thick dark border, while the light side has a thick white border.

Those extra-dark areas scattered around all of the lines in the image are what creates the "harsh" look in the image. In a sense, those halos are extra image data your eye has to consider. They essentially add a completely different type of "noise" to the image, making it more jarring.

Unfortunately, there's little to be done about oversharpening, which means it's always best to err on the side of not sharpening enough, because you can always add more later.

Exposure Problems

As with a film camera, if you choose a bad exposure on a digital camera, you'll get a bad image. Although modern automatic light-metering systems are sophisticated and often do a good job, they can still make mistakes, particularly if they aren't used properly. The meters in most cameras have tendencies, and experience will usually help you predict how your camera's meter might respond to a particular lighting situation.

In addition to controlling how generally bright or dark your image is, your exposure choice will also affect the detail in different parts of your image. Figure 4.8 shows three different exposures of the same image. The first image shows an underexposed image, which lacks details in its shadow areas. Exposure and detail are a matter of taste, of course, and one could easily argue that it doesn't matter that there are no shadow details. However, if you were hoping for a different level of contrast in the image—one that might reveal some detail in those dark areas—you'd be out of luck with this picture.

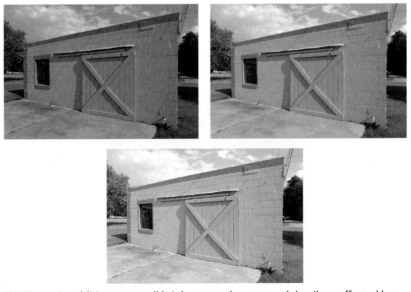

FIGURE 4.8   In addition to overall brightness, color tone and detail are affected by changes in exposure, as you can see in this example where we go from underexposed, through the camera's recommended exposure, and finally to an overexposed image.

The second image was shot with the camera's recommended metering. It provides a good balance of shadow and highlight detail, evidence that the camera does a good job of metering in bright daylight. The third image was overexposed, yielding an image that has the most detail in its shadow areas but no detail in its highlights. Again, you might prefer the darker or lighter image. The point is to recognize how a camera's metering and exposure choice can affect detail and overall results. Typically, overexposed highlights are never attractive (unless you're going for a very overblown, high-key effect in your image), because when an area overexposes, it loses all detail, becoming a flat field of white pixels.

Exposure choice also controls what color the tones in your image will be, a subject we'll explore in great detail in Chapter 7, "Shooting".

Lens Distortion

On a typical zoom lens, you'll most likely find a little distortion at the extreme ends of the lens. When you zoom all the way in (to full telephoto), you might notice *pincushion distortion*, which causes straight lines to bend inward. More common is *barrel distortion*, which you'll encounter only at extreme wide angles. As you might expect, barrel distortion causes vertical and horizontal lines to bend outward. (See Figure 4.9.)

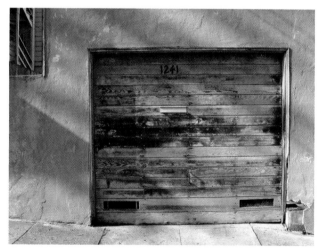

FIGURE 4.9   Wide-angle lenses often suffer from a bit of barrel distortion. Although it's slight in this image, you can see it along the top of the garage door.

Very wide-angle lenses are always going to have some distortion, and in many cases, these types of distortions are going to be concealed by the subject matter of your image. It's only when you have very strong horizontal and vertical lines—a horizon or the top or sides of buildings, for example—that these problems will become apparent.

Wide-angle lenses can also be susceptible to *vignetting*, a darkening that appears in the corners of the image. Sometimes, vignetting can be subtle, so you may not notice it until you see a few images shot with that lens. Vignetting is also sometimes desirable, as it focuses attention on the center of your image, although it's usually better to shoot with a clean lens and add vignettes later, using your image-editing software (it's easier to add a vignette than it is to remove it).

Posterization

A good digital camera captures a very large range of tones and colors. Obviously, having the capability to reproduce a large variety of hues means you can more accurately represent colors you find in the real world. Just as importantly, though, this assortment of tones allows you to create very smooth gradients and transitions from one tone to another. This allows you to create realistic-looking, smooth shadows and highlights.

Posterizing is the process of reducing the number of tones in an image. The image retains its dynamic range—that is, the brightest and darkest tones remain the same—but the number of intervening tones is reduced.

Figure 4.10 shows a grayscale ramp that goes from black to white, using 256 different shades. The second image shows the same ramp from black to white, but it has been posterized down to 16 colors.

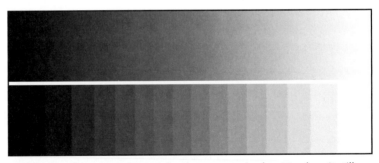

FIGURE 4.10   This grayscale ramp has been posterized to 16 colors. It still spans black to white, but there are now only 16 gradations between full black and full white. Posterizing is the process of reducing the number of tones that are used to represent an image, and posterization is especially ugly in areas of transition like a gradient.

Unless you're using a camera phone, or buying the absolute *cheapest* digital camera you can find, you probably won't have posterization problems with the images that come straight from your camera. After a little editing, though, you may be able to spot some posterization problems in your image, like the ones in Figure 4.11.

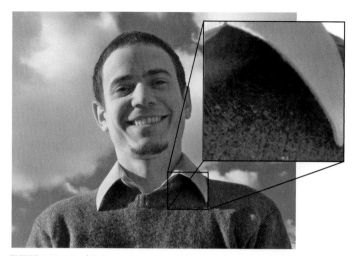

FIGURE 4.11   In this image, you can see posterization of shadow tones underneath the man's shirt collar. This posterization has occurred because of the amount of tonal adjustment we applied to the image. We pushed our edit far enough that we "used up" a lot of the image data.

You'll learn more about why this happens, and how to prevent it, in Chapter 11, "Correcting Tone and Color."

Good or Bad, Who Can Tell Why?

Sometimes, an image just looks bad, and there's no real reason why. Sure, you can look for color casts, aberrations, and contrast troubles, but often there are simply indefinable combinations of all of these things that cause an image to just look "wrong."

Similarly, an image might be full of technical mistakes but still be a good image. Some of the most famous, most important photographs in history exhibit many of the "problems" just discussed, and yet they're still masterfully conceived and executed. Before you spend too much time obsessing over technical details, step back from the image and examine it as a whole. Ultimately, your goal is to evoke an emotional response from the viewer. An image might be riddled with technical problems, but still be emotionally compelling.

Of course, before you can start breaking the rules, you have to learn them, so being able to spot the troubles we covered in this chapter is a valuable skill. What's more, it is important to know a camera's technical shortcomings so you can work around them or, sometimes, exploit them, as in Figure 4.12, a low-resolution, grainy, technically bad image that is still nice to look at.

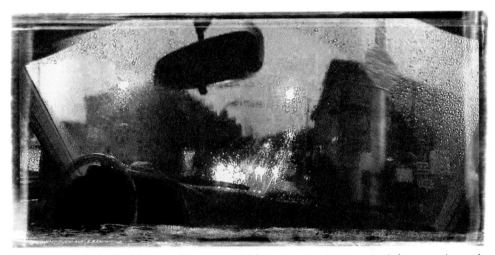

FIGURE 4.12   Technically, this image has many mistakes—uneven exposure, weird perspective and distortion, visible seams from the process of stitching it together from individual images, and of course, the extreme noise. Nevertheless, despite its technical flaws, it's a good image. It's always important to remember that image quality cannot be quantified down to a checklist of flaws.

CHOOSING A DIGITAL CAMERA

In This Chapter

- Budget
- Point-and-Shoot or SLR
- Resolution
- Point-and-Shoot Lens Specifications
- Basic Controls
- Camera Design
- Features
- What's in the Box?
- Special Features
- Accessories
- What Should I Buy?

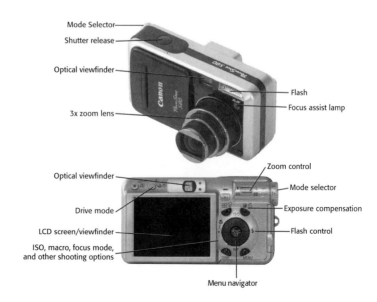

Mode Selector

Shutter release

Optical viewfinder

3x zoom lens

Flash

Focus assist lamp

Zoom control

Optical viewfinder

Mode selector

Drive mode

Exposure compensation

LCD screen/viewfinder

Flash control

ISO, macro, focus mode, and other shooting options

Menu navigator

If you're shopping for a digital camera, whether it's because you don't have one, or because you need to upgrade, this chapter should help you understand the questions and concerns you need to address when considering a particular model. There are no specific recommendations or reviews in this chapter. Rather, the goal here is to help you understand more about how a camera works, and what the various features are that you'll have to choose from, so you can learn to evaluate cameras on your own.

Before you head out to the store, though, you need to accept one painful fact: the camera you buy will be replaced very soon by a newer model. Waiting for the next generation isn't going to help, because there's going to be another generation right after that one, and another one after that, and so on. However, this sad fact doesn't have to be as depressing as it might seem.

The good news is that the digital camera market has matured to the point where the level of advancement from one generation to another is not as marked as it used to be. Back when the new generation meant a change from 1 megapixel to 2 megapixels, waiting around made sense. But these days, when the change is from 8 to 10 megapixels, or no change in resolution but the addition of new features, then the evolutionary advancement between generations isn't so critical. In fact, these days, new models are sometimes *inferior* to the previous generation.

As with computer gear, if you don't need a camera right away, then wait, because you might get more for your money later. But if you're ready to buy, start your research now. Many great cameras are out there, so there's no reason to put off picking one of them!

In this chapter, we take a fairly straightforward approach to choosing a camera:

1. First, determine how much you're willing to spend. Your goal is to get the best camera you can for your budget. *Best* is defined as the balance of features that serves your particular needs.
2. Next, decide whether you are looking for an SLR or point-and-shoot camera. If you can't make this decision right away, that's fine. It will probably become apparent pretty soon after you start comparing cameras, or maybe even as you read further into the chapter.
3. Next, determine what resolution you need for the type of output you're creating.
4. Among the cameras with the right price and resolution, select the ones that have the shooting features and controls you want.
5. Of those cameras, make your final choice based on which model delivers the best image quality.

This last point will be your most crucial criteria. If you've narrowed your choice to two cameras, and one has great features but the other produces better pictures, you should go with the second camera. Of course, it's frustrating not to get everything you want in a camera, but you can work around most feature deficiencies. Trying to work around bad image quality is much more difficult.

BUDGET

For most people, the first limiting factor in a digital camera purchasing decision is going to be price. Before you make any other choices or evaluations, you should decide how much you're willing to spend. Digital cameras run the gamut from cheapo $100 point-and-shoots, to professional-level SLRs costing thousands of dollars, so it's important to zero in on a price range you can afford. Bear in mind that you may have to buy some extra accessories in addition to the camera—storage cards, rechargeable batteries, lenses, printer, camera case—so don't forget to factor these expenses into your budget.

Once you've selected a price range, your goal is to find the best camera that can be had for that price. *Best* is a subjective term, of course—if portability is your main concern, a high-resolution professional camera with a super telephoto lens is not going to be the best option. After you've selected a price point, you're ready to begin evaluating the camera's features.

POINT-AND-SHOOT OR SLR

As with film cameras, the digital camera market is divided into two major categories: point-and-shoot cameras and *single lens reflect*, or *SLR* cameras. While both types of cameras share many features, and both are capable of producing great image quality, they vary significantly in their price, the way you use them, and their capabilities.

You don't have to choose one or the other right away, but most people usually have some idea fairly early on that they're looking for one or the other. Although you can change your mind at any time, if you can decide sooner rather than later that you're looking for one or the other, you'll have an easier time quickly narrowing the field of candidates.

Point-and-shoots and SLRs share many features and characteristics, and we'll cover those in detail, but first let's look at how they differ.

Point-and-Shoots

The term *point-and-shoot* implies "lower quality" or "underfeatured," but don't be prejudiced by this term. These days, point-and-shoot digital cameras can have pro-quality lenses, extensive feature sets, and can produce excellent images.

Point-and-shoots typically have three features that differentiate them from their SLR cousins. First, they have fixed, rather than interchangeable, lenses. Fortunately, these days, all point-and-shoots have zoom lenses, and some offer an extremely wide zoom range.

Second, point-and-shoots have smaller image sensors than SLRs. A smaller sensor means that you'll take an image quality hit, usually in the form of more noise. However, as you'll see once you start examining cameras, some point-and-shoots can produce images comparable to some SLRs.

Finally, point-and-shoots and SLRs use very different kinds of viewfinders. With a point-and-shoot, you can use the camera's LCD screen as a viewfinder, and you might have an optional optical rangefinder viewfinder. Increasingly, more and more point-and-shoots are offering only LCD viewfinders. We'll have much more to say about viewfinders later in this chapter.

Because they usually have smaller sensors and lenses, point-and-shoot cameras can be made very very small, and come in a huge array of designs and sizes. (See Figure 5.1.)

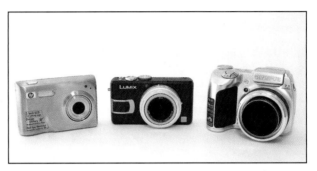

FIGURE 5.1   Point-and-shoot cameras run the gamut, from tiny, easily pocketable cameras, to larger units with longer lenses, more controls, and advanced features.

Thanks to their small sensors and fixed lenses, camera makers can build point-and-shoot cameras with designs that would be impossible to achieve with a film-based camera. For example, some point-and-shoots have viewfinders that rotate independently of the lens, allowing for easy waist-level or over-the-head shooting. Twisting bodies, internal zoom lenses, and many other radical options are possible with a point-and-shoot camera. All this means that you can find cameras tailored to very specific types of shooting, from simple snapshot cameras to full-featured cameras with controls that outperform some SLRs. Point-and-shoot cameras can also be made very quiet, making them ideal for shooting in locations where a loud shutter noise is inappropriate.

While point-and-shoot cameras often provide full manual controls, they also excel at, well, point-and-shoot-type snapshots. The current generation of point-and-shoots provides the latest advances in autofocus and autoexposure tools, making them ideal for "run-and-gun" shooting, where you only have one chance to capture a particular moment.

These days, point-and-shoots also contain other features SLRs can't provide, such as video modes. What's more, most point-and-shoots pack built-in macro capabilities that would require a separate, expensive macro lens if you were shooting with an SLR.

Although shapes and designs may vary, most digital point-and-shoots will have anatomical features similar to those shown in Figure 5.2.

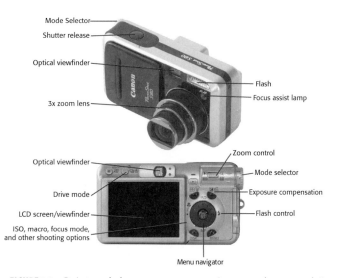

Mode Selector

Shutter release

Optical viewfinder

3x zoom lens

Flash

Focus assist lamp

Optical viewfinder

Drive mode

LCD screen/viewfinder

ISO, macro, focus mode, and other shooting options

Zoom control

Mode selector

Exposure compensation

Flash control

Menu navigator

FIGURE 5.2   Point-and-shoot cameras come in many shapes and sizes, but most will offer some combination of the following features.

SLRs

Single Lens Reflex means that your camera's viewfinder uses the same lens that is used to focus light onto the focal plane. By comparison, the optical viewfinder on a point-and-shoot uses one lens for the viewfinder and another lens to expose the focal plane. The advantage of an SLR is that what you see is usually very close to what you'll get in your final image, in terms of cropping (most quality SLR viewfinders show 95% of the image that will actually be captured). In addition, you'll be able to see the effects of any filters or other lens attachments directly in the viewfinder.

A point-and-shoot camera's LCD screen also uses the camera's lens, but in every case, you'll find the viewfinder in an SLR to be much brighter and clearer than what you'll see on an LCD screen. There are other important viewfinder differences, which we'll discuss later.

Almost all digital SLRs use removable lenses, meaning you aren't locked in to a particular focal length range when you buy the camera. In addition, you can add specialty lenses such as tilt-and-shift lenses for architectural photography, or telescope mounts of astronomical photography. The ability to change lenses also means you can improve image quality by investing in better (although more expensive) lenses at any time.

Most SLR manufacturers have their own proprietary lens mounting scheme, so when you choose a particular SLR body, you're also buying into a particular lens system. You'll want to evaluate the lenses available for each system when picking a camera, a subject we'll discuss at length later.

Don't Forget about Third-Party Lenses

In addition to the lenses made by specific camera manufacturers for their own lens systems, there are also very good third-party lenses made by companies such as Tamron and Sigma. Offering lenses for Canon, Nikon, and several other systems, these companies make very good lens alternatives, often at lower prices. When lens hunting, don't forget to consider these options.

The removable lens mounts on SLR cameras require a fairly large camera body, which means that the camera has enough room to hold a larger sensor. Larger sensors usually mean better image quality, because the individual photosites on the sensor can be larger, and therefore more efficient at gathering light. As we'll see later, the larger sensors in an SLR also make it possible to shoot images with shallower depth of field than what you can achieve with a point-and-shoot.

SLRs also offer other more professional features than their point-and-shoot counterparts, such as higher resolution sensors, more sophisticated focus mechanisms, faster burst shooting, the ability to shoot raw, advanced external flash systems, body designs tailored to rugged environments, and higher ISO settings. (See Figure 5.3.) Finally, most SLRs offer very speedy all-around performance. Image processing, menu navigation, file writing, and image playback are often much faster on an SLR than on a point-and-shoot camera.

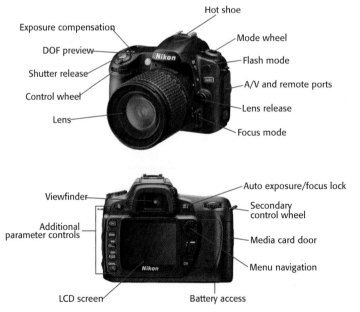

FIGURE 5.3 Most SLRs feature a design similar to this Nikon D80, and some variation of these controls. On some cameras, some of these features are accessible through dedicated buttons, while on other cameras, these features are controlled via menu options.

On the downside, SLRs usually won't offer the option to shoot movies, and because their lenses are removable, they're more prone to collecting *sensor dust*, which can appear on your image as specks and smudges (but can be cleaned off). In addition, very few SLRs offer the option to use the LCD screen as a viewfinder. At the time of this writing, Olympus sells a few SLRs with this feature, and Canon sells one very high-end SLR with this option.

Shooting with an SLR represents a very different kind of shooting, wherein you look through the camera's viewfinder to block out the rest of the world and focus on your shot. While you can take exceptional images with a point-and-shoot, an SLR offers more control, power, and versatility than any point-and-shoot.

In the rest of this chapter, we will discuss all of the issues and features you need to consider when shopping for a digital camera of any kind, in addition to providing tips and guidelines for evaluating each feature. To begin, we'll look at the very guts of the camera and weigh the merits of different image sensors. Where appropriate, we'll provide separate discussions for SLRs and point-and-shoots.

RESOLUTION

As you've probably already discovered, there are *many* digital cameras out there. The quickest way to winnow the field of possibilities is to focus on cameras with a particular resolution. Why not just buy the most resolution you can afford? *Because resolution is not the final arbiter of image quality!* If you learn nothing else from this chapter, take that maxim to heart. Obviously, more pixels mean more detail, which should mean a better picture. However, it doesn't always work this way because the *quality* of the pixels being captured is every bit as important as the *number* of pixels being captured. As such, pixel count alone is not a measure of a camera's quality. Consequently, it's important not to get caught up in the "resolution wars" many vendors wage with each other.

So how do you choose? By considering how you'll most likely be outputting your images. If you need to regularly create 13" × 19" prints, (or bigger), you definitely need a higher resolution camera. However, if you spend the bulk of your time printing out 4" × 6" prints or posting to the Web, you'll be able to get away with less resolution. The fact is, there's a lot you can do with just 3 or 4 megapixels. And don't worry—if you commit to a 4-megapixel camera, it doesn't mean that you absolutely can't output a larger print. As you'll see later, it is possible to scale up an image, albeit with a loss of some quality.

 ### *You Say You Want a Resolution*

If you're confused about the concept of resolution, check out Digital 101: A Few Basic Ideas, in Chapter 1, "Introduction".

Resolution can be a tricky number because many vendors make their resolution claims based on the total number of pixels on the camera's image sensor, when, in fact, the camera doesn't use all of those pixels. (See Figure 5.4.) For example, the Olympus SP-510 Ultra Zoom uses a CCD sensor with a resolution of 7.4 megapixels, but the camera's maximum image size is only 3,072 × 2,304, or 7,077,888 pixels. So where'd the other 300,000 pixels go? Some are masked away to deliver the 4:3 image proportions Olympus wanted, whereas others are needed by the camera for internal functions such as determining black levels and for demosaicing the pixels along the edge of the frame. (Remember, the camera determines the color of each pixel by examining the pixels around it. So, there needs to be some extra pixels beyond the effective edge of the frame.) Olympus only claims a resolution of 7.1 megapixels for the SP-510 UZ, but other vendors are not always so honest. Therefore, if you're a resolution stickler, be sure to check the number of pixels being used, or the *effective pixel count.*

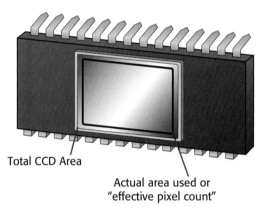

Total CCD Area

Actual area used or
"effective pixel count"

FIGURE 5.4 The actual number of pixels a CCD uses is often smaller than the total number of pixels it provides.

FOVEON®—FULL COLOR WITHOUT INTERPOLATING

In Chapter 2, How a Digital Ca mera Works," you learned that digital cameras perceive color by analyzing a group of pixels to determine the color of every single pixel in your image. This complex mechanism is necessary because the individual pixels in most sensors can read only light and dark, not color. Foveon, Inc., has developed an image sensor that uses a completely different approach. Their unique X3® image sensor has separate red, green, and blue sensors at each photosite, meaning that each pixel in the sensor can read full color, *with no demosaicing necessary.*

In theory, this setup eliminates any number of color artifacts and problems that derive from the color interpolation required by every other type of image sensor.

→

So, why should you even consider a camera equipped with anything else? Because the simple fact is, if you compare a Foveon-equipped camera with a competing CCD- or CMOS-equipped camera, you'll probably find that Foveon hasn't yet caught up to the other technologies. CCD and CMOS have decades of research and engineering behind them. Foveon is a technology with issues of its own. It's certainly possible that in the future, this technology will win out, but in the meantime, image quality and feature set—not potential coolness of the underlying technology—are still the benchmarks for camera value.

However, some good Foveon-equipped cameras out there are certainly worth your consideration.

Choosing a Resolution

As mentioned previously, the quickest way to narrow your digital camera search is to zero in on a resolution that's suitable to the type of output you're going to produce. Simply put, to make a quality print of a particular size you need a certain number of pixels. We'll talk about resolution (and why you can get away with lower resolution as your print size gets bigger) in much more detail in Chapter 16, "Output." For now, you can use Figure 16.18 as a guideline.

Note that these numbers are not hard and fast. If you pick a 3.3-megapixel camera, that doesn't mean it's impossible for you to print an image larger than 5" × 7"; it just means that you will start to see a softening and lack of sharpness as you enlarge past 5" × 7". Whether this lack of sharpness will matter depends on how picky you are and the types of shots you're taking.

Unfortunately, you can't always frame your image exactly as you want it in your final print. If you can't get close enough to your subject and don't have a long enough telephoto lens on your camera, you may have to shoot your image and crop it later. So, even if you never expect to print anything larger than, say, 5" × 7", you might still want to bump up one resolution class, so your images will have enough pixels to allow you to crop but still print at 5" × 7".

BLOWING UP YOUR IMAGES

With modern imaging software, you don't have to settle for the resolution provided by your camera. Through interpolation (also called *resampling*), you can use your image-editing software to enlarge your pictures. Therefore, when we say that a typical 3-megapixel camera can print a 4" × 6" picture, we mean that it can do so without any post-processing. You can, of course, print much larger than this by up-sampling your images.

However, you can enlarge a picture only so far before you begin to see interpolation artifacts. (See Figure 5.5.) Obviously, the more resolution you start with, the better the results.

→

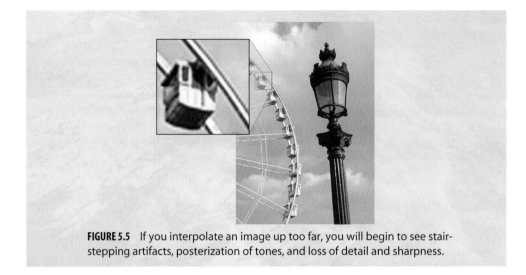

FIGURE 5.5   If you interpolate an image up too far, you will begin to see stair-stepping artifacts, posterization of tones, and loss of detail and sharpness.

How Much Bigger Is That Extra Megapixel?

If you're considering spending the extra money for a camera with higher resolution, it's worth doing a little math. A 50 percent increase in the number of pixels in a camera adds only 22.5 percent more print area. This is the difference between an 8" × 10" print and a 10" × 12" print. Therefore, the extra resolution won't give you substantially bigger prints. However, if your camera and optics are good enough, higher resolution can give you better detail. You can see the difference in relative image sizes in Figure 16.18, which also shows you what size output you can reasonably expect to achieve with a given resolution. Figure 5.6 shows the typical pixel dimensions for specific resolutions.

2.1 megapixels - 1600 x 1200
3.14 megapixels - 2048 x 1536
3.8 megapixels - 2272 x 1704
4.92 megapixels - 2560 x 1920
5.0 megapixels - 2592 x 1944
6.3 megapixels - 3072 x 2048
8.3 megapixels - 3264 x 2448
11 megapixels - 4,064 x 2,704
13.7 megapixels - 4500 x 3000

FIGURE 5.6   Before you decide that you need a particular resolution, it's important to understand that the difference between one resolution and another is not always as large as it might seem. Depending on how big you want to print, you might find that you don't need to spend the extra money on extra pixels.

Buy Some Media before Shopping

Because a camera's LCD screen is too small to accurately judge a camera's performance, consider buying your own media card. You can then take the card to your local camera store, use it in a few different cameras, and then examine the results at home. When you finally buy a camera, you can always reuse the card.

Sensor Size and Focal Length

Image sensors, whether CCD or CMOS, can be very small—as small as 1/4". Should you be concerned about the physical size of the sensor if it packs the resolution you want? In many cases, yes, because smaller sensors often suffer an image quality hit due to their reduced size.

As explained in Chapter 2, the surface of an image sensor is divided into a grid of pixels. On a larger sensor, each pixel is physically larger than those of a smaller sensor. Larger pixels are capable of collecting more light, which means they are usually more color-accurate than smaller pixels. In addition, on a smaller sensor, where the pixels are packed more closely together, there is a greater chance of electron spillage and blooming (see Chapter 4, "Evaluating an Image"), which can appear as weird color artifacts in your images. Finally, larger pixels result in a better signal-to-noise ratio, resulting in images with less noise.

Building a lens that can focus onto a very small area can be difficult, so lens quality becomes *more* important when the image sensor is very small, and as you increase pixel density on a sensor of any size. These are just some of the reasons why raw pixel count is not necessarily a measure of a camera's imaging quality.

At the time of this writing, digital SLR cameras are topping out at 16.7 megapixels. Some theorize that there is no need for resolution to go any higher than this because the physical size of the individual pixels is beyond the resolving power of the best SLR lenses now available. In other words, we have reached the point where lens technology, not image sensor technology, is now the limiting factor on high-end SLR cameras.

If this is true, future improvements in image sensor technology will not involve more pixels, but will be made by crafting sensors with the same resolutions we have today but with larger pixels.

Unfortunately, image sensors are difficult to make, so it's more cost effective for a manufacturer to create physically smaller chips.

For a point-and-shoot camera, sensor size is not really an issue you need to consider when buying a camera. If your sensor has troubles related to its size, you'll discover them when you evaluate the camera's image quality.

Focal Length Multipliers

All lenses project a circular image onto the focal plane. The film or image sensor that's sitting on the focal plane records a rectangular crop from the middle of that circle. Obviously, a larger sensor records a larger crop. (See Figure 5.7)

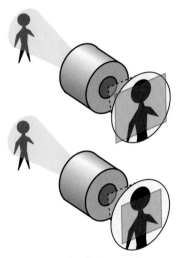

FIGURE 5.7 Your lens projects a circular image, but your camera's image sensor crops a rectangular portion out of that image. The amount that is cropped depends on the size of the sensor. This is why different sensor sizes yield different field of views for any given focal length.

Because of this, the same lens placed on a camera with a different sensor size will yield a different field of view.

The 35 mm frame size has been the standard for so long that most people tend to "think" in terms of 35 mm when they consider a particular focal length. So, a 50 mm lens is considered a "normal" lens, while a 200 mm is considered telephoto, and 28 mm is considered wide angle. However, as you just learned, if you place those same lenses on cameras with smaller sensors, they'll have the narrower field of view of a more telephoto lens. Therefore, when you place a 50 mm lens on a camera with a smaller sensor, it might end up having the field of view of a 70 mm lens on a 35 mm camera.

For example, the sensor in a point-and-shoot camera is so small, camera makers can get away with using lenses that have very short focal lengths—usually in the 8–15 mm range. In 35 mm terms, 8–15 mm is insanely wide-angle. Therefore, to learn what the equivalent focal length is in terms of a 35 mm camera, you must multiply the actual focal length by a *multiplication factor* to determine the 35 mm focal length equivalency.

Fortunately, with point-and-shoot cameras, if your manual doesn't list the multiplication factor, it will probably list the equivalent 35 mm focal length range.

It's very important to understand that the lens won't have the same magnification as its 35 mm equivalent; it will simply show the same field of view. For example, a true 75 mm lens on a 35 mm camera will have different optical properties than a lens with an equivalent 75 mm crop on a camera with a smaller sensor.

All point-and-shoots, and most digital SLRs, have sensors that are smaller than a 35 mm frame, so you'll probably need to spend some time figuring out the equivalent focal length ranges of any cameras you're considering.

Full-Frame Sensors vs. Reduced-Frame Sensors

If you're shopping for an SLR, you will eventually encounter the "full frame" debate. Currently, a handful of digital SLRs have sensors that are the same size as a frame of 35 mm film. Other digital SLRs use a sensor that's roughly the same size as a piece of APS film. These differences in size have a few effects on image quality—some noticeable, some more theoretical.

As discussed in the previous section, an SLR with a reduced-frame sensor will have a *focal length multiplier* listed somewhere in the camera's manual. You'll multiply the focal length of any lens you attach to that camera by the focal length multiplier to learn the equivalent crop in 35 mm terms. For example, most Nikon SLRs have a focal length multiplier of 1.5. A 50 mm lens placed on one of these cameras will have the same crop as a 75 mm lens on a full frame camera (50 * 1.5).

This cropping factor can be very handy for shooters who like using very long telephoto lenses. For example, if you stick a 300 mm lens on a Canon EOS Digital Rebel, which has a 1.6x focal length multiplier, you'll have the same crop as a 480 mm lens. If you like shooting with wide-angle lenses, though, things are a different story. A 24 mm lens—a very wide lens on a full-frame camera—will have a full-frame equivalent crop of 36 mm—not very wide.

Fortunately, many camera vendors have responded to this problem by making lenses specially engineered for their cameras that have smaller sensors. Canon, for example, makes a 10–22 mm lens that yields a 16–35 mm equivalent range. These lenses will not work on a full frame sensor, because they don't project a large enough image. Note, however, that full-frame lenses will work just fine on a reduced sensor camera.

Canon's denotes their "digital specific" lenses with the EF-S label, Nikon with the DX label.

Until recently, the lack of wide-angle lenses was one of the best reasons to opt for a full-frame digital SLR. However, full-frame SLRs are significantly more expensive than their reduced-frame counterparts. Now that camera manufacturers are selling wide-angle lenses that work with reduced-frame sensors, why might you want a full-frame camera?

First, with a full-frame camera, you don't need to do any calculation to figure out the equivalent crop. If you're used to thinking in terms of 35 mm focal lengths, this is a welcome convenience. Full-frame cameras have larger sensors, which allow for much higher resolutions—the *lowest* resolution full-frame camera currently available is the 13-megapixel Canon EOS 5D. Just as importantly, in terms of image quality, larger sensors also allow for much larger pixels, resulting in better signal-to-noise ratio. With their larger sensor size, it's also possible to get slightly shallower depth of field with a full-frame camera. Finally, full-frame cameras also typically have larger, brighter viewfinders than their APS-sized cousins, and many feature high-end features such as rugged weatherproofing.

You'll pay a premium for this extra functionality, though. At the time of this writing, the cheapest full-frame digital SLR has a list price of $3300. However, that's just the beginning of the price difference. Because of their extra resolution, full-frame cameras are *very* unforgiving of mediocre lenses. If you want to get the best quality you can out of your expensive camera, you'll need to buy fairly expensive lenses to go with it. And, since you're shooting higher resolution images, you'll need more storage.

As a lens gets longer and wider, it gets harder to engineer. Lenses engineered for a reduced sensor size can be smaller, lighter, and therefore less expensive than their full-frame counterparts *without* sacrificing image quality. This is not to say that all reduced-frame lenses are exceptional, but some are, and they come at a very reasonable cost.

Full-frame camera bodies are also physically larger than reduced-frame SLR bodies. Because of the larger sensor, a full-frame camera must have a larger mirror, and larger pentaprism. All of this makes for a camera that is noticeably bigger and heavier. Since you'll also be buying larger lenses, your entire camera kit will probably be significantly heavier than a reduced-sensor kit with equivalent lenses.

Finally, if you do lots of extreme telephoto work—wildlife or sports shooting, for example—you might want to stick with a reduced-frame sensor. Because a reduced-frame sensor has more tightly packed pixels, you'll possibly get better detail on objects that are small in the frame.

Many people are confused about the full-frame versus reduced-frame debate. They feel that the industry will ultimately go toward all full-frame cameras, so investing in special "digital" lenses is a waste of money. Canon has definitely fed fuel to this idea by releasing the 5D, the most affordable full-frame SLR yet seen. At the same time, though, they have continued to produce new digital specific lenses, indicating they're not going to be abandoning their digital lens mount system anytime soon. Meanwhile, Nikon has steadfastly stated that they have no plans to release a full-frame camera, but the rumor mill suggests otherwise.

The 35 mm frame size (on which the "full frame" sensor is based) was not created because of any special advantage or theoretical necessity; it's just something we've all become accustomed to. Sure, you can put more, larger pixels on it, but the 5D offers no better signal-to-noise ratio than Canon's reduced frame EOS 30D. If what you need is a very high resolution SLR, then full frame is currently your best option; just be prepared to spend more money, and carry more weight.

POINT-AND-SHOOT LENS SPECIFICATIONS

If you're shopping for a point-and-shoot camera, you'll want to make some lens decisions fairly early on. You can't remove the lens on a point-and-shoot camera, so you need to pick a camera with a lens that will allow you to do the type of shooting you want to do.

Ideally, we all want a single lens with a focal length that goes from extremely wide to extremely telephoto, delivers excellent quality with a wide aperture across its range, and yet is small enough to fit in a camera the size of a credit card. Unfortunately, such technology doesn't yet exist, so you'll have to make some compromises.

If you want a camera with an extremely long zoom range, you'll have to give up on small size, as longer lenses require a bigger camera body.

Note, however, that camera manufacturers have adapted a convention used by the video camera industry and now typically specify the focal length of a lens by a multiplication factor. So, you'll see cameras that have a 3x zoom lens, or a 10x zoom, or something in between. This is not particularly useful information, as it doesn't tell you which focal lengths are covered by that specific range.

In general, it's safe to assume that a 3x or 4x zoom lens will give you something like the equivalent of a 35 to 135 mm lens on a 35 mm film camera. A 10x zoom lens will usually offer you something more like a 28–200 mm lens on a 35 mm camera. However, these are approximations, and you'll want to check the camera's spec sheet for more info.

If you shoot wildlife and sporting events, or if you simply like shooting things that are far away, you'll want a lens with a longer telephoto reach. If you shoot architecture, street scenes, or prefer shooting wide angle, you'll want a lens that can zoom out to a short focal length. The typical 3x or 4x zoom will provide an excellent "walk-around" range that will cover most of the typical shooting situations.

Once you've determined what focal length you want, you'll probably find that you've weeded out some cameras, either because they have more lens than you need, or not enough. If you're feeling frustrated because you've found a camera you *adore* but it doesn't have the extreme focal length ranges you want, check a little farther and see if it supports any kind of lens extensions. Many point-and-shoots offer wide-angle and telephoto adapters that can greatly extend the range of your camera.

Later in this chapter, we'll cover the details of evaluating the quality of a specific lens.

INTERNAL AND EXTERNAL LENSES

One thing to consider when point-and-shoot shopping is the configuration of the camera's lens. Some point-and-shoot cameras like the Canon S80 shown in Figure 5.2 have telescoping lenses that close up to be flush with their bodies. Other cameras have lenses that protrude from the camera even when closed. Still other cameras have zoom lenses that are oriented vertically *within* the camera's body (see Figure 5.8). A mirror at the top of the lens allows the vertically mounted lens to look out the front of the camera. If you want a camera with the smallest possible profile, you'll probably want a lens that retracts completely into the camera, or is completely contained within the camera. When considering a retractable lens, pay close attention to how quickly it extends and retracts, as this will have a bearing on how quickly you can take a shot.

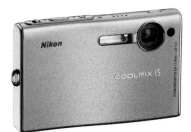

FIGURE 5.8   When selecting a point-and-shoot camera, you'll want to give some thought to whether the lens protrudes from the camera body. This Nikon S5 has a lens that is positioned vertically within the camera body, and so remains completely self-contained.

BASIC CONTROLS

Once you've narrowed your search to a particular resolution class, you're ready to start considering the features, controls, and designs of specific cameras. This stage of your decision centers on the specifics of what you need for the type of shooting you like to do, and your personal preference for camera feel and—let's face it—what's cool.

Exposure Control

After resolution, the next demarcation in the digital camera market is the degree of exposure control provided by the camera. In other words, are you looking for a simple, fully automatic snapshot camera? Or do you expect a more advanced camera with extra control? Or perhaps you don't know from extra control and would like a snapshot camera with some extra manual controls that will let you grow into a more advanced level of photography.

In the old days of film cameras (circa 20 years ago), you had to pay a lot of extra money to get a camera that offered completely automatic operation. Now, every digital camera offers complete automation, and you have to pay a lot of money for a camera that offers any manual controls.

Typically, cameras that offer more control also offer higher-quality lenses and, therefore, better image quality. Vendors figure that users who are serious enough about photography to understand manual overrides are serious enough to want higher quality components in their camera.

So, what do we mean by manual control? If you read Chapter 3, "Basic Photography: A Quick Primer," you got an introduction to the concept of shutter speed, aperture, ISO, and exposure control. A camera with more sophisticated controls will provide you with several options for taking control of exposure decisions. Presented next are the shooting options you can expect to find on a camera, both point-and-shoots and SLRs. How many of these options are necessary depends on your photographic needs.

Auto Mode

Most digital cameras provide a fully automatic mode that makes the camera function as a simple snapshot camera. In this mode, *every* decision about your next shot will be made by the camera. Shutter speed, aperture, ISO, white balance, focus—even whether to use the flash—are all determined by the camera. If you want to override any of these, you're out of luck. If you don't know anything about photography, auto mode is a great way to immediately start taking pictures. Fortunately, these days the auto features built in to most cameras are very good.

Program Mode

Most digital cameras provide a *program mode,* which gives you a little more control than the fully automatic mode. While shutter speed and aperture will be calculated automatically, the camera might provide a few options for overriding these decisions. In addition, you'll have the option to manually change ISO, white balance, focus, and flash. Depending on the quality of the camera's automation mechanisms, this might be the only mode you need for 80 percent of your shooting. And, depending on your camera's controls, you might find that you can easily get access to all necessary manual overrides, meaning you might not ever need to switch out of program mode.

However, automatic routines don't always make choices that yield the *best* result. They often make choices that yield an *average* result. In a tricky lighting situation, average results are nothing to sneeze at. However, there might be times when the camera's estimations are simply wrong for the situation. It is these times when you'll want some additional shooting control.

Preset Exposure Modes

In addition to a fully automatic program mode, almost all digital cameras these days offer a selection of preset exposure modes. These modes don't do any type of magic processing; they simply favor—or lock the camera into—particular apertures and shutter speeds that are appropriate to certain situations. Most cameras with preset exposures include variations on the following modes:

Landscape: Cancels the flash, locks focus on infinity, and typically uses as small an aperture as possible for maximum depth of field.

Portrait: Favors wider apertures to produce a softer background.

Pan-focus: Provides settings intended for really fast shooting. Focal length is locked on full wide; focus is kept at infinity. This mode essentially turns your camera into a speedy, fixed-focus camera.

Fast shutter: Forces a large aperture to facilitate a fast shutter speed; sometimes called "Sports."

Night: Uses slow shutter speeds for dimly lit scenes, and typically fires the flash to provide some foreground illumination. Sometimes called "Slow sync." Many cameras let you choose whether to fire the flash at the beginning or end of the exposure. (See Figure 7.50.)

Sand and Snow: Intentionally overexposes the scene so that snow is rendered white instead of gray. This mode will make more sense when you learn about light meters in Chapter 7, "Shooting." Sometimes called "Beach."

Although these modes provide no facility for fine-tuning, they do let you bias the camera's decision-making process in a direction that might be more appropriate for your current shooting situation.

Priority Modes

Priority modes are where the real power lies for the serious photographer. With these modes, your camera gives up some of its autopilot mechanisms and lets you call the shots. For maximum creative control, you'll want to have at least one of the following shooting modes in addition to the camera's automatic mode:

Aperture priority: *Aperture priority mode* lets you select the aperture you want to use, leaving the selection of an appropriate shutter speed up to the camera. When you are looking at a camera's aperture priority mode, pay particular attention to the range of f-stops available. You want an aperture priority control that will let you pick any of the camera's possible apertures.

Shutter priority: *Shutter priority mode* is the opposite of aperture priority mode. Pick a shutter speed, and the camera will automatically select the right aperture.

Manual: In true *manual mode*, you can set both the aperture and shutter speed, giving you full control over the camera's exposure.

When evaluating the manual modes on a camera, be sure the controls for both aperture and shutter speed are easy to use and convenient. You don't want to miss a shot because you couldn't figure out how to change the camera's aperture, or because it took too long to set the shutter speed. In addition, make sure the camera displays some type of meter reading while you're changing your settings; otherwise, it will be impossible to know if you're over- or underexposing.

If you know that you're never going to adjust an aperture or shutter speed setting, you simply don't need priority or manual modes. This decision will immediately eliminate some more cameras from your buying decision. Similarly, if you know that you want to be able to override automatic exposure settings, you can also eliminate some cameras from your field of view.

Now you're ready to start looking at some of the other exposure features the camera offers. These are controls you need to think about, no matter what level of photographer you are and what types of pictures you most often take.

Program Shift

As you learned in Chapter 3, many combinations of shutter speeds and apertures yield an equivalent exposure. Many cameras provide a simple control that lets you automatically cycle through all reciprocal exposures after the camera has metered.

With a Program Shift control, you can meter your scene and then simply flip through all equivalent exposures until you find one that better suits your photographic intent. If you want a fast-moving object to appear blurry, for example, you can cycle through to an exposure combination that uses a slower shutter speed. Similarly, if you want an image with a shallow depth of field, you can cycle through to an exposure that uses a wider aperture. Automatic reciprocity allows you to have a fine degree of exposure control without having to resort to a priority or manual mode. (See Figure 5.9.)

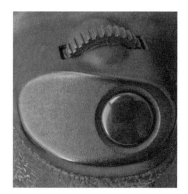

FIGURE 5.9 On Canon digital SLRs, the control wheel located just behind the shutter button allows you to automatically cycle through all reciprocal exposures after the camera has metered.

Exposure Compensation

Exposure compensation controls let you force the camera to over- or underexpose by a certain number of stops (or fractions of stops) without having to worry about actual apertures and shutter speeds. With exposure compensation controls you can, for example, tell the camera to underexpose by half a stop, and it will find a way to do so that still yields a good exposure. These controls are powerful and will often be the only exposure controls you'll need to use, even if you're a serious photographer. We'll discuss them in great detail in Chapter 7, "Shooting" and Chapter 8, "Metering and Exposure."

Together, automatic reciprocity and exposure compensation controls provide all the manual control you'll need for most situations. When you are evaluating a camera, take a quick look to see how these controls are implemented. You'll be using them a lot, so make sure they're easy to use, and that you can find them by feel without having to take your eyes off the viewfinder. You'll also want to ensure that both controls provide good feedback, allowing you to easily see settings as you change them. Finally, be certain that the exposure compensation control provides at least two stops of adjustment in both directions. Most controls let you adjust in 1/3-stop or 1/2-stop increments. (See Figure 5.10.)

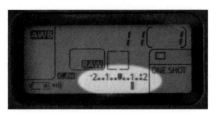

FIGURE 5.10 This display shows a typical exposure compensation readout. Here, you can see that we've dialed in +1 stop of exposure compensation.

White Balance

White balance is not actually part of the exposure process. However, because it's a parameter you'll want to consider while shooting, we're going to discuss it alongside the exposure controls. The sooner you get into the habit of remembering to think about white balance, the better off you'll be.

White balancing is the process of calibrating your camera so it can correctly interpret colors under the type of light in which you're shooting. We'll discuss white balance in great detail in Chapter 7. When you are assessing a camera, though, you'll want to consider the following:

- In addition to an automatic white balance control, find out if the camera offers separate settings for daylight, fluorescent, and tungsten. Some systems provide white balance presets that are measured in degrees Kelvin (5500°K, for example). This is fine as long as you know which *color temperatures* relate to which kinds of light. (See Figure 7.31.)
- For maximum flexibility, you'll want a manual white balance control that lets you set white balance for your particular situation by focusing the white balance system onto a white object. Make sure these controls are easy to get to, because you'll be using them often.
- Does the camera use a through-the-lens (TTL) white balance system, or an external white-balance sensor? Ideally, you want a TTL white balance system for better accuracy.
- Many cameras offer "white balance fine tuning," a slider that lets you tweak the color parameters of the camera's preset white balance modes. This fine-tuning lets you compensate for weaknesses in the camera's built-in settings, and for unusual lighting situations.

Finally, you'll want to look at the quality of the camera's white balance. Take some sample pictures using the appropriate white balance settings and check for odd color casts. If possible, test the auto white balance mechanism under mixed lighting. Chapter 7 will give you a better idea of what to expect when white balance goes wrong.

Metering

Whether you're shooting on full automatic or calculating your exposures by hand, if you don't have a decent light meter you'll end up with the wrong exposure. The modern light meter is an incredibly sophisticated device, and many camera vendors have not scrimped on adding high-caliber, state-of-the-art metering systems to their digital cameras.

Arguing which company's metering software is better is a discussion far too technical for this book. Fortunately, metering systems from the major digital camera makers come with years of refinements and are all generally excellent. However, you'll probably find that metering systems from different companies have different characteristics and tendencies. Some might consistently meter shadows well, whereas others might excel at midtones or highlights. The good news is that a meter's tendencies will usually be consistent, meaning that over time, you will come to learn how your meter will handle specific situations, and of course, you can always adjust your images in post-production.

Most higher quality cameras include a selection of different metering modes. (See Figure 5.11.) These modes typically break down into variations of the following categories:

Matrix (sometimes called multisegment): A *matrix (multisegment) metering* system divides the imaging area into a grid, or matrix, and meters the light coming from each cell. These readings are then analyzed and averaged to calculate the ideal exposure for the shot.

Center-weight metering: A variation of matrix metering, *center-weight metering* also divides the image area into a grid, but lends more "weight" to the readings from the middle of the image.

Spot metering: A *spot meter* reads only a single area in your image, usually the center. A spot meter lets you deal with complex lighting situations or tricky backlighting.

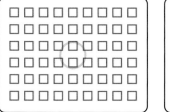 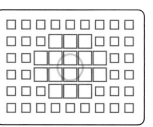 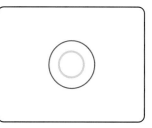

FIGURE 5.11 Most cameras offer some combination of three metering types. From left to right, *matrix*, which averages meterings from across the frame; *center-weight*, which meters across the frame but gives more emphasis to the middle cells; and *spot metering*, which meters a single area in the center of the image.

As with white-balance sensors, you want a camera that uses TTL light metering rather than a meter that's external to the lens. With an external meter, your camera will not be able to accurately account for any filters or lens attachments you might be using.

Most cameras include some mix of the three systems described previously. To test them, try shooting in complex lighting situations (dark foreground with a bright background and vice versa; darkly shadowed areas; and areas with lots of bright highlights) and see how the camera chooses to meter. Does it preserve shadows? Does it blow out highlights? Most important, does it do these things consistently? Before testing a metering system, it's a good idea to read the metering and exposure sections in Chapter 7.

ISO Control

With a film camera, you're limited to a particular film speed for an entire roll of film. With a digital camera, you can adjust the sensitivity of your camera on a shot-by-shot basis, by changing its ISO—giving you options film shooters never dreamed of.

Most digital cameras have a standard ISO rating somewhere between 80 and 100. In other words, these cameras have a light sensitivity that is roughly equivalent to film rated at 100 ISO. Many digital cameras allow you to increase their ISO rating, typically offering a choice of 100, 200, or 400. Some cameras offer a slower ISO 50 speed, whereas higher end cameras can go as high as 3200. These faster, more sensitive modes allow you to shoot in lower light without using a flash (which is ideal for situations where a flash is inappropriate), and allow you to use faster shutter speeds and smaller apertures in bright daylight. However, just as faster film produces grainier images, higher ISO settings in a digital camera produce images with much more noise.

The ideal camera provides an automatic ISO mechanism (that is, it automatically selects a faster ISO when there is not enough light) and manual selection of ISO. Be sure to look at images shot with different ISOs to get a sense of how noisy the camera becomes at higher speeds.

Because you can change ISO from shot to shot, ISO serves as a third exposure parameter (after shutter speed and aperture). As such, you ideally want an ISO control that is easy to access and provides a clear indication of what the current ISO is so you don't shoot indoors at ISO 400 and then forget to change back to a slower speed when shooting outdoors, because you'll be introducing extra grain into your images.

Live Histogram

You're going to learn much more about histograms—a type of graph of your exposure—in later chapters. Histograms are an essential tool for determining if you've chosen the correct exposure when shooting. On many cameras, you must take a picture before you can examine its histogram. However, many point-and-shoot cameras now provide live histogram displays that can be used while shooting. (See Figure 5.12.)

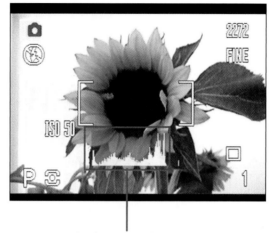

Live histogram display

FIGURE 5.12   A live histogram display (shown here directly beneath the focusing target) is an excellent exposure tool that makes it much easier to determine the correct exposure. A live histogram is particularly useful for cameras that lack optical viewfinders, because LCD viewfinders don't always provide a full view of an image's dynamic range.

Although not a feature for the typical snapshot photographer, if you have more serious photographic goals, a live histogram can be a handy, although not essential, feature.

Exposure Locks and Panoramas

Panoramic shooting is a great way to capture broad vistas without having to spring for a fancy wide-angle lens or adapter. Although you might have experimented with shooting panoramas with your film camera, your digital camera is a much better tool for creating collaged (panoramic) images, thanks to powerful stitching software you can use to process your images.

We'll discuss panoramic shooting in more detail in Chapter 9, "Special Shooting." When you buy a camera, it's worth trying to get one that has a *panoramic* or *exposure lock* mode. Exposure lock simply means that after you take the first image, the camera locks its exposure and shoots the rest of your panoramic series using those same settings to ensure even exposure across the entire image.

Some cameras offer a special *stitch assist* mode that provides visual cues to ease panoramic shooting. These modes often work with special software that can automatically stitch an image as it's transferred to your computer. Although such automation is nice, it's not required for high-quality panoramic shooting.

Exposure lock can also be handy in normal shooting situations when you want to meter off one part of an image and then reframe your shot. You can do this on most cameras by pressing the shutter button, but you'll lock focus and exposure. A dedicated exposure lock lets you independently control exposure and focus.

Depth-of-Field Preview Button

Many SLRs have a depth-of-field preview button that lets you see an approximation of the depth of field you will achieve with your current exposure settings. If you like shooting with depth-of-field effects, this can be an essential feature. Make sure the button is easy to reach. You'll learn more about depth-of-field preview in Chapter 8.

Selectable Color Space

As discussed in Chapter 2, there are many different ways of modeling and representing color. Each model has a particular gamut of colors it can display. The available gamut is referred to as a *color space*. You'll learn more about color spaces later. For now, all you need to know is that some color spaces are better than others are, and many cameras offer a choice. Ideally, you want a camera that provides an assortment of color spaces, including Adobe RGB. Most cameras will shoot in the sRGB color space.

CAMERA DESIGN

By this stage, you should know whether you're favoring an SLR or a point-and-shoot, have an idea of what resolution you want, and know what basic exposure features you need to have for the type of shooting you do. You can further reduce the field of candidates by making some basic decisions about the physical design of the camera you want. These considerations range from the physical size of the camera, to the quality of the viewfinder, to the layout of the camera's controls. Like any tool, a camera will be of dubious value if it is poorly designed and difficult to use.

With the elimination of film—and all the film-handling mechanics a film camera requires—it's possible to make a digital camera that provides a size, body design, and features that film photographers of 10 years ago would never have dreamed of. Consequently, camera makers find themselves trying to balance the old against the new. Sometimes the balance works, and sometimes it doesn't.

When considering a camera's design, you will evaluate size, comfort, and features. However, camera selection also involves trying to find a camera that facilitates your style of shooting. If you're shopping for a point-and-shoot, you'll need to think about what kind of focal length range you usually need. Do you frequently shoot subjects that require a telephoto lens? Then you'll be looking at larger cameras. Is small size and easy portability your primary concern? Then you'll be looking at cameras with smaller lenses. Viewfinder concerns will also be a huge consideration when shopping for a point-and-shoot. All of these issues will inform the camera's overall design.

If you're shopping for a digital SLR, you won't have such a wide variety of camera designs from which to choose. There will be plenty of features that inform your decision, and we'll cover all of them. However, when it comes to basic design, you'll mostly be looking at differences in size and control layout.

The design of your camera's body influences how easily and quickly you can get to the camera's controls and settings. Therefore, you want a camera with a design

that makes sense to you and allows you to "feel" your way around without having to take your eye off your subject.

Size

Probably your first concern when considering the physical specs of a camera is its size. Are you looking for a tiny camera that will fit in a shirt pocket, or are you willing to carry something bigger? Although tiny and portable is great, there's a price to pay with a smaller camera, because smaller units typically lack the features and controls of larger models. On the other hand, a camera doesn't do you any good if you don't have it with you, so small cameras definitely gain points for the fact that you're simply more likely to carry them. (See Figure 5.13.)

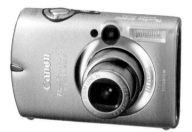

FIGURE 5.13   These days, you can get a very good digital camera in just about any size. Tiny pocket-size cameras such as the Canon Powershot SD900 Digital Elph pack high-resolution sensors and very good lenses that produce excellent images, but lack some more sophisticated controls.

Larger cameras typically sport better viewfinders, often better lenses, have more controls, and are usually a little easier to shoot with. The larger size makes for an easier grip, whereas the heavier weight can make it easier to shoot steady, sharp images.

As digital camera technology progresses, vendors are integrating more and more functions into custom chip sets that can be easily dropped into any camera. For example, the Canon DIGIC® image-processing chip first appeared in some of their higher end cameras as a single-chip solution for all of the cameras' image-processing needs. This chip soon migrated down to the lower end of Canon's lineup, bringing high-end features to less-expensive cameras.

Many other vendors have followed suit, meaning you can now get a low-priced ($300–$400) mid-sized camera that offers the same program and manual modes as a higher end camera. What separates these models from their higher end brethren? Although high-end and low-end cameras now share more and more features and body designs, higher end cameras still sport better, more expensive lenses and often have additional high-end controls, as we'll see later.

One of the most important considerations to weigh when considering a particular camera is: can you hold it comfortably for long periods of time? You don't want a camera that is so small that you'll easily drop it, nor do you want a camera that's so large that your hands will cramp up after a few hours of shooting. Before you purchase any camera, you should get your hands on it, and make sure you can comfortably handle it.

Body Design

Because film cameras have to have a mechanism for rolling film from one spool, across the focal plane, and onto another spool, they all have a basic design that is roughly the same. Digital cameras don't have this limitation. Because image sensors are so small, they can be tucked away into just about any part of a camera's body. This means that digital cameras can have radically different shapes and designs from traditional film cameras.

Consider, for example, the Nikon Coolpix S4. (See Figure 5.14.) The latest in a series of similarly designed Coolpix cameras, the S4 holds its lens, flash, and sensor in one housing, and its LCD screen, processor, and controls in another. The lens tilts up and down, affording you a wide range of viewing angles, thus allowing you to use the camera while holding it over your head, at waist level, or up to your eye.

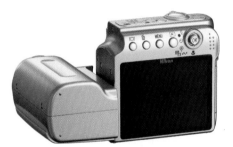

FIGURE 5.14   The Nikon S4 provides a split body design that houses the LCD and camera controls in a swiveling chassis held separate from the lens and image sensor.

These days, most cameras employ a typical boxy design reminiscent of point-and-shoot film cameras. (See Figure 5.15.) However, even within this traditional design, vendors often add some extra variations such as tilt-out LCD screens that provide the same shooting flexibility as the Nikon Coolpix P4.

As you learned earlier, a digital camera takes pictures using the same basic mechanisms as a film camera: light is focused by a lens onto an image sensor, which captures an image and stores it on a memory card. Obviously, as with a film camera, you need some way of "aiming" the camera so you can see what the camera is seeing, to compose your shot. This is, of course, the role of the camera's viewfinder.

Viewfinders

There are three types of viewfinders. Point-and-shoot cameras will have a rangefinder viewfinder, an LCD viewfinder, or both, while an SLR has a through-the-lens (or, *TTL*) viewfinder. Each type has its own advantages and disadvantages.

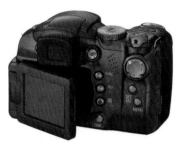

FIGURE 5.15   Many point-and-shoot cameras offer traditional, boxy camera designs but with unique improvements such as tilt-and-swivel LCD screens that provide incredible shooting flexibility, such as this Canon PowerShot S3 IS.

Rangefinder Viewfinders

In a rangefinder camera, the image sensor is positioned directly behind the lens. An additional, smaller lens positioned above the main lens provides you with a view of your scene. In other words, the camera looks through one lens while you look through another. (See Figure 5.16.)

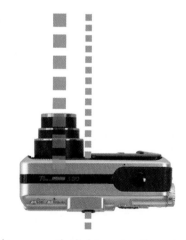

FIGURE 5.16   In a rangefinder camera, the light passing through the camera's lens falls onto the focal plane. The viewfinder uses a completely different light path, meaning that what you're seeing in your viewfinder is not exactly what's landing on the image sensor.

Because they are optically less sophisticated, rangefinder systems are much easier to build than other viewfinder systems. On the downside, because you're not looking through the same lens the image sensor is looking through, you're not necessarily seeing the exact image that will be recorded. If you're using lens filters or extensions—such as a telephoto or wide-angle extension—you won't be able to see the effects of these lens add-ons through your viewfinder.

Also, because the viewfinder is positioned above or to the side of the imaging lens (or sometimes, a little of each), you might have trouble with *parallax* when shooting objects that are very close. Just as something very close to your face appears in a slightly different position when you close one or the other eye, objects very close to your camera will appear in a different position in your viewfinder than they will in your final image.

The viewfinder lens is referred to as the *optical viewfinder,* but most rangefinder cameras also let you use the camera's LCD screen as a viewfinder. More on these in a moment.

Unfortunately, most vendors don't put much effort into their optical viewfinders, so you won't have a lot of options when you shop around. When testing an optical viewfinder, check for simple issues such as clarity and distortion. Does the viewfinder provide an image that is clear and easy to see? Most cameras also include one or two status lights within their optical viewfinders—one to tell you the camera has focused, and another to tell you the flash is ready. Make sure these lights are easy to see within the viewfinder and are visible in bright daylight.

You'll also want to be sure the viewfinder provides some type of focusing target such as *crosshairs*, and if you'll be doing a lot of macro photography, you'll probably want some parallax guides. (See Figure 5.17.)

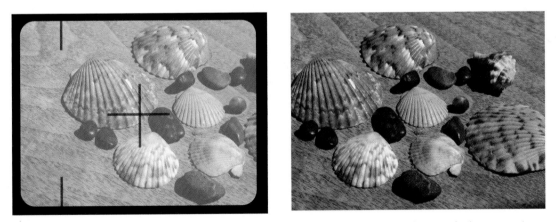

FIGURE 5.17 When you shoot at close range, what you see through the viewfinder of a rangefinder camera is not what your camera will actually shoot. Parallax guides give you an indication of where the real edges of the image are. The image on the left shows the view through the viewfinder, and the image on the right shows the resulting picture. Notice that the parallax lines allow you to correctly frame the left side of the image, even though you can't see the right side (because you're too close to the subject). If a camera's viewfinder is above the lens rather than next to it, the camera will exhibit parallax shift vertically rather than horizontally.

The most important thing to know about the optical viewfinders on rangefinder cameras is that they rarely provide good coverage. That is, they don't show you the same field of view the camera's lens is seeing. On average, an optical viewfinder will

display about 85 percent of the final image, although some can go as low as 65 or 70 percent. (See Figure 5.18.) By comparison, LCD viewfinders and the viewfinders in high-quality SLRs deliver about 95 percent coverage.

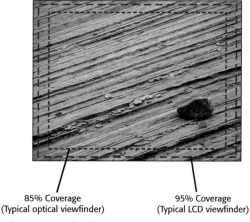

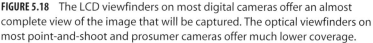

85% Coverage
(Typical optical viewfinder)

95% Coverage
(Typical LCD viewfinder)

FIGURE 5.18   The LCD viewfinders on most digital cameras offer an almost complete view of the image that will be captured. The optical viewfinders on most point-and-shoot and prosumer cameras offer much lower coverage.

Because you're seeing a smaller-than-actual-size image, you don't have to worry about accidentally cropping something out of your frame, but you will have to crop your image later to get the same framing you saw when you looked through the viewfinder. Since you have limited resolution in your camera, optical viewfinders can be frustrating in that they don't allow you to make the best use of all the pixels at your disposal.

If you wear glasses, look for a *diopter* adjustment next to the optical viewfinder. (See Figure 5.19.) This is a small wheel that allows you to adjust the optical viewfinder to keep it in focus.

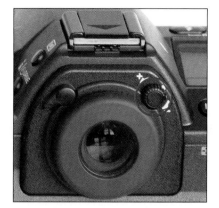

FIGURE 5.19   A diopter wheel lets you adjust your optical viewfinder to compensate for your own vision.

Many vendors model their digital rangefinder cameras off the same rangefinder designs they use for the point-and-shoot 35 mm and APS film cameras. As such, you might feel comfortable and familiar with a rangefinder camera; familiarity makes for quick learning. These types of cameras can also be made very small, making it simple to carry them anywhere. Because these designs span the spectrum from low-end to high-end, you don't have to compromise image quality to get an easy-to-use, possibly familiar digital camera.

LCD Viewfinders

All point-and-shoot cameras include the capability to use their LCD screens as a viewfinder. With the LCD viewfinder, you'll have much more flexibility in the way you shoot because you can position the camera wherever you want. Moreover, because the image on the LCD is coming directly off the camera's image sensor, you get to see a close approximation of your final image. It's not an exact image because your camera might do some processing (color correction, sharpening, noise reduction, and so forth) of the image data before saving. If you're using any lens filters or lens attachments, though, you'll be able to see their effects on the LCD.

The downside to LCD viewfinders is that images in them can be difficult, if not impossible, to see in direct sunlight. Similarly, shooting in very dark situations can be difficult, because the camera's image sensor may not be able to resolve enough detail to make a clear image. (This doesn't mean the camera still can't take a legible image by using a long exposure. It just means you'll have a difficult time framing that image.) Also troublesome is that LCD screens can be battery hungry.

The biggest problem with an LCD viewfinder has to do with composition and dynamic range. Your eye has the ability to see a tremendous range of light to dark. Current camera technology, whether digital or film, can only record about half of this range. Consequently, a big part of your decision-making process when shooting and editing is to decide what you want to capture from the full range of brightness your eye can perceive.

When you look through an optical viewfinder, you perceive the full dynamic range of the scene. You can then make any relevant exposure decisions, which will allow you to capture the scene in the way you want. The image shown on your camera's LCD viewfinder is generated by the camera's image sensor, which means it has a more limited dynamic range than your eye has. As such, you won't see the full range of tones that are present in your scene. Most cameras will adjust the image on the LCD viewfinder to protect the highlights—that is, to allow you to still see detail in the brightest parts of the image. This means that shadow areas will probably turn completely black. (Figure 5.20.)

This can greatly complicate composition on an LCD, because you simply can't see all the details in your image. Photographers who have only worked with digital cameras usually don't notice this difference, but if you're coming from a film background (even a point-and-shoot film background), making the switch to an LCD viewfinder can be tricky.

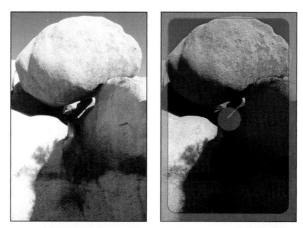

FIGURE 5.20   The image on the left shows how this scene looks to your eye. The image on the right shows how it looks through the more limited dynamic range of an LCD viewfinder. Since you can't see all the details, it can be more difficult to judge composition while looking at the viewfinder.

LCD-ONLY CAMERAS

Some cameras eschew the optical viewfinder/LCD combo in favor of an LCD-only approach. Available in a range of resolutions and packing vast arrays of features, these cameras often offer the most radical departures in camera design.

When considering an LCD-only camera, you'll need to weigh all the same factors you would with any other type of camera, but you'll probably want to put a little extra emphasis on assessing the quality of the camera's LCD screen. After all, because this is your only way of framing a shot, you'll want to be certain it provides a good view.

Evaluating an LCD Screen

While the built-in LCD screen is one of the great advantages of a digital camera, a bad LCD screen can actually be an impediment to good results, especially if your camera only provides an LCD viewfinder. When you evaluate a camera, be sure to consider the following issues regarding the LCD screen:

How big is the LCD?   When it comes to LCD viewfinders, bigger is better. Most LCDs range between 1 1/2 and 3 inches (measured diagonally).

How bright is the LCD, and how visible is it in bright sunlight?   Brighter is better because it will make the screen easier to read in direct sunlight. *Transreflective LCD screens* use a combination of backlighting and reflected ambient light to create an image that is very clear in bright sunlight. If you plan to do a lot of outdoor photography, this feature is valuable.

How good is the refresh rate?   The frequency with which the camera updates its LCD viewfinder is referred to as the *refresh rate*. A camera with a low refresh rate will deliver a stuttery image in the viewfinder. A low re-fresh rate can also cause smeared color artifacts and lower resolution.

How does the LCD viewfinder perform in low light? If you plan to do a lot of night shooting, you'll probably need a camera with both an LCD and an optical viewfinder, because there's a good chance that images in your LCD screen will appear black in low-light situations. Some cameras, though, offer special modes that artificially brighten the image in low light. If you spend most of your time photographing in the dark, this will be a worth-while feature to seek out.

How good is the coverage on the LCD? Most LCD viewfinders show an image that is 95 percent to 98 percent of the image that will actually be shot. Any less than this should be considered a liability.

Does the LCD have an antireflective coating? This feature can make a big difference when you are shooting in bright sunlight, because it will greatly cut down on glare on the LCD.

Does the LCD offer a brightness control? Many cameras feature LCD screens with adjustable brightness. Although a brighter screen uses more power, it can be easier to see in direct sunlight.

You'll also want to consider the physical design of the LCD. Most cameras sim-ply have their LCD screens mounted on the back of the camera body, but as you saw earlier, some models place the LCD on a swiveling panel that can be flipped out, away from the camera.

Viewfinder Hoods

Although the quality of LCD viewfinders has greatly improved, it can still be difficult to see them in bright sunlight. Special hoods that fit over the LCD screen, such as the Hoodman (Figure 5.21), offer a simple, portable solution for reducing glare in direct sunlight. For more information, check out www.completedigitalphotography.com/hoodman/.

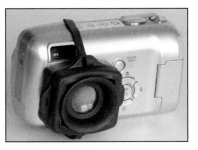

FIGURE 5.21 Hoodman, USA produces numerous LCD hood accessories that make your camera's LCD screen much easier to see in bright daylight. In addition to shielding the screen, many Hoodmans also include built-in magnifiers that produce a larger image.

Single Lens Reflex (SLR) Viewfinders

In an SLR, the image sensor is also positioned directly behind the lens. However, unlike a rangefinder or LCD-only camera, in an SLR a mirror is positioned between the lens and the image sensor. (The shutter sits between the mirror and the sensor.) This mirror reflects the light coming through the lens up into a prism, which bounces the light out through the eyepiece. When you press the shutter button, the mirror flips up, so that the light coming through the lens passes onto the image sensor. (See Figure 5.22.)

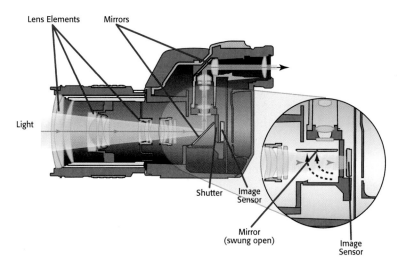

FIGURE 5.22 In an SLR camera, light passing through the lens is bounced off a mirror and up into the viewfinder. This *through-the-lens* (TTL) light path ensures that you are seeing the same thing the camera sees. When you press the shutter-release button, the mirror is flipped up so the light can pass onto the image sensor.

The movement of the mirror is what causes your viewfinder to black out when you press the shutter release. (With the mirror pulled up, your viewfinder is no longer being fed the light that's coming through the lens.) Because they look directly through the lens, SLR viewfinders present a much higher-quality view than a rangefinder, which looks through separate, low-quality optics. The result is a viewfinder that is usually brighter and clearer than the optical viewfinders on a typical rangefinder camera.

In addition, because you are looking through the same lens the image sensor looks through, you can see the effects of any filters or lens extensions you may have installed on your lens, and you don't have to worry about parallax. You also typically get better coverage from an SLR viewfinder than you do from the optical viewfinder found on a rangefinder camera. Finally, SLR viewfinders usually include status displays that show exposure information and other camera settings. Because you can see your image and all your settings in the same viewfinder, you're free to concentrate on your image.

However, there can be a downside. One of the great advantages of digital cameras is the capability to use the LCD on the back of the camera as a viewfinder. This is achieved by pulling the "live" image off the image sensor and passing it to the screen. In an SLR, though, there *is* no light hitting the image sensor until you press the shutter release. Therefore, on almost all SLRs, you can't use the LCD as a viewfinder.

Several years ago, Olympus created the first SLR whose LCD could be used as a viewfinder. This camera worked by using a beam splitter to pass some of the light coming through the lens on to the LCD. Current Olympus SLRs still provide this functionality, but now use a separate LCD mounted above the mirror. If you absolutely need the capability to use the SLR as a viewfinder (perhaps because you do a lot of studio photography, macro work, or want to be able to shoot at waist level), you'll want to spend a lot of time examining Olympus' offerings. Sony and Canon now also offer SLRs with similar capabilities.

When evaluating an SLR viewfinder, you'll want to consider how bright the viewfinder is, how big it is, and whether its brightness extends evenly from edge to edge and corner to corner. You'll also want to pay attention to what type of status display is shown in the viewfinder. Ideally, you want to see at least shutter speed, aperture, ISO, and exposure compensation in the display.

Finally, some SLRs allow you to change the *focusing screen*. The focusing screen is the flat translucent plane onto which the image in the viewfinder is projected. Some focusing screens have markings or textures that are intended to serve as focusing aids. In a camera with interchangeable focusing screens, you can replace the default screen with one that is perfectly clear. This can be an essential feature if you intend to do a lot of manual focusing, or specialized shooting such as astro-photography.

ELECTRONIC TTL VIEWFINDERS: THE "OTHER" SLR

Many cameras have an SLR appearance, but don't actually have a true single-lens reflex design. Although these cameras have a viewfinder positioned just like a real SLR, the viewfinder is not optical. Rather, it is an electronic viewfinder—a little LCD screen—just like you'd find on a video camcorder. These electronic TTL viewfinders show the exact same image as the LCD screen on the back of the camera. Although this is a terrific advantage over the typical optical viewfinder found on a rangefinder camera, it is far inferior to a true SLR viewfinder.

Electronic TTL viewfinders lack the clarity and resolution of a true SLR viewfinder, which makes manually focusing extremely difficult, and can be distracting when framing. They're often difficult to see in bright light, and many of them freeze their displays while the camera is autofocusing, which makes it very difficult to track moving action. In addition, the lack of clarity and freezing image can be a distraction in your picture-taking process.

$\rightarrow$

In addition, because they're limited by the performance of the camera's imaging chip, electronic viewfinders inherently have a lower dynamic range than an optical viewfinder. Although this means that the viewfinder will show a truer representation of the range the camera can capture, it also means you're not seeing the full range of colors that are actually there, which might hamper your process of deciding which colors you want to capture.

To their credit, they offer extensive feedback of the camera's current settings and, unlike an external LCD screen, can be seen in bright sunlight. You'll want to evaluate these viewfinders just as you would any other LCD screen. If you're set on a camera with an electronic viewfinder, try to find one that also offers a live histogram feature. Because you'll be looking at an inferior image, you'll need all the technical feedback you can get.

What We Know So Far

Keeping in mind the questions we've outlined so far, you should have narrowed your decision based on the following criteria and decisions:

- You've made a budget and determined your price point.
- You should have selected a resolution.
- You've made some decisions about the basic control and exposure options you want.
- You've identified the size of camera you're looking for.
- You know whether you want an SLR or a point-and-shoot camera.
- If you're shopping for a point-and-shoot, you've identified the focal length range you want to have.
- Based on your understanding of the advantages and disadvantages of different viewfinder systems and how they relate to your photographic style, you should have further refined your search.

In other words, you should have narrowed your selections to cameras with a particular resolution, of a particular size, and design.

Now you're ready to start evaluating the individual features of each camera you'll consider. No matter what resolution, size, or style of camera, the next section will give you an idea of what features you might want to look for and how to evaluate them when you find them. There are many features available, but if you've resolved the previous criteria, you've done most of the difficult work of selecting a camera.

"HOW ABOUT USING MY DIGITAL VIDEO CAMERA?"

Your digital video (DV) camera probably has a "still" or "picture" mode of some kind. These modes usually record a still image over several seconds of videotape or, alternatively, record it to a removable flash card. For the user who needs both stills and video, this might seem like an ideal solution, because you only need to carry one device.

→

Video cameras, however, typically shoot still images that are far inferior to even an inexpensive digital still camera. First, even though many video cameras are now offering still modes of one or two megapixels, this is far less than even an inexpensive digital still camera. Moreover, because these devices are primarily concerned with recording video, and because video is very low resolution compared to a digital still image, the typical video camera does not have to have a particularly great lens. Even though it might have a high-resolution sensor, it may not have a lens that can really take advantage of it. Second, the images are usually interlaced, meaning they are composed of two alternating, interwoven images (unless your camera has a progressive scan mode). In addition, if the image is being stored on tape, the image will be compressed using DV compression. Third, a video camera is designed and optimized to produce images for the NTSC or PAL color gamut, color spaces that are more limited than what a digital still camera can produce. They also tend to oversharpen images to compensate for the low resolution of broadcast television. Fourth, DV cameras use rectangular pixels, so you might have to correct all your images to compensate for the change to the square pixels of your computer monitor. Finally, if your camera stores images on tape, you'll face a workflow hassle when you're ready to pull out your images. All in all, it's best to use a video camera for video. Buy a still camera for your still images, unless you're going for a somewhat degraded, video look.

However, many still cameras are now offering excellent video modes that are capable of recording full-screen, 30-frames-per-second video with sound. Obviously, you can't shoot for hours, but for grabbing the occasional video clip without sacrificing still-image quality, a still camera that shoots video is definitely a better option than a video camera that shoots still images.

"OKAY, THEN HOW ABOUT MY CAMERA PHONE?"

While Nikon and Canon may be the big names in photography, Nokia still sells more cameras than both of them combined. If you bought a cell phone in the last few years, the odds are good that it has a camera on it. Camera phone resolutions are increasing all the time, with some vendors touting 5-megapixel phone cameras.

Hopefully by this point, you recognize that just because a phone has a 5-megapixel imaging chip doesn't mean it's a good camera. Camera phones have tiny, plastic lenses, no dedicated image processing circuitry, and must heavily compress their images due to limited onboard storage.

You can take attractive pictures with a camera phone, but they'll be attractive because of their flat, smeared color and "lo-fi" look. While tiny camera phones may one day be a substitute for a "real" camera, they're still a long way from being a serious photographic tool.

FEATURES

It used to be that when you bought a camera, you got a device that took pictures. Well, not anymore! Now when you buy a camera, you get a device that takes pictures of many different sizes, with many different color options and effects, using many different automated tools, and that might even shoot full-resolution video with sound. Sure, you might not need *all* these features, but for quality work, you will need many of them. Consequently, it's important to spend some time considering the quality and performance of the various hardware and software systems onboard any camera you're considering.

In this section, we're going to work through all the major options found on today's cameras. In the process, you'll get a better idea of whether each feature is valuable to you, and will learn some criteria by which you can evaluate each option.

Lenses

Your camera's lens is where the whole imaging process starts. (Actually, your light source is where the whole imaging process starts, but let's forget about that for the moment.) If you have an inferior lens that can't do a good job of focusing light onto the camera's focal plane, the quality of the camera's image sensor and internal processing software won't really matter.

If you're shopping for a point-and-shoot camera, there's some good news, thanks to the small sensor sizes used in digital point-and-shoots. Because a lens doesn't have to project a very big image to cover the very small image sensors used in point-and-shoot digital cameras, point-and-shoot lenses can be much shorter, and of much smaller diameter, than a lens for a 35 mm camera. This is great news for lens designers, because it's much easier to correct aberrations in shorter lenses with small diameters. Consequently, point-and-shoot cameras—even inexpensive ones—tend to have very good lenses. Often, the lens on a point-and-shoot digital camera will be far superior to the lens on a point-and-shoot film camera, meaning that you'll usually get *better* results from a low-end digital camera than from a low-end film camera. Of course, there are exceptions, but in general, you can expect to find point-and-shoots packing decent to very good lenses.

WANT TO SHOOT SHALLOW DEPTH OF FIELD? YOU MAY HAVE TO GET AN SLR.

As you'll learn in Chapter 7, the amount of depth of field in an image is affected by the sensor size of your camera. If you want to shoot with very shallow depth of field (to create a portrait with a blurry background, for example), you're going to have a hard time doing so with a point-and-shoot camera, do to their tiny image sensors. This is one reason you might want to consider an SLR.

If you're shopping for an SLR, you have good news of a different variety: because you can change the lenses on your camera, you have many more options in terms of quality, features, and focal lengths. What's more, you don't have to commit to a particular feature set or quality when you make your initial purchase. If you're on a budget, you can select a starter lens to begin with, and then upgrade with better lenses later.

Evaluating Lens Image Quality

As with other features, you should test the quality of a lens before you commit to buying a particular camera (or a particular lens, if you have an SLR). The easiest way to test a lens is to shoot some images with it and look for aberrations and image-quality troubles. There are a number of different types of lens aberrations ranging from *astigmatism* to *comas,* but in a modern, high-quality lens, you need to worry about only a few types of issues. When you look for aberrations or image-quality troubles, be sure to test the lens throughout its zoom range. When evaluating a lens, consider the following:

- First, check for general **focus and sharpness**. How well does the lens render fine detail? Are the corners of the image as sharp as the middle? Be sure to check throughout the camera's zoom range. Often, as you zoom to a wider (shorter) focal length, the camera will have more trouble maintaining sharpness from corner to corner. Also, try shooting with a number of different apertures. Most cameras have an aperture "sweet spot" that yields the best focus—it's often two stops down from its widest aperture.
- Does the lens have trouble with **chromatic aberrations**? (See Chapter 4 for more on what this problem looks like.) Shooting trees or telephone wires against a bright sky is often a good way to force chromatic aberrations. This problem usually occurs only at wider—sometimes fully wide—angles. Even the best lens can suffer from chromatic aberration, so don't immediately discount a camera if you see some purple or red fringing around an object. Rather, try to assess how severe the problem is, how extreme your shooting situation is (in other words, will you realistically be shooting in such a situation very often), and whether the problem is actually bad enough to show up in your final output, whatever it may be.
- **Vignetting** is a darkening of the image around the edges and corners that usually occurs at the extremes of the camera's zoom range. Look for changes in brightness across the image and throughout the zoom range.
- **Barrel and pincushion distortions** (Figure 4.9) are spatial distortions of your image that are similar to a funhouse mirror. **Barrel distortion** causes a straight vertical line to be bowed outward toward the edges of the frame; **pincushion distortion** causes a straight vertical line to be bowed inward toward the middle of the frame. These distortions are more prevalent at the wide angles of your zoom lens and will definitely occur if you attach a telephoto, wide-angle, or **fisheye** attachment to your lens.

- The **contrast** produced by a lens might vary when you are using smaller apertures. Try shooting some high-contrast areas using the widest and narrowest apertures of the lens.
- Wider-angle lenses are more prone to **lens flares**. (See Figure 5.23.) Zoom the lens to its widest angle and shoot some tests into bright light sources (but never point a camera directly at the sun!) to test for flares. If a lens has a propensity to flare, be aware that you can often prevent flares through the use of a lens hood.

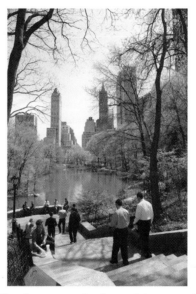

FIGURE 5.23   This lens flare is an example of one of the types of flares that can occur as light bounces around inside the lens. Better lenses are less prone to flaring.

- Lens quality can also affect **color reproduction**. If you find that a camera tends to shoot images that are a little "warm" or "cold," the trouble might be in the lens.

It is impossible to eliminate all aberrations in a lens. Your goal in testing a lens is to determine what kinds of troubles it has, how bad those troubles are, if you think they will affect the type of shooting you tend to do, and if you can work around them. For example, all aberrations except for distortions can be reduced by stopping down the lens, and many kinds of distortion can be eliminated using special software.

When looking at cameras, you'll often see specifications that describe a lens as being *aspherical*. This simply means that the lens is not a perfectly round hemisphere. Aspherical lenses contain some nonspherical elements that are designed to eliminate certain aberrations. You might also see that a lens has some type of *coating* on it that usually serves to reduce reflections and flares.

In addition to the quality issues described previously, you'll want to consider the following lens features when evaluating a point-and-shoot camera:

What is the focal length range of the lens? You can't change lenses on a point-and-shoot camera, so you're stuck with whatever focal length range the built-in lens has. For maximum flexibility, you'll want as wide a range as possible; however, this will probably mean buying a bigger camera. Think about the type of shooting you like to do, and make sure your candidate cameras offer a focal length range that will support your shooting style.

Does the lens support add-on extensions? Some point-and-shoot lenses support add-on extensions such as telephoto or wide-angle adapters. These can often provide you with the extra focal length range you need, without having to go to a larger camera with a bigger lens. If you think you'll want such extensions, be sure to consider how easy they are to attach and remove when evaluating the camera.

Does the lens have threads? A *threaded lens* allows you to add filters, which can be essential for achieving certain effects. Some cameras require a special adapter for attaching threaded components. If you're considering such a camera, be sure to add in the cost of the extra adapter, and try to determine how easy it is to attach and remove. In addition, find out if you have to re-move your attachments before you can remove the adapter, because these actions will make the camera a bit more difficult to use.

Does the camera have an electronic or manual zoom control? On a longer lens, a manual zoom mechanism—usually a rotatable ring on the camera's lens—is better than an electronic mechanism because it allows for a finer degree of control, faster zooming, and less use of battery power. On smaller cameras, manual zoom controls are simply not possible.

Is the camera's zoom control proportional? A *proportional zoom control* varies zoom speed depending on how far you push the zoom button. In other words, if you push the zoom control just a little way "in," the lens zooms in slowly. If you press it a long way "in," the lens zooms in quickly. Proportional zoom controls make it easier to make fine adjustments and to quickly get the lens zoomed to the area you're targeting.

Interchangeable Lenses

If you have opted for a digital SLR that supports interchangeable lenses, your lens evaluations are going to be more complicated simply because you have so many more choices. You'll have the option to use lenses that can go much wider or much more telephoto than what you'll find on cameras with built-in lenses. You'll have options for many different zoom ranges, and *prime* lenses—non-zoom lenses of a fixed focal length. And, of course, you'll be able to choose from a selection of lenses with drastically varied quality.

When evaluating a lens for a digital SLR camera, you'll want to consider all the same issues discussed in the previous section. In addition, however, you'll need to weigh the following factors particular to interchangeable lenses:

Focal length: Whether you're looking at a zoom or prime lens, your first concern is to get a lens that provides the focal length you want. If your camera has an image sensor that's smaller than a piece of 35 mm film (and currently, almost all digital SLRs have smaller image sensors), remember that the effective crop of any lens will be narrower than it would be on a 35 mm camera. For example, many Canon EOS SLRs have a focal length multiplier of 1.6x, meaning any lens you use will have an effective crop that is 1.6 times greater than it would be if mounted on a 35 mm camera.

Image stabilized: Many lenses include image stabilization hardware. These mechanisms track the jitter you produce with your hands and automatically alter certain optical properties of the lens to counteract the effects of that jitter. Therefore, if you jitter to the left, the lens alters itself to bend the light passing through the lens back to the right to counteract the jitter. Image stabilization is not meant to be a substitute for a tripod. Instead, it provides enough stability to make it easier to frame a shot when using an extremely telephoto lens, and can allow you to shoot in much lower light, with slower shutter speeds, without worrying about hand shake. Stabilized lenses will often rate the degree of stabilization in terms of a number of stops. For example, a lens that provides three stops' worth of stabilization will let you shoot with a shutter speed that is three stops slower than what you would normally expect for that focal length. We'll discuss this in more detail in Chapter 7.

Size of the lens: Obviously, you'll want to consider the size and weight of a lens, simply to assess whether you really want to lug it around with you. With a very large-diameter lens—such as an extreme wide-angle lens—you'll want to also check to see if the lens casts a shadow when used with the camera's on-board flash.

A reduced-sensor SLR can be very generous to a lens. For example, some wide-angle lenses are susceptible to lens flares and vignetting around the edges and corners. However, because a reduced-sensor SLR captures only the middle portion of the lens, these troubles are often cropped away. (If you're using a lens designed for a reduced-sized sensor, you'll be capturing edge-to-edge and will need to check the edges for flares and vignetting.)

That said, a cheaper lens that fares sufficiently on a 35 mm film camera might not perform as well on a high-res digital camera, simply because a high-res camera requires a lens that can focus well to a very tiny area.

STABILIZED SENSORS

While some vendors, such as Canon and Nikon, make lenses that have built-in stabilizing mechanisms, a few vendors, such as Sony and Pentax, have opted to stabilize the *image sensor* itself. The sensor sits on a movable plate that can be shifted from side to side and

→

up and down to compensate for any jitter introduced by your hand. The advantage of a stabilized sensor is that it will work with any lens you attach to the camera. The disadvantage is that stabilization mechanisms usually need to be tweaked to a particular focal length for optimal performance. Consequently, you'll typically find that sensor stabilization methods don't yield as much stabilizing effect as stabilized lenses. In addition, with a stabilized sensor, the stabilization is happening *after* you've looked at the image, which means that a stabilized sensor offers no advantage when trying to shoot with an extremely telephoto lens. A stabilized lens, on the other hand, provides a steady view while framing, which can make telephoto shooting much easier.

Check Your Speed

Whether you're looking at an SLR with removable lenses or a point-and-shoot, you'll want to give a little thought to lens speed. As discussed in Chapter 3, the "speed" of a lens simply refers to the widest aperture to which it can be opened. Therefore, a lens that can open to f/1.2 is a very fast lens. With such a wide aperture, it can gather a lot of light in a short amount of time, meaning you can use faster shutter speeds. In addition, you can shoot with shallower depth of field.

Zoom lenses typically have an aperture range that corresponds to their focal length. So, you might see a zoom lens that lists its speed as f4–5.6. This means it's f/4 at the wide end, and 5.6 at the telephoto end. You probably won't be able to find a point-and-shoot camera with a zoom lens that's a constant speed across its range. In fact, you probably won't have many options, speed-wise, when shopping for a point-and-shoot. However, your depth of field options are limited on a point-and-shoot anyway, due to the smaller sensor size.

If you're shopping for a lens for an SLR, you have many more speed options. In general, speed differences will be one of the primary factors that impact a lens' price. For example, Canon sells an excellent 50 mm f/1.8 lens for under $100. Their 50 mm f/1.4 lens, though, sells for several hundred dollars. Making a fast lens is not easy, so you'll pay a price for it. In addition, faster zoom lenses are usually much larger than their speedier counterparts. Therefore, if you want speedy lenses, you'll need to balance price/weight against slower speed.

Another option is to shoot with prime lenses, which allow you to buy a speedy lens in a smaller package. You won't have a choice of focal lengths, of course, and you'll still pay a premium.

Bokeh. A very fast lens will be capable of shooting with shallow depth of field. How shallow will vary depending on the focal length of the lens and the size of your image sensor. You'll use shallow depth of field when you want to blur out the background behind a subject to isolate that subject, and bring more attention to it. Believe it or not, different lenses blur with different qualities. You might think that blur is just blur, but some lenses generate a prettier, smoother blur with no weird artifacts or shapes. The term *bokeh* simply refers to the quality of the out-of-focus areas in an image. Bokeh is a completely subjective quality, with no real definition or quantifiable attributes. So, when you hear people speaking about a lens having "great bokeh," they simply mean that the quality of its background blur is very attractive to them.

OF DIGITAL LENSES

As you saw in Figure 5.22, the very rear element of a lens does not extend all the way to the focal plane of a camera. You have to have room for the shutter and, in the case of an SLR camera, the mirror that bounces light up into the viewfinder. However, if you can position a lens closer to the focal plane, you can make a lens smaller (which often equates to higher quality, since there's less glass in the lens). Because of this, some camera makers have created new lens mounts for their digital SLRs. Canon's EOS-S-compatible SLR bodies, and Nikon's DX-compatible SLR bodies both use a smaller mirror, which means there's more space inside the camera. Thanks to this extra space, S and DX lenses can have a rear element that extends further into the camera, and thus closer to the image sensor. (All this is possible because digital image sensors are smaller than 35 mm film, so the lens doesn't have to cover as big an area.) At the time of writing, both the S and DX series provide an excellent selection of high-quality lenses. Fortunately, S- and DX-compatible cameras also work fine with any "normal" lenses designed for a full-frame sensor.

LENS ATTACHMENTS

Many digital cameras that have built-in lenses include support for lens attachments. These additional lens elements screw onto lens threads or attach to other special mounting devices on the lens. For a camera that doesn't have interchangeable lenses, such attachments provide a way for you to add extra wide-angle or telephoto power to your camera.

When buying any lens attachment, evaluate it carefully, checking for all the aberrations and potential problems discussed earlier. Many third-party attachments use inferior optics that yield lousy image quality.

In addition, pay attention to the following:

- Does the attachment block the optical viewfinder? Some attachments are large enough that they will obscure part of the optical viewfinder, making it difficult to frame your shot.
- Does the attachment cast a shadow when used with the camera's on-board flash?
- Does the attachment require a special adapter or step-up ring? If so, you'll need to be sure to buy one.

Finally, you'll also want to see how easy it is to attach and remove the device, including any adapters or step-up rings it might require.

A camera that supports lens attachments can be a less-expensive, and smaller, alternative to a full-blown SLR with interchangeable lenses.

Lens Rental

If you're shopping for lenses for your SLR, consider renting the lenses you're considering. Many photo stores rent SLR lenses at daily or weekly rates, which can be a great way to try out a lens and make an informed buying decision. If you don't have a rental house in your area, consider renting online from services like www.rentglass.com.

Digital Zoom

Loosely related to lenses are the *digital zooms* provided by most cameras. Evaluating a digital zoom feature is a simple two-step process:

Step 1: Turn off the digital zoom feature.
Step 2: Don't ever turn it on again.

That's it! You're done and can now go on to consider other features.

The fact is that most digital zoom features do a terrible job of acting like a zoom lens. Obviously, the camera cannot digitally increase its focal length, so these features work by cropping the image, and then scaling that cropped area up to the full size of the frame. The problem with most digital zooms is that they use bad interpolation algorithms when they scale up, so they tend to produce jagged, blocky images. Consequently, rather than using a digital zoom, it's much better to shoot the image with your camera's maximum optical zoom, and then crop and enlarge it yourself using an image editor. Most image editors provide more sophisticated interpolation options.

There are three occasions when a digital zoom can prove useful:

- If you don't have any image-editing software that is capable of cropping and up-sampling.
- If you don't want to magnify the JPEG artifacts in your image. Because the camera enlarges your image *before* compressing, digital zooms don't worsen any JPEG artifacts. Enlarging the image in an image editor will.
- If you're shooting at one of the camera's lower resolutions, a digital zoom may help. Most of the time, when you shoot at a lower resolution, the camera simply shoots at full resolution and then downsamples. Because there's more resolution to start with, using a digital zoom on a lower-resolution image often produces fine results.

If you must use a digital zoom feature, you ideally want to have one that offers good interpolation and provides a continuous range of zooming rather than fixed zoom ratios.

Focus

No matter how much you spend on a camera, you're going to get a camera with an autofocus feature. Believe it or not, using the autofocus mechanism properly is one of the biggest problems new users face when they first start shooting. Fortunately, all these mechanisms work the same way.

Using the camera's viewfinder, you place the focusing target (usually the middle of the viewfinder) on the object in your scene you want to have in focus. (See Figure 5.24.) When you press the shutter release button halfway, the camera measures the distance to that object and *locks the focus*; pressing the button the rest of the way will take the picture. (If your camera has a fixed-focus lens, you can skip this section.)

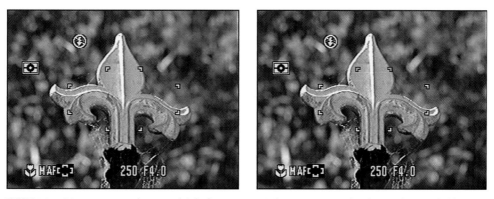

FIGURE 5.24   Many cameras have multiple focus spots. When you press the shutter button halfway, the camera determines which focus spot is on your subject, automatically focuses the lens to that point, and locks the focus. Here, the camera has selected the upper focus spot.

We'll discuss all the concerns and practices of using an autofocus system in Chapter 7. When you choose a camera, though, look for the following items:

Passive versus active autofocus: Autofocus systems that use a *passive* TTL system determine focus by looking through the lens. *Active autofocus* mechanisms employ a separate sensor outside the lens to measure distance; focus is then set accordingly. *Passive autofocus* systems are usually more accurate and have the advantage of working with lens extensions and attachments.

Focus-assist lamp: The downside to most passive TTL autofocus mechanisms is that they don't work well (or at all) in low-contrast situations. A *focus-assist lamp* (sometimes called an *autofocus-assist lamp*) is a white or red light that the camera automatically shines into your scene when there isn't enough contrast to lock focus. Look for a focus-assist lamp that can be deactivated for more discreet shooting.

Number of autofocus points: Although less-expensive cameras will always use the middle of the viewfinder as the autofocus "target," fancier cameras will usually provide several autofocus points that can be used for determining focus. The camera tries to assess what elements in the scene need to be in focus (that is, what's in the foreground and what's in the background), and selects an autofocus point accordingly. These systems often provide much more accurate focus, but they can make mistakes, so look for a camera that has the option to select an autofocus point manually or to default to a center point for focusing. Because autofocus mechanisms are typically more sensitive to horizontal features, having more image points can make up for this lack of sensitivity to vertical elements and improve the camera's capability to focus. Also, if your camera has a servo-tracking feature (the capability to automatically track and focus a moving object), having more autofocus points will result in better tracking.

Number of autofocus steps: With more autofocus steps, there are more locations a lens can set itself to in order to get focused. However, as we'll see in Chapter 7, this doesn't necessarily mean the camera will do a better job of focusing.

Special focusing aids: Through the early days of digital photography, camera makers simply migrated many systems over from their film cameras. The autofocus, and metering systems they had already built for 35 mm cameras, moved easily into their digital counterparts. These systems have been improved on over the years, but vendors have also found new ways to take advantage of the LCD screens and computing power built in to digital camera. Many cameras now feature special autofocus features that can automatically detect faces in your scene, and use that information to determine correct focus point. These systems are easy enough to evaluate: just try them. If you find that you can consistently get good focus, in varying degrees of light, and with complex compositions—your subject off-center, multiple people in one shot, etc.—there's no reason not to embrace these new technologies. However, you'll still want the option to turn these features off and return to a typical autofocus system.

Continuous Autofocus

Some cameras offer a *continuous autofocus*, which constantly refocuses as you move the camera. The advantage to this mechanism is that when you're finally ready to shoot, the camera might already be in focus. If you're considering a camera with a continuous autofocus feature, make sure it's possible to disable the feature because you might need to occasionally turn it off to save your battery.

Some cameras are now sporting a variation of continuous autofocus that automatically starts the continuous autofocus mechanism when the camera is not moving. The idea is that if the camera has stopped moving, it's probably because you're trying to line up a shot. The advantage of these systems over continuous autofocus is that they're more battery efficient because they're not continuously focus hunting.

Manual Focus

Manual focus can be a boon for times when your camera's autofocus mechanism can't lock focus, or when you want to force the camera to focus on something in particular. Unfortunately, most point-and-shoot digital cameras don't have an old-fashioned, lens-mounted manual focus ring. Instead, they typically use a special menu option that requires you to dial in the distance to your subject or use buttons on your camera to manually focus the lens. Although these controls are adequate, the lack of high-quality viewfinders on most point-and-shoots can make manual focusing difficult or impossible.

At the very least, try to get a camera that has a manual infinity focus lock. This will allow you to lock the focus on infinity, which can be a real battery and time-saver when you know you'll be shooting objects that are far away.

Shutters and Apertures

Your camera's shutter and iris controls allow you to change exposure to control the brightness or darkness of your image, and the depth of field and motion-stopping power. Whereas film cameras have mechanical irises and shutters—actual metal, cloth, or plastic mechanisms that open and close—digital cameras often use different methods, such as electronic shutters, for exposing the image sensor. Rather than having a mechanism that opens and closes in front of the sensor, a camera with an electronic shutter simply turns its image sensor on and off for the appropriate length of time. One shutter mechanism is not necessarily better than another, as long as the camera offers the shutter-speed control you need to take the kind of shots you want.

All digital cameras offer an *automatic exposure* feature, which will automatically calculate the appropriate shutter speed and aperture at the time you take a picture. Some cameras, though, also offer manual controls for shutter speed and aperture. When you are assessing a camera's manual overrides, make sure the camera offers a good range of shutter speeds—ideally ranging from a few seconds to at least 1/500th of a second. It's also nice to have a *bulb mode,* which makes the camera leave its shutter open for as long as you hold down the shutter release button. On many cameras, bulb mode is only accessible through a remote, either wired or wireless.

As in a film camera, the aperture in a digital camera is controlled by an iris, an interlocking set of metal blades whose opening can expand or contract to make a bigger or smaller aperture. Many small point-and-shoot digital cameras have only two apertures, usually f2.8 and f5.6 or f8 and f11. These cameras make up for their lack of aperture options by varying shutter speed. Although this configuration doesn't limit the conditions under which you can shoot, it does possibly hobble your creative possibilities. Ideally, you want a camera with more aperture options.

Alternately, some small cameras use their iris as a shutter, simply snapping it open and closed to make an exposure. The downside to this scheme is that at higher shutter speeds, the camera might require you to use smaller apertures, because a wider aperture would take too long to close and would prevent the camera from achieving the desired shutter speed. Again, if you want maximum creative flexibility, this type of mechanism might be too limiting.

Also, some cameras limit their minimum aperture to f8 in an effort to avoid certain diffraction artifacts caused by the camera's lens. The automatic meters in these cameras, therefore, tend to favor wide-open apertures. These factors can limit your creative flexibility, so you might want to do a little investigation when evaluating a camera.

On an SLR, you won't need to worry about any of these issues. SLRs have real shutters and apertures and offer a much larger range of shutter speeds and apertures. In general, most SLRs will offer far more shutter speed range than you'll need for most shooting situations. If you know you need a fast shutter speed for the type of shooting you do, you'll want to weigh that into your decision. Many SLRs offer shutter speeds up to 1/8000th of a second.

Similarly, if you like doing long exposure work—for low-light shooting, infrared, or astrophotography, for example—you'll want to choose a camera with a bulb mode. You might also want to check into the camera's remote control options. For long exposure work, a remote control that offers a shutter lock can be essential.

Image Control

In a film camera, once you select a type of film, you're stuck with the characteristics of that film until you shoot the entire roll. Different digital cameras have particular imaging characteristics, but most include a number of controls that let you fine-tune how you want the camera to process and store images.

Image Resolution and Compression Controls

Almost all digital cameras offer a choice of resolutions. In addition to the camera's maximum resolution, most cameras offer lower-resolution options that allow you to fit more images onto the camera's storage card. Even though you might have spent the extra money for a 7- or 8-megapixel camera, you might not always need to shoot at full resolution. For example, if you need to shoot images for the Web (and you're *sure* you'll never want to print them), your storage will go much farther if you shoot at *VGA* or *XGA* resolution (that is, 640 × 480 pixels or 800 × 600 pixels, respectively) than if you shoot at the camera's full resolution.

For maximum flexibility, you want to choose a camera that provides a range of switchable resolutions. Most cameras offer at least full resolution, an intermediate resolution, and two Web-quality low resolutions (usually VGA and XGA).

Put Your Money Where Your Storage Goes

Nowadays, digital camera storage is so cheap that there's really no reason not to always shoot at the highest resolution your camera provides. In other words, instead of trying to conserve space on your storage card, just buy some additional cards. By shooting at full resolution, you'll have the option to enlarge parts of your images, and if you decide later that you want to print your images, you'll have the resolution you need to get a good print.

Image Compression

Compression can save a tremendous amount of storage space, but can also adversely affect image quality. Ideally, your camera will offer a range of compression settings, from a high-quality JPEG compression to a really squeezed, low-quality JPEG compression that yields very small files. JPEG compressors that deliver 3:1 or 4:1 compression ratios are considered high quality. Lower-quality JPEG compression typically provides ratios of 10:1 or 20:1.

Compression settings are not something you'll change often. In fact, you'll probably change them only if you start to run out of storage. Ideally, you want a camera that offers the flexibility to mix and match different image sizes and compression settings. At the very least, you want two or three compression settings for each resolution setting on the camera.

On many digital cameras, the best-quality JPEG settings are so good that they're indistinguishable from uncompressed images. Nevertheless, certain shooting conditions leave your images especially susceptible to JPEG artifacts. Areas of complex contrast, such as foliage and leaves, and areas of broad, flat color, such as skies, are often prone to bad artifacting. Having an uncompressed option can be a lifesaver if you find yourself shooting under these circumstances.

Raw Files and Uncompressed Files

If image quality is your highest concern and storage is of little consequence, you'll want to get a camera that can also store an uncompressed image, usually a raw, or TIFF file. Although these files are typically very large—roughly 8 megabytes for a raw file on an 8-megapixel camera—they offer many advantages over JPEG files.

Remember that your camera works by taking data from the pixels on the image sensor (which is usually 12 or 14 bits of data per pixel) and interpolating it up to 16 bits per pixel before processing, compressing, and storing it on your camera's storage card. In raw mode, the camera stores the *original* information that came directly off the sensor. Since raw files are not downsampled to 8 bits of color per pixel, the way JPEG files are, they preserve all the color information your camera is capable of capturing.

If a camera doesn't have a raw mode, it might provide a TIFF mode. However, because raw data has not been interpolated (you do the interpolation later, using your computer), it's usually significantly smaller than a full, uncompressed TIFF file. For example, a raw 2048 × 1536 pixel image usually comes out to around 3.9 MB, whereas a 2048 × 1536 TIFF image typically weighs in around 9.4 MB. TIFF files don't offer the editing flexibility and options raw files provide, but they *are* free from compression artifacts.

If you're not sure if you want to make the leap into working with raw files, you might want to look for a camera that can save raw and JPEG files at the same time. In this mode, when you shoot a picture, a raw file, and a normal JPEG file that has been processed according to your camera's current settings, are stored on your card. If you need to quickly review or use an image, you can simply use the JPEG file. For more serious editing work, you can turn to the raw file when you're ready.

Because raw files are so large, some cameras simply can't muster the processing power to do anything else while they're writing a raw file to a storage card. After shooting a raw image, these cameras will lock up and not be capable of shooting another image until the raw file is stored. Obviously, this is hardly conducive to rapid shooting. So, if you plan to shoot lots of raw files, be sure to try a few shots in raw mode to see how quickly the camera can handle repetitive raw shooting.

We'll discuss raw files in more detail in Chapter 12, "Raw Conversion."

Macro Mode

Most point-and-shoot digital cameras include a special macro mode for shooting extremely close objects. (See Figure 9.19.) Digital point-and-shoot cameras fare much better than most 35 mm cameras when it comes to macro photography. Because they have tiny lenses with a deep depth of field, digital macro photographers have a focus advantage over cameras with larger lenses. Some digital cameras can focus on an object as close as 2 cm away! In addition, movable LCD screens can make the physical process of macro photography much simpler.

When evaluating a macro mode, try to get a sense for how close you can get the camera to your subject and still lock focus. Also, some macro modes have a focal length "sweet spot." That is, you'll get better results when you zoom the lens to a particular part of its zoom range. Some cameras provide a meter that indicates when you're in the ideal macro zone.

Sharpness, Saturation, and Contrast Controls

Many digital cameras include adjustable levels of sharpness, saturation, and contrast. Technically, these settings have nothing to do with exposure. Rather, they control the post-processing your camera performs before storing the image. The idea of "too much" sharpening might seem strange at first, but as you saw in Chapter 4, it is possible to oversharpen an image. Similarly, the default settings on some cameras yield images that can be oversaturated. Adjusting these parameters lets you tailor your camera to your personal tastes and to the needs of particular shooting situations. (See Figure 5.25.)

Aspect Ratio

The ratio of an image's length to its width is called the *aspect ratio*. Most point-and-shoot digital cameras use the same 4:3 aspect ratio your computer screen and television use, but some—and almost all SLRs—use the 3:2 aspect ratio of 35 mm film. (See Figure 5.26.)

Some cameras offer a choice of either aspect ratio. (See Figure 5.27.) However, many of these cameras achieve the wider 3:2 aspect ratio by simply shooting a cropped version of the camera's native 4:3 ratio. Therefore, when you shoot 3:2, you're shooting lower-resolution images. It's often better to simply shoot 4:3 and crop the image later. If you prefer a particular aspect ratio, you'll want to choose a camera that can shoot with those dimensions.

Some cameras even offer the option of an extremely wide 16:9 aspect ratio (the same as HD TV). Many of these cameras achieve 16:9 through a crop of their original 4:3 image, but *some* cameras, such as the Panasonic Lumix LX 2, have a true 16:9

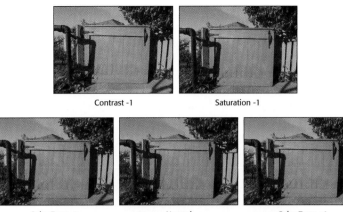

Contrast -1   Saturation -1

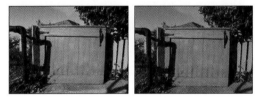

Color Tone -1   Normal   Color Tone +1

Contrast +1   Saturation +1

FIGURE 5.25   If your camera supports different contrast, saturation, and/or color settings, you can dramatically change the camera's color qualities. All photos shown here were shot using full-automatic mode. The only difference was the change in settings noted beneath each image.

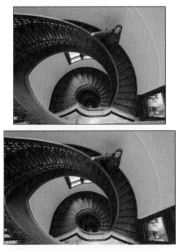

FIGURE 5.26   Most digital cameras use the same 4:3 aspect ratio as your computer monitor. Some cameras offer the 3:2 aspect ratio of 35 mm film.

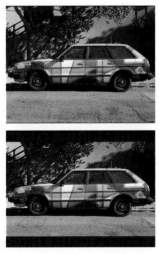

FIGURE 5.27   Some cameras offer a choice of aspect ratios. Usually, the wider choice is nothing more than a cropped version of the normal 4:3 aspect ratio. It is better to shoot full-screen and do the cropping later.

image sensor. A switch on the front of the lens lets you easily change from 16:9 to 3:2 or 4:3. The camera is at its maximum resolution when shooting at 16:9, and at lower, cropped resolutions when shooting at the smaller aspect ratios.

Flash

No matter what level of camera you are considering, most units will have a built-in flash. Obviously, bigger cameras will have a larger, more powerful flash unit, but even small cameras can offer good flash hardware.

Flash photography is one of the most difficult things for any camera to handle, and digital cameras are no exception. Consequently, it's important to carefully evaluate a camera's flash system before you buy.

There are a few simple issues to clarify up front:

What is the range of the flash? Because of their small size, most built-in flashes have a range of only around 10 to 15 feet. Although this is fine for most snapshot situations, for more serious work you'll need additional lighting. If you're looking at a particular small camera, pay close attention to flash coverage. Because smaller cameras have such small flash units, it's sometimes difficult for them to cover even a mid-sized room with their built-in flash.

Does the flash produce a color cast? Do some simple flash tests to ensure that flash pictures are not plagued by weird color casts. Unfortunately, some cameras have trouble calculating a proper white balance when shooting with a flash.

Does the camera have a hot shoe or external flash sync connection? For maximum flash flexibility and control, you want a *hot shoe* for connecting an external flash. (See Figure 5.28.) These standard connections are usually designed to work with specific flash units made by the manufacturer. If the camera doesn't have an actual hot shoe (or is too small to have one), look for a connection for an *external flash sync*, which will allow you to connect an external flash (again, usually a specific model) to the camera using a small cable. You'll probably need to buy some type of bracket to hold the flash.

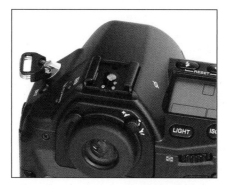

FIGURE 5.28   For serious flash work, you'll want a camera with a hot shoe or external flash sync connector.

Where is the internal flash positioned? Ideally, you want a flash that is as far from the lens as possible. If the flash is too close to the lens, the camera will be more susceptible to the red-eye effect. We'll discuss this in more detail in Chapter 14, "Imaging Tactics."

What flash modes does the camera offer? Look for a camera that offers a completely automatic mode, where the camera decides when to use the flash; a *force flash* or *fill flash* mode, which allows you to force the flash to fire to provide a slight fill light; and a *red-eye reduction* mode, which reduces the chance of red-eye in your image by first firing a short flash to close down the irises in the eyes of your subject. Many cameras also offer a *slow sync* mode that lets you combine flash photography with long shutter speeds to capture more background detail when shooting in low light. Be sure the camera lets you specify whether the flash fires at the beginning or end of the exposure. And, of course, you want the capability to turn off the flash altogether.

Does the camera offer control over flash intensity? Many cameras let you control how strong the flash will be by specifying a *flash exposure compensation*, usually measured in f-stops, or fractions of a stop. Given the difficulty many cameras have with flash metering, this manual override can be essential to getting good flash photos.

How quickly does the flash recycle? Try to get a feel for how frequently you can fire the flash. This will vary depending on how strong the camera's batteries are, but some flashes are simply faster at recharging than others.

In addition to the physical specifications of the camera's flash, you'll want to assess how well the camera meters and white balances when you use the flash. The best test of a flash's performance is to shoot pictures of people's faces indoors under a slight mix of lighting. The human eye is well tuned to flesh tones, so pictures of faces make a good test of how well a flash system is reproducing color.

Look at the overall exposure of your image. A poor flash system will overexpose the highlights, resulting in bright white smears instead of smoothly gradated highlights. Skin tones will often go pale or wash out when they are shot with a less-capable flash system. A flash that is too bright will also cast harsh shadows across and behind your subject.

Look at the overall color tone of the image. Is there a color cast of some kind? If you're in a room with strong lights (usually incandescent, or tungsten, lights), your camera might choose to favor those lights when it white balances, resulting in an image with slightly blue highlights. If your image ends up with a slight yellow cast to its highlights, the camera probably favored the on-board flash when it was white balancing.

If your camera has a special manual white balance setting for use with a flash, be sure to switch to that setting and try a few shots. You might get better results.

SLR shoppers will want to consider the external flash systems that are available for each candidate camera. In addition to the usual price and power concerns, you'll also want to consider these issues:

- Does the camera offer TTL metering with the hot shoe?
- Can multiple external flash units be used in a master/slave configuration? If so, can the camera's built-in flash be used as a master?

- Does the flash have a zoom capability that can read distance information from your camera's lens?
- Can the flash be swiveled and tilted? At the very least, you want a tilt for bouncing the flash off the ceiling. With a swivel, you'll have the additional option of bouncing the flash off walls and other reflectors.

You'll learn a lot more about flash photography in Chapter 9. Before you invest in an external flash system, take the time to read that chapter.

Body Design and Construction

You'll want to spend some time considering the body design and construction of your potential purchase. Poor design can make a camera's controls difficult to use, which can often cause you to miss shots. And, of course, flimsier construction can shorten the life of your camera.

Modern cameras can be made of any number of materials, from metal to carbon fiber to aluminum to plastic. Obviously, sturdier materials are more durable (and usually feel better in terms of finish and heft), but even a predominantly plastic body can hold up well in rough conditions.

When you are assessing a camera, try to get a feel for the quality of its build. If you lightly squeeze it, does it creak or does it feel solid? A creaky camera might just get creakier—and possibly more fragile—as its screws and joints loosen. If the camera has a split body or flip-out LCD screen, try to get an idea of the durability of the swiveling mechanism. Will it hold up to normal use, or might it wear out?

Digital cameras can often have strange designs, so make sure your camera sports a finish and moldings that make it comfortable to hold onto and difficult to drop. Finger moldings and rubberized components can make an otherwise odd shape comfortable to hold. If you're a nature photographer who spends a lot of time shooting in cold weather, you may want to consider how easy the camera is to operate with gloves, and whether it has water-resistant seals and seams. Smaller cameras can be particularly difficult to hold onto and use comfortably, so spend some time determining how comfortable the camera is to use with one or both hands, and make certain it includes a wrist strap.

Doors and port covers can be especially fragile components. Check the battery compartment door and media card door for durability and easy access. (See Figure 5.29.) You'll be using these mechanisms *a lot*, so make sure they can stand up to repeated openings and closings. In addition, make sure you can get to them in a hurry if you need to, even when the camera is mounted on a tripod. Rubber or plastic port covers (such as what might go over a battery charging port or a USB port) are often the flimsiest part of a camera. Try to get a feeling for the weaknesses of these covers. Although you won't be able to improve them, they might at least last a bit longer if you are aware of how easily they can be broken off.

Heft is often a concern for more serious photographers. A heavier camera, although a bit of a pain to lug around, is usually easier to shoot with, because extra weight makes for a more stable shot. If you're used to a film camera with a good deal of weight, you might want to look for the same thing in a digital camera.

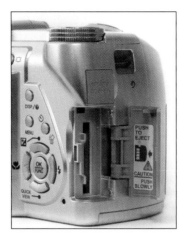

FIGURE 5.29 Pay attention to the doors and covers a camera uses for its media, batteries, and ports. You'll be opening and closing these a lot, so make sure they're sturdy and durable.

Finally, try to get an idea as to how much of the camera's body and internal chassis are made of metal. As we'll see in Chapter 9, heat can greatly degrade image quality, and components such as LCD screens and large-capacity memory cards can produce a lot of heat. Metal substructures and chassis can serve to dissipate heat that might otherwise affect image quality.

Status LCDs

Not to be confused with your camera's full-color viewfinder/playback LCD is the small status LCD that might be present on the top of the camera. These screens are used for displaying current camera settings and the number of shots remaining.

Some cameras skip these displays and assume you'll simply get this information from the viewfinder LCD. However, if you're in bright sunlight or if your batteries are running low, you might not want to activate your main LCD just to find out if your flash is turned on. Most important, having a permanent display of camera status makes for faster, more convenient shooting.

Figure 5.30 shows a typical, full-featured status LCD.

If a camera *does* use its main LCD as a status display, you'll want to check that it displays the status information you want. Also, if the camera has an optical viewfinder, be sure you can easily turn the LCD screen off when shooting, so the glare doesn't corrupt your field of view. Finally, make sure the screen is visible and readable in direct sunlight.

Tripod Mount

This might seem like a superfluous item to bring up for discussion, but a poor tripod mount can really mess up a shoot, if you're trying particular techniques. Any

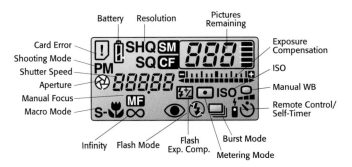

Battery   Resolution   Pictures Remaining

Card Error
Shooting Mode
Shutter Speed
Aperture
Manual Focus
Macro Mode

Exposure Compensation
ISO
Manual WB
Remote Control/Self-Timer

Infinity   Flash Mode   Flash Exp. Comp.   Burst Mode   Metering Mode

FIGURE 5.30   You'll want your camera's LCD status display to show a full range of status and setting information. When you're shooting on the go, you don't want to have to dig into the camera's menu system to check on a particular setting.

experienced photographer will tell you that there is a difference between a good tripod mount and a bad one. The following features make for a good tripod mount:

Metal construction: A tripod mount is a simple screw socket recessed into the bottom of the camera. (Some tripod mounts also include additional stabilizing holes.) If the screw socket is made of plastic, it can be very easy to strip out the screw threads by forcing the tripod in at the wrong angle. Even if you're always very careful, fragile plastic threads can wear out with repeated use. Look for a metal screw mount.

Positioned along the lens axis: Ideally, you want a tripod mount that is positioned so the camera will pan (rotate) around the axis of its focal plane. (See Figure 5.31.) Such a tripod is required for shooting panoramas. If you're not serious about panoramic shooting, though, an off-axis tripod mount shouldn't be a deal-breaker.

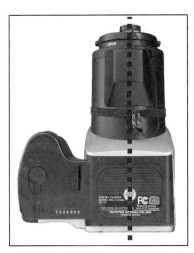

FIGURE 5.31   Ideally, you want a tripod mount that lies on the same axis as the lens.

Positioned so you can remove the batteries and media: Once you put a camera on a tripod for a shoot, you don't want to have to dismount it to change batteries or storage media. Make sure the battery and media doors are unblocked when the camera is tripod mounted.

Image Buffering

As you'll recall from Chapter 2, after a digital camera exposes its CCD, the image data is passed to a special on-board computer for processing. After it is interpolated for color, white balanced, sharpened, and de-noised (among other things), the data is compressed and then stored on the camera's storage device. All this processing can take a lot of time, which means your camera can be too busy to take any more pictures.

Fortunately, most cameras include special memory buffers (and sometimes separate processors) to handle the processing of an image, which frees up the camera to shoot again immediately. Ideally, you want an *image buffer* that can hold at least five or six full-resolution shots. Odds are that you won't be shooting more than that in quick succession, but if you are, you'll need to use a special "continuous" shooting mode.

Continuous Shooting

Many cameras offer special modes for shooting a rapid series—or *burst*—of images. With speeds varying from a single frame to 5 to 10 frames per second, these features are ideal for shooting sports or fast-moving objects. But burst shooting is handy for more than just sports or nature photography. Shooting bursts of people is the best way to capture a particular moment or the best expression. By shooting a burst, you can grab a series of frames, and then pick the best one of the bunch.

Referred to as *burst, continuous*, or *drive mode*, continuous shooting modes usually work just like an autowinder on a film camera. Just press the shutter button, hold it down, and the camera will shoot as quickly as it can. (See Figure 5.32.)

Note that some cameras can achieve their full burst speed only when they are shooting at a lower resolution. If you want full print quality from your burst images, make sure your camera's continuous mode supports the full resolution of your camera. Note, too, that some cameras can shoot up to only a certain number of shots before they have to stop and flush the series of images out to storage. Be sure to investigate the maximum number of burst shots that can be taken at once.

Continuous Flash Shots

Most cameras can't use a flash when shooting in continuous mode, because there isn't enough time for the flash to recharge. However, some cameras can manage roughly one frame per second when shooting with the built-in flash. If you have a job that needs continuous flash shots, keep an eye out for this feature.

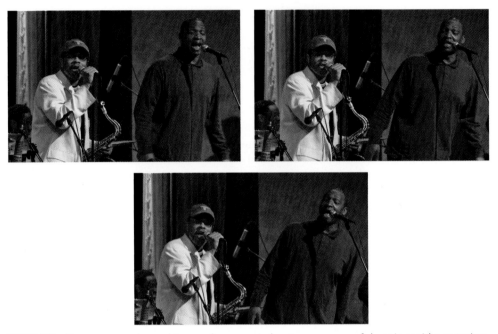

FIGURE 5.32 If your camera has a drive mode, you can shoot a sequence of shots in rapid succession. Not all cameras support burst shooting at full resolution.

Movie Mode

Many digital cameras offer the capability to shoot movies, in either AVI, QuickTime, or MPEG format. Most cameras provide movie modes that can shoot 640 × 480 video at 30 frames per second including sound, with a duration that's limited only by the amount of storage space on your card. In addition, the compression used in these modes is often better than what you'll get out of a DV video camera!

Most movie modes work the same way: you simply press the shutter button and the camera begins recording; press it again and recording stops.

When you are assessing a camera's movie mode, you'll want to look at maximum frame size, maximum recording time, and quality of the compression. In addition, you might want to see if the camera can zoom while recording video—many cameras cannot zoom in video mode. If you want maximum flexibility when shooting video, you might want this feature. However, if you're really serious about video, you should buy a video camera, rather than hinging your still camera buying decision on video features.

Finally, note that some cameras require special flash cards rated for a specific speed to record video. These cards are usually a little pricier. So, if you want to ensure video capability, you may need to choose your storage card very carefully.

Black and White

Many digital cameras offer special black-and-white modes for shooting grayscale images. Because you can use your image-editing program to convert a color image to grayscale, and because a black-and-white image takes the same amount of storage space as a color image does, you might wonder why you would want to shoot in black and white. After all, isn't it better to shoot in color and have the *option* of black-and-white images later?

The biggest advantage of a dedicated black-and-white mode is that it lets you immediately see your image in black and white. Learning to visualize scenes in black and white can be difficult, so having an on-the-fly black-and-white view of a scene can be very helpful for the beginning shooter. Some cameras even offer built-in processing that mimics the types of lens filters film photographers have traditionally used to improve contrast in black-and-white photos.

Finally, if speedy grayscale workflow is essential, and you don't want to spend time performing conversions by hand, a camera with a built-in black-and-white mode can be very handy.

Self-Timers and Remote Controls

At some point, you've probably owned a film camera that had a self-timer on it. You know: you set the timer and then run as fast as you can to try to get in the shot and look natural in the five seconds or so you have before the camera fires. Most digital cameras have the same type of feature.

Some cameras also offer wired or wireless remote controls that provide zoom and shutter controls. (See Figure 5.33.) These remotes facilitate self-portraits, and serve as a shutter release for long-exposure images. If remote operation is important to you, consider the following:

- Make sure the range of the remote is long enough for your typical remote-shooting jobs.
- For wireless remotes, you'll ideally want to have an infrared sensor on both the front and back of your camera.
- If you will be using your camera to run slide shows (through the camera's video out port), you'll want remote playback control and shooting control.
- Some remotes offer a time-lapse feature (sometimes referred to as an *intervalometer*), which will automatically take a shot at a given interval. Some intervalometers also let you specify the number of shots you want taken at each interval. This allows you to perform time-lapse bracketed sequence, when used in conjunction with your camera's autobracketing mode.
- Some remotes also offer a long-exposure timer that allows you to take longer exposures than you can manage with the camera alone. (In other words, these remotes provide a *bulb* mode to cameras that might not otherwise have them.)

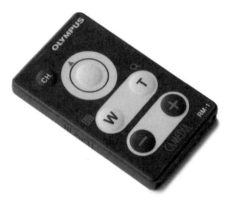

FIGURE 5.33   A wireless remote control lets you shoot hands-free, just as you would with a cable release on a film camera.

Camera Timings—or, Is Your Camera Speedy Enough to Get the Shots You Want?

Great image quality doesn't do you any good if your camera is too slow to get the shots you need. Because a digital camera must do so much calculating and processing to create an image, it's easy for it to get bogged down in ways film cameras can't. You'll *definitely* want to consider the speed and performance of a camera before you buy one. In addition to the speed of the menu system, be sure to consider and measure the following:

Boot time: How long does it take the camera to boot up? Ideally, you'll want a camera that boots up instantly, or as close to instantly as you can get, as this will afford you a better chance of getting a shot in a hurry. Check to see if the camera offers a low-power sleep mode, and test how long it takes the camera to wake up. One of the downsides to cameras with an extending lens is that they take a while to boot up because they have to take the time to extend the lens. In addition, you might not feel comfortable walking around with the camera in sleep mode, because the lens will still be extended. However, if you shut down the camera to retract the lens, you'll be forced to wait through a boot cycle when you're ready to shoot again. Consequently, for cameras with extending lenses, it's imperative to take note of boot time. You should find that most SLRs boot up nearly instantaneously.

Prefocus time: When you press your camera's shutter release halfway down, the camera will perform all its autofocusing, metering, and white balancing. (We'll discuss this *prefocusing* step more in Chapter 7.) When you test a camera, try to get a sense of how quickly it can perform these prefocusing steps.

Shutter lag: Some digital cameras have a noticeable lag between the time you press the shutter release and the time the camera actually takes a picture, even if you've already prefocused. If the *shutter lag* is long enough, you might miss the moment you were trying to capture. This is probably the most important performance characteristic to assess before you buy.

Recycling: Be sure to check how long it takes the camera to *recycle* itself after you take a shot. Ideally, you'll want to be able to shoot again immediately. Most modern cameras can recycle right away by storing the previous image in a memory buffer. When the buffer is full, you'll have to wait for it to flush out to the storage card. Be sure to test the camera's performance both before and after the buffer has filled.

Playback Options

You'll be spending a lot of time reviewing images using your camera's playback options, especially when you're in the field. Consequently, it's worth taking a little time to explore a camera's playback features. Are they easy to use? How quickly can you switch from record to playback mode?

In addition to general usability, look for the following features:

A *thumbnail* view that lets you view multiple images on-screen at once: This feature can greatly speed navigation of a large media card. (See Figure 5.34.)

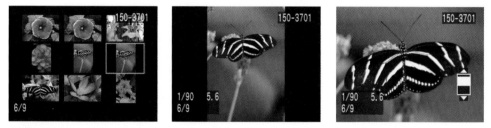

FIGURE 5.34   A thumbnail view lets you quickly see the contents of your media card. Some cameras also allow you to zoom in to an image and pan around it, making it easier to check focus and depth of field.

Zoom features that let you zoom in on an image and pan around: A good zoom feature can be a great way to ensure a shot was in focus. For panning about an image, a smooth pan is much better than a camera that restricts you to looking at specific "quadrants" of an image.

Easy deletion and locking of features: You want a speedy interface for deleting single or multiple images. When you have to free up space on a card, you don't want to miss a shot because your camera's interface is too complex.

Some cameras also offer features that automatically rotate the image so that it's upright, whether you shot it vertically or horizontally. This feature is of questionable advantage when using the camera's playback mode—after all, it's not too hard to simply tilt your camera. Most cameras store this rotation information with the picture. If your image editor or cataloging program can read it, it will automatically rotate your image.

Other cameras feature printing commands that let you print to special printers designed to work with your camera. Such features can turn your digital camera into an instant camera, but for serious work, you'll want more image-editing and printing control.

Finally, as you'll see in Chapter 8, *histograms* (computer-generated graphs of the distribution of tones in an image) can be a great exposure calculation aid. Many cameras can display a histogram of an image you've already shot. (See Figure 5.35.)

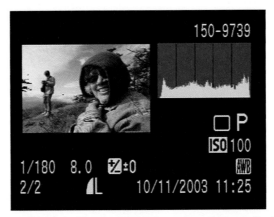

FIGURE 5.35   As you'll learn in Chapter 8, having a camera that can display a histogram is an invaluable aid for using your camera's manual exposure features.

This feature is valuable if you plan to use any manual exposure features.

Storage and Input/Output

A digital camera isn't much good if you can't get your pictures out of it. Fortunately, most cameras come equipped with a number of interfaces for moving your pictures to another device.

Transferring and Viewing Images

Today, almost all cameras come equipped with a USB connector of some kind, along with a cable to connect the camera's USB port to the standard USB port on your computer. USB is a good interface that makes for reasonably quick transfer of images. Some cameras also provide remote camera control through the USB port. If you need a computer-operated camera (either for time-lapse or other automated operations), be sure your camera's software supports remote operation.

Note that smaller cameras often achieve their small size by leaving off the USB port. Instead, they provide a special dock in which you can place the camera. You then connect the dock to your computer. There's no penalty for this, performance-wise, but it is an extra piece of gear you'll have to carry if you want image-transfer capability on the road.

USB-2 and FireWire are better alternatives to USB-1, simply because they're much faster interfaces. However, you'll find FireWire ports only on higher-end cameras, and even there it's somewhat rare. If you're concerned about transfer time, don't worry. There are plenty of ways to move images to your computer speedily.

Transfer Software

Your camera will come bundled with software for transferring images to and from your camera. Some units come with a simple *TWAIN driver* that can be used from within your editing package, whereas others offer standalone applications that allow for *media cataloging*, simple editing, and printing. Many computer operating systems (such as Apple's OS X, and Windows XP and Vista) offer automatic image transfer through a system called *Picture Transport Protocol (PTP)*. With these systems, any time you plug a camera into your computer, the OS automatically transfers all the images in the camera to your hard drive.

We'll discuss transfer software in more detail in Chapter 6, "Building a Workstation."

Video Input/Output

Most cameras provide a special video output port that lets you connect your camera to a television to view your images. Although televisions don't provide nearly enough *dynamic range* to view your images in all their glory, they do seem to be everywhere, providing a convenient way to review images when you are traveling. A video connection can also provide a convenient way to present a slide show of images, and most cameras offer some type of automatic slide-show feature that allows you to step through all the images on your camera.

Because not all countries use the same video standard, make sure you get a camera that supports the appropriate standard. Most cameras come in either NTSC or PAL versions.

Storage

Film is a clever invention because it can both capture and store an image. An image sensor, on the other hand, can only capture an image. Consequently, once your camera is done *sampling* and processing an image, it needs a place to put it.

Today, pretty much all cameras use some form of *flash memory* card. These are small wafer-like cards that house a type of RAM that doesn't require a constant stream of power (that is, it is *nonvolatile*). Therefore, after your camera has recorded an image, you can shut off the power without worrying about what has been stored on the memory card.

Flash memory cards (or just "flash cards") are a great solution to the digital camera storage problem. They're small, they can hold huge amounts of data (up to 16 GB in some cases), and can be easily swapped with other cards, just like a roll of film.

With higher-capacity cards costing less and less, it can be tempting to invest in a single card with loads of space. Bear in mind, though, that a large card is something of an "all your eggs in one basket" situation. If that card crashes, you lose everything. As such, you might consider investing, for example, in two 1 GB cards rather than a single 2 GB card. One advantage of a large-capacity card is that you won't have to interrupt your shooting to change cards. For event shooting—weddings, concerts, performances—choosing a bigger card can keep you from missing shots while you change media.

How Much Do You Need?

How much storage you need depends largely on your shooting conditions, how many pictures you typically take, how big your camera's images are, and what level of compression you're using. Obviously, if you're shooting in a computer-equipped studio, storage is less of a concern because you can dump your pictures to disk as you shoot. Similarly, if you're in the field with your laptop, you'll be able to clear your camera's storage as it fills. However, if you're planning a three-month trip through the Amazon (or even a three-hour trip to the zoo, and you tend to be shutter-happy), storage might be a bit of a concern.

If you're like most people, when you shoot film you probably take 36 exposures and get back three or four shots you like—maybe. Digital cameras are no different. For every 40 or so images you shoot, you'll maybe want to keep a third of them. However, with a digital camera, you don't have to wait until you've shot all 40 before you decide which ones you want to keep. Rather, you can delete the bad pictures as soon as you've taken them. Consequently, digital camera storage goes a little further than an equivalent number of film exposures because you'll be more selective along the way.

Unfortunately, experience is the only way to find out what your storage needs are. It's safe to assume that on a typical 2- or 3-megapixel camera, a 32 MB card will get you two dozen high-quality images. Start with this estimate and try to get an idea for what this translates into in terms of "keeper" images. Then, make sure you have an appropriate amount of storage before embarking on an important shoot.

If you're working with a higher-resolution camera, you'll need to carry more storage. With an 8-megapixel camera you'll get approximately 260 high-quality JPEG images on a 1 GB card, and roughly 100 raw images.

Currently, there are several major competing flash memory standards. For the most part, there's little practical difference between these formats, but some are more popular than others, and that can sometimes translate into cheaper card prices, and a greater number of available sizes. However, at the time of writing, flash cards are roughly the same price/megabyte no matter which format you choose.

Probably the only reason to choose a camera with a specific media type is if you need a particular capacity. For example, CompactFlash cards currently have larger capacities than any other medium. If you're going to be backcountry shooting for an extended period, larger cards will give you more shooting capacity. (Another alternative is to use a "digital wallet" device, which we'll discuss in the next chapter.)

Size Does Matter

Although vendors usually measure their flash cards in terms of megabytes, many vendors define a megabyte as being 1,000,000 bytes. Your computer, on the other hand, defines a megabyte as being 1,048,576 bytes. Therefore, when you stick a flash card in your computer, it might display a slightly smaller capacity than what you were expecting.

Although people will make arguments for one format over another, there's really not much difference. They are all equally reliable, equally speedy, and (mostly) equivalently priced.

Media Tips

There are a few things you should know about removable media. Obviously, these cards are fragile, so treat them with care. Also, consider the following issues:

- The number of images a card can hold depends on the resolution and compression settings with which you're currently shooting. These vary greatly from camera to camera, so you'll need to consult the camera's manual to find these statistics.
- The bigger the card's capacity, the more power it takes to keep it running. Consequently, in theory, smaller cards use less battery. Although it's difficult to tell if this has any bearing in the real world, switching to a smaller-capacity card when your batteries run low might garner you a few extra shots.
- Larger-capacity cards generate more heat. If you're using a tiny camera, which tends to get hot simply because of its design, it might be worth sticking to smaller-capacity cards. As you'll see later, excess heat can make your images noisier.
- If something goes wrong with a larger-capacity card, you'll lose more images than you would if you had been using a smaller-capacity card. Therefore, it might be worth buying a number of smaller cards instead of one big one.
- X-rays don't seem to matter, so feel free to take your camera with you to the airport, dentist, or thoracic surgeon.

WHAT'S IN THE BOX?

When you buy a camera, you'll want to consider everything you're getting for your money, so take some time to assess what else is bundled with your camera. (See Figure 5.36.)

Don't expect to get a huge media card with your camera. If the card that came with your camera seems small (if it came with one at all), that's probably because it is. Because of the economies of scale, adding a bigger card would usually raise the price of the camera by more than it would cost you to buy a bigger card on your own. Therefore, you should plan to buy some additional media along with your camera.

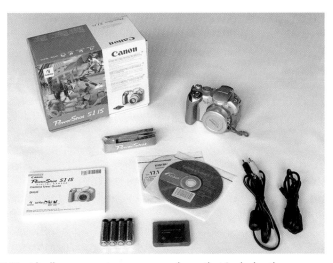

FIGURE 5.36   Ideally, you want a camera package that includes these components.

Batteries

What with the image sensor, the LCD screen, the media drive, the flash, and the motorized zoom lens, the typical digital camera demands a *lot* of power. Your camera will use one of two different battery systems: a proprietary (custom) battery, or batteries of standard size (usually AA).

Proprietary batteries: More and more vendors are using special proprietary (custom) battery packs in their cameras. The advantage to these is that they usually provide extremely long life and include special controllers that can provide accurate charge estimates, and special power-saving operations. What's more, these batteries tend to be smaller and lighter than an equivalent amount of AA or AAA batteries. On the downside, custom batteries require custom chargers, so if your battery dies in the field, you can't just run down to the corner store and buy another. Of course, you can protect yourself against this eventuality by buying an extra battery for your camera. Note that there are now many third-party battery options available for most popular digital cameras. These batteries usually offer equivalent performance and longevity at a *substantially* lower price. Even if you're wary of the quality of these batteries, they're usually so cheap that it's worth buying one just to try it out. (Camera vendors may tell you that using third-party batteries can damage your camera, although I've never personally experienced any troubles.)

Standard-size rechargeable batteries: Offering the same battery technology as a proprietary battery, standard-size rechargeable batteries offer much longer life than normal, nonrechargeable alkaline batteries, and have the advantage of universality. As better battery technology comes along (as long as it comes along in the same size), you can drop these batteries into your camera. Standard-size rechargeables are much cheaper than proprietary designs, are readily available, and in a pinch can always be replaced by alkaline batteries.

In addition to sizes, there are a number of different battery technologies available.

Alkaline batteries: Alkaline batteries are really not good for much when it comes to a digital camera. In some cases, you'll be hard-pressed to get half a dozen shots out of a set of alkalines before they are too weak to be used. Digital cameras have very specific power requirements, and as soon as a set of alkalines drops below those levels, the camera will register them as dead. You can usually continue to use them for a while in a lower-power device such as a radio or tape player. In general, use alkalines only when you absolutely have to. The cost, waste, and environmental impact just aren't worth it.

NiCAD (Nickel Cadmium) batteries: NiCADs don't deliver a lot of power, and need to be drained completely before you recharge them or they will develop a "memory" that will prevent them from being completely recharged. They're a bad choice for your digital camera.

NiMH (Nickel-Metal-Hydride) batteries: *NiMH batteries* are relatively inexpensive (usually $25 to $30 for a set of four, plus another $15 or $25 for a charger), powerful, quick to recharge, and lack a memory. In addition, NiMH batteries are more environmentally friendly than either NiCADs or alkalines. NiMH batteries are the ideal choice for the digital camera owner. In fact, buy a few sets—one for your camera, an extra set to go in your pocket, and a set to go in your recharger.

L-Ion (Lithium Ion) batteries: *L-Ion batteries* are also a good choice, although not as prevalent, and are sometimes more expensive. You can often find chargers that will charge both NiMH and L-Ion batteries.

Lithium batteries: Lithium batteries are not rechargeable but offer a lot of power for a long time. Roughly the shape of two AA-size batteries stuck together, you'll need to be sure your camera can use Lithium batteries. Although strong and long lasting, they're still disposable and are usually rather pricey.

When you shop for a recharger, you might want to consider its strength. Some chargers can recharge faster than others—in some cases, as fast as 15 or 20 minutes. In general, any recharger will probably serve you just fine. If you plan to travel to other countries, look for a recharger that can work with a range of input voltages. We'll discuss battery use, management, and performance in more detail in Chapter 7.

SPECIAL FEATURES

On top of the many features we just discussed, many vendors pack their cameras with special, unique features that can be a boon or a burden to the digital photographer. With their on-board computers and automatic functions, digital cameras can perform many tricks film cameras can't. Listed next are some unique features you might encounter in your camera shopping. Some of these features are great; others are rather silly.

Time-lapse (intervalometer): Unfortunately, only a few cameras offer a time-lapse feature that lets you program the camera to automatically shoot a picture at a predefined interval. A good time-lapse feature will let you specify an interval ranging from a few seconds to a few days. For documenting slow processes, creating animations, or producing high-quality time-lapse video, a time-lapse feature is essential. Some cameras provide time-lapse features through an external remote control.

Remote computer control: Some cameras include software that lets you control your camera from your computer via the same serial or USB link the camera uses to download images. If you need to take pictures in harsh, industrial conditions, or want to leave your camera unattended, this feature might be the answer.

Autobracketing: As we'll see in Chapter 8, *bracketing* is the process of shooting the same image with slightly different exposure settings to help ensure you get a good shot. Many cameras now feature an *autobracketing* feature that will automatically shoot four or five images with slightly different exposures each time you press the shutter release.

Dust reduction: Because the lenses on many SLRs are removable, it's possible for dust to get inside the camera. More and more cameras are including built-in dust-reduction systems that automatically shake the camera sensor (or a plate in front of the camera sensor) or use other tricks to keep the sensor clean. You won't choose a camera simply because it has a dust-reduction feature, but ending up with a camera that has one is a great convenience.

White-balance bracketing: Similar to exposure bracketing, white-balance bracketing automatically shoots a series of frames with slightly altered white balance in each shot. For tricky lighting situations where you're unsure of what the proper white balance should be, this feature can help you get the right color. However, it's not a deal-breaking feature you absolutely have to have.

Focus bracketing: This feature does the same thing as exposure or white-balance bracketing, but alters the focus slightly in each shot. To be honest, this is kind of a silly feature. It's probably most useful if you do a lot of macro photography, a situation where proper focus can often be difficult.

Voice annotation: Although the capability to record and store small voice annotations (comments) with each image is not a tremendously useful feature, some applications—real estate photography, for example—can benefit from it. Remember that it will use up storage on your media card, so you'll want to buy more storage or shoot at a lower-quality level (or both).

Best-shot selection: Some cameras include a "best-shot selector" that automatically shoots a series of images when you press the shutter button, analyzes them to determine which one is best, saves that one, and throws out the rest. This feature is best used in tricky macro situations where it can be difficult to hold the camera steady enough to get a clear shot. (Best-shot selection seems to work by simply selecting the largest file as the best. Because the sharpest image will compress the least, the file with the largest size is most likely the sharpest.)

In-camera effects: Many cameras offer special effects features that can automatically *solarize*, tint, or turn your images into negatives. There are even cameras now that will make your subject look thinner! These are, of course, all tasks that can be performed in your computer with a great deal more control. It's almost always better to skip these features and shoot the cleanest, best-looking image you can.

Neutral density filter: A neutral density (ND) filter is normally a physical filter you attach to a camera's lens. It cuts the intensity of the light entering the lens without altering the light's color. ND filters can be useful for bright situations where you'd like to have a little more aperture or shutter-speed latitude. Some cameras now include an internal ND filter that can be activated automatically or manually. Although somewhat rare, it can be a handy feature.

Noise reduction: Some cameras include special noise-reduction modes that kick in automatically during longer exposures. Such schemes can often greatly improve the quality of low-light shots.

Pixel mapping: It is possible for a pixel on your camera's image sensor to die or "get stuck." Some cameras now feature *pixel mapping* features that will cause the camera to analyze its image sensor and map out any dead pixels. The camera will then interpolate the missing pixels when it produces the final image.

User sets: User sets allow you to define different combinations of features that can be quickly accessed by simply changing feature sets. For example, you might define a particular configuration for indoor flash photography and another for outdoor manual exposures.

Automatic image rotation: Some cameras are able to detect whether you're holding the camera in *portrait* or *landscape* orientation (that is, vertically or horizontally), and can mark the image as being rotated or not. When you play back the image on the camera, it will be automatically rotated. Having the image rotated on the camera is actually not that useful, because it's easy enough to rotate the camera. However, if you use an image editor that can read image rotation information, the image will be automatically rotated when you open it.

Custom tone curves: In Chapter 2, you learned that before your camera saves an image, it applies a mathematical curve to the data in your image to correct for the fact that your camera records data in a linear fashion. Some higher-end cameras let you manually create custom tone curves that can be downloaded to the camera, giving you precise control over the camera's contrast and color response. Presently, this feature is found only on very high-end professional digital SLRs.

ACCESSORIES

A good camera bag is essential, and there are many many options available from vendors such as LowePro, Tenba, Tamrack, M-Rock, Kiesel, and others. Everyone has his or her own idea of what makes a good bag, but your first consideration is that it can hold the gear you want to carry for a particular shoot, which these days might include a computer, a camera, and lenses. If you're shooting with an SLR, you might find that you need multiple bags for different camera configurations. For example, on a day of street shooting, you may find that you don't need your macro and telephoto lenses, while on a day hike you might prefer to carry only certain prime lenses. The best advice for bag buying is to get your hands on the bag ahead of time. If the bag you want isn't available in a nearby store, consider a mail-order house that provides a good return policy.

Tripods

A tripod can be a must-have accessory for many different types of shooting. If you need to shoot with long exposure times that preclude handholding (a topic we'll discuss in Chapter 7), you'll need a tripod. Even if you're shooting at hand-holdable speed, if you're very concerned about sharpness, you'll want to shoot with a tripod. While it may seem that a fast shutter speed is too quick to capture any camera movement, even the tiniest amount can produce a noticeable lack of sharpness if you intend to blow up your images to a very large size.

A cheap tripod is better than no tripod at all, and there are plenty of options available from vendors such as Slik and Bogen. Most $100 or sub-hundred dollar tripods include a built-in head that provides separate controls for locking the pan and tilt axes.

When considering a tripod, you'll want to assess the following factors:

Weight. How heavy is the tripod? Heavier tripods provide more stability, but if a tripod is so heavy that you're less likely to carry it, it doesn't provide much value. If you will only be using a tripod in a studio, you can go for a heavier tripod, but if you plan to carry your tripod on long trips or all-day hikes, you'll want to consider an aluminum or carbon fiber tripod to save weight.

Carrying capacity. You'll want to note exactly how much weight the tripod is designed to hold. This amount will need to include the weight of your camera, heaviest lens, and the head (if the tripod doesn't have a built-in head). Many tripods are designed to hold heavy, large-format cameras with expensive lenses. Fortunately, most digital cameras are much smaller and so require a much lighter tripod.

Built-in head. If the tripod has a built-in head, you'll want to assess how stable it is. An inferior head will still have a little bit of movement and flex even when all the axes are locked down. Also, check to see if the camera stays where you want it when you lock it down. In other words, after positioning your camera and then locking the pan and tilt locks, does the camera stay in that exact spot, or is there a little droop? Droop is always frustrating.

Removable head. More expensive tripods don't provide a head; instead, they include only a mount onto which you attach a head you buy separately. A tripod with a removable head offers several advantages. First, it allows you to choose precisely the type of head you want (more on heads in a moment), and allows you to use different heads for different situations. This can be especially useful if you want your tripod to do double-duty as a video tripod. (See Figure 5.37.)

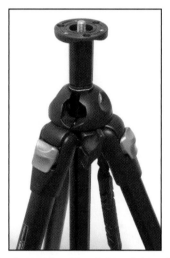

FIGURE 5.37   This Manfrotto tripod has lightweight carbon fiber legs, a mount for a removable head, and a center column for additional height.

Center column. Some tripods have an additional center column that can be raised above the top of the tripod itself. While this can get you extra height, be aware that a center column basically turns your tripod into a monopod, albeit a very stable one. Still, if you're shooting in very windy conditions, you may not want to use the center column. Therefore, this will need to factor into your assessment of the usable height of the tripod.

Height. Tripods come in many different heights, the trade-off being that a tripod that can go higher will be more comfortable to shoot with (less stooping to look through the viewfinder), allow more flexibility (shooting from a greater variety of altitudes), but will be larger and heavier. Therefore, you'll want to carefully consider weight and portability when choosing a tripod height.

On some tripods, the center column is removable, so you don't have to carry it if you don't want to. These tripods also often allow you to fit the center column into a horizontal orientation, allowing you to shoot straight down or straight up. (See Figure 5.38.)

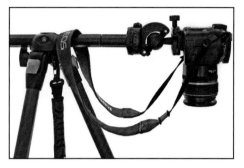

FIGURE 5.38 The capability to remove the center column allows you to lighten the tripod, and many tripods let you remount the center column in a horizontal position for shooting straight up or down.

Legs that can be extended to 90°. Some tripods allow you to extend the legs to an angle greater than 90°. This allows you to put the tripod on uneven terrain, and makes it possible to get the camera into any position you need.

Number of leg segments. Some tripods have two leg segments, some have three, and some have four. The more segments there are, the thinner the legs are, and thinner legs can mean potentially less stability. However, a tripod with more segments will collapse into a smaller, easier-to-carry package. So, you'll need to balance carryability versus stability. If you regularly shoot in very windy conditions, you'll probably want a sturdier tripod. However, you usually get into very windy conditions by hiking, which means you'll want a lighter tripod. You'll simply have to decide how much you're willing to carry. However, for extra stability, you'll want to look for a weight hook.

Weight hook. Many tripods offer a hook at the bottom of their center column, which allows you to hang a weight for greater stability. Many photographers carry empty sandbags they can fill up in the field (if you're in the wild you can just use dirt; if you're in an urban area, you can find a nearby hotel and try to sneak off with some ashtray sand), but you might find that your camera bag itself offers plenty of weight.

Tripod Heads

If you've opted for a tripod that doesn't have a built-in head, you'll need to purchase a head in addition to the tripod itself. Tripod heads fall into two major categories: pan and tilt, and ball heads. A pan and tilt head provides separate locks and controls that let you lock down either the pan or tilt axis so you can independently move either axis. (See Figure 5.39.)

Pan and tilt heads are great for situations where you need a very fine degree of positional control. You can first position one axis, lock it down, and then position the other. The downside to pan and tilt heads is that they're usually larger, and so are heavier and more difficult to carry, and a cheap pan and tilt head can suffer from the same "drooping" problems as an all-in-one tripod.

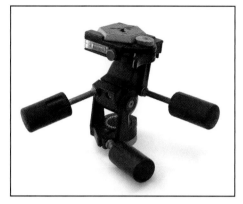

FIGURE 5.39   A pan and tilt head allows you to independently tilt, pan, and swivel the camera. Because you can lock down any axis, it's very easy to make controlled camera moves.

A ball head uses a simple ball-and-socket mechanism that allows the camera to be positioned in just about any orientation. (See Figure 5.40.) The advantage of a ball head is that the ball locking mechanism is very simple, which means it's usually very stable. Once you lock the camera down, it won't droop or drift. In addition, a ball head provides far fewer moving parts, and so is less likely to break and is easier to keep clean.

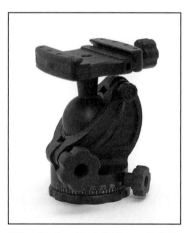

FIGURE 5.40   A ball head like this AcraTech Ultimate Ball Head allows you to freely position the camera in any orientation. Even inexpensive ball heads are very stable, and most are fairly lightweight, when compared to pan and tilt heads.

The downside to a ball head is that it's very difficult to move the camera on just one axis. For example, you might get the camera positioned with the tilt you want, but then realize that it's not quite level. Trying to level the camera might alter your tilt. Ideally, you'll want a ball head with a separate pan axis, which rotates the entire head, allowing you to isolate your panning moves.

Most ball heads have a notch cut into the side, so you can tilt your camera into a vertical position for shooting in portrait orientation. However, note that if you have a very heavy camera, this can throw off the center of gravity on your tripod. An L-bracket mount will allow you to position your camera on the ball head in either portrait or landscape orientation. Obviously, you'll need a bracket that fits your head and camera, and doesn't get in the way of your battery or media card doors. Also, you'll ideally want a bracket that isn't too heavy.

No matter what kind of head you're shopping for, you'll want to consider the following:

- **Weight.** You're already carrying a camera, lenses, and a tripod, and now you have to throw in a tripod head as well. Even a smallish head can weigh a pound or more, so you'll want to consider your options carefully.
- **Carrying capacity.** Like a tripod, a tripod head has a maximum load it was designed to bear. Make certain the head you're considering can hold your camera and heaviest lens.
- **Mounting bracket.** Most tripod heads (removable or nonremovable) have a mounting bracket that attaches to your camera. You can leave this bracket on your camera all the time, allowing for quick and easy mounting of the camera onto your tripod. When assessing an all-in-one tripod or tripod head, consider the size and weight of the mounting bracket. If it's something you can't leave on your camera all the time, it may not be the best choice. Mounting and unmounting a bracket can be a hassle, and might make you less inclined to use your tripod.

If a tripod head doesn't have a mounting bracket, offering instead just a screw, you'll have to screw the tripod onto the camera (or vice versa), which can be cumbersome and time consuming.

Tiny Tripods and Alternative Heads

If you have a small camera, there's no need for a big bulky tripod and head. Many vendors make tiny tabletop tripods that are ideal for stabilizing everything from compact point-and-shoots to mid-size SLRs. Tabletop tripods are lightweight and can easily fit in a back pocket. Set them up on a wall or pile of rocks and you have a good substitute for a full-size tripod.

Some vendors also make special ball heads designed specifically for small cameras. These often make more sense than a much heavier head designed to support far more weight than you need. (See Figure 5.41.)

Many other types of camera mounts exist, from suction cup mounts you can stick on a window, to special car mounts for shooting out of a car, or new designs such as the Jobi Gorillapod, which has multiple jointed legs that can wrap around poles, trees, furniture, and more.

Finally, many photographers swear by the simple beanbag. A beanbag sized just a little smaller than your camera will keep your camera steady, and will conform to the base of your camera to provide good support on any type of terrain.

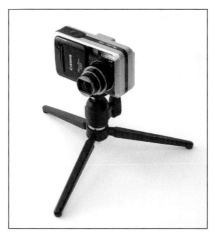

FIGURE 5.41   You can use a tiny tripod for point-and-shoot or SLRs. For times when it's not possible to carry a big tripod, or when you need to get your camera into a difficult spot, desktop tripods can be a lifesaver.

Sensor Cleaning

As discussed earlier, if you're using a digital SLR, at some point you will probably encounter the problem of sensor dust. Because the lens on an SLR is removable, it's possible for dust to get inside the camera body, and collect on the sensor. Sensor dust will appear in your images as smudges or black specks, and you can tell if you have a sensor dust problem if you have a smudge or speck that appears in the same place in every image. (See Figure 5.42.)

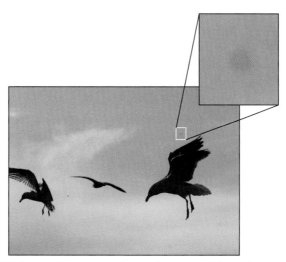

FIGURE 5.42   Sensor dust appears in your image as dark specks or smudges. With care and some special tools, you can clean your sensor.

Many cameras now include special built-in sensor cleaning mechanisms, but if yours doesn't, or if your does and you've been in a particularly dusty situation, you may be faced with the problem of sensor cleaning.

Determining if you have a dirty sensor. Sometimes, what appears to be sensor dust might actually just be something on your lens. Your first step when cleaning is to determine if your sensor actually needs to be cleaned. The easiest way to do this is to put your camera in manual focus, point it at a blank white wall (or clear blue sky), defocus the lens, and take a picture. Bring this image into your image editor and increase the contrast using a Levels adjustment (you'll learn how to do this in Chapter 11, "Correcting Tone and Color)." Any dust problems should be readily apparent.

Cleaning your sensor. Sensor cleaning is not to be taken lightly. The image sensor in your camera is an extremely critical component, and you don't want to do anything that might damage it.

Never, ever, use compressed air to clean your sensor! The propellants used in cans of compressed air can leave a physical residue that can permanently mar your sensor.

To clean your sensor, you'll need special cleaning tools, and a little time. If you're not comfortable with this type of endeavor, you can send your camera to its manufacturer for cleaning.

There are two types of cleaning: dry and wet. Dry cleaning involves using a special brush to remove debris from your sensor, while wet cleaning involves special swabs and chemicals for removing particularly stubborn particles. You can find both types of products, and excellent sensor cleaning tutorials, at *www.visibledust.com*. The Visible Dust Corporation has a long history of making cleaning materials for high-end microscopes and other optical devices, and their products are top notch.

Prevention. With just a little effort you can keep your sensor from *getting* dusty in the first place. Most of the dust that lands on your sensor is delivered by the end of the lens. So, keeping your lenses clean is a good way to keep your sensor clean. Before you go out on a shoot, use a blower bulb or blower brush (but never compressed air) to blow out the camera end of your lens.

Built-in Sensor Cleaning

Some cameras include built-in sensor cleaning mechanisms that automatically shake the sensor, or a clear plate in front of the sensor, every time you turn the camera on or off. For the most part, these mechanisms are ineffective. At the time of this writing, Olympus' Sonic Wave Filter technology is the best, but you shouldn't base your buying decision on any of these sensor cleaning mechanisms. They don't hurt anything, but they're not a reason to choose a particular camera.

When changing lenses, try to use gravity in your favor. Keep the camera pointed down, and don't remove one lens until you have the other lens in-hand, ready to attach. It might feel like it requires three hands, but if you hang the camera around your neck and practice, you'll develop the coordination to make speedy lens changes.

Some people also claim that turning off your camera before changing lenses will reduce the chances of dust getting on the sensor. Because your sensor has a static charge when powered up, the argument goes, it can attract dust. Whether this charge dissipates immediately upon powering down is unclear. Unfortunately, there's no easy way to test this hypothesis, but if you're trying to be very cautious about dust, go ahead and power down the camera before any lens changes.

If you have lots of dust problems when you first get your camera, this might be because some of the materials inside the sensor chamber are shedding residues of different kinds. This should abate after a few months.

Other Accessories

In later chapters, we'll look at other accessories such as white balance aids, flash diffusers, and more.

WHAT SHOULD I BUY?

As you've seen, choosing a digital camera involves balancing and compromising on a number of different features and technical considerations. If you've followed the procedure outlined throughout this chapter, you should have made the following decisions:

- What resolution do you need?
- How much exposure control do you need? Fully automatic, or a mix of automatic and manual controls?
- What type of camera are you looking for? Tiny pocketable camera? Mid-sized point-and-shoot? Pro-level SLR?
- What features do you need?

Each of these steps should further reduce the field of possibilities, making your buying options simpler as you make each decision. Here are some of the baseline features and capabilities you should look for:

- Resolution that's appropriate for your intended output medium. Although it's simple to follow the "more is better" approach when choosing a resolution, this isn't always the case. If you're not sure about the resolution needs of your intended output medium, see Chapter 16, "Output."
- Satisfactory (or better) image quality. Always defer to image quality as the ultimate arbiter of camera value, because when the shooting's over (no matter how

easy or difficult it was), if you don't have a decent image, you've wasted your time.

- For maximum creative flexibility, look for manual exposure and priority modes.
- Exposure compensation controls that are easy to access.
- Manual white balance control is a must for ensuring color quality.
- Adjustable ISOs guarantee that you'll be able to shoot under different lighting conditions.
- At the very least, your camera should have two metering modes: a matrix metering mode and a spot meter.
- Controls and body design you find comfortable and will facilitate the way you like to shoot. This includes the shape and feel of the camera, the quality and coverage of the unit's viewfinder(s), the focal length of the lens (in other words, does the lens provide the wide angles or telephoto qualities you want), the right type of storage and connectivity, and support for any external flash units you might want to use.

Obviously, your needs might go far beyond this, but these items will help to ensure you can get the shots you want.

Wondering about a Specific Camera?

The goal of this chapter was to give you the skills to evaluate cameras on your own, so that even as technology changes and improves, you can still make an intelligent decision about what makes a good camera. Nevertheless, it's always nice to get other opinions about particular models. To check out reviews of some of the latest digital cameras, look at www.completedigitalphotography.com.

CHAPTER

6 BUILDING A WORKSTATION

In This Chapter

- Choosing an Operating System
- Building Your System
- Software
- Accessories
- Preparing Your Monitor
- Ready! Aim!

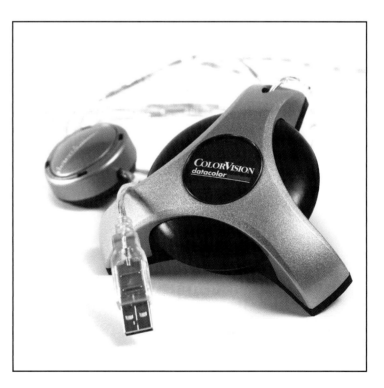

Ask any experienced film photographer and he or she will tell you that shooting the picture is only half the work of taking a photograph. The other half occurs in the darkroom where you exercise precise control over developing and printing techniques to achieve the results you imagined when you were shooting. Digital photography is no different—but, of course, there's no darkroom involved. Whereas film photographers rely on rooms full of enlargers, plumbing, and photographic chemicals, the digital photographer needs a decent computer, a lot of storage, some image-processing software, and a printer.

In this chapter, we'll explore the issues and questions you need to resolve when you construct a workstation for processing your digital images. Although we discuss computer hardware and image-editing software in this chapter, printers and other output devices will be covered separately in Chapter 16, "Output."

Your first step in assembling a workstation is one you might have already taken: select an operating system.

Choosing an Operating System

If you're interested in digital photography, you probably already own a computer and so have already chosen an operating system (OS). If you haven't, or if you're thinking of upgrading, or if you simply don't like your operating system, then it's time to make a choice. Because the OS you choose will affect all your other buying decisions, it's the first issue to consider.

As far as digital photography is concerned, OS choice is really a matter of preference. Whether you choose a Macintosh or Windows computer, you'll get pretty much the same capability and spend about the same amount of money. The main differences between them are in their interfaces, but a discussion of the strengths and weakness of each system is far beyond the scope of this book. Rather, this chapter will simply cover the issues that are relevant to digital photographers.

Macintosh

The Macintosh is where mainstream digital image editing began. Photoshop and its first competitors were originally written for the Mac OS between 1988 and 1990, providing Apple® and its developers with 15 years to tweak and refine their image-processing capabilities.

All Macs ship with internal USB-2 and Firewire ports, and some include Firewire 800 connections. As such, you won't have any trouble connecting cameras, card readers, or external drives to your Mac. OS X can automatically recognize and download images from just about any camera you plug into it. What's more, every Mac comes preinstalled with iPhoto™, a free, very good image-cataloging and printing application with an exceptional interface, that has no counterpart in the Windows world.

Both the Mac and Windows provide access to platform-specific software, so if there's an image-editing or cataloging program you're especially interested in, you may need to choose the platform that supports that program. For example, Apple's Aperture is an excellent photography workflow and editing tool that is only available for the Mac.

Windows

The main advantage of Windows over the Mac OS is that it is ubiquitous. Consequently, you probably won't ever have trouble finding a service bureau that can handle your Windows-based files. Similarly, repair shops and new equipment are often easier to find and less expensive because the Windows realm is more competitive.

The main disadvantage to a Windows-based computer is that it is more difficult to maintain. With more complicated hardware and software setups, you might spend a lot more time fidgeting with your computer than working with your images. However, like OS X, Window XP and Vista include automatic image-downloading features that will take care of moving your pictures onto your computer whenever you plug in a camera or insert a media card.

For the type of work covered in this book, your only real concern is the capability to run a capable image-editing program, so either a Mac or a Windows computer should work just fine for your digital darkroom forays.

Building Your System

Once you've chosen an OS, you're ready to select a computer. Your hardware concerns are mostly the same no matter which OS you use. When you select a computer, you'll want to pay particular attention to the following items:

- RAM
- Processor speed
- Storage
- Monitors
- Input/output options
- Graphics card

Of course, you'll probably be using your computer for more than just processing images, so if you have other concerns (perhaps you'll also be using it for editing video, making music, and checking email), you'll need to factor in the particular requirements of those tasks as well.

RAM

Although a fast processor is essential for good image-editing performance, of greater concern is the amount of random access memory (RAM) in your computer. High-resolution digital photos can be very memory hungry, and if you start performing complex effects, your memory needs will go even higher. As such, the amount of RAM installed in your computer will have a huge effect on image-editing performance.

For editing images in Photoshop, Adobe recommends a RAM size equal to two to three times the size of your typical image. Although your image might be only 8 MB, your RAM requirements can actually be much higher once you start using some of the more memory-hungry features in Photoshop, such as layers, complex filters, or the History palette. For maximum performance, you'll want a RAM level closer to 20 times the size of your image. In addition, remember that your OS and other applications will also need some memory, so don't base your RAM needs on Photoshop alone.

In the end, if you're on a budget, you might want to consider paying for a slightly slower, less-expensive processor and putting the money you save into more RAM. (See Figure 6.1.)

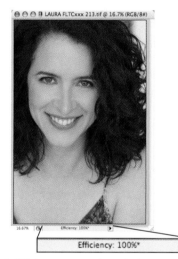

FIGURE 6.1   If Photoshop's Efficiency meter drops below 100 percent, you know that it can no longer keep all of its image data in RAM. Less than 100 percent efficiency means it must spool information to disk, which leads to slower performance. Keeping an eye on the Efficiency gauge is a good way to determine if your system could use more RAM.

Fortunately, RAM is cheap, so you should be able to easily outfit your computer with at least the recommended RAM spec provided by your image-editing applications. Of course, you can always add more RAM later, if you find out that your current memory capacity is too low.

Processor Speed

These days, even the slowest processors are fast enough for most image-editing work. If you're in a high-pressure production environment where you need to crank out images in a hurry, it's worth investing a little more for a faster CPU. For most tasks, however, you can get by with a fairly average (by today's standards) processor.

Nowadays, pretty much any machine you buy is going to be more than powerful enough for your image-editing needs.

Storage

The bad news is that digital images can take up a lot of space. The good news is that hard disk storage is really cheap. Simply put, the more storage you have, the better. Bear in mind that you'll need space for your OS, your image-editing applications, and any other software you plan on using, and that's all *before* you've shot any pictures. A 100 GB drive will keep you editing for a long time.

You'll also want some type of storage for backing up and for transporting images to service bureaus. Recordable CDs and DVDs offer the best price per megabyte, and almost every computer has a CD/DVD-ROM drive. Additional external hard drives are also a good option (Figure 6.2). External FireWire and USB drives are small, hot-swappable (meaning they can be plugged and unplugged without restarting the computer), and score over recordable CDs because they are rewritable.

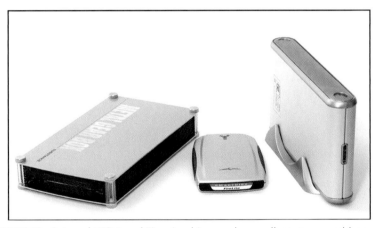

FIGURE 6.2 External USB-2 and Firewire drives make excellent storage add-ons, for backup or additional workspace. Small, 2.5" drives, like the one in the center, can take their power from the same cable that is used to connect the drive to the computer, making them ideal for taking on the road. Larger drives require separate power, but offer much larger capacities, and better price per gigabyte.

CDR or CDRW

Some recordable CD drives can also create rewritable discs using special, more expensive rewritable media. CDRWs are great for storing copies of work in progress. Backing up in-progress works to a reusable CDRW while you're working and then to a normal CD when you're finished is a great way to prevent the confusion of having multiple versions of a work-in-progress.

Monitors

You're going to be spending a lot of time staring at your computer screen so it's important to choose wisely when you select a monitor. In addition to the usual questions of brightness, sharpness, and contrast, as a digital photographer you should be particularly choosy about color reproduction. How picky you depends largely on the final destination of your photos.

If you're shooting for the Web, color fidelity is less of a concern because there is no *color calibration* system for the Web. That is, even though you might have the color set perfectly on your screen, there's no telling what the image will look like on someone else's monitor. Therefore, simply choose a monitor that looks good to you and is comfortable to use.

If print is your final destination, get ready to spend some additional money. For serious print work (that is, commercial press-ready print work), you're going to want a high-quality monitor, and you'll want a hardware calibrator. (We'll discuss hardware calibration in more detail later in this chapter.)

Of course, you'll need a video card to feed a signal to your monitor. If your computer doesn't already have a video card, you'll want to consider the following when you shop:

What resolutions does it support? For most image-editing work, you want to be sure you're using a video card that supports 1024 × 768 pixels. Because of the palette-heavy interfaces of most image-editing programs, a screen with a resolution less than 1024 × 786 can feel uncomfortably cramped.

Note

Some programs have minimum resolution requirements. You'll want to check the documentation of your image editor to make certain that you're choosing a video card that can drive the software you want to use.

What color depth does it support? Or, how much *video RAM (VRAM)* does it have? The number of colors that a video card can simultaneously display is known as its *color depth*. Color depth is also referred to as *bit depth* because more bits per pixel means more simultaneous colors. The amount of video RAM installed on the card determines both the color depth and resolution that the card can display. Make sure that your card can support millions of colors (or *24-bit color*) at your desired resolution. These days, any new video card that you buy will support 24-bit color.

Does it provide any acceleration? Some video cards include special co-processors for accelerating both two-dimensional (2D) and three-dimensional (3D) performance. 2D acceleration can mean that scrolling and screen redrawing will be much faster; 3D acceleration will greatly improve your computer's performance when you're working in a 3D modeling and animation package. In general, hardware acceleration is not required for image editing, though some programs such as Apple's Aperture *do* require hardware acceleration. Consult your software's hardware requirements for more details.

LCD vs. CRT

Probably your first, and most important decision when monitor shopping will be to choose between an LCD display and a CRT display. (CRT stands for *cathode ray tube* and basically means a "traditional" monitor with a picture tube, rather than a flat panel of liquid crystal diodes.) A few years ago, this was a fairly simple decision because CRTs were much higher quality than LCD screens. Nowadays, not only are LCD screens suitable for print work, you'll probably be hard-pressed to find a high-quality CRT display. More and more manufacturers have bailed out of the market, especially at the high end.

Extremely high-quality CRTs often yield slightly better shadow detail than do LCD screens, while LCD's almost always provide better sharpness. CRT's also sometimes provide separate inputs and adjustments for the red, green, and blue channels. This can make it much easier to calibrate and adjust the display.

When assessing a CRT, you'll want to check the edges of the screen for any convergence troubles (slight red, green, or blue fringing around pixels) and for distortion problems—slight bulging or pinching of the image. If the front of the screen is curved, check the edges of the screen for softness and distortion.

LCD quality has improved tremendously over the last couple of years, with the latest models providing near-CRT color gamuts and contrast ratios. What's more, LCDs are typically *much* smaller than a CRT that provides the same screen size, and they lack some of the questionable health issues of cathode ray tubes. Most importantly, though, high-quality LCDs no longer have the viewing angle troubles that they used to have. When evaluating an LCD screen, be sure to look for:

- Consistency of color and contrast from different viewing angles.
- Even brightness across the front of the screen. In particular, pay attention to the corners.

By the time you read this, a new LCD technology may be widely available, which uses separate red, green, and blue LEDs for the backlight of the screen, making for a wider color gamut, and more even illumination across the surface of the screen. These "wide gamut" LCDs offer the promise of exceptionally good display at very reasonable prices.

Whether you're shopping for an LCD or CRT, you'll need to consider the following issues:

Size: The physical area of your screen is largely a subjective choice. Do you prefer squinting at a smaller image on a 15" monitor, or bathing in the radiation of a 30" CRT? Whatever size fits your ocular preference and desktop space is the size that's right for you.

Frequency: The refresh rate—the frequency with which a monitor's screen is redrawn—is measured in hertz (Hz). The higher the number, the more frequently the screen refreshes. The more frequent the refresh, the less flicker a screen will have. Ideally, you want a screen that supports multiple frequencies and different resolutions. Higher frequency is better.

Interface: Does the monitor provide an interface that's compatible with your video card? Different interfaces include VGA, DVI, and ADC. You'll usually want to give some thought to the type of monitor you plan on using *before* you buy a video card, as not all video cards are capable of driving the native resolutions provided by some exceptionally large LCD screens.

WHAT ABOUT A LAPTOP?

The ideal computer choice for a digital photographer is a good, high-powered laptop. Because it is portable, a laptop computer allows you to edit, retouch, and print your images anywhere, and makes for a great mass storage device for those extended digital photography expeditions.

For the most part, choosing a laptop computer involves all of the same processor, RAM, and storage considerations as choosing a desktop.

In addition to the performance concerns discussed previously, you'll want to look for the following features:

- **A very good screen.** Follow the same guidelines listed in the previous section for assessing the quality of a laptop's screen. As with a desktop computer, you'll want a resolution of at least 1024 × 768.
- **A video out port.** The ideal laptop setup is to use your laptop LCD screen in the field, and a high-quality monitor when you're back home. At the very least, a video out port will allow you to take your computer to a service bureau and connect to a monitor there for final proofing. Using a two-monitor system (the laptop's LCD screen and an additional external monitor) can also make your virtual workspace more comfortable. You can, for example, keep all of your image editor's tool palettes on your laptop's LCD screen and your image on your CRT. If this sounds like the ideal situation for you, be sure to check that the laptop shows one desktop across both screens, and doesn't simply mirror the same image on both.
- **USB, FireWire, or serial ports.** Be sure to get a computer that provides the type of port that your camera uses. Currently, most cameras connect through a USB-2 port, while some higher-end cameras use FireWire. Much older cameras will use USB-1 or even old-style serial connectors.
- **A PC card or ExpressCard/34 slot.** With either of these types of peripheral slots, you'll have a simple, quick way to transfer images to your computer. Using an adapter such as the one shown in Figure 6.3, you can simply insert the media from your camera directly into your laptop. These types of adapters are currently available for all removable formats.

Finally, you'll want to consider size and weight when you shop for a laptop. Remember that you're already going to be carrying a bag of camera gear, so you don't want to weigh yourself down even more with a computer that's too heavy.

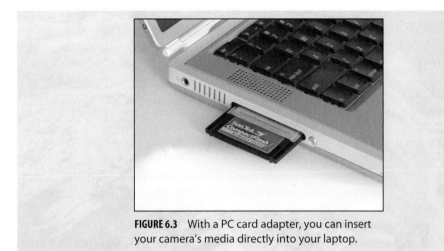

FIGURE 6.3   With a PC card adapter, you can insert your camera's media directly into your laptop.

SOFTWARE

These days, even lay people understand that digital image editing software can do things that would have been incredibly difficult or impossible in a traditional darkroom. People who have never picked up a digital camera will speak of images being "Photoshopped." And while it's true that good image-editing software is now an essential part of the photographer's toolkit, it's important to understand that corrections and adjustments are just one part of your post-production workflow.

The process of sorting, organizing, and selecting your choice images is often a bigger part of your workflow than any type of special effects or digital correction. In fact, as we'll discuss throughout the remainder of this book, if you do your job right while you're shooting, then you won't have to do much—if any—correction and manipulation later.

Fortunately, software vendors have come to recognize this, and there are now several excellent "workflow" applications that help with the sorting and organization part of your workflow, while also providing image editing, and often a way to launch into a more advanced image editor.

We'll discuss post-production workflow in detail in Chapter 10, "Workflow," however the basic workflow goes like this: import your images from your camera or media card; identify the select images that you want to output; apply metadata and keywords to your images; edit and correct your selects; output your images; back up and archive.

With your operating system, you can transfer your images and organize them into folders or directories, but modern workflow tools such as Adobe Photoshop Lightroom and Apple's Aperture offer powerful comparison and organization tools that will make your post-production much simpler.

While these tools offer image-editing features, you might also want an additional editing program such as Adobe Photoshop or Photoshop Elements, and you might need some additional utilities such as panoramic stitching programs, high dynamic range processing programs, and backup applications.

In the rest of this chapter, we'll discuss what you should consider when evaluating each of these types of applications.

Workflow Applications

Workflow applications are a new class of digital photography post-production tool. Apple was the first to market with such a tool when they released Aperture in November of 2005. Adobe followed with Photoshop Lightroom in January of 2007. Both of these programs provide a single application that allows you to import, sort and compare images; apply metadata; edit images, process raw files, export electronic files, create web galleries, and print. What's more, both programs provide an image library system that allows you to create and maintain a searchable, sortable archive of *all* of your images, not just one shoot or folder full of images.

You could, of course, perform all of these tasks using a multitude of other applications, but the integration provided by both Aperture and Lightroom makes for a much more streamlined, flexible, and efficient post-production workflow. What's more, both of these programs allow you to use the exact same workflow whether you're working with JPEG, TIFF, or raw files. Both programs have their strengths, meaning you'll want to take a little time to evaluate each.

Photoshop Lightroom. Available for both Mac and Windows, and priced at $299, Photoshop Lightroom offers importing, sorting, comparing, organizing, keywording, editing, raw conversion, web page output, and printing, all in a single application that provides different virtual "rooms" for each task (Figure 6.4). Lightroom's strongest advantages are some excellent editing tools not found in other editing applications, (Photoshop CS3, excepted) and raw shooters will be pleased to find that Lightroom includes the latest version of Photoshop Camera Raw for raw conversion. This means it yields professional-quality results, supports a tremendous number of raw formats, and provides all the tools you expect to find in a good raw converter.

Current users of Photoshop Camera Raw will find it easy to switch to Lightroom, while the huge number of third-party websites and books devoted to the product make it possible for novices to quickly get up to speed.

You can download a free 30-day, fully functional trial version of Lightroom for Mac or Windows at *www.adobe.com/go/trylightroom*.

Aperture. Apple invented the photography workflow genre with Aperture, an excellent Mac-only product that combines all of the expected workflow features, and adds book printing, a unique interactive "light table," automatic backup, tethered shooting, multicard importing, scriptability, and more. Aperture's raw converter is first-rate and it includes very good editing tools (Figure 6.5). It's biggest strength, though, is its exceptional interface, which allows for a fluid, ever-changing workflow. With Aperture, you're never stuck in any particular mode, making it easy to work the way you want to work, and the way that is best for the particular images that you're processing.

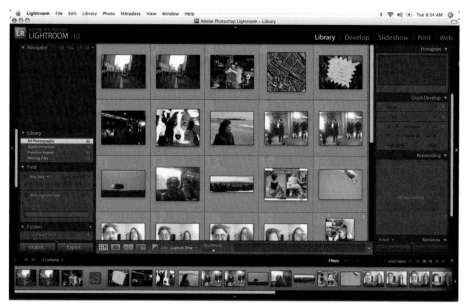

FIGURE 6.4   Adobe Photoshop Lightroom provides a single application that offers an integrated environment for importing, sorting, applying metadata, editing, and output.

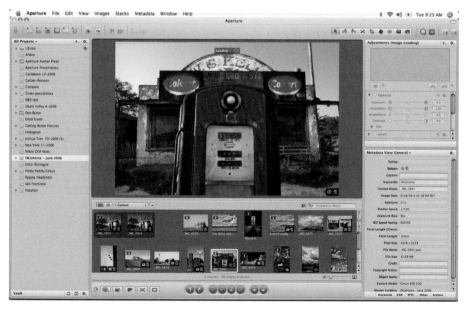

FIGURE 6.5   Apple's Aperture offers a full assortment of workflow tools wrapped up in an excellent, fluid, non-modal interface.

Aperture performs much of its editing work using the graphics processing unit on your computer's video card. As such, it's very important to check that your Mac is Aperture compatible. A free 30-day trail version is available for download at *www.apple.com/aperture/*.

Finally, it's worth noting that both Aperture and Lightroom offer non-destructive editing, a topic we'll cover in more detail later in this chapter.

APPLE iPHOTO

If you're a Mac user, you have another workflow management option, in the form of iPhoto. Bundled free with all new Macs, or available separately as part of iLife, (which includes video editing, DVD authoring, and blogging software) iPhoto is an excellent image management, editing, organization, and output tool (Figure 6.6). Rather like "Aperture lite" iPhoto provides all of the workflow management features that most users will need including importing, organizing, keywording, editing, and output. iPhoto supports JPEGs and raw files, providing you with the same workflow no matter what type of file you're working with. If you're a Mac user, it's worth giving iPhoto a close look before you invest in any additional software.

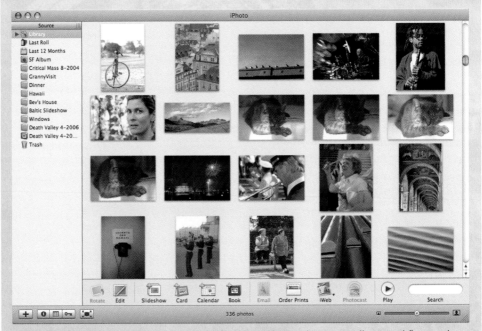

FIGURE 6.6   Apple's iPhoto is bundled with all Macs and provides an excellent workflow and editing solution. Because it's free, and very capable, it's worth taking a close look at iPhoto before investing in other software.

Raw converter compatibility

If you plan on using raw, then you'll need to be sure that your raw conversion or workflow application supports your particular camera. A raw converter must have a special profile for each specific type of raw-capable camera. If your application doesn't specifically say that it works with the raw files from your camera of choice, then you'll need to consider a different program. Right now, Photoshop Camera Raw (which is built in to Photoshop, Photoshop Elements, and Photoshop Lightroom) supports far more camera types than any other converter, though any of the major raw conversion apps will support all of the popular cameras.

Most vendors are diligent about releasing updates to support cameras as they're released, but it can sometimes take a while for these updates to appear.

Browsing and Cataloging Applications

Loosely related to workflow applications are applications that allow you to browse a folder full of images. With a browser, you can view thumbnails and previews of your images, perform batch renaming; add, view, and edit metadata; and organize images into subfolders. Many browsers also offer import features, raw conversion, and batch processing capabilities that allow you to speed up your workflow. Some browser programs offer limited image-editing and correction tools, but most assume that you'll perform serious editing in a dedicated image-editing program.

A browser serves as a halfway point between your image editor and the file manager that's built in to your operating system. While a browser provides viewing, editing, and metadata controls that aren't available in your file manager, it still relies on the directory system and file architecture provided by your OS. By comparison, workflow applications like Lightroom and Aperture maintain their own database of images and provide a single integrated environment for your entire workflow, including cataloging.

If you don't want to commit to a workflow application, then a browser program will be an essential tool for viewing, sorting, and launching images into your image editor. Some cross-platform browser applications include:

Adobe Bridge, which ships with the Adobe Creative Suite 2, and Creative Suite 3, provides all of the browser features you'd expect, wrapped up in an interface that integrates seamlessly with the other apps in the Adobe Creative Suite (Photoshop, Illustrator, InDesign, etc.). What's more, it provides access to Photoshop Camera Raw for raw conversion and offers excellent batch processing capabilities (see Figure 6.7).

CameraBits PhotoMechanic provides most of the features you'd want in a browser including capturing, renaming, raw conversion, metadata editing, and much more. In addition, the program provides batch processing features, the ability to import from multiple cards simultaneously, and extremely fast performance. If you work on short deadlines, or have older hardware, Photo Mechanic's speedy performance might be the deal-making feature for you.

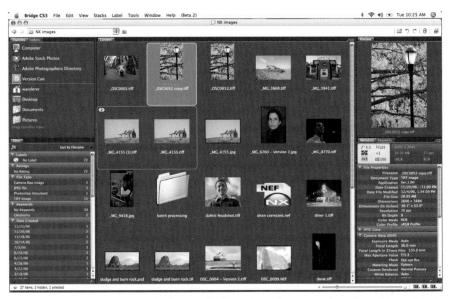

FIGURE 6.7   Adobe Bridge, which ships with Photoshop Elements, Photoshop CS2 and CS3 provides file browsing, file renaming, metadata editing, raw conversion, and more, making it a great foundation for JPEG or raw workflows.

A cataloging application allows you to create a catalog of any folder or volume. The catalog can contain thumbnails of images, metadata, keywords, and a pointer to each image's original location. With a cataloging application you can create searchable, browseable catalogs of images that you have archived on off-line media such as optical disks or external hard drives. What's more, you can give these catalog files to clients and friends, so that they can easily browse your collection.

Some very good cross-platform catalog programs that provide all the expected cataloging features include:

Extensis Portfolio, which offers excellent features including the ability to view full-screen previews of any cataloged image; support for dozens of raw formats; batch file conversion features; one-click CD archiving; folder syncing, and excellent web publishing features.

iView MediaPro also provides excellent cataloging features with superb web output, very speedy performance, the ability to create stand-alone viewer documents, and much more. At the time of this writing, the future of iView MediaPro is a little fuzzy, as the company has been bought by Microsoft. Keep an eye on Microsoft's web site for more details.

Canto Cumulus is a high-end cataloging system that offers a sophisticated client/server architecture that is ideal for workgroups and large publishing organizations. If you want to create complex multiuser photo/print production workflows, then Cumulus might be the tool for you.

NONDESTRUCTIVE EDITING

In Chapters 1, "Introduction," and Chapter 2, "How a Digital Camera Works" you learned that an image is composed of a number of pixels represented by numeric values. In most image editors, when you make an adjustment, the color values of the adjusted pixels are altered to reflect your changes. In a *nondestructive editing* system, actual pixel values are never altered. Instead, a description of any edit that you make is stored in a list. Any time the computer needs to display, output, or print the image, the original pixel values are processed according to the instructions stored in the list of edits. (See Figure 6.8).

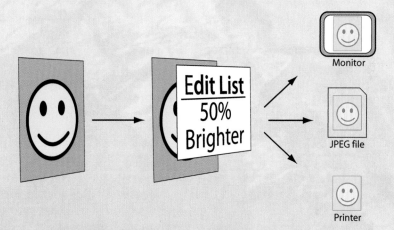

FIGURE 6.8   In a nondestructive editing system, all edits that you make are kept in a list. In real time, the editing software takes your original image data, processes it according to the instructions in the list, and then outputs it to whatever destination you need. This process happens continuously as you make edits and changes.

The advantage of a nondestructive editing system is that you can undo any edit at any time. You can also go back and alter the *parameters* of any edit at any time, making a nondestructive system far more flexible than a destructive editor. Photoshop's Adjustment Layers (which you'll learn about in detail in Chapter 13, "Building Your Editing Arsenal") are a form of nondestructive editing. Apple's Aperture, Adobe Photoshop Lightroom, and Nikon Capture NX offer completely non-destructive editing.

Image-Editing Applications

Workflow applications like Lightroom and Aperture provide all the editing power that you'll need for 80 to 90% of your images (and perhaps all of the editing power that you'll ever need, depending on the types of images you like to make). Browser programs such as Photo Mechanic, and consumer applications like Apple's iPhoto might also provide most, if not all, of the editing power that you'll want.

When it comes time for more complex edits, though, you might very well need to step up to a more powerful image editor. The main advantage of a higher-end editor is that it allows you to use selections, masks, and compositing operations to constrain your editing operations to specific parts of your image. With these features you can, for example, adjust the contrast or color in one part of your image, while leaving the rest alone.

Advanced image editors also provide lots of different color and tonal adjustment tools, providing you with far more editing power. Here are a few of your image editing options:

Adobe Photoshop is, of course, the standard-bearer for advanced image editors. The program offers an enormous selection of tools, wrapped up in a very good interface, and all of it built on top of an excellent color engine that yields professional-quality results. You'll be hard-pressed to find a feature that Photoshop doesn't have, and if you do manage to find one, you'll probably be able to hunt down a third-party Photoshop plug-in that adds that feature to the program. While this depth of functionality makes Photoshop hard to beat in head-to-head feature comparisons, it also makes for a program that can be fairly intimidating.

Photoshop is not just for photographers. The program has extensive web development features, prepress features, compositing and special effects features, scientific analysis features, and more. The fact is, most photographers don't need most of the features included in the program. Fortunately, if you keep this in mind as you learn Photoshop, you should find that you can safely ignore the features you don't need. You can easily customize Photoshop's interface to hide the features you don't want.

Photoshop is an industry unto itself, so you should have no trouble finding all sorts of resources for learning the program, from books to web sites, to training videos to classes. In Chapters 11 through 15, we'll be covering a lot of image-editing basics that should help you with most of your Photoshop chores.

Photoshop Elements is a stripped down, under-$100 version of Photoshop that offers all of the essential photography features that you'll need. Photoshop Elements uses an interface similar to Photoshop CS's interface, so you get all of the advantages of Photoshop's UI design, as well as most of the higher-end package's most important features and performance characteristics. What you *don't* get are some important tools that you may or may not need. For example, Elements lacks the capability to work with CMYK images—the type of images you need to create if you're going to output to a professional offset press. You cannot use Elements to edit and view individual color channels. As you'll see later, this can be important, because channel editing is a necessary feature for creating certain types of effects. Elements does not have a Curves control, but if you shoot raw images, your raw conversion software might offer Curves controls of its own. Finally, Elements does not include some of Photoshop CS's more advanced editing tools such as high-end masking tools, and automation capabilities.

In general, Elements is probably enough power for most of your image-processing needs. Whether it's right for you should become more apparent as you learn more about the techniques and theories presented later in the book. Some of the tricks shown in later chapters are not possible in Elements, but it's still a great way to get into Photoshop. If you need more power later, you can always upgrade to the full version, which shares most of the Elements interface.

Adobe provides a time-limited, fully functional evaluation copy of Photoshop Elements, that's free to download. For more info, see *www.completedigitalphotography. com/pselements*.

Nikon Capture NX is a new edition to the high-end image-editing field. While Nikon has offered a version of Capture for years, that program was intended simply as a raw converter. Nikon Capture NX allows you to process Nikon raw files, but it also lets you work with TIFF and JPEG images. Capture NX provides all of the editing power that most users will need, and it wraps up this power in a unique interface that combines non-destructive editing with some unique selective-editing tools (Fiure 6.9). The biggest strength of Capture NX is that you don't have to hassle with complex masking tools. Using the program's powerful UPoint tools, you can create sophisticated masks with just one or two clicks. If you're new to image editing, you'll find Capture NX's tools far easier to use than Photoshop, while experienced editors will probably be surprised at how much faster Capture NX's masking tools are to use.

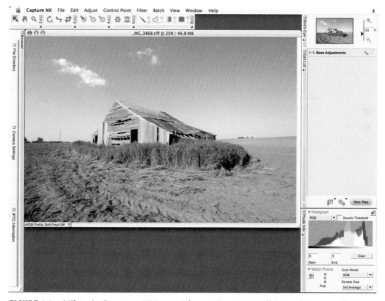

FIGURE 6.9   Nikon's Capture NX provides unique, excellent editing tools that will appeal to any users who like to make selective edits. Not just for Nikon users, Capture NX can read and write TIFF and JPEG files.

If you use a non-Nikon camera and like to shoot raw then you'll still need a raw converter application, but you may find that Capture NX is a great addition to your digital arsenal.

Image-Editing Features

If you decide to use something other than the applications mentioned here, you'll want to look for the features described in the next sections.

Levels and Curves Controls. There's no better, easier way to adjust contrast, color, and saturation than with Levels. Although your program's interface might vary somewhat, make sure that its Levels features include the controls and adjustments that are highlighted in Figures 6.10a and 6.10b.

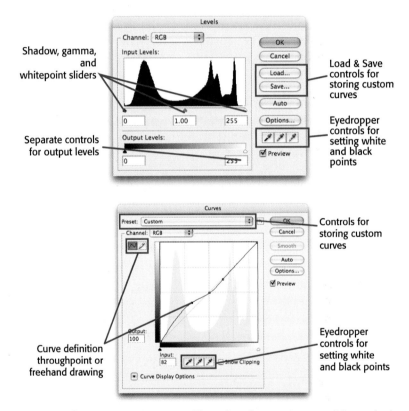

FIGURE 6.10 If you're not going to use Photoshop for your image-editing tasks, be sure that the program you choose offers Levels and Curves dialog boxes similar to the ones shown here. You will learn more about these controls later in this book.

Curves controls also provide a tremendous amount of power, but are more complicate to learn and use. These days, many programs provide easier alternatives to curves, but if you have some experience with a curves interface, then you'll want to ensure your image editor has a curves feature.

Good Selection/Masking Controls. Whether you'll be using your image editor for *all* of your editing chores, or to supplement a separate workflow tool, you'll want the ability to easily create selections (sometimes called masks) so that you can constrain your edits to a specific part of your image. Look for selection tools that can automatically select based on color or tone, and that allow you to easily add to or subtract from a selection.

Good Paintbrush and Clone Tools. For retouching, you must have a good set of paintbrushes. Make sure your program supports pressure-sensitive tablets for more natural-looking brushstrokes. A *Clone* (sometimes called Rubber Stamp) tool is absolutely essential for everything from erasing artifacts to touching up images. Although nowadays this shouldn't be too much of a concern, make sure that your program's paintbrushes are antialiased (that is, they have soft edges).

Sharpening filters. Sharpening is an essential last step before printing, so you'll want to ensure that your image editor of choice provides at least an Unsharp Mask sharpening feature.

Blur and Noise Filters. You'll use these two basic filters for many everyday editing chores, so make sure your application provides some equivalent.

File Format Support. TIFF, JPEG, GIF, BMP, and ideally Photoshop (PSD) are the bare minimum file formats that your application should support. Obviously, if your job requires specific file formats, you'll want to be sure your application supports those as well.

Raw support. If you plan on shooting in raw format, a topic that we'll discuss in detail in Chapter 12, "Raw Conversion" then you'll need a program that provides raw conversion. Your camera probably shipped with one, but you may prefer to have a raw converter that's integrated into your image editor.

Shadow/Highlight control. In Chapter 14, "Imaging Tactics," you're going to learn about a special tonal adjustment control called Shadow/Highlight. This *adaptive* allows for simple, automatic adjustment of shadow and highlight details. Photoshop, Photoshop Elements, Lightroom, Aperture, and Capture NX all provide such a control now, and it is rapidly becoming a standard part of any post-production workflow.

Other features

If your editor of choice provides those essential features, you'll next want to look for these additional features.

Support for Photoshop Plug-Ins. You can expand and extend an editor's features through the use of special *plug-ins*, small bits of code that can be added to an application. There are a huge-number of Photoshop plug-ins that allow you to do everything from blurring an image to adding 3D objects. Many digital cameras interface with your computer through a Photoshop *Acquire Plug-in,* a special piece of software that lets Photoshop communicate with your camera through a serial, USB, or FireWire cable. If your camera requires the use of such a plug-in, you'll definitely need an image editor that supports Photoshop's plug-in format and that is compatible with your plug-in of choice.

Support for Multiple Color Spaces. Although your camera and desktop printer both operate in RGB color space, you might need other color spaces for specific tasks. Commercial printers usually require documents to be in CMYK color, whereas some corrections and adjustments are easier to perform in L*A*B color. If you do a lot of black-and-white work, you might want the capability to make *duotones, tritones,* and *quadtones*.

Access to Individual Color Channels. There are some corrections and adjustments that can only be performed by working on specific color channels. (See Figure 6.11.)

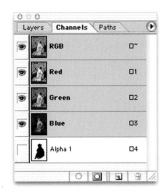

FIGURE 6.11 Though not essential, the ability to edit individual color channels can help you with some types of edits.

The tutorials and examples included in this book use all of the features discussed here. Even if your program of choice provides different approaches to these features, you should be able to follow along with the tutorials and examples.

WHAT ABOUT THE SOFTWARE THAT SHIPPED WITH MY CAMERA?

Most cameras ship with some combination of image editing, importing, and image browsing software. If your camera can shoot in raw format, then it might also include a raw conversion program of some kind. Some cameras are bundled with popular apps such as Photoshop Elements, but most include proprietary applications developed by the camera manufacturer.

In general, it's safe to say that these bundled apps are not as good as many inexpensive third-party alternatives. However, if you can't afford or don't have access to other applications, the bundled software will probably work fine.

Panoramic Software

In Chapter 9, "Special Shooting," we'll discuss panoramic shooting, the process of shooting a series of image "tiles" that can be *stitched* together to create a seamless panorama. If your camera didn't ship with stitching software, you'll need to buy some.

HDR Shooting

Chapter 9 will also cover the process of High Dynamic Range imaging, a special shooting and processing technique that allows you to capture images with a much greater range of brightness. You'll need special software to process these types of images.

File Recovery Software

Alas, there might come a time when you accidentally erase an image, or an entire card full of images, without realizing that you haven't backed them up to your computer. Fortunately, there are a few programs that can often recover your images intact, as long as you haven't already recorded new images onto the card.

Although you might already own file recovery software such as Norton Utilities®, it's important to note that such programs usually can't recognize removable media such as CompactFlash cards or Memory Sticks. For these types of media you need special recovery software such as PhotoRescue™. Available for Mac and Windows, a demo version can be downloaded from *www.photorescue.com/datarescue*. Although the program is well-designed and very effective, you will, hopefully, never need to use it.

ACCESSORIES

There are a few accessory items that can make your life with your digital camera easier, the most convenient one being a media drive that supports the type of media used by your camera. (See Figure 6.12.) These drives typically connect through your computer's USB or FireWire port. Insert your camera's media into the drive's slot and it will appear on your desktop as another volume, allowing you to drag and drop images onto your computer's hard drive. These drives are usually faster than transferring files from your camera via a cable and don't require you to use your camera's battery power.

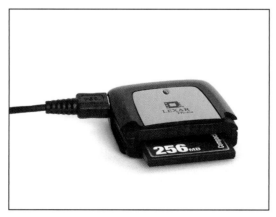

FIGURE 6.12   A CompactFlash or SmartMedia drive provides a simple, quick way to get your images into your computer. In addition to saving time, you'll save camera-battery power.

If your camera uses a USB cable to connect to your computer, and if you already have a number of USB devices installed, you might need to get a USB or FireWire hub. Offering multiple ports, hubs make it possible to connect several devices simultaneously.

PREPARING YOUR MONITOR

Editing and correcting images digitally is a lot easier than using traditional darkroom techniques, but there are still some technical challenges you have to wrestle with. The biggest of these is the issue of getting the colors on your printer to match the colors on your screen. As you may have already discovered, prints can often look very different from the image on your computer monitor. *Monitor profiling and calibration* is the process of tuning your system so that your printed output better matches what you see on-screen. How much effort to spend on this process depends on how picky you are, what kind of workflow you expect to have, and what kind of gear you use.

Fortunately, there's been a lot of good work done on improving color consistency from screen to print, so getting good results from your printer is not as complicated as it used to be. With the current generation of printer drivers from Epson®, Canon, and HP®, you can get very good results by simply using the automatic color-correction features built in to the printer drivers. Note that these drivers probably won't produce prints that exactly match the color on your monitor, but you'll also probably find that with practice, you'll learn how things on your screen correspond to what comes out of your printer. For example, you'll get better at eyeballing when shadows in an image are too dark.

However, your screen will never *exactly* match your printed output, simply because the two technologies are very different. Your monitor and printer use different primary colors that mix together in very different ways. Adding to the problem is the fact that your monitor is a self-illuminated display that generates its own light, while a photographic print is a reflective media that bounces light from another source. Finally, your monitor probably has a much wider gamut, or range of displayable colors, than does any printer that you'll find.

All of these parameters combine to create a very tricky situation for your computer. Trying to display an image in the same way it will print is very tough. As such, you'll never get your monitor and prints to exactly match. However, with a little care, you can get them very close, which means you can greatly reduce the number of test prints that you need to make.

If you've ever worked in a darkroom, you know that it takes a fair number of test prints to discover exactly what printing exposure is best for a particular image. The same is true when printing digitally, but it's possible to greatly reduce the number of test prints. If you're frustrated with the wasted ink and paper that you have to go through to make test prints, just bear in mind that it's still much more cost effective than working in a chemical darkroom. And, as the technology improves we may one day have much better screen-to-printer fidelity.

Tip

If all you're looking for is snapshot output, then you may be better off using an online printing service, or a drugstore service. These often deliver simple 4" x 6" output at a much more affordable rate than you can get from your desktop printer.

In the following section, we'll discuss monitor profiling, and a few basics of color management. We'll have much more to say about this subject in Chapter 16, when we discuss printing.

A Little More Color Theory

As you saw in Chapter 2, light mixes together in an additive process so that as colors are added together they appear more and more white. Ink, on the other hand, mixes in a subtractive manner. That is, as colors are mixed they appear darker. While the primary colors of light—the fundamental colors from which all other colors can be made—are red, green, and blue, the primary colors of ink are cyan, magenta, and yellow. (See Figure 6.13.)

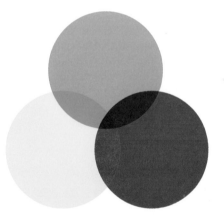

FIGURE 6.13   The primary colors of ink: cyan, magenta, and yellow. These colors differ from the primary colors of light—red, green, and blue—that your camera uses to create images. This difference is one of the things that makes monitor/printer calibration so complicated.

This difference in the way colors are made is what makes accurate calibration of your monitor and printer so difficult. Each time you print, your computer has to figure out how to take your image—which it represents as a combination of red, green, and blue light—and convert it into the mix of cyan, magenta, and yellow ink that your printer expects.

Special K

As you might already know, color printing uses four colors: cyan, magenta, yellow, and black. Black is not a primary color, of course, but black ink is added to the mix because it is impossible to create perfectly pure ink pigments. Therefore, although the theory says that if you mix cyan, magenta, and yellow together you will eventually get black, the truth is you'll just get very dark brown because of impurities in the color pigments of your inks. Adding a little black ink is the only way to get true black. This is why most color printing is a four-color process called CMYK.

As if converting colors between these two different color spaces wasn't difficult enough, accurate color reproduction is further complicated by the fact that not every monitor is the same. If you've ever looked at a wall of TVs in an appliance store, you've seen that an image can vary greatly even between identical models. There are a number of reasons why, ranging from differences in color adjustments on each set, to differences in age, to differences in manufacturing. Computer monitors vary in the same way, which is why a digital image or Web page on your monitor might look completely different on someone else's monitor.

Printers have their own collection of troubles. Each manufacturer might take a different approach to reproducing colors, and different brands of ink and types of paper have their own unique color qualities as well. Further complicating matters is the fact that different printing technologies can use completely different approaches to reproducing color. Some printers use four colors, some add extra colors to reproduce lighter tones, some use ink, some use solid wax, and so on.

Fortunately, with just a few simple steps, you can greatly improve color consistency.

Profiling and Calibrating Your Monitor

To improve color consistency across multiple devices, a group of camera, software, and display vendors created the International Color Consortium. The ICC has defined a standard method of profiling printers and monitors. An ICC profile contains a description of the color and contrast properties of a device, and these descriptions can be used by software in your computer to adjust color on-the-fly as it passes from one device to another. The color in your document is never actually altered. Instead, it is temporarily modified to try to preserve consistency from one device to another. Consequently, your image should appear consistent as you move it from computer to computer, and from screen to printer.

This type of color management only works well when you have accurate, high-quality profiles for your monitor and printer. We'll detail printer profiles in Chapter 16. Right now, it's time to consider your monitor profile.

The Macintosh operating system includes a software monitor calibrator that lets you create a monitor profile by eye (Go to System Preferences > Displays, click on the Color tab, then press the Calibrate button and follow the on-screen instructions). If you're using Photoshop on Windows, then you can use the Adobe Gamma application included with Photoshop to create a monitor profile by eye. These programs yield profiles that are better than using no profile at all, but if you're going to bother with color management, it's best to use a hardware profiler to create a monitor profile.

There are several relatively inexpensive profilers on the market, ranging from the $79 Pantone Huey, or ColorByte Spyder2express to more expensive systems such as the $170 Spyder2Suite (Figure 6.14), $279 Spyder2Pro, or the $250 Gretag-Macbeth Eye-One Display2.

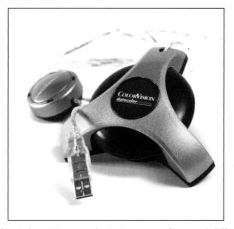

FIGURE 6.14   The ColorVision Spyder is just one of several different monitor calibrator/profilers. After hanging the device in front of your monitor, you use special included software to automatically build a profile.

All of these devices provide a piece of hardware that you attach or hang in front of your monitor. The included software then uses the device to measure the color and contrast properties of your monitor, and then generates a profile that you install on your computer. The higher-priced profilers do a better job than the less expensive units, and their software provides more configuration options. However, even a $79 device will be better than no calibration, or "eyeballed" calibration. The money you invest in a calibrator will more than pay for itself in saved ink and paper.

All of these devices include detailed instructions on their use, as well as guides for getting better results. In general the process is automatic and painless, and you'll probably want to reprofile at least once a month (more if your monitor is older).

MONITOR CALIBRATION TIPS

Before you calibrate your monitor, whether by eye or with a hardware calibrator, let the monitor warm up for half an hour or so. This will give it time to get up to its usual operating temperature. For best results, turn down the lights in the room and block any reflections or glare that might be striking the monitor.

Set your desktop background or pattern to a neutral gray. (When you do any precise color manipulation or editing, you should set your desktop to gray to keep your eyes from getting confused.) If you want to get really picky, it's a good idea to move any large, brightly colored objects out of your field of view. In general, you want your working space to be neutrally colored.

READY! AIM!

If you read and considered the last two chapters and have made all of the relevant purchases, then you have everything you need to start shooting! The next section of the book (Chapters 7 through 9) deals exclusively with shooting and, for the most part, won't involve your computer very much. Don't worry, though, you'll get plenty of mouse time starting in Chapter 10.

7

SHOOTING

In This Chapter

- Seeing, Interpreting, and Composing an Image
- Five Practices for Better Shooting
- Initial Camera Settings
- Building a Shot
- Simple Flash Photography
- Power and Storage Management
- And That's Just the Beginning!

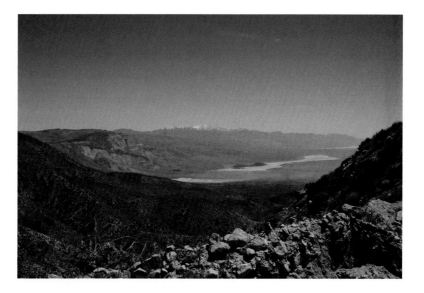

According to Ansel Adams, when famed photographer Margaret Bourke-White was shooting, she would simply set her camera on 1/100th of a second and then shoot the same image over and over using every aperture her camera could manage. This, combined with her gift for composition, ensured that at least one of her images would come out the way she envisioned.

If you're like most people, you probably find yourself shooting whole rolls of film (or cards full of images) hoping that one or two of the pictures will be "keepers." Unfortunately, no camera technology can guarantee that you'll always shoot great images, but there are a number of things you can do to improve your chances of getting images you like, and digital cameras offer a number of creative advantages that make it easier to take good shots.

Although digital cameras make Bourke-White's approach far more cost-effective, a much better practice is to spend some time learning how to intelligently use the tools and features found on your camera to ensure you can get a good shot with only one or two exposures.

The study of photography covers two major domains: craft, which is the button pushing—the study of the mechanics of making a good image; and artistry, which encompasses the study of recognizing and understanding what makes a good image. In this book we're going to focus mostly on the craft side of things, so you don't have to employ a Bourke-White approach. Before we get into that, though, we're going to take a quick look at some of the "artistic" issues all photographers face. Artistry is a skill and a discipline just like any other, and it can be practiced and improved upon with some simple effort and time.

Seeing, Interpreting, and Composing an Image

Your eyes work a lot like your camera. A lens in your eyeball focuses light onto a light-sensitive area at the back of your eye. This area translates the light exposure it receives into luminance and chrominance signals and transmits these to the brain along the optic nerve.

There are four types of light-sensitive cells on the back of your eye. In the very center of the light-sensitive area of your eye sit the cones—color sensitive cells that cover a tiny area about 1 mm in diameter. This area, the *fovea*, is the part of your eye that registers color and sharp focus. There are three types of cones, one type sensitive to red light, another to green, and another to blue—the same color primaries most digital image sensors use to make a full-color image.

Surrounding the fovea are the rods, which are so light sensitive that it only takes one to detect a single photon of light (once your eyes are adapted to the dark). However, rods are only sensitive to luminance changes, they cannot register color at all. Consequently, rod vision is luminance vision only, and it makes up the majority of the light-sensitive area of your eye. As light fades, the cones in your eyes become less effective, and the rods take over. This is why, as it gets darker, you perceive less color.

Thanks to the extreme sensitivity of the rods in your eyes, you can perceive a tremendous range of lightness values—far more than any digital or film camera. Because your camera is sensitive to a far narrower range of brightness, you'll often have to make some decisions about which particular range of light you want to capture from a scene. We'll discuss this in more detail when we cover exposure.

Your rod vision is not terribly well focused. In fact, because it's your cone vision that is focused, the actual focused part of your field of view is very small. Hold your arm out fully extended and point your thumb straight up. The area covered by the tip of your thumb to the first joint is, roughly, the only part of your field of view that is in focus. Now hold your thumb up against one of the paragraphs of text in this book and lock your eyes on the end of your thumb. Without moving your eyes, using only peripheral vision, try to read any of the text around your thumb. You'll probably find that most, if not all of it, is out of focus. Your thumb is actually covering up the only focused part of your field of view.

You don't usually notice this limited field of focus because you subconsciously move your eyes about to "sample" the focus from different areas of your field of view. Your brain then assembles all these samples into an overall sense of focus.

Your brain plays a huge part in the way you see the world. So huge, in fact, that it's possible to have perfectly functional eyes, but still be blind if you've suffered certain kinds of neurological damage. While your eyes collect and measure light, and then pass the results to the brain via the optic nerve, it's up to the brain to interpret these signals to create a final perception. To do this, your brain maps an expectation of the current scene onto the information it receives from your eyes. Sometimes, the brain's expectations do not fully correlate with the signals being sent by the eyes, resulting in a visual "disconnect," sometimes known as an *optical illusion*.

Figure 7.1 shows a very common optical illusion.

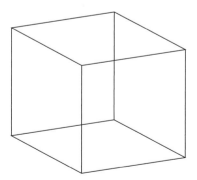

FIGURE 7.1 Although these are just a pattern of two-dimensional lines, your brain knows enough about their overall shape to assume they represent a three-dimensional object—a cube. And so, your brain tries to perceive a sense of depth in the image. However, the brain isn't entirely correct—the illustration is only two-dimensional, and there isn't enough information in the image to correctly render a fully realized cube, so the cube appears to flip back and forth as your brain tries to reconcile the lines to its expectation of the shape they represent.

Figure 7.2 shows another example, an optical illusion created by MIT researcher Edward H. Adelson.

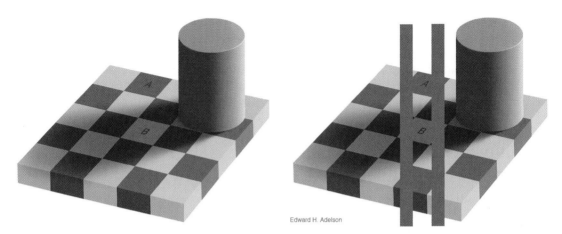

Edward H. Adelson

FIGURE 7.2   While the checkered squares appear to be alternating colors, squares A and B are actually the same color. However, your brain "corrects" the B square to make it fit an expectation that isn't true. The lower figure shows that the two squares are actually the same color.

While these illusions are interesting, they also serve to reveal one of the biggest artistic barriers you'll face as a photographer: the difference between *looking* and *seeing*.

Looking vs. Seeing

You experience a tremendous amount of visual stimulation during a typical day. I'm not talking about media—although with all the books, magazines, TV shows, movies, and Web pages out there, there's plenty of that. I'm referring to the regular amount of stimulus you experience as you wend your way through a normal day's activities. But although you may have to *look* at a huge assortment of people, places, and objects during the course of a day, you don't actually have to *see* very many of those objects to successfully survive and thrive in the world.

For example, consider the process of running a typical errand in town, either in a car or on foot. As you travel about, you will be acutely aware of dozens, or even hundreds of cars, and possibly dozens or hundreds of people. Not to mention bicyclists, baby strollers, and many other things. If the day goes well, you will successfully navigate alongside, in-between, and past all these cars and people without ever colliding with one. Although you will engage in a complex choreography with these objects, when you get home you will most likely be hard-pressed to describe the details of the majority—if any—of these vehicles or people.

There might be one or two cars (or people) you took note of because they were particularly attractive or unusual looking, but you will have perceived most of the cars you looked at as simple generic objects. Upon returning home, you might not register any of them as specific types of vehicles, and instead report, "traffic was really heavy today." In a sense, you're not seeing the trees for the forest.

You can, of course, recognize a car as a car without having to examine it in great detail. Because your brain projects an expectation and understanding of "car" onto the visual stimulus it receives when you look at a car, you don't have to actually stop and examine the object to discover that it has wheels, windows, headlights, and cup holders. By contrast, a young child might actually have to acutely examine the object, but as you grow older you amass a wealth of experience that allows you to perceive the world in a very abbreviated manner. We usually perceive our environment in an iconic, semiotic way—with little acknowledgment of the visual details—because this allows us to move more quickly and efficiently through the day.

While this ability to look at objects without seeing them makes it easier to efficiently perform your everyday tasks, it's anathema to the process of good photography. For example, when going to mail a letter, we don't have to carefully examine each and every store we pass to determine which one is the post office. We can easily pass them all without registering any details until we come to the one with the flag and mailbox out front. While this ability is great for trying to get to the post office before it closes, it also means that you might have walked right past a potentially compelling photograph, because you were not actually having to *see* anything you were looking at.

Consequently, one of your most difficult goals as a photographer is to learn to spend less time looking, and more time seeing. As you learn to do this, your level of photographic artistry will increase, regardless of your current craftsmanship.

Represent!

We've all probably experienced something like this: you're standing somewhere spectacular, like the edge of the Grand Canyon, and you think, "This is so amazing, I *must* take a picture of it!" You pull out your camera, hold it up to the scene, and capture a few images. Later, at home, you look at your prints, only to be disappointed. "I dunno, somehow, I remember it being bigger—grander," you think.

The fact is: *no one* can take a photo that will make the viewers feel like they're standing on the edge of the Grand Canyon. It's simply not possible any more than it's possible for a dancer to choreograph a dance that will make someone feel like he or she is standing at the Grand Canyon. Although it appears that you can capture an incredibly believable facsimile of a scene, photography is a *representational* medium. Your live experience of the Grand Canyon involves much more than the simple visual stimulation you're receiving. First, it involves a very *complex* visual stimulus—a 3D, panoramic stimulus with far more color and brightness information than your camera can capture. In addition, all of your other senses are mixed in as well.

However, although you may not be able to create a photograph that truly recreates the experience of standing in a particular location, you *can* create a photo that evokes *some* of the feeling you had. Your job as a photographer is to determine what it is about that moment that is compelling to you. Is it the size? The color? The sense of geologic time you can see in the striated colors of the rocks? Or perhaps it's the people you're with, or simply something about the way the light is playing off of a particular rock formation. Rather than trying to capture the entire experience of where you're standing, you need to try to identify a more refined feeling of what it is about that moment that compels you. Then, you need to employ your craft skills to figure out how to represent that feeling in a flat, two-dimensional photo. Photography is a representational medium, not a literal duplication of an experience.

Alfred Hitchcock once described drama as "life with all the boring parts removed." Dramatists very often take a normal, everyday event and blow it up into drama. They exaggerate some things, remove others, and make up others to create a representation of something the audience will respond to. Photography is the same way.

For example, last year I was in Death Valley. Because parts of Death Valley are below sea level, there is an interesting phenomenon where sand blows off of the surrounding mountains, hits the weird air currents of the valleys that sit below sea level, and immediately falls to the ground, to form giant sand dunes. There are four such dune fields in the park, and when you see them from afar, they're quite striking. The dunes are huge, and when viewed from above, you get a tremendous sense of scale—you can imagine the sand flying off the mountain to be deposited on the valley floor.

One morning, I was driving out of the mountains and came across such a vista. I grabbed my camera and took the picture shown in Figure 7.3.

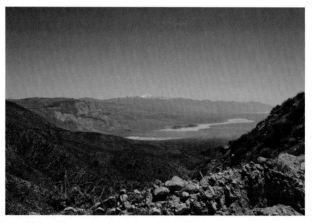

FIGURE 7.3   This isn't much of a picture. There's no real composition, and nothing for the eye to follow. What's more, the majestic dune field in the distance appears as a fairly boring, small patch of beige near the bottom of the image. The picture in no way captures what I was seeing and feeling.

So, I drove down to the valley floor to get closer to the dunes, and took the picture shown in Figure 7.4.

The next day, storm clouds blew in, and I hiked into the dunes themselves. Being *in* a dune field is a unique experience. The scenery is a constantly shifting play

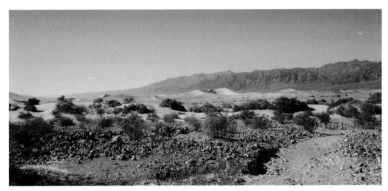

FIGURE 7.4   This isn't much better. There's no sense of scale, and still no real composition to speak of. Your eye doesn't know how to "read" the image, and it's not particularly evocative of anything.

of geometry, and the mountains of sand are huge. All these factors add up to a profound sense of otherworldliness. I took my time, worked my subject, and shot the image shown in Figure 7.5.

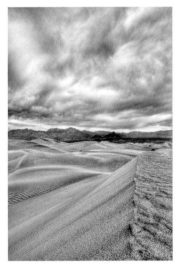

FIGURE 7.5   Finally, by getting into the dunes themselves, and working the shot, I came up with something that may not show a broad vista of scenery, but still captures the feeling of the place.

I can say with a fair degree of certainty that it didn't look *exactly* like the image in Figure 7.5. However, it did *feel* like that image—mysterious, beautiful, and strange. So, although that photo is not a literal image of the sand dunes, it still effectively captures something about the "truth" of the experience I had there. This is your goal as a photographer.

Not just for "artists"

If you're thinking, "I'm not interested in having a gallery opening, I just want to take better pictures of my kids," don't worry. The things that make a good photo, and the artistic and craft issues you face as a photographer are the same whether you're shooting your family, or fine art shots.

Warming Up

While everyone knows that you need to stretch before exercise, and warm up before playing a musical instrument, people don't often think about warming up before shooting pictures. However, if you've been sitting in your office all day, or haven't picked up your camera in a while, you shouldn't expect to be able to go out in the world in a way that is "open" to potential images. In other words, you shouldn't expect to be able to see right away.

Here are a few exercises you can do to warm up before shooting. These may sound like they have nothing to do with seeing, or with photography, but they usually do a pretty good job of getting your visual sense going. I learned these exercises while working with theatrical improvisers, a group of people who need to be very tuned in to their environment and their senses.

Wrong name. Before you go out, spend about five minutes walking around the room, pointing at objects and naming them the wrong thing—out loud. Don't worry about what you name them. You'll end up free associating, and probably working through categories of objects. Concentrate on looking at the object, and then giving it a different name. This exercise forces you to really see things, and breaks you out of your abbreviated, iconic view of the world. When you've done this for a few minutes, stop and look around the room. Some people perceive a brightening of colors, others a greater sense of depth or strong outlines around objects.

Peripheral vision exercise. At some point as you head out to your shoot—or at any time if you're just street shooting—down the street, lock your eyes straight ahead and try not to move them. Pick out an object in the distance, in your periphery. It can be a car, a house, a street sign—anything at all. As you walk toward the object, try to become aware of as many details of the object as you can without looking directly at it. When you have finally reached the object, stop and look at it. You'll probably see it in extreme detail.

Take a test shot. If you do nothing else to warm up, at least do this: as soon as you step out the door, take out your camera and take a picture. It doesn't matter what you shoot—your foot, your hand, the stop sign across the street—just take a picture. This will at least remind your hands and eyes of what you're up to, and get you started thinking in terms of the camera frame.

Making an Image

There will be occasions when a great picture simply presents itself. Maybe you're standing in the right place at the right time just as the light turns perfect over a particularly striking vista. Most photos, though, have to be *made*. That is, you first have to recognize them, and then choose a composition and exposure that yields a compelling, evocative result. Developing your ability to see will help you recognize images, and will help you better understand the best way to represent them. Employing your composition skills, exposure understanding, and other aspects of your craft will help you capture the image you envision.

In the Beginning…

All photos begin with light. Very often, it is simply the light you will find compelling in a scene, not the actual subject matter. For example, you may choose to shoot a landscape not because the landscape itself is particularly compelling, but because the light playing off it is. Good light can turn an otherwise pedestrian scene or subject into something interesting, as you can see in Figure 7.6.

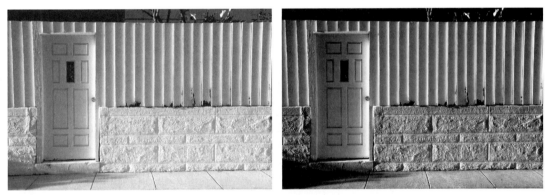

FIGURE 7.6 While the first shot in this figure is not especially interesting, as the light changed the scene became increasingly dynamic. Quality of light is very often the defining characteristic of a scene.

As you learned earlier, your eye packs far more luminance-sensitive cells than it does color-sensitive cells. As such, it is much more sensitive to contrast than it is to color. As we'll see once we start editing, your eye drinks up contrast in an image, and contrasty light is usually far more compelling than flat light.

Sunlight yields more contrast when it is shining from a low angle. So, early morning and late afternoon light is far more interesting than the light of mid-day. Low-angle light casts longer shadows, which makes for surfaces that have more texture and visible detail. In the middle of the day, when the sun is shining straight down, there is very little shadowing, resulting in a flat, boring look.

You'll often work with existing light in two ways. When you find an area of particularly compelling light, stop to see if there's any type of picture to be had there. As you explore the area, maybe you'll find a texture or subject that is worth shooting, since it is in good light. Conversely, if you're out and about and discover a particularly interesting subject, try to assess if better light will fall onto it at some point. Perhaps the sun will pass out of shadow and illuminate your subject in a more interesting manner.

The light of the early morning and late afternoon changes *very* quickly, which can work both for you and against you. If you see something that isn't particularly well lit, it might change very soon. At the same time, when you see the image you want, you might have to work very quickly to capture it, before you lose the light.

In the spring and fall, when the sun doesn't climb very high in the sky, you'll find good light during more of the day. The specific hours will vary depending on your latitude.

All that said, just because it's raining or dingy doesn't mean there aren't still good photos to be had. Sometimes, too much contrast can be a bad thing, as it can serve to make your image harsh and complex. Also, shooting when there is less contrast affords you the opportunity of adding more contrast where you want it, later on. We'll explore this in more detail in our post-production chapters.

Composition

Just because something looks cool in real life, doesn't mean you can simply point a camera at it and get a good picture. Unlike the real world, a photograph is bounded by a frame—the edge of the photo itself. When looking at a photo, the viewer "reads" the contents of that frame to try to determine and understand what it is you're showing them. The simplest definition of composition is that it's simply the way you frame your scene, but good composition means much more than simply choosing a way to crop the world to fit into a rectangle.

Good composition is the process of arranging forms and tones in a way that is pleasing, and guides the viewer's eye to bring attention to your subject. Good composition can also reveal things in the scene viewers might not notice on their own—repetitive patterns, a play of light and shadow, or even a feeling about the particular moment you're photographing.

There are no hard and fast rules that will guarantee good composition all the time, but there are some guidelines you can follow that will usually improve your shots. These guidelines can be mixed and matched and, of course, they can be ignored and abandoned. Every image is its own unique challenge, but in general you'll want to consider the following when composing a shot.

Balance. Elements in your shot have different "weights." A heavy element on one side of the frame might need to be balanced by an element on the opposite side of the frame. For example, in Figure 7.7, the two large birds on the left are balanced by the smaller bird on the right. The smaller bird manages to create balance because it is positioned far in the lower right corner. This shifts the center of balance to a different place in the image, just as a real weight would.

If we remove the left-hand bird from the image, as shown in Figure 7.8, the picture falls out of balance. Now the two left-hand birds are simply positioned oddly in the frame, flying out of the picture with a big empty space behind them.

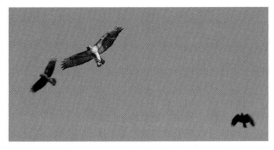

FIGURE 7.7 The elements in this image are positioned in a balanced way in the frame. Each has a "weight" that balances the other.

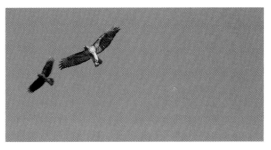

FIGURE 7.8 If we remove the bird on the right side, the image is no longer balanced—the left side is too heavy.

Placing something in the dead center of the frame can also create a balance, as shown in Figure 7.9. This is not often the most interesting composition, but in this case it works fairly well because of the hills on either side that guide the viewer's attention to the middle of the frame.

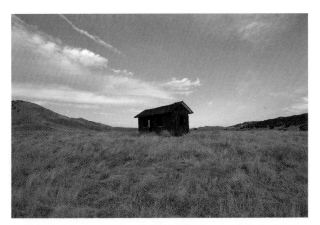

FIGURE 7.9 Balance can even be created by placing an element in the center of the image. Here, the sloping hills on either side serve to create an even balance.

Finally, balance is not created just with geometry. You can also balance tones against each other. For example, in Figure 7.10, the dark tones on the left side of the image are balanced by the light tones on the right side. The bicyclist on the right side of the image also adds some additional weight. People are always very compositionally "weighty," and the addition of a person almost always makes a scene more compelling.

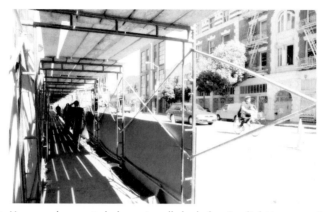

FIGURE 7.10   You can also create balance tonally by balancing light tones against dark tones. Here, the dark left of the frame is balanced by the lighter right half of the frame.

The rule of thirds. You can often achieve good composition by dividing your image into thirds and placing elements on your scene at the *intersection* of any of the grid lines. In Figure 7.11, the geometric components of the scene have been placed accordingly.

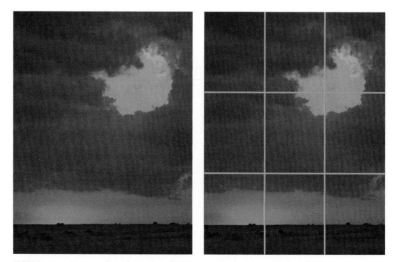

FIGURE 7.11   To employ the rule of thirds, you divide your image into equal thirds, and try to place elements close to the intersections of the divisions.

Repetition. Repeating patterns are often very interesting, like the repeating pattern of the fence you saw in Figure 7.6. Figure 7.12 shows another image with some simple repetition.

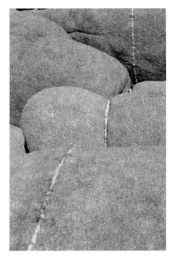

FIGURE 7.12   Repeating forms—geometric or tonal—
are often interesting, and make for good composition.

Geometry. Geometric patterns are also often very compelling (and often include an element of repetition). Figure 7.13 is composed around a number of interlocking and overlapping triangles.

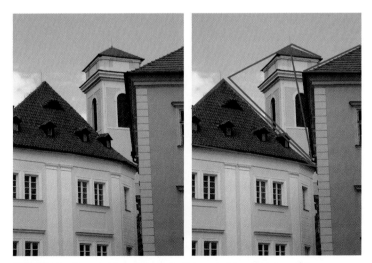

FIGURE 7.13   Geometric patterns, in this case triangles, are often
compositionally interesting, and usually have an element of repetition.

Lines. Like geometry, strong lines often make for good composition, especially strong diagonal lines. Figure 7.14 is a prime example of this, with the rock included to break up the repetition and to provide a focus for the eye (note too, that it's mostly placed according to the rule of thirds).

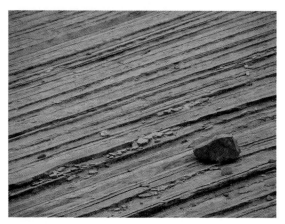

FIGURE 7.14   Strong lines make good compositional elements. This image obviously also has strong repetition.

Figure 7.15 is another example of diagonal lines, although not necessarily so literal. The wires, the lines of the sidewalk, and the repeating telephone poles all create a sense of lines receding to a vanishing point.

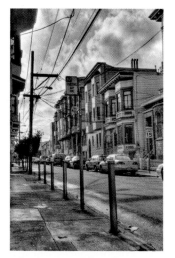

FIGURE 7.15   Line and geometric elements don't have to be overly pronounced or literal. This image has a strong sense of diagonal lines.

Curvy lines are also often interesting, such as the path shown in Figure 7.16. This image also features a tonal balance. By placing the dark path more to the right, we balance the dark tones of the path with the large bright area to the left.

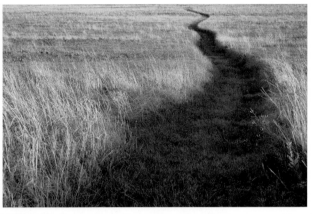

FIGURE 7.16   Strong curvy lines also make effective compositional images.

Mixing and matching. As you've seen in many of these images, you can mix and match different compositional elements and ideas, combining them to create a stronger effect.

Over time, you will internalize these ideas and find yourself employing them by feel. That is, you'll simply find that a particular composition feels right because it is properly balanced and composed. Until then, you'll want to try practicing with these concepts.

Portrait Composition

There are a few very simple compositional guidelines you can follow to take better people pictures. Whether shooting candids or posed portraits, remember the following:

Watch your headroom. While the image in Figure 7.17 includes a nice shot of the woman, there's really no need for all that space above her head. It doesn't reveal anything about her location, and takes up a lot of space that could be used to present her larger.

Lead your subject. When your subjects are looking off-frame, "lead" them by letting us see where they're looking (Figure 7.18).

Don't be afraid to crop tight. There's often nothing wrong with cutting off part of someone's head. A tightly cropped image is more personal, and brings more focus to the subject (Figure 7.19).

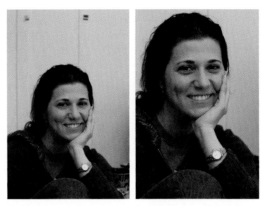

FIGURE 7.17   The left image has too much headroom. Since the space above her doesn't reveal anything about her location, it's wasted. A better approach is to frame tighter, so that more of the image is used to show her.

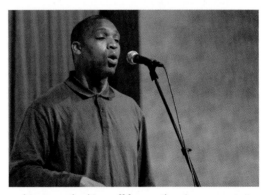

FIGURE 7.18   When subjects are looking off frame, the viewer wants to see what's in front of them. "Lead" your subjects by revealing the direction in which they're looking.

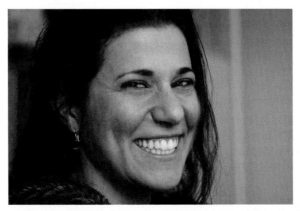

FIGURE 7.19   You don't have to show someone's entire face or body. Don't be afraid to crop tight to create a more intimate, personal shot.

Always remember: the most essential part of any portrait is the eyes. Make sure they're in focus and well composed. Cropping the eyes and lips is usually a bad idea, and cropping people at the joints can often be awkward as well.

Exercise: Composition

One of the great things about composition is that you can often correct it after the fact. The crop tool in your image editor gives you the capability to recompose and change the balance of your images. Ideally, you want to get your composition as right as possible inside your camera, to save post-production time, and to maximize the use of your image sensor. But, there will be times when cropping is the only way to get the shot you want.

Cropping is also a great way to practice composition. Find the `Cropping Tutorial.pdf` document in the Tutorials/Chapter 7 folder on the companion CD-ROM, and print it out. On it you will find a collection of pictures shot by some vacationing tourists. With a pen, mark a new crop for the image you think makes it look better. If you don't think it needs a crop, leave it alone. When you're finished, watch the Cropping Tutorial.mov to see how I recropped the images.

ON THE CD

FIVE PRACTICES FOR BETTER SHOOTING

While practicing "seeing" may seem abstract, it is something you can work at and improve. Composition is something you will always continue to explore and refine, as you will with your understanding of exposure. At the same time, there are some other practices you can employ to improve the quality of your images.

Seeing *In* the Camera, not *Through* the Camera

The brain has an amazing ability to focus your attention on something within your field of view. So much so, that it becomes very easy to not notice all the other things that *are* in your field of view.

For example, while walking downtown in San Francisco one day, I spotted the scene shown in Figure 7.20.

It may not look like much in the picture because, well, it's not. There's no real composition, and nothing for your eye to follow. Mostly, it looks a photo of an empty parking space. Granted, this is often a photo-worthy event in San Francisco, but while standing at the scene, what I was really struck by was the building with the tall façade in the distance. I found it striking for some reason, and then noticed that the strong rectangular shape of that building was balanced by the round turret of the building across the street.

In other words, my attention was focused on a very small part of my field of view, and completely ignored all the clutter around it. Holding a camera up to my face didn't change this perception—my brain continued to focus my attention on one small part of what was in the frame. So, when shooting, it's very important to

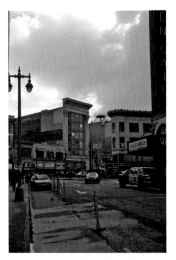

FIGURE 7.20   While walking down the street in San Francisco one day, I came across this scene.

pay attention to the image that is being shown in the viewfinder—see *that* image, not the small part your brain might be paying attention to.

The best way to guard against this is to trace your eyes around the edge of the frame before you press the shutter button. This will make you pay attention to other elements in your shot, and will also help you notice any strange intersections in your composition—telephone poles sticking out of people's heads, and that sort of thing.

Work the Subject

We've all done this: while walking down the street, something catches your eye that you think will make a great picture. So, you stop where you are, compose your shot, calculate your exposure, and fire away. Now think about it: what are the odds that you just happened to be standing in the one ideal spot to take a photo of whatever the thing is you saw? Of course, if it's a fleeting moment, you might very well have been in the only place possible to get the shot, but if it's something more persistent, there's a very good chance that there's a better place from which to build your shot.

To carry on from the previous example, after coming across the scene I described earlier, I zoomed in and started to take some pictures of the two buildings I had spotted. I shot several different frames from slightly varying distance, some with cars passing in front and some without. You can see a few of the results in Figure 7.21.

One of the great advantages of digital photography, of course, is that we can see our compositions right away, by looking at the LCD screen on the back of the camera. A quick check of my shot showed me something I was having trouble seeing through the viewfinder: the two buildings were too far apart to reveal the contrasting geometries I had noticed. This, again, is an example of my brain focusing my attention on something in the scene that wasn't actually being captured by my composition.

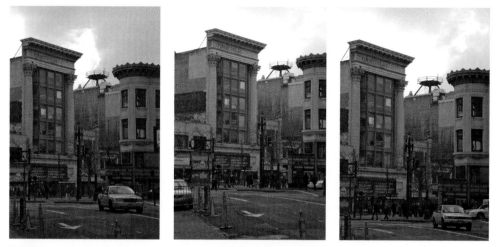

FIGURE 7.21   To attack this scene, I tried a number of different shots, from slightly different positions, with and without cars.

So, I moved across the street and tried a few more frames, and finally ended up with a composition I liked, the one in Figure 7.22. While I was shooting, I was visualizing the scene in black and white, and was choosing an exposure that would allow me to render the final image in a particular way. We'll look at that process in Chapter 14, "Imaging Tactics," when we discuss black-and-white conversion.

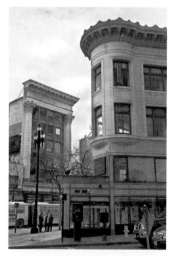

FIGURE 7.22   To get the scene I wanted, I finally had to move across the street and try a few more shots and angles.

The point is that you have to *work* your subject. Move around, try it from different angles—get closer, get farther, stand on your toes, get down on your knees, try different focal lengths. Figure 7.23 shows another example, a series of images of the great jazz drummer Jack DeJohnette. This scene had to be worked for quite a while to find a combination of interesting composition, good facial expression, and dynamic movement. I finally decided on the final shot, an image I shot using a LensBaby, a cool SLR attachment you can learn more about at *www.lensbabies.com*.

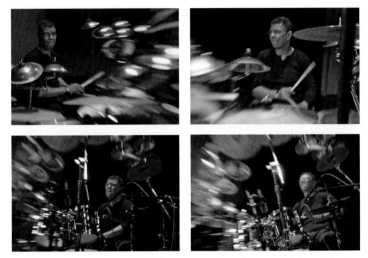

FIGURE 7.23   It took a number of experiments with composition and camera position, and a lot of frames containing different positions and facial expressions, to get a shot I liked.

Many people think that professional photographers go out, shoot 30 frames, and return home with 30 great shots. They don't. They work their shot, trying different angles, exposures, and ideas. Very often, they don't know which the idea is best until they get home and look at their images. The more you work your shot, the more choice you'll have when you get to post-production.

BURST MODE

As mentioned earlier, burst mode (sometimes referred to as drive mode) is a great way to improve your chances of catching a particular moment. It can also be essential for shooting complex group scenes where it's difficult to keep track of everyone's facial expression.

However, don't become too reliant on burst mode. Learning to shoot in single frame mode is a very important skill that will greatly improve your ability to recognize the "decisive moment" in a scene. What's more, depending on the speed of your camera's burst feature, the decisive moment may happen between frames. Consequently, being practiced at recognizing, anticipating, and capturing single frames can be an essential skill.

Narrative

Narrative is the process of telling a story. Narrative is a fairly simple thing to understand when you're writing or shooting video, because it's possible to convey a series of events that have a beginning, middle, and end. In photography, it can be a little more ephemeral.

Obviously, you can shoot multiple images to create a *diptych* or *triptych* that tells a straightforward story. But a single frame can also have a narrative. An image of a small child next to a broken vase tells a definite story of something that has just transpired. The image in Figure 7.24 also conveys a narrative, the promise of a big concert.

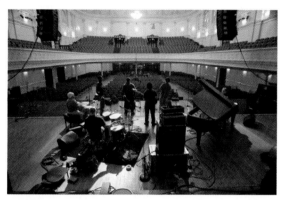

FIGURE 7.24   Although a single frame, this image tells the story of an impending event.

When trying to construct a photographic narrative, it's important to think about what information is required to tell your story. For example, this image from the same shoot simply shows clarinet player Don Byron. We don't know where he is, if he's playing with anyone else, whether he's preparing to play, or finishing. (See Figure 7.25.)

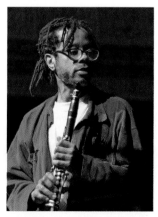

FIGURE 7.25   This figure doesn't convey quite as much narrative, because we can't tell the location, the nature of the event, whether he's finished playing, or going to play, and so on.

As we've learned, the viewer will project a lot of information into a scene. An empty, lit concert hall implies rehearsal, which probably means daytime, which means there's going to be a show happening in the future. As a photographer, you can use the viewers' automatic projections to build a story, as long as you give them enough clues to point them in the right direction.

Simplify

The less complex shot is almost always the better shot. We don't mean the shot that was easier to shoot, but the shot that contains fewer elements, so the viewer's eye is easily directed to the subject at hand. Good photography is a subtractive process. Where painters start with a blank canvas and get to add whatever they want, photographers start with the entire world and have to try to figure out ways to hide and remove elements from a scene, to reduce it to the bare essentials that convey their photographic idea. And so we choose our camera position very carefully, we crop, we make particular exposure choices, and we edit and adjust our images, all to reveal certain elements of a scene.

It's very rare that you won't get a better picture by moving closer to your subject. This is often the easiest way to simplify your composition and remove unwanted elements. When that isn't possible, think about other ways to streamline your image: post-production cropping, exposing to bring attention to one element or another, and so on. You'll learn more about these processes later in the book.

Don't Be Afraid

It may sound strange to talk about fear in terms of shooting photos. After all, unless you're shooting in particularly harrowing conditions there's no real risk involved in photography. Nevertheless, most people still employ risk management behavior while shooting. To get good images, you have to have the courage to try something new, to experiment, and to consider compositions and ideas you might not have shot before.

Why are people afraid to try new shots? Sometimes, it's because they're in public and are afraid of looking stupid. Don't worry about this. Most people in public are so busy worrying about whether *they* look stupid that they don't have time to notice what you may or may not be doing with your camera.

More often, the fear of trying new shots is the fear of coming home to find that you shot bad photos. Whether you experiment wildly or not, accept this right now: *the majority of the images* any *photographer takes are not keepers! And some are outright bad!*

You probably have a "comfort zone" of some kind, a type of shot you have been pleased with in the past. So you will continue to shoot this type of shot because, even if you're bored with it, you won't get home later and end up feeling discouraged by having taken something "bad" or "stupid."

When you work a subject as described in the previous section, you will get a lot of unusable images, possibly some "stupid" ones, and maybe some "bad" ones. And none of that has any relationship to your skill as a photographer. Working a subject is just like sketching, and just as not every line in a sketch is the "correct" line, not every photo you take is the "correct" photo, but they all serve to help you zone in on the keeper shot. However, many times you won't get that keeper image if you don't have the nerve to try some new ideas. So shoot a little extra—shoot on impulse and take chances. After all, you can always delete them later.

Equipment Doesn't Always Matter

Photography gear is so cool and so much fun that it can be very easy to think that buying more of it will make you a better photographer. It won't. Don't get me wrong, some cameras take images that are much sharper, and possess much more vibrant color than other cameras, but you can take a good picture with *any* camera. For example, Figure 7.26 shows a three-image panorama shot with an old 640 × 480, first-generation digital camera.

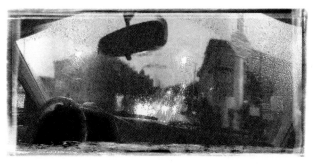

FIGURE 7.26   It's possible to take good images with *any* type of camera. Don't fall back on the excuse that you just need better gear to be a better photographer.

If you are editing an image and find a technical flaw you feel truly compromises the image—maybe the edges are soft, or the high-contrast areas suffer from distracting color fringes—you might want to invest in some different gear. Or, if you find that what would have made the image great is if you'd been able to shoot with a wider angle, or shallower depth of field, expanding your toolbox might be a reasonable idea. But if you think that any one piece of gear is going to make you take more interesting photos, you're wrong. Henri Cartier-Bresson, arguably the most influential photographer of the 20th century, shot most of his images with a 35 mm camera with a fixed, 50 mm lens. No autofocus, no autometering, no autowinding, and only one focal length. The cheapest decent digital point-and-shoot offers more features and flexibility.

If you want to take better pictures, spend your worry on light and seeing, not on gear envy.

Practice

As mentioned earlier, all the disciplines and theories we've been discussing are things you can improve at. However, improving takes practice—concentrated, focused practice. If you shoot regularly, you *will* become a better photographer. Don't force yourself—if you aren't able to be present, and "see" while practicing, the practice won't do you any good, but you should try to get out with your camera as often as you can.

Remember, too, that you need to be able to shoot in your own backyard. If you think you can't practice until you go on vacation, or until you're somewhere "interesting," you're mistaken. If you can't shoot at home, on your own block, you're not going to be able to shoot in Paris, or the Amazon rainforest, or Antarctica. It's not the place you're in, it's what you're able to see, and seeing takes practice.

One of the easiest ways to practice is to give yourself an assignment. Sometimes, if you just go out in the world and look for images, it's difficult to see anything. When you have the whole world to choose from, where do you start? An assignment or project can help give you focus, and narrow the range of possibilities, which will help you see more images.

Some possibilities for assignments or projects include:

Choose a subject you care deeply about. Interested in old architecture? Then define an old architecture project of some kind. Concerned about the homeless? Fascinated by the local bird population? Any of these make excellent subjects for a photo assignment.

Choose a simple word or phrase. "Beauty and the best," "My cup runneth over," "Look before you leap." There's no right or wrong to any of these topics, so you can interpret them however you like.

A particular type of object. Stoplights, for example. Obviously, pictures of bunches of stoplights may not be interesting, but many events happen *around* stoplights that might be very compelling. A particular object can often provide a context and structure for your shooting.

A geographic area. Sometimes, confining your photo safaris to a particular location can help refine your eye. For example, while working on this book I've been spending so much time *writing* about photography that I haven't had a lot of time for actual shooting. When this happens, I decide to work on my Three Blocks project—images taken within three blocks of my house. Three blocks provide enough space for variety, but are close enough that I can easily duck out for 30 or 45 minutes to do some shooting, without falling *too* far behind on my deadline. (Let's face it, very often there's no question of being behind, it's just a matter of degree.)

A project can often be "an inch wide and a mile deep." Set a limited goal to give yourself direction and then explore that goal in great detail.

Finally, *remember to look through the camera!* This may sound like strange advice; often we go out to shoot and feel pressured to deliver images, or we've been working hard and forget to warm up, so we're not really seeing. We hurry through the world with an "okay, I'm ready to shoot, bring on the images" kind of attitude. Very often, you can't recognize an image until you look through the camera's viewfinder. What appears to be an empty, boring tableau might actually be full of complex interesting compositions once you see the scene through your camera viewfinder.

While out walking about, if something even remotely interesting catches your eye—a play of the light, a compositional idea, an interesting color—look at the scene through your camera. You still don't have to take a picture, but you may be surprised to find a composition you didn't see before. When the impulse of an image hits, there's very often something there if you dig into the scene and work it.

INITIAL CAMERA SETTINGS

Your camera provides many controls and settings. At first, keeping track of all of them can feel overwhelming. Fortunately, many of the settings on your camera are not "everyday" settings. Rather, they're basic configuration parameters you'll probably change once and then rarely touch again. In this section, we'll look at these types of settings, and discuss how to configure them.

Image Size and Compression

Your camera probably allows you to select from a number of different size and compression settings. Nowadays, with storage so cheap, there's almost no reason not to shoot at full resolution with the best quality compression, even if you're shooting for the Web. Sure, full-resolution images have to be resized before being posted to the Web, but the extra resolution gives you the option of later repurposing your images for print, or for cropping and enlarging just part of the image. As such, when you first get your camera, you'll most likely set resolution and compression to their highest-quality settings, and then leave them there.

However, there are some times when you might want to change these settings. If you're on a long shoot and you begin to run out of storage, for example. Or, if you're shooting for a particular workflow—such as for the Web or for a small print size—and you don't want to spend a lot of time resizing your images later.

Image size is simply the dimensions, in pixels, of the image the camera will create. A 3-megapixel camera, for example, typically offers a maximum resolution of roughly 2048 × 1536 pixels, along with options for shooting in XGA resolution (1024 × 768 pixels) and VGA resolution (640 × 480 pixels).

Which size is the "correct" size depends on how you will output your images. If your images are destined for the Web, you might be able to get away with 640 × 480 resolution. The correct image size for print depends on the type of printer to which you'll be outputting, and the final print size of your image. We'll discuss these issues in detail in Chapter 16, "Output."

When it comes to compression, it's best to always shoot with the lowest level (highest quality), particularly if you're shooting images that don't fare well under JPEG compression. (See Chapter 2, "How a Digital Camera Works.") JPEG artifacts are difficult, if not impossible, to remove later, so it's best to avoid them altogether. If you're shooting in raw format, this won't be a concern.

Obviously, choosing the largest image size with the lowest compression setting means you won't be able to fit as many images onto your storage medium. If you run short on storage when you're in the field, you might want to switch to different image size and compression settings:

- If your destination is the Web, you can afford to lower the camera's resolution (and hope you never want to print any of your images).
- If your final destination is print, you should keep your resolution the same but increase your compression (and hope the artifacting isn't too bad).

Money Can Buy Photographic Happiness

Storage is one of those few problems you can easily solve by spending additional money. If you want to ensure you can always shoot at the highest quality your camera allows, you should invest in more storage.

Some cameras do not allow you to adjust image size and compression separately. Instead, they'll offer a menu of predefined combinations. In Figure 7.27, the camera shows options for full resolution with high quality (low compression), full resolution with low quality (high compression), the same options for medium and small resolution, and finally raw format. Next are options for raw format, plus a separate JPEG file, then finally raw only.

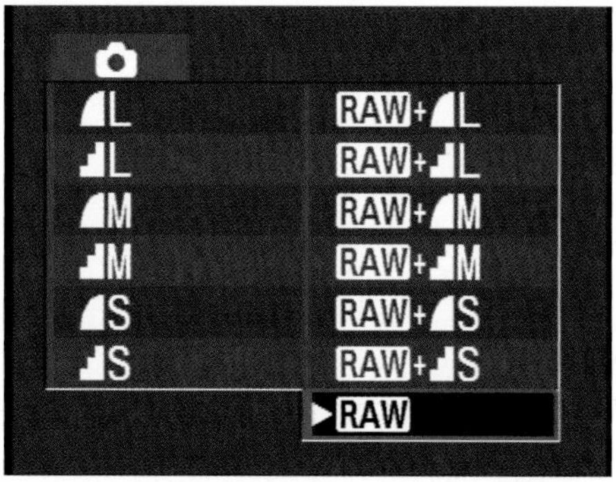

FIGURE 7.27   A typical image-size menu. You can select between three different sizes, each with a choice of two compression (quality) settings, raw format plus a JPEG, or just raw format.

File Format

Although JPEG is the format of choice for all digital cameras, many models also offer some additional uncompressed formats. Uncompressed files take up substantially more space than JPEGs, but are free from the blocky artifacts JPEG images sometimes possess. They might also afford you more editing latitude and allow some edits that simply aren't possible in JPEG files. Your camera probably supports either or both of the following formats:

TIFF: TIFF files are a standard, uncompressed file format that just about every graphics program can read. The easiest way to determine the size difference between shooting in TIFF and shooting in JPEG is to stick an empty card into your camera and note how many pictures are available in JPEG format. Now, switch to TIFF format and note the remaining pictures. It will probably be much lower. TIFF files are useful for those times when you want to greatly enlarge an area or part of an area and simply can't afford to see any JPEG artifacts.

Raw: If your camera supports it, raw is the preferred choice for uncompressed shooting. In Chapter 2, "How a Digital Camera Works," you learned about the advantages and differences of raw shooting. We'll cover raw exposure in Chapter 8, "Metering and Exposure," and raw processing in Chapter 12, "Raw Conversion." If you don't want to shoot in JPEG format, and your camera offers both TIFF and raw options, it's better to choose raw. Raw files are smaller than TIFF files and offer much more editing flexibility.

Raw + JPEG: Some cameras can simultaneously store images in raw and JPEG mode. We'll discuss the merits and drawbacks of this in Chapter 12.

You'll probably rarely change image size and compression, unless you start to run out of storage. You might change file format more often, although beginning digital photographers might want to stick with JPEG before complicating matters with raw options.

With these configurations in place, you're ready to consider the settings you'll change more often, sometimes even with every shot.

Image Processing Parameters

Most cameras provide special menu options for controlling some image processing functions such as contrast, saturation, and sharpness. These adjustments are applied to JPEG or TIFF files in-camera, after you shoot. They're really nothing more than the same type of image-editing operations you might perform on your own later, using your image editor on your computer. In most cases, these options offer a simple slider control that gives you a choice of three to five different levels for each setting.

The advantage of these options is that if you regularly find yourself making a particular change in post-production—increasing or decreasing the saturation, bumping up the contrast, sharpening your images—you might be able to adjust these parameters so you don't have to perform these additional editing steps. This can greatly simplify your post-production workflow. Just as you used to choose a particular type of film for its contrast and color characteristics, you can use these settings so your camera shoots images with a particular look.

The downside to these settings is that they sometimes "use up" some of your editing latitude, meaning that, later, you won't be able to make as many edits before encountering certain types of artifacts. We'll cover this concept in more detail in Chapter 11, "Correcting Tone and Color."

Sharpening is a particularly dangerous setting, because it's impossible to remove *over*sharpening from an image.

Try some test shots with different settings, and you'll probably find a set of parameters you like. You'll probably find that you can leave your camera at those settings from then on, and will rarely alter these parameters.

Of course, if you want to change these features regularly, that's fine. You might, for example, discover that one contrast setting works very well indoors, while another works better outdoors. Or, perhaps you have a job where the client wants images to look older. In that case, you might choose to dial down the saturation for the duration of the shoot.

Many cameras provide the option to store sets of parameters, so you can quickly reconfigure an entire batch of settings with a single menu option.

Remember: If you're shooting raw, these parameters have no effect. However, the image that's displayed on your camera's LCD after you shoot *might* be processed with these settings. As such, it can appear that changing these types of settings is altering your raw file. They're not. They're simply altering the image the camera builds for playback.

BUILDING A SHOT

So far, we've discussed how to be more attuned to potential images; how to compose a scene to create a well-balanced, compelling shot; how to practice your composition and shooting skills; and how to configure your camera's initial basic parameters. We discussed the difference between art and craft in photography, and so far have mostly covered the art side of things. Now it's time to head into the craft—the actual button pushing and decision making that will happen when you have found a scene and are ready to start trying to make a picture of it.

Many decisions must be made when you take a shot, and your camera is capable of making many of them for you. Nevertheless, you must pay attention to bias it toward better decisions, to ensure that it's making good choices, and to understand when it may be time to take some control away from the camera.

In this section, we're going to look at the process of building a shot. The steps you go through when you've spotted a scene and want to try to capture it. You won't always have time to work methodically through each of these steps, and as you improve and gain more experience, many of these steps will come automatically—you won't even have to think about them.

Deciding to Shoot

Earlier, we talked about how to recognize a shot. Shot recognition will happen in different ways depending on the type of shooting you're doing. If you're shooting an event—a wedding or birthday party, for example—your recognition will probably come very quickly, as you move amongst the crowd looking for nicely balanced compositions, good moments, and compelling expressions. If you're shooting on the street, you might also happen upon split-second moments that require more reflex than thought.

But there might be other types of street shooting that require more considera-tion. Perhaps the light has fallen on a particular location in a beautiful way, and you want to try to work that location to take advantage. Landscape shooting can be the same way: you spot the beautiful vista and then try to figure out what the picture is.

Depending on the pace and style of shooting, the way you decide to shoot will vary. Sometimes, you'll have to move quickly and fire reflexively, while trying to keep one eye trained on your settings. At other times, you will have had an impulse that a potential shot lies before you, and you'll have to work to determine what the shot is.

In either case, you'll need to consider all of the following decisions.

Choosing a Mode

Your digital camera probably has a number of shooting modes that dictate what ex-posure decisions will be made by the camera and what decisions will be left up to you. Your first task when you approach a shot, therefore, is to choose the appropri-ate shooting mode. (See Figure 7.28.)

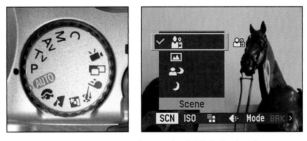

FIGURE 7.28   Some cameras have physical dials that let you select different shooting modes; others require a trip into the camera's menu system to change modes.

Very often, the subject matter or style of shooting will immediately dictate a mode. For example, when shooting an event you may walk into the room and real-ize the light is very low, and you will need to choose a mode that allows you control of shutter speed, to guarantee sharp images. You'll probably stick with that mode for the duration of the shoot. Or perhaps you're off to shoot a social occasion with good lighting, and so decide to choose a mode that will allow you control of aperture, so you can choose to blur out the background behind people.

For some subjects, you may try several different modes as you work the shot and change your idea of what it should be. For example, you might start out on fully automatic mode, and then realize later that to capture the image you want, you need more control.

Often, shooting on full automatic will be all you need to do. (And don't worry, shooting on automatic doesn't mean you're a wimpy photographer.) Every photo-graphic situation is unique, of course, but there are some general guidelines you can follow to determine when you should use each shooting mode. As you learn more about photography, and your camera in general, you'll get a better idea of which mode to choose.

Full Automatic

Most automatic modes take care of everything. They select a white balance, ISO, shutter speed, and aperture, and choose whether to use the flash. Automatic modes usually also let you select a metering mode, if your camera offers a choice. For the most part, the automatic mode on your camera will do a good job in just about any situation. If you're in a hurry to catch a fleeting action, this might be your best bet. Or, if you're simply tired of thinking about your camera all the time and just want to take a picture, go with automatic mode.

Program Mode

Program mode offers most of the automatic functionality of a fully automatic mode—auto white balancing, light metering, exposure choice—but allows you to override some options. On most cameras, program mode will let you make your own selection of ISO, white balance, and exposure compensation. Some will even let you cycle through reciprocal exposures to choose a shutter speed/aperture combination that's more appropriate to your desired image. For most shooting tasks, the simple manual overrides provided by program mode are all you'll ever need.

The first priority of your camera's light meter is to get you an image that is well exposed in terms of brightness—not so dark that you can't see details, and not so bright that details have blown out to complete white. It achieves this by selecting a shutter speed and aperture, and possibly by changing the ISO. It will always prioritize shutter speed, to try to guarantee a speed that is fast enough to prevent blurring caused by camera shake.

In a dark situation, it may not be able to do this. For those times, you might want to shift to a mode that allows for manual shutter speed control, to guarantee a shake-preventing shutter speed. Similarly, if you *want* blur in your image—blur you can control— you'll want to use a manual shutter speed mode. As already mentioned, if you want control of aperture for your creative intent, you'll want to switch to a manual aperture mode.

Shutter Priority and Aperture Priority Modes

Automatic modes can yield excellent results, but they also make certain assumptions about how you want your image to look. For example, in automatic mode, your images will be evenly exposed, and the camera will try to defer to faster shutter speeds to stop motion. As already mentioned, there will be times when these assumptions will be wrong. For those times, you might want to switch to a priority mode.

Shutter priority mode lets you select the shutter speed you'd like to use. The camera then selects an appropriate aperture. Shutter priority is ideal for times when you have to freeze motion, such as capturing action at a sporting event, because it lets you force the camera to shoot with a particular (fast, in the case of sports) shutter speed. Similarly, there might be other times when you want to ensure that a speeding object looks blurry in your final image, and so will choose a slow shutter speed.

Aperture priority mode works the same way, but allows you to select an aperture and leaves the choice of shutter speed up to the camera. Aperture priority modes give you control over the *depth of field* in your image, allowing you to control how much of the image is in focus. (See Figure 7.29.)

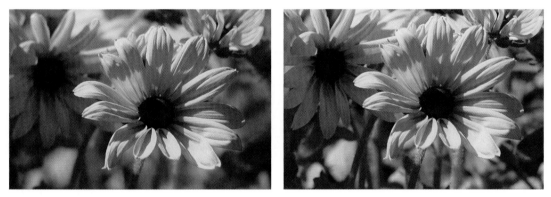

FIGURE 7.29 By changing the camera's aperture, we can control the depth of field in an image. Note the difference in background in these two images. The lower image has a much deeper depth of field, resulting in a more focused background, whereas the upper image has a shallow depth of field, resulting in a blurry, softly focused background. These images were shot with reciprocal exposures—only the aperture changed.

Most shutter and aperture priority modes also yield control of ISO and white balance. In Chapter 8, "Metering and Exposure," you'll learn much more about how to use these modes.

Manual Mode

As you would expect, full manual mode gives you control of everything. Although this might seem like the ultimate "power user" mode, you might find that you often need control of only one exposure parameter or the other, and so you will use a priority mode. However, manual mode is a must for maximum creative freedom and for handling difficult lighting situations.

Special Shooting Modes

Some cameras offer special shooting modes for specific circumstances. In these modes, certain features are preset. For example, landscape modes typically fix the focus on infinity and select smaller apertures to ensure maximum depth of field. Sometimes, these special modes are the only way to gain access to certain features such as slow-sync flash (which we'll discuss later). Before you use any of these modes, however, check the camera's documentation and be sure you understand the settings that might be affected.

As you learn more about the decisions you'll make when you shoot, choosing a mode will become more obvious. Because this book won't cover how to use the controls of specific cameras, it's important for you to spend some time learning how the various modes on your camera work.

White Balance

Different types of light shine with different color qualities. Direct sunlight, for example, is very blue, while tungsten light is very orange. One of the amazing characteristics of your eyes is that as you move among all of these different types of light, you still perceive colors in the same way. Blue looks blue whether you're in sunlight or a lamp-lit room. Your eyes can even understand mixed lighting conditions—sunlight shining through a window into a fluorescent-lit room, for example.

Unlike your eyes, a digital image sensor is not as sophisticated. As you move from one type of light to another, shooting pictures, the same color might appear very different from one photo to the next, as the lighting conditions change. An image sensor simply captures light and passes it to the camera's onboard computer for processing. It's up to that computer to interpret the color correctly for the particular type of light in which you are shooting. For it to correctly perform this interpretation, the camera's computer needs to determine, or be told, what type of light is striking your subject. Fortunately, there's a very easy way to perform this calibration.

As you learned in grade school, white light is composed of every other color. Therefore, if a camera can accurately reproduce white, it can accurately represent any other color. *White balancing* is the process of determining what, in your scene, is white. Once your camera knows what is supposed to be white, it can determine the type of light in your scene and accurately reproduce any other color. Figure 7.30 shows the same scene shot several times, each with a different white balance setting.

YOU SAY "COLOR," I SAY "COLOR TEMPERATURE"

The color of a specific light is measured as a temperature using the Kelvin scale. For example, direct sunlight has a color temperature of 5500°K. You will often see photographers referring to the *color temperature* of a light source, and your camera's white balance setting might even prompt you to enter the color temperature of the current light.

The reason light color is defined as temperature is because of something called *black body radiation*. If you heat a black object, it will begin to change color. As it gets hotter, it will progress through a spectrum of colors from red through orange, then yellow, white, and blue-white. The color corresponds to the temperature to which the object has been heated. This, then, is why light is measured as a temperature.

One thing to note, as the temperature increases, the color shifts toward blue. So, higher temperatures actually yield colors we traditionally refer to as "cooler."

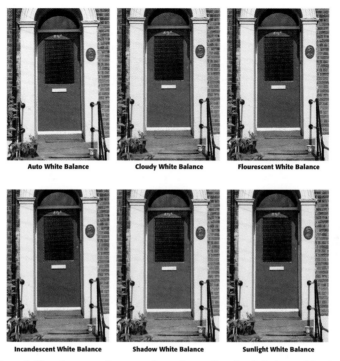

| Auto White Balance | Cloudy White Balance | Flourescent White Balance |

| Incandescent White Balance | Shadow White Balance | Sunlight White Balance |

FIGURE 7.30   Although film photographers need to select a film that is balanced for the type of light in which they'll be shooting, digital photographers need to make certain their cameras are properly white-balanced for the current light. Use the wrong white-balance setting, and your images will have strange color casts that can be difficult to remove.

Setting White Balance

Every time you take your camera into a new lighting situation, you need to consider how to best white balance for that light. Proper white balance is essential to getting accurate color, and the only equivalent it has in the film world is the choice you make when you buy a particular type of film. Consequently, whether you're new to photography or you're an experienced film photographer, *you must learn to start thinking about white balance!*

All cameras have an automatic white-balance feature and, depending on the quality of your camera, this might be all you need to use to get accurate white balance. The simplest automatic white-balance mechanisms look for the brightest point in your shot, assume that that point is white, and then use that point as a reference to balance accordingly. More sophisticated automatic white balancers perform a complex analysis of many different areas in your image. Both mechanisms are surprisingly effective, and you'll almost always yield very good color when shooting in direct sunlight, and decent color in other lighting conditions. However, even a few clouds can confuse an auto-white-balance mechanism, and in other types of light you may find that your auto white balance works very poorly. So, even with the best cameras, you'll very often need to switch out of auto-white-balance mode.

Fortunately, most cameras offer preset configurations for different lighting conditions—Daylight, Tungsten, Fluorescent, and possibly a Cloudy or Overcast setting. (Tungsten is sometimes called "Incandescent" or "Indoors.") Because there are two different temperatures of fluorescent lights—"cool white" and "warm white"—some cameras offer separate settings for each fluorescent color.

Other cameras will actually specify white balance presets in degrees Kelvin. Be sure you understand which setting corresponds to which type of light. (See Figure 7.31.)

White Balance in K°		
3000°K	-	White Tungsten
3700°K	-	Yellow Tungsten
4000°K	-	Flourescent
4500°K	-	Flourescent
5500°K	-	Sunlight
6500°K	-	Cloudy
7500°K	-	Shade

FIGURE 7.31 Some cameras use manual white-balance controls that are measured in degrees Kelvin. If your camera simply presents a list of temperatures, here are the types of lights to which those temperatures correspond.

These white-balance presets are usually more accurate than automatic white balance in the situations for which they're designed. However, you can't always be sure that your lighting situation is exactly the color temperature your camera's preset is expecting. For these situations, some cameras offer white balance fine-tuning that allows you to alter a preset white balance to be warmer or cooler.

Manual White Balance

So, in general you can expect your camera's auto white balance to do very well in direct sunlight. For other instances you have white balance presets, which may not be tuned exactly right for the light you're trying to shoot in. Therefore, for the absolute best results under any lighting situation—and especially under mixed lighting—you'll want to use your camera's manual white balance.

To use a manual white-balance control, hold a white object—such as a piece of paper—in front of the camera, and activate the camera's manual white-balance feature. The camera will calculate a white balance based on the light in your scene.

Measure the Right Light with the Right White

When you manually white balance, be sure to hold your white card in the light that is hitting your subject. This is particularly critical in a studio situation where your camera might be sitting in very different light from your subject.

On some cameras, you set manual white balance by pointing the camera at a white object and then pressing a special button. On others, you take a picture of the white object and then tell the camera to use that image as the white reference. The advantage to the second approach is that you can store white pictures shot in different lighting situations and switch between them very easily. Check your camera's manual for more details.

For example, Figure 7.32 shows an image shot with auto white balance in the shade. The color is not wildly out of whack, but it's too cool and the flesh tones are not accurate. In the second image, the model held up a piece of white paper, and the camera's manual white balance feature was used to calculate white balance. The third image was taken using that manual white balance setting. As you can see, it's much warmer, with more accurate flesh tones.

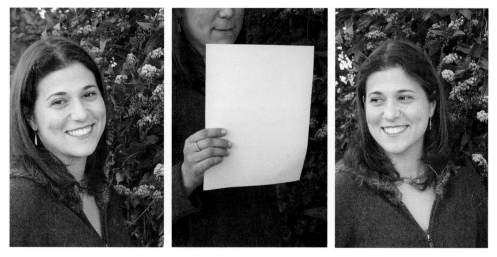

FIGURE 7.32   The first image was shot with auto white balance. For the second image, we had the model hold up a white piece of paper. We told the camera to use this image to set a manual white balance, and took the third image, which is much more accurate.

For this technique to work, the white piece of paper *must* be in the same light as your subject. For example, in Figure 7.32 the camera could have been positioned in direct sunlight. If the paper was held directly in front of the camera, we would have ended up with a white balance calculation based on direct sun rather than on shade.

Take some test pictures with your camera to learn more about its white-balance peculiarities. This will give you a better idea of when you need to white balance manually.

Change Manual White Balance Every Time You Change Light

Once you've manually white balanced, you can continue to use that white balance setting as long as your lighting doesn't change. If your lighting changes, you'll need to white balance again.

White Balance Aids

While the manual white balance image in Figure 7.32 looks much better, it's still not perfect. Overall, the color is a little yellowish. While manual white balance is almost always better than auto, there are some simple things you can do to improve it even more.

The ExpoDisc shown in Figure 7.33 is a white-balance aid that works in conjunction with your camera's manual white balance. When you're ready to manually white balance, you place the ExpoDisc over the end of your lens and point your camera at your light source. Then, you take a white-balance reference shot. This shot is then used as the source of your manual white balance. Really, the ExpoDisc is nothing more than a substitute for a white piece of paper. However, the white balance derived from the Expo-Disc generate shot is usually much more accurate than what you'll get off a piece of paper, as you can see in Figure 7.34.

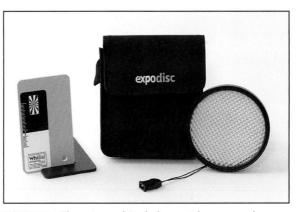

FIGURE 7.33 These two white-balance aids can greatly improve the accuracy of your manual white-balance operations. On the left is the WhiBal white-balance reference card, and on the right is the ExpoDisc.

ExpoDiscs range in price from $99 to $130 depending on the size you need, and you can learn more about them—including detailed tutorials on how to use them—at *www.expodisc.com*.

While the ExpoDisc lets you get accurate color right out of the camera, it requires you to position the camera at your subject's location, and then point back to your light source. This can be difficult if your light source is an on-camera flash. A white balance reference card such as the WhiBal card shown in Figure 7.33 provides

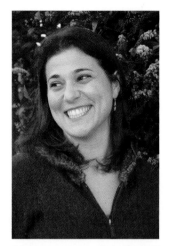

FIGURE 7.34   For this image, we used the ExpoDisc to perform our manual white balance. As you can see, it's more accurate than the in-camera manual white balance shown in Figure 7.32.

a simple way to correct white balance *after* you've taken the shot. To use the WhiBal card, you place it within your light field, just as you do with a normal white-balance reference, and then take a picture using auto white balance. Then, remove the card and shoot your shots, also using auto white balance. (See Figure 7.35.) Later, you use your image editor to correct the white balance using your reference image. We'll discuss how to do this in Chapters 11 and 12.

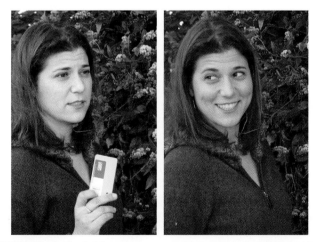

FIGURE 7.35   In the left image, our model is holding the WhiBal white-balance reference. We took a picture, and then removed the card. In our image editor, we used that reference image to correct the color in the right-hand image, resulting in a very accurate white balance.

A white balance reference card even works well for street shooting. If you find yourself in a weird lighting situation, just hold the card in front of the camera and take a shot. You can later use that image to correct the other shots you shoot in that light. (See Figure 7.36.)

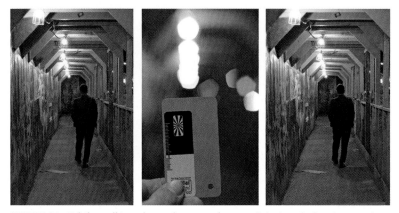

FIGURE 7.36   While walking down the street late at night I took the shot on the left. Because I knew that auto white balance would be inaccurate, I immediately held up my WhiBal card and took a shot of it. Later, I used the WhiBal image to correct the color in my original shot.

The WhiBal card is available from *www.whibal.com* and sells for around $30.

Bad White Balance

You might be tempted to assume that you don't have to worry about correct white balance because you can always use your image editor to correct white-balance troubles. This is sometimes true, but it can take a lot of work to correct a bad white balance. (See Figure 7.37.) The color shifts that occur from incorrect white balance don't affect all of the colors in an image equally—the highlights in an image might be shifted more than the shadows. Consequently, you won't be able to do a simple global correction. Moreover, as you'll see later, by the time you're done correcting the white balance, you might have used up enough of your image's dynamic range that it will be difficult to perform further corrections and adjustments without introducing artifacts. In the end, it's best to shoot with the most accurate white balance your camera can manage.

If you're shooting in raw mode, you might feel like you don't need to worry about white balance, since raw files allow you to set white balance after the fact, without using up any of your editing latitude. This is true, but shooting with bad white balance means you'll have to do a lot of editing and adjustment later. Shooting as cleanly as possible in-camera will greatly speed your workflow. Also, just because raw images allow for fine white-balance control, it can still be difficult to determine the correct white balance.

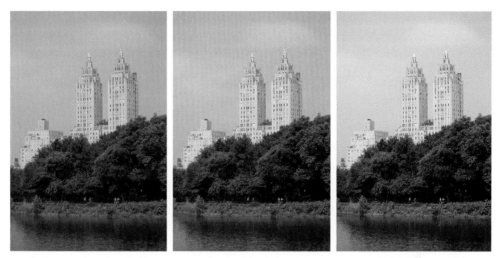

FIGURE 7.37   The left image was accidentally shot with Tungsten white balance (instead of auto, or daylight). The middle image shows our attempts to correct the color. Although the image is improved, completely removing the bad color casts is extremely difficult and results in an image with bad posterizing artifacts (which are difficult to see at this print size). The right image was shot with a correct white balance. As you can see, white-balance choice is not to be taken lightly, because correcting it later is extremely difficult.

No matter what format you're shooting in, you may decide that you don't need to worry about white balance because you're ultimately going for a stylized look, not realistic color. That's fine, but you never know how you might want to repurpose your images later. Having accurate white balance will give you a record of what the real color was, and still allow you to perform your stylized adjustments.

Metering

You're going to be reading a lot about metering later in this chapter and in Chapter 8. For now, simply be aware that your camera provides different metering choices. It probably defaults to some form of matrix metering, which will be the best option for most shooting situations. If you change your meter to another setting, be sure to remember to change it back when you change shooting situations.

ISOs

As you saw in Chapter 3, "Basic Photography: A Quick Primer," a digital camera's sensitivity to light is measured using the same ISO scale used by film cameras. As ISO rating increases, the camera becomes more light sensitive, and a more light-sensitive camera offers different creative possibilities. In addition to allowing you to shoot using less light, a higher ISO rating allows you to use smaller apertures and higher shutter speeds when shooting bright daylight.

Although the most common ISO speeds are 100, 200, and 400, higher-end models can go as high as 3200 ISO while some cameras offer a super slow ISO 50.

There is a price to pay for this increased sensitivity, though. As explained in Chapter 2, as you increase ISO, your images will get noisier. Consequently, you'll want to keep your ISO setting as low as possible. (See Figures 4.2 and 4.3 for examples of noise.)

Some cameras handle this extra noise better than others, producing fine-grained, monochromatic noise that almost looks like the increased grain you'd find in high-speed film. Higher-end cameras often don't show a noticeable increase in noise until around ISO 800. Other cameras, though, produce increased noise that is quite ugly. In Chapter 14, "Imaging Tactics," we'll look at some methods for trying to remove noise from your images.

Cameras with very low ISOs produce images with very little noise. However, shooting at ISO 50 is only practical in bright sunlight or with a tripod.

Keep an Eye on Your ISO

Most cameras remember your last ISO setting, even after you've turned off the camera. Therefore, if you spent a long night shooting at ISO 800, don't forget to check your ISO setting the next day, before you go out shooting in bright daylight. Although your camera will be able to shoot in daylight at ISO 800, your images might be overexposed; they will certainly be noisier than at a slower speed, and your shutter speeds will be very high.

Framing and Focusing

Earlier in this chapter, we discussed a number of guidelines for good composition—where to place things in frame to create a balanced, pleasing image. How you choose to frame the scene has an obvious impact on its composition. However, your choice of focal length and camera position will also have a great impact on your composition, as they both greatly affect the sense of space and depth in your scene.

Focal Length

The great thing about a zoom lens is that it provides tremendous flexibility when you frame a shot. Without changing your position, you can quickly zoom in to a subject to get a tighter view and a different framing. However, it's important to recognize that as you zoom, many things change in your image besides the field of view and magnification. A zoom lens is more than just a convenience. The ability to select a focal length lets you greatly alter the sense of space in your composition.

It's easy to think of your zoom lens as a big magnifying glass and, to a degree, it is. As you zoom in, your subject appears larger and larger. This is why digital camera manufacturers label their lenses with a magnification factor—2x, 3x, and so forth. However, a few other things happen to your image when you zoom.

As you go to a longer focal length (zoom in), your field of view gets narrower. The human eye has a field of view of about 50° to 55°. This is considered a "normal" field of view, and any lens that produces a 50° to 55° viewing angle is said to be a *normal lens*.

More important, though, is to pay attention to the way your perception of the depth in your scene changes. Consider the images in Figure 7.38.

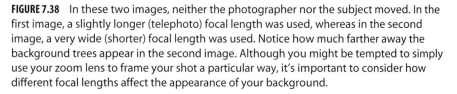

FIGURE 7.38   In these two images, neither the photographer nor the subject moved. In the first image, a slightly longer (telephoto) focal length was used, whereas in the second image, a very wide (shorter) focal length was used. Notice how much farther away the background trees appear in the second image. Although you might be tempted to simply use your zoom lens to frame your shot a particular way, it's important to consider how different focal lengths affect the appearance of your background.

Both of these images were shot from the same location. The only thing that changed between shots was the focal length of the lens. In addition to the framing and the size of the subject, notice how the background appears much farther away in the wide-angle image. In general, the wide-angle image has a much greater sense of depth. Now look at the two images in Figure 7.39.

In these two images, the subject remained in the same place, but the photographer moved farther away and used a different focal length to keep the images framed identically. Notice how much closer the tables and chairs look in the second image. As the photographer moved back and zoomed in, the depth in the image became compressed, resulting in the background elements appearing closer.

As you can see, both field of view and the sense of depth in an image are functions of the position of your camera and the focal length you choose to use. These two factors combine to create a very different sense of depth and space. Photography textbooks for the last 150 years (including previous editions of this book) have explained that this change happens because as you change focal lengths, different parts of your image are magnified by different amounts. *This is not true!* All lenses magnify by the same amount. The change in perspective occurs because of your changing camera position, and the field of view differences provided by different focal lengths.

Controlling depth and perspective in your scene is yet another creative option you have available. Next time you're shooting a location, consider how you want to

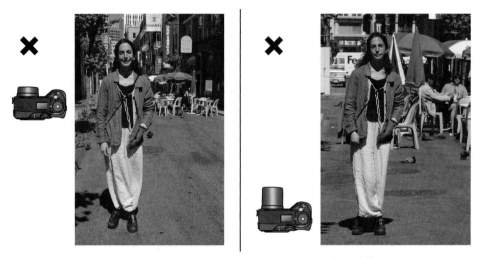

FIGURE 7.39   Although these two images are framed the same, notice how different the backgrounds are. In the left image, the camera was positioned close to the subject and zoomed out, whereas in the right image, the camera was pulled back and zoomed in. Note how much closer the background chairs appear in the telephoto (right) image. The sense of depth in the scene changes as we change our camera position and corresponding focal length. In general, the entire sense of space differs in the two images, even though the subject didn't move.

represent that space. Do you want it cramped and claustrophobic? Or deep and expansive? Choose your camera position and focal length accordingly.

To see proof of this claim that all lenses magnify by equal amounts, take a look at the `Camera Position.pdf` *movie located in the Chapter 7 folder of the companion CD-ROM.*

ON THE CD

Portrait Distortion. At some point, you've probably looked at a photograph of yourself and thought, "That doesn't really look like me." One reason for the poor result might be that the photographer used a wide-angle lens. Shooting a portrait with a wide-angle lens can be problematic because of the weird perspective it provides. Check out the pictures in Figure 7.40. The image on the left was shot with a slightly telephoto lens and really does look like the actual person. The image on the right is not such a good likeness. The nose is too big, and the ears have been rendered too small. In addition, the distance between the nose and ears—the depth of the picture—is too long. (Of course, although the picture on the right is less literally correct, it might be a better expression of the person's true character. This is a creative, interpretive choice you get to make while shooting.)

Typically, portrait photographers use a slightly telephoto lens. Some even use special "portrait" lenses that have some spherical aberration designed into the lens. These aberrations tend to soften the detail in the image to improve skin tones.

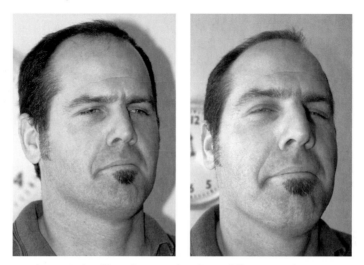

FIGURE 7.40   A change in focal length can make a huge difference in the appearance of your subject. The image on the left was shot with a long (telephoto) focal length. Next, we zoomed out and moved closer to our subject to produce the oddly distorted image on the right. (As in the previous example, note how the depth in the telephoto image appears different. The clock over the man's shoulder appears much closer in the left image.)

Geometric Distortion

Most zoom lenses exhibit some form of barrel or pincushion distortion when zoomed to either of their extremes. These distortions will show up as curves and warps around the edges and corners of your image. (You can see an example in Figure 4.9.)

When you find yourself at the limits of your zoom range, check the edges of your image to see if there's any distortion. If there is, and you can live with it, then by all means take the shot. If it bothers you, you might need to reposition your camera and select a new focal length. If the distortion isn't too bad, you might be able to remove it with your image-editing software, as we'll see in Chapter 11. Barrel distortion is especially prevalent when shooting macro photographs, because you tend to be zoomed out all the way and positioned very close to your subject. It's not necessarily a problem, but it's good to keep an eye out for it while you're shooting. If you get an unacceptable level of distortion, you may want to zoom in some and go for a shot that isn't as close to your subject.

One Way to Avoid Embarrassment

If you're using a rangefinder camera with an optical viewfinder, note that, because you aren't looking through the camera's imaging lens, it is actually possible to shoot with the lens cap on. Some cameras are smart enough to warn you, but others will let you blithely go along shooting black frames. Be sure to double-check! If your subject is pointing and laughing at you, there's a good chance that it's because your lens cap is on, or you're having a bad hair day.

Cutting Down on Lens Flares

Figure 5.23 shows the type of flaring that can occur with some lenses. Typically, lenses with wider diameters are more prone to flaring. There are several ways to eliminate flares, the easiest being to simply hold your hand above the lens (or put a sunshade on your lens) to block the flare-causing light. Circular polarizers will also help reduce flare, although at the expense of f-stops.

Prefocusing/Focusing

Your digital camera invariably has an automatic focus, but you still need to give some thought to focusing. Your camera's autofocus mechanism has to make some decisions about what it thinks it should focus on. If it makes the wrong choice, your picture will be out of focus. Unfortunately, your LCD screen is too small to provide an accurate gauge of focus, so you may not know your picture is out of focus until you get back to your computer. Consequently, it's a good idea to understand the workings of your camera's autofocus system so you can use it effectively.

No matter what type of system your camera uses for determining focus, the process of focusing is the same: you frame your shot and press the shutter down halfway. The camera will calculate and lock focus (and calculate exposure and auto white balance), and then beep or show a light to indicate that it's ready. Pressing the button the rest of the way will take the picture using the focus, exposure, and white balance settings the camera has calculated. This process, called *prefocusing*, is identical to the way autofocus mechanisms work in film cameras.

Although this system is simple to use, photographers who are new to autofocus cameras can be quickly frustrated by what seems to be an extreme lag between the time they push the button and the time the camera actually takes a picture. This *shutter lag* usually occurs because the photographer is simply pressing the button down all the way to take the picture, rather than pressing down the button halfway and giving the camera a chance to prefocus. By pressing down the button all the way, you're asking the camera to focus, calculate exposure, and figure out white balance all in the instant you want to take the picture. *Neglecting to prefocus is the biggest mistake that beginning autofocus photographers make, and can lead to a great deal of frustrating, missed photos. Get in the habit of prefocusing!*

Prefocusing might sound like an inconvenience, but it's really no more trouble than what you'd have to do with a manually focused camera, except that instead of focusing manually, the camera is focusing for you.

Shutter Lag Even with Prefocusing

As you saw in Chapter 5, "Choosing a Digital Camera," some cameras have a bit of a shutter lag, even if you've already pressed down the shutter release halfway to go through the prefocusing step. Unfortunately, there's really nothing you can do to work around this problem except to learn how long the lag is so you can try to anticipate when you need to press the shutter to capture the action you want. Another option is to switch to your camera's burst mode and shoot a series of images with the hope that one of them will capture the moment you were looking for. If your subject is far away, consider using your camera's landscape mode, which locks focus on infinity, eliminating the need for focusing when the shutter is pressed halfway.

Your camera might also have a continuous autofocus mechanism, which automatically focuses every time you move or zoom the camera. With continuous autofocus, your camera stands a much better chance of being ready to shoot at any time. However, it can also drain your battery and sometimes be distracting, because you will constantly hear the lens working. If your camera has a speedy autofocus, you might find little advantage to a continuous mechanism.

Some cameras also feature a *focus-tracking*, or *servo-tracking*, feature that can automatically track a moving object and keep it in focus for as long as you hold down the shutter button halfway. For sports and nature photography, this feature can help to ensure that you're always ready to get the shot.

Most digital cameras employ one of two different autofocus mechanisms, each with its own strengths and weaknesses.

Active Autofocus

Although less popular than it used to be, some lower-end cameras still provide *active autofocus* mechanisms because they're typically the cheapest system to implement. An active autofocus mechanism works by using an infrared beam to measure the distance to your subject; your camera then sets the focus accordingly. It's called an "active" system because the camera is actively emitting a signal in an effort to measure distance. The easiest way to tell if your camera uses an active system is to look at the technical specifications included in your camera's manual.

Although active autofocus mechanisms work fairly well, they have a number of limitations.

- You must have a clear line of sight between you and your subject. Bars in a zoo, fence posts, or other obstructions can keep the camera from accurately measuring distance.
- Because the infrared beam is not originating from the lens, the camera might not correctly calculate focus if you're using any type of lens attachment, such as a wide-angle or telephoto adapter. Consequently, most cameras with active autofocus mechanisms don't provide for such attachments.
- If you're standing close to another strong infrared source—such as a hot campfire or a birthday cake covered with candles—the heat from that source can confuse the camera's autofocus mechanism.
- On the positive side, active autofocus systems work just fine in the dark.

Passive Autofocus

Most cameras use a *passive autofocus* system, sometimes called a *contrast detection* system. You should be able to find out what type of system your camera uses by simply looking at the specifications table in your camera's manual. For example, your camera might specify its autofocus system as a "*TTL* contrast detection autofocus."

Contrast-detecting autofocus systems work by focusing the lens until the image has as much contrast as possible. The idea is that a low-contrast image is a blurry image. Therefore, by increasing contrast, the camera increases sharpness. The top image in Figure 7.41 shows an out-of-focus image. Look at the individual pixels up close and you'll see that there is very little change from one pixel to the next. That is, the pixels have little contrast between them. In the bottom image in Figure 7.41, a sharp image, you can see that individual pixels have a more dramatic change in contrast from pixel to pixel.

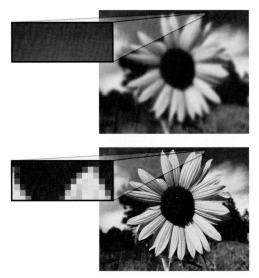

FIGURE 7.41   If you look closely at the pixels in the top, blurry image, you'll see that there is very little change in tone from one to the next. That is, there is little contrast between them. In the bottom image, there is a big contrast change from pixel to pixel. This is why searching for high contrast is a good way to detect focus.

When you press the shutter release halfway, a passive autofocus camera takes an initial reading of the contrast in your shot. It then focuses the lens closer and checks the contrast again. If contrast has increased, the camera continues focusing inward until the contrast decreases. With a decrease in focus, the camera knows it has gone too far and can step back to the correct focus. Obviously, many variables can affect this process, such as the camera's capability to detect contrast, the precision with which it can move its lens, and the speed at which it can go through the entire procedure. Theoretically, a camera with more autofocus steps can achieve a more precise focus position and, therefore, achieve better focus. However, point-and-shoot digital cameras typically have *very* deep depths of field, so tiny changes in focus usually aren't that important. Moreover, most of the steps in an autofocus system are centered around very close (macro) ranges, where they tend to be needed, and where depth of field offers less compensation, so a camera that provides more autofocus steps will not yield significantly better performance in everyday use.

Contrast detection is largely a function of the available light in your scene. If the area in which you're pointing your camera is too dark, or is uniformly colored, your camera won't be able to detect any contrast and will be unable to determine focus. Today, most cameras include an automatic *focus-assist lamp* (also known as an *auto-focus-assist lamp*) that shines a light onto your scene if the camera can detect focus. By lighting up the scene, your camera's autofocus mechanism can "see" better. Some cameras use a normal white-light focus-assist lamp, whereas others use a less-intrusive red lamp. Some cameras will use their built-in flash, firing a rapid series of short bursts to illuminate the scene enough to detect focus.

A passive autofocus mechanism has many advantages, including:

- Because they look through the camera's lens, passive auto-focus systems work with any filters or lens attachments you might be using.
- They're simply analyzing what the camera is seeing, so they can work through windows, water, or other transparent materials.
- They have no distance limitation, although your camera's auto-focus-assist lamp will have some type of limiting distance.
- Unlike non-TTL active systems, you can be sure that a passive system is focusing on something that's actually in the camera's field of view.

On the downside, passive systems do require light in your scene and a subject that has enough detail to produce contrast. However, these limitations are minor, and, as you'll see later, you can usually work around them using one of several techniques.

ADVANCED AUTOFOCUS MECHANISMS

If you have a higher-end digital SLR, your camera might use a more advanced form of aut-ofocus called *phase difference*, or *phase detection*. Phase detection autofocus is a passive TTL metering system that uses a complex arrangement of prisms and two tiny CCD arrays that are placed next to the focal plane. Both CCDs see the same part of the image, but one CCD looks through the left edge of the lens and the other looks through the right edge.

When the lens is focused too close, the image in the left edge of the CCD will be slightly to the left of the right-edge CCD. When the lens is focused too far, the opposite oc-curs. By analyzing the two images and determining the difference in shift between them, the camera can calculate which way to move the lens and how far it needs to go.

As with other autofocus systems, the quality of a phase difference system depends on its capability to quickly and accurately control the lens motor, and to detect what area needs to be in focus.

→

Phase difference systems are incredibly accurate and generally speedy. In addition, many of these systems are capable of focusing in near darkness. On the downside, some phase difference autofocus mechanisms become less reliable at apertures below f5.6, because as the aperture gets smaller, the CCDs lose their line of sight out of the lens and the mechanism can become confused. In general, though, these systems, whether single- or multispot, are by far the most accurate, quickest autofocus mechanisms available.

Focus Spots

Obviously, you want your autofocusing system to focus on the subject of your image, not on something else in the scene. Therefore, your camera has a *focusing zone* or *spot* that determines which part of the image will be analyzed for focus. Most cameras simply use a small area in the middle of the frame as the focus target. Sometimes this area is marked with crosshairs or a box.

However, if your subject isn't in the middle of the frame, there's a good chance your camera is going to focus on the background of your image, leaving the foreground soft or outright blurry.

Because your subject isn't always in the middle of your image, most cameras offer multiple focus zones. A camera with multiple focus spots analyzes several different points in your image to determine where your subject might be. Once it has decided, it analyzes the focus spot or spots closest to that subject to calculate focus. (See Figure 7.42.) This process allows you to frame your image as you like without having to worry about your subject being in the middle of the frame. However, it's important to pay attention to where the camera is focusing, because the autofocus mechanism might pick the wrong subject. When the camera locks focus, your camera will illuminate or flash the focus point it chose. Get in the habit of paying attention to its choice. If it chooses the wrong spot, you'll need to try again.

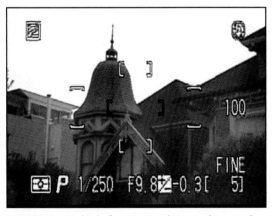

FIGURE 7.42   Multiple focus zones let you choose where the camera's autofocus mechanism will look when it determines focus.

Some cameras now employ face-detection algorithms that can detect where people are in the frame, and then automatically select a nearby focus point. The camera will usually indicate which face it has chosen, and which corresponding focus point it has decided to use.

Because automatic mechanisms can't always choose the correct focus point, most cameras let you manually select a focus point to ensure that your autofocus mechanism analyzes the right area. You should have some type of control that will let you cycle through each of the camera's focus points.

Most cameras with multispot autofocus mechanisms also allow you to put the camera into a single, *center-spot focusing* mode (sometimes called *spot focus*), which forces the camera to behave like a normal single-spot autofocus camera. Very often, single-spot focus is the most reliable, fastest way to focus when creating an unusual composition.

For example, if you're set for center focus and you want to focus on something on the right side of the frame, you can simply point the camera's focusing target (usually the middle of the frame) at that object, press your shutter button halfway to lock focus, hold it, *and then reframe your shot* to your desired framing. When you press the button the rest of the way, the camera will take the picture using the focus it initially calculated. Figure 7.43 shows an example of this method.

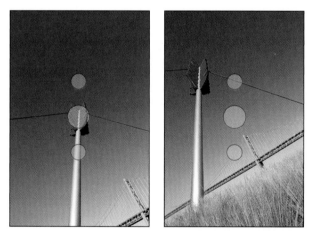

FIGURE 7.43   To keep the camera from focusing on the sky, the camera's focusing target was pointed at the lamppost, and the shutter release was pressed down halfway to lock focus. The image was reframed, and the picture was shot with the correct focus.

Be aware, though, that there are some potential pitfalls to this technique.

In addition to calculating focus, when you press down your shutter button halfway, your camera calculates exposure and white balance (if you're using automatic white balance). If the lighting in your frame is substantially different after you reframe from what it was when you locked focus, your camera's exposure could be off. (As you'll see in the next chapter, you can sometimes use this exposure change to your advantage.)

Camera manufacturers have come up with two solutions for these problems. The first is a separate *exposure lock* button that allows you to lock your camera's exposure and focus independently. Different exposure lock features work in different ways, but most allow you to do something like this: frame your shot, measure and lock the exposure, move your camera and lock focus on your subject, and then return to your final framing with everything ready to go. As we'll see later, exposure lock is also necessary for taking good panoramic shots.

If your camera uses a TTL contrast-detection focusing system, the center focusing spot (no matter how many focus zones the camera has) is usually a *dual-axis zone*. That is, it examines contrast along both a horizontal and vertical axis. If the camera has multiple focus spots, there's a good chance that the other zones are *single-axis zones*, which measure only contrast (and, therefore, focus) along a horizontal axis. For locking focus on horizontal subjects, such as horizons, a single-axis zone can be problematic. For these situations, you might want to force the camera to use its center, dual-axis zone.

If there's any one rule to using an autofocus camera—whether a single-spot or multispot focusing system—it's simply to pay attention. Don't just assume the camera will be able to calculate everything accurately. If your camera has a single-spot focusing system that sometimes requires you to lock focus and reframe, be sure to look for any potential metering and white-balance troubles before you shoot. If your camera has a multispot focusing system, be certain it has chosen the correct subject and focusing zone.

What to Do If Your Autofocus Won't Lock Focus

If you're using a contrast-detecting autofocus system, there will be times when it won't be able to lock focus. Shooting in low light is especially problematic, because there might not be enough contrast in your scene for the camera to detect focus. Hopefully, the camera has an automatic focus-assist lamp that will activate to light the scene. If the focus-assist lamp lights up and the camera still can't focus, try moving the camera slightly. You might illuminate something that has enough contrast for the camera to be able to focus, but be careful the camera doesn't focus on something at the wrong distance.

Autofocus mechanisms can even get confused in bright daylight if your camera is pointed at something with low contrast. In Figure 7.44, you can see that the middle of the frame is filled with an object that is a solid color (the lamp). In this case, the lamp had so little contrast that the camera's contrast-detecting autofocus system was unable to focus. By tilting the camera up so the focusing target sits on top of a part of the lamp with more contrast, the autofocus mechanism can find and lock focus. After locking focus, we tilted the camera back down to our desired framing, as shown in the image on the right. Always be certain to choose an area with more contrast that's at the same distance as the area you want to focus on.

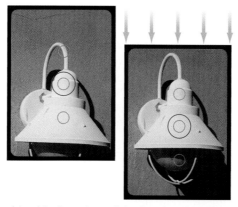

FIGURE 7.44 Because this white lamp is a solid color, there's little contrast for a camera's contrast-detecting autofocus mechanism to detect. To get the camera to lock focus, you must frame the shot at a point where there is some contrast, lock focus, and then reframe. (Be sure you lock on a point that's the same distance away as your subject.)

Manual Focus

Your camera's autofocus system is probably all the focusing control you'll ever need. However, if you run into a situation where your camera can't autofocus and you can't work around it, or if you have a particularly "creative" shot you want to compose, you might need to resort to your camera's manual focus. (This is assuming that you're using a prosumer-type camera that lacks interchangeable lenses with focus rings. If you're using an SLR, you can easily switch between automatic and manual focus.)

Unfortunately, manual focus features on non-SLR digital cameras leave a *lot* to be desired. Between poorly designed controls and viewfinders that lack focusing aids, getting an accurate manual focus out of your camera can be difficult. A few years ago, most digital cameras simply offered you a choice of distances. Consequently, in addition to trying to estimate the distance to your subject, you had to hope that the camera provided a preset focus distance that was close to what you needed.

Some digital cameras still work this way, but most manual-focus mechanisms are now more robust, letting you smoothly move throughout the focus range of your camera. However, determining when you've achieved focus is still difficult, because neither your camera's LCD screen nor optical viewfinder will be good enough to let you see focus.

Fortunately, because of their small sensor size, and because their auto exposure mechanisms are sometimes biased toward smaller apertures, you often don't have to worry about your focus being dead on, because your depth of field will be very deep.

Even if your camera doesn't have a full manual-focus control, it probably has a preset control for locking focus at infinity. This can be a handy feature for landscape photography or for other times when your subject is far away. Lock your camera's focus at infinity and it will perform faster—it won't be trying to autofocus—and your batteries might last a little longer as the camera won't be moving the lens.

Metering

A lot happens when you press your camera's shutter button halfway down. The camera focuses, calculates white balance (if you're set for auto white balance), and uses its light meter to measure the light in your scene, and to calculate a proper exposure. Exposure is simply the combination of shutter speed and aperture settings that will be used when you press the shutter button the rest of the way down, exposing the image sensor to light.

Determining the correct exposure can be a complex process that balances many variables ranging from the practical necessities of getting a visible image to the artistic possibilities you can control by varying one parameter or another. Chapter 8 will deal exclusively with metering and exposures. For now, we're going to assume that you're leaving your camera set to an automatic exposure mode, so you don't have to worry too much about metering.

That said, there are still some things to keep an eye on when using your camera's automatic metering modes.

> **Watch that shutter speed!** Unless it's a very small point-and-shoot, your camera probably has some kind of display that shows current exposure settings. These settings are displayed once the camera has calculated an exposure (which, of course, doesn't happen until you press the shutter button halfway down).

If you're using a camera with an LCD viewfinder, the exposure settings will probably be displayed somewhere on the LCD screen. If you're using an SLR, the exposure settings should be shown inside the camera's viewfinder, and possibly on an external LCD status screen. You're looking for two numbers; one will be the shutter speed and will probably appear as a fraction: 1/125, 1/250, 1/60, and so on. These indicate the length of the shutter speed in seconds. Some cameras simply display the denominator (125, 250, 60), and expect you to understand that this represents a fraction of a second.

The other number you're looking for is the aperture value—8, 11, 16, 22, and so on. Sometimes, these will be displayed with an "f" in front of them (f.8, f.11, f.16), and sometimes just as a simple value. Most cameras display shutter speed first and then aperture. (See Figure 7.45.)

In a full manual mode, you may not have any option for changing these values, but it's still worth keeping an eye on the shutter speed to determine if it's practical to shoot handheld. If your shutter speed is too slow, handholding your camera may not be a good idea, because the natural jitter in your body will result in a softening (or outright blurring) of your image.

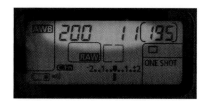

FIGURE 7.45   Here, our camera indicates that it has calculated an exposure of 1/200th of a second, at f.11.

Some point-and-shoot cameras will display a warning icon (usually a hand with "shake lines" around it) when they think you're in danger of shooting with a shutter speed that might result in shake-induced blur.

Obviously, if you're shooting on a stable tripod, this is of little concern, as the tripod will hold your camera steady throughout the long exposure. However, if you're shooting a fast-moving subject, you may want to keep an eye on your shutter speed to try to determine if your shutter speed is fast enough to freeze motion.

In either of these situations, if you decide the auto-selected shutter speed is not practical, you'll want to use a manual control to select a new speed. We'll cover such controls in-depth in the next chapter.

Calculating a Safe Shutter Speed for Handholding

The generally accepted rule for what makes a shutter speed acceptable for handheld shooting is to simply take 1 over your current focal length. So, if you're shooting with a 50 mm lens (or a zoom lens set to 50 mm), you shouldn't shoot any slower than 1/50th of a second. If you're shooting with a 200 mm lens, you shouldn't shoot with a shutter speed slower than 1/200th.

The idea is that, as the image is magnified when you zoom in, so too is any motion within the frame. So, you have to use a faster shutter speed as you go to a longer focal length.

On a point-and-shoot camera, you may not have a readout that tells what your current focal length is. However, these cameras will usually have a handholding warning indicator, as described above.

If you're shooting with a digital SLR, you'll be able to determine your current focal length by simply looking at your lens. However, as you learned in Chapter 5, lenses on a digital SLR are often subject to a focal length multiplier that changes the effective crop of the lens at a given focal length. So, if your lens has a focal length multiplier of 1.6, you'll first need to multiply your current focal length by 1.6, and then perform your calculation. If you're using an image-stabilized lens, you'll need to adjust for the number of additional stops provided by your stabilizer. (See Figure 7.46.)

Putting It All Together

The processes we've defined in this section are not necessarily performed in the straight linear order we have described here. Obviously, you'll need to frame *before*

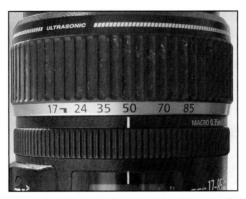

FIGURE 7.46   This 17–85 mm lens is currently set to a focal length of 50 mm. However, this lens is attached to a Canon EOS SLR that has a focal length multiple of 1.6. Therefore, the crop of this lens is equivalent to 50 × 1.6, or 80 m. Our minimum shutter speed for sharp handheld shooting is 1/80th of a second. However, because the lens has a 3-stop image stabilizing system, we might be able to get away with shooting as low as 1/20th.

you press the shutter button, but on some images you'll move back and forth between several of these steps. For example, you might choose an initial mode with one idea in mind, and then, as you try different frames and compositions, realize you need to switch to a different mode. As you work in this mode, you may realize that you need to switch to a different ISO to facilitate the exposure you want. As you work the shot further, you may find still other ideas that require different settings. Remember: don't be afraid to keep working the shot and experimenting with different ideas.

SIMPLE FLASH PHOTOGRAPHY

Using your camera's built-in flash is pretty simple: just turn it on and let the camera worry about when and how much to fire it. Using your camera's built-in flash *well* is a bit more difficult. Unfortunately, the small flash units provided by most cameras are low powered, and because of their positioning on the camera, they don't often produce very flattering light. However, your camera's built-in flash does have its uses, and with a little knowledge, you can get it to yield good results.

When you shoot a picture using your flash, many things happen in a short amount of time. First, the camera opens its shutter and begins exposing the image sensor according to the settings defined by you or your camera's light meter. Then, the camera turns on the lamp in its flash unit. With the lamp on, the camera begins measuring the flash illumination that is bouncing off the subject and returning to the camera. In this way, the camera can meter the light of the flash while it's flashing. When it has decided that the flash has cast enough illumination, it shuts off the flash, finishes the exposure, and closes the shutter.

Flash Modes

Most digital cameras provide several different flash modes. If you're shooting in a fully automatic mode, your camera will try to determine, on the fly, whether the flash is needed. If it deems the flash necessary, it will fire it for the appropriate amount of time. In addition to this mode, your camera probably provides the following:

Fill: This mode uses the flash to fill in shadows. It is typically used for backlit situations or other instances where you're shooting in bright light but your subject is in shadow. Usually, the camera uses a lower power flash setting so as not to overexpose the shadows in your image.

Red-eye reduction: The "red-eye" effect (see Figure 7.47) occurs when the light from your flash bounces off the retinas of your subject's eyes as he or she looks into the lens. If the flash on your camera is placed close to the lens, there's a much better chance of getting red-eye, because it's easier for the light to bounce straight back into the lens. Red-eye reduction modes work by firing a flash, or the camera's auto-focus-assist lamp, to close the subject's pupils. When you use these modes, be sure to inform your subject that there will be two flashes. Otherwise, your subject might move or close his or her eyes after the first firing. Whether you're shooting with or without a red-eye reduction flash, moving slightly to one side before you shoot can prevent your subjects from looking directly into the camera's lens. You can also try turning on all the lights in the room in an attempt to narrow everyone's pupils.

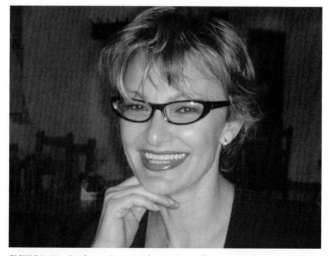

FIGURE 7.47   Red-eye is prevalent in small cameras because of the position of the flash. Fortunately, correcting the problem is fairly simple using tools found in most image editors.

Ol' Blue, er, Red Eyes...

Generally, people with lighter-colored eyes are more susceptible to red-eye in photographs than people with darker-colored eyes. Probably the worst red-eye situation is shooting a blue-eyed person in a dark room. When you shoot lighter-eyed people, it's a good idea to take the time to review your images on your camera's LCD. If your camera has a zoom feature in its playback mode, zoom in and check out the eyes. You might find you need to reshoot.

Cancel: This feature simply deactivates the flash. This isn't exactly a mode, but it is important for times when you're shooting in an area where a flash is not appropriate or when you want to handle low light in a different way.

Spend some time using the different flash modes on your camera to learn their characteristics. In particular, determine if the flash consistently over- or underexposes, and if it tends to produce odd color casts. If so, you might want to adjust its settings as described in this section.

After the flash has fired, any leftover charge is saved for the next firing. Consequently, your flash's recycle time can vary depending on how much it had to fire. In other words, you'll get faster recycle times when you use your flash in brighter light, because the flash won't have to fire for as long and, hence, won't have to recharge as much.

One problem with onboard flashes is that they're really not positioned to provide flattering light. Our eyes are used to a strong overhead light source, so flashing a bright light directly in front of a subject usually produces a somewhat weird lighting perspective. In addition, a poor flash exposure can result in harsh lighting with overblown highlights and hard-edged black shadows if the flash fired too much, or an underexposed image if the flash fired too little. (See Figure 7.48.)

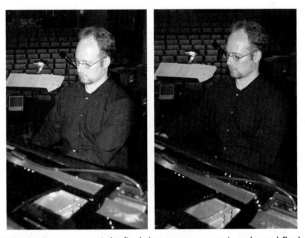

FIGURE 7.48   At times, you might find that your camera's onboard flash creates harshly lit scenes with blown-out highlights. Flash exposure compensation lets you dial down the power of the flash for better exposure.

Fortunately, many cameras offer flash power adjustment controls—sometimes called *flash exposure compensation*—that let you increase or decrease the power of the flash by one or two stops in either direction. After a test shot, you might find that your camera's flash is too strong. Dialing down the power by a stop or so might be enough to produce a much better exposure.

Remember that your camera's flash has a limited range, usually no more than 10 or 15 feet. Consequently, as your focal length increases, your flash's effectiveness decreases. That is, if you zoom in on an object 20 feet away, don't expect your flash to do a great job of illuminating it. Increasing the flash power by a couple of stops might improve your flash performance at these distances.

Flash White Balance

Your flash is usually not the only source of light in a room. In most cases, you'll be shooting flash photos in a room that also contains incandescent or fluorescent lights and maybe even sunlight. All of these light sources can serve to create a complex, mixed-lighting situation that requires a special white balance.

Some cameras have a separate white-balance setting for flash that can often correct color-cast problems, but on most cameras, manual or automatic white balance will yield the best results.

To get an idea of your how your camera white balances when you use the flash, take some test flash pictures indoors under normal incandescent (tungsten) lighting using the camera's automatic white balance. If the images come out with a slightly blue cast or if the highlights are blue, the camera's white balance chose to favor the room's tungsten lighting. If the images come out a little yellow or have yellow highlights, the camera white-balanced in favor of the flash.

There's little you can do about these color casts. Sometimes, dialing down the flash's power will reduce the effect, or you can try to filter your flash. If you find blue highlights in your flash pictures, buy some yellow filter material at your camera store and tape a piece of it over your flash. This will balance your flash for tungsten, making it better match the indoor lighting (which your camera is white-balancing for anyway).

When Should You Use Your Flash?

Most people assume that you use flash when it's dark and turn it off when you're back in bright light, or daylight. While this is occasionally true, you can also argue that it's often the exact opposite of correct flash philosophy.

When you shoot with a flash, your camera chooses an exposure that's appropriate for exposing the flash-illuminated area—which is usually a fairly small zone in front of the camera. Because the camera is exposing for the bright illumination in the flash zone, everything outside that zone will be underexposed, resulting in your background appearing as a dark limbo space.

If you're gunning for a quick snapshot, this may be your only option. But, if you have more time, you should consider two other possibilities.

High-ISO low-light shooting. As you've already learned, as you increase your camera's ISO, it becomes more sensitive to light, which means you can shoot in lower light. Shooting in low light without your flash will produce a more natural-looking scene, but you might have to shoot with a slower shutter speed, which will mean you'll run more risk of having blurring due to camera shake, and your subject moving.

If your camera has a shutter priority mode, try locking the shutter speed on something that offers good motion stopping power—1/30th or 1/45th. Your images might still come out too dark, but you'll be able to brighten them later.

If you're shooting a subject that isn't moving, you can use your camera's recommended shutter speed, as long as you have a way to stabilize your tripod. We'll discuss tripods in detail in the next chapter. (See Figure 7.49.)

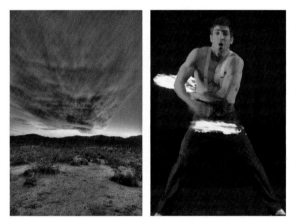

FIGURE 7.49   Raising your camera's ISO makes it possible to shoot in situations that would otherwise be impossible or inappropriate. For this sunset, we set the camera on ISO 1600, mounted it on a tripod, and used a long exposure. For this flame juggler, we set for ISO 1600, put the camera on aperture priority, and shot at a 50th of a second to ensure good motion stopping.

Of course, any time you switch to a higher ISO you'll run the risk of increased noise in your images. In addition to producing noisier images, at longer shutter speeds, many of the individual pixels in the camera's sensor might begin to behave strangely, sometimes getting "stuck" so they appear bright white.

Some cameras employ special noise-reduction schemes when you shoot at speeds longer than one second. Most of these schemes employ some form of *dark frame subtraction*. When this feature is enabled, any time you shoot an image with an exposure longer than one second, the camera automatically shoots a second frame, this time with the shutter closed. Because the exposure is the same, the pixels in the camera's sensor have time to malfunction exactly as they did in the first image. However, because the shutter is closed, the resulting black frame is essentially a photograph of only the stuck, noisy pixels from the first image. The camera then combines the images, essentially subtracting the second frame from the first. Because the second frame contains only the noise, the resulting image is much cleaner.

If your camera doesn't have such a feature, you can perform it yourself by simply putting your lens cap on and taking a second image with the same exposure settings. In Photoshop, you can subtract the black frame from the image frame. You'll find a PDF file detailing how to do this in the Tutorials/Chapter 7 folder of the companion CD-ROM.

The amount of noise in an image is strongly affected by the temperature of the camera's image sensor, so be sure to shoot your dark frame right away to ensure that both images are shot with the camera at the same temperature. A difference of even one or two degrees will result in enough change in noise that the technique won't work.

ISO choice when shooting long-exposure images can be a bit tricky. On the one hand, you might want to shoot with a higher ISO to reduce the shutter speed, and avoid stuck pixels. On the other hand, shooting with a higher ISO introduces high ISO noise. So, you might want to try both techniques and see which one ends up noisier.

Shooting Outside at Night? Cool Your Camera Before You Shoot.

The noise a digital camera produces is directly related to the temperature of the camera's image sensor. For every 6°F to 8°F increase in the temperature of the sensor, the noise will double. Therefore, if you know you're going to be shooting long exposures outside, take your camera out 20 to 30 minutes early and let it cool down to the outside temperature. As the camera cools, you should see a marked decrease in noise. Do not try to cool down your camera by putting it in the refrigerator or putting it on ice! Cooling it too quickly can cause damaging condensation to form inside the camera.

Stabilize Your Camera when Shooting with Slow Shutter Speeds

When shooting with slow shutter speeds, you'll want to reduce the possibility of camera shake by using a tripod or other stabilization technique. We'll discuss this topic in more detail in Chapter 9, "Special Shooting."

Slow sync flash mode. One problem with using flash in very low light is that, while the flash is capable of properly exposing your foreground, everything in the background lies out of range of the flash, and ends up so underexposed as to be completely dark. (See Figure 7.50.)

Most cameras offer a special *slow sync* mode that uses a combination of a flash and a slow shutter speed to properly expose the foreground and background. The flash exposes the foreground, freezing any motion, while the slow shutter speed allows the camera to capture a good exposure of the background. (See Figure 7.51.)

On most cameras, slow sync is a special scene mode—just like landscape or portrait—that you select from the scene mode control.

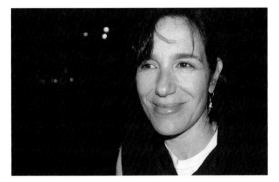

FIGURE 7.50 This exterior night shot was illuminated only by our flash. Although it did a good job of exposing our subject, nothing in the background is visible, because the camera chose a shutter speed that was appropriate only for the flash-illuminated woman.

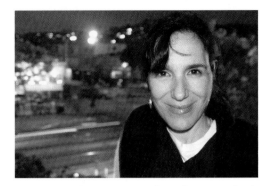

FIGURE 7.51 This image was shot a few seconds after Figure 7.50, using the camera's slow-sync mode. The flash was fired to illuminate the subject and freeze her motion, but the shutter was left open for several seconds to capture the background, resulting in an image that reveals far more detail.

On a higher-end camera that doesn't offer a scene mode, or if you're using an external flash, you usually achieve slow sync effects by putting the camera in manual or priority mode. Consult the documentation for your camera or flash for details.

When shooting people using slow sync mode, be sure to tell them to hold still *after* the flash fires. Many times, people will start moving after the flash has fired, while the long exposure is still going. This can result in weird blurs in your image.

Many slow sync modes offer the choice of *first curtain* or *second curtain* sync. This simply denotes whether the flash will fire before or after the long exposure, allowing you to control where you might want blur in your image.

Fill flash. When shooting outside, you'll often find that the sky is much brighter than your subject. Most matrix metering systems will favor the sky when metering, causing your subject to be rendered too dark. If your camera has a spot meter, you can work around this problem by spot-metering off your foreground subject, which will cause the background to overexpose and wash out completely.

A better solution is to activate your camera's fill flash. This will throw enough light on your foreground that the camera will properly expose both the foreground and background (assuming your foreground is within range of your flash). (See Figure 7.52.)

This is the same practice you'll use in a brightly lit room to counter any backlighting caused by bright windows. Fill flash is also great for subjects who are wearing hats or are shaded by overhanging trees or other foreground objects. Usually, the bright outdoor light will be so strong that your flash will provide a rather soft fill light, with none of the harsh shadows you might see indoors or in lower light.

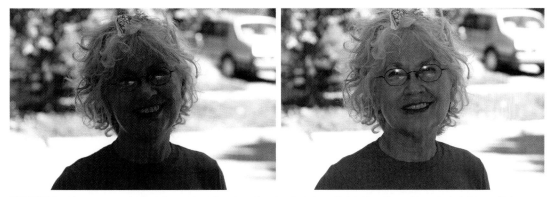

FIGURE 7.52   Your camera's flash is not just for shooting in dark, low-light situations. Even in bright sunlight, you might sometimes need to use your camera's flash to compensate for a bright background or for shadow-producing hats, trees, or buildings.

POWER AND STORAGE MANAGEMENT

Film cameras do have one marked advantage over digital cameras: they don't *have* to have batteries. With an all-manual film camera, all you need is film (as long as you don't want a light meter), making it simple to go on long photographic excursions without carrying batteries, battery chargers, and laptop computers.

Digital cameras are not so efficient. For a few days of shooting, you probably won't have to worry too much about batteries and storage when you use your digital camera, unless you're very shutter happy or have a tiny storage card. For long trips, though, you'll want to make some effort to conserve and maximize both batteries and storage.

Feel the Power

The easiest way to allay your power fears is simply to buy lots of batteries. If your camera uses a custom, proprietary battery, buy an extra. If your camera didn't ship with an external charger (that is, you have to recharge batteries in the camera), you might want to spring for a charger as well.

If your camera uses AA-size batteries, pick up two sets of NiMH rechargeables and a charger. NiMH batteries don't usually reach their full level of performance until they've been charged a couple of times, so make sure to give them good strong charges the first few times you recharge them. Unlike NiCAD batteries, you don't have to drain NiMH batteries before you charge them because they have no "memory effect," so after the second recharging, feel free to "top them off" before you go shooting. Be aware, though, that NiMH batteries will lose their charge over time, whether they're in or out of your camera. A month on the shelf is often enough for them to drain completely, so if you haven't used your batteries in a while, be sure to give them a good charge. In addition, once they're fully charged, take them out of the charger. Leaving the batteries in the charger, constantly recharging, can shorten their life.

Obviously, when you travel abroad, you'll need to buy the appropriate adapters and converters to power your charger, and any other equipment you might choose to bring along.

Even with a spare set of batteries, it's a good idea to get in the habit of shooting with an eye toward battery conservation. The two systems on your camera that use the most power are the LCD screen and the flash. If your camera has only an LCD viewfinder (or if you prefer using the LCD viewfinder), you might want to conserve power by limiting the amount of time you spend reviewing images on the LCD screen.

Your camera probably has a sleep mode that causes it to switch to a low-power setting if you don't use it for a while. Try to get a feel for how long it takes the camera to wake up. You might need to wait an extra two to five seconds if your camera has gone into its sleep mode. Most cameras doze off if you don't use them for 30 seconds. This is fine for everyday, snapshot shooting, but can be a real bother if you're shooting portraits or other studio work that requires a long setup. For these occasions, you might want to change the sleep time to its maximum (15 to 30 minutes). If you know you're going to be away from the camera for a bit, turn off the LCD screen to conserve power.

Over time, you'll get a better idea of how many pictures you can expect to get from a set of batteries. However, there will still be times when your batteries will wane before you're done shooting. For these instances, you might want to employ some of the following battery-saving measures:

- Switch off your camera's LCD and use the optical viewfinder. If your camera doesn't have an optical viewfinder, turn off the LCD whenever you're not framing a shot. In addition, if your camera's LCD provides a backlight that can be turned off, turn it off.
- Some cameras include a "review" setting that lets you specify how long an image will be displayed on the LCD after you shoot. Turn off this review, or at least set it to its smallest value.
- Try to avoid flash pictures. If you have to shoot in low light, switch to a higher ISO, or try long exposures from a tripod.
- Turning your camera off and on often uses more power than simply letting it sleep. (Turning it off and on usually causes the camera to zoom the lens a lot.) Unless you know it will be a while until your next shot, simply let your camera sleep.
- If your camera offers manual focus and zoom features, switch to these.

- If your camera doesn't offer a usable manual focus, but you know your pictures will all be shot at the same distance (infinity, for example), lock the camera's focus on infinity. Keeping the camera from autofocusing will save a tiny bit of power.
- If you need to transfer pictures to a computer in the field, don't use your camera's cable connection. Use a media drive or PC card adapter instead.

Finally, be aware that cold temperatures will noticeably shorten battery life. If you're shooting outside in below-freezing temperatures, your batteries will probably die quickly. You can often squeeze a little more power out of them by taking them out of the camera and warming them up inside your pocket. This might sound hard to believe, but it's true. A few minutes inside your coat can often get you an additional dozen pictures. Don't put the whole camera in your pocket—this will most likely fog up your lens. (See the cold weather tips in Chapter 9, "Special Shooting.") Lithium batteries (not to be confused with L-Ion rechargeables) often stand up much better to cold weather than do NiMH or alkaline batteries.

Alternative Charging Options

While plugging into a wall is a quick and easy way to charge your batteries, there isn't always a wall around to plug into. If you're going to be traveling in more primitive conditions, you might want to consider some alternative charging options.

A car charger will let you power your camera's charger off a normal car cigarette lighter socket, and you should be able to order one directly from the manufacturer if you can't find one at your local camera store (or online).

For the ultimate in camera energy independence, consider a solar charger like the one shown in Figure 7.53. This Solio can charge your camera, cell phone, PDA, iPod, and more, and provides a way to keep your camera running even if you're far from a power grid. You can find out more at *www.solio.com*.

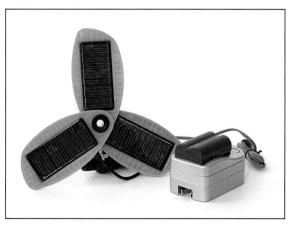

FIGURE 7.53   If you have a car charger for your camera battery, you can probably charge your battery using the Solio portable solar charger.

Media Baron

Earlier in this chapter, you read about some image size/compression strategies for saving media. Although these practices can make your storage go farther, the ideal solution is simply to buy more media cards. The price of media cards continues to drop, but if you tend to shoot *lots* of images, or if you're planning an extended trip, consider some of these storage alternatives.

Laptop Computers

For longer trips, take a laptop computer. In addition to giving you a place to store images, you'll have a complete darkroom with you. With a laptop and your favorite image-editing application, you can assess right away whether your day's shooting was successful and determine if you need to reshoot something.

Portable Battery-Powered Hard Drives

If you don't feel like lugging around your laptop computer, consider a standalone battery-powered hard drive device such as the Epson P-5000® shown in Figure 7.54. Measuring roughly the same size as a paperback book, these battery-powered devices contain a hard drive, a media slot, and an LCD screen. Simply insert the media from your camera into the slot, and you can back up your images to the internal drive. You can then put the card back into your camera, erase it, and start shooting again. These types of devices also allow you to view and delete images, build slideshows that can be output to a TV via a standard video out port, and even listen to MP3s. Because they're built around standard laptop computer hard drives, these types of devices deliver a much cheaper price-per-megabyte than any type of flash

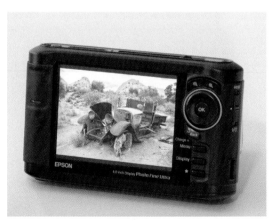

FIGURE 7.54 The Epson P-5000 provides up to 80 GB of portable battery-powered storage providing a small, high-capacity location to offload your images, letting you free your storage cards for more shooting. The P-5000 lets you view and delete JPEG or raw files, listen to MP3s, and watch movies!

card. Although bigger and heavier than a handful of flash cards, they offer a tremendous amount of storage in less space than a full-blown laptop. Less-expensive models are available that lack an LCD screen for reviewing your images.

Blank CDs, Cables, and PC Adapters

Finally, you can simply carry around some blank CD-ROMs and all of your camera's connectivity options. Then, you need only to find a service bureau, an Internet café, or a friend with a computer to burn your camera's images to your blanks. Obviously, your service bureau or friend will need a CD burner and the appropriate port. If they're running an older operating system that doesn't automatically download images, you'll need to bring the transfer software provided with your camera.

Hedge Your Bets by Offloading

Even if you have a very large storage card—one that can hold all the pictures you might conceivably need to shoot—it's still a good idea to offload some images from time to time. Media cards can crash, so backing up to another form of media is a good way to ensure you won't lose all your images in the event of a storage crash. If you have the space, consider making more than one backup.

AND THAT'S JUST THE BEGINNING!

The automatic modes on many digital cameras can do an extraordinary job of metering, white balancing, and shooting. Even the best photographic algorithms can be fooled, however, and none of them really knows how to do anything but take "correct" pictures. For tricky lighting situations, or for times when you want to break the rules, you're going to have to take control of your camera—and that's the subject of the next chapter.

8

METERING AND EXPOSURE

In This Chapter

- What You Can Do with Exposure Adjustments
- How to Adjust Exposure
- In-Camera Histograms
- Bracketing
- Exposing for Raw
- Exposing to Avoid Chromatic Aberration (Purple Fringing)
- Taking Control

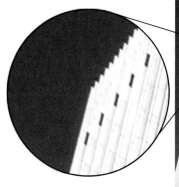

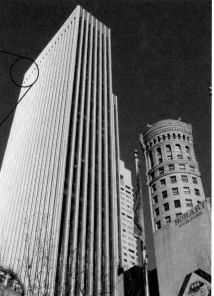

A t the simplest level, your exposure choice governs whether your image will be too bright or too dark. In this regard, your camera's automatic meter will almost always do a good job of keeping your image well-exposed, but your choice of exposure also provides a tremendous degree of creative control. Understanding your light meter, and the effects of different exposure decisions, is an essential step to moving beyond simple snapshot photography. In this chapter, we'll explore metering and exposure in great detail. You'll learn what types of effects you can create with different exposure settings, and how you change exposure settings using the various controls on your camera.

In these days of fancy digital image editors, many people think, "Why should I worry so much about exposure? I can just fix it in the computer later." That may or may not be true depending on your shooting situation, but whether it is or not, it's also important to understand the limitations of digital image editing.

If you've ever used a tape recorder or video camera to record someone's voice, you know that if he or she is standing on the other side of the room, you may get bad-sounding audio. Later, maybe you can turn the volume up louder to try to hear that person, but it still won't sound very good. Photography is the same way: if you don't capture high-quality data, no amount of image editing will be able to fix the problems in your image. Also, as you'll learn in Chapter 11, "Correcting Tone and Color," a finite amount of editing can be performed on an image before ugly artifacts begin to appear. If you get the exposure right in-camera, you won't have to make these types of broad, potentially damaging edits.

Finally: image editing takes time. Shooting with an accurate exposure will mean less post-production work and a more efficient workflow.

WHAT YOU CAN DO WITH EXPOSURE ADJUSTMENTS

Some of today's advanced metering systems go far beyond simple light metering and offer a level of sophistication that's roughly akin to having an experienced photographer with a spot meter standing by your side.

However, like all automated systems, the light meters in your camera have to make certain assumptions, and most meters assume you want to take a "correct" photograph. That is, most cameras will produce images with good tone and contrast and with the subject clearly in focus. There will be times, however, when you might disagree with your camera about what the subject of your image is. Or, you might have different ideas about focus, contrast, or tone.

In these instances, you need to throw your camera into manual override and start making some exposure decisions on your own. Manual exposure controls allow you to create images that are very different from what your camera's automatic features might deem "correct." They also allow you to shoot higher-quality images by affording you more control of the color and contrast your camera will produce.

Your exposure choice determines more than just how bright or dark your image will be. By changing your camera's exposure, you can alter four characteristics of an image:

- Motion control
- Depth of field
- Tonality
- Detail

In the next section, you're going to learn what these different characteristics look like, how you might use them, and which exposure parameters affect them. Later in this chapter, we'll look at *how* you can make the types of exposure adjustments that are necessary to achieve the effects we'll see here.

To get the most out of this chapter, you'll need to have an understanding of the reciprocity concepts discussed in Chapter 3, "Basic Photography: A Quick Primer," and the basic metering theory introduced in Chapter 7, "Shooting."

Motion Control

Controlling motion in your image—that is, controlling how much your camera freezes motion as opposed to letting it blur—is an intuitive process. Use a higher, faster shutter speed to freeze motion, and use a lower speed to let things blur. Once you dip below the appropriate handheld speed for your current focal length, you'll need a tripod to hold the camera steady; otherwise, camera shake will introduce unwanted blur into your image. (See Figure 8.1.) We discussed calculating a handheld shutter speed in Chapter 7.

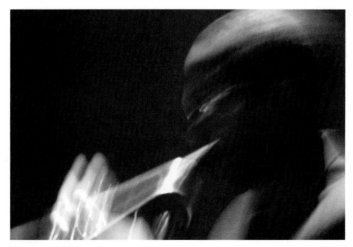

FIGURE 8.1   Normally, your camera aims to freeze motion by using a fast shutter speed. By choosing slower speeds, you can introduce blur into your images.

As discussed earlier, slow shutter speeds are also handy for shooting in very low light. See "When Should You Use Your Flash?" in Chapter 7.

Depth of Field

Depth of field is the measure of how deep the focused area of your image will be. In an image with deep depth of field, everything will be in focus. A shallower depth of field will yield blurry backgrounds or foregrounds.

There will be times when you want everything in your image to be in focus. For example, in a landscape shot you'll usually want the entire scene to be in focus. Similarly, in a shot of a large group of people, or a close-up shot of an object, you'll want deep depth of field to ensure that all the details of the people or object are in focus.

For other images, you might want a shallow depth of field, to bring focus to one part of your image. The most common example of this is a portrait, where you choose to shoot with a shallow depth of field so the background of the image is soft and indistinct while your subject remains sharply focused. This serves to focus attention on your subject. Remember, part of your job as a photographer is to figure out how to guide the viewers' eye and their attention. Control of depth of field is one of the most powerful tools you have for doing this.

It is important to understand that the depth of field in an image is centered on the area on which you are focusing. In other words, if you currently have a depth of field that is about 10 feet deep, that doesn't mean that things farther than 10 feet from your lens will be out of focus. Rather, it means that things *within 10 feet of the point on which you are focusing* will be in focus.

Figure 8.2 shows the same image shot with varying depths of field.

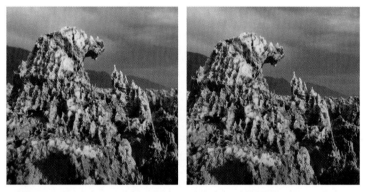

FIGURE 8.2   The left image has shallower depth of field than the right image. Elements both in front of and behind the salt formation are out of focus. In the image on the right, we stepped down to a smaller aperture to achieve deeper depth of field. The left image was shot at f/4.5, while the right image was shot at f/11.

Apparent depth of field is a function of three parameters: aperture size, focal length, and sensor size. *Larger apertures and longer focal lengths yield shallower apparent depths of field.* Therefore, if you want to shoot very shallow depth of field, you'll want to choose a lower f-stop, and zoom in as far as possible. Obviously, as you zoom in you may need to change your shooting location. For shallower depth of field, you'll want to use a smaller aperture. We'll discuss deep depth of field in more detail in the landscape shooting section of the next chapter.

In general, when you're closer to your image, the distribution of depth of field in front of and behind your subject will be fairly even. That is, there will be a roughly equal distance of focused area in front of and behind your subject. As you move farther away from your subject, the area of blurred focus will extend more behind than in front. The generally accepted rule of thumb is one-third in front, and two-thirds behind.

DEPTH OF FIELD WITH POINT-AND-SHOOT CAMERAS

If you have some experience with 35 mm or larger formats, it is important to realize that because of the tiny focal lengths found on most point-and-shoot digital cameras (which are inherent to the small designs of those cameras), depth of field is much deeper than you might be used to. On a typical point-and-shoot digital camera, the depth of field produced by an f5.6 aperture works out to be more like the depth of field produced by an f16 aperture on a 35 mm camera. This is great news for users who want really deep depths of field. However, photographers who are used to being able to separate foregrounds from backgrounds using very shallow depths of field might be frustrated. (See Figure 8.3.)

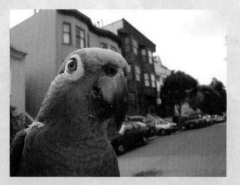

FIGURE 8.3 Most digital cameras are not capable of capturing very shallow depth of field. Although this is great for maintaining sharp focus, you might be frustrated if you want to intentionally blur out the background. The slight blurring of the background in this image is about the most you can expect from a point-and-shoot digital camera.

If you're using a digital SLR with interchangeable lenses, you'll have an easier time achieving very shallow depths of field. Although the sensor in a digital SLR is usually smaller than a piece of 35 mm film, the longer focal lengths provided by an SLR's larger lenses make for shorter depths of field.

Focal Length Only Appears to Affect Depth of Field

There is a long-held, long-taught belief that longer focal lengths yield a shallower depth of field. This isn't true. Longer focal lengths yield an apparently shallower depth of field. You can learn more about this by reading Focal Length and Depth of Field.pdf *in the chapter 8 folder on the companion CD-ROM. For all intents and purposes, though, when you want an image that appears to have shallower depth of field, use a longer focal length.*

NEUTRAL DENSITY FILTERS FOR SHALLOW DEPTH OF FIELD IN BRIGHT LIGHT

No matter what type of camera you have, it can be difficult to achieve shallow depth of field in bright daylight, because you won't be able to open the aperture wider without overexposing. If your camera provides very fast shutter speeds, you might be able to compensate for the larger aperture. If not, you might want to consider using *neutral density filters,* special filters that screw onto the end of your lens and serve to cut down the amount of light entering your lens, without altering the light's color. By cutting down the light, you might find that you have some extra flexibility with regard to exposure.

Neutral density filters are usually rated using an ND scale, where .1ND equals 1/3 stop. Therefore, a .3ND filter will reduce the incoming light by one full stop. Neutral density filters can be stacked on top of one another to selectively add or subtract more stops. However, even the best filters are not optically perfect, so it's better to use as few as possible to reduce the chance of introducing optical aberrations into your lens system. In other words, if you want a 1-stop filter, use a single .3ND filter instead of three .1ND filters.

Here's a great neutral density-filtering trick: say you want to photograph a building on a busy street corner at noon, but you don't want to include any of the people who are pouring into and out of the building. Stack up a few neutral density filters until you have an 8- to 10-stop filter. This will increase your exposure time to 10 or 15 minutes, meaning that anything that's not stationary for at least that long won't be included in the shot. Obviously, you'll need a camera that provides a manual shutter speed control and allows for such long exposures. When the exposure is finished, you'll have an image of just the building.

Shutter Speed and Depth of Field

Because of the reciprocal nature of apertures and shutter speeds (see Chapter 3, "Basic Photography: A Quick Primer"), you can trade depth of field for more motion-stopping power. That is, you can go to a wider aperture (less depth of field) to use a higher shutter speed (more motion stopping). Conversely, you can switch to a slower shutter speed (less motion stopping) to use a smaller aperture (more depth of field).

These are the types of trade-offs you need to consider when you choose your exposure settings. Because there can be many different aperture/shutter combinations that will work for a given lighting situation, understanding the effects of different combinations will allow you more creative freedom.

Nearsighted?

If you are nearsighted enough to need glasses, try this quick little depth-of-field experiment. Take off your glasses and curl up your index finger against your thumb. You should be able to curl your finger tight enough to create a tiny little hole in the curve of your index finger. If you look through the hole without your glasses, you will probably find that everything is in focus. This hole is a very tiny aperture and, therefore, provides very deep depth of field— deep enough, in fact, that it can correct your vision. On the downside, it doesn't let a lot of light through, so unless you're in bright daylight, you might not be able to see anything well enough to determine if it's in focus. The next time you're confused about how aperture relates to depth of field, remember this test.

Tonal Control

Through your exposure choice, you can also control the tone and color of objects in your image. It's often necessary to make such tonal control decisions to get your camera to accurately reproduce the tone and color in your image, because of the way your light meter works.

It's very important to understand that the light meter on a typical point-and-shoot, prosumer, or even most higher-end cameras *cannot* tell you anything about the colors in your scene, how much contrast there is, or how to preserve all the detail that's present. In other words, your light meter doesn't tell you (or your camera) the *best* exposure for the scene you are shooting. Rather, your light meter simply tells you an *adequate* exposure for the scene you are shooting—one that will not grossly over- or underexpose your image. In many cases, you will take your meter's adequate reading as a starting point and build from there into the best exposure.

The photographic process is complicated by the fact that your eyes can see a much greater range of light to dark—and far more color—than can your digital or film camera. Your eyes' greater sensitivity to light is one of the reasons why it's difficult to capture a photo that looks like the actual scene—your camera simply can't record all the light your eyes can detect.

As you learned in Chapter 3, each time you change your aperture or your shutter speed setting by one full stop, you are doubling or halving the amount of light that hits the focal plane. Open your aperture by a stop, and the amount of light doubles. Close it one stop, and the amount of light is halved. In other words, a "stop" is a measure of light. The human eye can perceive a range of about 30 stops of light, whereas a digital camera can typically capture only 10 to 12 stops of light. Therefore, when shooting a picture, you have to decide which 10 to 12 stops you want to capture. These days, a good light meter will almost always pick a range of stops that yields a good image, when shooting in a bright, evenly lit situation. At other times, things can be more complicated.

For example, consider Figure 8.4. In real life, the bottom of the canyon and the blue of the sky were visible to the eye. However, because the camera could capture only some of the range of light, it was not possible to shoot a single exposure that would properly expose both the depths of the canyon and the bright sky above. So, although we can see detail in the sky in the first image, we see no detail in the canyon. In the second image, we have the exact opposite problem. When metering, you'll sometimes have to choose which areas of tone detail you want to preserve.

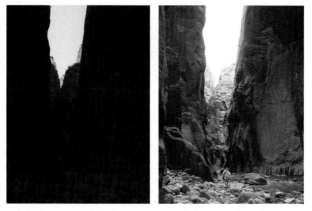

FIGURE 8.4   Because of the huge range of light to dark in this canyon, it was not possible to take a single exposure that captured both the bottom of the canyon and the sky above. In Chapter 14, "Imaging Tactics," you'll see one way to solve this particular exposure problem.

Your light meter does only one thing: it measures the *luminance* of the light reflected by your subject. Whether it measures the luminance of the entire scene or just a part of it depends on the type of meter you are using.

Figure 8.5 shows a grid with an equal number of black and white squares. If you were to measure this grid with a light meter, you would find that it is reflecting 18 percent of the light that is striking it. (Yes, it might seem like it should be reflecting 50 percent of the light, but it's not.) The luminance of most scenes averages out to be the same as this grid—that is, most scenes in the real world reflect 18 percent of the light that strikes them. Because this is a measure only of luminance (not color), you can also think of this 18 percent reflectance as a shade of gray. Therefore, this particular gray shade is known to photographers as *18 percent gray*, or *middle gray*.

The most important thing to know about your camera's light meter is that *it always assumes it is pointed at something that is 18 percent gray*. In other words, your light meter calculates an exposure recommendation that will accurately reproduce middle gray under your current lighting. Because a typical scene reflects 18 percent of the light that hits it, this assumption is usually fairly accurate. Obviously, if the lighting in your scene suddenly changes, the readings will no longer be accurate (even if the scene is still reflecting 18 percent of that light), and you'll have to remeter.

However, because your scene might not be exactly 18 percent gray, to get the best results from your light meter, you'll want to meter off something that is middle gray,

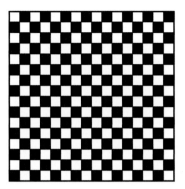

FIGURE 8.5 Although each of these squares is black or white,
the entire field of squares meters as 18 percent, or middle gray.

such as an 18 percent gray card. Readily available at any photo supply store, you can simply place this card in your scene and use it as the subject for your metering.

Unfortunately, although 18 percent gray is often a good assumption, it's not always correct. For example, the upper image in Figure 8.6 was shot using the camera's default metering. The image is neither too bright nor too dark—in other words, the meter did a good job of picking a range of stops that yields a good result. However, the black statue appears a little grayer than it did in real life. This is because the camera is *assuming* the statue is gray, and so is calculating an exposure that will correctly render the statue as *gray*.

In the lower figure, we underexposed the image to render the statue in its true, blacker tone. (Note that by underexposing we also got a better rendering of the brightly lit columns in the background. Because they're not overexposed anymore, you can see more detail on them.) In other words, we took the camera's initial metering as a starting point, and then modified it to capture a range of tones that is more accurate.

Note that this adjustment does not mean that there's something wrong with our light meter. The light meter was actually doing what it's supposed to do.

Just as we underexposed to restore the blacks in the image, if you're shooting something white—or if you're in a white environment, such as snow—you'll need to overexpose to correctly render white objects as white, rather than as middle gray.

Colors have a luminance—or tone—just as black-and-white images do and, therefore, need the same type of compensation for accurate reproduction. For example, look at Figure 8.7. The left image was shot with the camera's recommended metering, whereas the right image was underexposed by a third of a stop because the red color of the scooter was a bit darker than 18 percent gray. Simply put, by overexposing your images, your colors will become lighter; underexposing will make your colors darker. Such adjustments allow you to either restore the right color to the objects in your scene, or intentionally boost or decrease the saturation of objects within your scene.

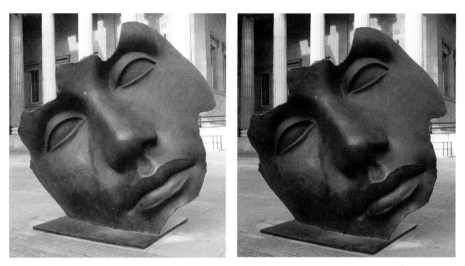

FIGURE 8.6 Although the top image looks good, the camera's default metering did not render the statue in its true black tone. By underexposing, we were able to produce a truer representation in the bottom image.

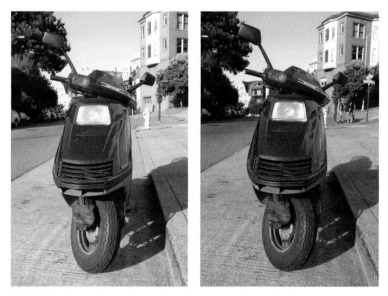

FIGURE 8.7 Through careful choice of exposure when shooting, you can capture images with better color saturation.

As stated earlier, your camera's light meter generates exposure settings that create an adequate picture. In general, your camera's meter will yield images with good color and proper exposure throughout the shadows and highlights. However, because of your light meter's assumptions, your picture might come out lacking details in some highlights or shadows. Or, it might look a little flat, because darker or lighter tones will all be rendered as middle tones. With some simple exposure adjustments, you can turn these images from adequate to exceptional, yielding images with improved color accuracy, contrast, and saturation (or tonal accuracy and contrast, if you're shooting black and white).

Note that the way you choose to create an over- or underexposure has no impact on the overall tonal adjustment. If you choose to change shutter speed, aperture, or some combination of both, you'll get the same tonal alteration in your final image. Which method you choose might depend on other exposure needs you have—motion stopping or depth of field, for example. You'll learn more about this when we cover exposure controls later in this chapter.

Details, Details

Earlier, you learned that some autofocus mechanisms work by detecting contrast within an image. The fact that more contrast means sharper focus—and therefore, more detail—is an important concept to remember when you choose an exposure for an image.

Figure 8.8 shows the same image shot with a range of exposures. Notice how the level of detail and sense of texture change from exposure to exposure.

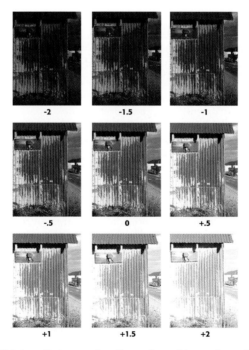

FIGURE 8.8   This heavily textured wall was shot with a variety of exposure-compensation settings. In addition to looking brighter or darker, notice how the level of detail and texture change with different exposure settings.

As you can see, in the underexposed images, many of the dark parts of texture are getting lost in the dark shadows. Conversely, in the overexposed images, many of the bright parts of texture are getting lost in the bright highlights. Fine texture and detail are often defined by the small highlight and shadow areas on the texture's surface. Consequently, you'll want to expose to reveal these highlights and shadows. In general, to preserve texture, you'll want to capture as broad a tonal range as you can, a topic we'll discuss in more detail later in this chapter.

Lower Your Camera's Sharpening

Sometimes, when shooting JPEG images in high-contrast situations, you can get better tonal range by setting your camera's contrast or sharpening setting to low (assuming your camera has a contrast or sharpening setting). As you've seen, an image with more sharpness has greater contrast between individual pixels. This can sometimes mean less tonal range, because more pixels are represented by high-contrast shades than by a broad range of tones. All cameras are different, of course, so do some experimenting with your camera's sharpness controls. Take some test shots with identical exposure settings but different sharpness settings, and examine the resulting histograms to learn how each setting affects tonal range.

HOW TO ADJUST EXPOSURE

As you've just seen, by altering exposure, you can adjust everything from the focus and sharpness in your image, to the color and tone of objects. In the previous section, we examined how you can change shutter speed to control motion-stopping power, aperture to control depth of field, and overall exposure to alter tones and detail in an image. However, we didn't speak at all to the subject of *how* you actually make these changes on your camera.

Because your light meter is the key to all exposure calculations and operations, we're going to take a quick look at the metering systems your camera might have before jumping into an examination of exposure controls.

Meters

Your camera probably offers a choice of different metering modes. These are usually selected from a button on the camera's body, or from a menu within the camera's menu system. (Note that if you're in a fully automatic shooting mode, you probably cannot change the metering mode.) To shoot a well-exposed image, you need to choose a metering mode that's right for your scene.

Matrix metering. A *matrix meter* (sometimes called a *multisegment meter*) divides your image into a grid and takes a separate meter reading for each cell in the grid. These cells are then analyzed to determine an exposure setting. Matrix metering is the best choice for most situations and is certainly the best option when you're simply trying to get a quick shot using your camera's automatic features. However, as you saw earlier, there will be times when you'll need to make some adjustments to your matrix meter reading. You might need to over- or underexpose to restore proper tone to your images, or you might need to bias the camera in a particular direction if you're shooting a scene that has more than a dozen stops of tonal values.

Center-weighted metering. A variation of matrix metering, *center-weighted metering* also divides your image into a grid of cells, but when analyzing the readings, a center-weighted metering system gives preference to the cells in the middle of the image. Typically, the middle 80 percent of the cells are considered more important than the outlying regions.

Center-weighted metering is designed for those times when your subject is in the middle of your frame, and your background contains bright lights, dark shadows, or other extreme lighting situations that might throw off the metering in the center of your image.

Spot metering. A *spot meter* measures only a small area of your image, usually the center. The metering from this area is the only information used to calculate an exposure. The most common use for a spot meter is for dealing with extremely backlit situations—a person standing in front of a window, for example—that would normally cause your camera to underexpose your foreground. Spot meters can also be handy with dark backgrounds, such as the one shown in Figure 8.9. In the left image, the background is deeply shadowed and has lost detail. By activating the camera's spot meter and metering off the shadowy background, the camera produces an image with much better shadow detail. Unfortunately, some foreground detail and color saturation was washed out in the process.

Performers on a stage are often excellent candidates for center-weight and spot metering.

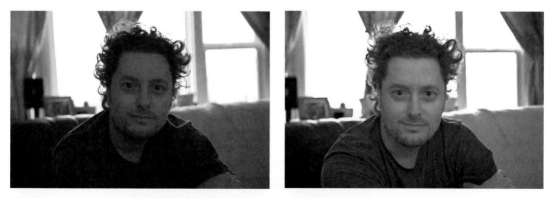

FIGURE 8.9 We shot the left image with matrix metering. Because the camera included the bright windows in its metering calculations, the foreground ended up underexposed. In the right image, we switched to center-weight metering, which did a better job of accurately exposing our subject.

Adjusting Exposure

As you've seen, there are many creative options to weigh and decisions to make when you choose an exposure for an image. For example, you might know that you want a shallow depth of field, so you will select a wide aperture. However, perhaps your images include many dark-colored objects that you feel need to be underexposed. At this point, you would probably choose to adopt a shorter shutter speed—rather than a smaller aperture—to preserve your shallow depth of field. Of course, if there are some fast-moving objects in your scene you were hoping to blur, you'll have to consider just how much you can slow down your shutter speed. All these different factors must be weighed and balanced.

Once you've made your decisions, you can begin to use your camera's settings to adjust your exposure accordingly. Fortunately, even if you have a less-expensive camera, you probably have enough controls to make some simple adjustments.

In this section, we'll cover all the ways you can adjust exposure on your digital camera. Which adjustments to make will depend on your image, of course, and which controls to use to make your adjustment will depend on which exposure characteristics you want to change and which you want to preserve.

Exposure Compensation

These days, almost all digital cameras, from simple point-and-shoots to high-end digital SLRs, provide exposure compensation controls. Even some camera phones now include an exposure compensation feature!

An exposure compensation control lets you specify an amount of over- or underexposure. Most cameras let you adjust exposure compensation in 1/2 or 1/3-stop increments, and allow you to over- or underexpose by up to two stops. (See Figure 8.10.)

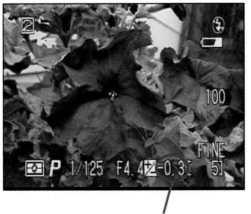

Exposure Compensation Display

FIGURE 8.10 Most cameras simply indicate exposure compensation with a numeric readout of the current amount of compensation (in this case, –.3 stops).

What's great about exposure compensation is that it lets you think in purely relative terms with no concern for specific shutter speed or aperture. So, for example, if you think your scene needs to be overexposed by a stop to properly render some white objects, simply press the + exposure button twice (assuming your exposure compensation increments in half stops). Your camera will meter as normal to determine its usual adequate exposure, but will then shoot at one stop over that exposure. Exposure compensation controls are the quickest and easiest way (and on some cameras, the only way) to make exposure adjustments.

On many cameras, the fully automatic mode will not provide access to exposure compensation, so you'll have to switch to program mode (or your camera's equivalent).

Most cameras try to achieve the requested change in exposure by changing shutter speed. When this isn't possible, either because the camera's shutter can't go any faster or because slowing the shutter speed would risk blurring the image, the camera will make changes to aperture. Sometimes, the camera will make slight changes to both shutter speed and aperture. Fortunately, these changes are usually minor enough that you won't see any change in the camera's capability to freeze motion or in the image's depth of field.

If you want to force exposure compensation to alter a specific parameter, put your camera into the appropriate priority mode. For example, if your camera is in shutter priority mode, any exposure compensation adjustments will be made by altering aperture. In aperture priority, compensation will be achieved through shutter speed changes.

Exposure compensation controls are powerful tools, and you will continue to use them even after you've learned some of the other exposure controls at your disposal. Get comfortable with your camera's exposure compensation controls, learn how to use them quickly, and begin learning how to recognize how much compensation is necessary for different situations. Because there are no hard-and-fast rules for over- or underexposing, you have to go out and practice!

Program Shift

Many cameras allow you to automatically cycle through reciprocal exposure settings after the camera has metered, allowing you to easily scroll through all the other aperture and shutter speed combinations that yield the same exposure as what the camera has just metered. In this way, you can quickly choose an equivalent exposure with a shutter speed or aperture that is more to your taste.

For example, if you're shooting a scene and decide you want shallower depth of field, press your shutter button down halfway to meter, and then use your program shift control to cycle through to an equivalent exposure with a wide aperture.

Note that because these are reciprocal exposure settings, they will still yield the same middle gray exposure as the camera's initial setting. If you want to over- or underexpose, you'll have to perform those adjustments separately. (See Figure 8.11.) A program shift feature combined with the camera's exposure compensation controls usually provides all the manual control you'll ever need, because you can usually achieve any exposure you want by using these simple adjustments.

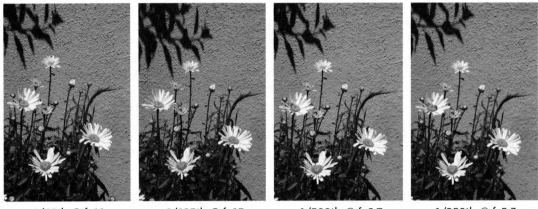

| 1/60th @ f. 19 | 1/125th @ f. 13 | 1/500th @ f. 6.7 | 1/250th @ f. 5.3 |

FIGURE 8.11 A large series of images of the same subject matter, each shot with a reciprocal setting.

CONTROLLING EXPOSURE WITH YOUR LIGHT METER

Using a built-in light meter, you can force an over- or underexposure by pointing the camera at something darker or lighter. Meter off a darker subject, and your camera will overexpose. Meter off a lighter subject, and you'll get an underexposure. (See Figure 8.12.) However, because your camera will probably lock focus at the same time as exposure, you'll need to be certain you are metering off something that is at the same distance as the image you would like to have in focus, or use your camera's exposure lock feature (if it has one).

Priority and Manual Modes

Priority modes provide a great balance of manual control with some automatic assistance. Typically, you'll select shutter priority when you want to control motion, and aperture priority when you want to control depth of field. You can select either aperture or shutter for tonal changes. Alternatively, you can combine a priority mode with your camera's exposure compensation controls. For example, you might use a shutter priority mode to ensure the motion control you want, but then use exposure compensation controls to intentionally over- or underexpose. (See Figure 8.13.)

Using a priority mode is simple: just select the aperture or shutter speed that's appropriate for what you're trying to achieve, and let the camera calculate the other value. Most cameras will warn you when they think you've chosen an exposure

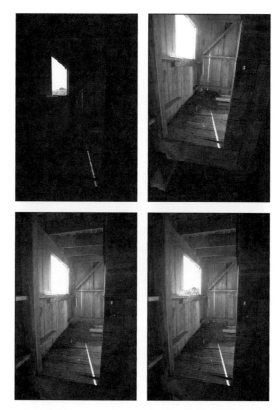

FIGURE 8.12   The upper-left image was exposed using the camera's default metering, which obviously biased itself toward the bright window, leaving the rest of the room in darkness. By tilting the camera down, we were able to force the camera to more accurately meter for the dark tones in the image, resulting in the lower-left picture. Finally, we cut the properly exposed window from the dark frame and then composited it with the well-exposed image to produce the final composite shown in the lower right.

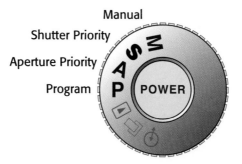

Manual

Shutter Priority

Aperture Priority

Program

FIGURE 8.13   Most cameras offer a simple dial or switch for changing the camera from full automatic mode to a priority or completely manual mode.

combination that will result in over- or underexposure. Don't worry, the camera will still shoot the picture; it's just trying to tell you that your settings don't conform to its idea of a good picture. Check your manual for details on how your camera indicates a bad exposure combination.

Full manual modes give you control of both aperture and shutter speed and offer more flexibility than any other shooting mode. However, because some digital cameras have cumbersome manual controls, you might find it easier to simply use a priority mode.

DEPTH-OF-FIELD PREVIEW

If your SLR has a depth-of-field preview button (Figure 8.14), you can use it to get an idea for the depth of field that will be provided by your current exposure settings. Normally, your camera's iris is open as wide as it will go, regardless of the aperture choice you've made. This allows you to see a bright, clear view through the viewfinder. When you press the shutter release to take a picture, the iris is closed down to your desired setting, and then reopens to full wide after the picture is taken. Obviously, this all happens in a fraction of a second.

If you've chosen a small aperture, the depth of field in your final image may be shallower than what you see when you look through the viewfinder. If you press your depth-of-field preview button (after metering and setting your desired aperture), the aperture will close down and stay closed as long as you hold the button. This allows you to see the image through the actual aperture you will use. However, with the iris stopped down, your viewfinder will become much dimmer, which can make it hard to see your image at all, much less notice depth of field.

Give your eyes time to adjust to the dimmer viewfinder, and if need be, cover your other eye with your hand to give yourself as dark a viewing environment at possible. As your eyes adjust, you should be able to get a better sense of the depth of field in the image.

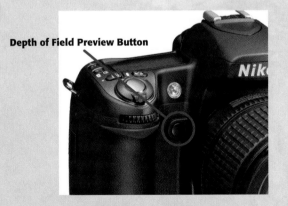

Depth of Field Preview Button

FIGURE 8.14   Like most SLRs, this Nikon D80 has a depth-of-field preview button, which allows you to see the actual depth of field in your scene. Not all DOF preview controls are in this location. Check your camera manual for details.

ISO Control

When you put a roll of film in a film camera, you're stuck with that film's ISO rating for the entire roll. Most digital cameras, though, allow you to change the ISO for each picture you take. Higher ISOs mean you can take pictures in less light, but you can also look at ISO adjustments as an additional exposure control.

ISO 200 is twice as sensitive to light as ISO 100 is. Moreover, as you might expect, ISO 400 is twice as sensitive as ISO 200 and four times as sensitive as ISO 100. As you learned earlier, every doubling of light is measured as a stop. Therefore, when you change from ISO 100 to 200, it's as if you've opened your camera's aperture one more stop or cut your shutter speed in half. This extra stop can often be what you need to save a shot.

For example, let's say you're shooting at dusk at ISO 100 and you have your camera's aperture open pretty wide to reduce depth of field. Unfortunately, with your current aperture, your meter has recommended a shutter speed of 1/15th of a second, too slow to be shooting handheld. Although you left your tripod at home, you don't have to compromise your depth of field choice. Just increase your ISO to 200 to pick up an extra stop, allowing you to set your shutter to 1/30th, or ISO 400 to get up to 1/60th of a second.

Or, maybe you're shooting a football game on a somewhat cloudy day, and even with your aperture open all the way, the fastest shutter speed your meter recommends is 1/60th. Crank the ISO up to 200 or 400 and you can shoot as fast as 1/250th for plenty of action-stopping power.

Of course, as you increase ISO rating, you'll be increasing the amount of noise in your image. Different cameras produce different amounts and qualities of noise, so you'll want to experiment with your camera to determine if you can accept the noise it produces at higher ISOs.

Tiny ISO Changes

Some cameras that only have a few apertures will make tiny changes to ISO sensitivity to create additional stops, usually without introducing noticeable noise.

Just as there is a reciprocal relationship between aperture and shutter speed, when you start manipulating ISO you must think of reciprocity between all three factors. As you increase ISO, you might need to close your aperture or increase your shutter speed.

Intermediate ISOs

Some cameras now allow you to manually switch to fractional stop ISOs. So, instead of 100, 200, 400, you might have 100, 125, 160, 200, 250, 320, and 400. Each of these steps represents a change of 1/3 of a stop. With these fractional stops, you can boost your ISO by only as much as you need to get the extra shutter speed or aperture latitude you want, without incurring any more noise than you have to.

ELECTRONIC VIEWFINDERS AND METERING

In Chapter 5, "Choosing a Digital Camera," we discussed how LCD screens and electronic viewfinders show a limited view of the dynamic range in your scene. While your eye can see a huge range of light to dark, your camera can only capture a fraction of that range, and the image shown on your camera's LCD is even more limited.

When using an LCD or electronic viewfinder, therefore, it's very important to keep one eye on the actual scene. This will help you better assess what tones you have to work with, and will remind you that there might be more detail in the scene than your camera is showing you.

Of course, you can also just take a shot and look at the resulting image on your screen to assess whether you got what you want. If not, you can adjust your exposure and try again. The important thing is simply to be aware that your LCD viewfinder is showing you a narrower range of tones than what the camera will actually capture.

IN-CAMERA HISTOGRAMS

First the bad news: the LCD viewfinder on your camera will greatly increase the brightness and possibly color contrast and saturation in any image you view. This is because the camera's designers want to ensure that the image on the viewfinder is visible in bright, direct sunlight. Because of this, your camera's LCD screen does not actually present an accurate representation of what the colors and tones in your image actually look like. This means that when you shoot an image and then look at the results on the viewfinder, you won't necessarily be able to spot over- or under-exposure, or assess contrast and color.

The good news is that if your camera includes a built-in histogram, you can easily determine if your image has certain exposure problems. Not all cameras have histograms, but your camera's manual should make it easy to determine how to activate the histogram view for any image you've taken.

Figure 8.15 shows a histogram display from a Canon SLR. In addition to displaying the histogram, the thumbnail display flashes any areas that have clipped highlights or shadows.

We'll be spending a lot of time with histograms when we start post-production, so an understanding of the use of a histogram is very important.

Don't Know Much about Histograms

A *histogram* is a simple graph of the distribution of all the tones in your image. Histograms can be easily created by most image-editing applications and are a great way to understand exposure.

Look at Figure 8.16 and its accompanying histogram.

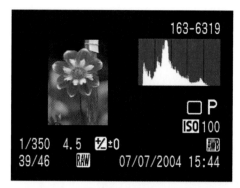

FIGURE 8.15   Many cameras can display a histogram of any image you've shot. In addition to this histogram, this display from a Canon SLR shows date, time, and all exposure parameters. In over- or underexposed images, the display also flashes areas in the image thumbnail that are "clipped" in the histogram.

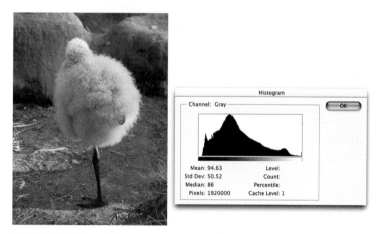

FIGURE 8.16   With a histogram, you can analyze your images to determine which type of exposure corrections they might need.

A histogram, such as the one shown in Figure 8.16, is simply a bar chart showing how much of each shade of gray is present in the image, with each vertical line representing one shade. Black is at the far left, and white is at the far right.

From the histogram, you can see that the image in Figure 8.6 is fairly well exposed. It has a good range of tones from black to light gray, which means it has a lot of contrast. Most of the tones are distributed toward the lower end because of the dark grays and shadows in the background. However, even though the background is dark, there is still a good range of middle gray tones and lighter tones from the gray of the baby flamingo.

Notice that the shadow areas do not *clip*. That is, they curve down to nothing by the time the graph reaches the left side. This means that the shadowy details in the image have not gone to solid black. In fact, there is very little solid black in the image at all. This is an indication that there is plenty of detail in the shadow areas. Also notice that there are a large number of tones overall, meaning the image has a good dynamic range and, therefore, a lot of editing potential. Although the brighter areas are a little weak, we can correct for this in our image editor.

Now, look at Figure 8.17.

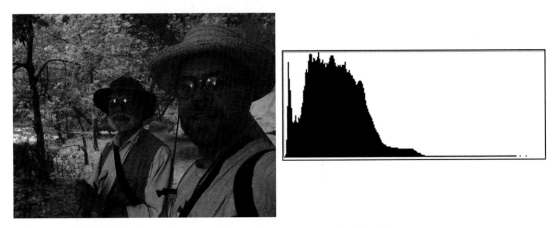

FIGURE 8.17   An underexposed image has a very characteristic histogram.

You can probably tell by looking at Figure 8.17 that the image is underexposed, but the histogram still provides some interesting information. As you can see, there is no white in this image at all and very little medium gray, but at the lower end there is a preponderance of solid black. Notice that the shadow areas don't curve down to black as they do in Figure 8.16. Rather, they are "clipped" off the edge of the histogram—the image is so dark and underexposed that many of the darkest tones have piled up in the darkest tone. In a well-exposed image, the shadow areas would be spread over a large number of darker tones, with only a little solid black. If you look in the shadow areas of the image, you'll see that they look completely black, rather than having any variation or range in their dark tones. In other words, the shadows have lost detail.

In a grayscale image, a histogram is literally a graph of the gray tones in an image. As you saw in Chapter 7, colors have a tone that roughly corresponds to the tonal qualities of a shade of gray. When you take a histogram of a color image, such as the one in Figure 8.15, the resulting graph shows a composite of the red, green, and blue channels in the image. The practical upshot is a graph that is still an accurate gauge of the contrast and tonal information in your image.

An image that is overexposed will exhibit a similar histogram but weighted on the other end, with tones grouped in the white areas and with clipped highlights. (See Figure 8.18.)

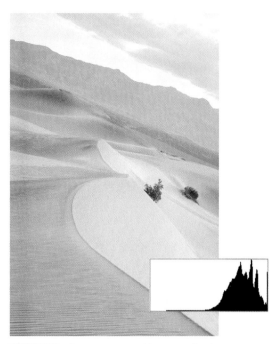

FIGURE 8.18   An overexposed image—the tones are weighted to the right of the histogram. In this image, you can see that the highlights are clipped—they get cut off by the right side of the histogram.

The histogram is an exceptional exposure tool for shooting in a difficult lighting situation. Set your exposure, shoot a test shot, and then take a quick look at the image's histogram. If you see clipped highlights or shadows, you'll need to try a different exposure and shoot again. (If your camera has a live histogram feature like the one shown in Figure 5.12, you can watch the histogram *while* you change exposures.)

Assessing Contrast

In addition to spotting over- and underexposure problems, you can use your camera's histogram to determine the amount of contrast in an image. Take a look at Figure 8.19.

The image has little contrast and appears "flat." A quick look at the histogram shows why. Most of the tones are grouped in the middle of the graph—they don't cover a broad range.

After consulting this histogram, you would know that it was worth trying a second, additional exposure, this time with a little bit of underexposure. In addition to eliminating the slight amount of highlight clipping visible on the right edge of the histogram, it would place more tones in the lower, shadow part of the histogram, most likely resulting in more data spread across the graph—that is, more contrast.

Note, though, that some images show a low-contrast histogram because they actually don't have much contrast in them. The histogram for Figure 8.20, for example, shows mostly dark tones. There's not a huge range of tonal information in the image because the image is mostly dark background. So, there's no way we could actually capture more contrast from this image. However, our histogram can still tell us whether we've clipped the highlights or shadows.

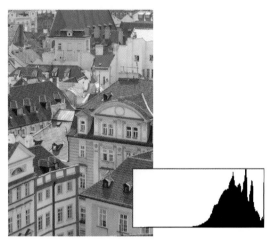

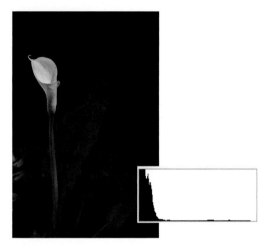

FIGURE 8.19 In a low-contrast image, the tones will be in the center of the histogram. Notice the lack of dark black or light gray tones.

FIGURE 8.20 This histogram shows low contrast because there's simply not much contrast in this image. It's mostly dark background.

Don't Worry about the Shape of the Histogram

There is no right or wrong shape to a histogram, so don't worry about the overall shape of the pile of tones. As long as you have good contrast, and nothing's clipping, you have a healthy histogram. Bear in mind that some images are low-contrast scenes, so getting a very contrasty histogram may not be possible.

Examining Color

Your histogram can't tell you too much about the color in your image, but if your camera displays a three-channel histogram, you might be able to get a sense for bad white balance. A three-channel histogram simply shows a separate histogram for each color channel (red, green, and blue). If the three channels are way out of registration, there's a chance your image has a white balance problem. Note, though, that this is a difficult thing to assess, because sometimes images simply have very different amounts of different colors, which can also skew your histogram.

RECORDING YOUR EXPOSURE SETTINGS

To really understand exposure, how it works, and what decisions to make, you must practice. However, for your practice to do you any good, you need a record of what exposure settings you used in any particular image. In the old days, you had to carry around a notebook and record your exposure settings by hand. You can still do that, of course, and make any other notes you feel are important to remember, but the odds are that your camera will remember your settings for you, because most digital cameras record a number of parameters when an image is stored to disk. Figure 8.21 shows the information stored by a Nikon point-and-shoot camera.

This information is stored using a standard format called *Exchangeable Image File (EXIF)*, which was created by the Japan Electronic Industry Development Association in 1995. If your digital camera is EXIF compatible (and most are), all its files are EXIF files, whether they use JPEG or TIFF compression.

The great thing about EXIF files is that their image data can be read by any program, even if that program isn't specifically EXIF compatible. The EXIF data is simply stored in the header information of the file, so any application that can read JPEG or TIFF files can still read an EXIF-compatible file.

These days, most image-editing, cataloging, and browsing applications allow you to look at an image's EXIF data (as shown in Figure 8.22). As you'll see, this data is often very helpful when editing.

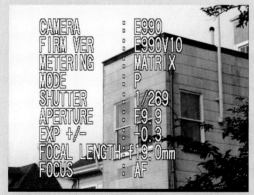

FIGURE 8.21   Most cameras will store a record of all the parameters you used for each shot. This data is stored with the file and can be read using special software.

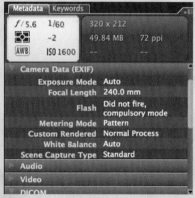

FIGURE 8.22   Adobe Bridge CS3 displays an EXIF readout for each image you select.

BRACKETING

While it's important to understand all the exposure theory we've discussed here, there's a very simple practice you can employ to help ensure you get a correct exposure, no matter what shooting situation you're in.

Bracketing is the process of shooting extra exposures above and below your target exposure to provide yourself a margin of error in your exposure calculation. If you've made a somewhat accurate, educated guess about exposure, one of your bracketed images will most likely be good, even if your original guess was off. Bracketing is a tried-and-true practice of film photographers, but it's much easier with a digital camera.

The easiest way to bracket is with your exposure compensation control. Take a shot, then dial in an underexposure, and shoot again. Then do the same with an overexposure. There's no right or wrong exposure interval to use, and you can shoot as many images as you want.

As always, with exposure compensation you'll have no way to control *how* the camera achieves its over- or underexposure, so you may want to switch to a priority mode.

Many digital cameras offer *autobracketing* features, which let the camera take care of bracketing for you. For example, Figure 8.23 shows the Auto Exposure Bracketing menu control from a Canon digital SLR, which lets you dial in a bracketing range. Here, we've chosen a three-step bracket with 1-stop intervals. When you press the shutter, the camera will shoot an image at the recommended metering, and then automatically adjust for 1-stop of overexposure. This setting will be used for the next shot, while the shot after that will automatically be set for 1 stop of underexposure.

If you activate the camera's drive (or burst) mode, you can simply press and hold the shutter release for three shots, and the camera will shoot an autobracketed set.

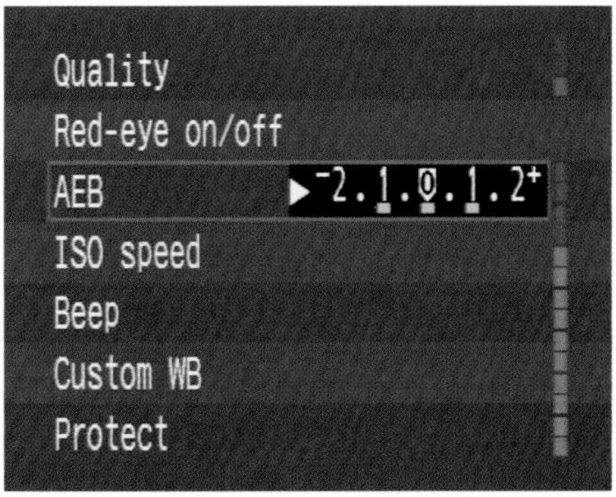

FIGURE 8.23   If your camera has an autobracketing feature, you can set it to automatically shoot a series of bracketed exposures.

Saving Space While Bracketing

With digital bracketing, you don't have to worry about the waste and expense of shooting extra film. However, if storage is a concern, you might want to examine your bracketed set. After shooting, quickly check the histogram for each image using your camera's LCD. You can then throw out the images that are obviously poorly exposed.

When autobracketing, your camera will employ its usual procedure for determining whether it should achieve its exposure adjustment through shutter speed changes, aperture, or both. If you want to force changes to use specific aperture or shutter speed adjustments, you'll need to put your camera into a priority mode, and configure accordingly.

JPEG EXPOSURE TIPS

If you're shooting in JPEG mode, here are two simple things to keep in mind when choosing an exposure:

- Protect your highlights! Overexposed highlights are ugly! They're big empty areas of white that are boring and distracting. So, when choosing an exposure, be sure to protect your highlights. While you want to have shadow detail, it's always better to risk losing shadow detail to be sure you've protected your highlights. A dark, black shadow will be less noticeable and distracting than a blown-out highlight.
- Usually, a slight bit of underexposure will yield slightly better saturation. In typical, even daylight and indoor situations, leaving your camera set to −.3 stops will produce slightly "punchier" images. However, if you're in a bright location, or shooting something with a lot of white, you'll want to adjust your exposure accordingly.

Obviously, these two factors must be balanced with any other exposure concerns you're balancing (depth of field, motion stopping, tone mapping, and so on).

EXPOSING FOR RAW

If you're shooting in raw mode, you'll want to calculate your exposure adjustments a little differently than you do when shooting JPEG. In Chapter 2, "How a Digital Camera Works," you learned about the differences between raw and JPEG images. As you'll recall, one of the image processing steps that occurs inside your camera when you shoot in JPEG mode is *gamma correction*—the process of applying a mathematical curve to the image's tones to adjust them so the highlight and shadow areas look more like the way your eye sees the world. This step is necessary due to the fact that your eye sees tonal information in a nonlinear fashion, while your camera has a linear response.

Film also has a nonlinear response to light. Because of this, when you're shooting JPEG you can choose to make the same types of exposure decisions you would choose when you're shooting film.

Raw files must also be gamma corrected to create a nice-looking image, but this gamma correction step happens *after* you shoot, when you're converting your raw image using your raw conversion software. The raw file that gets stored on your camera's media card is an un-gamma-corrected linear file, and you can exploit this fact when you choose an exposure, so as to shoot images with a little more editing latitude, and less shadow noise.

How Your Camera Responds to Light

In Chapter 2, you learned about the difference between linear and nonlinear light response. Your camera has a linear response, which means that when it begins capturing an image, it first measures the brightest values in your scene. That brightest stop's-worth of light takes up *half* of the dynamic range of the sensor.

In other words, if your camera can capture 4096 levels of brightness, 2048 of those levels will be used to represent the brightest stop in your image.

Half of what's left over after that will go into representing the next brightest stop, half of what's left over from that will go into the next, and so on and so forth for 10 to 12 stops' worth of light (or whatever the range of your camera is). Figure 8.24 shows a visual representation of this concept.

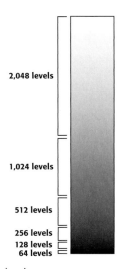

FIGURE 8.24   Half of the data your camera captures goes into representing the brightest shot in your image. When shooting raw, you can exploit this fact to shoot images with lower noise.

The practical upshot of this is that by the time you get to the darkest areas in your image, you may have very few levels left to represent that information. This can result in shadows that are posterized and noisy. Meanwhile, the brightest stop in your image will be very data-rich, with plenty of subtle shadings and tones.

Therefore, when shooting raw, it's often advisable to shoot with some *overexposure* to bias the camera toward capturing more data in the tonal range for which it stores the most data. Later, in your image editor, you can redistribute these tones, to push them down into the shadow parts of your image to create good shadows. The result will be shadows with far less noise, and possibly fewer posterization artifacts. (You'll learn how to perform this adjustment in Chapter 12, "Raw Conversion.")

Your Overexposure Safety Net

The thought of risking overexposure can be frightening because, as described earlier, when you overexpose a highlight it turns to a distracting blob of empty white. However, very often when you overexpose you don't actually overexpose, or clip, all *three* color channels. Sometimes, you only overexpose one or two color channels. If you're using a raw converter that offers a highlight recovery feature, the converter can use the one or two remaining, intact channels to rebuild the information that was clipped from the overexposed channels. (See Figure 8.25.)

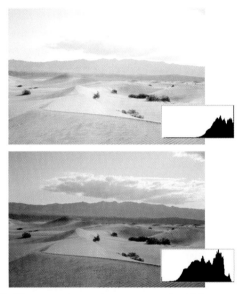

FIGURE 8.25   The upper image is overexposed, which you can tell by looking at both the histogram, which is clipped on the right, and the clouds in the image, which have blown out to complete white. In the upper image, we've used the highlight recovery capability of our raw converter to recover most of the details in the clouds.

In addition, your camera might capture additional "headroom" above and beyond the data that is used to create the image you see. This data is necessary for some of the interpolation calculations the raw converter must perform. This headroom is stored inside the raw file along with the regular image data. A raw converter that can perform highlight recovery can often reach into this information to rebuild blown highlights.

Most good raw converters these days offer highlight recovery capabilities. Photoshop Camera Raw, Aperture, Lightroom, Nikon Capture NX, Capture One, and others all offer this feature, and you'll learn how to use it in Chapter 12.

The practical upshot of this additional capability is that you have a bit of a safety net when overexposing. If you go too far, there's a chance you'll be able to recover any accidental clipping that occurs.

With that said, you still want to be careful about exposure. You can't just set your camera on +2 stops of overexposure and think you'll get all sorts of great data. Ideally, you want to ride close to the edge of overexposure without clipping.

If your goal is to capture a darker image, it's still a good idea to use some slight overexposure. Again, you'll rebuild your dark areas with the data-rich tones you collect in the brighter areas of your image.

Some Assembly Required

When you use this technique, your images will not look very good straight out of the camera, because you're shooting with the intention of applying some post-processing adjustments. As such, your images will possibly be washed out and overexposed. So, if speedy workflow is your priority, then it's better to expose normally.

How Much Overexposure Is Enough?

There are no hard-and-fast rules for overexposure when exposing for raw, and the correct amount will vary depending on the brightness in your scene. An image with lots of bright specular highlights—such as rippling waves, or metallic glints—will probably afford less latitude for overexposure than other scenes. Very often, though, you'll find that you can overexpose by at least a full stop, sometimes more.

Unfortunately, your camera's histogram is not especially useful for this technique. To show a histogram of a raw image, your camera first has to make a JPEG of the image. It then produces a histogram of that JPEG image (the JPEG image is not stored). JPEG images, as you learned, are gamma corrected, so they are nonlinear images.

The resulting histogram will usually show highlight clipping *before* it has actually occurred in your raw file. Sometimes, there can be as much as 1.5 to 2 stops of additional latitude beyond what the histogram will show you for a raw file. As an experiment, shoot some images with your camera and then take them into your raw converter, but leave the images on the camera's card. Compare the histogram your raw converter generates to the camera's histogram, and you'll probably notice a difference on the bright end of things.

If Ever There Was a Time to Autobracket...

If the thought of bad exposure scares you, just remember that you can always bracket! Any camera that offers raw support probably also has an autobracketing feature. Get a big storage card and get in the habit of bracketing your shots until your comfortable with the amount of overexposure you want to use.

If you're still confused, don't worry; this technique will make more sense once you've done some raw conversion, and explored the "back end" of shooting raw. We'll cover all the details in Chapter 12.

EXPOSING TO AVOID CHROMATIC ABERRATION (PURPLE FRINGING)

If your camera has a problem with purple fringing (as discussed in Chapter 5), or if you're shooting with an SLR using a lens that has this problem, there are some things you can do to reduce the chance of this artifact occurring. (See Figure 8.26.)

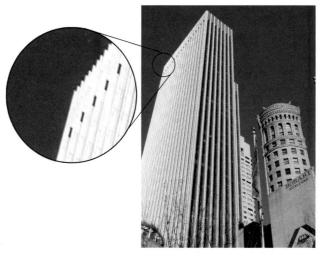

FIGURE 8.26   Some digital cameras suffer from a type of color aberration that causes purple fringing along areas of high contrast in an image.

Purple fringing usually occurs when you shoot into a high-contrast situation using a very wide angle (or close to it). For these reasons, landscape shots usually suffer the most from purple fringing. Skies often create troublesome contrast situations, and landscapes typically prompt you to use a wide angle. Trees are also particularly bad subjects when it comes to purple fringing. Because they typically have a bright sky behind them, and because they include so many high-contrast details, you'll often find that shots taken from beneath a tree or through a tree (for example, on a horizon) will have bad purple fringing around the small foliage details.

If you're in such a situation and you know that the lens on your camera is subject to this problem (not all lenses will be), try the following solutions:

- Zoom in to a longer focal length. In fact, shooting several images at different focal lengths might be best.
- If you can't get a framing you like without shooting at full wide, try closing down your camera's aperture. You will, of course, have to adjust your shutter speed appropriately. Be careful if you make this adjustment using your camera's exposure compensation controls, because they won't necessarily compensate with an aperture adjustment. It's better to use your camera's manual controls (or program shift control, if your camera has one).

- Some lenses exhibit purple fringing only at the edges of their photographs. If this seems to be true of your camera, try to frame the image so particularly trouble-some subject matter (trees, bright shapes, fine details) are away from the edge of the frame.

Obviously, no matter how careful you are, you won't always be able to avoid these artifacts. As you might expect, there are some ways to remove these problems using your image-editing program. You'll learn some purple fringe removal techniques in Chapter 14.

TAKING CONTROL

The good news about many of the techniques and ideas described in this chapter is that you probably won't always have to rely on them, or concern yourself with them. The fact is, modern digital camera meters and preprogrammed modes are *very* good. Nevertheless, if you're serious about photography, there will be times when taking control will be the only way to get the shot you envision. After reading this chapter, you should be comfortable with the concepts of manual exposure, and you should understand how your camera meters. Most important, you should know how to use and read a histogram, because we'll be relying heavily on histograms later in the book.

SPECIAL SHOOTING

In This Chapter

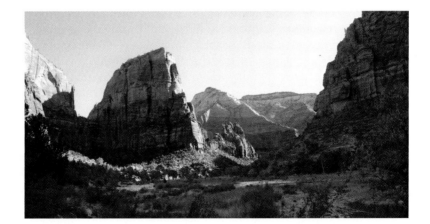

A t the end of the Apollo 11 moon landing, Neil Armstrong and Buzz Aldrin blasted off from the moon in their tiny lunar module, aiming for a rendezvous with crewmate Michael Collins in the orbiting *Columbia* service module. As the tiny speck of a spaceship rose up from the moon, ground controllers recorded Collins saying, "I got the Earth coming up behind you—it's fantastic!" Back on Earth, after the rocks and spacesuits and Hasselblad cameras were all unloaded, and the film was developed, Armstrong and Aldrin were able to see what Collins had been so excited about: a photograph of the earth rising above the moon, with the lunar lander flying close by in the foreground. In other words, a single picture encompassing all of humanity except for one man: Mike Collins, the photographer.

Like all the astronauts, in addition to having the "right stuff," Collins had to have a comfortable knowledge of basic photographic principles. A quarter of a million miles from Earth, he still had to worry about f-stops, shutter speeds, and film stocks in addition to worrying about asphyxiation, burning up on reentry, and drowning in the ocean.

Hopefully, you won't ever have to face such photographic concerns. However, it is important to realize that certain types of photography require special equipment, techniques, and preparation. In the case of lunar photography, you would need a massive government-funded space program in addition to your digital camera and a decent computer. Web photography, on the other hand, requires a camera with appropriate resolution and a good understanding of how your images will be sized and compressed for delivery.

In this chapter, you'll learn about all types of special shooting considerations, ranging from shooting in black and white to shooting in extreme weather.

STABLE SHOOTING

No matter what your shooting conditions, from simple street or event shooting to more complex shooting in harsh environments, keeping your camera stable is an essential part of shooting sharp images and having maximum creative control.

Many people believe that if you're shooting with a fast shutter speed, you don't have to worry about camera stability, but camera shake can impact your images at even very fast shutter speeds. What's more, camera stability becomes more important if you're shooting with a camera that has a very high pixel count. A camera with 10 or 12 megapixels is capable of revealing the softness that can be caused by very fine camera shake and vibration.

While tripods and monopods are the obvious solutions for stabilizing your camera (and we'll talk about shooting with these devices later in this section), there are also tricks you can employ when shooting handheld to achieve better stability. As you practice your handheld shooting, you'll get more adept at keeping your camera steady. Here are some tips you can use to improve your camera stability when hand-holding.

Keep your elbows in. Holding your elbows against your sides provides much better stability than holding them out, away from your body. (See Figure 9.1.)

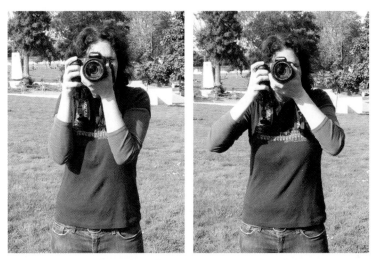

FIGURE 9.1   Always keep your elbows against your sides. This gives you a much more stable shooting position. When your elbows are away from your body, it's much harder to stabilize the camera.

This is especially true when shooting with the camera in portrait orientation. When shooting vertically, many people use the position shown in Figure 9.2. If you turn the camera the other way, though, you can keep your elbows against your body for great stability. It's also more comfortable, albeit it doesn't give you that cool "gotta get the shot" look.

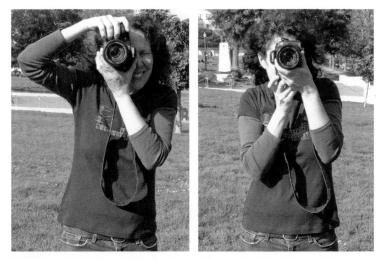

FIGURE 9.2   The "elbows in" rule also applies to shooting in portrait mode. In the right-hand image, the photographer has a much more stable position than she does in the left, with her elbows akimbo.

Don't hold your breath. When hand-holding is particularly difficult—shooting with a very long focal length, or very slow shutter speed, or both, for example—some people hold their breath while shooting. This can actually make you jitterier. Breathe normally, and try to press the shutter as you're exhaling.

Squeeze the shutter button, don't jab it. Sometimes, the greatest amount of camera movement occurs when you press the shutter release, since you're actually pushing against the camera at that moment. If you're pre-focusing (which you should be doing, and which you learned about in Chapter 7, "Shooting"), you already have the shutter button halfway down. Getting it the rest of the way should be a very simple, very small motion.

Use an image-stabilized lens. If you're shooting with a higher-end camera that supports interchangeable lenses, spend the extra money for image-stabilized lenses.

Beware of diffraction effects—watch your aperture. As you stop your lens down (that is, go to a higher f.stop number), *diffraction* effects can occur that result in a loss of sharpness. In some instances, these can occur noticeably as soon as f.11. In other lenses, they're not a problem until smaller apertures, such as f.16. Whether the softness is a problem or not depends on how you will be outputting. If you're going out to low-res Web images, or small prints, the diffraction softening may not be an issue. Nevertheless, it's worth doing a few tests with your camera to determine how small you can take your aperture before you notice an unacceptable loss of sharpness.

Learn about sharpness at different focal lengths. As with aperture, some focal length choices will impact sharpness. Some lenses don't produce even edge-to-edge sharpness across their range, so you'll want to experiment with your lens to determine if there is any sharpness falloff at particular focal lengths. This doesn't mean that you'll always avoid these focal lengths, but if you're shooting an image in which sharpness is critical, such an understanding of sharpness might prompt you to choose a different focal length and camera position.

Shooting with a Tripod

For maximum stability, you'll want to shoot with a tripod. We covered tripod buying in Chapter 5, "Choosing a Digital Camera," and so have already discussed questions of weight versus stability. Once you have a tripod, there are a few things to keep in mind when using it.

Use a remote control or self-timer. As long as your camera is on a tripod, you might as well get your potentially shaky hands completely off the camera by using a remote control or the camera's built-in self-timer.

Don't use the center column if you don't have to. If you can get your camera to the height you want using the legs, do that rather than use the center column. With the center column extended, your camera is not as stable as when it's resting directly on top of the main platform.

When in muddy, dirty terrain, extend the tripod legs from the lowest segment first. This will ensure that the majority of the leg latches are lifted off the ground, away from the mud and dirt that could gum up the latch workings.

Make sure the tripod is level. Some tripods have a built-in level. If yours doesn't, you need to pay particular attention to horizontal lines in your image to ensure they're level. Yes, you can straighten an image in post-production, but straightening requires a crop, which means you're effectively shooting at lower resolution. If you're shooting with a ball head, remember that just because the tripod is level, the head may be askew.

Pay attention to wind. Wind can cause vibration in even the heaviest tripod. If you're shooting in a very windy environment, you will most likely not want to use the center column.

Use the weight hook. Hang your camera bag or a sandbag from the weight hook at the bottom of the center column (if there is one) for additional stability. (See Figure 9.3.)

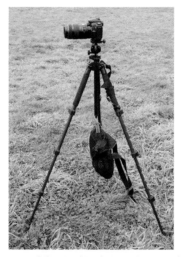

FIGURE 9.3   For extra stability in this shot, we've attached the weight hook to the bottom of the camera, and hung our camera bag from the hook. Note, too, that we have not elevated the center column.

Make sure the camera's not front-heavy. If you have an especially big lens on the camera, and the tripod is on uneven terrain, be sure the tripod is stable before taking your hands off the camera. You don't want a heavy lens to tip the entire apparatus forward. Also, be sure the tripod is not in danger of tipping or being blown over if you leave it unattended.

When appropriate, use mirror lockup. If you're shooting a long-exposure using a digital SLR, activate the camera's mirror lockup feature, if it has one.

This feature prevents small extra vibrations caused by the mirror flipping up and down.

Finally, the best advice for shooting with a tripod is to remember to take the tripod. If your tripod is so big, heavy, or unwieldy that you don't ever take it shooting, maybe you should consider getting a smaller, lighter tripod. Even though a smaller tripod offers less height and stability than a large tripod, if it means you'll carry it more often, it's a more useful piece of gear.

MONOPODS

A monopod does not provide as much stability as a tripod, but they're usually lighter and easier to carry, so there's often a better chance you'll take a monopod with you. Monopods are also ideal in situations where you need stability but don't have the time or space to set up and move a tripod from place to place. Sporting events and live shows are ideal situations for monopod use. Monopods are also extremely handy if you're shooting with a heavy lens. In addition to providing more stability, the monopod will give your arms and hands a break when you're shooting.

BLACK-AND-WHITE PHOTOGRAPHY

All digital cameras produce color images, but some of the most famous images in history were shot with black-and-white film. In fact, because your eyes are so much more sensitive to luminance than they are to color, a black-and-white photo actually contains everything your eye needs to represent a scene. The option to shoot in black and white is an important tool in the photographer's creative toolbox. Color is often distracting and unnecessary, and black-and-white images allow you to explore geometry, tone, light, and shadow in ways that aren't possible with color images.

If you want to shoot black-and-white images with your digital camera, you have two options: you can shoot in color and convert to black and white later, a topic we'll cover in great detail in Chapter 14, "Imaging Tactics;" or, if your camera provides one, you can shoot in a special black-and-white mode.

The advantage to shooting in black-and-white mode is simple convenience. You don't have to perform any extra conversion later. In addition, you can see your image in black and white right on the camera's LCD screen, which makes visualizing in black and white much easier.

The downside to a built-in black-and-white mode is that you usually don't have much, if any, control over the black-and-white conversion. As you'll see in Chapter 14, black-and-white conversion is not an objective science. An infinite number of black-and-white images can be derived from a color image, and which one is "correct" is a subjective decision. Therefore, performing your black-and-white conversions by hand will give you far more control over the final image.

Use Raw + JPEG for Black-and-White Shooting

If your camera has the capability to shoot raw and JPEG files simultaneously, consider using this mode, and configuring the JPEG image to be black and white. When you shoot, your camera will show the black-and-white JPEG, so you can immediately see the image in black and white, but you'll still have the raw file for performing your own custom black-and-white conversion later. Not all cameras have both of these features—check your camera manual for details.

Seeing in Black and White

One of the most difficult things about shooting in black and white is recognizing potential images. You see the world in color, so trying to imagine it in black and white can be hard. There are plenty of times when an image that looks good in color will also look good in black and white, so you'll often find good black-and-white images by simply looking for the usual markings of a good shot.

There are other images, though, that make great black-and-white images, but aren't so interesting in color. These images can be difficult to see, given your color view of the world.

BLACK-AND-WHITE SHOOTING

It used to be that if you were a hobbyist photographer, you *had* to shoot in black and white. Color darkrooms were very expensive, and black-and-white film was far cheaper than color. Nowadays, you can spend $100 on a photo printer and have a very affordable color print lab right on your desktop. Because of the ubiquity and affordability of color, many beginning digital photographers never go through the black-and-white phase that used to be required of all photography students.

In the last few years, several desktop printers have come to market offering excellent black-and-white printing capabilities, and you'll learn about those in Chapter 16, "Output." Now that there are affordable black-and-white output options for digital photographers, there's nothing to stop you from pursuing black and white with your digital camera.

As an exercise, spend the next week shooting only black and white. Forcing yourself to give up color offers several things:

- Shooting black and white requires you to pay attention to luminance, tone, geometry, and texture. When you work with black and white, you might find yourself hunting for a very different type of image than what you look for when shooting color. This can greatly expand your shooting repertoire.
- Because you see in color, trying to recognize and previsualize potential black-and-white scenes is a very good way to force yourself into "seeing" the world around you. Black-and-white shooting gets your visual sense going in a very active way.

- Since black-and-white images are often driven by form and tone, they become very good composition exercises. As you shoot more black and white, you may find your composition skills developing in new ways. (See Figure 9.4.)

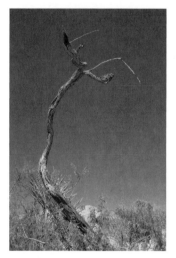

FIGURE 9.4   Black-and-white shooting forces you (or sometimes frees you) to concentrate on formal compositional ideas like geometry, line, tone, and shadow.

Finally, black and white is simply a very different way of seeing the world. After a while, you may find that some images look *more* real in black and white than they do in color. Stripped of their color, they can achieve an immediacy you can't achieve in color. Black and white is a form of abstraction that can be very powerful. As discussed earlier, abstraction can serve to engage the viewers, as it asks them to conjure certain details on their own.

Infrared Photography

Infrared light is not visible to the human eye. However, special infrared-sensitive films can be used to capture infrared light, allowing you to capture scenes in a very different . . . er, light. Skies and foliage are particularly well suited to infrared photography—leafy greens will appear white and skies will be rendered with much more contrast. With the use of an infrared filter that you attach to the end of your lens, you might be able to perform infrared photography with your digital camera. (See Figure 9.5.)

Most image sensors are so sensitive to infrared light that camera makers have to put a strong infrared "cut" filter between the lens and the sensor. Without this filter, the sensor will yield images with very strong color casts. Despite these filters, though, some infrared does get passed through to the camera's sensor, allowing you to use your digital camera for infrared photography. Unfortunately, there's no hard-and-fast rule for how strong a camera's IR filter is—the only way to find out is to ex-

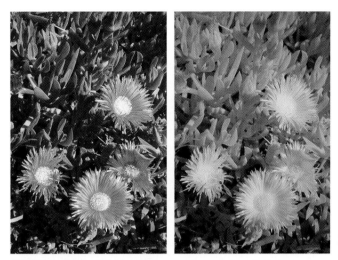

FIGURE 9.5   With an infrared filter, you can capture just the near-infrared spectrum of light. In infrared, vegetation appears very bright whereas skies turn very dark.

periment. Before investing in an infrared filter, you can get a rough idea of a camera's infrared sensitivity with the help of the remote control from a TV, VCR, or stereo. Just point the remote at the camera's lens, press and hold a button on the remote, and take a picture. If the camera can see the light of the remote (Figure 9.6),

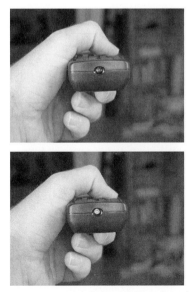

FIGURE 9.6   You can get a pretty good idea of the infrared capabilities of your camera by taking a picture of a remote control's infrared emitter. Note that, in the second image, the remote's emitter is "lit up" with infrared light.

you'll know that the sensor is picking up some IR. The brighter the light, the better your camera will be for infrared shooting.

A number of filters are available for infrared photography, but the most popular are the Kodak® Wratten™ 89b, 87, and 87C filters. Hoya® makes two filters, the R72 and RM72, which are equivalent to the Kodak 89B. B+W® also make Wratten equivalents, the 092 and 093.

The right filter is partly a matter of taste, because different filters yield different levels of contrast. Depending on your camera's infrared sensitivity, you'll need either a brighter or darker filter. Note that infrared filters are expensive, and the larger the diameter, the more you'll have to pay. Before buying a particular filter, you might want to poke around some of the more popular digital photography online forums for advice from other users who have shot infrared with your type of camera. If you can't find any usable advice, you'll simply have to experiment with different filters. Because they are so dark, you can expect infrared filters to cut 4 to 10 stops from the available light! That means you'll be using very long exposures even in bright daylight. Obviously, a tripod is essential for infrared photography. To pick up some extra stops (and reduce lengthy exposure times), you can set your camera to a higher ISO, but this will make your images noisier. Typically, Wratten 87 exposures in bright daylight at ISO 200 start at around five seconds. Because the filter can confuse your camera's light meter, you might have to do a little experimenting to find the right exposure.

When shooting film, infrared photographers often have to worry about the infrared filter causing a focus shift that can result in the camera focusing beyond its focal plane. Fortunately, the deep depths of field of a typical consumer digital camera greatly reduce the chances of focus troubles. Just to be safe, though, you might as well lock your camera on infinity when you shoot landscapes, and if you seem to be having focusing troubles, put your camera in manual mode and decrease the aperture to increase depth of field.

Also, bear in mind that because of the long exposure times, shooting moving objects or landscapes on a windy day can be problematic, as your results can be smeared or soft.

You don't have to have a black-and-white mode on your camera to shoot infrared images. When you shoot color through an infrared filter, most images will appear in brick red and cyan tones, rather like a duotone. (See Figure 9.7.) You can easily convert these to grayscale later.

Because of the bright light required, you'll typically shoot infrared only outdoors. Any incandescent objects—glowing coals, molten metal—will emit a lot of infrared radiation. The thermal radiation produced by the human body, however, is way beyond the sensitivity of the near-infrared capabilities provided by your camera.

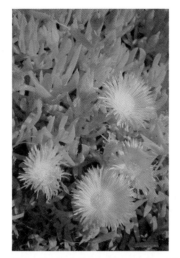

FIGURE 9.7   Even if you're shooting with an infrared filter, the image that comes out of your camera will still be in color, and will need a good amount of processing, and grayscale conversion.

EXTERNAL FLASH

While built-in flashes offer convenience, they also suffer from some significant liabilities:

Range. Built-in flashes are usually very small and so have very limited range. Once your subject goes beyond 10 feet, most built-in flashes are useless.

Propensity to red-eye. Because they're positioned so close to the lens, most built-in flashes are very prone to producing red-eye effects.

Unflattering position. Because light almost always comes from overhead, firing a flash directly into someone's face rarely looks natural. Shadows get cast in weird places, skin tones pick up unusual highlights, and dark shadows get thrown behind the person's head.

No creative control. Since built-in flashes can't be moved, you have very little control over your lighting effects.

Slow recycle times. Most built-in flashes take several seconds to recycle, which can often be long enough that you'll miss some shots.

With an external flash, you can eliminate all these concerns. Granted, you'll have to spend some money, and you'll have a little more gear to carry, but if you regularly shoot in situations that require a flash, you'll find an immediate improvement in your images if you use an external flash. To use an external flash, you must have a camera with a flash *hot shoe*.

What to Look for in an External Flash

Shopping for an external flash is pretty easy because there usually aren't too many options available for a specific camera model. While you can use almost any flash with almost any camera, you'll want to immediately refine your selection to flash units designed specifically for your camera. These models will integrate very tightly with the camera's metering system, which will make for much easier, better-quality flash exposure.

Once you've zeroed in on the models built for your camera, you'll want to consider the following:

Power. All flashes have a *guide number* that tells how much output they provide. Higher numbers will yield a longer range, but will also result in a physically larger flash unit. Think about the type of flash work you do, and decide if you really need a flash with a huge reach, or if you can get away with a smaller, less-expensive unit.

TTL metering. If you're looking at a flash designed specifically for your camera, it will most likely have *through-the-lens* metering. If it *doesn't*, you'll want to consider going with a different unit.

Zoom. If you're looking at a flash unit designed specifically for your camera, it should offer the capability to automatically zoom based on the focal length you've set your lens to. If you're shooting with an SLR, be aware that not all lenses transmit focal length information back to the camera. If some of your lenses don't, a flash zoom feature won't be of any use when you shoot with those lenses.

Tilt and swivel. You want a flash head that can at least tilt, and ideally you want one that can swivel. As you'll see in the next section, the capability to tilt and swivel to bounce the flash off walls, ceilings, and reflectors allows you a tremendous amount of creative freedom. (See Figure 9.8.)

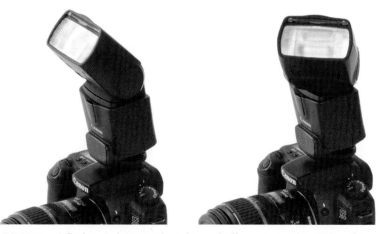

FIGURE 9.8 A flash unit that can tilt and swivel offers many more options for creating flash shots with natural-looking lighting.

Exposure compensation control. While your camera probably provides an exposure compensation control that will work with an external flash system, having such a control on-board the flash is often a great convenience. Look for a control that's easy to access and use.

Slave control. If you think you might want to eventually work into multiple-flash lighting setups, you'll want a flash system that allows one flash to trigger other, multiple slave flashes. This topic is beyond the scope of this book, but it's something to consider if your want to buy a flash that will grow with your shooting needs.

Fortunately, Canon, Nikon, Sony, Olympus, and Pentax all make very good flash systems, so you should end up with a full-featured flash unit no matter what you buy. Your main choice will simply be to decide about the level of flash power you want.

Shooting with External Flash

So, now that you've bought the thing, what can you do with it? Right off the bat, you'll probably notice that your external flash produces *much* more illumination than your camera's built-in flash. In fact, you may find that you regularly need to use flash exposure compensation to dial back the power a little bit. If your flash images look a little too "hot," you'll need to try lowering the flash exposure.

The most significant advantage of an external flash is the capability to bounce its light off other surfaces. In general, the light sources we're used to seeing the world under are very large and diffuse. Your flash, by comparison, is a small, point light source, and so creates a very harsh light. However, if you tilt the flash so its light bounces off the ceiling, *the ceiling* becomes the source of illumination for your scene. (See Figure 9.9).

On most flashes with tilt, the camera automatically adjusts its exposure to adjust for the amount of tilt you have on your flash. As long as you're using a flash with automatic TTL metering, the camera will be able to adjust flash exposure as you tilt and swivel the flash. Nevertheless, you'll want to keep an eye on your histogram, and see if your flash exposure is correct. If it's not bright enough, use a positive flash exposure compensation. If it's too bright, set your flash exposure compensation lower.

Direct flash has the advantage of "flattening" facial features. Notice in the direct flash image in Figure 9.9 that there are no shadows under his eyes or eyebrows. This can often be a good thing, as it affords you a way to, for example, reduce the apparent size of someone's nose. However, you'll run the risk of picking up dark shadows under the chin, as our model has in Figure 9.9.

If your flash can swivel, and tilt, you can bounce the flash off walls, or reflectors to create side lighting effects, which allow you more control over the shadows in your image.

Tilting and swiveling also allows you to easily reposition the direction of the flash as you change from portrait to landscape mode. (See Figure 9.10.)

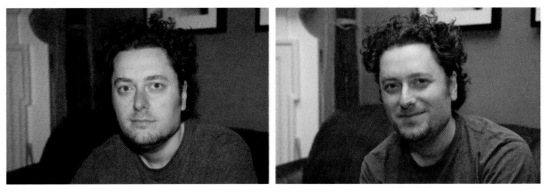

FIGURE 9.9   In the upper image, we've fired the flash directly at our subject, resulting in a harsh front-lighting. In the second image, we bounced the flash on the ceiling. In addition to being less harsh, we can see more contour on his face, and the background gets illuminated.

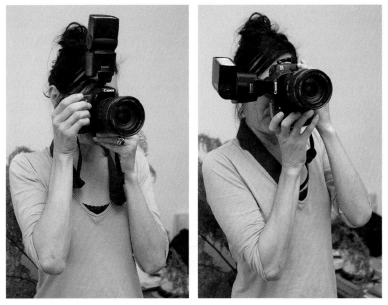

FIGURE 9.10   If your flash can tilt and swivel, it's easy to keep it pointed at the ceiling as you change from portrait to landscape orientation.

Getting Your Flash Off the Camera

Like any light source, an external flash will cast a shadow behind your subject (assuming there's something there for the shadow to be cast onto). Perhaps you've noticed this before in flash pictures—a dark shadow behind your subject. (See Figure 9.11.)

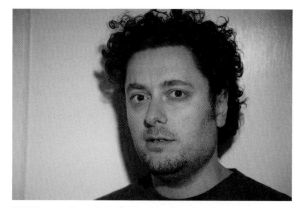

FIGURE 9.11   People in flash pictures often have annoying shadows behind them.

In the case of a picture like Figure 9.11, you can try to get the person to move away from the wall, but this isn't always possible, especially when you're shooting candid shots.

Using an *off-camera flash cable* or a *flash bracket*, you can raise the flash up higher, so the person's shadow will be cast lower. This will often result in your subject's body hiding the shadow, as in Figure 9.12.

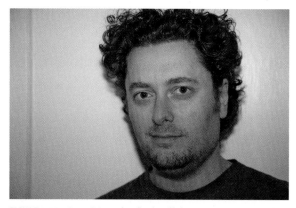

FIGURE 9.12   By raising the flash off the camera, using a bracket or off-camera cable, we can try to hide the shadow with the subject's body.

An off-camera flash cable simply provides an extension cord that allows you to hold the flash away from the camera, usually higher, although you can also position it from side to side to create different lighting effects. A flash bracket serves to raise the flash off the camera, but allows you to continue shooting with both hands for greater stability and shooting flexibility. (See Figure 9.13.)

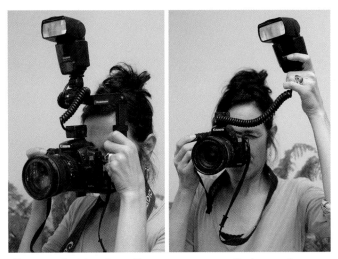

FIGURE 9.13   Off-camera flash brackets allow you to get your flash away from your camera and into a position that will allow you to reduce annoying shadows behind your subject. If you don't have a bracket, you can use an off-camera cable, and simply hold the flash in a better position. (Note that, to use a flash bracket, you must have an off-camera flash cable.)

Slow Sync Flash

In Chapter 7, we looked at special slow sync flash modes that can be used with your camera's built-in flash. On many cameras, the same slow sync shooting mode you use with the built-in flash will work with your external flash. If it doesn't, or if your camera doesn't have such a mode, you'll need to use a priority mode.

Set your camera on either aperture or shutter priority mode. The camera will meter for the ambient light in the scene, and will choose an exposure that will properly expose your scene. But, it will then fire the flash to illuminate the foreground in your scene. The result will be an image with a flash-illuminated foreground and a properly exposed background. (See Figure 7.51.)

As mentioned in Chapter 7, if the camera chooses a very slow shutter speed, your backgrounds can end up blurry.

Why Can't I Use a Fast Shutter Speed?

All cameras have a maximum shutter speed they can use with a flash. These typically vary from 1/90ᵗʰ of a second up to 1/250ᵗʰ of a second on higher-end cameras. This is sometimes referred to as flash sync or x-sync speed.

For many low-light situations, using manual exposure with your external flash is the best way to go. Put your camera in manual mode, set your shutter speed to 1/30ᵗʰ of a second, and your aperture to f/5.6. Your flash will be used to illuminate your foreground elements, and the longer shutter speed will help to better expose your backgrounds. If you're shooting scenes with a lot of motion, 1/30th of a second might result in your subjects being blurred. Consider switching to a higher ISO—say, 200—so you can change your shutter speed by one stop, to 1/60th of a second.

As you can see in Figure 7.51, the flash-illuminated foreground in a slow-sync image has a very different color temperature than the long-exposure background. If this bugs you, you can try placing a *gel,* or colored filter, over your flash to balance its output so that it's the same color temperature as the background.

Flash Diffusers

A flash diffuser can be very useful when shooting crowds of people. A diffuser such as the Gary Fong LightSphere creates a very even, diffuse fill light that does a very good job of illuminating crowds of people. Priced around $50, these small, easily packed accessories are a great add-on for any flash user. Check out *www.garyfong.com* for details and sample pictures.

Because of the instant feedback provided by your digital camera, learning to shoot with an external flash is much easier than it is with a film camera. Find yourself a subject—still life or portrait—and spend some time practicing. As with any situation, don't forget to "work" your subject. Try different flash positions, tilts, swivels, and exposure compensations.

CONTROLLING AVAILABLE LIGHT

While electronic flashes are easy to use and provide you with a tremendous amount of creative control, you can often achieve all the lighting control you need by simply working with available light and simple reflectors and diffusers.

It's hard to beat the sun as a light source. It's bright, it's there for up to half the day, it produces a strong even light, and it's a great color that both your eyes and camera are well adapted to. The problem with sunlight is that there are times when there's too much of it. When shooting in bright sunlight, one of your biggest problems will be to *reduce* the amount of light hitting your subject, so you can lessen the amount of contrast in the scene.

For portraits, this will result in a reduction of dark shadows under eyes, a lessening of lines and wrinkles, and a smoothing of skin texture. For other subjects, it means more even color and contrast and a generally more even exposure.

Figure 9.14 shows a portrait that was shot in direct sunlight. While the scene is nicely lit, the shadows in the image are very strong, and overall the image is *too* contrasty.

What we really needed was for a cloud to pass over the sun to cut the intensity of the light. While this is not an unreasonable thing to expect in San Francisco, on this afternoon it didn't happen, so we had to employ the use of a portable cloud, in the form of a large diffuser.

Diffusers are simply large pieces of white cloth that serve to diffuse light, casting a very soft shadow. Diffusers come in many varieties. The best are round diffusers

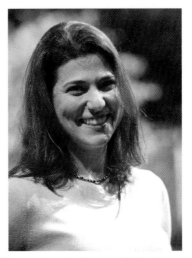

FIGURE 9.14   This image, shot in direct sunlight, is too contrasty. The dark shadows created by the intense light are unflattering and distracting.

that easily collapse to become very portable. Photoflex (*www.photoflex.com*) makes diffusers in many different sizes and colors, but you can find similar reflectors from a number of other vendors.

To use a diffuser to attack our high contrast problem, we simply mounted the diffuser on a pole (also available from Photoflex) and held it above our subject to cast a shadow onto her face. (See Figure 9.15.)

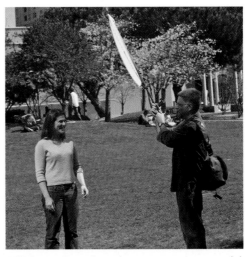

FIGURE 9.15   To reduce the contrast on our model, we held a diffuser above her to cast a soft shadow onto her face.

With our "cloud" in place, the harsh shadows on our model's face were greatly reduced, making for a more flattering light. (See Figure 9.16.)

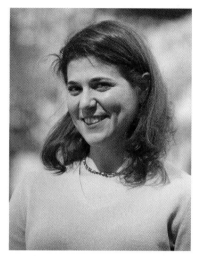

FIGURE 9.16   With the diffuser in place, the shadows on our model's face are now far less harsh.

Our work is not finished, though. While the shadows are softer, there's still a pronounced shadow under her chin, and in her eyes. We can eliminate these by using a reflector to bounce some light up into her face. (See Figure 9.17.)

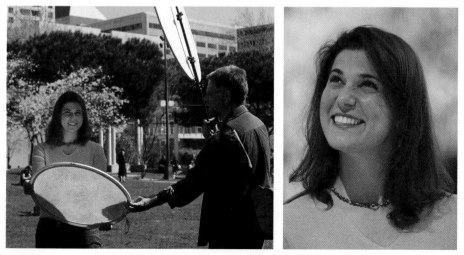

FIGURE 9.17   Here, we're using a diffuser to soften the light striking the model, and a reflector to bounce some light back into her face, from below. By controlling and redirecting the light, we can eliminate shadows to produce the portrait shown on the right.

Collapsible reflectors are easy to carry, and come in a variety of colors including white, silver, and gold. White reflectors create a very natural-looking even fill, while silver and gold reflectors move more light, with gold warming the light along the way. The Photoflex 5-in-1 includes zip-over covers that allow you to easily change the color of the reflector.

Although not as easy to carry, big pieces of white cardboard, paper, or foamcore will work just as well for creating a white fill.

Another way to handle harsh, contrasty lighting is to shoot *into* the sun. Position your subject with her back to the sun, and you will be shooting from within her shadow. This will serve to cut a lot of the harshness *and* you'll get a nice rim light, or halo. If you add a reflector in front, you can have a rim light and even lighting on her face. (See Figure 9.18.)

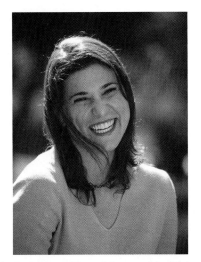

FIGURE 9.18   For this shot, we positioned the model with her back to the sun, to create a halo around her head, and then used a reflector to illuminate her face.

You can use these same techniques for shooting flowers and other still lifes, provided they're small enough to cover with a diffuser.

MACRO PHOTOGRAPHY

Although the term *macro photography* would seem to describe a process of photographing very large objects, it's actually the opposite. With your digital camera's macro feature, you can take high-quality images of extremely small things.

Digital point-and-shoot cameras are particularly well suited to macro photography. They generally have excellent optics, which make for sharp, clear images, and their low light sensitivity means you can get them into small spaces to capture images up close. The macro features of some cameras allow for amazingly close shots—as close as one inch in some cases! (See Figure 9.19.)

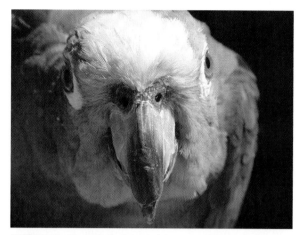

FIGURE 9.19 Your digital camera's macro feature lets you take close-up photos that would require a very expensive lens if you were shooting with a film camera.

If you're shooting with a digital SLR, you'll need to buy a special macro lens. You'll want to consider all the same lens factors that were discussed in Chapter 5.

No matter what type of camera or macro lens you're using, you'll face the same issues when taking your macro shots.

Finding the Optimal Macro Focal Length

Most point-and-shoot macro features are optimized for a particular range of focal lengths. Although most cameras will let you shoot macro pictures with your lens zoomed to any point, you'll get much better results if you put your camera in the macro "sweet spot." For some cameras, this is full wide, while for others it's somewhere else in the zoom range. Some cameras won't focus at all in macro mode unless they are set within a particular focal range. Cameras that usually require you to be in a specific zoom range will usually have some kind of indicator in the viewfinder that will show when you're in the optimal macro focus range.

Macro Focusing

Your camera's autofocus mechanism should work normally when you shoot in macro mode. However, be aware that at very close distances, even slight, subtle changes in camera position can ruin your focus.

When shooting macro photographs, your camera must be extremely close to your subject, which means that you and your camera will be blocking out much of the light in your scene. Because of the low light levels, you'll have to use a slower shutter speed. Therefore, to get the best results when you focus at macro distances, use a tripod. Doing so will ensure that the camera remains steady in the event of a slow shutter speed, and will prevent you from accidentally making slight movements after the camera has already focused. (A tabletop tripod like the one shown in Figure 5.41 can be ideal for macro shooting.) You can also increase the camera's ISO to give it some latitude to select a faster shutter speed.

If you don't have a tripod, consider activating your camera's continuous autofocus feature, if it has one. This will help keep the image in focus even if you accidentally jiggle the camera.

It's usually easier to hold the camera steady if you *don't* try to press the camera's zoom buttons. Instead of using the camera's zoom controls to frame your shot, simply move the camera in and out. At macro distances, you won't have to move it very far to get a reframing.

The best rule of thumb is simply to work quickly. Get the image framed, prefocus, and then shoot right away. Finally, just to be safe, shoot a few frames. If your first is out of focus, perhaps the second or third will be okay. If your camera has a drive mode (also known as *burst mode* or *continuous mode*) that is capable of shooting at the resolution you want, consider turning it on. If you're facing a difficult macro shot, shooting a burst of images will improve your chances of getting a good image.

Some Nikon cameras include a unique "Best Shot Selection" feature that is ideal for macro photography. This feature shoots a burst of images and tries to identify the one that is in sharpest focus. The others are automatically discarded.

Poor Depth of Field

Be warned that when you are in macro mode, your camera will have a *very* shallow depth of field. Although this can create very nice effects and excellent isolation of your subject, if your subject is large enough, you might have trouble keeping all of it in focus.

Consider the image in Figure 9.20.

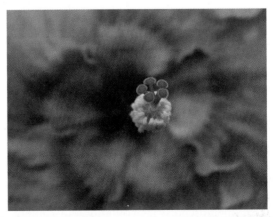

FIGURE 9.20   This flower was shot with the camera's macro mode. Although it's not a particularly large flower, it is deep enough that, at macro photography distances, the image has a depth of field problem. The flower's stamen is in focus, but the petals are blurry.

The depth of field in this image is so shallow that the flower's petals are out of focus. In fact, the depth of field is short enough that this image might have been better served by switching out of macro mode, pulling the camera back, zooming in, and shooting the image normally. Another option would have been to autofocus on the petals and reframe the shot. However, the stamen in the center of the flower would then be out of focus.

If you're shooting a flat subject, depth of field won't be a problem, of course. If you're shooting something that's even a few inches deep, though, you need to think about which parts will be in focus. Judging depth of field on your camera's LCD can be very difficult, because the screen is simply too small to reveal which parts of your subject are in focus. Sometimes, you can use your camera's playback zoom feature to examine different parts of your image up close. Even with a 4x magnification, however, you still probably won't be able to see subtle changes in focus. If you're concerned about depth of field, your best option is to protect yourself by shooting multiple shots with a number of different focal lengths—including some nonmacro shots. You should also take some shots with your autofocus locked onto different parts of the subject.

If you're shooting a flat subject, try to keep the camera parallel to the plane of your subject. Any tilt will introduce extra depth into your image. Those areas of depth might be rendered blurry by your camera's shallow depth of field.

Improved Macro Depth of Field

You can get improved depth of field in your macro shots by post-processing using special software. See "Deep Focus Software" in the next section, or if you have an SLR, you can consider using a tilt and shift lens, also covered in the next section.

LANDSCAPE PHOTOGRAPHY

While landscape photography is not significantly different from any other type of shooting—you still have to find your subject, calculate an exposure, and work the scene to find the shot that's right—there are a few things to keep in mind when shooting landscapes.

While it might be tempting to just use the widest angle you can, to capture as broad a vista as possible, bear in mind that as you go wider, the objects in your scene will become smaller and less distinct. You're not going to be able to take a single image that encompasses your entire field of view, so try to find a slice of that vista that is compelling. You'll need to employ all the same compositional ideas we discussed in Chapter 7 as you strive to create an image that is balanced.

While you might find occasions to shoot with shallow depth of field, in most landscape shots you'll want to ensure that everything in the shot is in focus. The great landscape works of Ansel Adams and others are notable partly because of the photographers' attention to focus. With great detail throughout the image, you really feel like you can walk right into the picture.

Exposing for Extreme Depth of Field

Obviously, to get deep depth of field you'll want to use a smaller aperture (high f-stop number). This will require a longer shutter speed, so you might need to use a tripod, depending on the circumstances.

However, even with the deep depth of field provided by a small aperture, it's still possible for your image to have focus problems. Remember, your depth of field is centered on the point you focus on, and there's less depth of field in *front* of that point, and much more behind. This difference increases as you focus farther away. So, when you shoot a landscape and focus on distant mountains (which usually means that you're focusing on infinity), there's a chance that your foreground will be out of focus because there's not enough depth of field in front of your focus point to render near details in sharp focus.

Every lens has a *hyperfocal distance*. When you focus your lens on infinity, the nearest point that is also "acceptably sharp" is the hyperfocal distance, and this distance changes with your aperture setting. (See Figure 9.21.)

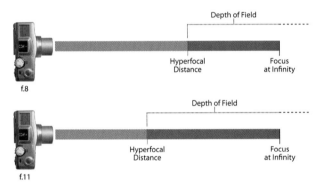

FIGURE 9.21 When focused on infinity, at a given aperture, the hyperfocal distance is the nearest point that is acceptably sharp.

When focused on infinity, your depth of field extends from the hyperfocal distance to infinity and, possibly, beyond. This "beyond" distance can be considered wasted depth of field because, obviously, there's nothing beyond infinity, and there might be a considerable amount of foreground that's not within your depth of field.

If you set the camera's focus to the hyperfocal distance, your depth of field will extend from half of the hyperfocal distance to infinity—a much deeper depth of field. (See Figure 9.22.)

In the old days, lenses included markings that let you identify the depth of field range for any aperture/focus combination. Today, zoom lenses and point-and-shoot cameras lack these markings, as do many prime lenses, meaning it's much more difficult to make these kinds of depth of field calculations. However, making these calculations well was always somewhat difficult, as they required a good ability for estimating distance.

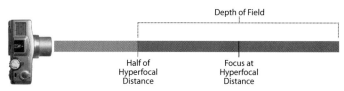

FIGURE 9.22   You'll get deeper depth of field by focusing on a point that's half of the hyperfocal distance from the camera. This will keep you from "wasting" depth of field behind infinity.

However, whether you have lens markings or not (or understand any of the theory), there are some simple rules you can follow to ensure deep depth of field in your landscape images.

Think about where you're focusing. When you focus on the horizon, or another point in the very far distance, there's a good chance that you'll lose depth of field in the near foreground. If you are unable to calculate the exact hyperfocal distance for your lens, focus on a point halfway to two thirds of the distance to the farthest point in the scene. You can do this by selecting a different focus point, or by using the focus and reframe technique we discussed in Chapter 7.

Remember the 1/3rd 2/3rds rule. In typical landscape situations, one-third of your range of depth of field falls in front of your point of focus, and two-thirds behind.

Bracket your apertures. As you already know, smaller apertures yield deeper depth of field. However, if you simply set your camera on the smallest aperture, you'll run the risk of incurring *diffraction artifacts*, which can result in a softening of your image. You may find that you lose as much sharpness in diffraction as you were hoping to gain from depth of field control. To be safe, take several shots varying with different-sized apertures.

Bracket your focus. As you can see, your choice of focus point is critical to getting the deepest possible depth of field. To be safe, take a few shots with the same aperture at varying focal distances. This will improve your chances that one of them will have very deep focus.

As discussed earlier, if you're shooting with a point-and-shoot camera, you will inherently have deeper depth of field than you will on a camera that uses a bigger sensor. Consequently, these issues might not be as critical.

Portable Depth of Field Calculators

If you have a Palm or Windows Mobile device, you can get small apps that will perform depth of field calculations for you. With both Focus+ for the Palm and DOF 1.0 for Pocket PC, you enter your current focus distance and aperture, and the software yields depth of field and hyperfocal distance. Both apps are easily found with a Google search.

If you're shooting in low light, shooting with deep depth of field becomes more complicated. The small apertures you need will require longer shutter speeds and higher ISO settings, both of which will lead to increased noise. For these situations, you might want to consider one of the following two options.

USING A-DEP ON CANON SLRs

Some Canon digital SLRs include a special shooting mode called A-DEP, which can automatically calculate an exposure that will yield the deepest depth of field. You'll find A-DEP alongside the camera's other shooting modes. Frame and focus just as you normally would. The camera will automatically measure the distance to the nearest and farthest points, and select a focus distance and aperture that will yield the deepest depth of field. After prefocusing, you can use the Depth of Field Preview button to see how much depth of field you have.

A-DEP can work well, but you might want to experiment with it to get an idea of its effectiveness.

Tilt and Shift Lenses

If you're using an SLR, you have another option for capturing deep focus, which is to use a tilt and shift lens. These lenses allow you to shift the front and back planes of the lens in different ways to correct for perspective distortion and to ensure that things near the lens and far away are in focus. Shooting with tilt and shift lenses takes more time, as you can't autofocus, and metering can sometimes be a little more complicated. In addition, these types of lenses are usually pretty pricey.

Tilt and shift lenses are also commonly used in architecture and product photography, because they allow you to reduce or eliminate perspective distortion. (See Figure 9.23.)

Deep-Focus Software

Finally, you have one more option for shooting images with deep focus. Software programs such as Helicon Focus allow you to achieve deep focus by combining multiple images shot with different focal points. You set your aperture to one setting, and then shoot multiple frames, each focused to a different distance. Helicon Focus can then combine them into one completely focused image. Obviously, this software is not usable for moving subject matter.

This type of software is also ideal for macro photos, and you can learn more about Helicon Focus at *www.heliconfilter.com*.

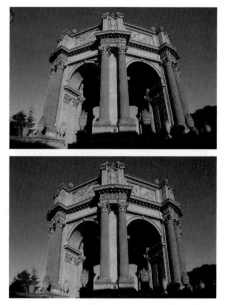

FIGURE 9.23   In addition to controlling depth of field, you can use a tilt and shift lens to adjust perspective, allowing you to straighten horizontal or vertical lines.

SHOOTING PANORAMAS

No matter how wide your lens, there will be times when you want to shoot a vista that simply can't be captured with a single image. However, by shooting a series of images that overlap, and then using special panoramic stitching software, you can create panoramic images that encompass a much wider field of view than you can capture within a single shot. (See Figure 9.24.)

Panoramic software can take a series of overlapping images and stitch them together to create a single image. (See Figure 9.25.)

Besides hiding the seams of an image, panoramic software corrects the perspective of each image by essentially mapping the images onto the inside of a giant virtual cylinder. The curvature of the imaginary cylinder corrects the perspective troubles in your image.

In addition to printing wide panoramic prints of your images, you can deliver your panoramas as *virtual reality (VR)* movies that present a window onto your panoramic scene and allow users to "navigate" the scene by pivoting and tilting their view. (See Figure 9.26.)

You'll learn all about stitching in Chapter 15, "Special Effects," but getting a good-looking panorama begins with your shoot.

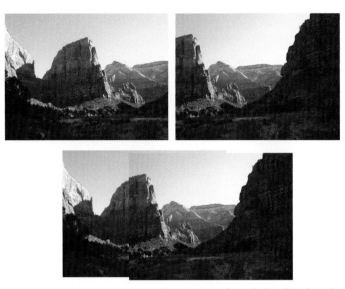

FIGURE 9.24   These two images were shot separately with the idea that they would be stitched into a panorama. Panoramic images can be stitched together from any number of overlapping images.

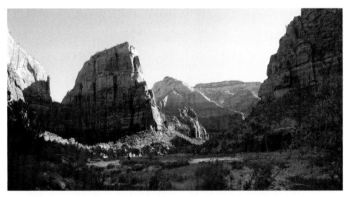

FIGURE 9.25   Here, the two images in Figure 9.24 have been stitched together to create a single, seamless image.

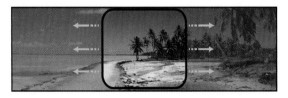

FIGURE 9.26   If you store your images as VR movies, users can use special viewing software to pan and tilt around your scene. With more advanced authoring tools, you can build fully navigable VR environments.

Preparing Your Camera

You can use any focal length to shoot a panorama; however, your focal length choice *will* affect your final image, just as you learned in Chapter 7. With a longer focal length, objects that are more distant will appear larger in your final image; however, you'll see less foreground. With a shorter focal length, you'll see more foreground, but distant objects might be very tiny. (See Figure 9.27.) However, as your focal length increases, the number of shots required to shoot your panorama will increase. If you need to work in a hurry because of changing weather, or moving subject matter, you may be better off with a wider angle that will allow you to shoot fewer frames.

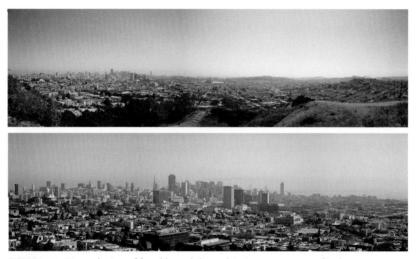

FIGURE 9.27   Your choice of focal length has a big impact on your final panorama. In the upper image, we used a shorter focal length, which allowed us to shoot a wider panorama with fewer shots, but left the buildings in the shot very small. In the lower image, we used a longer focal length, which obscured much of the foreground, but rendered the distant objects larger.

Note that shorter focal lengths are more prone to vignetting, which can lead to visible seams in the final panorama. Also, wider angles are more prone to flares, which can be difficult to manage when panning across a wide range of brightness values.

Panoramas can be shot in either portrait or landscape mode. Portrait mode will allow you to capture more vertical details (such as sky or foreground) but will also require more shots, because a portrait image is not as wide as a landscape image.

One disadvantage of having to shoot *more* frames is that more frames mean more opportunity for mistakes in your final image. Each time you shoot an additional frame, you create at least one additional seam, and seams are where artifacts and troubles can develop.

There are two ways to shoot panoramas: the correct way, which involves a lot of special equipment but produces very precise, accurate images for stitching; and the sloppy way, which can be more prone to error, but can still produce fine results.

Proper Panoramic Panning

The most critical part of shooting a panorama is properly panning the camera and overlapping your separate frames.

For best results, mount your camera on a tripod and set the tripod to be level. Note that if your camera's tripod mount is positioned off-axis (Figure 9.28) from your lens, you're not going to be able to use your tripod for shooting full 360° panoramas. Because of the off-axis rotation, the ends of your panoramas won't necessarily fit together. For smaller panoramas, though, you should be fine no matter how your tripod mount is positioned.

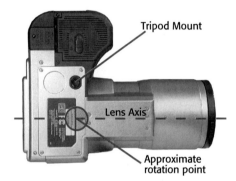

Tripod Mount

Lens Axis

Approximate rotation point

FIGURE 9.28   If your camera's tripod mount is off-axis from the rotational center of the lens, you'll have a hard time shooting full 360° panoramas from a tripod.

When you shoot with the camera handheld, remember to pivot the *camera*, not your head or body. Your eyes are a few inches in front of the center of rotation of your neck, and your camera's image sensor will be even further removed from your neck or body's rotation, meaning that if you simply turn your head or body, you'll actually be rotating around a point several inches *behind* the camera. Therefore, between shots, rotate the *camera* properly and then—if necessary—reposition your body behind the camera's new position. Your main concern when you rotate the camera is to keep its bottom parallel to the ground. If you tilt the camera in addition to rotating it, you'll run into some problems when you are stitching. (See Figure 9.29.)

When you pivot the camera, remember that your images must *overlap,* not sit adjacent to each other. Most stitching software recommends a 15 to 30 percent overlap between images, and some vendors recommend a 50 percent overlap. Many cameras feature panoramic assist modes that offer on-screen cues as to how much you need to overlap. If your camera has such a feature, it's definitely worth using. A little experience with your stitching program will give you a better idea of how images need to overlap.

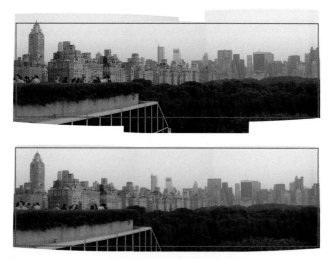

FIGURE 9.29 If you don't keep the bottom of the camera level as you rotate it, you'll end up with lots of unusable, wasted content in your final panorama that will have to be cropped. When your camera is level, you end up with more usable image for your final crop.

If you're a stickler for extreme precision, or if you're shooting full 360° panoramas for use as VR movies, you're going to have to do a little more work when you shoot to ensure your source images are accurate enough to yield the results you want. You will absolutely need a tripod (preferably one with a built-in level), and you'll probably want to invest in a panoramic tripod head. A panoramic head is a special mount that attaches to your tripod and includes preset rotation controls that allow you to quickly rotate your camera by a specified amount. Such heads typically sell for $100 to $300 (depending on the size of the camera they must support), and are worth the money if you do a lot of panoramas. (See Figure 9.30.) (See *www.completedigitalphotography.com/tripodmounts* for more info.)

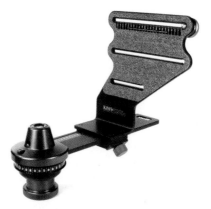

FIGURE 9.30 This panoramic tripod head properly positions your camera for extremely accurate panorama shooting.

To ensure you're rotating your camera precisely around its focal plane, you'll want to identify the camera's *nodal point*, the optical center of the camera's lens. (See Figure 9.31.) Most panoramic mounts include special adjustments for ensuring that the camera's nodal point is positioned directly above the tripod's axis of rotation, even if the camera's tripod mount is off-center. If your camera's nodal point is not marked, you might have to do a little experimentation to determine the best axis around which to rotate the camera.

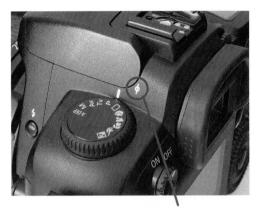

Nodal Point Marker

FIGURE 9.31   Most SLRs (and some higher-end point-and-shoots) will indicate their nodal point with this marking.

Panoramic Exposure

Because you will be pointing your camera in many different directions as you shoot a panorama, it's important to plan your exposure ahead of time. Your goal is to have an even exposure across all the images in your panorama so seams are not visible.

In general, if you have more than a one- or two-stop difference in exposure between two adjacent images, you're going to see a band along the seam when the panorama is stitched.

In an evenly lit scene, such as the one in Figure 9.24, maintaining exposure is fairly simple, because there are no dramatic changes in lighting between one frame and the next. However, you still need to keep an eye on your exposure, especially if you're using your camera's automatic exposure mechanism. For example, because the first frame contains more sky, your camera might choose an exposure that's a little different from what it selects in the second frame. If the exposures are too far apart, a seam will be visible in the final panorama.

If your camera provides an exposure lock feature, you can lock your exposure after the first frame, to ensure the second frame is exposed with the same values. Or, you can meter off a more intermediate part of the image, lock that exposure, and then shoot each individual frame with that metering. If your camera includes a panoramic assist mode of some kind, it will automatically lock the exposure after each frame.

If you're shooting a scene that encompasses a bright light on one end (say, the sun, or the lamp in a room) and ambient light or dark shadow on the other end (Figure 9.32), things are going to be a bit more complicated. The simplest way to handle this situation is to shoot the same way you would an evenly lit scene: choose an intermediate exposure, lock your camera's exposure settings, and then shoot your panorama. Your bright light source will be overexposed, but your midtones and shadows will probably be okay (unless you have some exceptionally dark areas). However, despite these potential issues, your finished panorama will be evenly exposed and free of banding.

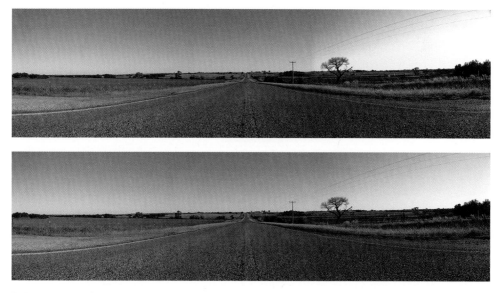

FIGURE 9.32 Landscape panoramas often present a difficult exposure problem because, invariably, the sun is sitting at one end or the other of your scene. In the top image, we let the camera meter for each of the four frames we shot. Unfortunately, when we stitched, the rightmost end (the side the sun was on) ended up heavily overexposed, thus spoiling our stitch. For the lower image, we pointed straight ahead—to what would be our middle frame—metered, and then locked the exposure using our camera's exposure lock. We then reframed for our leftmost image, focused, shot, and then rotated to shoot each of our three other frames. The uniform exposure made for a more successful stitching operation.

If you're willing to do a little more work, take an initial, intermediate exposure reading and lock it into your camera. Then, for frames that are significantly brighter or darker, use your camera's exposure compensation control to over- or underexpose on particularly bright or dark frames. To prevent banding, keep your compensations to within 1/2 to 1 1/2 stops.

Shoot with Care

When you shoot around people, animals, or other moving objects, pay attention to where you position the seams of your image. A person who is present in one image and gone in the next might turn partially transparent if he or she falls on a seam in the final panorama. (See Figure 9.33.)

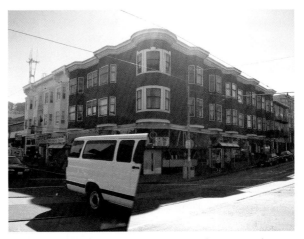

FIGURE 9.33   When shooting a panorama, be certain that moving images do not fall on a seam, or you'll end up with weird, split objects in your final panorama.

If the objects in your panorama are moving in a particular direction, shoot in the opposite direction. That is, if a person is walking across your scene from right to left, shoot your images from left to right. This is assuming that you don't *want* to see multiple copies of the person across your panoramic field of view. If you *do*, then by all means, shoot from right to left and ensure that the person is in the middle of each shot when you shoot. (See Figure 9.34.)

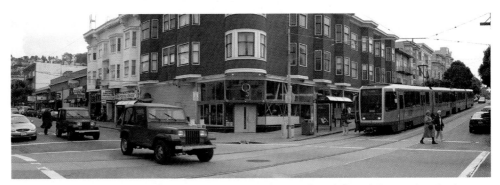

FIGURE 9.34   Because we were shooting our panorama images from left to right, we shot the Jeep twice. Consequently, when stitched, there are two identical Jeeps in the shot.

Finally, learn to think of the panoramic process as a complex—but free—super-wide-angle lens. Don't just use panoramas for capturing wide vistas; use them for any occasion when you'd like to have a wide-angle or fisheye lens. (See Figure 9.35.)

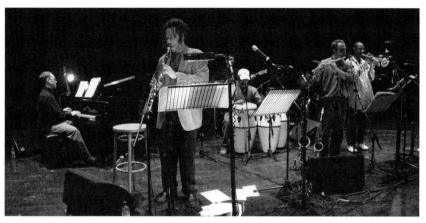

FIGURE 9.35 Panoramas aren't just for landscapes. Think about shooting them any time you would normally opt for a wide-angle—or even fisheye—lens.

Also, remember that you *can* shoot panoramas vertically. Just as with a horizontal panorama, shoot a frame, then rotate the camera upward (or downward if you started at the top of the scene), and shoot additional frames. (See Figure 9.36.) You'll need to consider the same exposure issues you face with a horizontal panorama. We'll discuss vertical stitching in Chapter 15.

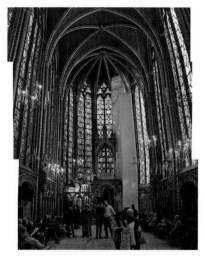

FIGURE 9.36 Panoramas can also be shot vertically. This three-shot panorama was shot from bottom to top, and then stitched using normal panoramic stitching software.

SPECIAL PANORAMA ATTACHMENTS

If you regularly need to shoot panoramic images, you might want to invest in a special, single-shot panoramic attachment. Products such as the Kaidan® 360 One VR adapter allow you to shoot full 360° panoramic images with a single shot from your digital camera.

These contraptions work by positioning a parabolic mirror in front of the lens. When the camera—with the device—is pointed straight up, the mirror reflects a full 360° down into your camera lens. The resulting image requires special "dewarping" software (included with the device) to dewarp the image into a normal panoramic picture. As with any other 360° panorama, these files can be used to create a QuickTime VR movie in addition to simple panoramic images.

For more information, check out *www.completedigitalphotography.com/360One*.

Collaging

While panoramic stitching software is a great way to shoot wide panoramic vistas, that doesn't mean you shouldn't forget about the old techniques people used to use to create panoramas, and collages. Layering overlapping images on top of one another *without* stitching allows you to create stylized representations of a scene without the seamless perfection of a computer-stitched panorama.

Figure 9.37 shows a collage of a Roman amphitheater created by graphic designer Kalonica McQuesten.

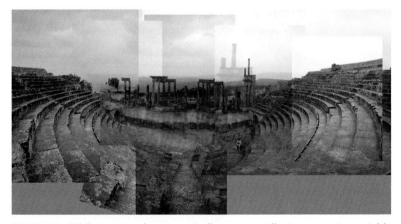

FIGURE 9.37   While not seamless or optically correct, collaging sometimes yields more evocative effects than does panoramic stitching.

She shot "coverage" of the scene by shooting many overlapping images of the entire scene, not just of a single panoramic swath. These were layered on top of each other in Photoshop, and special selection masks were used to alter the transparency in different places within the image. You'll learn about this type of masking in Chapter 14.

Collaging is also a great way to salvage panoramas that don't stitch properly.

High-Dynamic Range (HDR) Imaging

As already discussed, your eye can perceive a much greater dynamic range than your camera can. In other words, your eye can register far more tones from dark to light. If you find yourself in a scene with a very extreme dynamic range, like the one shown in Figure 8.4, you have a few options. First, you can elect to capture just one part of the scene—either light or dark—and let the other part of the scene plunge into shadow, or blow out to complete white. Depending on the nature of the shot, and your composition, this can end up looking like a very stylized abstraction.

If you're going for more realism, you can shoot two images—one exposed to capture the lighter parts of the image, and the other exposed to capture the darker parts. You can then composite these two images using compositing software. In Chapter 14, we'll explore how to composite the two images shown in Figure 8.4.

This type of compositing can vary in difficulty depending on the content of your scene. Fine details such as leaves, or complex transparent textures, can be extremely difficult and time-consuming to composite. In some cases, getting a good composite might be impossible.

Over the last few years, a new post-processing technology has developed that allows you to capture the full dynamic range of a scene by shooting multiple images, which are then combined using special software to create a high-dynamic range image. (See Figure 9.38.)

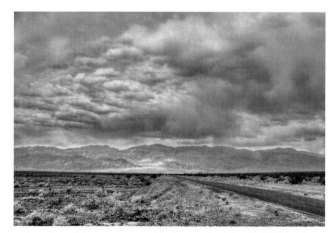

FIGURE 9.38   This high-dynamic range image has extreme detail throughout its tonal range. Foreground, sky, and shadows are all well-exposed, yielding an image that includes far more than the normal 8 to 10 stops' worth of range.

In an HDR image, different tones are automatically selected from each of your source images to produce a final image with a full range of tones. HDR images can have dark shadows *and* bright highlights, each culled from a different source image.

Shooting and processing HDR images is not difficult, but there are a few caveats to accept before you begin:

- Because HDR images require multiple source images, each shot with a different exposure, shooting HDR imagery of moving subjects is not possible.
- A little bit of HDR goes a long way. Sometimes, HDR images end up looking "too" real, and many people do not like the hyper-reality of HDR. We'll discuss HDR processing in detail in Chapter 15.
- HDR requires a camera with raw capability, and an aperture priority mode.
- Because you must shoot multiple images with identical framing, HDR requires a tripod.

Shooting HDR

Your goal when shooting HDR is to shoot a series of identically framed images, each exposed 1 stop apart. Because you don't want any change in depth of field between the images, you'll want to shoot in aperture priority mode, to ensure your aperture doesn't change from one shot to the next, as a change in aperture could result in a variation in depth of field.

To shoot an HDR image:

1. Mount your camera on your tripod and frame your shot.
2. Set your camera to shoot in raw mode.
3. Set your camera to aperture priority, and dial in an exposure compensation of –2.
4. Shoot the first image, and then change exposure compensation to –1. Shoot the next image and continue shooting until you've shot frames at 0 exposure compensation, +1 stop, and +2 stops. (See Figure 9.39.)

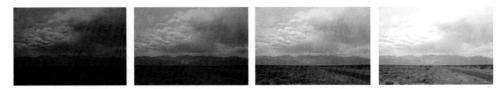

FIGURE 9.39   These source images were used to create the HDR image in Figure 9.38.

That's all you need to do. You'll need to employ all the camera stabilization techniques discussed in this chapter to achieve maximum stability.

If you're shooting a scene with clouds, bear in mind that if it's windy, the clouds might move between shots, resulting in blurry skies. So, you'll want to work as quickly as possible. To speed things up, you can consider using your camera's autobracketing features with drive mode. However, if your camera only allows a 3-stop bracket, you'll need to do two different bursts, one at –2, –1, and 0, and another at 0, +1, and +2. Obviously, you'll discard one of the images shot with 0 exposure compensation.

One caveat to be aware of when using drive mode: it can often cause your camera to shake enough that your images will be slightly out of registration. So, you might want to try both an autobracket/drive mode series of shots, and a manually adjusted series of shots.

Finally, as we'll see in Chapter 15, some HDR processing applications can automatically align images to compensate for registration troubles. However, although these mechanisms can work very well, they can also fail, so it's better to shoot the most stable source imagery you can manage.

With your images shot, you'll need to transfer them to your computer and process them with HDR software. See Chapter 15 for more details.

UNDERWATER PHOTOGRAPHY

Thanks to their small size and excellent low-light capabilities, digital cameras make for excellent underwater photography. To shoot underwater, you'll first need an enclosure for your camera. Some camera vendors make their own underwater housing, but if yours doesn't, you can probably find a third-party housing. You want to be sure to get a housing designed for your specific model of camera. An ill-fitting housing might leak, which would, obviously, be very bad. A good housing will provide access to all the camera's menus and controls, and if you plan to do a lot of underwater photography, you should consider the availability of underwater housings when you're shopping for a camera.

Once you have a housing, your next step will be to get underwater. Each type of housing will be rated to be safe to a specific depth, so make sure you don't exceed the capabilities of your housing.

Today, many point-and-shoot cameras have special white balance settings for shooting underwater. If yours has one, give it a try. It can be dim and murky underwater, so you may need to switch to a higher ISO. In many cases, you'll be using the camera's flash, which means you can stick to a lower ISO setting. Depending on your subject matter, you might need to use your macro setting. (See Figure 9.40.)

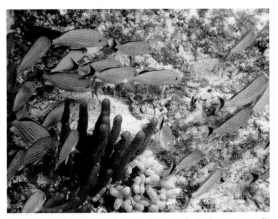

FIGURE 9.40   Thanks to their low-light sensitivity, digital cameras allow for excellent underwater photography. You'll need a special housing designed for your specific camera. Image Copyright © 2007 by Derrick Story.

TETHERED SHOOTING

Your in-camera histogram provides an excellent way to judge your exposure, while your camera's LCD screen lets you see your exact composition. Your computer, though, provides a much better view of your images, and far more powerful analysis tools. Tethered shooting is the process of connecting your camera to your computer *while* shooting. As you shoot, the images are automatically moved to the computer and displayed so you can see them on your computer screen right away. This allows you to more easily assess focus, color, and tone, and adjust your shot and reshoot.

Tethered shooting is ideal for studio work, but you can also use it in the field as long as you're willing to lug along the extra gear. Most cameras capable of tethered shooting ship with software that handles the real-time transfer to the computer. For more details, consult the software manual that came with your camera.

Tethered Shooting with Aperture

If you're an Aperture user who shoots with a Canon SLR, you can download the Aperture Hot Folder Automator workflow from http://automator.us/aperture/example-04.html. This simple package lets you shoot tethered, directly into Aperture.

USING FILTERS

Lens filters can be used for everything from creating special effects to correcting image problems, but before you can start using a filter, you have to figure out how to get it onto your camera.

First, check the lens on your camera for lens threads; if it isn't threaded, you won't be able to attach any filters, unless the camera provides some kind of filter adapter that attaches using some other kind of mount. The filter size for your lens is probably written on the end of the lens. (See Figure 9.41.) If not, check your manual.

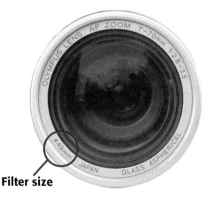

Filter size

FIGURE 9.41   If your lens has threads, you can find out what size filters you need by looking for a thread-size marking on the end of your lens. The lens shown here needs 49 mm filters.

When you buy filters, be sure to get filters that have the same thread size as your lens. Most filters will have threads of their own, which will allow you to stack filters.

Other filters might not be available in the right size for your lens, and so might require the use of a *step-up ring,* a simple adapter that screws onto the front of your lens and provides a bigger (or sometimes smaller) set of threads for accepting filters with different thread sizes. Be careful with step-up rings, though—if they're too big, they might block your camera's metering sensors, flash, or optical viewfinder.

Lens filters are completely flat, meaning they don't add any magnification power to your lens. Although optically they are simpler than a lens, you still want to be careful about your choice of filter. There *is* a difference between a $100 ultraviolet filter and a $35 ultraviolet filter. Just as an element in your lens can introduce aberrations, a poorly made filter can introduce flares and color shifts. Although it can be tempting to go for the less-expensive filter, spend a little time researching the more costly competition. You might find there is a big difference in image quality.

Types of Filters

In Chapter 8, "Metering and Exposure," you read about neutral density filters, non-colored filters that you can use to cut out a few stops' worth of light to increase your exposure options. In addition, earlier in this chapter you read about infrared filters that can be used to photograph objects in infrared light. There are many other types of filters—too many to cover here. However, if there were a group of "essential" filters, it would probably include the following:

Polarizers: *Polarizers* allow light that is polarized only in a particular direction to pass through your lens. The practical upshot is that polarizers can completely remove distracting reflections from water, glass, or other shiny surfaces. To use a polarizer, you simply attach it to the end of your lens and rotate it until the reflections are gone. Polarizers can also be used to increase the contrast in skies and clouds. (See Figure 9.42.)

Ultraviolet filters: Ultraviolet filters are used to cut down on haze and other atmospheric conditions that can sometimes result in color shifts in your image.

Contrast filters: You can increase contrast and saturation in your images by using simple colored *contrast filters.* Yellow filters will typically darken skies and shadows, and yellow-green and red filters will increase such contrast even further. Conversely, blue filters will lighten skies and darken green foliage and trees.

Graduated neutral density filters: These filters cut the light from one half of the lens while leaving the other half untouched. A graduated filter provides another way to shoot high dynamic range landscape scenes. With the graduated filter, you can reduce the exposure of the sky, allowing you to get a more even exposure in the sky and foreground.

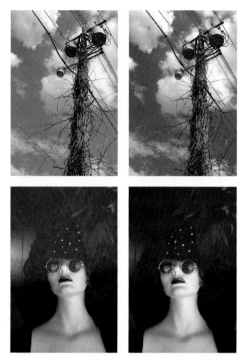

FIGURE 9.42 These images show the difference in shooting with and without a circular polarizing filter. In the top images, you can see how a polarizer lets you control the color and contrast of skies and clouds, whereas the bottom images show how you can use a polarizer to eliminate reflections. No post-processing was applied to any of these images.

Effects filters: There are any number of *effects filters*, ranging from filters that will render bright lights as starbursts to filters that will soften, or haze, an image. Major filter manufacturers such as Tiffen®, B+W, and Hoya publish complete, detailed catalogs of all their filter options.

UV filters: Ultraviolet filters cut out the little bit of ultraviolet light that makes it through the atmosphere. With a film camera, UV light can sometimes lend a blue cast to your images. This is not really a concern with digital cameras, but UV filters still serve a valuable purpose in that they protect your lens. If you drop the lens, slip and fall, or crash the lens into something, a filter can bear the brunt of the damage, usually leaving the lens unharmed. UV filters also offer great protection in harsh environments such as beaches, or in wet environments where you need to be able to quickly wipe off the lens without worrying about scratching the front element. When shopping for a UV filter (or Skylight filter, a variant of the normal UV filter), don't settle for anything but a multicoated filter, which helps reduce glare, and helps with light transmission, resulting in a brighter image.

Clear filters: If you're only interested in protecting your lens, then you might want to consider a clear filter which serves no function but to shield the front element of your lens. In addition to protecting it from scratches, a filter can also prevent dust from getting inside the lens.

If your camera does not have a TTL light meter, you're going to have to do some manual compensating when you use a filter. Because the metered light is not passing through the filter, the meter will lead you to underexpose. Most filters will have a documented *filter factor*, which will inform you of the exposure compensation (in stops) required when you use that filter.

Similarly, if your camera does not use a TTL white-balance system, your white balance might not be properly adjusted for the filter's effect. The only way to find out for sure is to do a little experimenting.

Obviously, if your camera is not an SLR, you won't see the effects of the filter when you look through the camera's optical viewfinder. Switch to the camera's LCD.

In general, except for polarizing filters, you can use your image editor to achieve all the effects that can be created with lens filters. Lens filters have the great advantage of not requiring additional edits, so if you know you need an effect, and can achieve it with filters, this will greatly speed your workflow. However, if you shoot "clean" images and add filter effects later, you'll also have the option of repurposing that image for nonfiltered uses.

Lens Extensions for Point-and-Shoot Cameras

Some point-and-shoot cameras support screw-on lens extensions that attach to your camera's filter threads, or to a special bayonet mount on the front of the camera, to create a more telephoto or wide-angle lens. As with filters, these extensions might require a step-up ring. Also note that some cameras require you to choose special settings—usually accessed through a menu option—when using a lens extension. If you don't let the camera know that an extension is attached, its focus and metering operations can become confused.

Spend some time experimenting with your camera's extensions to determine their idiosyncrasies. For example, some lenses might have bad barrel or pincushion distortion or vignetting problems.

Finally, if the extension or step-up ring is very large, it might obscure the camera's optical viewfinder or onboard flash. If the extension protrudes too far in front of the flash, it will cast a shadow when you take the shot. Usually, the only solution is to use an external flash.

SHOOTING IN EXTREME CONDITIONS

One great advantage of film cameras over digital cameras is that they can be incredibly simple machines and, thus, very durable. Because all the imaging and storage technology in a film camera is contained in the film, the camera itself can be little more than a box. This is not true with a digital camera, which requires batteries, silicon chips, LCD screens, and many more potentially fragile components.

When you shoot in extreme heat or cold, or in very wet or dusty situations, you need to take a number of precautions to ensure you don't damage your camera. Obviously, as with any mechanical apparatus, dirt, dust, sand, water, and extreme temperatures are definite hazards.

If you do a lot of shooting in extreme weather, you might want to consider a weather-resistant camera. Whether you need a simple point-and-shoot or full-blown SLR, there are cameras available that include special weatherproof seals around their controls and extra durable bodies for photographing in harsh conditions.

Dirt, Dust, Sand, and Digital Cameras

Be particularly cautious about dirt, dust, and sand, because even if it doesn't get inside the camera, a single grain of sand can be abrasive enough to scratch your lens. With their deep depths of field, minor lens scratches on a point-and-shoot camera are usually nothing to worry about, but why take chances?

If you have an SLR with very expensive lenses, you'll want to consider a UV filter for trips into dusty conditions, for the lens protection it will provide. Remember to always buy multicoated filters. Anything less can impact the optics of your lens.

Water and Digital Cameras

Digital cameras and water definitely do not mix. Although a few sprinkles are nothing to worry about, you absolutely do *not* want to submerge your camera. The rule of thumb for manual film cameras has always been: if it falls in the water, grab the camera and put it in a bucket of that same water. Keeping a film camera submerged will prevent rust until you can get the bucket and camera to a repairperson who can take it apart, clean it, and dry it. (Of course, carrying a bucket in your camera bag can be a bit of a hassle.)

Unfortunately, this doesn't apply to today's electronics-laden digital and film cameras. If your camera goes in the drink, fish it out immediately and do everything you can to get it dry. Immediately remove the battery and media card; open all port covers, lids, and flaps, and wipe off any water you can see, no matter how small. Set the camera in a warm place and do *not* turn it on until you're sure the camera has had time to dry, both inside and out. At the least, give it a couple of days to dry.

If you know you're going to be using your camera in potentially wet situations (kayaking, canoeing, taking your convertible to the car wash), consider buying a *drybag*—a sealable, waterproof bag that will keep your camera dry even if it gets submerged.

Your camera should be fine in light rain, as long as it doesn't get completely soaked. If you plan to spend all day in the rain, or are shooting in very heavy rain, try sticking your camera in a Ziploc® bag. You'll still be able to access the controls, and you can always cut a hole for the lens. (See Figure 9.43.)

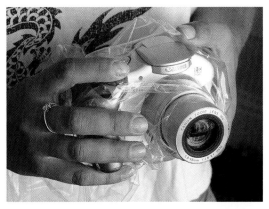

FIGURE 9.43   If you're shooting in light rain, consider using a Ziploc bag to protect your camera. Be warned, though, that your camera is very sensitive to cold and damp.

The Camera that Came In from the Cold

Shooting in cold weather presents a number of problems for the digital photographer. First, there are the LCDs on your camera. Remember that the "L" in LCD stands for liquid. As temperatures drop, your LCD will become far less "L," and the last thing you want is for it to turn into a solid crystal display. Although the LCD won't necessarily be damaged by cold weather, it might prove to be unusable.

Other, smaller, electronic components might actually be damaged if you try to use them in cold weather. Extreme cold might cause small electronic components to expand or contract enough that using them will cause them to break. Your camera's documentation should list a range of operating temperatures and, although you *might* be able to push these an extra 20° on the cold end, it's safe to say that such use won't be covered by your warranty.

Even if you're shooting within your camera's proscribed operating temperatures, be very careful when you move the camera from cold temperatures to warm. Walking into a heated house from a day of shooting in the snow can cause potentially damaging condensation to form inside the camera. If you know you're going to be shooting in cold weather, take a Ziploc bag with you. Before you go into a warm building, put the camera in the bag and zip it up. Once inside, give the camera 20 or 30 minutes to warm up to room temperature before you let it out of the bag. If you don't have a bag, be sure not to turn it on until any condensation has had time to evaporate.

If the temperature is cold enough to freeze your camera, it's probably cold enough that you'll be wearing gloves. Because gloves tend to reduce your manual dexterity, be absolutely certain your camera has a neck or wrist strap and that it's securely attached to some part of your body.

In addition, if you're shooting in icy, slippery conditions where you might be prone to falling, attach a UV filter to the end of your lens. This will add an extra level of scratch and shatter protection that might save your lens in the event of a fall.

As discussed in Chapter 7, batteries can be greatly affected by cold weather. Take a look at the cold-weather battery tips in Chapter 7 in the section "Power and Storage Management."

Hot Weather and Digital Cameras

Hot weather can also affect your camera. As mentioned earlier, as your camera heats up, noise in your images increases. If you're shooting in hot weather, this can cause a visible increase of stuck pixel noise—bright white pixels scattered about your image. This is especially problematic if you're in a hot environment, in direct sunlight, with a black camera.

You might also notice the LCD screen acting a little sluggish. Screen redraw might look weird, and some or all of the screen might appear black. Many LCD screens are not reliable above 32°C (90°F). Turn off your camera and try to get it somewhere where it can cool down. If you must shoot in high temperatures, consider keeping your camera in some type of dry cooler (an ice chest with some blue ice) until you're ready to shoot.

If you haven't exceeded the camera's recommended operating temperature, but your LCD has overheated and isn't working, it's probably safe to keep shooting using the camera's optical viewfinder (if it has one). Turn off the picture-review function because your LCD won't be visible anyway.

Changing Lenses in Hostile Conditions

If you're shooting with an SLR, you're going to want to be very careful about how you change lenses in hostile conditions. By "hostile," I mean situations that are prone to producing dust and debris that can get on your image sensor. Such conditions might not actually be hostile to *you* but they can leave image-marring grunge on your sense that will have to be cleaned off.

For example, if you're at the beach, or in a dusty abandoned factory, you'll want to be very careful about changing lenses. The easiest way to handle such situations is to *not* change lenses. Try to select a general-purpose lens before you go into these environments, and limit yourself to only that lens.

If you must change lenses in such situations, remember these tips:

- Have the new lens ready *before* you remove the old lens. You want the camera lensless for as little time as possible. While this can sometimes feel like it requires three hands, if you hang the camera around your neck while you handle your new lens, you should be able to easily swap lenses very quickly.

- Try to keep the camera pointed down before you change lenses. Keeping the camera pointed down will protect the opening to the sensor chamber, and will allow gravity to work in your favor.
- Don't take the end cap off the lens until you're ready to mount the lens on your camera. Remember: most sensor dust is transferred to the camera by the lens. Therefore, keeping your lens clean is the best way to keep your sensor clean.

If your sensor does get dusty, you'll need to clean it using the techniques discussed in Chapter 5. You'll probably also need to remove the dust in your images using the techniques covered in Chapter 14.

ASTRO-PHOTOGRAPHY

Although you might not have the massive space program necessary to shoot like the Apollo astronauts, there's no reason why you can't photograph the same subject matter. The Hubble Telescope, after all, is really just a giant, orbiting digital camera. Because of its extreme sensitivity to light, your digital camera is an ideal tool for photographing astronomical objects through a telescope. (See Figure 9.44.) In fact, many astronomers find that even cheap $100 Web cameras produce good astro photos.

In addition to providing you with a way to record your astronomical observations, your digital camera can help you capture images of subjects you normally can't see, and can let you see those objects in color. Your eye has to gather a lot of light to discern the color of an object, and it simply cannot gather light fast enough to see the color of objects millions of miles (or light years) away. Because your digital camera can sit and gather light for a long time, it can resolve the color of objects that would appear black and white if you simply looked at them through a telescope.

Some quick astro-photography tips include:

- Obviously, you'll have to buy a lens mount that will allow you to attach your camera to your telescope. There are many such mounts and adapters; check with your telescope dealer or camera manufacturer for details. You might need a number of different step-up rings and adapters depending on the type of camera and telescope you have.
- Your camera will need to have a manual mode that allows for shutter and aperture control and provides for long exposures (greater than 30 seconds). Your light meter will be useless for this type of photography, so you'll be doing everything manually.
- To prevent vibration, you'll want to use a remote control or self-timer to fire your camera's shutter release. In addition, if your camera has a mirror lockup feature, use it, because this will further reduce camera vibration when you shoot.
- As your camera gets warmer, the noise in your images will increase. Let your camera cool down outside before you start shooting. As your camera cools, its propensity for noise will decrease.

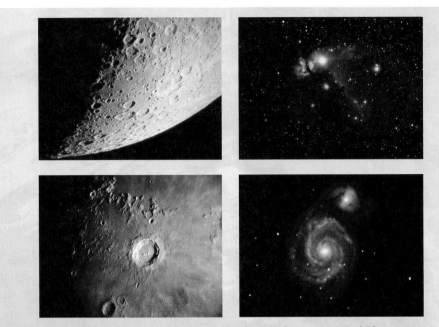

FIGURE 9.44 These four images show what can be done with a 2-megapixel Olympus 2020 digital camera and a good telescope. The lunar photos on the left were shot by Greg Konkel. The photos of Saturn and the Whirlpool galaxy were shot by Gary Honis using a custom-modified, air-cooled Olympus camera. For a detailed description of their techniques—and many more excellent pictures—check out *www.completedigitalphotography.com/astro.*

HALFWAY THERE

Like a film camera, to get the best prints from your digital camera, you'll need to manipulate your image to turn its tonal information into the image you originally envisioned. That process begins by making some preparations on your computer. In Chapter 10, "Workflow," you will learn how to transfer your images to your computer and how to configure your image-editing software.

10

WORKFLOW

In This Chapter

- Post-Production Workflow
- Apple Aperture and Adobe Photoshop Lightroom
- Learning More

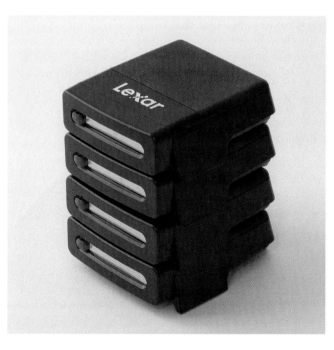

In the rest of this book, you will learn about what happens after you've finished shooting. From color correcting to editing to printing, the following chapters will cover the processes that have traditionally happened in the darkroom but now happen inside your computer.

Of course, one of the reasons we all love digital photography is the ease with which it makes it possible to get images off our cameras, into our computers, and out into the world. One of the other great advantages of digital over film is that it really doesn't cost anything to shoot, so you can experiment and explore with much less concern than you ever could with film. As such, the process of managing all those images as you move them from your camera to your computer, edit them, and then output them can quickly become overwhelming.

Workflow is the process of managing this whole business. The workflow you choose will govern how you import images, how you keep them organized, how you edit and correct them, tag them with searchable metadata, output them, and archive them for safekeeping. When I wrote the last edition of this book, you had to use separate applications for most of these tasks, and then find a way to manage your image files yourself as they passed from point to point throughout your workflow.

You can still work that way, of course, and for many people it's the best choice. However, since the last edition, an entirely new category of photo workflow software has appeared that can perform much of this work for you. Apple defined this new software niche with their Aperture application, and Adobe was quick to follow with Lightroom. Both programs provide excellent workflow options, and we'll look at them in this chapter, along with several other workflow tools. First, let's define exactly what needs to happen in a typical workflow.

POST-PRODUCTION WORKFLOW

If you're coming from a wet darkroom background, this whole "workflow" discussion may seem a little strange. But even in a chemical darkroom, you have a workflow, a method for keeping track of your negatives and prints, and the custom instructions you might come up with for printing those images. As much as anything else, defining a workflow is a process of figuring out how to stay organized, both in your current project and as your library of archived images grows.

While your camera probably came with some software manufactured by your camera vendor, this software is almost always second-rate, so you'll probably want to find a different method for managing your post-shoot workflow.

Whether you choose to handle your workflow using a dedicated workflow application, or a combination of applications, you'll probably find that your typical post-production process goes something like this:

Import. Before you can do anything else, you need to get your images off your camera's media card. It doesn't really matter if you choose to import your images directly from your camera using a cable, or from a storage card using a media card reader. However, importing directly from your camera will drain your camera battery.

Renaming and organizing. If you use multiple applications for managing your workflow, you probably use your operating system's file manager to rename your images and to organize them into folders. There's no right or wrong way to name and organize your files, so do whatever makes the most sense to you and feel free to experiment with different schemes. If you use a dedicated workflow application like Aperture or Lightroom, you'll probably skip this step.

Metadata tagging and keywording. Metadata tags are simple bits of text that can be stored in your image file. There are several different kinds of metadata tags. As you've already learned, your camera stores EXIF metadata tags to record the parameters that were used for shooting. IPTC metadata is a standard set of metadata tags that let you record copyright information, keywords, location, and many other pieces of standardized information. Metadata tagging and keywording can be an essential step for the long-term organization of your image archive. For example, with categorical keywords assigned to your images, you'll later be able to easily search for images that fit a particular description. With metadata and keywords stored in your image, you aren't limited to organizing only by filename.

Selecting your pick images. You'll typically shoot far more images than you will actually deliver or use. There's no reason to spend time correcting and editing images that aren't going to make the cut for final delivery, so once you've tagged and keyworded your images, you're ready to start selecting your *pick* images—the "keeper" or "hero" images you'll pass on to the rest of your workflow. Note that some people swap this step with the last one, figuring they'll delete any images that don't get selected as picks, so there's no reason wasting time keywording and tagging nonpick images. Other people feel it's a mistake to delete any images, as you never know what you might need later. Storage is cheap these days, and workflow tools make it easier to manage large numbers of images, so there's little reason not to keep your secondary images.

Correct and edit. Now you're ready to perform any corrections, edits, or special effects you have in mind. This stage can involve anything from the simplest contrast and tone adjustments to complex compositing and filtering operations. If speedy workflow is a must, you'll try to minimize this step by shooting your images so they're as correct as possible when they come out of the camera.

Output. With your images edited, you're ready to output to your final media. This step often involves sharpening and resizing steps. You'll then print your images, or save them as files for electronic delivery via email, the web, or disk.

Archiving and backup. Accidents happen, and you don't want to lose images in a disk crash, so you'll want to archive your project once you've delivered your final images. Archiving can be achieved by copying images to a second hard drive, burning them to optical media, or uploading them to a server.

Cataloging. As you amass more images, you'll want a way to browse and search your ever-growing library, so you'll want to catalog the archived volumes you create so you can find your images later.

These are the steps you'll take with just about any type of photo work you do. Obviously, there will be times when you might quickly grab a shot or two and move them into your computer to quickly edit and output them, without needing to go through the rigmarole of an entire workflow. However, for most shoots, you'll perform some variation of the workflow just described.

If you're working with a client, you may find yourself performing the last part of the workflow a little bit differently. For example, you might have a quick Output step before the Correct and Edit step, so you can post your pick images to the Web for client approval. If they don't like some images, you'll want to select alternates and output again. When they sign off on the images, *then* you can start editing, and post a final Web gallery of edited images for approval. If they like those, you'll do your final output to electronic files, print, or whatever your client may need.

If you're delivering electronic files (for, say, publishing in a magazine), you may have to use particular naming conventions. You'll have a specific naming step at some part of your workflow to get your files renamed properly.

Some people like to do an initial archive immediately after they import images into their computer. This gives them a backup copy of all their original files. In addition to security in the event of drive trouble, this also provides a fallback plan should they end up creating edits they don't like.

Different types of images, and different types of jobs, might require slightly different variations of the workflow described here. Consequently, you'll probably find yourself regularly making little tweaks and adjustments to the way you do things, both because you'll need to experiment to work out the best workflow for you, and to tailor your workflow to your current needs.

RAW WORKFLOW

Just a few years ago, if you were a raw shooter, your workflow issues were quite a bit more complicated, because you had the extra step of raw conversion to consider. Fortunately, nowadays things are much simpler thanks to new software tools that let you treat your raw images just like JPEG images. As such, depending on the software you choose to use, you might not have to perform a separate raw conversion step in your workflow.

You'll learn the details of raw conversion in Chapter 12, "Raw Conversion," but we'll be discussing some software options for raw shooters as we move through the rest of our workflow discussion.

In the rest of this section, we'll take a closer look at the software options available for each step of the workflow described previously.

Importing

Importing (some people call this step *ingesting*, but that sounds a little too biological for me) is simply the process of copying images from your camera's media card to your computer. You can do this by hand using the file manager in your operating system, or you can use special software to do it for you. Both the Mac OS and Windows can automatically recognize most cameras and media card readers and will automatically copy your images to your hard drive.

On Windows, the Camera and Scanner Wizard will take care of managing the transfer process. It will show you thumbnails of the images on the card and let you pick which ones you want to copy, and a destination to copy them to.

On the Mac OS, plugging in a camera or media card will launch an application called Image Capture, which also lets you select, rotate, and crop images, and choose a destination. In the Image Capture Preferences, you can elect to launch a different application when a camera or media card is inserted. So, you might choose to launch iPhoto, Aperture, Adobe Bridge, or another program that can copy images. (See Figure 10.1.)

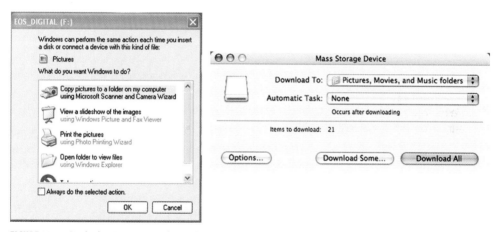

FIGURE 10.1   Both the Mac OS and Windows can automatically transfer images for you any time you plug in a camera or card reader.

Reformat, Don't Erase

Most cameras offer an option to erase all images, and some importing programs such as Aperture and Lightroom offer to erase your card after importing. Most of the time, these options are fine, but erasing all images can sometimes result in a scrambled directory structure on the card that can result in the risk of future lost images. Reformatting a card in the camera is a much safer, more reliable way to erase the images from a card.

MULTICARD IMPORTING

PhotoMechanic and Aperture allow you to import from multiple card readers simultaneously. You'll need card readers that can be daisy-chained together, like the Lexar Professional Compact Flash Readers shown in Figure 10.2. Load up the card readers and both programs will cycle through each reader, importing as normal. Multicard import allows you to perform a massive amount of importing without having to babysit your computer.

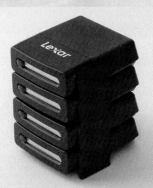

FIGURE 10.2 Using these Lexar CompactFlash Firewire readers and Aperture or PhotoMechanic, you can import multiple CompactFlash cards with a single command

Renaming and Organizing

Depending on your workflow, your archiving scheme, and your final output needs, you might need to rename your image files. Your camera generates fairly meaningless names, of course, but if you'll be searching and sorting your images using any kind of thumbnail viewer, filenames may not be so relevant. If you like to search for specific images by filename, you'll probably want to rename. Some people use elaborate naming schemes that include shoot dates, project numbers, and so on.

If you tag your images with metadata and keywords, filenames aren't so important, as you can search your image library for specific metadata tags. Similarly, if your operating system lets you search by date, you may not need to include dates in your naming schemes. The decision to rename might become easier for you after we've considered some of the other workflow steps.

Adobe Bridge provides very good batch renaming commands, as does CameraBits PhotoMechanic, Nikon Capture NX, Apple Aperture, and Adobe Lightroom.

When it comes to organizing, you can choose to arrange your images into folders and subfolders using your file manager. Image browsers like Adobe Bridge and PhotoMechanic can help you with this step, too. If you're using a program like iPhoto, Aperture, or Lightroom, you will have organizational tools within those programs; underlying folder structure might not be so critical to your workflow with those applications.

Metadata Tagging and Keywording

Good metadata and keywords can make it much easier to keep your image archive sorted and organized, and can greatly simplify the task of finding images later. If you're posting images to the Web, you will at least want to add your copyright and ownership metadata. If you're serious about maintaining a large library of images, you'll want to apply keywords as well.

You can use any keywording scheme you want, but it's best to start with broad categories you can tag all your images with, and then add more specific categories for specific shoots. For example, you might make very broad keywords such as "Interior" and "Exterior," "Travel," "Landscapes," "Family," and "Candids." So, if you're on vacation and you take a nice candid shot inside a cathedral, you would tag that image with Travel, Candids, and Interior. As you shoot images of specific family members, you might want to create keywords with those people's names. Similarly, you might want to create specific keywords for subject matter: Animals, Architecture, Forest, Desert, Dessert, Entrees, and so on. There's no right or wrong to keywording, but it is of little value if you don't keep a consistent set of keywords, and you don't take the trouble to tag your images.

File browsers such as Adobe Bridge and Photo Mechanic provide very good keywording and metadata editing tools, as do image catalogers such as Extensis Portfolio. Adobe Photoshop, iPhoto, Lightroom, and Apple Aperture also provide very good keywording and metadata tools. (See Figure 10.3.)

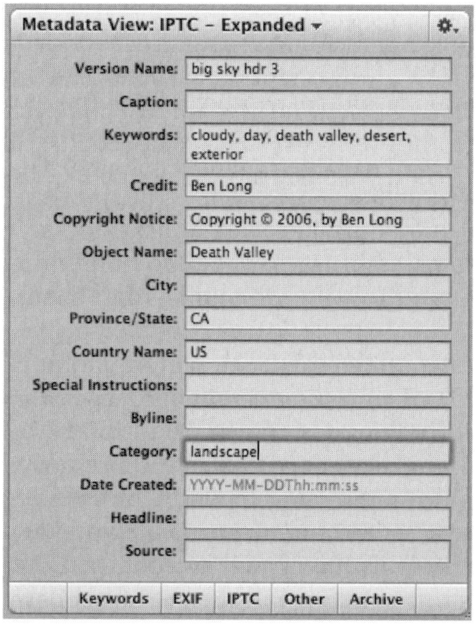

FIGURE 10.3 As with other workflow, cataloging, and browsing applications, Aperture provides you with a simple interface for adding and editing metadata.

Selecting Your Pick Images

As mentioned earlier, you won't want to edit and adjust *every* image you shoot. Instead, you'll want to pick only the "keeper" images that should be passed on to the rest of your workflow. Selecting your picks is usually a simple process of browsing through thumbnails or preview images to compare different shots and find the ones you like best. Usually, you give the pick images some kind of rating that indicates they're the best image (five stars, or something like that, depending on the browser you're using).

While searching for the best images, you'll also want to apply ratings to alternate images—four stars to the second best, for example—so you can easily find alternative images when you need them.

Picking your selects is much easier if you're using an application that provides a compare feature; that is, some way to view images side by side. Ideally, you also want a zoom or magnifying tool to view the images at 100 percent to check sharpness and detail. Aperture provides excellent comparison tools, as does Lightroom, and Adobe Bridge CS3. Other image browsers such as iPhoto and PhotoMechanic also make good tools for picking your select images.

If you shoot raw, you'll want to be sure to pick a tool that can display thumbnails and previews of your raw images without requiring any kind of complex conversion step. All the applications mentioned here can do that.

Correct and Edit

After selecting your pick images, you're ready to start editing and correcting. Which software to choose for this depends on the amount of work your images will need. If your images only need simple tonal corrections, your image browser might be able to make these for you. If you need to make more complex edits, you may need to go to a more advanced image editor. Your browser software probably provides a convenient way to launch images into an external editor. If it doesn't, you might want to consider a new browser.

Apple Aperture and Adobe Photoshop Lightroom both provide a full suite of raw conversion and image editing tools, and these will probably be all you need for most of your image editing chores. We'll be dealing extensively with image editing in Chapters 11 through 15.

Don't Forget Photoshop Elements

When we mention Photoshop in these descriptions, we mean either the Creative Suite version of Photoshop, or the much more affordable Photoshop Elements, which offers all the Photoshop features most users need.

Output

Output covers everything from printing your images, to posting Web pages, to emailing pictures, to creating files that can be given to a friend, publisher, or printer. Depending on the editing you've been doing, you'll probably output your images using your image editor or your workflow application. If you're using your image editor, you'll have to take care of resizing and saving in the appropriate format. If you're using a workflow management tool or file browser, you might have options for automatically outputting Web galleries and email, complete with automatic resizing.

Output will be discussed in detail in Chapter 16, "Output."

Archiving and Backup

With your work complete, you'll want to make backup copies of your edited images, and your original files (if you haven't already). You can create backups by simply copying images to another drive, or by burning them onto optical media such as recordable CDs and DVDs. When a project is completely finished, you might want to back up all the images and remove them from your drive to free up space.

You'll probably want to keep many of your pick images on your drive for easier access, so you can create portfolios and prints with less hassle.

When backing up your images, you'll want to exercise all the same concerns as when backing up any kind of digital data. For extra safety, you'll want multiple backups, and you'll want to check your backup media from time to time to ensure it's still readable. Some people have expressed concern over the longevity of optical media such as recordable CDs and DVDs, so you might want to periodically recopy your backup disks onto new media.

To perform your backups, you can use the file manager in your OS, CD burning software, or backup software. Apple's Aperture includes a built-in progressive backup system that makes archiving and backup simple and painless.

Cataloging

If you've archived images to another drive or to optical disks, you'll want a way to keep track of the images on each backup volume. A cataloging program such as Extensis Portfolio is the easiest way to do this. Cataloging programs differ from file browsers such as Adobe Bridge in that they actually store a document that contains thumbnails of all the images on a specific volume. You can browse this document even if the original volume is not online, and you can perform searches of metadata, keywords, and filenames to easily find the image you're looking for. For maintaining a large library, cataloging software is essential.

APPLE APERTURE AND ADOBE PHOTOSHOP LIGHTROOM

Now that you've identified and spec'ed out the different parts of your workflow, you might be wondering what software you'll use for each step. While you could use a separate application for each of the steps outlined earlier with the advent of Apple Aperture and Adobe Photoshop Lightroom, you now have the option of using a single application that can perform every step in your workflow. These programs can save you a tremendous amount of housekeeping, and lead you to a very streamlined, efficient workflow.

Whether you're using Lightroom on the Mac or Windows, or using Aperture on your Mac, there are some fundamental ideas and concepts you need to grasp to get the most out of those programs.

Aperture and Lightroom Philosophy 101

Whether you use Aperture or Lightroom, (and whether you use Lightroom on the Mac or Windows operating systems) one of the most common mistakes you're liable to make when you first adopt either program is to assume these programs are meant as simple image editor replacements. If you think of these programs this way, you will continue to import your images by hand, organize them using the file manager in your operating system, and then, when you're ready to compare some images, or perform some edits, you'll try to move those images into either of these programs. If you try this approach with either program, you'll quickly find that your workflow is more complex and cumbersome than ever before.

Unlike a straight image editor, these programs are not intended to sit on top of your OS file manager; they're designed to completely *replace* your operating system's file manager. While your file manager might do a fine job of organizing your images into folders, renaming files, and letting you copy and back up files, it doesn't offer any of the extra functionality you need as a photographer. You can't compare images, or search metadata, or view your images at 100 percent. In the real world, you don't organize your bank statements using the same system you use to organize your photos, so why should you expect that the same tool on your computer will serve both purposes?

The reason these programs can't sit on top of your file system is that to use them, you first have to import your images into *their* library systems. So, it's not a matter of simply opening an image in either program every time you want to knock off a few edits. Instead, you have to import the image before you can perform any edits. For these programs to work, you have to give your workflow over to them. The first part of your workflow needs to be to let either of these programs import your images into its library. Then you can easily compare, sort, rate, edit, and output.

If this sounds like a big hassle, bear in mind that you have to import your image onto your drive anyway, so it's not like it's adding a step. And, you'll probably quickly find that the benefits far outweigh the initial confusion of this new way of working. *Because* these systems have their own libraries, they are able to offer functionality, like multiple versions, that you can't get using a normal, file manager–based workflow.

The good news is that you can back out of either system at any time, with your data completely intact. Therefore, there's really no risk involved in trying either of these applications.

This Philosophy also Applies to iPhoto

If you're a Mac user using iPhoto, you'll find that the same philosophy applies there. iPhoto also expects you to import its images into your library system, and it takes care of the same kind of file management overhead and housekeeping chores Aperture and Lightroom address.

Libraries: Embedded or Referenced?

Both Aperture and Lightroom (and, incidentally, iPhoto 6) allow you to import images in two ways: as embedded (sometimes called *managed*) images, or as referenced images. When you choose to import an image as an embedded image, the image is copied into a special folder on your hard drive. This is not a folder that you are ever expected to deal with directly. Instead, Aperture and Lightroom sock your images away in this library folder, so they can always know where the images are, and manage them accordingly. If you ever need a copy of the image, you ask the program to give you one, and it copies the image to the location you specify.

When you import an image as a referenced image, the original file is left in its original location, and a pointer to that file is stored in the program's library. This pointer is analogous to an alias on the Mac, or a shortcut in Windows. Your original image file remains in a place where you can see it and manipulate it (move it, copy it, launch it into other applications), *and* it can still be found by Aperture or Lightroom.

The advantage of embedded images is that the application always knows where they are. It's impossible to break the link, so the application can do a seamless job of managing your images. In Aperture, embedded images also have the advantage of being included in the automatic backup process that's built in to the program.

The advantage of referenced images is that they are in a normal part of your file system, where you can easily access them if you want to manipulate them in another program, or copy or move them. The downside is that if you're not careful, you can easily break the link between them and Aperture or Lightroom.

Both programs allow you to mix and match your importing choices on an image-by-image basis, so you don't have to commit to either approach. Some things to consider, though:

- If you keep your library on an external drive (both programs allow you to specify the location of the library through a simple preference change) so you can easily move it from one computer to another (say, from your desktop to a laptop), embedded images (sometimes referred to as "managed") will probably be the best way for you to go, as this will ensure your library always has access to the images you've imported into it.
- If you need to use your images in other programs, such as video editors or 3D modeling programs, importing as references will be the best solution. Similarly, if you sometimes want to try using different raw converters to convert your raw files, importing your raw files as references will make it much easier to quickly try different raw conversions.

Nondestructive Editing

Both of these programs employ nondestructive editing systems, which allow for a great deal of flexibility. If you're not sure what this means, review the *Nondestructive Editing* section in Chapter 6, "Building a Workstation." This is a key concept to internalize if you decide to use either of these applications.

COLOR MANAGEMENT SYSTEMS

As discussed in Chapter 6, color management software allows you to try to preserve consistent color from one monitor to another, and from your screen to your printer. If you do nothing else color management-wise, you'll want to calibrate and profile your monitor as described in Chapter 6. For accurate printing, you'll want to pay attention to the profiles you install for your printer. We'll cover this topic in more detail in Chapter 16.

ON THE CD

In the meantime, if you'd like to learn a little more about color management, check out the PDF "Color Management Systems" located in the Chapter 10 folder of the companion CD-ROM.

ON THE CD

If you're a Photoshop user, you might also want to tweak some of Photoshop's color preferences. You can learn more about this in the PDF "Photoshop's Color Settings" also located in the Chapter 10 folder of the companion disc.

LEARNING MORE

We've discussed many different applications in this chapter, from image editors to image catalogers to CD burners to applications that handle all of the aforementioned. Obviously, each of these applications is complex in its own right, and you'll need to devote some study to each. A comprehensive explanation of all the issues involved in all these different programs is beyond the scope of this book, but hopefully the general guidelines, questions, and issues raised here will help you sort through the choice of applications available to you, and make it easier for you to zero in on the questions you'll need to answer as you dive into the process of developing a workflow that works for you.

By this point, you should know how to get your images out of your camera, sort them, tag them with metadata, and select the images you want to correct and edit. Correction and editing will be our topics for the next five chapters, before we move on to final output.

11

CORRECTING TONE AND COLOR

In This Chapter

- Histograms Revisited
- Cropping and Distortion Correction
- Correcting Tone
- Should You Worry About Data Loss?
- Curves
- Levels and Curves and Color
- Hue/Saturation
- The Story So Far

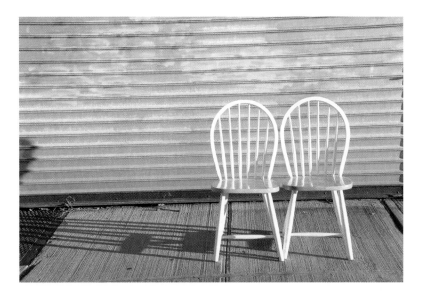

In general, you'll want to try to calculate exposures that will allow you to capture "finished" images directly in your camera. For the sake of expediency, it's almost always better to get your images exposed right when you shoot. However, there will be times when conditions don't allow for an ideal exposure, and other times when the image you see in your head is impossible to produce without additional editing. Finally, there will also be times when you simply mess up and don't choose the right exposure, or a moment presents itself so quickly that you don't have time to adjust exposure to the ideal. For all these times, you'll want to turn to your image editor.

With your image-editing software, you can perform some amazing manipulations (some would say "deceptions") of your images. The most useful features of your image editor, however, are not its capabilities to alter the content of an image, but its capabilities to alter the tone and color so the image—no matter what its content—looks better in final output. Sometimes, you'll use these features to correct the exposure you initially shot, and at other times, you'll use these features to *finish* the image you originally shot.

In terms of fundamental image editing, little has changed since the first edition of this book. The main tools you'll use to achieve your adjustments are Levels and Curves controls. These two tools provide very similar functionality using two different interfaces. Most image-editing programs include a Levels adjustment, and higher-end applications include both Levels and Curves. For the purposes of these tutorials, you can use any application that provides Levels and Curves. These tutorials are built around Photoshop. Even if you won't regularly be using a Curves-equipped image editor, it's worth going through the Curves tutorials simply for the theory that is explained.

To get started, let's quickly revisit the histograms you saw in Chapter 8, "Metering and Exposure," and look at how the information in the histogram is manipulated by the Levels control.

About the Tutorials in This Chapter

The tutorials in this chapter are all built around Photoshop CS3. However, in most cases we've also detailed the equivalent features in other image editors. Photoshop's tools and interfaces have been widely imitated (and, in some cases, improved) in other applications, so you shouldn't have any trouble following along in your image editor of choice. If you're using an earlier version of Photoshop, you'll see some differences in interface, but the controls and steps described here should still work.

You can download a 30-day, full-featured trial version of Photoshop from www.adobe. com/downloads. This will provide everything you need to perform the tutorials. If you'd like to check out some Photoshop alternatives, you might want to download the trial version of Adobe Photoshop Lightroom from that same link, or a trial version of Nikon Capture NX, which you can download at http://nikonimaging.com/global/products/software/capturenx/ nxsp/download.htm. If you're a Mac user, you'll want to give Aperture a try. You can download a trial version from www.apple.com/aperture.

HISTOGRAMS REVISITED

In Chapter 8, you learned about histograms—graphical representations of the tonal values within an image. If you'll recall, a histogram is essentially just a bar chart of the distribution of different colors and tones in a picture. Most cameras can produce histograms of images you've shot, making it easier to determine if you have over- or underexposed an image while you're in the field.

Your image editor can also produce a histogram of an image. Consider the image in Figure 11.1.

Figure 11.1 is a simple gradient from black to white, created using the Photoshop Gradient tool. The histogram confirms that the image goes from complete black to complete white, with most of the tones distributed at either end of the spectrum. You can also see from the histogram that there is a lot of contrast in this image—that is, the range of black to white covers the entire spectrum of the histogram.

Now look at Figure 11.2.

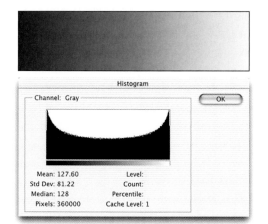

FIGURE 11.1   This gradient from black to white yields a simple histogram.

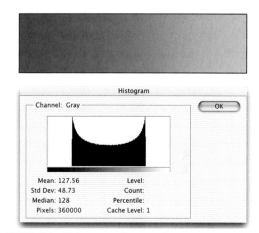

FIGURE 11.2   This grayscale ramp from 80 percent black to 20 percent black yields a histogram similar to the one shown in Figure 11.1, but the tones are centered in the middle of the spectrum.

Also created in Photoshop, this gradient was specified as having a range from 80 percent black to 20 percent black instead of pure black to pure white. If you look at the histogram, you can see that the tones in the image fall in the middle of the graph. There are no dark or completely black tones, nor are there any light or completely white tones. In other words, there's not much contrast in this gradient—the range from lightest to darkest is very small.

The histogram represents a graph of all the tones in your image. Therefore, before you start adjusting the image, you want to make sure your image does not contain any tones you're not interested in, as these will alter your histogram. So, before we start our tonal edits, we'll want to perform any cropping edits, so our histogram only shows the tones we will ultimately be interested in, rather than including tones that will ultimately be cropped away.

WHY IS THE HISTOGRAM OF A GRAY RAMP CURVED?

If a grayscale ramp is just a progression from black to white, why does the histogram show more data at the dark and light end of the scale? Remember, your eyes don't see things in a linear fashion; they expand highlights and shadows to reveal more tones and detail in bright and dark areas, so the edges of the histogram accurately show more tonal information there.

CROPPING AND DISTORTION CORRECTION

It may not be the most technically impressive tool in your digital toolbox, but over time, you'll probably find that your image editor's crop tool is one of the most powerful editing features at your disposal. With it, you can actually recompose your image after you've shot it.

Cropping is a very important first step because, in addition to changing the composition of your image, when you crop you will also remove tones from your image, which will affect your final histogram. For example, you might crop out areas of overexposed highlights, which will greatly change the appearance of your histogram. As you'll see later, this will ease your editing process.

In Chapter 7, "Shooting," you performed a cropping exercise on paper as a way of exploring composition. You'll apply those same ideas when you use the crop tool in your image editor.

In this section, we're going to look at the crop tool in Photoshop, but you'll find the same features we describe here in the crop tools provided by Aperture, Lightroom, Nikon Capture NX, iPhoto, and others.

TUTORIAL 11.1   CROPPING AN IMAGE

The hardest part of cropping is simply to decide what kind of crop you want. Using an actual crop tool is fairly simple. Fortunately, most crop tools make it easy to explore different crops. We'll be using Photoshop for this tutorial, but you should be able to follow along in any editing program that has a crop tool.

Step 1: Open the Image

ON THE CD

In your image editor, open the image *crop me.jpg* located in the Tutorials/Chapter 11 folder on the companion disc. (See Figure 11.3.) The focus of this image should be the birds on the telephone wire, which, with the telephone pole look sort of like musical notes. Because I didn't have a long enough lens, I shot this image with the intention of cropping it later. I tilted the camera to straighten out the telephone wires, but now we need to crop out a lot of extraneous detail.

Step 2: Drag out a Crop

Select the Crop tool. In Photoshop, you can do this by simply pressing C. Click to define the upper left corner of the crop you want, and then drag out a rectangle to define the crop. (See Figure 11.4.)

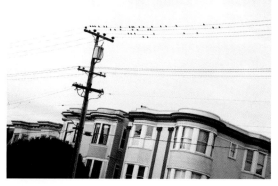

FIGURE 11.3 We didn't have a long enough lens to get this shot framed the way we wanted, so we'll use the Crop tool to recompose it.

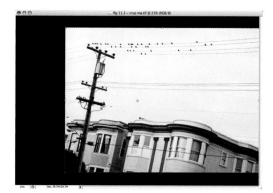

FIGURE 11.4 Using the Crop tool, drag out an initial crop. It doesn't matter if you don't get it correct right away, as you can correct it later.

Step 3: Adjust the Crop

A rectangle of dotted lines will be displayed to indicate where the image will be cropped. In Photoshop, you also have the option of masking out the uncropped part of your image. Blocking out the uncropped areas makes it much easier to tell what your finished, cropped image will look like. In the Control Bar at the top of the screen, you can define the color and opacity of the crop mask, which Adobe calls the *Shield*. (See Figure 11.5.)

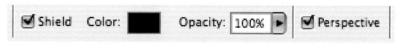

FIGURE 11.5 In Photoshop CS2 and CS3, you can specify how you want the cropped area of your image to be masked.

One advantage of using a semiopaque shield is that you can see what else is in the image. Personally, I like a solid shield so I can focus on just the cropped image.

The crop rectangle provides control handles at the corners, and in the middle of each edge. You can drag these to reshape the crop. Click the bottom handle and drag up to crop out the tree. Make any other adjustments you want. (See Figure 11.6.)

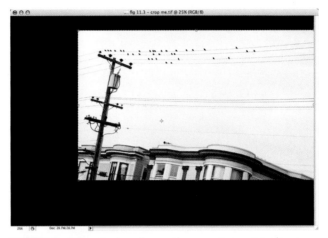

FIGURE 11.6   Using the handles on the cropping rectangle, you can resize your crop.

Step 4: Make the Crop

Press Return, or double-click within the crop rectangle to accept the crop. Your image will be cropped and will appear in a new, smaller window.

Sometimes, it can be hard to tell if you like a crop until you've accepted it. If you decide it's *not* what you want, undo and try again. If you're using a nondestructive editor like Aperture, Lightroom, or Capture NX, you can readjust your crop at any time, meaning you're never committed to a specific crop, as you are in a destructive editor.

In this example, we performed a free-form crop. That is, our final image has a different aspect ratio from our original. There will be times, though, when you want to ensure that your final result has specific proportions. For example, if you're cropping to fit a specific design or layout, or if you're planning to print at a particular size, you'll want to constrain your crop to a specific aspect ratio.

Step 5: Revert to the Previously Saved Version

We want to try a different crop of this image. Choose File > Revert to return to the original, previously saved version.

Step 6: Configure the Crop Tool

Our goal is to print this image out on a 4" × 6" piece of paper, so we want to ensure that our final image has the proper proportions. Select the Crop tool. On Photoshop's Control Bar, enter 6 in the Width field, and 4 in the Height field. (See Figure 11.7.)

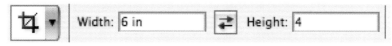

FIGURE 11.7 With the Crop tool selected, the Photoshop Control Bar lets you specify an aspect ratio for cropping.

Step 7: Make Your Initial Crop

Click and drag to define a cropping rectangle, as you did before. This time, your crop will be constrained to a rectangle with a 6:4 aspect ratio (or, 3:2, if you prefer thinking that way).

Step 8: Adjust the Crop

When working with a constrained tool, it can be difficult to nail the crop exactly right on the first try. Fortunately, after you've defined an initial crop, you can then click within the cropping rectangle and drag the crop around to position it. (See Figure 11.8.)

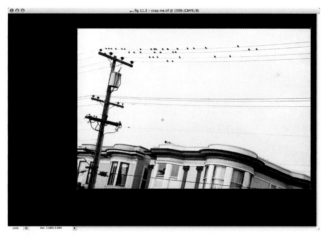

FIGURE 11.8 This crop has been automatically constrained for 4" × 6" output (a 3:2 aspect ratio).

Step 9: Make the Crop

As before, press Return or double-click within the cropping rectangle to make the crop.

The crop tools in the image editors we've discussed here have predefined constraints that you can select for easily cropping to specific aspect ratios. For example, in Photoshop, you open the Crop menu on the Control Bar to access the predefined cropping constraints. (See Figure 11.9.)

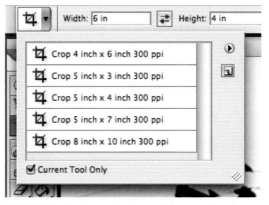

FIGURE 11.9   Most crop tools provide an option for selecting predefined cropping aspect ratios. Shown here is Photoshop's Crop Tool menu, which provides simple access to specific crop constraints.

Remember that you don't *have* to crop to the same aspect ratio your camera shoots, or to any of the preset aspect ratios in your image editor. Very often, the best crop for an image has an unusual aspect ratio. Landscapes often look better with a long, skinny, panoramic crop, while other situations might call for a narrow, vertical crop. The crop tool allows for great creativity so don't be afraid to experiment.

Don't hesitate to play around with different crops. The capability to drag and re-shape a crop on the fly makes it possible to easily see the possibilities of different croppings. If you're working with a nondestructive editor that can create different versions of an image (like Aperture, Lightroom, or Capture NX), you can easily create different versions cropped in different ways.

Straightening

No matter how careful you are when you shoot, your images won't always be perfectly level. Determining what's straight when you're shooting can be difficult, especially if you're shooting on unlevel, hilly terrain. A tripod with a level can help, but this isn't always an option. Straightening is an edit you should perform early in your editing pipeline because it requires a crop.

TUTORIAL 11.2   STRAIGHTENING AN IMAGE

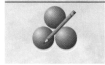

Ideally, you'll want to shoot your images straight, in-camera. Since straightening also requires you to crop your image, when you straighten, you'll end up lowering the pixel count of your image if you have to straighten the image later. Nevertheless, there will be times when you'll need to straighten an image, because you were sloppy when shooting, or conditions didn't allow you to shoot level, or because it was difficult to tell what was level while you were at the shoot.

Photoshop, Aperture, Lightroom, and Capture NX all have very good straightening tools, as does Photoshop Elements. Photoshop CS's straighten feature is actually the most complicated of any of these products, so we'll be covering it here.

Step 1: Open the Image

ON THE CD Open the image `Straighten Me.tif`, located in the Tutorials/Chapter 11 folder on the companion CD-ROM. (See Figure 11.10.)

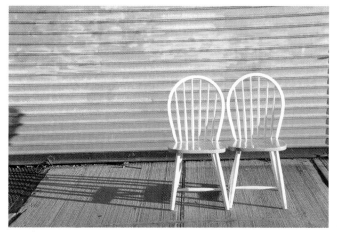

FIGURE 11.10   This image needs to be straightened, a task that can be performed using Photoshop's Ruler tool.

Step 2: Select the Ruler Tool

Photoshop doesn't have an actual straighten tool, but you can use the Ruler tool to automatically straighten an image. The Ruler tool lives in the Tool palette in the same cell as the Eyedropper tool. (See Figure 11.11.)

> *Selecting the Ruler from the Keyboard*
>
> *The keyboard shortcut for the Ruler, and all the other tools that live in the same menu, is I. If you press Shift-I repeatedly, you'll cycle through the Eyedropper, Color Sampler, Ruler, and Count tools. All Photoshop tools work this way. For example, L is the shortcut for the Lasso tool. Pressing Shift-L will cycle through all the various lasso tools.*

Step 3: Define a Straight Edge

Click with the Ruler tool on one end of something in the image that should be straight, such as the bottom of the metal garage door. While holding down the

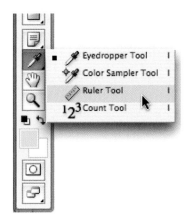

FIGURE 11.11 Click and hold on the Eyedropper tool to open a pop-up menu containing, among other things, the Ruler tool.

mouse button, drag to the other end of the garage door bottom. A straight line will be superimposed over the image.

Step 4: Rotate the Image

Choose Image/Rotate Canvas/Arbitrary, and Photoshop will present the Rotate Canvas dialog box. The Angle field, which specifies how much the image should be rotated, will automatically be filled in with whatever value is required to straighten the line you defined with the Measure tool. (See Figure 11.12.) Click OK, and your image will be rotated.

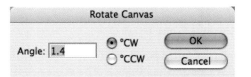

FIGURE 11.12 When you open the arbitrary rotate dialog after using the Ruler tool, Photoshop automatically fills in the rotation amount with a value that will straighten your image.

Step 5: Crop the Image

After rotating, your image will no longer be rectangular. Photoshop will have automatically changed the canvas size to encompass the entire, now askew image. (See Figure 11.13.) Obviously, the extra white space is not especially desirable, so you'll need to crop your image to produce a final, straightened image. (See Figure 11.14.)

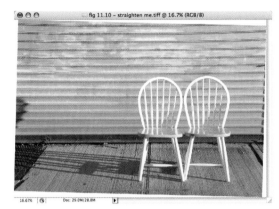

FIGURE 11.13 After straightening, the image will need a crop.

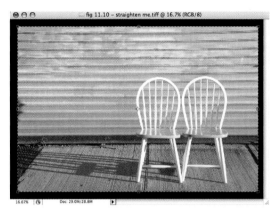

FIGURE 11.14 The final, straightened, and cropped image.

Nonwhite Background

The background of the rotated image will appear in whatever color you have currently set as the background color. By default, it will be white.

Aperture, Lightroom, and Capture NX provide excellent straightening tools that perform rotation and cropping at the same time, making for a simpler straightening process. And of course, since these are nondestructive editing systems, you can adjust your straightening at any time.

Correcting Geometric Distortion

There are certain types of geometric distortions you need to correct early in your workflow because they will also require a crop. And, if you're a stickler for geometric accuracy, you may want to try your geometric corrections right away, because if it turns out that you *can't* correct your image to your liking, you'll want to know that early so you won't waste time on other edits.

Barrel and pincushion distortions are simple geometric distortions that occur in images shot with extreme wide-angle or telephoto lenses. If you had to zoom way out when you were shooting your image, there's a good chance the vertical and horizontal lines in your picture will be bowed outward. Conversely, if your lens was zoomed in all the way, there's a chance your image will be bowed inward. If you're using a wide-angle or fisheye attachment on your lens, your images will almost certainly be distorted (unless you're using a *rectilinear* wide-angle lens on a digital SLR).

These distortions don't occur in all lenses—in fact, the lack of them is the mark of a very good lens—and even lenses that *do* have trouble with geometric distortion probably exhibit these issues only in specific, somewhat rare, circumstances. If you find yourself facing distortion problems, you can easily correct them using Photoshop CS2, or CS3.

TUTORIAL 11.3   CORRECTING BARREL AND PINCUSHION DISTORTION IN PHOTOSHOP CS2/CS3

Photoshop CS2 and CS3 provide an excellent tool for correcting all kinds of lens distortions. We'll be looking at all its features throughout this chapter, but first we're going to look at how to correct barrel and pincushion distortion.

Step 1: Open the Image

ON THE CD

Open the image graphwall.tiff, located in the Tutorials/Chapter 11/Lens Distortion folder on the companion disc. (See Figure 11.15.)

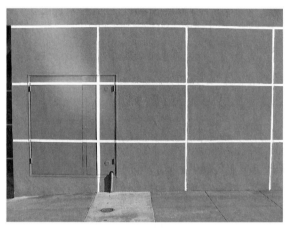

FIGURE 11.15 This image suffers from barrel distortion, a problem we can easily correct in Photoshop.

Step 2: Apply the Lens Correction Filter

Choose Filter > Distort > Lens Correction to open the Lens Correction filter. This filter provides a number of tools for correcting various lens issues. (See Figure 11.16.)

Step 3: Configure the Filter

The Lens Correction filter provides some simple utility functions we need to configure for our correction. The Grid that is superimposed over the image can be toggled on and off using the Show Grid checkbox. However, the grid is a handy reference for determining when we've restored our lines to true vertical and horizontal, so we want to leave it on. The grid density is a little high, though, so enter 32 in the Size box to make a grid with squares that are twice as big. This will make it easier to see our image.

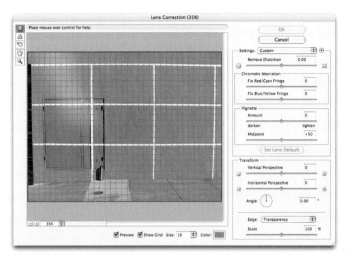

FIGURE 11.16   We'll use Photoshop's Lens Correction filter to eliminate the barrel distortion in our image.

Step 4: Remove the Barrel Distortion

The Remove Distortion slider at the top of the Settings pane allows you to easily correct either barrel or pincushion distortion. Slide it to the right to correct the barrel distortion. A value of +3 should do it. (See Figure 11.17.)

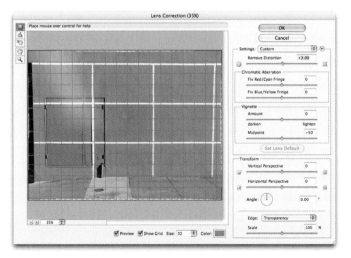

FIGURE 11.17   By simply sliding the Remove Distortion slider to the right, you can remove the barrel distortion from this image. To correct pincushion distortion, slide to the left.

Click OK and you're done—that's all there is to it! Note that if you had to remove a *lot* of distortion, your image may require a crop, which you can now perform as normal, using the Crop tool.

Straighten with Lens Correction

The Lens Correction filter also provides a Straighten tool, which you'll find in the small toolbar on the left side of the filter window. (See Figure 11.18.) This tool works just like the Ruler tool—simply drag to define a line that should be straight. When you release the mouse button, your image will automatically be straightened. However, it will still need a crop. If you're using an earlier version of Photoshop, you'll need to use the procedure described earlier.

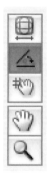

FIGURE 11.18   You can also use the Lens Correction filter to straighten an image, by selecting the Straighten tool.

If you're using an older version of Photoshop that doesn't provide a Lens Correction filter, you might still be able to perform some barrel and pincushion distortion. Check out the Lens Distortion.pdf document located in the Tutorials/Chapter 11/Lens Distortion folder on the companion disc.

ON THE CD

Correcting Perspective

There might be times when you want to adjust the perspective in an image, most commonly if you're shooting architecture. For example, when you're standing at street level shooting up at a building, the top of the building will be narrower than the bottom. This is another edit you want to perform early in your workflow because it requires cropping.

If your image editor provides free distortion tools that allow you to stretch and squash parts of an image, you can try to perform a horizontal stretch on the top of the image to make the top of the building the same width as the bottom.

If you have Photoshop CS2 or CS3, the easiest way to correct perspective is to use the same Lens Correction filter you used in the last tutorial.

TUTORIAL 11.4   **CORRECTING PERSPECTIVE IN PHOTOSHOP CS2/CS3**

Using the Lens Correction filter, we'll correct the perspective in a simple architectural snapshot.

Step 1: Open the Image

ON THE CD

Open the image Perspective Correx.tif in the Chapter 11 folder of the companion disc. (See Figure 11.19.) Shot from street level, this image has a strong perspective "distortion" that results in the top of the building appearing smaller than the bottom. This is, of course, how the building actually looked at street level. However, when walking down the street, you would most likely recognize the building's rectangular shape, which has been lost due to the perspective shift. Using the Lens Correction filter, we can adjust the image to reduce the perspective and restore the building to a stronger rectangular shape.

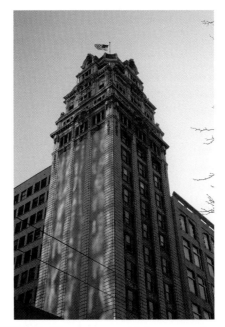

FIGURE 11.19   We can correct this image to adjust the perspective distortion so it looks more rectangular.

Step 2: Apply the Lens Correction Filter

Choose Filter > Distort > Lens Correction to invoke the Lens Correction filter, which you should be familiar with by now. As before, change the grid size to make the grid less coarse. Enter 64 in the Size field.

Step 3: Adjust the Perspective

The Transform section of controls allows you to alter the perspective of your image. Essentially, these tools let you rotate your image as if it were projected onto a flat plane. As the image tilts, the perspective will lessen. However, the resulting image will require a crop.

For this image, you only need to worry about the Vertical Perspective slider. Slide the Vertical Perspective to the left. As you do, the bottom of the image will tilt "backward" so that the bottom of the image is farther away from the top of the image. Actually, you're correcting the perspective in the image by introducing a *different* perspective.

You can use the grid lines as a reference to determine when you've corrected the image enough to return the vertical lines to true vertical. (See Figure 11.20.)

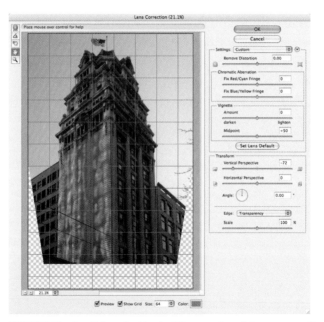

FIGURE 11.20 By sliding the Vertical Perspective slider, we can tilt the image enough to correct the perspective distortion.

Click OK to accept the change.

Step 4: Crop the Image

After the perspective adjustment, the image needs to be cropped to remove the extra space introduced by the perspective correction. Obviously, you will have to remove a fair amount of image data to get a good crop. (See Figure 11.21.)

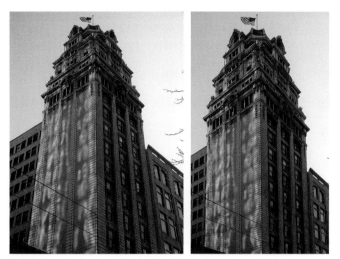

FIGURE 11.21   After your perspective adjustment, you'll need to crop your image back to a rectangle. Here you can see our final before and after.

Correcting Chromatic Aberrations

Chromatic aberrations are the weird purple, red, or blue fringes that can appear along high contrast lines, usually at the edges of your images. They are most often caused by lens distortions that prevent all wavelengths of light from being focused equally. Correcting chromatic aberrations doesn't require a crop, but it is something you might want to do early on, because if you *can't* correct these troubles, you may decide the image isn't worth further edits.

The easiest way to correct chromatic aberration is to go, once again, to the Lens Correction filter.

TUTORIAL 11.5   CORRECTING CHROMATIC ABERRATION WITH PHOTOSHOP CS2/CS3

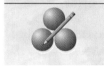

Figure 11.22 shows an image with some chromatic aberration troubles. While they may not appear obvious at the print size used in this book, when printed out at 8" × 10", the pink fringe along the edge of the rocks is very annoying. We'll use the Lens Correction filter to eliminate the fringe.

Step 1: Open the Image

ON THE CD

Open the Image `Chrom Ab Trouble.tif`, located in the Tutorials/Chapter 11 folder on the companion disc.

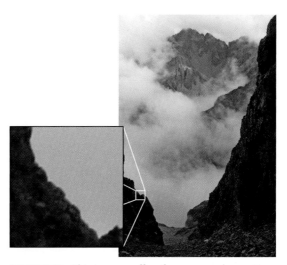

FIGURE 11.22   This image suffers from some chromatic aberration troubles we'll correct with the Lens Correction filter.

Step 2: Apply the Lens Correction Filter

This should feel familiar to you if you've been working through the other tutorials. For this correction, there's no need for the reference grid. Since it obscures the view and slows down your computer, deactivate it by unchecking the Show Grid button at the bottom of the Lens Correction filter.

Step 3: Arrange Your View

Using the magnifying glass tool located in the toolbar in the upper left corner of the Lens Distortion window, zoom in to 100%, centered around the rocks on the left side of the image, where a pronounced pink fringe is visible.

Step 4: Correct the Aberration

The two Chromatic Aberration sliders let you address different colors of fringe. They work by changing the registration of different color channels, to reduce a particular fringe-y color. Slide the Fix Red/Cyan Fringe slider to the right. You may have to wait a moment to see a change, because it can take a while for the filter to calculate its results, but at around +15, you should see your fringe disappear. (See Figure 11.23.)

When using the fringe correction sliders, be careful that you don't push them too far, as you might end up producing entirely new, different colored fringes in other locations. Just keep a close eye on your image as you make your adjustment. In Chapter 14, "Imaging Tactics," we'll look at an additional way to remove chromatic aberrations, which you can perform in any editor that lets you perform selective saturation adjustments.

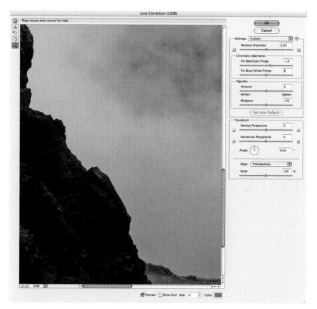

FIGURE 11.23   With a simple adjustment of the Fix Red/Cyan Fringe slider, we can eliminate the pink color fringe from the edge of the rocks.

With your geometric corrections out of the way, and your image cropped, you're ready to begin your tonal corrections.

Correcting Vignetting

The Lens Correction filter offers one more feature, which is the capability to correct vignetting, the darkening of corners that can sometimes occur with wide-angle lenses. Use the Amount slider to control how much lighter or darker to make the corners, and the Midpoint slider to control how large an adjustment is made in the corners.

CORRECTING TONE

Tonal correction is simply the process of ensuring that the contrast in your image is good—the blacks, whites, and other gray levels look the way you want them to look. Very often, tonal corrections are the only adjustments your image will need. With a simple tonal change, you can take an otherwise dull, hazy image and turn it into a scene that pops off the page.

Because colors also have a tone, many of your color problems will disappear with tonal correction. There are many different tonal correction tools, and you may find that you use some for some images, and others for other images. However, the tool you will probably find yourself using most often is a Levels adjustment, which can be found in all major image editors.

Levels

In Chapter 8, and earlier in this chapter, you spent some time reading histograms. From the histogram, you saw that you can easily determine when an image is too dark, too bright, or lacks contrast. What you cannot do with a histogram, however, is correct these problems.

A Levels control lets you alter the value of the blackest and whitest points in your image, and make the midtones brighter or darker. Most importantly, you can adjust any of these regions without affecting the others. So, for example, you can brighten dark areas without also brightening highlights.

We're going to begin our Levels work by correcting the grayscale ramp we saw in Figure 11.2. As you'll recall, this image suffers from low contrast. The brightest areas aren't white, and the darkest areas aren't black, which means that, overall, there's not much range from the darkest tone to the lightest. Fortunately, if your image editor has a Levels control, you have a solution to these problems. The Photoshop Levels control can be opened by clicking Image > Adjust > Levels, or by pressing Command/Control-L. Aperture, Lightroom, Capture NX and iPhoto—and most other image editing programs—also offer a Levels adjustment that works like the one we'll see here. The Levels dialog box is shown in Figure 11.24.

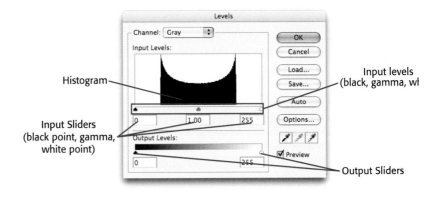

FIGURE 11.24 The Photoshop Levels dialog box offers a number of features. Right now, you'll be using only the histogram, input sliders, and Input Levels fields.

First, you can see that a Levels control is built around a histogram of your image. The Levels dialog in Figure 11.24 shows the histogram from the grayscale ramp we saw in Figure 11.2. Directly beneath the histogram are three *input sliders*. The left slider shows the position of black in the histogram—that is, it points at the location on the graph that represents 100 percent black. The right slider shows the position of white, while the middle slider shows the *gamma*, the midpoint of the tonal range.

The Input Levels fields above the histogram are simply numeric readouts of the positions of the three input sliders—0 represents black, white is represented by 255, and shades of gray are somewhere in between.

The easiest way to understand what these sliders do is to use them. Therefore, let's go back to the image shown in Figure 11.2 and try to correct it so it looks like the one shown in Figure 11.1.

TUTORIAL 11.6   USING LEVELS INPUT SLIDERS

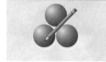

Our goal is to correct the grayscale ramp shown in Figure 11.2 so it has better black and white values and improved overall contrast; we want it to look like the smooth gradient in Figure 11.1. Although we'll be using Photoshop for this example, you can easily follow along in any image editor that provides a Levels control.

Step 1: Open the Image

ON THE CD

Open the file grayramp.tif, located in the Tutorials/Chapter11 folder on the companion CD-ROM. Once the image is up, open your Levels control. In Photoshop, choose Image > Adjustments > Levels.

If you're using Aperture, iPhoto, or Lightroom, you'll need to import the grayramp.tif *file into your library.*

Step 2: Adjust the Black Point

As you can see from the histogram in the Levels dialog box shown in Figure 11.24, the darkest tone in this image is not full black, but is closer to 80 percent black. Make sure the Preview checkbox in the Levels dialog box is checked. Drag the black triangle at the far left of the histogram to the right until it is directly beneath the left value of the histogram. (See Figure 11.25.) The black point readout should be around 52.

Now look at your image. The left side—that is, the black side—of the grayscale ramp should be black. With our Levels adjustment, solid black is no longer at 0 on the histogram—it's now at 52. (Remember, the histogram is a graph of values from 0 to 255.) Therefore, everything to the left of our new black point is considered black. Notice that our gamma point—the middle slider—has automatically moved to the right to preserve the relationship between black, midpoint, and white.

Look at the right side of the image and notice that the lightest value has not changed. This is one of the great advantages of the Levels adjustment—it allows us to edit different parts of the tonal range independently, while preserving the tonal relationships in our image.

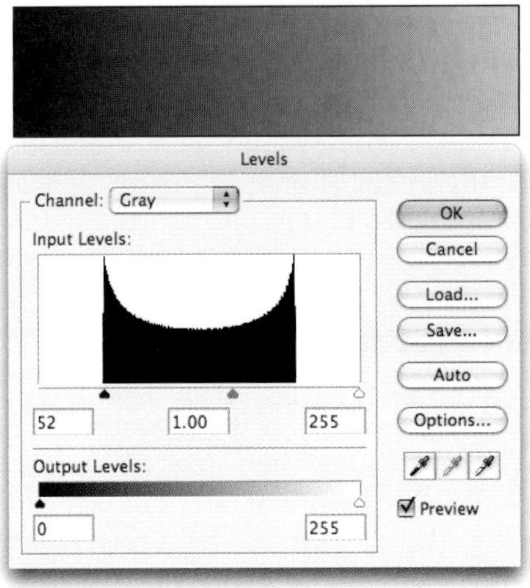

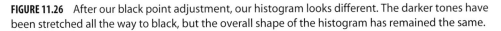

FIGURE 11.25   Setting the black point using the Levels control results in a gray ramp with correct black levels.

To understand this better, click OK to accept the changes. Now, open the Levels control again to see a new histogram of the image. (See Figure 11.26.)

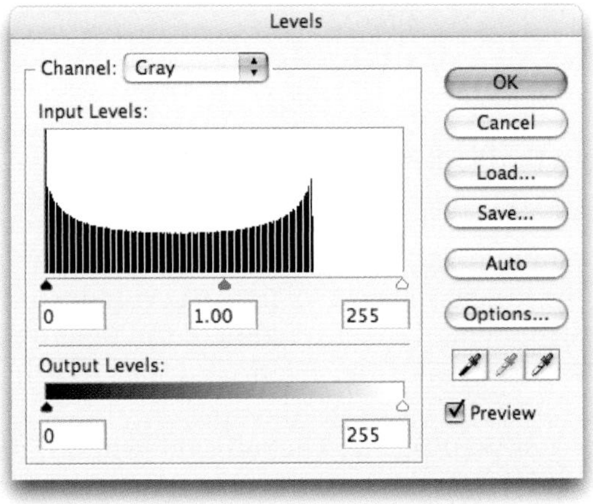

FIGURE 11.26   After our black point adjustment, our histogram looks different. The darker tones have been stretched all the way to black, but the overall shape of the histogram has remained the same.

You might be a little surprised to see that the histogram looks different than it did when you closed the Levels box before. Remember that after you performed your black point adjustment, the image still had a full range of tones from 0 to 255. This histogram is a graph of those new, adjusted tones.

As you can see, some bars are missing, indicating that we've lost some data. This makes sense when you think about what your black point adjustment did. You moved the black point in to indicate the value you wanted to be black. The Levels control placed that value at 0 and stretched all the values between 0 and your midpoint (the gamma slider) to fill the space. Unfortunately, there wasn't enough data to fill the space, so some tonal values were left empty. To make the absence of those tones less noticeable, Photoshop has spaced these missing tones across the tonal spectrum.

The good news is that the distribution of tones within the image—as represented by the shape of the histogram—has been preserved, so the ramp still has the progression from black to white we want.

Step 3: Adjust the White Point

Now we need to do the same thing to the white point that we did to the black point. Open your Levels control and take another look at your histogram. The white values in your image—the right of the grayscale ramp—are not really white, they're light gray.

Drag the white slider to the left so it points to the right data in the image. The white point display should read approximately 190. (See Figure 11.27.)

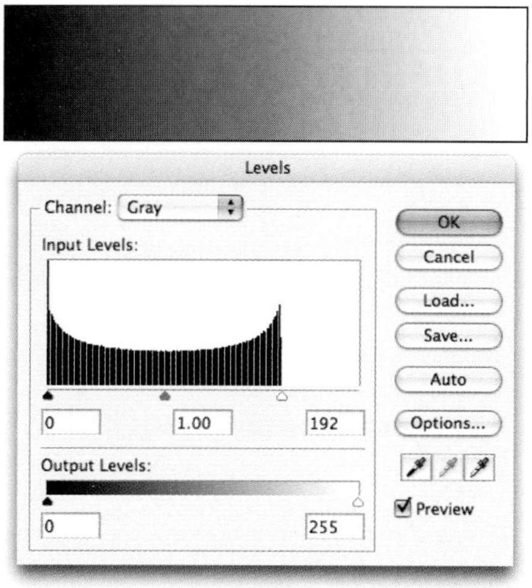

FIGURE 11.27   After adjusting the white point, your Levels dialog box should look something like this.

Now look at the right side of your image. It should be a brighter white. The good news is that your shadows are still nice and dark! As with the black point adjustment, adjusting your white point also adjusted the midpoint, to keep the relationship between the white point and midpoint the same. The black point was left untouched.

Clicking the Auto button in the Levels dialog box does the same thing you just did in these two steps. It moves the black point to the leftmost tonal value in the histogram, and moves the white point to the rightmost value. Why not just use Auto every time? Because sometimes, the rightmost point on your histogram is not what you want as white in your image. It might be a specular highlight or bright flare, whereas true white is further to the left. You might also find that, for printing purposes, you sometimes want to leave a little "headroom" above and below your tonal range.

The Load and Save buttons allow you to save your Levels adjustments for reuse later. For example, if you've shot a series of images in the same lighting or exposure situation, you might find that the same Levels adjustment is appropriate to all of them. In this case, you could save a Levels adjustment that could be loaded and applied to all your images.

Click OK to accept your new white point, and then open the Levels dialog box again to see the new histogram. (See Figure 11.28.) As with the black point adjustment, we've lost some more image data, but as before, we've preserved the overall tonal distribution in our image.

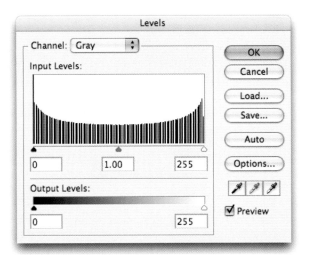

FIGURE 11.28   After adjusting our white point, a new histogram shows that we have lost some data, but notice that the overall distribution of tones has retained its original shape.

Step 4: Play with the Gamma Slider

This particular image doesn't need a gamma adjustment, but there are some interesting things to learn by moving it around and observing the results. Slide the gamma slider to the left and watch what happens to your image. (See Figure 11.29.)

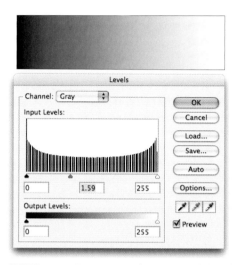

FIGURE 11.29   As we move the gamma slider, the midtones in our image shift toward black or white.

As you move it, the midtones in your image become much lighter. Slide it back to the right, past its original location, and you'll see your midtones get darker. As you move the gamma slider, though, your black and white values stay locked down at black and white. Gamma lets you adjust the midtones of your image to shift contrast more toward shadows or toward highlights. With it, you can often bring more detail out of a shadowy area, but you'll never have to worry about your blacks or whites turning gray.

Type 1.0 into the gamma readout (the middle text box above the histogram) to return the gamma slider to its original location.

With the Levels dialog box still open, zoom in on your image. (In Photoshop, you can do this by pressing Command-+ on a Mac, or by pressing Ctrl-+ if you're using Windows.) Now, drag the gamma slider to the left. Again, you'll see your midtones lighten, but now watch what's happening in the shadow areas. If you look closely, you'll probably see some slight tone breaks.

Tone breaks are the result of the loss of data that results from the Levels control stretching the tonal values in your image. In other words, as you stretch the tonal values, Photoshop is discarding data and your image is posterizing. Drag the slider in the other direction and you'll begin to see banding in the highlights of your image as you darken the midtones, causing the highlights to stretch to fill in the now empty space.

Play around with these controls to get a feel for their effect, and to see how the image changes and degrades. These changes and problems are particularly easy to see in this document because it is a simple linear gradient.

PHOTOSHOP CS3'S PALETTE DOCKS

In Photoshop CS3, Adobe made a major change to the interface that controls palettes. Palettes now reside in special docks that can be easily collapsed, to allow for more efficient use of screen space. (See Figure 11.30.)

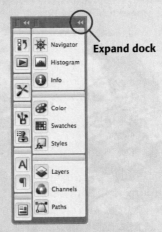

Expand dock

FIGURE 11.30 In Photoshop CS3, palettes are collected into collapsible palettes to help you better manage screen space.

Hovering your mouse over any icon in the dock will tell you which palette it opens. You can click on the icon for any palette to expand it and make it viewable, or you can click on the Expand Dock button at the top of each dock to expand all palettes to full size. Clicking on a palette or the Expand Dock button again will collapse the palette or dock.

In the tutorials in this book, we won't explicitly say when or if you should expand or collapse a dock, so you're on your own for managing your palettes and docks.

TUTORIAL 11.7   ADJUSTING A REAL-WORLD IMAGE

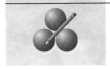

Using a Levels control on a real image is no different from the process you just performed on the grayscale ramp. You'll set your black and white points, and then adjust the gamma, or midpoint. In this tutorial, we're going to correct the image shown in Figure 11.31.

Step 1: Open the Image

ON THE CD

Open the image `Real World Levels.tif`, which is located in the Tutorials/Chapter 11 folder on the companion disc.

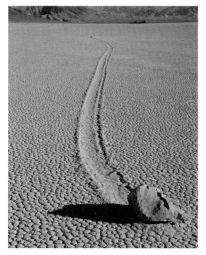

FIGURE 11.31   We didn't do a very good job with the exposure of this image when we shot it. It has a murky quality that stems from a lack of contrast.

Step 2: Examine the Histogram

Before you can begin making any corrections or adjustments, you need to devise a plan of attack, and the easiest way to do that is to examine your image's histogram. The histogram will help you determine what adjustments will be necessary, and in what order. This is why we made certain to perform any cropping operations right away. We need to be sure our histogram contains only relevant data.

Photoshop CS, CS2, and CS3 provide a Histogram palette that lets you see a histogram of the current image. If it's not already visible, you can open the Histogram palette by selecting Window > Histogram. (See Figure 11.32.)

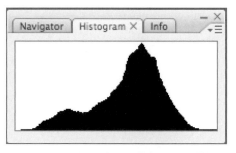

FIGURE 11.32   Photoshop's Histogram palette lets you see a histogram of the current image.

As you can see from the histogram, this image has some contrast problems. There's no black or white in the image. The lack of contrast is giving it an overall dull appearance.

Step 3: Set the Black Point

Choose Image > Adjustments > Levels, or press Command/Control-L to open the Levels dialog box. We're first going to set the black point in the image to restore the dark tones to their proper values. There's no objectively correct black point; you can set it to wherever you want depending on how much contrast you want to have in the image, and how worried you are about shadow detail (as you darken shadows, they'll lose detail). The Levels dialog box provides a handy utility for determining exactly which tones are clipped by your black point adjustment.

Hold down the Option/Alt key while you drag the Black point to the right. As soon as you begin to drag, your image will turn completely white. Don't worry; your picture hasn't been erased. As you continue to drag, any pixels that are getting clipped by your black point adjustment will be highlighted. This is referred to as a *threshold view*. (See Figure 11.33.)

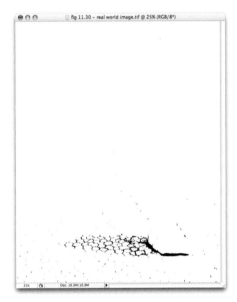

FIGURE 11.33   The threshold view in the Levels dialog makes it easy to see exactly which pixels are being clipped by your black point adjustment.

The first pixels to appear are the dark shadows directly beneath the rock. If you want, you can back off until these pixels are no longer visible, to guarantee you don't clip any tones. However, if the shadow underneath the rock turns completely black, it doesn't really matter since there's no meaningful detail in that part of the image anyway.

You can freely release and press the Option/Alt key to toggle in and out of Threshold view, allowing you to easily determine the effects of your black point adjustment.

We went for a fairly aggressive black point change, to produce stronger contrast in the image, and so set the Black point to 44. (See Figure 11.34.)

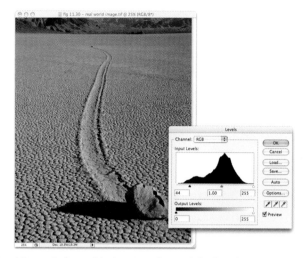

FIGURE 11.34   We settled on a black point of 44. While this clips some tones, they're not areas that contain important detail, and we wanted the stronger contrast.

Step 4: Set the White Point

You can use the same Threshold view when setting the white point—just hold down Option/Alt while dragging the white point slider to see a threshold view. In general, you can't push a white point adjustment as much as you can a black point adjustment, because clipped highlights are much more noticeable than clipped shadows. So, we set our white point to around 225. (See Figure 11.35.)

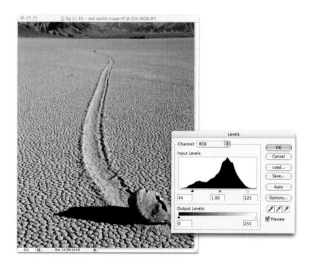

FIGURE 11.35   A white point of 225 brightens the image, removing some of the dullness, without blowing out any important details.

Step 5: Adjust the Midpoint

Our image already looks much better. The dull cast is gone, and there is a "punchier" level of contrast. However, we can improve the image a little more with a midpoint adjustment. In Figure 8.8, you saw how changes in exposure can alter the texture in an image. The dry lakebed in our scene has a very textured surface, and we'd like to play that up a little more.

The textury surface is composed of mid-range values. If we could darken some of those values, the texture would become more contrasty. Slide the midpoint slider to the right to about .79 to darken the midtones. (See Figure 11.36.)

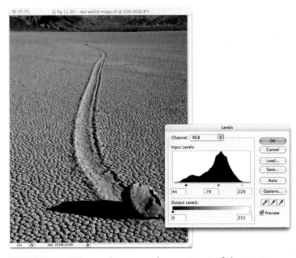

FIGURE 11.36   We can increase the contrast of the texture on the lakebed with a simple midpoint adjustment.

We've lost some detail in the rock shadow, but this is an acceptable loss to pick up the extra surface texture.

That's it! Click OK to accept the levels adjustment, and our image is corrected.

SHOULD YOU WORRY ABOUT DATA LOSS?

In the last two tutorials, you engaged in image-editing operations that removed data from your image. That really sounds like something you should be worried about, doesn't it? In some cases, it is.

Fortunately, the type of data loss you just saw was not readily apparent on-screen—you had to make a fairly extreme adjustment and zoom in very close to the image—and the data loss was certainly far too slight to appear in a printout.

However, if you were to make the change you just made, and then go back and make two or three more edits that also produced some data loss, your image might visibly degrade. This is why it's so important to capture as much data as you can *when you're shooting*. If your image has a lot of tonal range to begin with, you won't have to make adjustments that are too extreme when you're editing, and your image editor won't have to throw out so much data as it manipulates the image's tones. Controlling data loss is just one more reason why it's important to choose a good exposure when you take a picture.

Once you have your image in your image editor, you'll want to think carefully about your edits to minimize your data loss. When you are editing, try to achieve as much as possible with the fewest tonal corrections. In other words, don't use a Levels command to fix your black point, and then use an additional Levels command later to adjust your white point. Make your tonal corrections count by accomplishing as much as you can with each correction. (In the grayscale ramp tutorial, we used two separate commands, but that was only for the sake of getting to look at the intermediate histogram. Normally, we would have done the white and black point adjustments in one command.)

In Chapter 4, "Evaluating an Image," you learned about posterization. Posterization (sometimes referred to as *tone breaks*) is the key to knowing when you've exhausted your tonal range. Posterization is also a great way to tell if you should make an edit or not. Your image editor provides a huge number of options and alternatives. If you're wondering if you should make an edit, or if you're wondering how far to push an edit, check to see if the edit introduces any posterization. If it does, back off on the edit.

You saw an example of posterization in an image in Figure 4.11. Remember, though, that posterization that shows up on-screen may not be visible in print.

ANOTHER WAY TO THINK ABOUT EDITS

As you've seen, you can make some profound adjustments to your image using just the Levels tool. In the next section you'll see similar capabilities with the Curves tool, and later some other options. In the end, these tools all perform slight variations of the same function: they allow you to very selectively brighten or darken specific pixels in an image. Some of them allow you to brighten or darken only the red, green, or blue component, but still they all function by performing a controlled increasing or decreasing of pixel values.

When you adjusted the black point in the grayscale ramp, you told Photoshop to darken a specific set of tones in the image. Photoshop was smart enough to darken the tones by varying amounts to try to create a smooth transition from the adjusted to nonadjusted tones.

The histogram provides a great visual aid for this lightening and darkening—it allows you to think of the tones in your image as a quantity that can be pushed around to different parts of the tonal range. So, you might think of pushing tones down to fill in empty regions in the shadows. However, in the end, you're simply darkening tones that are already there so they fall onto a different place in the histogram.

CURVES

The Levels control provides the simplest way to perform the basic tonal adjustments you will regularly need to make, but it's not the answer for all corrections. Curves is a tool that can do everything Levels does, but also provides a few other capabilities. Unfortunately, Photoshop Elements does not provide a Curves control—Curves is one of the features that makes the full-blown Photoshop cost more—so if you're using Elements, you'll need to download and install the Photoshop CS3 demo from the Adobe Web site.

You can open the Curves dialog box by clicking Image > Adjust > Curves, or by pressing Command/Control-M.

Curves in Other Applications

Lightroom and Capture NX also provide curves.

A typical Curves interface (Figure 11.37) is really just a different interface to the same adjustments you were making with the Levels control.

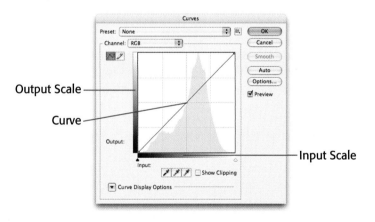

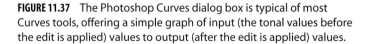

FIGURE 11.37 The Photoshop Curves dialog box is typical of most Curves tools, offering a simple graph of input (the tonal values before the edit is applied) values to output (after the edit is applied) values.

Like a Levels dialog, the Curves dialog box also presents a graph of the data in your image. Instead of graphing the distribution of tones, however, it shows a graph of the unaltered versus altered pixels in your image. The horizontal gray ramp along the bottom of the Curves dialog box represents the tones in your image before they are altered by the Curves command. The vertical gray ramp along the left side of the Curves dialog box represents the tones in your image *after* they are altered.

When you first open the Curves control, the Curves graph shows a 45° line from black to white, indicating that the input tones (the ones along the bottom) are identical to the output tones (the ones along the side). If you change the shape of the line, you change the correspondence of the input tones to the output tones. (See Figure 11.38.)

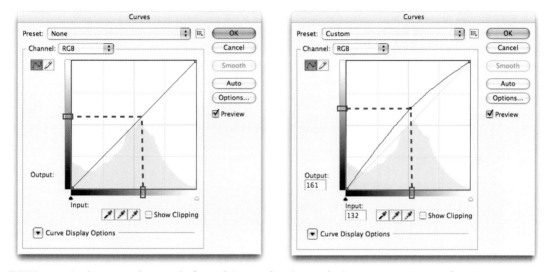

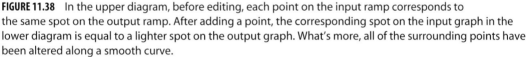

FIGURE 11.38   In the upper diagram, before editing, each point on the input ramp corresponds to the same spot on the output ramp. After adding a point, the corresponding spot on the input graph in the lower diagram is equal to a lighter spot on the output graph. What's more, all of the surrounding points have been altered along a smooth curve.

When you adjusted the black point using your Levels control, you told your image editor that there was a new value it should consider, black. The image editor then stretched and squeezed the values in your image to make your desired adjustment. The curve in the Curves dialog box, which starts out as a straight line, lets you clearly see how all the tones in your image are being stretched and squeezed. To redefine your black point using Curves, for example, you move the black part of the curve to a new location. Figure 11.39 shows the Curves adjustment required to turn the gray ramp shown in Figure 11.2 into the full ramp we saw in Figure 11.1. In other words, this curve performs the same correction we created earlier with the Levels control. (See Figure 11.37.) The black and white points—the ends of the curve—have been dragged inward, remapping the not-quite-black and not-quite-white tones in our image. All the other tones on the curve have been adjusted accordingly.

The main advantage of Curves is that, whereas Levels lets you edit the white, black, and midpoints of an image, Curves lets you edit as many points as you want.

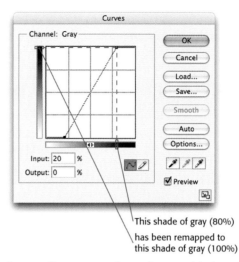

This shade of gray (80%) has been remapped to this shade of gray (100%)

FIGURE 11.39   This Curves adjustment performs the same black-and-white correction as the Levels adjustment you saw earlier, effectively turning the 80–20 gray ramp shown in Figure 11.2 into the black-to-white gray ramp you saw in Figure 11.1.

Would You Like a Histogram with That Curve?

Photoshop CS3 shows a histogram display behind the curve, making it easier to see which parts of the curve correspond to which parts of your histogram. Earlier versions of Photoshop do not include this feature. However, the Histogram palette included in Photoshop CS and CS2 (and several versions of Elements) solves this problem. Open the Histogram palette before you open the Curves dialog, and you'll be able to keep an eye on the histogram while you set up your Curves adjustment.

A QUICK WORD ABOUT TONE

When you are correcting and adjusting color, it's important to remember that when you add more red, green, or blue to an image, you're adding more light—your color will get lighter. In other words, some colors are inherently brighter than others. A pastel blue, for example, in addition to being a different hue and having a different saturation, is lighter than a dark red or dark blue. Therefore, if you perform adjustments that change the color in your image, you might be changing the overall lightness or darkness of your image.

TUTORIAL 11.8   CORRECTING TONE WITH CURVES

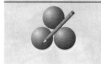

The easiest way to learn how the Curves control works is to try it. In this tutorial, we're going to use the Curves tool to color-correct an image.

Step 1: Open the Image

In Photoshop, open the image `prague.tif` located in the Tutorials/Chapter 11 folder on the companion CD-ROM. (See Figure 11.40.) As mentioned earlier, Photoshop Elements does not have a Curves control, so you'll need to use the full version of Photoshop for this tutorial. You can use any version of Photoshop for this lesson, or install the Photoshop demo included on the CD-ROM.

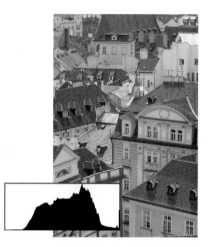

FIGURE 11.40   The histogram confirms what your eyes will tell you: this image is too dark and needs better contrast.

As you can see from the histogram, the image has a good amount of dynamic range. However, as is obvious from both the image and the histogram, the picture lacks contrast, so we need to reset the white and black points.

Step 2: Set the Black Point

Open the Curves dialog box. In Photoshop, you can open it by clicking Image > Adjust > Curves, or by pressing Command/Ctrl+M (Command if you're using a Macintosh, Control if you're using Windows). The black point on the curve is the point at the bottom of the 45° line. This point indicates that black on the input scale corresponds to black on the output scale. We want to change it so that dark gray—the darkest tone in the image—on the input scale corresponds to black on the output scale. Because the input scale goes horizontally from black to white, we need to move the black point to the right.

Click the black point and drag it to the right. If you have the Histogram palette open, you can watch the black point on the histogram shift to the left, indicating that we are effectively moving the darkest point toward black. Remember, we don't want to clip the blacks, so don't let the tones in the histogram fall off the left side. (See Figure 11.40.) When adjusted properly, the Input box should read approximately 35, and Output should stay at 0. With this move, you're saying that values at 35 or lower are equivalent to 0, or black. The dark areas in your image should now look black. What do those numbers mean? The 35 value you just selected in the Curves dialog box is equivalent to about 87 percent black (black is 0, white is 255).

Step 3: Set the White Point

Correcting the white point in this image is a bit trickier because, as you can see from the histogram, there is already some pure white information in the image. If we shift the white point, we will risk blowing out the highlights even further. However, the image could be a little brighter, so let's try a white point adjustment anyway.

The histogram indicates that there are some white pixels in the image already, so let's begin by identifying them, so we can keep an eye on them while making our adjustment. With the Curves dialog still open, click and drag the cursor around the image. The Curves dialog will display a small circle on the curve to indicate the value of the particular pixel you're pointing at. In this way, you can easily see which parts of the curve correspond to particular colors in your image. The white point is the point at the other end of the curve, in the top-right corner. As you drag around the image, you'll quickly see that the roof of the white building near the top-right of the image falls mostly near the white point of the curve. This is the area to watch while we edit. Although it's okay if it loses a little detail, we don't want to posterize it or blow it out completely.

Just as you moved the black point directly to the right, you want to move the white point directly to the left to indicate that light gray should become white.

Click the white point and drag it to the left until the Input box reads about 238. The Output value should still read 255. In other words, the value 238 has been stretched out to 255. (See Figure 11.41.) So far, this is no different from the type of adjustment you make when you move the black and white points in the Levels dialog.

With the black and white points adjusted, the image should have better contrast and be slightly brighter. We've sacrificed a little detail on the white roof, but it's not obtrusive. Now we're ready to make further corrections.

Step 4: Adjust the Gamma

In the Levels tutorial, you saw how you could use the midpoint, or "gamma," slider to adjust the midtones in an image. Because this image could use a little more contrast in the midtones, we're going to perform a gamma adjustment by adding a new point to our curve.

The gamma point is the point on the curve in the middle of the graph. Normally, it lies at the intersection of the two middle gridlines, but because of our white and

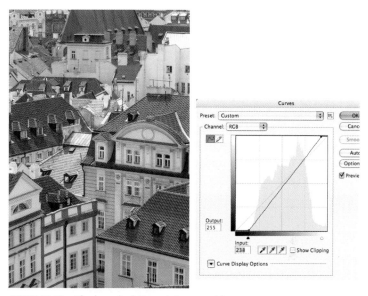

FIGURE 11.41   Black and white points are set in the Curves dialog box by sliding the endpoints toward the center of the graph.

black point adjustments, the midpoint has shifted down and to the right a bit. Move your pointer over the curve until the Input display reads about 132. This is roughly the midpoint. Now, click and drag down and to the right a tiny bit to darken the midtones. (See Figure 11.42.)

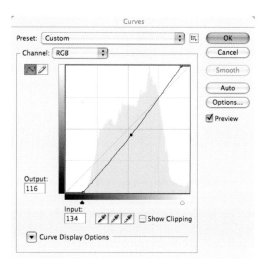

FIGURE 11.42   Gamma is adjusted by dragging the midpoint of the curve to lighten or darken the image.

As you move the point, notice that the curve changes shape. Remember when you tried to use the Brightness and Contrast controls and were hampered by the fact that your adjustments were applied evenly to the entire image? With Curves, as you can see, your adjustments create a smooth curve of change throughout the tonal range. What this means is that in addition to adjusting that single gamma point, you have adjusted the nearby points by varying degrees. Levels works the same way, but with Curves you can really see how other tones are affected. Click OK to accept your Curves adjustment.

Finally, you might want to perform a slight crop of the bottom of the image. Your finished image should look something like the one shown in Figure 11.43.

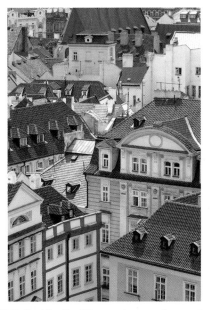

FIGURE 11.43   The final Prague image after setting white, black, and midpoints with the Curves tool.

WHICH SHOULD I USE? LEVELS OR CURVES?

Let's face it: Curves is confusing. What's more, getting competent with the Curves dialog takes a lot of practice. While hardcore editors swear by the Curves dialog, it can be a real pain to use. If you find yourself more comfortable working with the Levels dialog box, then by all means, use it instead of Curves. Not using Curves does not make you a wimpy photographer. Curves is ideal for times when you want to make an adjustment that only affects a tiny part of the tonal range in your image. However, as you'll see in Chapter 13, "Building Your Editing Arsenal," there are other ways to constrain edits.

→

In Aperture, you can activate a special Quarter Tones feature (Figure 11.44), which adds two additional points to the Levels control. This gives you the equivalent of a Curves control with 5 points on it. In addition, the three middle points allow you to move their upper handle, so you can specify exactly which part of the tonal range you want those points to operate on.

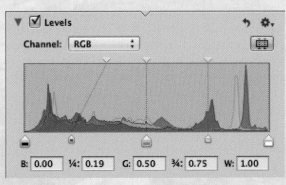

FIGURE 11.44   Aperture's Levels control lets you activate additional control points, and change which part of the histogram is affected by each point.

Lightroom provides a different workaround for simplifying Curves. In Lightroom, the Curves control has separate sliders beneath it that allow you to adjust the curve with a slider interface, rather than by dragging points (although you can edit with points as well). In addition, the Lightroom curve shows a shadowed preview of what the adjusted shape of the curve is at any particular point, making it easier to predict how the curve will change as you adjust it. (See Figure 11.45.)

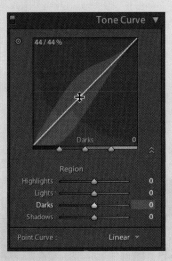

FIGURE 11.45   Lightroom's Tone Curve provides both point and slider controls, and innovative displays that make it easier to understand how the tone will change as you adjust it.

BRIGHTNESS AND CONTRAST

Some image editors, Photoshop included, provide a Brightness and Contrast control. These controls are like the brightness and contrast controls on a TV set. However, depending on the application you're using, you may not want to use this feature. In all versions of Photoshop prior to CS3, the Brightness and Contrast control was pretty much useless. Unlike Levels and Curves, Brightness and Contrast in older versions of Photoshop didn't let you independently adjust separate parts of the tonal range, making it virtually impossible to make the types of corrections we've seen in this chapter. With CS3, Adobe has fixed the Brightness and Contrast control, making it a far more useful tool. However, you'll still probably find Levels more flexible, and easier to use.

LEVELS AND CURVES AND COLOR

So far, you've seen how Levels and Curves controls can be used to adjust tone and contrast, whether in color or grayscale images. These tools, however, can also be used to adjust, correct, and change color. In previous chapters, you read about many ways in which color can go wrong when you shoot. Levels and Curves are two tools that allow you to fix color problems that arise from bad white balance, improper exposure, or a bad camera.

To understand how Levels and Curves affect color, you have to understand how color is stored in an image. In Chapter 2, "How a Digital Camera Works," you learned that digital cameras make color by combining red, green, and blue information. These separate red, green, and blue components are referred to as *color channels,* or just *channels,* and many image editors allow you to perform corrections and adjustments on these individual channels.

In Photoshop, you can access the different color channels through the Channels palette (click Window > Show Channels). The Channels palette includes separate rows for the Red, Green, and Blue channels, and for your image—the RGB channel. (See Figure 11.46.) By clicking each channel, you can view its contents.

If you click the Red channel in the Channels palette, you'll see a grayscale image that represents all the red in your image. Why is it grayscale? Because, if you'll recall, one *24-bit image* is made up of three separate *8-bit images,* and with 8-bit images you can have up to 256 shades of gray. When you look at an individual color channel, you're looking at the grayscale image where that particular component color information is stored. A bright white pixel in a Red channel equates to full red in your final image, because bright white has a value of 255, the maximum allowed in an 8-bit image. (See Figure 11.47.) Combine a bright red pixel in a Red channel with identical pixels in the Green and Blue channels and you'll have a white pixel in your final image, because full red, plus full green, plus full blue equals white.

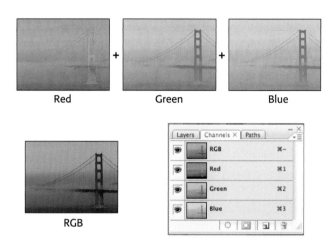

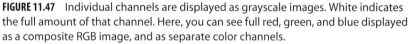

FIGURE 11.46   The Channels palette lets you view and edit the individual Red, Green, and Blue channels that make up your RGB documents.

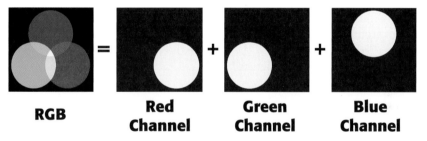

FIGURE 11.47   Individual channels are displayed as grayscale images. White indicates the full amount of that channel. Here, you can see full red, green, and blue displayed as a composite RGB image, and as separate color channels.

It's possible to edit the color channels directly, and there are a number of editing tricks you can employ that rely on individual channel edits. In addition, through the Channel pop-up in Photoshop's Levels and Curves dialog, you can perform Levels or Curves adjustments on specific color channels. When you view a channel in Photoshop, you can use all the editing, painting, and manipulation features you would normally use. This is a very handy feature for digital camera users, because digital cameras often have trouble with specific channels. For example, many cameras produce more noise in one channel than another. With your image editor, you can try to attack the noise in an individual channel directly by applying special noise-reducing filters or blurs—or even painting by hand—directly into that channel.

Similarly, you may find that the color in your final image is off because one particular channel is out of balance. When this happens, you can correct the color in your final image by manipulating an individual channel.

Depending on how you like to perform your edits, you may not find that you ever need to edit an individual channel directly. However, an understanding of separate channels is necessary to understand how certain color correction operations work, such as the one we'll see in the next tutorial.

TUTORIAL 11.9   CORRECTING A COLOR CAST

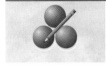

So far, you've used the levels control to adjust contrast and tone in an image by changing the white and black points. You've performed these adjustments by moving the white and black point sliders. Most Levels adjustments provide an additional way to set white and black points, and a way to easily neutralize color casts. In this tutorial, we'll explore both of these features.

Step 1: Open the Image

ON THE CD

In Photoshop, (or your image editor of choice) open the image `Tumbleweed.tif`, located in the Tutorials/Chapter 11 folder on the companion disc.

This image needs a contrast adjustment, but it also has a reddish color cast we'll need to correct. (See Figure 11.48.)

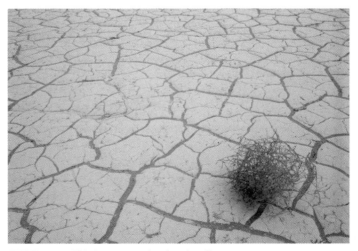

FIGURE 11.48   This image needs a levels adjustment to correct contrast, and its color cast.

Step 2: Open the Levels Dialog Box

Choose Image > Adjustments > Levels, or press Command/Control-L to open the Levels dialog box. From the histogram, you can see that the image lacks any true white—there's no data extending all the way to the right side of the histogram. As you learned in previous tutorials, you can adjust the white point slider to define a new white point, but you can also use the white point eyedropper, the rightmost eyedropper located directly beneath the Options button.

Step 3: Set the White Point

Click on the White Point eyedropper to activate it, and then click with the eyedropper on something in your image that is supposed to be white. (See Figure 11.49.)

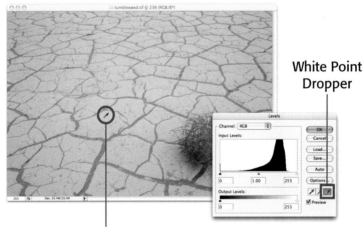

White Point
Dropper

Setting white point here

FIGURE 11.49   The White Point eyedropper lets you set the white point by simply clicking on something in your image that is supposed to be white. Here, you can see where we've chosen to click.

After setting the white point, the image will immediately look much better. (See Figure 11.50.)

Step 4: Correct the Color Cast

There are two other eyedroppers in the Levels dialog box. The Shadow dropper lets you set the black point of an image by simply clicking on something black—just as you corrected the white point by clicking on a white area. This image doesn't need a black point adjustment, because it's a somewhat low-contrast, very high-key image.

The middle dropper lets you define something in the image that is supposed to be neutral, or middle gray.

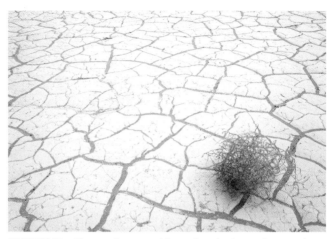

FIGURE 11.50 After setting our white point, the image has much better contrast, but it still has a slight reddish cast.

Select the Neutral eyedropper, and then click on one of the gray parts of the image, as shown in Figure 11.51.

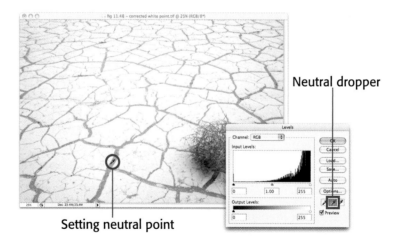
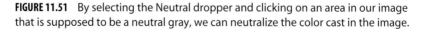

FIGURE 11.51 By selecting the Neutral dropper and clicking on an area in our image that is supposed to be a neutral gray, we can neutralize the color cast in the image.

When you use the neutral eyedropper to tell Photoshop that a particular pixel is supposed to be neutral, it automatically performs separate Levels adjustments on the individual red, green, and blue channels so the resulting tone is neutral. In a way, it's kind of like white balance. By setting the neutral point correctly, all the other colors fall into line and the color cast is eliminated.

Step 5: Click OK to Accept the Edits

If you like the new color, you're done with the image. If you don't like the new color—or if the color cast has changed—you might not have clicked on a pixel that was truly supposed to be neutral. Click again in a different place until you find a point that results in a neutral image.

All the eyedroppers work this way—if you don't like the initial result, simply click again in another location. You can also use the droppers and sliders interchangeably. So, you might set the white point with the dropper, but then set the black point with the slider. As you practice more with the Levels control, you'll get a better idea of which controls are best for particular operations.

When you're finished adjusting your image, click OK.

Bad White Balance in JPEG Images

This technique can also sometimes work for correcting bad white balance in JPEG images.

NEUTRALIZING IMAGES IN APERTURE, LIGHTROOM, AND CAPTURE NX

In Aperture, you can neutralize color casts using the Gray tint slider located in the Exposure adjustment (you might also find that the White Balance dropper will fix your color cast problems).

In Lightroom, you'll use the White Balance dropper, while in Capture NX, you use the Set Neutral Point dropper in the Levels & Curves edit.

TUTORIAL 11.10   CORRECTING COLOR WITH CURVES

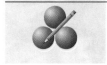

Whereas Levels lets you edit the black, white, and midpoints, with Curves you can set up to 14 different points at any location along the curve, allowing you to precisely edit particular tonal ranges. Earlier, you saw how to use Curves to achieve a Levels-like correction. In this tutorial, you're going to use Curves to perform a color correction that would be impossible with Levels.

Step 1: Open the Image

In Photoshop, open the image bud.tif located in the Tutorials/Chapter 11 folder on the companion CD-ROM. (See Figure 11.52.)

Step 2: Check the Histogram

A quick look at the histogram shows that our blacks are not clipped, meaning we don't really want to move the black point. Nevertheless, the image is too dark so the

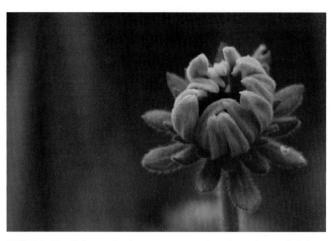

FIGURE 11.52   Using a single curves control, we're going to brighten this image, and adjust the color to make the yellow stand out a little more.

shadow areas are going to need to be lightened. As you've already seen, the background of the Curves dialog box provides a reference grid that shows midpoints and quarter-points along the curve. Click the bottom-left quarter-point and drag up to brighten the shadow areas. (See Figure 11.53.)

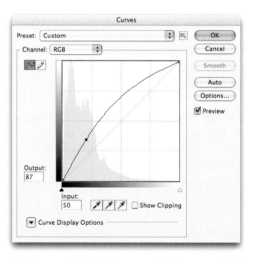

FIGURE 11.53   For this image, we're leaving our white and black points where they belong and beginning our editing by adding a point to brighten the shadow details.

There's no right or wrong place to start when correcting this image. However, it's usually a good idea to begin with either the highlights or shadow areas to map out the extremes of contrast in your image before you worry about the midtones.

Step 3: Adjust the White Point

With this single adjustment, the image already looks better, but we've lost a little contrast (a fact that is confirmed by the histogram). Lower contrast means less information between the black and white points, so we're going to restore our highlights by adding a point in the upper quarter of the curve. (See Figure 11.54.)

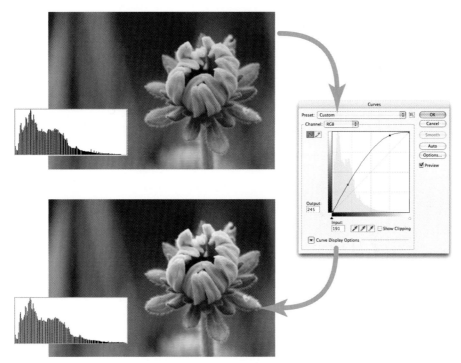

FIGURE 11.54   To restore some lost brightness, we apply another point in the highlight region of our curve. Our curve now has two additional points, and the contrast in the image is improved.

Step 4: Add Midpoint and Tweak

As is clearly visible in the Curves dialog, a change in one part of the curve can greatly affect another part of the curve. Consequently, correcting with curves is not usually a straight procedural process. You often have to move between points, tweaking and retweaking them as you reshape the curve into just the right shape. For this final step, we moved the first point to deepen the shadows a little more, and added an additional point to brighten some of the middle tones to produce the image in Figure 11.55.

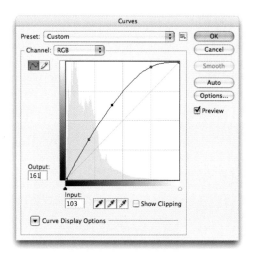

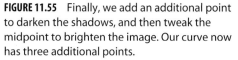

FIGURE 11.55   Finally, we add an additional point to darken the shadows, and then tweak the midpoint to brighten the image. Our curve now has three additional points.

Step 5: Warm Up the Flower

For our final correction, we want to add some warmth to the flower to separate its yellowish/green tone from the predominantly green background. Earlier, you saw how you could use the Channels palette in Photoshop to view individual color channels in your image. Because some edits are easier to perform on individual color channels than on the entire composite image, the Curves dialog allows you to adjust the curve of individual color channels. (Similarly, the Levels dialog lets you perform levels adjustments on individual color channels.)

Therefore, to warm up the flower, we want to add some red to the yellow tones that make up the flower. In the Curves dialog, open the Channel pop-up menu and select Red. You should see a new flat curve. Don't worry, the curve you just built is not gone—you can switch back to it by selecting RGB from the Channels pop-up menu. The Curves dialog lets you keep separate curves for each channel, plus the RGB composite.

Your goal is to shift the curve to the top left to add more red. However, you only want to move the part of the curve that contains the yellow information of the flower, so as not to adjust the red in the green tones of the background.

With the Curves dialog open, click in the image and drag it around. A circle will appear on the curve and move around as you drag the mouse. This circle is showing

you where the selected pixels map onto the curve. In this way, you can easily identify the part of the curve that needs editing.

Command-click (or Control-click if you're using Windows) on part of the yellow flower. Photoshop will automatically add a point to the part of the curve that
corresponds to this color. Drag this point up and to the left to add more red. This will
warm up the flower, but will also add a red cast to your image. To compensate for
this, add one point on each side of your first point, and drag them back down to flatten the curve. (See Figure 11.56.)

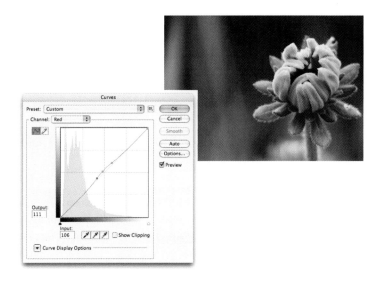

FIGURE 11.56   The final Red channel adjustment
shown here isolates a very small part of the curve
and boosts the red just a tiny bit, resulting in our
final image, which has a much warmer flower.

Learn your Curves Keyboard Shortcuts

*Photoshop's Curves dialog provides a number of keyboard controls that make it easier to
make tiny adjustments to control points on the curve. Consult Photoshop's built-in Help to
learn more about these.*

HUE/SATURATION

While both Levels and Curves are great for altering color and improving tone, when
it comes to adjusting the saturation of an image or altering a specific color, there is a

better choice: Hue/Saturation. In this tutorial, we're going to take a quick look at saturation adjustment using Hue/Saturation. Later, we'll see more about altering color using this powerful tool.

The goal of this tutorial is to fix up the image shown in Figure 11.57. While the image looks okay as-is, it's a little bit flat. We're going to use a saturation adjustment to give it more punch.

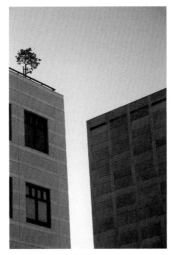

FIGURE 11.57   This image looks okay in terms of contrast and tone, but we want to liven it up a little.

TUTORIAL 11.11   ADJUSTING SATURATION

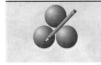

Step 1: Open the Image

In Photoshop, open the image `saturation buildings.tif` located in the Tutorials/Chapter 11 folder on the companion CD-ROM.

ON THE CD

Step 2: Perform Saturation Adjustment

In Photoshop, choose Image > Adjustments > Hue/Saturation, or press Command/Control-U. The Hue/Saturation dialog box appears.

Drag the Saturation slider to the right to about +35 to increase the saturation in the image. (See Figure 11.58.)

Using the Hue slider, you can choose to alter the hues in the image, or lighten or darken the image using the Lightness slider.

Step 3: Adjust the Saturation of the Blue Building

The Hue/Saturation dialog box also lets you make adjustments to specific color ranges.

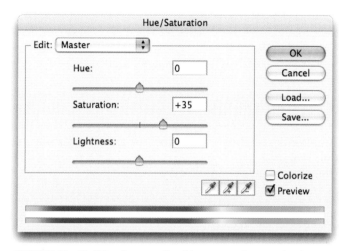

FIGURE 11.58   We'll begin our edit with an overall saturation increase.

From the Edit menu, choose Blues. Now, hold your mouse over the blue building. The pointer should change to an eyedropper. Click with the dropper on one of the darker blue tones on the building.

The color ramp at the bottom of the dialog box will immediately show you the range of colors you have selected. The name of that color range will now appear in the Edit menu. You are now configured to edit just the blue tones in the image (your original master adjustment is still there, and you can switch back to it by selecting Master from the Edit menu).

Drag the Saturation slider to the right to edit only the blue building. (See Figure 11.59.)

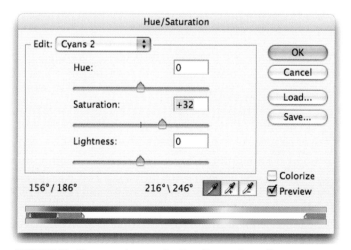

FIGURE 11.59   You can also use the Hue/Saturation adjustment to alter specific color ranges.

Step 4: Adjust the Yellow Building

Now select Reds from the Edit menu, and then click on the orange building to select its color range. Drag the Saturation slider to the right to increase the saturation of the orange building.

You can control how wide a range of colors is adjusted by dragging the sliders on either end of the color range selector. On each end are two sliders, an inner one and an outer one. The inner sliders control the range of tones that will be adjusted, while the outer sliders control the falloff, or transition zones, between the edited and unedited colors.

Your final image should look something like the one shown in Figure 11.60.

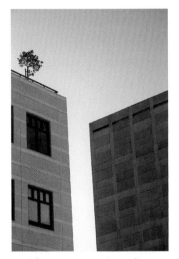

FIGURE 11.60 After our saturation adjustments, the final image has better, more saturated color.

You can also use the Hue/Saturation control to *reduce* the saturation in an image, which is often a good way to tone down distracting colors and tones that are just a little too "hot." Simply apply a negative Saturation adjustment to reduce saturation.

THE STORY SO FAR

At this point, you should feel very comfortable reading histograms to help assess what corrections are necessary in an image. You should also have a grasp on performing basic contrast and tone corrections using Levels and Curves, and should feel comfortable adjusting some of your own images. Before you head off to your photo archive, though, look at one more example that might save you a little frustration.

As you've already seen, you can use Levels, Curves, and Hue/Saturation to adjust the tones and colors in your image. However, it's important to note that even though Curves provides a lot of flexibility in terms of being able to limit your corrections to a particular color, there will still be times when you cannot set enough control points on the curve to constrain your edit to a particular part of the image.

Consider Figure 11.61. The two figures in the foreground are way too dark and need some major midtone adjustments. However, using Curves, there's no way we can select a part of the curve that targets only their midtones, because other parts of the image—the ground and the grass—fall on the same part of the curve. So, as we boost the midtones in the figures, we end up wrecking the contrast in the ground and grass and quickly posterizing it.

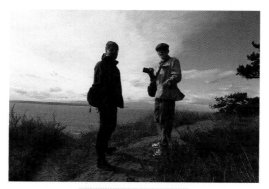

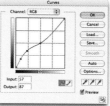

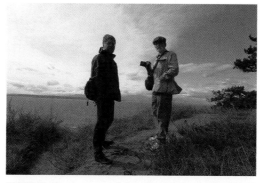

FIGURE 11.61   As powerful as the Curves tool is, it still doesn't provide a way for us to isolate only the tones in the two figures in the foreground. As such, there's no way to change their tones without also changing the tones in other parts of the image.

Remember that the points along the curve in the Curves dialog aren't related to a specific *part* of your image. Rather, they represent *all the pixels* in your image that have that color. Right now, we haven't covered the tools necessary to fix this particular image, but you'll get to them soon enough. In the meantime, try out some Levels and Curves adjustments on your own images to get a better feel for the effects of these tools.

RAW CONVERSION

In This Chapter

- Raw Workflow
- Raw Editing
- Copying Your Edits from One Image to Another
- Nondestructive raw workflow in Photoshop CS2/CS3
- What More Do You Need?

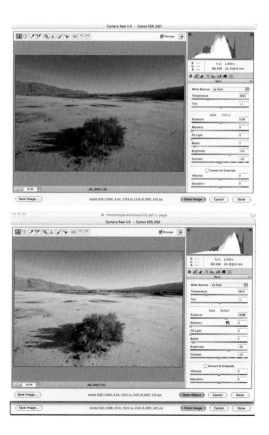

If you've made the decision to shoot raw, you'll have an extra step in your post-production workflow. As a raw shooter, you'll have to go through some form of raw conversion process. As you learned in Chapter 2, "How a Digital Camera Works," when you shoot in raw mode, all the processing that normally happens inside your camera is offloaded to your computer, where you have more control and flexibility. However, depending on the software you've chosen, raw conversion can make your editing workflow a little different from what it is when you shoot JPEG.

Fortunately, with programs like Aperture, Lightroom, iPhoto, Adobe Bridge, and Nikon Capture NX, raw workflow is now *much* easier than it used to be. In fact, you may find that your raw workflow is not any different from a JPEG workflow. However, when working with raw files, your editing options will differ from working with JPEG files because you have some additional tools and capabilities.

In this chapter, we'll explore all the specifics and strategies of raw conversion. You'll learn how best to approach your raw workflow and how to use your raw converter to edit and adjust your raw images.

RAW WORKFLOW

As with any workflow, your first post-production step as a raw shooter is to import your images from your camera's media card (or cards). You move raw files just like you do JPEG files, by copying them with a card reader, or by transferring them directly from your camera through a cable. If you're using a workflow application like Aperture, iPhoto, or Lightroom, those apps can import images directly from your card. Otherwise, you can use your OS's file manager to copy the images over.

As you learned in Chapter 10, "Workflow," one of your first workflow steps (after importing) is to sort through your images to find the keeper images you want to pass through to the editing and correction stage. In JPEG files, this is fairly simple because, these days, just about any application can read JPEG files. If you're using Mac OS X, you can open raw files in the Finder, just as you would a JPEG. Raw files are automatically opened in Preview so you can see a full-size preview of the image. However, as with any raw converter, the conversion software built in to the Mac OS doesn't support *all* raw formats. If you're using a very new, or much older camera, you may not be able to view raw files in Preview.

If you're a Windows user, some simple applications will allow you to view raw thumbnails and previews from within Windows Explorer. dpMagic (*www.dpmagic. com*) makes a free program for Windows XP and Vista™ called dpMagicCommunity that allows you to view thumbnails inside Windows Explorer. dpMagic Plus sells for $10 and adds full-screen preview, EXIF display, a histogram, and more. As with all raw converters, the dpMagic converters may or may not support your chosen camera, so you'll want to check the Web site to see if your camera is supported.

While viewing from the file manager can be handy, of far more utility are the browsers that are built in to the image-editing applications we've been talking about. With Aperture, Lightroom, Capture NX, iPhoto, and Adobe Bridge, you'll be able to easily browse and compare thumbnails of your raw images, just as you can with JPEG images.

All cameras store a low-res JPEG preview of your raw file inside the raw file itself. Many applications can show you this preview as a way of letting you quickly review your raw files. But most apps go a step farther and actually perform an initial raw conversion based on some automatic settings. These conversions usually yield a very good image—sometimes good enough that you won't need to perform any additional correction.

When contemplating your raw workflow, you'll want to consider the following notes, depending on what application you choose to use for your raw conversion.

Photoshop/Bridge. Adobe Photoshop uses a plug-in called Photoshop Camera Raw for its raw conversions. This plug-in is included with Photoshop, so you don't have to install anything else to use Photoshop for your raw conversions. Bridge is the file browser that's bundled with Photoshop, and it also uses Photoshop Camera Raw for raw conversion. Bridge lets you quickly and easily view thumbnails and previews of your raw images, and assign ratings and metadata. So, with Photoshop/Bridge, your workflow will be to copy your raw files to a folder on your drive, and then browse through that folder using Bridge. In Bridge, you can assign ratings and keywords, and then filter your view to only show images with a particular rating. In this way, you can easily choose your selects, and then view only those. (See Figure 12.1.)

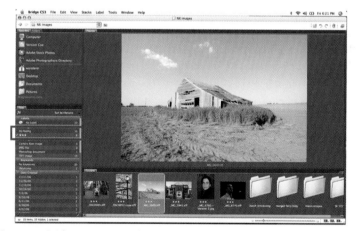

FIGURE 12.1   In Bridge, we can easily opt to filter our images to only view those that have a particular rating. This makes it easy to work with only our select images.

Bridge builds its thumbnails by performing a quick raw conversion on each file. When you're ready to work with a particular file, double-click on it, or press Return, and that file will open up in Photoshop Camera Raw. (See Figure 12.2.)

Camera Raw is a plug-in, not a standalone application. As such, it has to be hosted by another application. When you double-click on an image in Bridge, the

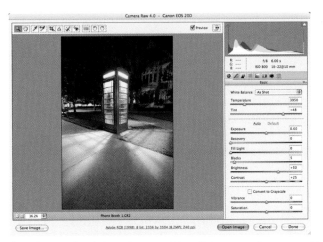

FIGURE 12.2 Photoshop Camera Raw's interface provides all the controls you need to convert your raw file. In fact, you may find that you don't need to perform *any* additional edits in Photoshop.

raw file is passed to Camera Raw, hosted by Photoshop. Alternately, you can select an image and press Command/Control-O to open that image in Camera Raw, hosted by *Bridge*. The capability to host Camera Raw in either application means you can let Photoshop batch process your raw files while you work in Bridge, or let Bridge batch process raw files while you work in Photoshop. For more information on Camera Raw workflow, practices, and editing, consult my book *Getting Started with Camera Raw*, which you can order from *www.completedigitalphotography.com*.

If you drag and drop a raw file onto Photoshop's icon, or choose File > Open from within Photoshop, and select a raw file, Photoshop will open that file with Camera Raw, just as if you had selected the file from within Bridge.

Aperture/Lightroom/iPhoto. Raw workflow is very straightforward with any of these apps because, workflow-wise, they treat raw files just like JPEG files. Import them into your library and you'll be able to immediately preview your images and begin comparing, rating, and picking. When you've chosen the images you like, you're ready to move on to editing.

Nikon Capture NX. Version 1 of Capture NX only works with Nikon raw files, so if you're using a different type of camera, you'll need to perform your raw conversion somewhere else before bringing your images into Capture NX for editing. If you're a Nikon shooter, though, Capture NX raw workflow is very simple. The program's built-in browser lets you view thumbnails of raw images, make comparisons, and then open images for editing.

Bundled raw converters. If your camera has raw capability, some kind of raw conversion software will most likely come bundled with the camera. You can use these apps to perform your raw conversions, and they very often include simple browsers that allow you to view thumbnails of your raw images. If your image editor of choice doesn't yet support your camera's raw format, these tools might be your only option. Your workflow will be to perform your raw conversion with one of these programs, save the result as a TIFF or Photoshop file, and then open that file in your image editor of choice.

No matter what application you choose, once you've selected the images you want to work with, you're ready to begin correcting and adjusting your images. If you're using Photoshop or your camera's bundled raw converter, you'll convert your image first, save it (usually as a TIFF or Photoshop file), and then perform any additional edits in your normal image editor. Your images won't always need additional editing after raw conversion, and in the rest of this chapter you'll get a better idea of which edits will be performed in your raw converter, and which will be performed later.

If you're working with Aperture, Lightroom, iPhoto, or Capture Raw, you won't have separate raw conversion/editing steps. In these programs, you can freely adjust raw conversion parameters alongside "normal" edits.

WHICH CAMERA RAW ARE YOU USING?

Different versions of Photoshop and Photoshop Elements support different versions of Camera Raw. So, if you're using an older version of Photoshop or Photoshop Elements, you may not be able to use the latest version of Camera Raw. In addition to not having access to the latest features, if you have to run an older version of Camera Raw, you probably won't have compatibility with the latest cameras. Unfortunately, the only way around this is to upgrade your copy of Photoshop.

DNG—The Adobe Digital Negative Specification

As you've learned, different cameras produce different types of raw files. Unlike JPEG or TIFF files, there is no generally accepted standard for raw. That means that anyone who wants to make a program to process raw files has to figure out how to decode each vendor's file format. Since most of these formats aren't published, this can be a very time-consuming, tedious process. This is also why raw converters must be updated every time a new raw-capable camera comes along.

Photoshop Camera Raw currently supports more raw formats than any other converter, which means that Adobe has done a lot of hard, diligent work in learning to process lots of raw formats. In an attempt to simplify the situation, Adobe has published the Adobe Digital Negative specification, an open standard for raw format data. Their hope was that camera manufacturers would embrace the digital negative spec, and create cameras that output digital negative files natively. So far, this hasn't happened. While one or two smaller vendors make a few cameras that can produce DNG files (the digital negative format), the big players—Canon, Nikon, Sony, Panasonic, Fuji—have largely stayed away from it.

Similarly, not many software vendors have embraced DNG. While Aperture offers DNG support, Apple's involvement in DNG has revealed that the format is not as universal and open as we would all like it to be.

Most vendors have stayed away from the format for the simple reason that Adobe is in control of it. While Adobe's interests seem purely benign, many companies fear investing time and energy in a technology controlled by one of their rivals. In the end, this is probably wise, and we will most likely not see a wide acceptance of DNG until a truly open standard—one controlled by a standards committee such as the ISO—is developed.

In the meantime, you can use the free Adobe DNG Converter to convert your raw files to DNG format. Why would you bother to do this? Currently, DNG files offer the following advantages:

- They guard against obsolescence. With your images in DNG format, you'll presumably always be able to open them, even if the giant international electronics conglomerate that made your camera goes out of business. Because DNG is an openly published standard, many people feel there will always be support for it.
- DNG files can include a copy of your original raw data, so you don't have to give up any extra proprietary information that may be buried inside.
- DNG files serve as a wrapper that holds both your original raw file, and the associated XMP data file (the list of raw conversion parameters Photoshop Camera Raw generates). This makes the files more easily moved, backed up, and emailed.

On the downside, converting to DNG takes time, consumes more storage, complicates your workflow, and, for the most part, doesn't buy you any new capabilities. For the time being, it's pretty safe to ignore DNG files, unless you have a specific workflow need they can help address.

RAW EDITING

Once you've picked the raw files you want to process, you're ready to start editing. If you're working with Photoshop, you'll open these images in Photoshop Camera Raw; if you're working with Aperture, you'll simply open the Adjustments HUD. In Lightroom, you'll move into the Develop module. No matter which raw converter you choose to use, you will find the same basic controls. These adjustments work the same way in all the raw converters we've discussed, and we'll cover them in detail before moving on to look at some of the unique controls provided by each app.

In Chapter 6, "Building a Workstation," you learned about nondestructive editing. This is an important concept to understand when working with raw files, as all raw converters employ a nondestructive paradigm.

Nondestructive Editing

Your raw converter provides tools that will let you alter exposure, white balance, color, and many other image parameters your camera adjusts automatically when you're shooting in JPEG mode. Some of these tools are no different than what you'll find in your regular editing program, while others provide capabilities you won't find when working with nonraw images in a normal editor. However, all the edits you make in your raw converter are nondestructive.

No matter what raw converter you use for your images, your original files are *never* altered. In fact, they really *can't* be, because they don't contain usable image data. So, there's no way for you to apply an edit that increases the contrast in a raw file, say, because the raw file doesn't have any finished image data.

Like any nondestructive editing system, your raw converter stores the adjustments you make as a separate list. In Aperture and Lightroom, this list is stored inside your library. Any time you want to view a particular file, the program looks up the edits you've made and applies them to that image. In Photoshop Camera Raw, you have a choice of storing your edits within an internal library, or as sidecar XMP files. These are simply small text files that are stored in the same directory as your raw file. Any time you open a raw file, Camera Raw looks to see if an XMP file exists, and then converts the raw file using any instructions stored in that file.

The Camera Raw Preferences dialog box provides a simple option for storing edits in the internal database, or as sidecar files (Figure 12.3). Sidecar files have the advantage that you can easily move them around with your images, so it's easy to pass raw files and sidecar files to other people, move them to other computers, back them up, or recover from a crash.

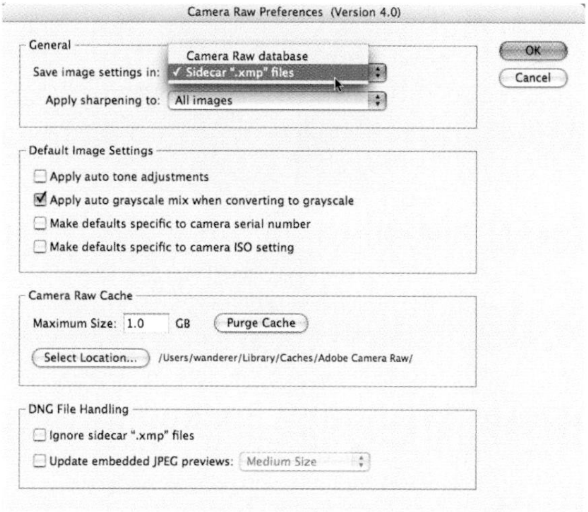

FIGURE 12.3   Using Camera Raw's Preferences dialog box, you can specify whether you want your edits stored in Camera Raw's internal database, or as separate, sidecar XMP files.

Basic Raw Adjustments

In general, you'll approach raw conversion the same way you approach any type of image editing: you'll begin with cropping and straightening, then correct the image's tone (white point, black point, and contrast), and then the color. If you're working with Aperture, Lightroom, Capture NX, or the most recent version of Camera Raw (version 4), you'll also be able to tackle dust, spot, and red-eye troubles. All versions of Camera Raw provide full access to the chromatic aberration and vignetting correction we saw earlier.

There is one slight workflow change you'll want to consider when working with raw files, and that is to address the white balance of the image before you begin any additional edits. In this section, we'll look at each of the basic raw conversion parameters, in the order you'll often want to employ them.

White Balance

As you learned in Chapter 2, when you shoot in JPEG mode, your camera adjusts the color in your image so it is properly *white balanced*, or calibrated for the color of the light under which you are shooting. When you shoot with raw, this adjustment is performed within your raw converter, so it's simple to change the white balance of your image *after* you shoot, during raw conversion.

Raw converters provide a simple White Balance slider that allows you to adjust the white balance in your image from blue to yellow. Simply move the slider back and forth to change the white balance, and overall color of your image. (See Figure 12.4.)

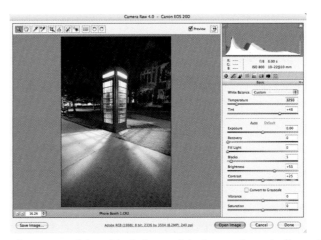
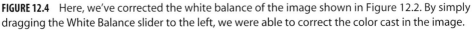

FIGURE 12.4 Here, we've corrected the white balance of the image shown in Figure 12.2. By simply dragging the White Balance slider to the left, we were able to correct the color cast in the image.

Because it's impossible to build a light source out of completely pure, refined substances, most man-made light sources have a little bit of a tint to them, which can often introduce slight color casts that can't be corrected with a simple white-balance adjustment. The Tint slider in your raw converter lets you adjust the color in your image from green to magenta, and is intended to allow you to correct any extra tint introduced by impurities in your light source.

In Chapter 11, "Correcting Tone and Color," you learned how data can be lost as you brighten and darken the tones in your image, pushing them from one part of the histogram to another. As you saw, if you stretch the tones in your image around too much, you begin to see tone breaks and other visible artifacts in your image. One of the great things about the white-balance control in your raw converter is that it's a completely "free" edit. No tones are used up as you make white-balance adjustments, because the raw converter simply changes its fundamental assumptions about the primary colors it uses to decode the color in your image. Therefore, if possible, you should make your color adjustments using the white-balance adjustment.

White-balance adjustments can also sometimes yield a change in contrast, so it's not a bad idea to perform your white-balance adjustment first, to get a better sense of the actual tone in your image. You can then move on to your tonal adjustments.

All the raw converters we've been talking about also include a White Balance eyedropper, which allows you to set white balance by clicking on a point in your image. The raw converter reads the color at this point, and uses that measurement as a basis for its white balance. While it may seem intuitive to click the dropper on something white, you actually want to click on something that is a neutral gray. In an image with really bad white balance, it can be difficult to tell what, if anything, in the scene was neutral gray. So, you may need to first use the sliders to get a ballpark white balance that renders your colors a little more accurate, and then use the dropper to zero in on something gray in your image.

A better approach is to use a white-balance card like the one discussed in Chapter 7, "Shooting." (See Figure 7.36.) As you'll recall, in this mixed-lighting night shot, I shot a second frame that included my WhiBal white-balance card. Because I know the WhiBal card is neutral, I can click on it with the White Balance dropper in my raw converter to calculate an accurate white balance. (See Figure 12.5.)

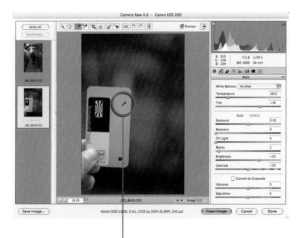

White-balance dropper

FIGURE 12.5 We're using Photoshop Camera Raw's white-balance dropper to sample our gray card. This will give us an accurate white balance, as you can see in Figure 7.36.

After clicking on the gray card, our white-balance will be set properly, and the Temperature and Tint sliders will have new values. However, so far all we've done is correct the white balance in the shot of our white-balance card—we also want correct white balance in our original shot. You can either take note of the new Temperature and Tint values and manually change them in your original image, or you can copy them into your original image, a process we'll explore later in this section.

Exposure

The Exposure slider in your raw converter allows you to adjust the overall exposure of your image and is analogous to the White Point slider in the Levels dialog box.

As you move the Exposure slider, your image will get brighter, just as when you move the White Point slider to the left in the Levels dialog. In Photoshop, Lightroom, and Aperture, as you move the Exposure slider you'll see your image change, and you'll see the tones in your histogram shift around. As with any type of adjustment, as you adjust exposure, you want to be very careful not to clip any of your highlight and shadow tones. (See Figure 12.6.)

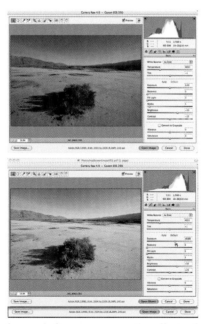

FIGURE 12.6   In this before and after, you can see the effects of a positive exposure adjustment. Our image is brighter, and our histogram shows a white-point change, just as we saw when adjusting the white point in the Levels dialog box.

Brightness

The Brightness slider is a midpoint, or gamma adjustment, that brightens or darkens the mid-tones in your image, without altering the white and black point. That said, it *is* still possible to clip highlights when using the Brightness control, so keep a close eye on the histogram while adjusting brightness.

Exposure and Brightness *both* provide the capability to lighten and darken your images, so why would you choose one over the other? We'll see the answer to that question shortly.

Blacks

If you're using Photoshop CS3 or Lightroom, you'll have a Blacks slider, which allows you to change the black point of your image. (In earlier versions of Photoshop, this was called *Shadows*.) Moving this slider to the right is the same as moving the black point in the Levels dialog to the right—your image will get darker.

If your raw converter doesn't have a Blacks control (or a Brightness slider), you can affect these same edits using a standard Levels or Curves adjustment.

Contrast

If you're using Photoshop Camera Raw, Lightroom, or Aperture, you'll have a Contrast slider. Dragging the Contrast slider to the right increases the contrast in your image, dragging it to the left decreases. This adjustment is simply performing a simultaneous black point and white point adjustment. The practical upshot is that you'll see the data in your histogram spread out farther, or squish tighter together. As with other adjustments, keep an eye out for clipping on both ends.

With these five controls you can perform the bulk of your tonal adjustments and color adjustments. (See Figure 12.7.) However, most raw converters provide some additional, important tools.

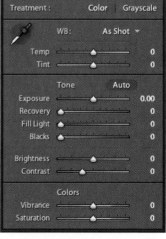

FIGURE 12.7   In Aperture and Lightroom, you'll find raw conversion controls similar to the ones we've seen here. Capture NX and most other raw converters also provide these types of controls.

Highlight Recovery

In Chapter 8, "Metering and Exposure," you learned an exposure strategy wherein you expose your images to try to capture as much data as possible from the brightest parts of your scene. This allows you to capture much more usable data, which allows you to make more edits before you see tone breaks and other image artifacts. However, the danger of this approach is that you run the risk of overexposure, which can lead to clipped, blown-out highlights.

As mentioned in Chapter 8, your raw converter probably has the capability to recover overexposed highlights when only one or two color channels are overexposed. This can often serve as a safety net when you end up pushing your exposures too far when shooting.

If all this sounds too good to be true, it isn't. At least, not completely. For example, Figure 12.8 shows an image with overexposed highlights. You can see from the histogram that the right side is heavily clipped. The clipped highlights are mostly in the sky, which has blown out to almost complete white.

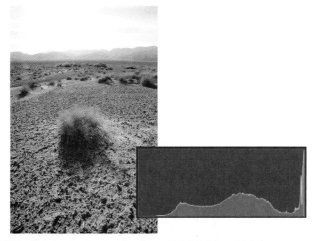

FIGURE 12.8 This image has badly clipped highlights, which have resulted in the sky being overexposed to almost complete white

After using the highlight recovery feature in Aperture, we produced the image shown in Figure 12.9. Note that Aperture was able to recover an amazing amount of detail in the overexposed area. Now, instead of a blank field of white sky, you can see textured clouds.

While Aperture did a great job of rebuilding much of the lost sky, some areas—especially around the sun—were completely clipped. These parts of the image could not be restored, and so are left overexposed. Sometimes, you'll be able to recover all your clipped highlights, and sometimes you'll only be able to recover some of them—it all depends on whether a highlight was partially or completely clipped. Also, some raw converters do a better job with highlight recovery than others.

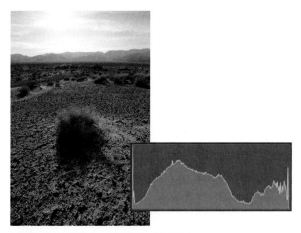

FIGURE 12.9   After performing highlight recovery, we have an image with restored detail in the sky.

In most raw converters you perform highlight recovery by simply sliding the Exposure slider to the left. As you slide, the spike on the right side of the histogram should get smaller, and the detail in your highlights should improve. You may have to underexpose your image a lot to recover all the highlights, but you can brighten it back up again using the Brightness slider.

This is one reason why you have both Exposure and Brightness controls. Since you'll sometimes be using the Exposure slider to *lower* the exposure in your image to recover highlights, you'll use the Brightness slider to brighten it back up again, with your new recovered highlights intact.

If you keep sliding to the left and your lost highlights don't reappear (and the corresponding white spike remains on the right side of the histogram), that particular area has been clipped in all three channels. A completely clipped highlight is simply lost, and there's nothing you can do about it.

After adjusting white balance, highlight recovery will probably be your next workflow step. Alternately, you may want to try recovering your highlights *before* you do anything else. After all, if you can't recover your highlights to your satisfaction, you might end up abandoning the image.

Once you've recovered any lost highlights, your image will probably be significantly darker, since you will have lowered the exposure of the image. Your next workflow step will be to try to restore brightness to the rest of the image, which you can do with the brightness control, or with a few other adjustments we'll see shortly.

Note that, while highlight recovery is a great tool, it's *not* a magic bullet. When you engage in a highlight recovery operation, your raw converter must perform a *tremendous* amount of interpolation. Simply put, it makes up a *lot* of data and, obviously, there will be times when it may not be able to do an especially good job of this. It's much better to try to expose to avoid clipped highlights than to rely on highlight recovery. Consult Chapter 8 if you're not clear on raw exposure strategies and how to implement them.

THE RECOVERY SLIDER

Photoshop Camera Raw 4.0 and Lightroom both provide a Recovery slider, which lets you recover clipped highlights without lowering the overall exposure of your image. While you can still perform highlight recovery with the Exposure slider, the Recovery slider means you won't have to later try to brighten your image to compensate for any darkening introduced by your highlight recovery operations. This can be a great timesaver, and can speed up your overall editing workflow.

Raw Exposure Strategy Revisited

Let's take another quick look at the raw exposure strategy we outlined in Chapter 8. As you'll recall, we explained that due to the nature of linear capture, your camera stores more tonal information in the brighter parts of your image than in the darker areas. As such, if you err on the side of overexposure, you capture tones into the areas where your camera stores the most data. The advantage of this technique is that you end up with data-rich images that can always be darkened to restore shadow information. The result is shadows with extremely low noise

The downside to this technique is that, out of the camera, your images will look washed out and overexposed. But, as you lower the exposure to darken the shadow tones back to where they're supposed to be, you'll be able to restore shadow tones without incurring noise. (See Figure 12.10.)

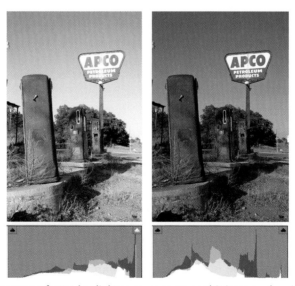

FIGURE 12.10   Because we performed a slight overexposure on this image, when it comes out of the camera it looks slightly washed out, with all of its tones gathered on the right side of the histogram. However, after a simple exposure adjustment in our raw converter, we can darken the tones to restore the image to a normal contrast ratio.

See Highlight Recovery in Action

On the companion disc, in the Chapter Tutorials/Chapter 12 folder, you'll find a QuickTime movie called Highlight Recovery.mov. *This short clip will show you another real-world highlight recovery example.*

Shadow/Highlight Adjustment

Photoshop Camera Raw 4.0, (the version of Camera Raw that is included in Photoshop CS3) Lightroom, Aperture, and Nikon Capture NX all include special *adaptive* tools for performing highlight recovery. Sometimes called *perceptual* adjustments, these tools let you automatically perform dramatic edits to only the shadows and highlights in an image without having to create complex selections or masks.

Consider the Levels control you used in Chapter 11. With the Levels adjustment, you can easily alter the values of specific tones in your image. However, when you change the value of a particular tone, *every* pixel in your image that has that tone will be adjusted. So, for example, maybe you feel that a shadow area in a portrait image needs to be lighter, so you use a Levels adjustment to brighten it, only to realize that the same adjustment also brightens the dark irises in your subject's eyes.

The problem is that the Levels adjustment doesn't know whether specific pixels are shadow tones or not. It simply alters all pixels that have a particular value.

Adaptive tools are more intelligent about the way they operate. When you use an adaptive Shadow tool to brighten shadows, your image editor analyzes your image to determine which pixels are shadows, and brightens only those. In addition, because shadows are usually bordered by a transition zone that blends into non-shadowy areas, an adaptive shadow tool "rolls off" the adjustment it applies to pixels bordering your shadow areas to create smooth transitions into nonaffected areas. (See Figure 12.11.)

An adaptive highlight control works the same way, but allows you to alter the values of highlight areas in your image. Your image editor automatically works to determine which tones in your image are highlight tones and only adjusts those.

Ultimately, both of these tools do nothing more than brighten or darken pixels in your image. Although they do a great job of determining *which* pixels to alter, you still need to keep an eye out for all the same artifacts you are wary of when using Levels or Curves.

Fill Light in Photoshop Camera Raw 4.0 and Lightroom

Photoshop Camera Raw version 4 and Lightroom both provide a Fill Light slider, which you can use to perform an adaptive shadow adjustment on your raw file. Adobe calls this control Fill Light because it creates an effect very similar to what you'd get if you fired a fill flash into your scene, but a little better. Shadows are brightened, but the highlights and brighter midtones in your image are left alone. This tool is just like the Shadows slider in Photoshop's Shadow/Highlight adjustment, which we'll learn more about in the next chapter.

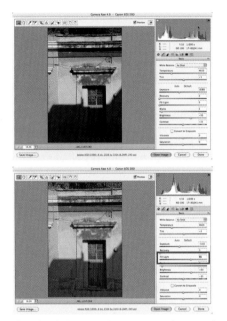

FIGURE 12.11   The Fill Light slider in Camera Raw 4.0 lets you brighten or darken only the shadow tones in your image. Here, you can see how it successfully identified the shadow in our image and brightened it without creating a conspicuous boundary between the adjusted and unadjusted areas.

Fill Light in Previous Versions of Photoshop Camera Raw

Previous versions of Camera Raw don't have a Fill Light slider, or any type of adaptive shadow control. So, if you're using an earlier version you'll have to wait and perform your shadow brightening in Photoshop. In the next chapter, you'll learn about the adaptive shadow tool that's built in to Photoshop CS, CS2, and CS3.

Highlights and Shadows in Aperture

In Aperture, you can use the Highlights and Shadows sliders to adaptively adjust both the highlights and shadows in your image. Both sliders provide additional options, which let you refine their effect, and we'll cover the details of these adjustments in the next chapter.

D-Lighting in Capture NX

In Nikon Capture NX, you'll find adaptive shadow control in the D-Lighting edit. Like the Fill Light slider in Camera Raw, you simply slide the D-Lighting slider to brighten shadow tones. Capture NX automatically calculates which tones in your image get adjusted.

Additional Adjustments in Photoshop Camera Raw 4.0

Both Lightroom and Camera Raw 4.0 provide a few additional controls. Because Lightroom is nondestructive, it doesn't really matter when you choose to use these commands. As discussed earlier, in Photoshop, raw conversion is a separate step from the rest of your edits. For speedier workflow, you might want to try to do as much processing as possible within Camera Raw itself, rather than waiting to perform edits in Photoshop. Except for white balance, there's no image-quality reason to perform edits in Camera Raw rather than Photoshop. There can be a workflow advantage to performing certain chores in Camera Raw, though, since Camera Raw has some handy batch processing features.

Depending on the version of Camera Raw you're using, you'll find these additional sliders:

Saturation (all versions): The Saturation slider allows you to increase or decrease the saturation of the colors in your image just as you would using the Hue/Saturation adjustment in Photoshop.

Vibrance (version 4): The Vibrance slider is akin to the Saturation slider, but only affects certain tones in your image, most notably primary colors. The Vibrance slider allows you to increase the saturation in your image without compromising flesh tones, something that's difficult to achieve with a normal Saturation slider. (See Figure 12.12.)

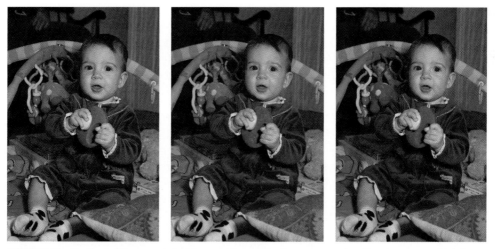

FIGURE 12.12   On the left is our original image. The center has seen a saturation increase, which has yielded stronger colors, but produced harsh flesh tones. The right image has had a strong Vibrance increase, which has boosted saturation while protecting the flesh tones.

Convert to Grayscale (version 4): The Convert to Grayscale checkbox allows you to convert your image to grayscale. You'll learn more about this feature in Chapter 15, "Special Effects."

Tone Curve (all versions): All versions of Photoshop Camera Raw provide a tab containing a tone curve. Just like the Curves adjustment you learned about in the last chapter, the Curve tab allows you to selectively brighten and darken specific tonal ranges in your image, and provides an additional level of adjustment power over the basic raw conversion sliders.

Sharpening and Noise Reduction: These sliders are not meant to replace the sharpening and noise reduction filters within Photoshop, which are very powerful tools. Rather, they're intended to provide an initial, subtle amount of adjustment. They allow you to restore some of the sharpness that's removed by the low-pass filter in your camera (see Chapter 2) without applying all the sharpening that may be required for your final output. In the Camera Raw Preferences dialog box (press Command/Control-K while in Camera Raw), you can set the Apply Sharpening To pop-up menu to specify that the sharpening settings should be applied to your final images, or only to the preview you see within Camera Raw. Setting to sharpening previews lets you work in Camera Raw with an approximation of what your final sharpening will be, but without actually sharpening your final image. You can sharpen your image by hand later, just as you always would.

Split Toning (version 4): Split Toning allows you to create duotone-like effects. The highlights in your images can be toned with one color, while the shadows can be toned with a separate color.

Lens Correction (all versions): Allows you to perform the same type of chromatic aberration and vignette correction you can perform with the Lens Correction filter in Photoshop CS2/3 (see Chapter 11 for more details).

Tools: In addition to these sliders, Camera Raw provides zoom and pan tools, a white-balance eyedropper, color samplers, crop and straighten tools, and rotate tools. In version 4, you'll also find red-eye reduction and retouching tools.

Workflow Options

As you learned in Chapter 2, a raw converter has to go through many steps to produce a final, usable image. In addition to calculating color and adjusting the image according to the settings you define using the raw conversion sliders discussed earlier, your final image has to be mapped into a specific color space and rendered at a given bit-depth. In Photoshop Camera Raw, you can control these steps in the workflow section of the Camera Raw dialog box. In Camera Raw 4.0, you can edit these parameters by clicking on the workflow options link at the bottom of the dialog. (See Figure 12.13.)

Bit Depth allows you to select either 8 or 16 bits per pixel. If you're ultimately going to save into a JPEG file, you'll want to select 8 bits. If you want to have as much editing latitude as possible—that is, to be able to make many adjustments before you see tone breaks and posterization— select 16 bits.

In Chapter 2, you also learned about color spaces. Camera Raw allows you to select among several color spaces. sRGB is the smallest, while ProPhoto RGB is the largest. Adobe RGB is a good general-purpose color space. While you might think it's best to simply choose the largest color space possible, there are times when a

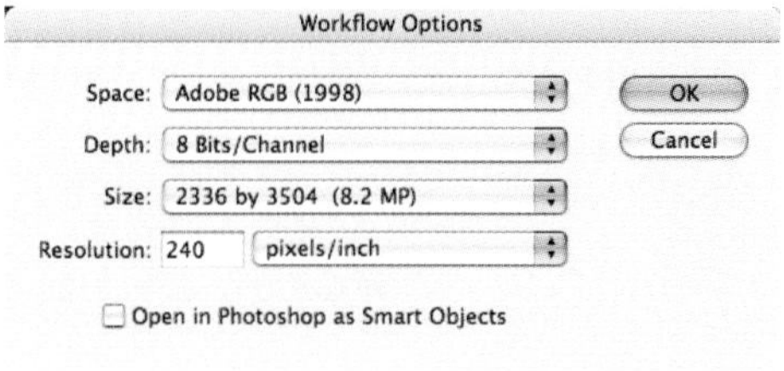

FIGURE 12.13   In Photoshop Camera Raw 4, you can adjust workflow options by clicking the workflow options link at the bottom of the Camera Raw dialog box. In previous versions of Camera Raw, these options are permanently displayed at the bottom of the main dialog.

larger color space can cause problems. If your image doesn't have a tremendous amount of color information in it, trying to stretch that data to fit into a larger color space will result in tone breaks and posterization. Fortunately, with a raw file you can easily try converting into different color spaces to test the results.

Camera Raw also allows you to specify pixel dimensions for the resulting file. This simply provides you with a quick way to produce a smaller image if your ultimate goal is Web output, email, or a smaller print size. You can perform this same resizing later using Photoshop's Image Size command.

Why Don't Lightroom, Aperture, and Capture NX Have These Features?

Since these three programs are nondestructive editors, they process your raw file in real time. As such, they don't ever need to write out a file in a particular size, color space, or bit depth until you decide to export to a specific file format. Consequently, you don't define these "workflow" parameters until you save an image out of one of these applications.

OPEN, SAVE, AND DONE

At the bottom of the Camera Raw window, you'll find Open, Save, and Done buttons (they sit in different places in different versions of Camera Raw). Each allows you to perform a different task with your processed image.

Open processes your image according to your settings and opens the resulting file in Photoshop.

Save processes your image and then saves the results in a standard TIFF, Photoshop, or JPEG file. Camera Raw even provides you with automatic naming options.

Both options also store the conversion parameters you specified in Camera Raw, either in Camera Raw's internal database or in a Sidecar XMP file, depending on how you've configured your Camera Raw preferences.

Done doesn't open or save the image, but simply stores the conversion parameters you've specified.

→

Because all these options store your conversion parameters, the next time you open the same raw file, Camera Raw will automatically show you your previous settings.

The final conversion can take time, so if you have a lot of images to process, it's often best to open them all in Camera Raw, set the settings for each image, Select All, and press Save. You can then walk away while Camera Raw makes its way through your images.

COPYING YOUR EDITS FROM ONE IMAGE TO ANOTHER

Because raw conversion is a nondestructive process—that is, because your edits are kept separate from the data—you can easily copy raw parameters you've specified for one raw image to a bunch of other raw images. White balance, exposure, brightness, and contrast adjustments, even cropping and straightening, can all be easily applied to multiple raw files. Very often, images shot under the same lighting conditions can be corrected using the same edits. Consequently, you might be able to quickly process an entire batch of images by editing the first image and then copying those settings to the other images in the batch.

Copying Raw Edits in Photoshop Camera Raw

If you're using Camera Raw, you have a few options for performing the same raw adjustments on multiple images. First, you can open several images simultaneously into Camera Raw. Each image will be displayed in a filmstrip view on the left side of the window. You can switch from one image to another by clicking on it. Click the Select All button, and then use the Synchronize button to synchronize your edits. (See Figure 12.14.)

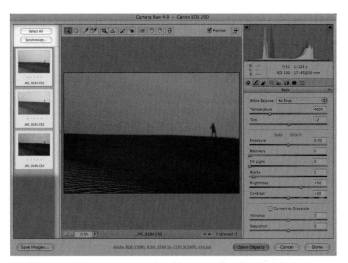

FIGURE 12.14   You can open several images simultaneously in Camera Raw, and then synchronize your edits between all of them.

Any edits you make will be applied to all the currently synchronized images. Synchronized images only remain synchronized during the current session. The next time you open the images, you'll have to resynchronize them.

You can also use Adobe Bridge to copy edits from one file to another. After you've made adjustments to one raw file, those edits can be copied and pasted onto another file.

If you're using Bridge CS3, select that image in Bridge and choose Edit > Develop Settings > Copy Camera Raw Settings to copy the settings from the selected file. Next, select the raw files you want to copy the settings to and choose Edit > Develop Settings > Paste Settings.

If you're using Bridge CS2, select the image whose settings you want to copy, and then choose Edit > Apply Camera Raw Settings > Copy Camera Raw Settings. Then, select the image(s) you want to apply the settings to and choose Edit > Apply Camera Raw Settings > Paste Camera Raw Settings.

Both versions also offer a "Previous Conversion" option in the same menu. This simply takes the last settings you applied to any image and applies them to the current selection of images. This saves you the trouble of doing a copy step, if the settings you want to copy were the ones you just applied.

Copying Edits in Aperture

In Aperture, you can use the Lift and Stamp tool to copy edits from one image to another. Select the Lift tool and then click on the image whose edits you want to copy. The Lift tool will automatically change into the Stamp tool. Click with the Stamp tool on any images you want to copy settings onto.

Copying Edits in Lightroom

Lightroom provides the same options as Camera Raw 4. By using the Edit > Develop Settings menu, you can easily copy edits from one image to another. This menu also lets you synchronize settings between images, and apply auto adjustments.

Copying Edits in Nikon Capture NX

In Capture NX, you'll find options for copying and pasting settings in the Batch menu located at the bottom of the Edit List palette.

WHAT MORE DO YOU NEED?

Raw conversion used to be a hassle, requiring a complex assortment of programs and a cumbersome workflow. Fortunately, with the current generation of tools, you can work with your raw files just as you would with JPEG, TIFF, or Photoshop files. What's more, if you've done a good job with your exposure, you may find that you don't need to perform any processing beyond your raw conversion settings.

Because it's possible to copy settings from one raw file to another, it's easy to create complex batch processing schemes that make short work of processing huge numbers of images. In this regard, working with raw files can actually be *easier* than working with JPEGs. We don't have the room here to detail the batch processing capabilities of every raw converter, but you can find out more by checking your program's documentation.

Once you've made your raw conversion, you'll be ready to consider any additional edits you might want to make. We'll cover these edits in the next two chapters. In Chapter 14, "Imaging Tactics," we'll also learn a method for working with raw files in Photoshop using a completely nondestructive workflow that will afford much greater editing flexibility.

13

BUILDING YOUR EDITING ARSENAL

In This Chapter

- What You'll Learn in This Chapter
- Brushes and Stamps
- Masks
- Layers
- Other Editing Tools

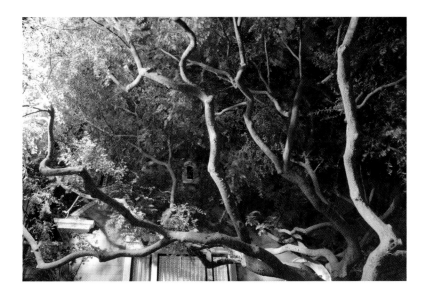

In Chapter 11, "Correcting Tone and Color," you learned about levels and curves, two important tools you'll use in almost all your everyday editing tasks. In this chapter, we're going to add to your toolbox by covering more of the basic tools and functions you'll use in everyday editing. These are the features you'll turn to again and again—in many different combinations—to perform your corrections, adjustments, and modifications. As in previous chapters, although the examples and tutorials in this chapter are built around Photoshop, any decent image editor should provide equivalent functions. Even if you're using a different image editor, you should have no trouble translating the workflows and approaches presented in this and the following chapters to your program of choice.

WHAT YOU'LL LEARN IN THIS CHAPTER

The image-editing market is fairly crowded with complex, powerful applications. It is far beyond the scope of any one book to detail the features of all these applications. However, bear in mind that many of these applications contain features you don't *need* as a photographer. For example, Photoshop contains tools for web designers, broadcast video producers, feature film special effects creators, prepress printing professionals, graphic artists, 3D modelers, scientists, and many other professions. Sure, it's called *Photo*shop, but it's really a general-purpose graphics application.

Because Photoshop has so many features, it's easy to become overwhelmed and intimidated by it. If that starts to happen, just remember that as a photographer, your needs will most often be fairly simple: tonal and color corrections, simple spot removal, perhaps some selective editing. Obviously, if you like to create very stylized images, you might perform more "special effects" type operations. In most cases, though, if you've done your in-camera work right, your image editing needs will be very simple, and there will be many Photoshop tools and techniques you'll never need to learn.

In this chapter, you'll learn about the image-editing tools that will concern you as a photographer. If your image editor provides additional features, you can probably ignore them for your basic photography work.

BRUSHES AND STAMPS

Many of the retouching and editing tasks performed in a real darkroom are dependent on brushes, masks, and paint. Your image editor is no different, except your brushes and tools are digital. To get good results from them, you still need a good hand, a trained eye, and well-designed tools—just as in a real darkroom.

The documentation that came with your image editor should offer plenty of information on how to use your editor's tools. In this section, therefore, you're going to learn what each tool is good for—you'll need to refer to your image editor's manual to learn the details of how to modify and adjust each tool. Being able to identify the right tool for a particular job will often save you a lot of time.

Brushes

Hopefully, your image editor includes a good assortment of paintbrushes and air-brushes. A good Brush tool offers an easy way to select different brush sizes and shapes, has *antialiased* (smooth) edges, pressure sensitivity when used with a drawing tablet, and variable opacity. (See Figure 13.1.)

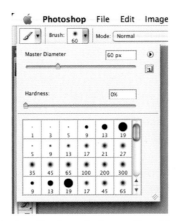

FIGURE 13.1   The Photoshop Brush controls—scattered between the Brush palette and the toolbar—let you select brush size, transfer mode, and opacity.

You'll use these tools for everything from painting out unwanted elements in a scene to performing certain types of color correction, creating masks, and "brushing in" different special effects.

To use a Brush tool well, you need—obviously—good hand-eye coordination and a feel for the brush. Your brush skills will develop over time and will be greatly aided by the use of a drawing tablet. In addition to providing a more intuitive interface, a drawing tablet is *much* easier on your hand than is a mouse. If you plan to do a lot of image editing, consider investing in an inexpensive pressure-sensitive drawing tablet such as the Wacom® tablet shown in Figure 13.2. At the time of writing, you can get a good Wacom pressure-sensitive tablet for less than $100.

You'll also want to spend some time learning the different keyboard shortcuts that augment your Brush tool. Learn your brush's features, including parameters such as opacity, *spacing*, and *repeat rate*.

If you're using Photoshop, you'll quickly become dependent on these brush-related keyboard shortcuts:

B: Selects the Brush tool.
Shift-B: Toggles between the Brush and the Pencil tools.
[: Shrinks the size of the current brush.
]: Enlarges the size of the current brush.

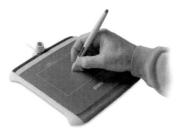

FIGURE 13.2   A pressure-sensitive drawing tablet such as this Wacom Graphire® is a must-have for serious image editing.

Brushes in Nondestructive Editors

If you're using a nondestructive editor like Aperture or Lightroom, you won't have brushes, because these programs don't manipulate individual pixels. Future versions of these applications may provide more brush-based capabilities. Capture NX, however, does give you some painting capability by allowing you to create color and mask layers within your document that can then be painted in or out using a brush.

Rubber Stamp or Clone

One of the most powerful—and seemingly magical—tools in your image-editing toolbox is a Rubber Stamp tool (also known as a Clone tool), which provides a brush that performs a localized copy from one part of your image to another, as you brush. (See Figure 13.3.)

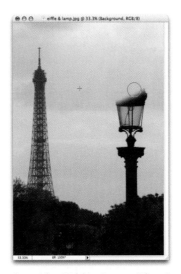

FIGURE 13.3   When you paint with a Rubber Stamp (Clone) tool, your image editor copies paint from your source area (the crosshairs) to your target area (the circle).

You'll use the Rubber Stamp tool for everything from removing dust and noise to painting things out of your image to painting things into your image. The advantage of a Rubber Stamp tool over normal copying and pasting is that the tool's brush-like behavior lets you achieve very smooth composites and edits.

In Photoshop, Change Your Painting Cursor

You'll have a much easier time with the Rubber Stamp tool, and all of Photoshop's Brush tools, if you make a simple change to Photoshop's preferences. In the Preferences dialog, select Display & Cursors, and then change Painting Cursors to Normal Brush Tip. This will show a cursor that's the exact size of your chosen brush, making it much easier to see the effect your brush strokes will have.

Study your Rubber Stamp tool's documentation to learn the difference between absolute and relative cloning, and how to set the tool's source and destination points. When you rubber-stamp an area, you want to know how to quickly select a source area, so it's imperative to learn the tool's controls.

Your image-editing application provides many more tools and functions, but you'll use the brushes and stamps the most. These are also tools that will not be heavily discussed or documented in the rest of this book. For the rest of these tutorials, it is assumed you know how to follow an instruction such as "Rubber-stamp out the telephone wires." If you don't know how to use these tools, consult your manual.

TUTORIAL 13.1   CLONING VIDEO TUTORIAL

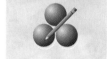

To learn more about cloning, watch the `Cloning Tutorial` movie located in the Tutorials/Chapter 13/Cloning folder on the companion CD-ROM. (See Figure 13.4.)

ON THE CD

Patch and Heal

Photoshop CS, CS2, CS3, and some versions of Elements include special variations on the normal Rubber Stamp tool. The Healing Brush works just like the Rubber Stamp tool, but with a bit more intelligence. Rather than copying pixels directly from the source location to your brush position, copied pixels are automatically adjusted for texture, lighting, transparency, and shading, so that your cloned pixels blend more seamlessly with the surrounding parts of your image. You can achieve the same results with a regular Rubber Stamp tool, but the Healing Brush is much easier to use. The Spot Healing Brush tool lets you instantly repair spots, dust, and other small, localized troubles with a single click. The Spot Healing Brush is especially useful for removing dust, slight lens flares, stuck pixels, and certain types of noise.

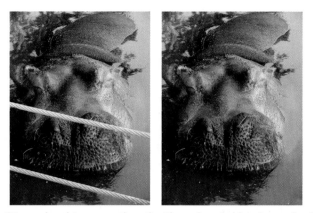

FIGURE 13.4 We used nothing more than the Photoshop Rubber Stamp (or Clone) tool to remove the wires from in front of this hippo. A Clone tool is a must for even the simplest touchups, so make sure you know how to use one. You can see how this image was corrected by watching the Cloning Tutorial movie located on the CD-ROM.

The Patch tool uses the same underlying technology as the Healing Brush tool, but it lets you patch an area by drawing around it with a lasso and then dragging that area over a part of your image that contains the texture you'd like to have in your selection. That texture is automatically copied and blended into your selection.

CLONING AND PATCHING IN APERTURE AND LIGHTROOM

With their initial release, neither Aperture nor Lightroom offers much in the way of brushing and painting. However, they do offer some simple cloning and patching tools that can be used for removing spots and dust from your image. These are *not* substitutes for a true Rubber Stamp tool—you won't be able to perform the types of edits you saw in the Cloning video. However, they will allow you to remove sensor dust and other spots and aberrations, and are sometimes useful for simple facial retouchings.

Consult the documentation to learn more about Aperture's *Spot and Patch* tool, and Lightroom's *Remove Spots* tool.

Dodge and Burn

In traditional darkroom work, dodging is the process of holding something in front of your print while it is being exposed in the enlarger, allowing you to underexpose a particular localized area. Burning is just the opposite—blocking out all of your image but one part to overexpose a particular localized area.

Both Photoshop and Photoshop Elements include excellent Dodge and Burn tools that work just like normal brushes. When you paint, the exposure of the underlying brushed part of the image is increased or decreased, depending on which tool you're using. Dodge and Burn tools are essential for facial retouchings, removing artifacts and blotches, increasing or decreasing exposure to add or remove emphasis from an area, and many other corrections, as you'll see in Chapter 15, "Special Effects."

MASKS

Masks are used for everything from compositing images together to constraining your edits and adjustments to particular parts of your image. Masks are much easier to understand once you realize that they are just like stencils you would use in a real darkroom or painting studio. The only difference is that, as you'll see, digital masks are much, much better.

Many photographers feel that masking is not such an important tool because they're not interested in creating weird special effects or wacky composites. Masking, however, can be an essential color-correction tool, allowing you to create adjustments and corrections that would otherwise be impossible. For example, if you want to color-correct only the background of an image, you might build a mask over the foreground elements. (See Figure 13.5.)

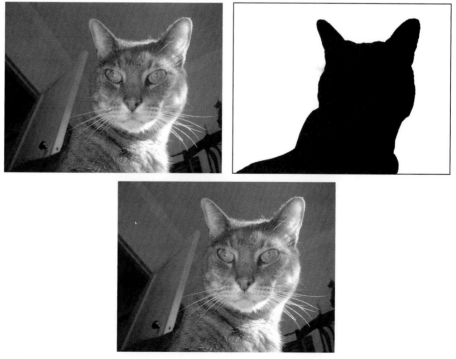

FIGURE 13.5   To correct the background of this image without altering the cat in the foreground, we created a mask that protects the cat during the Hue/Saturation adjustment that alters the background.

Similarly, a mask can serve as a stencil when you're combining separate images to create a single composite. If you want to superimpose a new element into an image, or replace a background image, good masking skills and tools are essential. (See Figure 13.6.)

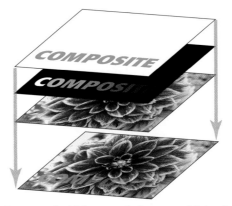

FIGURE 13.6   Masks are used to control which parts of a layer are visible when creating composites. You can think of a digital mask as sitting between two different elements in an image, to control how those two elements fit together. Similar to stencils, digital masks have the advantage of allowing for varying degrees of transparency. Although masks are essential for complex special effects work, they're also useful for basic color corrections and adjustments. Here, the top layer is being composited with the bottom layer, with a mask knocking out the background of the top layer so only the blue text gets combined with the flower.

Like many editing tasks, knowing how and when to use a mask is a skill. However, learning the basics of your masking tools is pretty simple once you understand a few simple concepts.

Mask Tools

Most image-editing applications offer many tools for creating masks, and you'll often find yourself using these tools in combination. Some tools, for example, are more appropriate for masking complex subjects, such as hair or fine detail. Other tools are more appropriate for masking geometric shapes or large areas of color. For building complex masks, you'll use a mixture of these tools.

Selection Tools

The simplest mask tools are the selection tools—the lasso and rectangular and circular marquees—that let you create basic selections by outlining areas of your image. You might not think of these as mask tools, but the selections they produce work just like a mask. Create a rectangular selection around an object, for example, and your editing tools will work only inside that selection. In other words, everything outside the selection is masked out. (See Figure 13.7.)

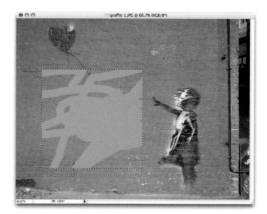

FIGURE 13.7   Creating a selection in your image editor is the easiest form of masking. Any operation—including simple paint strokes—are constrained within your selection. In other words, the selection is masking your image, just as a stencil would.

What makes these simple selection tools effective for complex masking is that most applications let you add and subtract from the selections you make. In Photoshop, for example, you can add to a selection by holding down the Shift key while you select more of the image. This method allows you to use different tools for different parts of your image. For example, you can use the Circle tool to select a curvy section of an object, then hold down the Shift key and use the Lasso tool to outline the rest of the object. (See Figure 13.8.)

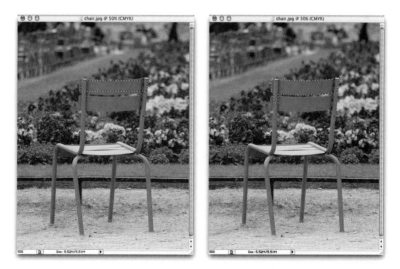

FIGURE 13.8   By holding down the Shift key when you use a selection tool, you can add to a selection. The capability to add to a selection allows you to use different tools to select different parts of an image. In this image, we used the Rectangular Marquee to select a rectangular-shaped area of the chair, and then the Lasso tool to trace around the edge detail.

Similarly, Photoshop lets you use the Option key (Alt if you're using Windows) to subtract from a selection. The ability to keep adding and subtracting to and from a selection with different tools is essential for building complex masks.

In the same family as the selection tools are Magic Wand tools that automatically hunt down similar colors to create selections automatically. As with other selection tools, Photoshop allows you to combine Magic Wand selections with selections made using other tools, by simply holding down the Shift or Option (Alt) keys.

No Masking or Selection in Aperture or Lightroom

At the time of writing, Aperture and Lightroom do not include any selection or masking. So, you have no way to mask edits within either of these programs. However, because both applications allow you to launch images into an external image editor, you can easily work your masking-capable editor into your Aperture or Lightroom workflows.

Mask Painting

The Photoshop QuickMask mode lets you create a mask by painting. (This feature is not included in Photoshop Elements.) To use QuickMask, click the QuickMask icon at the bottom of the main tool palette. In QuickMask mode, any areas you paint black will be selected when you exit QuickMask mode, and any areas you paint white will be unselected. (See Figure 13.9.)

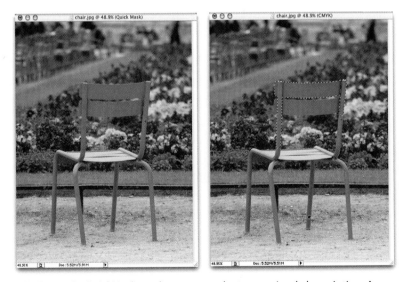

FIGURE 13.9   In QuickMask mode, you can select areas simply by painting. Areas painted red in QuickMask mode are selected when you switch back to normal mode. QuickMask is an easy way to make odd-shaped selections.

You can switch in and out of QuickMask mode as much as you like, meaning that you can combine its mask selection tools with your image editor's other masking and selection tools.

Color-Based Selection Tools

Many applications provide special tools for automatically selecting certain colors. Photoshop CS, for example, includes a Color Range command that can automatically select all occurrences of a particular color in an image. (See Figure 13.10.)

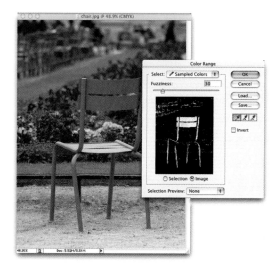

FIGURE 13.10   The Photoshop Color Range command lets you select all the occurrences of a particular color in your document.

Color Range will almost always select more pixels than you want, but the extra pixels can usually be easily removed with another selection tool.

QUICK SELECTION TOOL

Photoshop CS3 adds a powerful new selection option in the form of the Quick Selection tool. With it, you simply brush across an object you want to select. Photoshop automatically finds the edges of the object for you, and selects them. While it can't handle extremely fine detail like hair, and semitransparent objects, in many cases it builds very accurate masks, *very* quickly.

If you do a lot of masking work, the Quick Selection tool might be reason enough to upgrade to CS3. (See Figure 13.11.)

$\rightarrow$

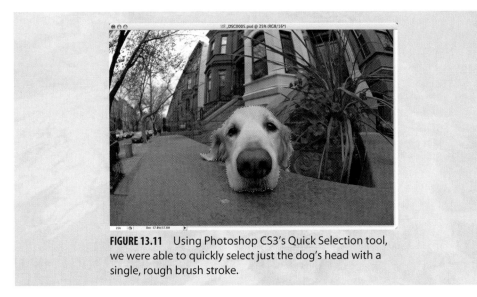

FIGURE 13.11   Using Photoshop CS3's Quick Selection tool, we were able to quickly select just the dog's head with a single, rough brush stroke.

Special Mask Tools

Some applications include special dedicated tools, such as the Photoshop Extract tool, which can perform complex extractions of difficult subjects, such as hair or transparent surfaces. (See Figure 13.12.) Extract doesn't create a mask, but it does let you isolate an image for compositing with another image.

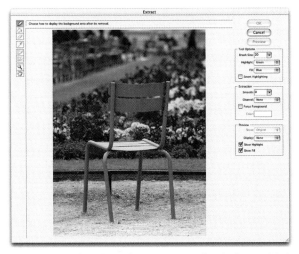

FIGURE 13.12   The Photoshop Extract tool includes sophisticated edge-detection capabilities for extracting part of an image. The result can then be composited with other images.

There are also several third-party masking plug-ins that can be added to any image editor that supports Photoshop plug-ins. Programs such as Corel® KnockOut, Extensis™ Mask Pro™ and Vertus FluidMask (Figure 13.13) provide a simple way of creating complex masks. If you find yourself consistently trying to mask difficult subjects such as hair or other objects with fine detail or transparency, it might be worthwhile to look into one of these options.

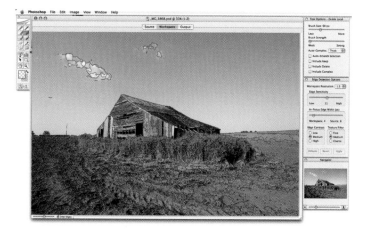

FIGURE 13.13   Masking plug-ins such as Vertus Fluid Mask allow you to create sophisticated masks with very simple tools. Fluid Mask does an excellent job of masking fine detail by first converting your images to vectors it can then easily manipulate.

Altering the Edge of a Selection

You usually don't want the border of a selection or mask to have a hard edge. Instead, you often want to *feather* or blur the edge of a selection so it blends smoothly into the background. This will make any edits or adjustments you make integrate more seamlessly into the rest of your document.

Photoshop and Photoshop Elements have long provided a Select > Feather Selection command that allows you to blur the edge of a selection by a specified number of pixels. In Photoshop CS3, Adobe has added the Refine Edge command, which provides a profound level of control for altering the edge of your selection, and previews of what your edge will look like when composited against a background. (See Figure 13.14.)

Saving Masks

Once you've used the various tools at your disposal to create a selection, you can save that selection as a mask for later use. In Photoshop, selections can be saved by clicking Select > Save Selection. At any time, you can use the Select > Load Selection command to restore your selection.

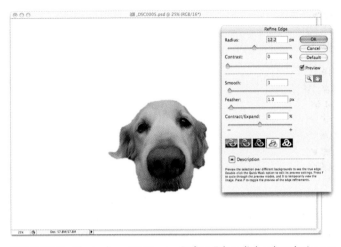

FIGURE 13.14 Photoshop CS3's new Refine Edge dialog box let's you easily feather and adjust the edge of a selection.

In Chapter 11, you saw how separate red, green, and blue channels are used to create a full-color image. You also saw that you can access and manipulate those individual color channels. Selections, or masks, are stored in a similar fashion. When you save a selection, your image editor creates a new channel in your document—called an *alpha channel*—and stores an image of your selection. (See Figure 13.15.)

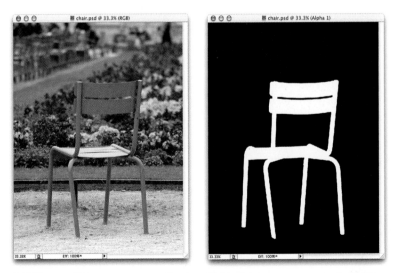

FIGURE 13.15 When you save a selection, Photoshop stores a grayscale, 8-bit alpha channel. Black areas of the image are masked, but white areas are not. If you load this alpha channel as a selection, the white area will be selected, just as if you had traced it with a Lasso—or any other selection—tool.

As you can see, any selection can be represented by a grayscale image—areas within the selection are stored as white pixels; areas outside are stored as black. (Another way of thinking of it is "black conceals, white reveals.") In Photoshop CS, you can create as many different selections as you want and store each in its own alpha channel. From the Channels palette, which you can open by clicking Window > Show Channels, you can access each mask by simply clicking its name. (See Figure 13.16.)

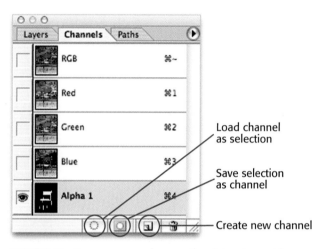

FIGURE 13.16   You can see and access the alpha channel from the Photoshop Channels palette.

Sort of Masked

So far, we've discussed masks as if they were simple stencils—edits are kept to either the inside or outside of the mask. Digital masks, however, are much more powerful than real-world masks, because in addition to masking an area, they can *partially* mask an area. Just as black pixels in a mask are completely opaque, gray pixels are only *partially* opaque, meaning you can use masks to apply effects and adjustments that vary across an image.

The easiest way to understand masks is to use them. In the following tutorial, you'll use a series of complex masks to alter an image.

TUTORIAL 13.2   CREATING COMPLEX MASKS

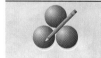

In this tutorial, you'll create and use a mask to perform a complex color correction. You won't be able to perform this tutorial in Photoshop Elements. But, even if you plan to use only Elements, it's worth working through this tutorial to get a better understanding of how masks work, and to learn about the Photoshop masking workflow.

Step 1: Open the Image

Open the image tree.jpg, located in the Tutorials/Chapter 13/Creating Complex Masks folder on the companion CD-ROM. (See Figure 13.17.) Your goal in this tutorial is to try to emphasize the foreground elements—the tree and the bent wrought-iron cage—by lightening the background. To edit the background without disturbing the foreground, therefore, you need to mask out the tree.

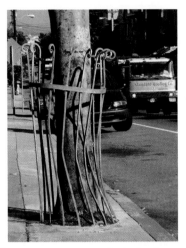

FIGURE 13.17   Because we want to edit the background of this image without disturbing the tree, we need to create a tree mask.

Step 2: Create a Mask

Using your choice of masking techniques, create a mask for the tree and the entire wrought-iron cage that surrounds the tree. Save the mask by clicking Select > Save Selection. To save time, the file tree with mask.psd has been included in the Tutorials/ Chapter 13/Creating Complex Masks folder. This image includes a prebuilt mask you can use for the rest of this tutorial. (See Figure 13.18.) (In case you're wondering, this mask was created by simply painting over the tree and fence using the Photoshop QuickMask tool.)

Step 3: Load the Mask

Before you can use a mask, you must load it. Open the Channels palette. You should see separate channels for red, green, blue, and your mask (called Alpha 1). At the bottom of the Channels palette are a series of buttons. The far left button is the Load Channel as Selection button. (See Figure 13.19.) Drag the Alpha 1 channel on top of this button; Photoshop will load the channel as a selection. (If you end up clicking the Alpha 1 channel, your document will switch to a view of that channel. Click the RGB channel at the top of the Channels palette to return to viewing the entire, full-color image. Then, try again to load your selection.)

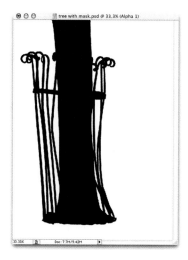

FIGURE 13.18 This mask was built using the QuickMask tool and is included in the Tutorials/Chapter 13/Creating Complex Masks folder.

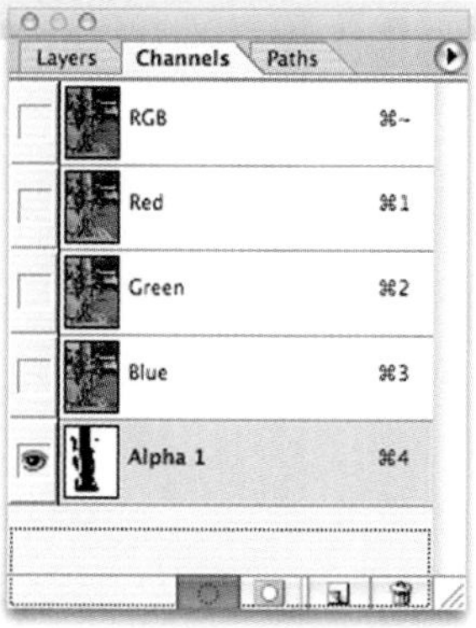

FIGURE 13.19 You can load a mask as a selection by dragging its icon in the Channels palette to the Load Channel as Selection button at the bottom of the Channels palette.

Sometimes, after loading a mask, it can be difficult to tell what is selected and what isn't. For example, with the tree mask loaded, it's difficult to tell whether the foreground or background is masked. To find out, click the Paintbrush tool and brush around on the image. You should see that the paint is going only into the background because the tree is completely masked. Click Undo to remove your brushstrokes. (If Undo doesn't undo all the strokes, use the History palette to remove the brushstrokes.) If the paint is going into the foreground, your mask is backward. From the Select menu, click Invert Selection to reverse your mask. Now when you brush, your paint should go into the foreground.

Step 4: Fade the Background

With your mask loaded, you can now start manipulating the background. If the goal is to emphasize the foreground, you should try lightening the background using a simple Levels command.

Click Image > Adjust > Levels to open the Levels dialog box. In previous tutorials, you used the Input controls exclusively and learned how they allow you to change the distribution of tones within your image. So far, though, your Levels adjustments have redistributed the tones in your image so they fit between full black and full white.

However, what if your printer can't print full black? Many offset printers can't hold more than 85 percent black—any more ink and they jam up. Therefore, Levels includes a pair of output sliders that allow you to adjust the limits of the tonal range in your image. The distribution of tones specified by the input levels remains the same.

Let's eliminate many of the darker tones without changing the tonal relationships in our image. Slide the left output slider to roughly the midpoint (around 126) and click OK. This step should create a faded background. (See Figure 13.20.)

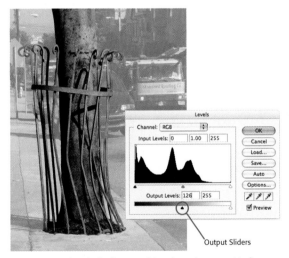

FIGURE 13.20 We've faded everything but the tree. Unfortunately, we've faded more than just what was behind the tree in the scene. The sidewalk in front of the tree has been faded as well.

Step 5: Assess the Change

Now it's time to assess if this was the right edit. With all those selection lines marching around, it can be difficult to see the image clearly. Click Select > Hide Selection to hide the selection lines; the selection is still active, you just can't see it. You can always click Select > Show Selection if you need to double-check that the selection is still active.

Sure enough, as we planned, the adjustment faded the background. Unfortunately, because we faded everything but the tree, our edit has also caused elements in front of the tree to fade. This is not really the desired effect. Click Undo to remove the Levels adjustment.

What we want is a Levels adjustment that won't affect the entire image uniformly, but will be stronger in parts of the image that appear farther away. It's time to create another mask.

Choose Deselect from the Select menu to deselect the current selection. We don't want anything selected right now.

Step 6: Create a Gradated Mask

Although you can use any number of selection tools to create masks, you can also paint them by hand, directly into an alpha channel. In the Channels palette, click the Create New Channels button (the second button from the right). A new channel will be created, selected, and filled with black.

Remember that black areas in a mask are completely opaque, white areas are completely transparent, and gray areas are somewhere in between. We want a mask that fades from fully opaque to fully transparent.

Set the foreground and background colors to black and white by clicking the Black/White switch next to the Photoshop color swatches in the main tool palette. (See Figure 13.21.)

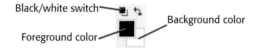

FIGURE 13.21   The Black/White switch lets you immediately set the foreground and background colors to black and white, respectively.

Now select the Gradient tool and drag from the top of the image to the bottom to create a complete black-to-white gradient. To make it easier to drag a straight vertical line, hold down the Shift key while dragging to constrain movement to 45° angles.

Step 7: Try the New Mask

Click the RGB channel in the Channels palette to switch back to full-color view. Now, load the new channel by dragging the Alpha 2 channel to the Load Channel as Selection button. A selection will appear that covers about half the image. Don't worry—Photoshop has loaded the complete mask; it's choosing to outline only areas that are more than 50 percent masked. Click Select > Hide Selection to hide the selection, and then apply the same Levels adjustment you did in Step 4. (See Figure 13.22.)

This is the effect we wanted—a lightening of the image that gets stronger from bottom to top. Unfortunately, the effect is no longer confined to just the background, it's fading the tree as well. Click Undo to remove the Levels adjustment, and let's make another new mask.

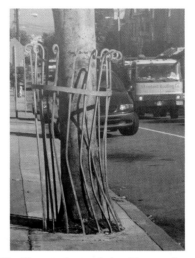

FIGURE 13.22   We get a better fade with a graduated mask, but now our tree is fading along with the background.

Step 8: Create Yet Another Mask

Go back to the Channels palette and delete the Alpha 2 channel by dragging it to the trash can at the bottom of the palette. Now make a new channel.

We want to create a gradient that fills the entire document *except* where the tree is. Unfortunately, the Gradient tool will fill the whole channel unless we *use the tree mask we already created*. Load the first mask (the tree) by dragging the Alpha 1 channel to the Load Channel as Selection button. You should see the outline of the tree mask.

Now, click on the Gradient tool and make a top-to-bottom, black-to-white gradient. You should end up with something like the mask shown in Figure 13.23. The tree is completely black, meaning it's completely masked and will not be affected by any editing operations, whereas the background is masked with a gradient, meaning the effect of any editing operations will vary from top to bottom. Click the RGB channel to view your color image.

Step 9: Fade the Background

Now, load your new mask by dragging it to the Load Channel as Selection button on the Channels palette, and apply your Levels adjustment. You should see a Levels change that affects only the background but varies from the bottom to the top of the image.

With this mask, you can now independently edit the foreground and background of your image. Try experimenting with different color corrections and filters. The image in Figure 13.24 has had a more severe Levels adjustment applied to it, and some subtle desaturations of the foreground and background. 🪓

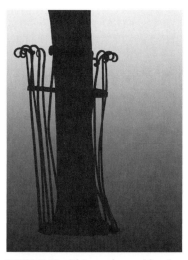

FIGURE 13.23   This mask provides the gradient we need to create our fade while masking out the tree.

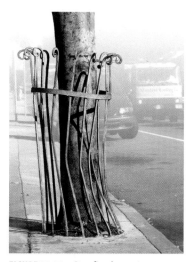

FIGURE 13.24   Our final tree image includes some extra color desaturations and levels adjustments.

MASKING IN NIKON CAPTURE NX

Capture NX provides many nice features, but one of the most important is its Upoint editing tools that make masking easier than in any other image-editing program. In Capture NX, when you want to create a mask, you click with the Color Control Point tool on the area you want to mask. Capture NX automatically analyzes the color you clicked on, and calculates and builds a mask. If that sounds too good to believe, believe it! The masking tools in Capture NX really work, and really are that easy to use. (See Figure 13.25.)

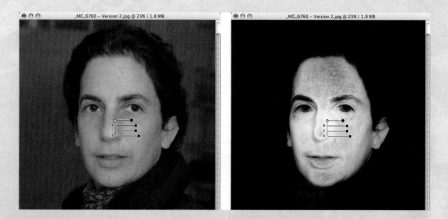

FIGURE 13.25   In Capture NX, we created the mask shown on the right with a single click of the Control Point tool. Capture NX automatically analyzes the image to create this complex mask.

> Novice image editors will find masking simple to pick up in Capture NX, while more experienced users will find they can create complex masks far more quickly than in any other program.

LAYERS

Layers are pretty easy to understand. If your image editor provides a layer facility, you'll be able to stack images—and parts of images—on top of each other within a document. A robust layer facility provides you with the ability to more easily make the types of corrections you saw in the last tutorial, and—if you structure your layers properly—allows you to go back and tweak your edits later.

Some Layer Basics

If your image editor provides layer controls, you'll need to spend some time learning how they work. Following are some of the basics of using the Layers control in Photoshop and Photoshop Elements. (Note that Layers weren't added to Photoshop until version 3. If you're using an earlier version, it's time to upgrade!)

Creating, Deleting, and Moving Layers

Fortunately, layer management is very simple in Photoshop or Photoshop Elements—you simply use the Layers palette. On the bottom of the palette are all the controls you need to create and delete layers. (See Figure 13.26.) Right now, you need to worry only about the Create layer and Delete layer buttons located on the right side of the palette.

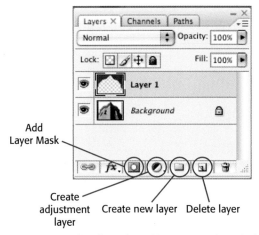

FIGURE 13.26 The Photoshop CS3 Layers palette includes simple button controls for creating and deleting layers.

When you create a new layer, it will appear as part of the layer stack in the palette. Because new layers are empty, your image won't look any different. All edits—whether painting, filters, or image adjustments—happen in the currently selected layer. Note that you can turn off the visibility of a layer by simply clicking its eye icon.

Layers that are higher in the Layers palette obscure any lower layers, and you can rearrange layers by dragging them up or down the stacking order. Note that you cannot change the order of the lowest layer—the Background—unless you double-click it to turn it into a normal, floating layer.

New layers are completely transparent, whereas the Background layer is completely opaque. (Obviously, as you paint into a layer, Photoshop changes the opacity of that part of the layer so your paint is visible.)

Opacity and Transfer Modes

You can change the opacity of the currently selected layer by simply sliding the Opacity control in the Layers palette back and forth.

You can also change how the currently selected layer interacts with layers that are lower in the stacking order by selecting a *blending* (or *transfer*) mode from the pop-up menu in the Layers palette. Normally, the pixels in a layer simply overwrite any pixels that are lower down the stack. By changing the blending mode, you tell Photoshop to mathematically combine pixels, instead of simply replacing lower pixels with higher pixels. (See Figure 13.27.)

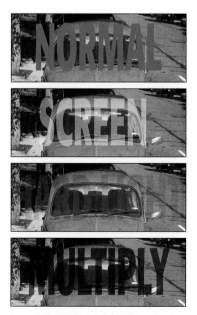

FIGURE 13.27 A few of Photoshop's blending modes, which control how one layer—in this case, the text—mixes with a lower layer.

As you work more with blending modes, you'll get a better idea of what they do. At first, don't worry about being able to predict their results. Just start playing around with them until you find the effect you like. You can lessen the effect of a mode by lowering that layer's opacity.

Blending modes are essential for creating some types of compositing effects. Figure 13.28 shows the creation of a virtual tattoo. When the tattoo image was layered directly on top of the body image, it looked like a simple overlay. Changing the tattoo layer's opacity helps some, but to create a realistic blending of the colors, we need to change the tattoo's transfer mode to Multiply.

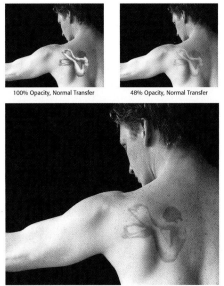

100% Opacity, Normal Transfer   48% Opacity, Normal Transfer

100% Opacity, Normal Transfer

FIGURE 13.28   To create this tattoo effect, we used a combination of an opacity change with a Multiply transfer mode to blend the tattoo layer with the skin.

In addition to compositing, you can use layer modes for hand-coloring grayscale images (Figure 13.29) and creating certain types of color corrections.

Watch That RAM!

As you add layers to your image, its RAM requirements will quickly skyrocket. Nothing affects Photoshop performance as much as RAM, so if you find your computer getting sluggish, it might be that Photoshop is running out of memory. The easiest way to shrink the RAM requirements of your document is to eliminate extra layers. If you think you've finished editing an individual layer, consider merging it with other layers using the Merge Linked or Merge Visible commands, located in the Layers menu.

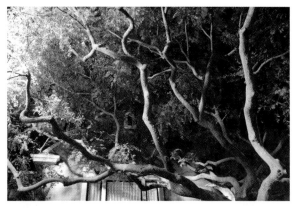

FIGURE 13.29 We created this hand-painted image by converting our photo to grayscale, and then hand-painting color into a new layer that was blended with our grayscale image using a transfer mode.

Adjustment Layers

One of the most powerful editing features in Photoshop and Photoshop Elements is their Adjustment layers, which let you apply Levels, Curves, and many other image-correction functions *as layers*. For example, when you add a Curves Adjustment layer to your document, Photoshop presents you with a normal Curves dialog box. You can adjust your image as desired but, when you click OK, instead of applying the Curves adjustment to the image—and altering the pixels in your document—it stores the adjustment in a new Adjustment layer that appears in your Layers palette. (See Figure 13.30.)

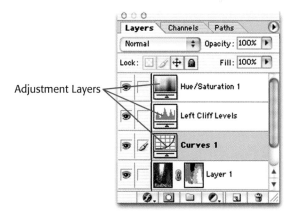

FIGURE 13.30 The top layers in this image are Adjustment layers. They apply, respectively, Hue/Saturation, Levels, and Curves adjustments to the underlying layer. Their settings can be altered or changed at any time.

An Adjustment layer affects all the layers beneath it. (You can constrain the effects of an Adjustment layer by grouping it with underlying layers; see the Photoshop online Help for details.) The real strength of Adjustment layers, though, is that you can go back at any time *and change the Adjustment layer's settings.* Therefore, if you decide at some point that you need a different Curves adjustment, you can simply double-click your Curves Adjustment layer and change its Curves parameters. In addition to providing flexible editing, Adjustment layers keep you from reapplying effects that result in data loss. You'll be using Adjustment layers extensively throughout the rest of this book.

Destructive versus Nondestructive Editing

If you open a Levels or Curves control (or any of the other adjustment tools mentioned in this chapter) and apply a change to your image, you are actually changing the original pixel data in your image. This is called destructive editing because you are destroying your original pixels. Adjustment layers do not affect your original data. Instead, they are adjustments that are applied on the fly to your image data as the data is written to the screen or output to a printer. These types of corrections are called nondestructive edits because your original image data is still there, allowing you to go back and change your edits and adjustments later. In programs like Aperture, Lightroom, and Capture NX, all edits are nondestructive. In Photoshop, only edits applied through Adjustment Layers are nondestructive.

Layer Masks

In the previous tutorial, you saw how alpha channels can be used to create masks. As powerful as alpha channels are, there is an easier way to perform many types of masking operations.

Photoshop CS allows you to attach a layer mask to any layer to create complex mask effects. From the Layers palette pop-up menu, you can choose to attach a layer mask to a layer. (See Figure 13.31.)

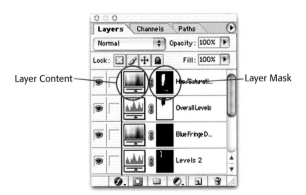

FIGURE 13.31 You can paint masking information directly into a layer's layer mask by clicking the layer mask thumbnail in the Layers palette.

Each layer entry in the Layers palette has a Document thumbnail and a Layer Mask thumbnail. You can click these thumbnails to switch between editing the layer or editing its layer mask. As you paint or edit a layer mask, you create masking information that works exactly like the alpha channel masks you saw earlier. Paint black into a layer mask, and the pixels in that part of the layer will be masked and, thus, invisible.

The complex masking effects you created in the previous tutorial could have also been created using Layer masks and Adjustment layers. The `Final Tree.psd` document on the companion CD-ROM (Tutorials/Chapter 13/Creating Complex Masks) includes all the Adjustment layers used to create the image shown in Figure 13.23.

ON THE CD

You'll get a lot of first-hand layer masking experience in the next chapter.

SIMPLIFYING PHOTOSHOP'S INTERFACE

As mentioned earlier, one of the things that makes Photoshop so complicated is that it contains features tailored to far more than simple photography. Fortunately, in the CS versions of Photoshop, you can streamline Photoshop's interface through the use of Workspaces, which allow you to highlight features tailored to a particular task.

From the Window > Workspace menu, you can select workspaces by task, or define your own workspace. For example, if you select the Color and Tonal Correction workspace, any menu items related to color and tonal correction will be highlighted, making it easier for you to ignore features you don't need.

Workspaces can also be used to control palette location, and to hide menu items. So, for example, you could completely deactivate menu items you don't need. Consult Photoshop's Help file for more info.

OTHER EDITING TOOLS

While the topics we've covered in this chapter are immediately useful for everyday editing tasks, they also form the foundation for much more complex corrections and edits you'll come to depend on for much of your normal editing work. In the next chapter, we'll learn how to build on the techniques you've learned here to create more sophisticated edits and corrections.

CHAPTER

14

IMAGING TACTICS

In This Chapter

- Editing Order
- Converting Color Images to Grayscale
- Finding Black-and-White Images
- Retouching
- Additional Editing Techniques
- Color Adjustment
- Editing
- Photoshop CS2/CS3 Smart Objects

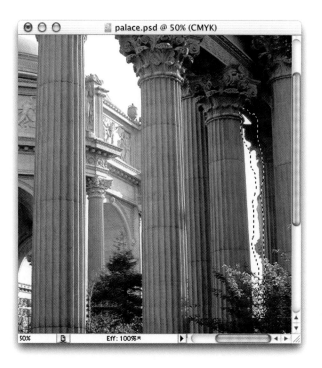

In this chapter, we're going to address specific image-editing problems you'll frequently encounter, and the workflow and order of operations you should use when editing and correcting. In the last chapter, you learned basic tonal and color correction. We'll build on those lessons in this chapter, refining your tonal adjustment skills and adding some important editing capabilities to your toolbox.

Because every editing task is different, it's difficult to create a comprehensive list of problems and solutions. Consequently, the tutorials in this chapter will also lead you through some low-level techniques that will help you approach and solve other problems you may run into on your own.

In addition to the printed tutorials, there are a few video tutorials included on the companion disc, and PDF files covering additional subjects. Ideally, these should be viewed in the order presented herein. Before we get started, we're going to take a look at the order of operations you'll want to consider when approaching your edits.

EDITING ORDER

For maximum flexibility and to preserve image quality, you'll usually want to perform your edits in a particular order. For example, you almost always want to apply any sharpening operations *after* you've performed all of your other corrections and edits. Because sharpening can be a very destructive operation, you want to do it only once, after you're sure nothing else in your image will change.

So far, if you've been following along in the book, you've performed your edits in a particular order. In the next two chapters you're going to learn many more additional editing tasks, and you'll want to be sure you perform these tasks at an appropriate stage in your editing workflow.

You'll typically perform your edits in this order:

Geometric corrections. These are the operations you learned about in Chapter 11, "Correcting Tone and Color," that can result in a crop in your image. You want to perform these functions first, to eliminate any irrelevant data from your image's histogram.

Tone and color corrections. These include the Levels and Curves operations you learned about in Chapter 11, and the tonal adjustments and white-balance correction you might perform in your raw conversion step. Often, these will be the only edits and corrections your image needs.

Grayscale conversion. If you ultimately plan to convert your image to grayscale, that adjustment will happen during your tone and color correction stage. We'll discuss grayscale conversion in more detail later in this chapter.

Retouching. If your image has any trouble with spots, sensor dust, or lens flares, you'll need to retouch those issues after your tonal corrections. We put tonal corrections first, because they sometimes reveal spots and dust you can't initially see.

Additional color and tonal corrections, special effects, compositing, facial retouching. Any additional edits come next. You'll learn about many of these techniques in this and the next chapter.

Noise reduction. If your image has any noise problems, you'll attack them now. Tone and color corrections can sometimes exaggerate noise troubles, so you want to have all your other edits out of the way before you take the time to address noise. There's another school of thought that says you should address the noise *first* before you do anything that might exaggerate it. On a particularly troublesome image, you might want to try it both ways.

Sizing, sharpening, and output. Your very last step is to resize and sharpen your image in preparation for output. We'll cover all these tasks in Chapter 16, "Output."

Obviously, this workflow is not carved in stone, and you'll often move back and forth between different steps, as some edits and adjustments will predicate a change or alteration in other edits and adjustments.

The ultimate goal of the workflow presented here is to preserve the highest-quality image data throughout your editing cycle. A slight variation is not going to destroy your image—in fact, you might do things very much out of order and still not see a difference. However, if you later want to make more edits, or different edits, you might wish you'd been a little more careful with your data.

You've already learned about geometric adjustments, basic tone, and basic color corrections. In the rest of this chapter, and in Chapter 15, "Special Effects," we'll look at the other operations described in this workflow, beginning with grayscale conversion.

Editing Order in a Nondestructive Editor

If you're working with Aperture, Lightroom, Capture NX, or any other nondestructive editor, order of edits is less important, because your edits will be applied in the correct order by the program at the time of output. However, it's still a good idea to work in the order described here. You'll want to crop before making tonal adjustments, to ensure a more relevant histogram, and you'll want to perform any geometric corrections and grayscale adjustments before you start editing in earnest, so you're editing on something closer to your final composition.

CONVERTING COLOR IMAGES TO GRAYSCALE

Although your camera might do a great job of reproducing color, there will be times when you want to convert your color images to grayscale, either for printing purposes or simply for artistic intent. There's a tricky thing about grayscale conversion, though, and that is that there is no "correct" gray tone that corresponds to any particular color. As such, grayscale conversion is very subjective, very much a matter of taste, and can change from image to image, depending on your artistic intent. For example, in some landscape images you might choose to render the sky with very dark tones, while in other images you might choose to render the sky with very light tones. (See Figure 14.1.)

In other words, an infinite number of grayscale images can be derived from any color image. There are also *many* ways to convert images to grayscale—far more than we can cover in this book, but we will look at a few alternatives.

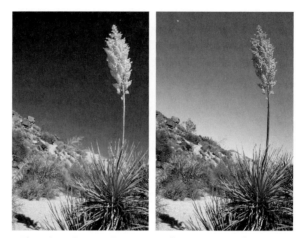

FIGURE 14.1   There's no "correct" gray tone that corresponds to a particular color value. As such, grayscale conversion can be very subjective. These two images were converted from the *same* color image, using different conversion settings. Which one is "correct" depends entirely on your personal preference.

Photoshop allows you to convert an image to grayscale simply by selecting a new color mode. (Image > Mode> Grayscale.) This type of conversion uses a stock recipe for mixing the image's red, green, and blue channels to produce a grayscale result. In theory, the recipe produces an image that is well suited to the eye's different color and luminance sensitivities.

Often, this is the best way to convert your image; however, you might find that the resulting image lacks solid blacks and bright whites. With its color removed, your image might be less "punchy." Fortunately, several other methods provide more control and, frequently, better results.

In many cases you might want to color-correct your image before using any of these methods. This might sound strange because you're just going to remove all the color, but an image with accurate color will usually produce a more pleasing grayscale image.

Back up Your Original

If you're using a destructive grayscale conversion method, you should make a backup copy of your original image. Although you might want a grayscale image now, you never know when you might need to go back to your original color version.

Channel Mixing

Photoshop, Aperture, Lightroom, and Capture NX all provide a variation on "channel mixing." As you've learned, your image editor can convert your image to a Grayscale mode by using a stock formula for combining the red, green, and blue channels in your image. Using a channel mixer, you can specify your own recipe for how the red, green, and blue channels should be combined.

As you mix more of a particular channel, those tones will get brighter. So, in a landscape scene with a big blue sky, if you mix in more of the blue channel, your sky will get lighter. How you choose to mix your channels will depend on the colors in your original image, and how light or dark you want them rendered.

For example, in Figure 14.1, the left-hand image was converted using a mix of 100% red, 0% green, and 0% blue. The right-hand image was created with a mix of 0% red, 91% green, and 100% blue. Fortunately, these controls are very interactive, so you don't need to be able to internally visualize the effects of different combinations. Understanding that a higher percentage of a particular channel equates to lighter shades of that range of tones will make your mixing efforts less random.

> **Photoshop CS/CS2/CS3.** In Photoshop, you access the Channel Mixer by choosing Image > Adjustments > Channel Mixer. In the Channel Mixer dialog box, check the Monochrome checkbox. Your image will change to grayscale, and you can now adjust the color sliders to select a channel mix you like. The Constant slider allows you to brighten or darken your image overall. The Photoshop Channel Mixer can also be applied as an Adjustment Layer, giving you the option of performing a nondestructive grayscale conversion.

> **Aperture.** In Aperture, you can convert an image to grayscale by adding a Monochrome Mixer adjustment. Select Monochrome Mixer from the Action menu in the Adjustments panel, or press Control-M. In the Monochrome Mixer, adjust the red, green, and blue sliders to taste.

> **Lightroom.** Lightroom provides an excellent variation on the Channel Mixer that works like the CS3 Black and White conversion described in the next section.

Note that with the Photoshop and Aperture channel mixers, you want to keep an eye on the total sum of your three channels. If the three channels add up to more than 100%, the overall exposure of your image will have increased, and you may have lost some highlights. If the sum of the channels is less than 100%, your image will have darkened.

Photoshop CS3 and Aperture also provide preset mixes that mimic the effect of using colored filters with traditional black-and-white film. For example, a red filter will usually produce a very contrasty image.

Channeling

If you're a Photoshop user, you might have discovered this already, but sometimes one of the individual color channels in your image actually makes for a very good grayscale image. Just click through the individual channels in the Channels palette and see which, if any, looks best. Depending on the color content of your image, any one of the channels might look good, although the Red and Blue channels might suffer from noise.

If you find a channel you like, simply click Image > Mode > Grayscale, and Photoshop will toss out the other channels, leaving you with a grayscale image of your chosen channel.

Converting to Luminance

In Photoshop, just as you can select a single color channel in RGB mode, you can convert your image to L*a*b mode and select just the Luminance channel. This will throw out all the color information in your image. After you convert to L*a*b mode, click the Lightness channel in the Channels palette and select Image > Mode > Grayscale. (See Figure 14.2.)

Desaturating an Image

You can perform a grayscale conversion by using the Saturation control to drain all the color out of your image. When your picture is completely desaturated, you'll have a grayscale image. Photoshop Camera Raw, Aperture, Lightroom, and Capture NX all provide a Saturation slider you can use for this effect. Photoshop also has a Desaturate command (Image > Adjust > Desaturate) that performs the same function. (See Figure 14.2.)

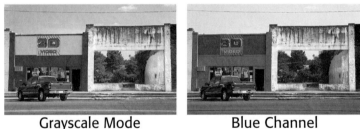

Grayscale Mode   Blue Channel

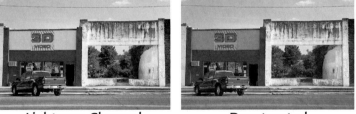

Lightness Channel   Desaturated

FIGURE 14.2 Here you can see the same image converted using a Photoshop Grayscale mode change, by selecting just the blue channel, by selecting just the Lightness channel (after converting to L*A*B color), and by desaturating.

Black and White

Photoshop CS3 provides an additional method for converting an image to grayscale. If you select Image > Adjustments > Black and White, you'll activate the Black and

White dialog box. (See Figure 14.3.) The Black and White adjustment is a souped-up, smarter version of the Channel Mixer. First, as you can see it offers far more color sliders. Next, it only alters actual colors, not component values. In the Channel mixer, when you adjust the Blue slider, for example, the blue component of all of the colors in your image are adjusted. In the Black and White dialog box, when you move the Blues slider, only pixels that are blue are affected. In addition to giving you more control, you don't have to worry about your total color percentages totaling 100%.

The coolest feature of the Black and White dialog box, though, is that you don't have to use its controls. Once you've invoked it, you can click on tones in your image and drag left or right to adjust their brightness.

Note too, that the Black and White adjustment can be applied as an Adjustment Layer. Simply choose Black and White from the New Adjustment Layer menu at the bottom of the Layers palette.

Lightroom provides the same controls for black-and-white conversion.

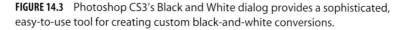

FIGURE 14.3   Photoshop CS3's Black and White dialog provides a sophisticated, easy-to-use tool for creating custom black-and-white conversions.

FINDING BLACK-AND-WHITE IMAGES

Learning to visualize the world in black and white is one of the most difficult tasks a black-and-white photographer faces. While we talked about this in Chapter 9, "Special Shooting," there's another way you can practice your black-and-white skills, and that's to look at the images you already have. Using your image browser or cataloger of choice, look through your existing library and try to identify any images you think might make good black-and-white candidates. Spend some time trying to visualize how the image might look in black and white, and what tones would be most evocative. Should it have a dark or light sky? Should it be super-contrasty, or washed out?

Once you've tried visualizing the image, open your image editor, and try a black-and-white conversion. See if the result looks like you imagined, and if your decisions about how to tone the different parts of your image were correct. Then, experiment with different conversions to see how the image changes.

RETOUCHING

With your initial tonal and color correction out of the way, and your image converted to grayscale, you're ready to start any basic retouching your image needs. While your picture might have looked clean at first glance, tonal adjustments can sometimes reveal flaws that need some touch-up.

Removing Dust and Spots

If you have a digital camera with removable lenses, it is possible for dust to get to your camera's sensor. Sensor dust will appear as dark blotches or spots on your final image. (See Chapter 5, "Choosing a Digital Camera," for sensor cleaning.)

Sensor dust sometimes looks just like the artifacts that appear when you have dust on your lens. (See Figure 14.4.) The easiest way to determine if the problem is with your sensor is to change the lens on your camera. If the artifact is still there, you know it has nothing to do with your lens.

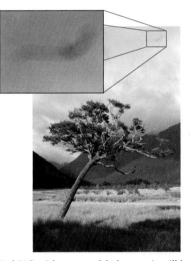

FIGURE 14.4 If you have a digital SLR with removable lenses, it will be possible for your camera to get dust or dirt on its sensor. If you notice strange smudges and blotches in your images— and they stay there even when you change lenses— it's probably time to clean your sensor.

No matter what kind of digital camera you have, a pixel or two on the CCD can go bad. If one of the pixels in your camera's sensor dies, your images will consistently have a white or blue spot at the location of the bad pixel. Unfortunately, there's nothing you can do to fix the camera, and most vendors won't replace or repair a camera with only one or two bad pixels.

For stuck pixels, or very dark dust and specks, you'll need to use your image editor's Clone or Rubber Stamp tool. For more on using the Clone tool, refer to the Cloning tutorial in Chapter 13, "Building Your Editing Arsenal."

If the dust in your image is light—more like a smudge than a speck—you might be able to use dodge tools to lighten the area. Photoshop's Healing Brush will also work for these types of problems, while the Spot Healing Brush provides an extremely simple one-click solution.

If you're using Aperture, the Spot and Patch tool will make short work of dust problems, while in Lightroom, you'll want to use the Remove Spots tool.

Removing Red-Eye

Because of their small size, many digital cameras are particularly prone to *red-eye*, that demonic look that can appear in your subjects' eyes when the flash from your camera has bounced off their retinas and back into the camera's lens. Although there are ways to avoid red-eye when you shoot (see Chapter 7, "Shooting"), there will still be times when you will face this problem in an image and need to remove it. *Pet-eye* is a variation of this that can cause dog and cat eyes to appear blue, or other incorrect colors. Some cameras now include built-in red-eye and pet-eye removal.

There are several effective methods for removing red-eye in your image editor. Which one to use depends mainly on the capabilities of your image-editing software.

Use a red-eye removal filter or tool. Many editing programs include special tools and filters for automatically removing red-eye. Photoshop (both the Elements and CS versions) have good red-eye reduction tools. If you're using an earlier version of Photoshop (7 or earlier), there are some good third-party plug-ins for performing red-eye removal. Aperture, Lightroom, iPhoto, and Capture NX also provide automatic red-eye reduction tools.

Desaturate the red area. Because the pupil turns red, and pupils are usually black or very dark brown, simply desaturating the red area will drain it of color and restore it to its normal dark tone. Select the affected area (you'll probably want to feather the edge of the selection by a pixel or two), and then use your desaturation method of choice. In Photoshop, you can use the Sponge tool or the Hue/Saturation dialog box.

Repaint the area by hand. If there's any natural color visible in your subject's eyes, you can try to select it with the Eyedropper tool and repaint the rest of the area with a paintbrush or pencil tool. This is probably the most difficult technique because you will need to be careful to preserve any highlights or catchlights in the subject's eyes. An eye without a glint of light does not look natural. Examine some non-red-eye flash photos to see what this highlight should look like.

Removing Color Fringing

In Chapter 8, "Metering and Exposure," you read about weird purple fringing artifacts that can occur when you shoot high-contrast areas with a wide-angle lens. Although opinions sometimes differ as to what causes these problems, everyone agrees that the results are ugly!

Earlier, you used Photoshop's Lens Correction filter to remove chromatic aberrations. If you're using an earlier version of Photoshop, or an image editor that doesn't have such a tool, or if Lens Correction didn't work, you'll need to try a different approach to removing these types of artifacts.

Most fringing artifacts can be eliminated with a simple Hue/Saturation Adjustment Layer. The idea is to simply target the color of the fringe and drain the saturation out of it to make it blend better with the background. The trick is to not mess up any of the other color in your image.

Desaturating a Chromatic Aberration

ON THE CD

Open the image `palace.jpg`, located in the Tutorials/Chapter 14 folder on the companion CD-ROM. The chromatic aberrations in this image are not terrible, but they are there. Look between the two rightmost columns and you'll see a nasty red fringe on the left side of the right column, and a bad green fringe on the right side of the left column. (See Figure 14.5.)

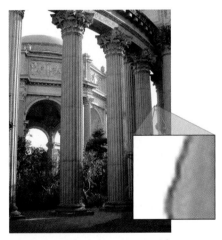

FIGURE 14.5   This image suffers from some bad fringing artifacts. In this tutorial, we'll remove them with some simple painting techniques.

Although the fringes aren't huge, the predominant colors in the image are red and green, so you'll have to be careful when you remove the extra colors.

TUTORIAL 14.1

Step 1: Select the First Fringe

Using the Marquee or Lasso tool, select the rightmost red fringe. You don't have to be precise in this selection; your main goal is to protect the other red tones in the image. (See Figure 14.6.)

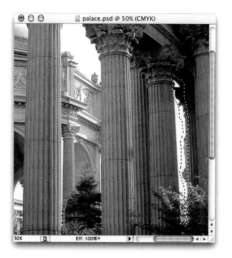

FIGURE 14.6   Use the Lasso tool to select the area of bad fringe in the image.

Step 2: Create a Hue/Saturation Adjustment Layer

With your selection active, use the Layers palette to create a new Hue/Saturation Adjustment layer. Notice that the Layers palette shows your Adjustment Layer with a Layer mask that matches your selection.

Step 3: Target the Offending Colors

Now you need to select the colors of the fringe. To do this, you'll need to zoom in to your document to see some individual pixels. Press Command and + (Control and + in Windows) a few times to zoom in to 200 percent. Because the fringe is kind of a pinkish-red, you want to limit the effects of the adjustment to reds. Select Reds from the Edit pop-up menu at the top of the Hue-Saturation dialog box.

Now you need to sample the color of the fringe in the image. Using the Eyedropper tool, select one of the very light-colored pink dots within the fringe. The color selection scale will shift to the left to encompass the color you sampled. Because the palace columns contain a lot of red, you want to narrow your red selection so as to not desaturate the columns. The color selection scale has four sliding controls, two on the left and two on the right. The inner sliders control the range of colors to select, whereas the outer controls create a color selection drop-off to ensure smooth color shifts.

Slide all four sliders inward to create a tight color selection. (See Figure 14.7.)

Step 4: Desaturate the Fringe

Now drag the Saturation slider to the left to suck some of the saturation out of the selected red tones. As they lose saturation, they may turn gray. If so, try backing off

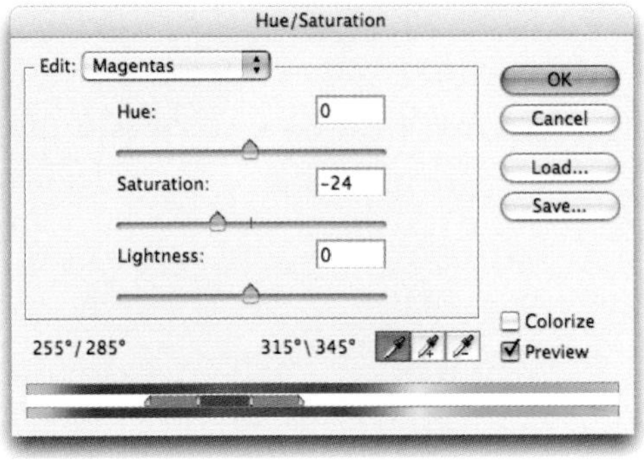

FIGURE 14.7   Targeting the fringe color.

on the desaturation by moving the Saturation slider back to the right, and instead add a little lightening by moving the Lightness slider to the right.

Step 5: Target More Colors

Although the image is probably looking better, there's still most likely a lot of red or pink. You want to now expand the target color range. Click the middle Eyedropper (the one with the + next to it), and click some of the remaining fringe colors. This process will add these colors to the range of colors being desaturated. You may have to go deep into the shadows of the columns to get all the colors. You may also have to adjust your Saturation and Lightness settings after you select more colors.

Step 6: Check the Results

When you're finished, click OK, and zoom out to check the results. In addition to looking at the quality of the fringe reduction, look closely at the surrounding area of your selection to ensure you haven't inadvertently desaturated any other parts of the column. If there's still visible fringing, double-click the Adjustment Layer to tweak your settings.

When you're done, do the same with the other fringe, but this time target the greens.

This approach will work for most chromatic aberrations, although you need to be careful. Sometimes, the color of your aberration will closely match the background of your image. For example, you'll frequently run into blue aberrations against a blue sky. Be sure to select your aberration first, to protect the rest of the sky. You'll also probably want to do less desaturation and more lightening to match the hue of the fringe to the sky.

Another approach to this problem is to use Photoshop's Sponge tool. The Sponge tool sits in the same slot of the tool palette as the Dodge and Burn tools. Configure the Sponge tool for 100% desaturation, set your brush size appropriately, and then brush along the colored fringes to desaturate them. Check Photoshop's built-in help for more information on using the Sponge tool.

Removing Fringes by Shrinking Channels

Fringes are often pure red, green, or blue colors. Consequently, they're often confined to an individual color channel. If you examine your individual channels and find this to be true, you can always go in and edit the channels directly.

Fringes sometimes look just like a misregistration from a printing press. That is, if your image has red fringing, it can often appear as if the Red channel has slipped out of registration with the Blue and Green channels. It hasn't, but you can try to correct it using the same procedures you would use to fix a misregistration.

1. Select the offending color channel.
2. Shrink it to "scoot" the fringe under the other color channels. You can do this by clicking Edit > Transform > Numeric and entering a tiny value—99.7 or 99.8, for example. This will reduce the size of the channel and hopefully hide the aberration.

After shrinking a channel, be sure to examine your image closely for any new artifacts that may have been introduced by the transformation. In particular, make sure no new fringing has developed in other parts of the image.

ADDITIONAL EDITING TECHNIQUES

While there is much you can do with the tone and color correction techniques we discussed in Chapter 11, and while you might be able to fix most of your image's problems during your raw conversion step, as discussed in Chapter 12, "Raw Conversion," some images will still demand additional edits. Sometimes, these will be additional color or tonal adjustments you can't make with the tools discussed so far; sometimes, these will be localized corrections—adjustments that are constrained to one part of your image; and sometimes these will be complex special effects involving radical retouchings, composites, and more. In the rest of this chapter, we're going to explore the more "everyday" techniques you'll need, including masking, noise reduction, and color correction. We will begin with another way to adjust tone in your image.

Adaptive Shadow/Highlight Correction

In Chapter 12, we introduced the concept of adaptive correction of shadows and highlights. Adaptive correction tools are able to automatically figure out which pixels in your image are shadows and which are highlights, and then brighten or darken just those areas. Photoshop Camera Raw and Lightroom provide a Fill Light slider that lets you automatically brighten shadows, while Photoshop provides a Shadow/Highlight adjustment. Aperture's equivalent is called Highlights and Shadows, while Capture NX's tool is called D-Lighting.

Shadows/Highlight in Photoshop CS2/CS3. To invoke the Shadow/Highlight tool, choose Image > Adjustments > Shadow/Highlights. By default, the Shadows/Highlights dialog box opens with a Shadows amount of 50, so you will see an immediate brightening of the shadows in your image. Move the Shadows slider to the desired setting. (See Figure 14.8.)

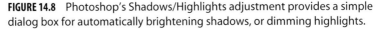

FIGURE 14.8   Photoshop's Shadows/Highlights adjustment provides a simple dialog box for automatically brightening shadows, or dimming highlights.

If you want to darken highlights in your image, slide the Highlights slider to the right. As with Shadows, the Shadows/Highlights tool will automatically determine which tones in your image are highlights.

Highlights and Shadows in Aperture. If you're using Aperture, you should have a Highlights and Shadows adjustment in the Adjustment pane by default. If not, you can add one by choosing Highlights and Shadows from the Action menu in the upper right corner of the Adjustments pane. Move the Highlights slider to the right to darken the highlights, and the Shadows slider to the right to lighten the shadows.

Photoshop, Aperture, and Lightroom all provide additional options for their adaptive shadow and highlight tools.

As discussed in Chapter 12, these adaptive tools intelligently roll off their adjustments through the transition zones that occur between shadows and midtones, and midtones and highlights. Using the extra options provided by each tool, you can gain more control over what constitutes a shadow and a highlight, and how much to roll off the adjustment through the transition zones. Consult your program's documentation for more details.

The most common use for these tools is when an image simply needs to be brightened up. In general, you'll find that you use these types of adaptive tools for two other common operations.

Fill flash. If you have images that should have been shot with a fill flash, but weren't, try hitting them with an adaptive shadow adjustment. You'll probably find that it often makes a good substitute for a fill flash, lightening shadows and generally evening out exposure. (See Figure 14.9.)

Reducing contrast. While we often strive to *increase* contrast through the use of exposure adjustments and image-editing techniques, there are times when an image can have too *much* contrast. For these instances, darkening highlights with an adaptive highlight adjustment while brightening shadows with an adaptive shadow adjustment can restore the overall contrast in an image back to something less harsh. (See Figure 4.10.)

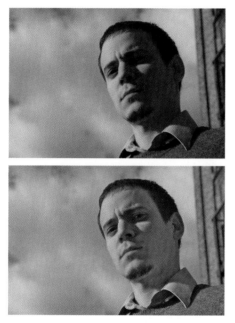

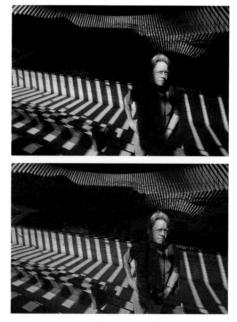

FIGURE 14.9   The top image should have been shot with a fill flash to illuminate the left side of this man's face. With an adaptive shadow adjustment, we can easily brighten the darker areas.

FIGURE 14.10   The upper image has too much contrast, so we used adaptive shadow and highlight adjustments to lighten the shadows and darken the highlights, to produce an image that's not as harsh.

NONDESTRUCTIVE SHADOW/HIGHLIGHT

While Photoshop provides Adjustment Layers for many of its effects and adjustments, the Shadow/Highlight adjustment is not one of them. Consequently, once you've applied it, you're stuck with it. If you'd rather have a less destructive way of applying the edit, try this:

→

1. Duplicate the layer you want to adjust with Shadows/Highlight. You can duplicate a layer in the Layers palette by dragging the layer to the New Layer button at the bottom of the palette.
2. Add the Shadows/Highlights adjustment to your duplicate layer.

Now, if you ever want to remove the adjustment, just throw out the duplicated, edited layer. If you want to *change* the amount of adjustment, throw out the duplicate, and reperform the entire duplicate/adjust operation.

Advanced Masking

Although Curves and Hue/Saturation allow you to limit your editing operations to specific tonal ranges, as you saw in Chapter 11 these tools don't allow you to constrain your edits and corrections to specific parts of an image. For this reason, and for the creation of composites and special effects, good masking skills are essential to effective color correction. In Chapter 12, you were introduced to alpha channel masks and Adjustment layers. In this section, we're going to show you how to create complex alpha channel masks using new methods that augment the masking skills you learned earlier.

Masking with Layer Masks

It's confession time: there is an easier way to perform some of the masking tasks you worked through in earlier chapters. However, even though the method you're about to learn facilitates simpler masking, it's important that you understand the masking concepts you explored earlier, both for the creation of more complex masks and to help you better understand our next topic.

In Chapter 13, you were introduced to Photoshop's Adjustment layers, special types of layers that don't contain image information but let you apply image adjustments in an easily editable manner. In addition to allowing you to adjust your edits after the fact, Adjustment layers also include powerful masking features in the form of Layer masks. The easiest way to learn how Layer masks work is with a quick tutorial. Note that this tutorial requires either Photoshop 7 or later, or Photoshop Elements 2 or later.

TUTORIAL 14.2

ON THE CD

Step 1: Open the Image

Open the image underexposed.jpg in the Tutorials/Chapter 13/ folder on the companion CD-ROM. Because of the camera's matrix metering, the foreground figures are very underexposed. (See Figure 14.11.) We can improve their contrast with a levels adjustment, but because the background—

especially the sky—is reasonably exposed, doing so would quickly blow out the clouds. We need to create a mask to limit our edits to only the figures in the foreground. As you learned in previous chapters, we could select the figures by outlining them with the selection tools (Lasso, Magic Wand, and so on), or paint over them in QuickMask mode, and then use that selection as a mask to constrain your Levels operation. We're going to take a very different approach for this image.

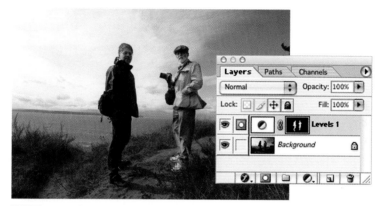

FIGURE 14.11 Our camera's matrix meter favored the sky in this image, resulting in the foreground figures being overexposed. (To avoid this problem, we should have used the camera's center-weight meter.)

Step 2: Create an Adjustment Layer

Add a new Levels Adjustment layer by opening the Adjustment Layer pop-up menu at the bottom of the Layers palette. (See Figure 14.12.) You might need to open the Layers palette if it's not visible. After creating the Adjustment layer, you will be immediately presented with a standard Levels dialog box. This is where you define what adjustment the Adjustment layer will make to your image. While looking *only at the figures,* make your adjustment to improve their exposure. This will adversely affect the background exposure, but don't worry about that right now. To heighten the contrast, you'll want to move both the black and white points, and you'll need a severe midtone adjustment to brighten their details. Consider a black point around 11, midpoint around 1.83, and a white point of roughly 234. Click OK when you're finished.

Step 3: Prepare Your Layer Mask

In the Layers palette, each Adjustment layer is represented by an icon that tells what type of adjustment it performs. Next to this icon is another icon that represents the Adjustment Layer's mask. (See Figure 14.13.) Each Adjustment layer has a built-in, associated alpha channel into which you can paint directly, just as you painted into an alpha channel in Chapter 12. If you paint black into the mask, the Adjustment layer will not affect those areas of the image. Select the Paint Bucket tool and choose black as your foreground color. Because we have the Adjustment layer's mask currently

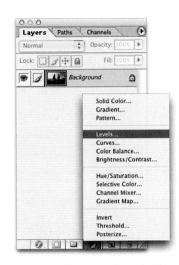

FIGURE 14.12   You can create an Adjustment layer in Photoshop CS or Elements by clicking the Add Adjustment Layer icon at the bottom of the Layers palette.

selected (you can tell because it has a black highlight around it in the Layers palette), painting operations will affect only the Adjustment Layer mask. With the Paint Bucket tool selected, click somewhere in your image to fill the Adjustment layer mask with black. Your image should return to its original state, because we have completely masked out the Adjustment layer. In other words, it's not affecting any part of your image.

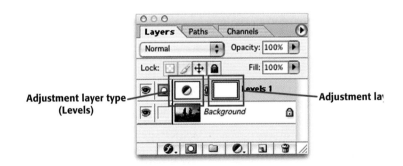

FIGURE 14.13   Adjustment layers show two icons in the Layers palette: one indicates what kind of Adjustment layer it is, the second shows a thumbnail of the Adjustment layer's mask.

Step 4: Paint in the Figures

Now select white as your foreground color and grab a Paintbrush tool. Begin painting on the figures in the image. As you brush, you will be punching a hole in that part of the layer mask, allowing the Adjustment layer's effect to filter down to your image. As such, the figures should brighten up according to your Levels adjustment. (See Figure 14.14.)

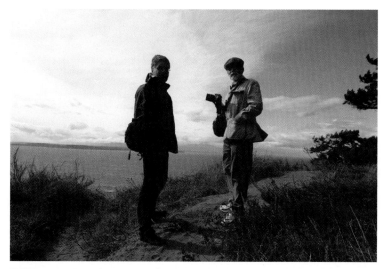

FIGURE 14.14   By painting into the Adjustment layer's mask, we can punch a hole in the mask, so the Adjustment layer's effect filters through only to the figures.

(If, at any time, you see actual paint going into your canvas, it means that you've clicked on the image thumbnail in the Layers palette. Click Undo, and then select the mask icon in your Adjustment layer.)

Step 5: Paint in the Foreground

The ground in the foreground could also use some adjustment, although not as much as what we applied to the figures. We could create another Adjustment Layer specifically tailored to the ground, but there's an easier way. Remember that in an alpha channel mask, black masks completely, white unmasks completely, and shades of gray fall somewhere in between. Adjustment layer masks work in the same way. So, if we want to apply only *half* the adjustment that we applied to the figures, we need to do nothing more than paint with a 50 percent gray color.

Select a roughly 50 percent gray foreground, and paint over the ground. (See Figure 14.15.) Note that you can use any painting tools. If you want to cover a large area quickly, grab the rectangular selection tool, select the bottom of the image, and then use the Edit > Fill command or Paint Bucket tool. You can then switch back to a paintbrush to paint the borders and fine detail.

Note that if you make any mistakes, you can simply grab the appropriate color— black, white, or gray—and repaint the damaged areas of your mask.

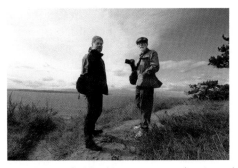

FIGURE 14.15   For our finished image, we used various shades of gray to paint more or less effect into different parts of the image.

The advantage of Adjustment layers with Layer masks is that you don't have to go through separate masking and filter steps. What's more, because your mask is dynamically applied to your Adjustment layer, you can go back and edit it at any time. With normal masking techniques, you'd have to make your mask, select it, apply your adjustment, and then, if it wasn't right, click Undo and then start over. We'll be returning to Layer masks again later to explore more functionality.

Image-Based Masks

As you've already seen, Photoshop has a number of excellent masking tools that let you paint, select, or outline masks. However, you've also seen that Photoshop has some great analysis tools that let you quickly identify particular tones and colors within an image. So, if the goal of masking is to select particular parts of an image, and Photoshop already knows how to identify particular colors, you should be able to use the image data that's in the image *to create masks*.

Consider the image in Figure 14.16.

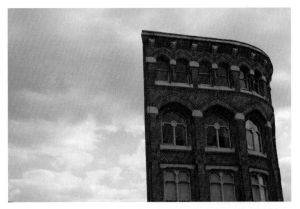

FIGURE 14.16   Because we metered to ensure the sky wouldn't blow out, the building in this picture ended up a little dark and dull. We want to apply a Levels adjustment to the building, without editing the sky at all.

As in our previous example, the building is underexposed, but the sky looks okay. We need to perform a midtone adjustment on the building, but if we open a Curves dialog box and click around with the Eyedropper tool, we'll find that the sky and the building share many midtone values. Therefore, if we start adjusting the building, there's a good chance we'll ruin the sky. A better choice is to build a mask for the building. This shape is simple enough that it wouldn't take too much work to paint it out—either into the mask of an Adjustment layer as we saw in the previous tutorial or using any of the other Photoshop selection tools.

However, because we want to achieve a slightly different effect, we're going to take a different approach. The texture of the building contains a wide variety of midtones of slight variation. To achieve better contrast on the building, we don't want to adjust all of those midtones uniformly. This means we need to create a very complex mask, which we're going to do using the image data that's already there. We know that we want to target the midtones. What's more, we know that alpha channel masks are simply 8-bit grayscale pictures. Photoshop, of course, is a great tool for creating 8-bit pictures, so we're going to create a modified version of our image that we will use to mask our original image.

Note that this tutorial is not possible using Photoshop Elements.

TUTORIAL 14.3

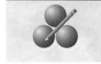

ON THE CD

Step 1: Open and Prepare Your Image

Open the file `Initial building.jpg` located in the Tutorials/Chapter 14 folder on the companion CD-ROM. This is the file we will ultimately edit. Right now, though, we want to make a copy of this file that we will manipulate into our mask. In Photoshop, click Image > Duplicate to create a new document containing the exact same image data. Now we want to convert this copy into a grayscale image. (Remember, this copy is going to become the basis for our mask, and masks are grayscale.) As you'll see in the next chapter, there are many ways to convert an image to grayscale. For this example, we're going to isolate the luminance information in the image, because we're interested in isolating the subtle changes in brightness on the surface of the building. Click Image > Mode > Lab to convert the image to L*a*b color mode. Rather than being represented by separate red, green, and blue channels, L*a*b images are represented by a lightness channel and two separate color channels. If you click the Lightness channel in the Channels palette, you should see a nice grayscale image.

Step 2: Create Your Mask

This Lightness channel will serve as a starting point for our alpha channel mask, but to use it, we need to move it to our original image. With the Lightness channel selected, open the pop-up menu in the top-right corner of the Channels palette and select Duplicate Channel. (See Figure 14.17.)

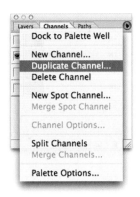

FIGURE 14.17   Open the Layers palette menu to access the Duplicate Channel command.

In the resulting dialog box, select initial building.tif from the Document pop-up menu in the Destination box. Then, click OK. Now close the copy—don't bother saving, because we won't need it for anything else—and return to your original document. Selected in the Channels palette should be the new alpha channel we just copied. Because it's selected, your image will appear in grayscale. You can drag this channel to the Load Channel as Selection button at the bottom of the Channels palette (just as you did in previous tutorials), and it will actually load as a selection. In other words, it's a perfectly usable mask. However, before we start using it, we want to make some modifications to it. If you loaded the mask as a selection, deselect it by pressing Command+D (Ctrl+D if you're using Windows).

Step 3: Adjust the Mask

As previously discussed, we want this mask to exclude the sky completely, because we're pleased with the sky exposure. We want to create a mask that focuses on the midtones. In an alpha channel mask, black areas are completely protected ("black conceals, white reveals"), so we know that if we can get the sky reduced to absolute black, it will be completely masked.

We've already learned about several tools that can be used to adjust tones within an image, and this grayscale mask is no different from any other image, so let's put our toolset to work. With the Alpha 1 channel selected, click Image > Adjustment > Curves to open the Curves dialog box. (We can't use a Curves Adjustment layer, because there's no way to limit an Adjustment layer to a particular channel.)

We know that for the time being, we don't want to alter our midtones, so click the midpoint to lock it down with a control point. We also know that the tones we want to darken are the brightest tones in the image, so bring the white point all the way to the bottom. (See Figure 14.18.)

This is a good starting point. Our building has not been masked at all, and the sky is much darker. However, it's not completely masked out. To eliminate it completely, we want to clip all its tones out of the curve, which we can do by moving our white point directly to the left. Don't be timid—slide it almost until it collides with the mid-

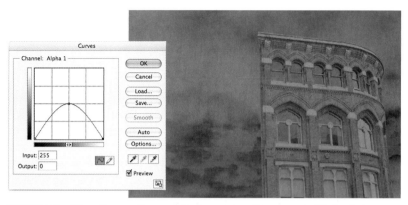

FIGURE 14.18   We will use a Curves adjustment to edit our mask. We begin by trying to reduce the sky to complete black, a process that begins by lowering the white point.

point. The sky will turn completely black, but our building will turn completely white. To correct the building, slide the midpoint to the left, to the next gridline.

Now you should have a gray building on a black background. If used as a mask, this mask would partially select the building, leaving the sky completely blocked. What should be apparent at this point is the procedure of using the Curves control to zero in on precisely the tones we want to mask.

Step 4: Finish the Mask

As it is right now, the building is not sufficiently selected. Remember, the whiter the building is, the more selected it is. Right now, with its predominantly middle-gray tones, this mask will not create a very strong selection—it's still mostly opaque. We want a higher-contrast mask, and so should adjust our curve accordingly. (See Figure 14.19.) We know that we want the white parts of the building to go whiter, so

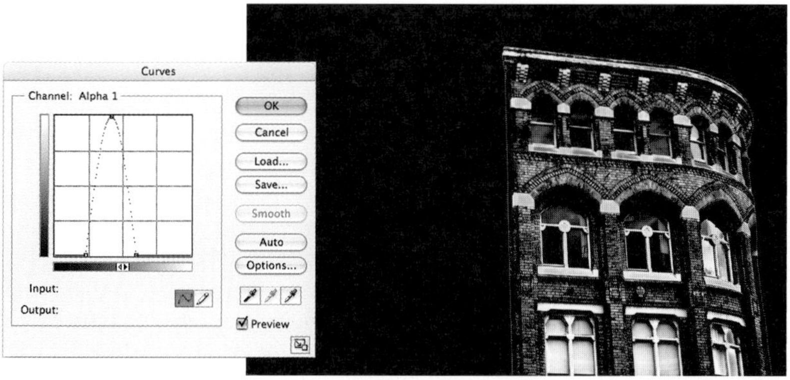

FIGURE 14.19   Our final curve results in a mask that isolates only certain midtones in the image.

we're keeping an eye on those areas of the mask and adjusting our midpoint to make them as white as possible.

Step 5: Load and Use the Mask

In the Channels palette, click RGB to return to viewing and editing the full image. Now load the new mask by dragging it to the Load Channel as Selection button at the bottom of the Channels palette. Press Command+H to hide the selection (Ctrl+H if you're using Windows), so it's easier to see our upcoming edits. If we've built our mask properly, we should have a selection that is grabbing only certain midtones in our image. At the beginning, we said that the building midtones needed to be brighter, so now that we've selected them, we're going to lighten them up.

In the Layers palette, create a new Levels Adjustment Layer. When you create a Layers Adjustment Layer with something already selected, Photoshop automatically uses that selection to create a Layer mask for the new Adjustment layer, meaning that our new Adjustment layer will affect only the areas defined by our mask.

In the Levels dialog box, increase the contrast of the image by shifting the white point to the left. As you move the sliders, you should see the midtones in the building brighten and change without altering the shadow tones or the sky. (See Figure 14.20.)

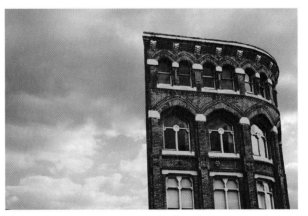

FIGURE 14.20   After loading our final mask, we can apply a Levels adjustment that is constrained to a specific range of midtones.

Step 6: Edit the Sky

After editing the building, you might decide that the sky could be a little more dramatic. Using the same technique, you can easily create a mask that protects the sky but knocks out the building. Create a new luminance channel from a duplicate of the image, copy that channel into your document, and then use a Curves adjustment to drastically increase the contrast of the mask, until the building is black and the sky is white. You probably won't be able to increase the contrast to the point where all the windows and details will go black, but you'll get a good edge on the building. You can quickly paint out the windows by hand. Then, load the new mask, and alter the sky to taste. The image in Figure 14.20 has had the contrast in the sky beefed up, using the mask shown in Figure 14.21. 🎨

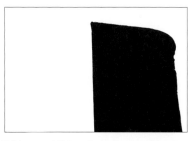

FIGURE 14.21   With an additional mask, we can edit only the sky to boost the contrast and make the clouds slightly more dramatic.

This technique of using adjusted, altered channels to create masks for editing is one we will return to for other operations. Although it may seem complex at first, as you gain more experience with masks, it will be easier to envision ways you can use your image itself to create usable masks.

COLOR ADJUSTMENT

So far, you've seen many examples of tonal corrections, and a few examples of localized color correction. Color correction used to be a bigger concern than it is now. As cameras have improved over the last few years, the need for complex, detailed color correction has waned. While you will occasionally need to adjust individual colors in an image (as we demonstrated in Chapter 11, see Figure 11.56), most of your color correction chores will be global adjustments, and most of these will be simple operations to correct color casts and white-balance troubles.

If you're shooting in raw mode, correcting white balance is very easy; just use the White Balance and Tint sliders as explained in Chapter 12.

If you're shooting in JPEG mode, correcting bad white balance can be more complicated.

Correcting a Bad White Balance in a JPEG File

ON THE CD

Open the Bad White Balance.tif image, located in the Tutorials > Chapter 14 folder on the companion disc. This scene shows a typical white-balance problem. We had been shooting indoors with an appropriate indoor white balance, and then went outside and started shooting in daylight. The resulting image has a bad blue cast. (See Figure 14.22.)

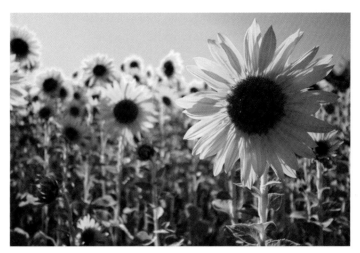

FIGURE 14.22 This image was shot with the wrong white balance, so we're going to have to do some work to get it back to something close to normal.

If we had been shooting in raw, correcting this image would be simple, and we could restore our color with great accuracy. Because we were shooting in JPEG mode, correcting the cast will be much more difficult, and we won't be able to restore to completely accurate.

TUTORIAL 14.4

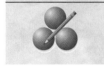

Step 1: Change the Histogram Display

If Photoshop's Histogram palette is not already open, open it now by choosing Window > Histogram.

In the upper-right corner of the Histogram palette is a small pop-up menu. Open this and choose All Channels View. The histogram display should now show the usual histogram, and separate histograms for the red, green, and blue channels. (See Figure 14.23.)

Notice how the separate channel histograms have wildly different shapes. The data in the Blue channel is bulked up on the left side, while the Green channel is more to the right, and the Red channel is spread across the entire range. As you can see, the Red channel has more data in it than the Blue or Green channels.

Step 2: Open the Levels Dialog Box

We're going to correct this image using Levels. Open the Levels dialog by choosing Image > Adjustments > Levels, or by pressing Command/Control-L. Sometimes, you can correct a bad white balance by selecting the Neutral eyedropper and then click-

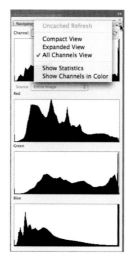

FIGURE 14.23   Using Photoshop's Histogram palette, we can get a view of the histograms for all three channels in the image. From these, we can see that the Red channel contains the most data.

ing on something in the image that is supposed to be neutral gray, as we saw in Chapter 11. There's nothing gray in this image, and the Neutral dropper is usually best for simple color casts, not wildly wrong white balance. We're going to have to use a more complex approach.

Step 3: Select the Red Channel

From the Channel pop-up menu, select Red. The histogram in the Levels dialog box now shows the Red histogram, and any changes we make will only affect the Red channel. We started with the Red channel because it has the most data in it. With more data, we'll be able to perform more editing without worrying about tone breaks or banding.

Step 4: Edit the Red Channel

This is a very bright, high-key image. We want more of our red data in the bright areas of the image, to warm up those areas. Slide the midpoint, or gamma, slider to the left to about 1.85. (See Figure 14.24.) This will cause our midtones to shift to the right. If this doesn't make sense, don't worry, you can always just fiddle with the slider to figure out which direction means more or less red.

Step 5: Edit the Green Channel

The image is already much better. However, while the sunflowers have a better, warmer color, the green stalks are now a little too red. Let's restore some green to them by editing the Green channel.

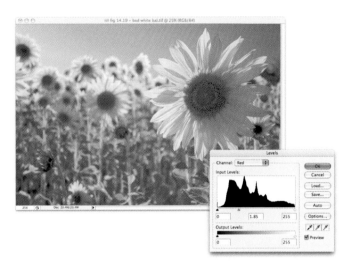

FIGURE 14.24   By adjusting the midpoint on the Red channel, we can warm up the image considerably, countering the ugly blue cast.

Change the Channel pop-up menu to Green.

Slide the midpoint slider to the left to about 1.37. This will restore a nice level of green to the flower stems, without compromising the yellow of the flower. (See Figure 14.25.)

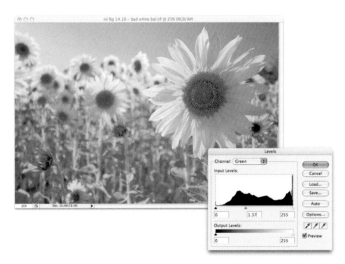

FIGURE 14.25   With a Green channel adjustment, we can restore the greens to the flower stems.

Step 6: Adjust Tone

Our color is much better, but the image also needs a general tone adjustment. Because we've been skewing our color channels around, the image has seen a change in brightness in some of its shadow tones.

Choose RGB from the Channel menu in the Levels dialog box. We can now perform a regular Levels adjustment to improve contrast. Slide the Black point slider to about 35 to darken the blacks in the image. (See Figure 14.26.)

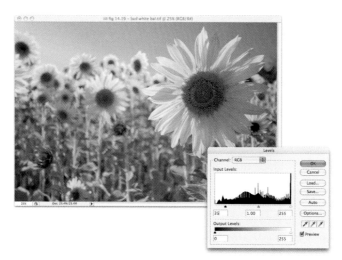

FIGURE 14.26   A black point adjustment will restore the contrast in our image.

Step 7: Click OK

Click OK to accept the Levels adjustment.

As you can see, you can perform separate adjustments to component channels, and to the entire composite RGB image with a single Levels command. The image still isn't perfectly accurate, but it has a much more natural look than it did before. Hopefully, the biggest lesson you'll take away from this discussion is to *always remember to consider white balance when you change lighting conditions!*

ON THE CD

More White Balance Correction

There are many different ways to approach any type of edit or correction, and which one you should use depends on the particulars of each image. For a different approach to solving a white-balance problem, take a look at the Eagle Color Correction.pdf *located in the Tutorials/Chapter 14/Eagle Color Correction folder on the companion CD. In this tutorial, we tackle another incorrect white-balance problem, as shown in Figure 14.27.*

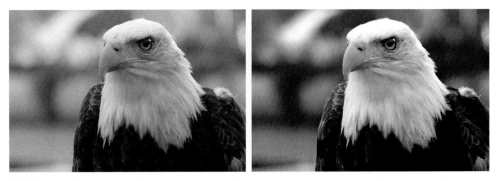

FIGURE 14.27 We corrected this problematic white balance using a number of techniques. The entire process is explained in a PDF file included on the companion CD-ROM.

Correcting Color with Layers

So far, all the color correction methods we've looked at have involved special tools such as Levels, Curves, or Hue/Saturation. However, you can make a number of adjustments simply by stacking layers on top of each other and then changing their opacity or blending method. For example, we took the image in Figure 14.28, duplicated its layer by dragging it to the Create a New Layer button at the bottom of the Layers palette, and then set the newly created top layer to Multiply. (See Figure 14.29.)

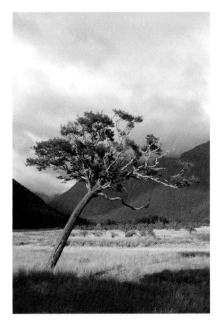

FIGURE 14.28 This image could use a bit of a saturation boost.
We could use the Hue/Saturation tool, but there's a simpler way.

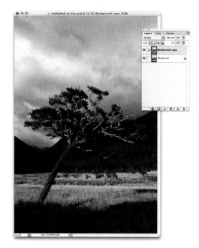

FIGURE 14.29   If we stack two copies of the image on top of each other, and set the transfer mode of the top layer to Multiply, we get a much more saturated image.

Together, the two images blend to create a much more saturated image with extreme contrast. You could achieve the same thing using Curves or Levels, and Hue/Saturation, but this technique is much faster.

However, our resulting image is a little too dark—fortunately, there's an easy way to tend to this.

Earlier, you saw how you could add a Layer Mask to an Adjustment layer to facilitate the painting of masking information directly into the Adjustment. Photoshop CS allows you to add Layer Masks to any other kind of layer. Simply select the layer to which you want to add a mask, click Layer > Add Layer Mask, and choose either Hide all or Reveal all, depending on whether you want the mask to be created completely black (hiding the entire layer) or completely white (revealing the entire layer). Now, just as you earlier painted into the Layer Mask using black, white, or shades of gray, you can paint into your top layer to reveal more or less of it. In this way, you can control how strong the blending effect is throughout different parts of your image.

In Figure 14.30, we created a Layer Mask on our top, "multiplying" image and painted our mask to apply the effect in varying degrees to various parts of the image—just as we did earlier, when we painted into the mask on an Adjustment Layer. We left the sky alone so it gets the full effect, but painted in varying degrees of effect on the grass. The most detailed painting occurred on the tree, where we used varying shades of gray to paint in differing amounts of shadows and highlights. Wherever we painted with white, we got the full, supersaturated multiply effect because we were allowing both images to appear at full strength. Painting with black yielded no effect whatsoever, whereas painting with a shade of gray introduced some in-between amount of effect. In this way, we were effectively able to paint in perfectly toned light or shadow wherever we wanted it. Bear in mind that there's no real science to this masking; we're simply painting where we want effect. The resulting mask shows how much we applied to different areas.

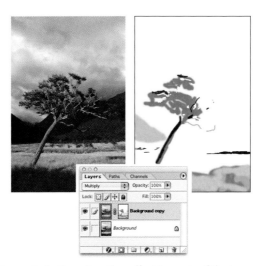

FIGURE 14.30   To constrain the saturation effect to parts of the image, we added a Layer Mask that allowed us to paint varying degrees of the effect into the image.

For lighter, underexposed images that lack punch, setting the top copy to Screen will often help boost the tone of the image.

Now consider Figure 14.31. Here, we've used the same pair of blended images, but this time we performed a Gaussian Blur on the top layer. Remember, changing the blending mode simply changes the mathematical operation that's used to determine what color each pixel is. So, rather than the upper pixel overwriting the lower pixel, the two pixels are combined using a mathematical process. In the case of Figure 14.31, the pixels' color values are multiplied. When we blur the top layer, parts of the upper image effectively go "out of registration" with the lower image, which has the effect of lowering the detail and sharpness in some areas but not in others. Overall color is preserved, though.

As in the previous example, we have used a Layer Mask to control the strength of our blurred effect. In other words, we've painted more of the blur into our image in some places than in others.

Combining layers by stacking and controlling blend modes and layer masks is a quick, easy, and powerful way to perform color corrections both image-wide and locally. What's more, you can combine this method with the corrections you learned earlier by applying adjustments to your upper, blending layer. You can use Levels, Curves, Hue/Saturation, or any other type of edit to one layer or the other. Or, you can attach an appropriate Adjustment layer to the layer you want to modify. By performing tonal adjustments to one layer, you can change the look of the final blended effect.

You can limit an Adjustment layer so it affects a specific layer rather than the entire image by stacking it directly above the layer you want to modify, linking it with that layer, and then grouping those layers together. In Figure 14.32, the Adjustment layer affects only the layer immediately beneath it. All the bottom layers are untouched.

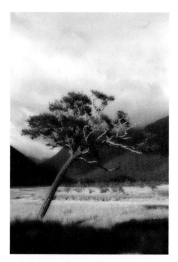

FIGURE 14.31   Here, we started with the same stack of layers but this time blurred the top, multiplied layer with a Gaussian Blur filter.

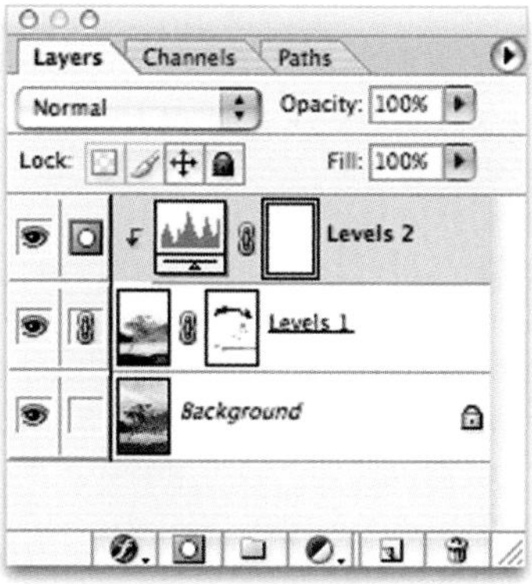

FIGURE 14.32   Using the Photoshop Layer Linking and Grouping features, you can constrain an Adjustment layer so it affects only specific layers.

EDITING

Your image is cleaned, your tone is corrected, your colors are adjusted—you have an image that is perfect raw material for your artistic license. Now is the time where you'll begin to create any composites or collages, or any radical touchups. Because you know that you've already removed any color fringes or other image artifacts, you can perform all your artistic edits without concern of duplicating artifacts.

After your edits, you may find that you need to tweak your color correction or tonal settings or perform another color correction pass to blend and smooth out your edits.

In the next chapter, you'll explore many of the things that might transpire in this editing stage, from compositing to adding texture and tone to your image. For now, let's concentrate on the remaining steps of your image-editing workflow.

Removing Noise

Noise is the most troublesome artifact to get rid of and, unfortunately, the most prevalent. Although modern digital cameras are getting much better in their capability to produce images with low noise, most will still generate some noise, particularly in shadow areas and bright skies, and especially when you shoot at higher ISOs.

Noise is produced by any number of components in your camera, ranging from the image sensor to the support circuits to the analog-to-digital converter. In Chapter 2, "How a Digital Camera Works," you saw how image sensors measure light by measuring the voltage of electrons released when light strikes a photo-sensitive metal. Unfortunately, the semiconductors used in your camera can generate electrical signals that are indistinguishable from the signals produced by your camera's sensor. These extra signals can leak into your image in the form of noise.

There are two types of noise you'll encounter in your image. *Luminance noise* does not alter the color in your image at all, but instead looks very similar to the static "snow" that you see on an untuned TV set. Luminance noise is almost always caused by the type of ambient electrical signals described previously. The good news is that it's not an unattractive noise—it looks a lot like traditional film grain—and although it might be easily visible on-screen, it probably won't show up in print.

Chrominance noise is more troublesome. If you see blue or red dots in an image—and these will be especially prevalent in low-light/high-ISO images—you have some chrominance noise to deal with. Many image sensors, especially CCDs, are more sensitive to red and infrared light than to blue light, so special filters are used to cut certain frequencies of red light to improve the blue response. (As discussed in Chapter 9, the strength of this filter will govern how capable the camera is at infrared photography.) Unfortunately, because the sensor is weak in its blue perception, the blue channel is the first thing to be compromised when you start amplifying the sensor signal to increase ISO. Consequently, on many cameras you'll see pronounced noise in the blue channel of an image. As such, chrominance noise is sometimes referred to as *blue channel noise*. (See Figure 14.33.)

In Chapter 2, you also learned that, because of the natural sensitivity of the human eye, there are twice as many green sensors on an image sensor as red and blue sensors. This means that the camera must perform much more interpolation for the red and blue color data than for the green color data. This interpolation can introduce further noise into the Blue or Red channels. The problem with trying to remove noise from an image is that there's no way to do it without altering your image. Removing luminance noise will tend to soften and smooth fine details, whereas trying to eliminate chrominance noise can alter the colors in your image. Noise reduction also often results in a loss of saturation.

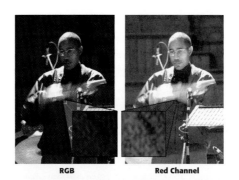

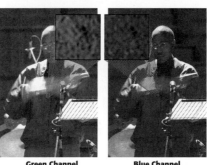

FIGURE 14.33   In a color image, different color channels can have different amounts of noise. Knowing which channels are noisiest can influence your noise-reduction strategies.

Nevertheless, a slightly softer or less-saturated image is usually preferable to an image covered with distracting, ugly noise.

If you're using Photoshop, it's fairly easy to identify which type of noise troubles you might be facing—simply look at the individual color channels. If you do, in fact, have a problem with Blue or Red channel noise, it will be very apparent by looking at the individual Blue and Red channels.

Noise-Reduction Software

These days, there are some excellent noise-reduction applications available, and some at extremely reasonable prices. In the end, no matter what type of noise troubles you're facing, getting a dedicated noise-reduction application is probably the easiest solution for eliminating noise.

Although there are many noise-reduction products out there, a list of the standouts follows. You can find links to demo versions of all these products at *www. completedigitalphotography.com/noisereduction*.

   Visual Infinity® Grain Surgery™: Available for Mac and Windows for $179. (See Figure 14.34.)

   PictureCode Noise Ninja: For Mac or Windows, this standalone program ships in a $29 8-bit version or a $69 16-bit version that includes batch processing.

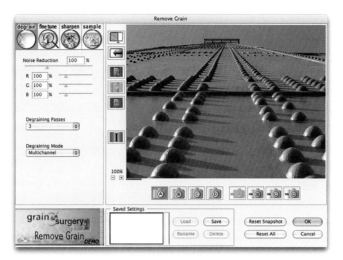

FIG 14.34   Grain Surgery provides sophisticated tools for targeting and removing noise, and adding noise and matching noise between different images—a necessary step when compositing images with differing noise qualities.

ABSoft® Neat Image: Available in several versions ranging from $30 to $75, this standalone Mac or Windows application is a little slow to process, but does very good work battling both luminance and chrominance noise.

Fred Miranda Noise Reducer ISOx Pro™: This $15 Photoshop action can be used on either the Mac or Windows versions of Photoshop 7 or later. It offers seven levels of noise reduction, and you can't beat the price, but it's a tad weak when compared to more expensive standalone packages. Still, it's a good solution at a fair price.

Don't expect these packages to turn noisy images into sharp, silky-smooth pictures. There will *always* be a price to pay for noise removal, usually in the form of reduced sharpness. However, these programs do a good job of trading ugly noise for softening and color shifts that are completely acceptable.

Removing Noise Manually

If you can't afford or don't have access to noise-reduction software—or if you're just the type of person who likes to take matters into your own hands—it is possible to reduce noise using your image-editing application. Although the techniques presented here are more time-intensive and not as sophisticated as what a standalone application will do, they can still be effective at improving a noisy image.

Before you can remove noise, you have to find it. In some images—particularly those shot at high ISOs—the noise will be strong enough that you won't have any trouble identifying it. In other images, noise might be less pronounced. Determining which parts of the image have noise problems will make it easier to develop a plan of attack.

Shadow areas are the most common locations for noise, even lighter shadows such as those found under a person's chin. Because low-light photos have many shadowed areas, you'll find much more noise in low-light images than in daytime images. Nevertheless, daylight skies are sometimes susceptible to noise, as are any flat, colored objects. When you identify noise, pay attention to what the noise looks like. Is it a simple grainy luminance noise, or is it loaded with specks of color?

Remember, don't obsess too much about fine-grained noise. Depending on your printer, you may not be able to see the noise anyway. Similarly, if you shoot with a high-resolution camera (four megapixels or better), you probably don't need to worry about slight noise that becomes visible when you zoom in to 100 percent. Although it may look bad on-screen, it will probably be minimized or completely invisible in print. If you're unsure of whether your noise is a problem, do a test print to see how bad the noise is. In addition, if you plan to greatly reduce the size of your image, there's a good chance that the noise in your image will be reduced or eliminated by the downsampling process.

Once you know where the noise is, you can begin to use any combination of the following procedures to remove it.

Reducing Noise with Median

What's annoying about noise is that it mucks up otherwise fine colors, so that a field of perfectly nice blue pixels is marred by weird pixels of other colors. However, you can use these correctly colored pixels to reduce noise by taking advantage of a couple of filters that are built in to Photoshop.

The first of these is the Median filter, located in the Filter > Noise menu. Median analyzes the pixels in an area to come up with a median statistical color value, which it then uses to adjust the color of each pixel. Figure 14.35 shows an image suffering from fairly typical sky noise. As you can see, it's predominantly a luminance noise and probably wouldn't show up in print. It's also a type of noise that will respond very well to Median filtering, so there's no reason not to try it.

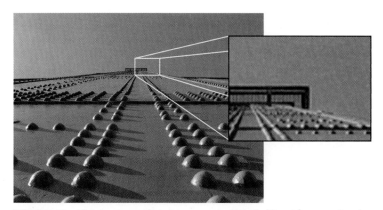

FIGURE 14.35   This image suffers from a typical kind of luminance noise that usually shows up in the Blue channel, making it especially prevalent in skies.

Since the noise is not visible in the bridge itself, we don't want to filter it, because Median can introduce softness into fine detail. A single click of Photoshop's Magic Wand selects most of the sky when used with a tolerance setting of 32. We then click Select > Similar, and Photoshop automatically grabs the rest of the blue in the image, leaving the bridge unselected. Finally, we activate the Median filter with a Radius of 3 and, as you can see in Figure 14.36, the noise is nicely smoothed out, with no loss of detail in the bridge, although there has been a slight overall change in the color of the sky.

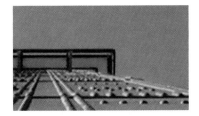

FIGURE 14.36   After running a 3-pixel Median filter over the selected sky, our image is much less noisy.

Protected Median Noise Reduction

In the previous example, we were able to easily constrain our noise reduction to the sky by using a simple selection. Because the Median filter can greatly soften fine detail, being able to filter only particular areas can be critical when removing noise. Unfortunately, not all images have such an easily selectable target area as the bridge picture we just used.

Figure 14.37 is a low-light, high-ISO image that suffers from a fair amount of both luminance and chrominance noise. If we apply a 1-pixel median blur to the image, we can successfully reduce the noise, but with a noticeable loss in sharpness. (See Figure 14.38.)

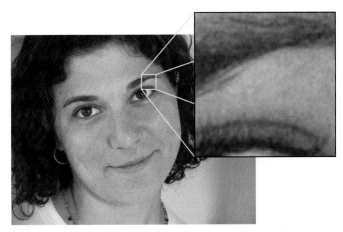

FIGURE 14.37   This image was shot with a higher ISO, resulting in an image with a fair amount of both luminance and chrominance noise.

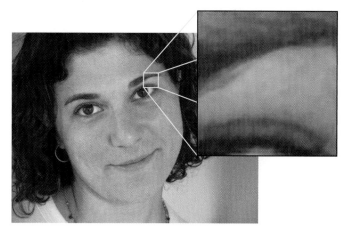

FIGURE 14.38   We can use the same Median filter technique to reduce the noise in this image, but we lose a conspicuous amount of sharpness.

Ideally, we would like to create a mask that protects all the edges in the image, so they don't suffer the blurring effect of the median filter. However, unlike our bridge image in the previous example, there are no simple areas of solid color we can easily select using Photoshop's normal selection tools.

Instead, we're going to pull a trick from earlier in the chapter, and use the image data itself to create a mask. Figure 14.39 shows a mask we created by duplicating the Green channel and then severely altering its contrast with a Levels adjustment. We then loaded this mask as a selection and applied a 1-pixel median filter through it. (See Figure 14.40.) As you can see, the mask protected many of the important hard edges, especially the eyes.

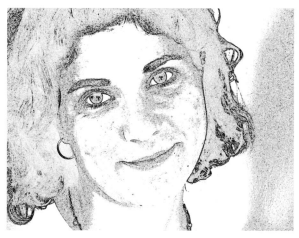

FIGURE 14.39   We selected the Green channel and applied a strong Levels Adjustment to alter the contrast to stark black and white. This mask will protect the edges of our image from the Median filter.

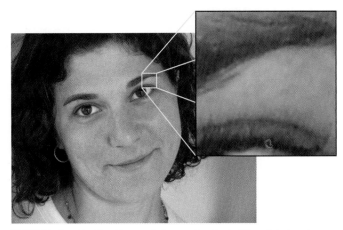

FIGURE 14.40   Our final image is less noisy, but still maintains sharpness around the eyes, and other hard-edged details.

Although we used a specially created luminance channel in the example in our earlier masking tutorial, duping the Green channel works fine for our purposes here. We simply want to create a map that shows the changes in contrast in the image, because contrast changes follow edge details and don't need all the fine luminance detail we wanted in our earlier example. Also, because we can get away with using the Green channel, we don't have to go through the extra step of duplicating the image to derive a new channel. Based on what you learned in the Advanced Masking section in this chapter, you should have no trouble pulling off this technique.

Noise Reduction in L*a*b Mode

As discussed earlier, L*a*b mode stores your image as three channels: a Luminance channel and two color channels. Just as you can attack the separate Red, Green, and Blue channels of an RGB image, L*a*b mode lets you selectively de-noise the color information in your image independent of the luminance. Converting to L*a*b mode and back again does result in a tiny bit of quality loss, but this loss will not be perceptible until you change modes a dozen times or so.

To reduce noise in L*a*b mode:

1. First, convert your image to L*a*b by clicking Image > Mode > Lab color.
2. In the Channels palette, switch to the A & B channel.
3. Use a Smart or Gaussian blur (or any of the averaging filters discussed earlier) to attack the noise. (See Figure 14.41.)
4. Now switch back to RGB.

Using Photoshop's History palette, you can easily jump back to the Blur operation to try different settings. This method of noise reduction often tends to reduce saturation in your image. Once you get back into RGB mode, you can use Hue/Saturation to try to restore lost saturation.

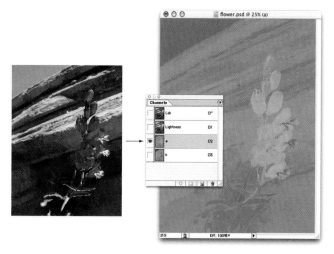

FIGURE 14.41   If you convert your image to L*a*b mode, you can attack the color information in your image independently of the lightness or detail of your image.

TUTORIAL 14.5   VIDEO TUTORIAL: PAINTING LIGHT AND SHADOW

ON THE CD

No matter what tools or procedures you choose to use when making your edits and corrections, one of the most important things to learn is to recognize the effect of light and shadow on your images. A photo is a flat object; the sense of depth in your scene comes from the interplay of light and dark. As you learn to think more like a painter who wrestles with adding or subtracting light from specific areas in a work, you'll find yourself creating more compelling adjustments and corrections. Located in the Tutorials/Chapter 14 folder of the companion CD-ROM is a tutorial movie (`Color Correction.mov`) that walks you through the process of adjusting the left image in Figure 14.42 so it looks like the right image. This tutorial will introduce you to the idea of thinking about your image edits as placement of light and shadow.

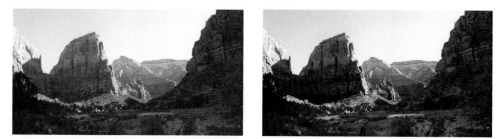

FIGURE 14.42   The left image doesn't look bad, but with some subtle color corrections, we can make it look much better. To learn how, watch the Color Correction video in the Tutorials/Chapter 14 folder of the companion CD-ROM.

Photoshop CS2/CS3 Smart Objects

Working with raw files in Photoshop is a two-step process. First, you convert the raw file into an editable file, and then you work with that file in Photoshop. Most of the time, this works just fine. However, if you start editing a converted raw image in Photoshop and then realize that maybe things would be easier if you had done your raw conversion with some different settings, things get more complicated. You have to throw out your file (and any edits you may have made to it), return to your original raw file, reconvert it, and start again on your additional edits. This is one of the advantages of a nondestructive editing system like Lightroom, Aperture, or Capture NX. At any time, you can adjust your raw conversion settings and all your "normal" edits.

With Photoshop CS2, Adobe added a new feature called Smart Objects, which allows you to achieve a more nondestructive workflow with your raw images.

Smart Objects are special layers that can contain references to vector files (like you might make in Adobe Illustrator), or regular bitmapped image data, or raw files. You treat these layers almost like any other layer, but at any time, you can alter the source data the Smart Layer points to. In the case of a Smart Object that contains a raw file, this means you can alter the original raw conversion at any time.

If this sounds complicated, don't worry, it's actually quite simple, as you'll see in the next tutorial.

TUTORIAL 14.6:   WORKING WITH SMART OBJECTS

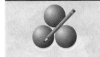

We're going to perform a few simple edits in Photoshop using a Smart Object that contains a raw file.

Step 1: Create the Smart Object

ON THE CD

Copy the file Smart Object.CR2 to your hard drive. You'll find it in the Tutorials > Chapter 14 folder of the companion disc. In Photoshop CS3, choose File > Open as Smart Object, and then select the file you copied to your hard drive. This file is a raw image shot with a Canon EOS 20D.

If you're using Photoshop CS2, you'll first need to create a new document with the same pixel dimensions as your raw file. If need be, open the raw file in Camera Raw first to take note of the pixel dimensions, then cancel out of Camera Raw and create your document. With your document created, choose File > Place and select the file you copied to your hard drive.

Step 2: Configure the Raw Conversion

Photoshop will open the file in Photoshop Camera Raw and present you with the standard Camera Raw dialog box. As always, Camera Raw provides suggested auto adjustments. These look good enough for now. (See Figure 14.43.)

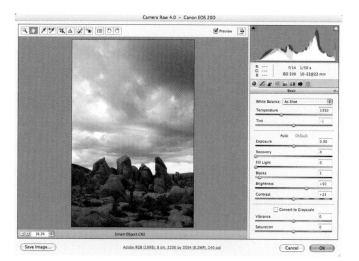

FIGURE 14.43   We opened this raw file as a Smart Object, which will allow us a truly nondestructive editing workflow. The default, auto settings look fine for our initial viewing.

Step 3: Open the File

Click OK in Camera Raw, and the processed file will open in Photoshop. Look at the Photoshop Layers palette. It should contain one entry that says Smart Object, and shows a thumbnail of your image.

If you're using CS2, the Raw file will be placed at the full width of your document and will initially provide control handles so you can scale the placed image. Double-click or press Return to accept the document as is. You now have a Raw file Smart Object.

If your document and the Raw file don't have the same aspect ratio, the canvas may have some extra space in it. Use Photoshop's Trim command (Image > Trim) to cut the canvas size down to match your image.

Step 4: Explore the Smart Object

Double-click on the icon of the Smart Object layer in the Layers palette. Your image will reopen in Camera Raw, *and you can now adjust any raw parameters you want!* (If you double-click anywhere else on the layer, you'll get the Layer Style dialog box. Cancel out of this and double-click on the icon for the layer.)

Unlike a normal layer, you cannot perform any pixel-level editing on a Smart Object, meaning you can't apply any adjustments directly to the layer, nor can you paint on the layer with the brushes, rubber stamp, or any other tool that needs to alter individual pixels.

However, you can work with Adjustment Layers, just like you would with a normal image, and you can also add Layer Masks to a Smart Object, meaning you can easily create composites that combine different conversions of the same raw file.

For example, this scene has a fairly large dynamic range, and it would be best to expose the sky separately from the foreground. We can easily do this by compositing two copies of the same Smart Object, with each processed slightly differently. Let's begin by adjusting this Smart Object to expose the sky the way we want it.

Step 5: Adjust the Smart Object

Let's increase the contrast in the sky to go for something a little more dramatic. We don't have to get it right the first time, obviously, because we can always come back and tweak it later. Set Exposure to –.95, and Contrast to +59. Click OK when finished.

Step 6: Duplicate the Smart Object

The image now has a more dramatic sky, but the foreground is too dark. We're going to create a copy of the Smart Object, and adjust the copy's exposure. From the Layer menu, choose Smart Objects > New Smart Object Via Copy. This creates a copy of our Smart Object, and this copy can have its own separate raw conversion parameters. Note that if you try to copy the Smart Object by using the normal duplicate layer commands, you'll end up with both copies having linked raw parameters.

Step 7: Adjust the Duplicate

In the Layers palette, double-click on the second Smart Object to open its raw conversion dialog box. We want to brighten the foreground. Set Exposure to +.25, and Contrast to +79. This will also brighten the sky, but don't worry about that right now. Click OK.

Step 8: Add a Layer Mask to the Copy

With the copy of the Smart Object selected, choose Layer > Layer Mask > Reveal All. This will create a Layer Mask that's full of white, meaning that right now, we're seeing all of the upper layer.

Step 9: Build Your Layer Mask

We're now going to use some of the same Layer Masking tricks we learned earlier. We're going to begin by filling most of the upper part of the layer mask with black, to reveal the sky from the lower layer. Set black as the foreground color and begin painting black over the sky. As you paint, you'll be filling the mask of the upper layer with black, blocking up those areas, and thus revealing the underlying layer. (See Figure 14.44.)

Don't paint all the way down to the rocks. Painting a clean mask around the rocks is very difficult, so we're going to take advantage of the fact that a cloudy sky is a diffuse, variable texture that can hide the boundary of our mask. Paint along the boundaries of some of the darker, lower clouds, so you can't see where the mask ends.

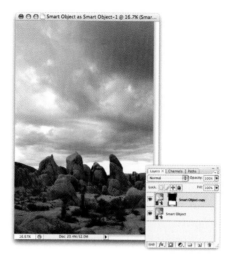

FIGURE 14.44   Using a Layer Mask, we can mask out the sky in the upper layer to reveal the better-exposed sky lying below.

Now we can refine our composite further.

Step 10: Fix the Sky

With our composite in place, we can now see that our sky adjustment is a little much. It looks a little too much like a fake sky composited into the background. Let's back off on our sky adjustment a little bit. Double-click on the Smart Object layer (the lower layer) to open the Camera Raw editor. Set Exposure to –.25 and Contrast to +30. This creates a more believable composite.

Step 11: Add Highlights to the Foreground

The foreground is a little flat, due to the flat lighting overhead. By painting in some highlights, we can add a little depth and dimension to the rocks. Click on the upper layer (Smart Object copy) and then add a new Levels Adjustment layer, by clicking the Create New Fill or Adjustment pop-up menu at the bottom of the Layers palette, and then selecting Levels. In the Levels dialog box that appears, drag the White point slider to the left to around 217. Click OK. The entire image will get brighter. We need to constrain the effects of our Levels adjustment layer with a Layer Mask.

Step 12: Build the Levels Layer Mask

Choose Edit > Fill. In the resulting dialog box, change the Use pop-up menu to Black, and then click OK. Your Levels Adjustment Layer will fill with black, blocking out all its effect.

Select white as your foreground color, select a smallish paintbrush, and begin painting white onto the bright sides of the rocks. This will add highlights to those areas and will create more of a sense of depth.

Step 13: Save the Image

Choose File > Save and then save the image in Photoshop format to your hard drive. At any time, you'll be able to return to this image and reedit any of the parameters we've been adjusting.

Step 14: Final Cleanup

There's some sensor dust in the clouds at the top of the image. You can remove this with the Rubber Stamp or Spot Healing Brush. However, since brushes won't work on Smart Objects, you first need to flatten the image. Choose Layer > Flatten Image. This will reduce your file to a regular, editable image layer. You can then use your technique of choice to touch up the dust areas. (See Figure 14.45.)

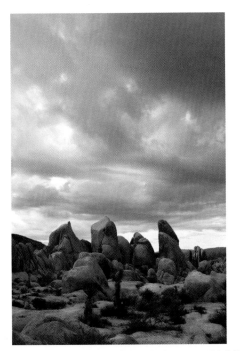

FIGURE 14.45   Our final rocks image after painting some highlights on the brighter rock faces, and then flattening and touching out the sensor dust.

Because we first saved a layered version, we still have an editable version of the document, if we want to make additional changes. 🎲

As you can see, while Smart Objects don't allow you to treat a raw document as a completely editable and paintable layer, they do provide a tremendous amount of flexibility when combined with Adjustment Layers, and Smart Object copies. Being able to work nondestructively can greatly ease your workflow and provide you with far more creative flexibility.

If you're using Photoshop CS3, note that you also have access to Smart Filters. Select a Smart Object layer and choose any filter from the Filter menu. That filter will be added as a Smart Layer, which simply means that it will be applied non-destructively. In the Layers palette, a new entry for that filter will appear, and you can double-click on that entry to adjust its parameters at any time. Note that Smart Filters only affect the Smart Object that they're attached to. They're not like Adjustment Layers, which affect everything lower in the Layer Stack.

Hopefully, in this chapter you've seen that good workflow is not just the process of following a particular order of operations; it also involves performing your edits and structuring your document in a way that makes it easy to make changes. When your document stays malleable, it makes each step of your post-processing workflow easier, because you don't have to worry about getting each setting right the first time.

In the next chapter, you'll learn more of the types of edits you can make during the editing phase of your workflow.

15

SPECIAL EFFECTS

In This Chapter

- Simulating Depth of Field
- Stitching Panoramas
- Applying Effects by Painting
- Creating "Hand-Tinted" Images
- Adding Texture, Grain, and "Film" Look
- Cleaning Portraits
- Compositing
- High Dynamic Range Imaging

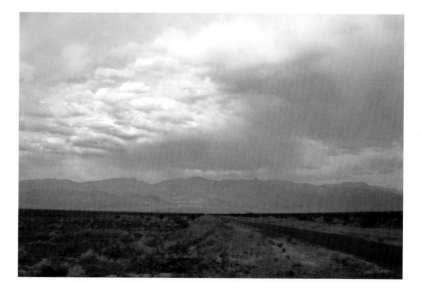

Your image editor is capable of much more than simple tonal corrections, of course. By now, you've probably already played with many of the filters and effects tools at your disposal, and have begun to see just how much you can manipulate an image.

In this chapter, you'll learn some of the more advanced editing operations that, as a digital photographer, you might want to use and explore. The lessons and examples in this chapter are not intended to help you create "trick photography" special effects. Rather, these techniques are intended to help you make up for deficiencies in your camera, to help you get good results from difficult shooting situations, and to help you make your images more "film like."

SIMULATING DEPTH OF FIELD

To the experienced photographer, one of the most frustrating things about a typical point-and-shoot digital camera is the deep depth of field. As you learned earlier, the tiny focal lengths on most prosumer cameras prohibit shallow depth-of-field effects. Fortunately, through some clever blurring, you can use your image editor to add a depth-of-field effect.

One of the most important things to remember about depth of field is that it is a *depth*. That is, the area in focus begins at one point and ends at another and is centered on either side of the plane of sharp focus. A shallow depth of field doesn't simply mean that your background will be blurry; it can also mean that part of your foreground will be blurry. In addition, different planes in your background will be more or less blurry, depending on how far away they are.

TUTORIAL 15.1	**SHORTENING DEPTH OF FIELD IN AN IMAGE**

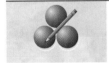

Figure 15.1 shows an image with very deep depth of field—everything in the image is in focus. In this tutorial, we're going to create a very shallow depth of field that will blur both the foreground and background.

Step 1: Open the Image

ON THE CD

Open the image cosmo.tif located in the Tutorials/Chapter 15 folder on the companion CD-ROM. In any portrait, you want the eyes of your subject to be in focus, so we're going to use the dog's eyes as the focal point of this shot. Your goal is to create an effect like the one shown in Figure 15.2.

Step 2: Prepare a Gradient

The blurring effect is actually very easy; we'll simply use the Gaussian Blur filter. However, we want the blur to increase gradually in both directions as it extends away from our focal point. Consequently, we need to apply our blur filter through a mask.

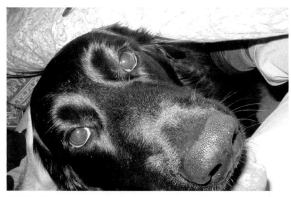

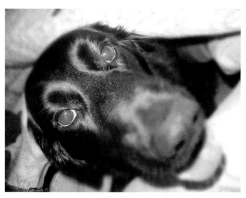

FIGURE 15.1   This image has a very deep depth of field. It's time to make it more shallow.

FIGURE 15.2   With some controlled blurring, we can create a shallow depth-of-field effect.

In the Channels palette, create a new channel by clicking the New Channel button at the bottom of the palette. Our masking needs are very simple for this project; a simple gradient should be all we need.

Type D on your keyboard to select black and white as your default foreground and background colors. Select the Gradient tool from the main tool palette (or press G to select it). Click the gradient sample on the Photoshop toolbar to open the Gradient Editor. Figure 15.3 shows the settings you will need.

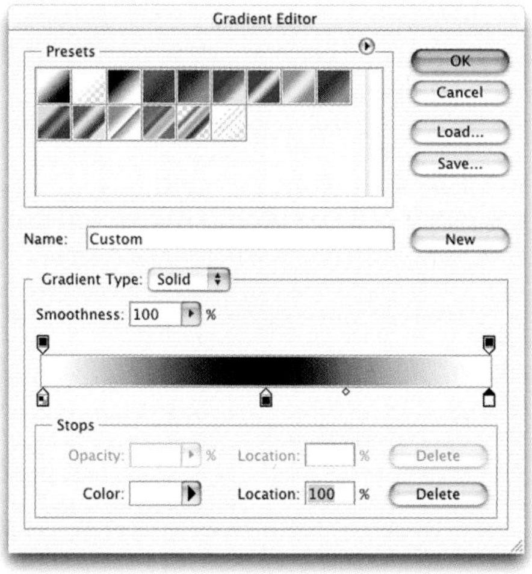

FIGURE 15.3   Use the Gradient Editor to build a custom gradient that can be used to create a depth mask.

You want a gradient that goes from white to black to white. On the gradient bar, double-click the bottom-left Color Stop and change its color to white. Change the bottom-right Color Stop to black, and drag it toward the center of the gradient until the location field reads 50%. Now, click the right end of the gradient sample to create a third swatch. Make sure its location is set to 100%, and then set its color to white. When you're finished, your gradient should like the one shown in Figure 15.3. Name the gradient, and click OK to save it.

Step 3: Apply the Gradient to Your Mask

With your new channel selected in the Channels palette, click the eyeball icon next to the RGB channel in the Channels palette. This will allow you to see your full-color image, and your alpha channel in red. (It's empty so you won't see any red yet, but once you start using the Gradient tool, things will change.) Because the alpha channel is selected (the RGB channels are only "eyeballed"), your actions will affect only your new alpha channel.

Drag the Gradient tool in a diagonal line from top-left to bottom-right to mask the dog's eyes. Your gradient will appear on-screen as a red tint over your image. Position your gradient so it looks like Figure 15.4. It might take a few tries, but each time you drag the Gradient tool, the new gradient will replace the old, so it's easy to quickly try many different gradients.

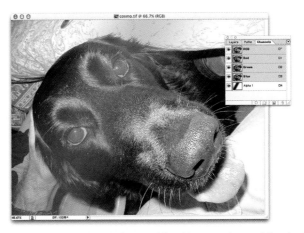

FIGURE 15.4   You want your gradient to blend in to and out of the dog's eyes.

Step 4: Apply the Blur

Remember, at this point, nothing has been selected; you've only created a mask by painting a gradient directly into an alpha channel. Now click the RGB channel to activate it, and drag your new alpha channel to the Load Channel as Selection button at the bottom of the dialog box to load your alpha channel as a selection. Apply a Gaussian Blur filter by clicking Filter/Blur/Gaussian Blur. Enter a Radius of 7 pixels. The foreground and background of your image should go blurry.

Although the effect looks good, the hand in the background looks conspicuously in focus. (See Figure 15.5.) It's on a deeper plane than the dog's eyes, so it should not be in focus. Undo the blur and click your alpha channel in the Channels palette to select it. We're going to do a little mask alteration.

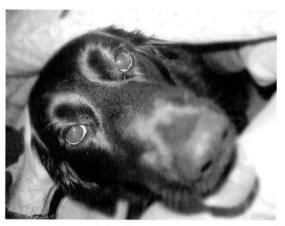

FIGURE 15.5   Although our blur is varying by the same amount, the hand and the dog's eyes are both in focus. Because the hand is actually farther away than the dog's eyes, it should be blurry.

Step 5: Alter Your Mask

Right now, the hand is not being blurred because it lies on the same line as our gradient—it is being masked. We want to unmask it so it will blur. Click the eyeball next to the RGB channel in the Channels palette so you can see your image and your mask.

The thumb is masked an appropriate amount; we just need to get the rest of the hand to match. Using the Eyedropper tool, click the thumb to sample its color. This is the color you'll use to paint the rest of your mask. Click the Paintbrush tool, and paint over the hand, up until it bumps the dog. Use a very soft-edged brush.

When you're finished, click the eyeball next to the RGB layer so you can see just your mask. It should look like something like Figure 15.6.

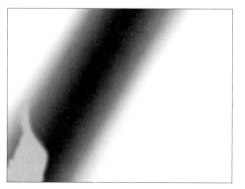

FIGURE 15.6   After editing, your new mask should look something like this.

Step 6: Apply Your Final Blur

Load your new mask and reapply your blur. Now your image should look something like Figure 15.2. With the hand blurred, the depth-of-field effect is much more realistic.

Blue Eyes?

The dog's eyes are blue because, just as human eyes reflect red when a flash is fired directly into them, dog eyes reflect blue. To remove the blue eyes, add a Saturation Adjustment Layer, set it to desaturate completely, and paint a mask to limit the Adjustment layer to only the dog's eyes. (See Figure 15.7.)

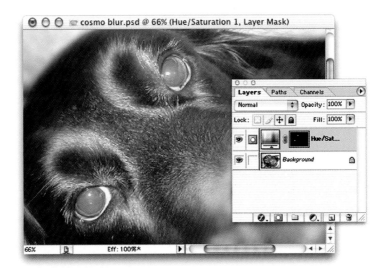

FIGURE 15.7   This dog is suffering from the canine equivalent of red-eye. You can attack the problem just as you would red-eye in a human. Use a Desaturation Adjustment layer to drain the blue color from his pupils.

Photoshop Lens Blur

If you're using Photoshop CS, CS2, or CS3 you can use the Lens Blur filter to add more realistic depth-of-field effects. (See Figure 15.8.) Like the technique you just learned, the Lens Blur filter can use an alpha channel as a map to guide how the image should be defocused. Unlike the technique you just saw, Lens Blur uses more sophisticated blurring algorithms that create defocused effects that look much more like the types of blurring you get in a camera lens. Although the bulk of your audience may not be able to notice the differences in different types of blur, if you're an experienced photographer or a stickler for realism, this tool is a great way to go.

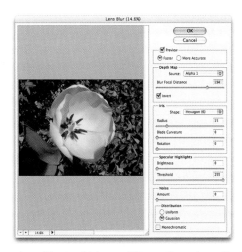

FIGURE 15.8   The Photoshop Lens Blur tool (choose Filter > Blur > Lens Blur) creates very realistic depth-of-field effects. As in the previous technique, you can create special masks to constrain its effects, but the filter creates a blur that looks much more like the blur created by a lens.

STITCHING PANORAMAS

In Chapter 9, "Special Shooting," you learned about panoramic images: multiple shots that can be stitched together to create wide, panoramic pictures. Good panoramas require some thought when you shoot, and sometimes require a little image editing before stitching.

Your camera probably came with stitching software (Figure 15.9), but if it didn't—or if you're not happy with it—consider a third-party alternative such as RealViz® Stitcher®.

No matter what software you use, your images might need a little cleanup before you start stitching. Variations in exposure from one image to the next can cause color banding and shift in your final panorama. Hopefully, you tried to compensate for this while shooting (see Chapter 9), but even the best-planned shots sometimes end up incorrectly exposed.

Before you stitch, open your panoramic shots and examine them for exposure differences. Are some images darker or lighter than others? Skies are particularly susceptible to saturation and hue changes from shot to shot. If you do see variations from one shot to the next, you'll need to color-correct your images. Typically, Levels or Curves adjustments are all you'll need. When you correct, consider the following:

- Choose the image you like most as a base image, and correct your other images to match.
- If the first or last image is very over- or underexposed (which sometimes happens because the sun is in the first or last image), consider throwing it out altogether and creating a smaller panorama.
- If you're having trouble matching tones and color from one image to the next, try stitching and then performing corrections on the completed panorama.

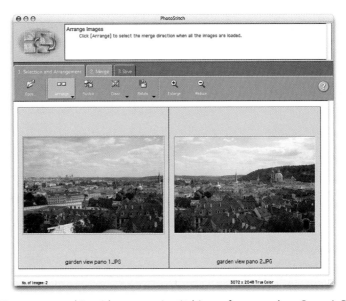

FIGURE 15.9   Many cameras ship with panoramic stitching software such as Canon's PhotoStitch, which can automatically stitch multiple, overlapping images into a single panoramic image.

Because you sometimes shoot panoramic images with your lens at its widest angle, your individual images might suffer from barrel distortion. *Don't* try to correct this before stitching—let the stitching software worry about that.

In addition, don't worry about spotting or removing dust or other aberrations. It's better to do this after you've stitched the panorama.

Some stitching programs offer a combination of automatic and manual controls. If your images were well shot (and after reading Chapter 9, how could they not be?), your program's automatic functions might be all you need. At other times, though, you might have to resort to manual control.

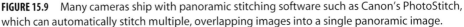

To use manual stitching controls, you simply find corresponding points within an image. These points are then used to guide the software's stitching efforts. Typically, you need to identify two pairs of points along each seam. Try to pick pairs of points that are close to the top or bottom of the image.

Finally, after stitching, your panoramic software might want to crop the image to eliminate uneven boundaries at the top and bottom of the image. These boundaries often create a nice frame and frequently include image elements you'd like to keep. Rather than letting your stitching software crop your panorama, leave the image uncropped. You can always crop it yourself in your image editor, or try to fill in missing information on your own to produce a larger usable image. (See Figure 15.10.)

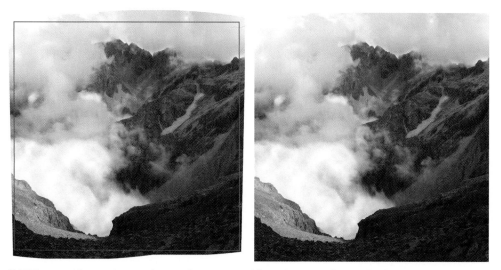

FIGURE 15.10　The top image shows where we would need to crop this stitched panorama to give it a square edge. However, rather than cropping, we decided to use the Rubber Stamp tool to clone in missing information to create a final, square image. With this technique, we get a slightly larger image.

Know Your Focal Length

Some stitching programs want to know the focal length of the lens (in 35 mm equivalency) that was used to shoot the panorama. If your camera has a fixed zoom lens, you might not know what the exact focal length was. You can use an EXIF reader to examine the header information in one of your images to determine the focal length you were using at the time of the shot. (See Chapter 8, "Metering and Exposure.") Some cameras store both actual focal length and 35 mm equivalent focal length in the EXIF header. If yours doesn't, you'll have to perform the 35 mm equivalency calculation on your own. (See Figure 15.11.)

After stitching, you might find that your image needs some more color correction. Again, skies can be especially problematic. If there is a color change from one image to the next, you'll see a short gradation along the seam of your panorama. Odds are that you won't be able to completely match the two images, but you might be able to create a smoother blend by adding a gradated Levels or Curves adjustment. Add the adjustment as an Adjustment layer, and use the Gradient tool to create a smooth transition.

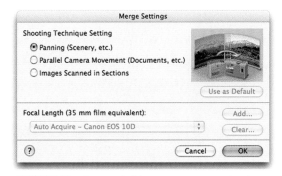

FIGURE 15.11   Some stitching programs need to know the focal length you were using when you shot your panoramic source images. Here, you can see that PhotoStitch has automatically determined the focal length.

STITCHING IN PHOTOSHOP

Photoshop CS and CS2 both provide a Photomerge feature (File > Automate > Photomerge) you can use to stitch images. In many cases, you'll probably find that this feature doesn't do as good a job as a dedicated stitching program. Consult Photoshop's online help for more info.

With CS3, Adobe has greatly improved the Photomerge feature by basing it on the new Auto-Align Layers and Auto-Blend Layers features that were added to CS3. Photomerge now produces excellent results, and the files it makes include masking information that makes it possible to easily modify the final merge. Consult Photoshop's online help for more details.

CREATING "HAND-TINTED" IMAGES

Traditional photo hand-tinting is a painstaking process involving special tints and a lot of hard work. Fortunately, creating such an effect in your image editor is fairly painless and involves little, or no, painting skill.

The following techniques allow you to create a hand-painted look or combination of grayscale/color images. The following procedures assume your image is already a grayscale image, either because it was shot that way or because you converted it to grayscale using one of the techniques discussed previously.

Painting with Light Opacity

The simplest way to tint an image is simply to paint over it using a brush with a very light (20 percent or lower) opacity. You can paint directly onto your image, but it will be difficult to make changes or corrections later. A better option is to create a second layer to hold the paint. If you choose this approach, set your brush to 100 percent opacity and change the opacity of the layer to 20 percent. This won't change the look of your results, but it will make it easier to repaint or change colors. What's more, it makes it possible to resample the colors you're using later. (You can simply set the layer opacity to 100 percent, and then sample using the Eyedropper tool.) You can even create separate layers for separate colors, making for easy color changes and opacity control of each color.

One problem with this approach is that it tends to lighten up shadow areas and generally lessen the contrast of your image. You can try to put some of that contrast back by stacking a Levels Adjustment Layer on the very top of your image, or you can choose to use a blending mode for your paint layer. Setting your painting layers to Multiply mode will cause your painted strokes to be multiplied with the underlying tones in your image. Because multiplying usually produces darker tones, your painted colors will darken, so you might have to overcompensate by choosing lighter colors. However, most of the shadow and contrast information in your image will be preserved. Figure 15.12 was hand-painted using multiplied paintbrushes.

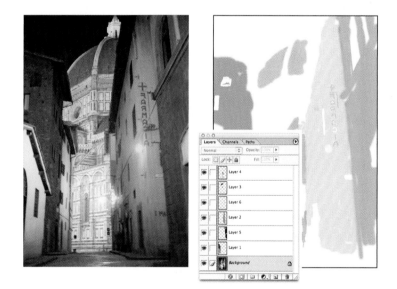

FIGURE 15.12   Originally a grayscale image, this picture was colored by painting into separate layers and adjusting the opacity of each color layer. The right image shows the isolated paint layer. As you can see, the actual painting is very simple.

Painting Desaturated Images

The easiest way to produce a hand-colored look is to start with a real color picture. Shoot a color image and then add a Hue/Saturation Adjustment Layer. In the Hue/Saturation dialog box, drag the Saturation slider all the way to the left to desaturate the image to grayscale.

With the Adjustment Layer selected, select a black paintbrush and begin painting over the parts of your image you would like to color. The paintbrush will mask those areas of the image, protecting them from the desaturation effect. Consequently, they'll return to their full saturation.

A fully saturated color element in the middle of a grayscale photo can sometimes look a little odd. After resaturating the elements of the image you want colored, add another Hue/Saturation Adjustment layer, and apply a little desaturation to the entire image to tone down the color elements. (Alternatively, sometimes it's better to *increase* the contrast between the color and grayscale areas. Use your new Hue/Saturation layer to increase the saturation of the color areas.) (See Figure 15.13.)

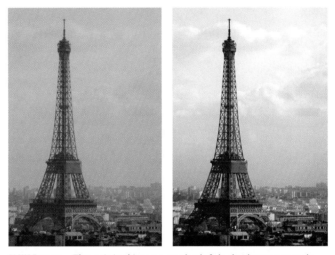

FIGURE 15.13 The original image on the left lacked some punch. We created the image on the right by boosting the saturation of the Eiffel Tower and by desaturating the sky to render it black and white, thus lending more focus to the foreground elements. Some additional color adjustments were performed to better integrate the foreground and background.

Painting with the History Brush

You can use the History brush to perform a variation of the previous method. Take a color image, convert it to grayscale, and then convert the grayscale image back to RGB. You'll still have a grayscale image, but because it's in RGB mode, it will be able to handle color information.

Select the History brush (available from the keyboard by pressing Y) and begin painting the areas you would like colored. The History brush paints using the information stored in the last History snapshot—the History palette shows a thumbnail view of that snapshot. If you haven't intentionally set a new snapshot, the History snapshot should be your original, color image.

As with the previous coloring scheme, you might end up with an image that has color elements that look a little conspicuous. Consider adding a Hue/Saturation Adjustment layer and then dialing down the saturation.

APPLYING EFFECTS BY PAINTING

The great advantage of Adjustment layers is that they allow you to change your mind later. At any time, you can double-click an Adjustment Layer to change its settings, disable its visibility to see what your image looks like without it, or delete it altogether. Moreover, as you've already seen, with the automatic masking that's built in to the Adjustment layer feature, you can easily create adjustments that are masked and constrained to a particular area.

Unfortunately, neither Photoshop nor Photoshop Elements provides Adjustment layers for many common operations such as sharpening, blurring, adding noise, or any of its fancier special effects filters.

However, now that you have some experience with layers, there's no reason you can't implement many additional effects in an Adjustment layer-like fashion. With a little thought and planning (and a fast computer with a lot of RAM), you can keep almost every edit you make on a separate, discreet layer so you can edit, hide, or remove it at any time. (See Figure 15.14.)

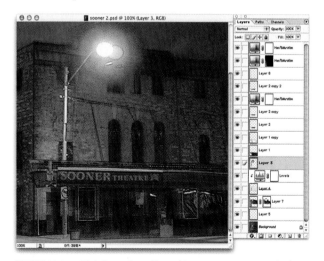

FIGURE 15.14   This heavily collaged image is composed of more than 25 layers, each of which contains a discreet painting or image-editing operation. With this type of structure, we can easily change or alter any edit we've made, at any time.

For example, if you need to paint onto an image, create a separate layer to hold your paint. This will allow you to repaint at any time, or get rid of your paint altogether, without affecting your original image. Throughout the rest of this book, we will be returning to this approach to editing, to control the placement of our edits and to preserve editability throughout our workflow.

ADDING TEXTURE, GRAIN, AND "FILM" LOOK

After spending all that time and money choosing the right digital camera, why in the world would you want to go to the trouble of making your images look like they were shot on film? Despite all the advantages of digital photography, film can have a texture and feel that is more attractive than what your digital camera might produce. Moreover, although they might not be conscious of it, most people are very used to the look of film.

There might also be times when you want to create a film-like look—possibly an old, beat-up film look—for stylistic purposes. Whatever the reason, there are a number of things you can do to make your digital images look more like film.

Before adding any texture or grain, take a look at the color and depth of field in your image. Professional film images are usually shot with larger cameras that afford a fine control over depth of field. Consider using one of the depth-of-field adjustment methods discussed earlier to shorten the depth of field in your image.

Many films have very particular color and contrast characteristics. Some produce images that are very saturated, whereas others yield colors that are more pastel. Most of the time, you can choose a color quality based on personal taste. However, if the image will be presented with images shot with a specific type of film, you might want to study that film with an eye toward mimicking its color characteristics. If you are trying to represent the look of black-and-white film, you'll most likely want to use the Channel Mixing method of grayscale conversion. You might also have to spend some time adjusting contrast with Levels and Curves.

All color and tone adjustments need to be performed before you add any texture or grain, because these effects can complicate your correction process.

Adding Grain

Film images have a noticeable grain caused by the clumps and particles of silver halide that are used to form an image. Films with faster ISOs have more grain, and different brands and formulations of film have different quantities and qualities of grain. Grain might sound like a bad thing, but it can actually be very beautiful, both for its inherent texture and because it serves to make the image a little more abstract, allowing the viewer's imagination to kick in.

The simplest way to add grain is with a noise filter. Photoshop includes a simple Add Noise command (Filter > Noise > Add Noise) that allows you to dial in different amounts of noise. (See Figure 15.15.)

Add Noise is a good choice for adding grain, but it does have limitations. First, it affects the entire image uniformly. In film, grain varies with the tone of the image, as silver halide crystals clump together more or less to form different tones. Consequently, a global Add Noise filter can leave the resulting image looking like it's being

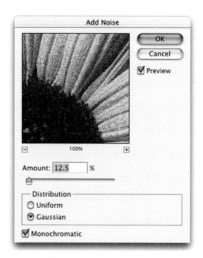

FIGURE 15.15   With your image editor's noise filters, you can create simple film-like grain.

viewed through a simple screen of noise. Second, once you add noise, it's there to stay. As you saw in the last chapter, removing noise is very difficult.

You can apply varying amounts of noise using one of the layering techniques described in the previous chapter. Duplicate the layer you want to noise up, and then apply the Add Noise filter. Configure the filter to add the maximum amount of noise you want in the image. Next, add a layer mask to the image, and fill it with black to completely eliminate your noise effect. You can now paint into the layer mask with various shades of gray to reveal varying amounts of your noise layer.

More recent versions of Photoshop also include a Grain filter (Filter > Texture > Grain), which allows you to add more complex, sophisticated forms of noise, including clumpy noise that often looks more like real film grain.

Grain and Texture Plug-ins

There are a number of Photoshop plug-ins designed specifically to replicate the look of film. Check out Alien Skin Exposure (www.alienskin.com/exposure) for an example of one such product. Exposure lets you select specific real-world film stocks. The plug-in then modifies your image to mimic the color qualities and grain textures of that particular film.

CLEANING PORTRAITS

No matter how young and fit you are, there will be times when a little digital makeover is just the thing to turn a decent portrait into an exceptional one. Facial re-touching can include everything from removing wrinkles and blemishes to altering shadow details to make facial contours less pronounced. As you've probably already guessed, Photoshop provides excellent tools for this type of cleanup. If you're using a different image editor, it probably has tools similar to the ones described here.

You mostly use two tools for the majority of your facial retouchings. The Rubber Stamp (or Clone) tool is good for completely removing features like dark wrinkles, assuming there's enough clear facial tone around the wrinkle to get a good clone. For the rest of your touchups, you'll use the Dodge tool. (See Figure 15.16.)

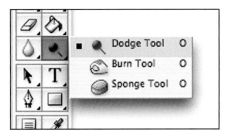

FIGURE 15.16 The Dodge and Burn tools in Photoshop and Photoshop Elements are essential retouching tools for removing lines and blemishes.

The Dodge and Burn tools let you brush lighter or darker "exposure" into any part of your image. With a few simple dodges, you can usually lighten wrinkles or other fine lines to make them less pronounced or to completely eliminate them. Dodge can also be used to lighten shadow areas to make contours less extreme. (See Figure 15.17.)

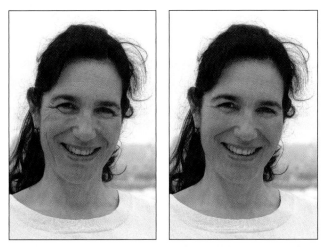

FIGURE 15.17 Using a combination of the Rubber Stamp and Dodge tools, and a separate blur layer, we retouched the image on the left to produce the result on the right.

For the retouching shown Figure 15.17, blemishes and discolorings were removed with the Dodge tool, as were most faint wrinkles. For larger wrinkles, the Dodge tool was used to lighten the wrinkle, and then the Clone tool was used to paint over the wrinkle with appropriate skin tone. The Dodge tool was also used to balance color overall. The whites of the eyes were dodged, and the teeth were whitened by using a Hue/Saturation layer. Finally, to selectively soften some skin tones, a copy of the image was created in a second layer and blurred with the Gaussian Blur filter. A Layer Mask was applied to the blurred layer, allowing us to paint blurred texture into some areas, leaving other details—eyes, eyebrows—sharp. The entire process took about 45 minutes.

The downside to dodging and burning is that, like any of Photoshop's painting tools, once you make the stroke, your pixels are altered and there's no way to change your mind later if you decide you need more or less of an effect. As we've explored in other sections of this book, many effects can be isolated into individual layers, allowing you to paint effects into your image in a nondestructive manner that allows you to reedit your image later.

Dodging and burning effects are no exception. To create a dodging and burning layer, add a new layer above the layer you want to edit, and change the layer's blending mode to Overlay. Painting into the layer with a color that's darker than 50 percent gray darkens the underlying image; painting with colors that are lighter than 50 percent gray will lighten the underlying image.

So, to remove a wrinkle, select a color that's lighter than 50 percent gray and begin brushing into your Overlay layer. For more control, it's best to lower the opacity of your paintbrush to around 20 or 30 percent, so you can paint in your effects gradually. If you make a mistake, you can simply use the eraser to erase your brushstrokes.

Healing Brush

If you're using a copy of Photoshop or Photoshop Elements that has a Healing Brush tool, you might find that it works very well for correcting certain types of facial blemishes.

COMPOSITING

Compositing—the collage-like process of layering multiple images together—is a mainstay of special effects work. Using the simple selection and layering tools discussed throughout this book, you can create all sorts of fantastic or surreal composites. In addition to doctoring photos, you can use compositing tools to solve more practical photographic concerns.

In Chapter 8, we explained how one way to handle the scene shown in Figure 8.4—a tricky exposure situation because of the extreme light and extreme dark—was to shoot two images, each metered separately, with the idea of sandwiching them together.

The same layer-stacking tricks you learned in previous chapters were used to create the composite shown in Figure 15.18. First, we stacked the two images on top of each other. Because we were not using a tripod for these shots, the images were not framed identically, so they were slightly out of registration. We lowered the opacity of the top image, and then selected the Move tool. With the arrow keys, we were able to nudge the image 1 pixel at a time until the images were properly registered. At that point, we returned the opacity of the top image to 100 percent.

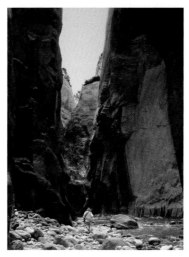

FIGURE 15.18   The final composite of the images we originally saw in Figure 8.4.

Next we added a Layer Mask to the top layer and began painting into it to control which parts of our top image were visible. Several other Adjustment layers were added to improve the effect and to provide color and tone correction. You can examine the final Photoshop file yourself, by copying it from the CD-ROM. You find the `canyon sandwich.psd` file located in the Tutorials/Chapter 15 folder.

HIGH DYNAMIC RANGE IMAGING

While the previous example showed a brute force method for combining different images to create a final shot with very wide dynamic range, in Chapter 9, we looked at another approach to capturing this kind of image. High Dynamic Range Imaging is the process of shooting multiple frames, each with a different exposure, and then merging these images using special software.

Photoshop CS2 and CS3 both provide special features for merging multiple source images into a single HDR image. Choosing File > Automate > Merge to HDR will open the Merge to HDR dialog box. (See Figure 15.19.)

Using the controls in this box, select your HDR source images, and then click OK. Photoshop will begin the merging process. You can also start an HDR Merge from within Bridge, by selecting the thumbnails of your source images, and then choosing Tools > Photoshop > Merge to HDR.

After some initial calculation, Photoshop will finally show its second Merge to HDR window, which will show you a rough approximation of the merged image, with the source images displayed in a filmstrip along the left-hand side. (See Figure 15.20.)

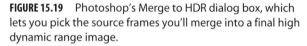

FIGURE 15.19   Photoshop's Merge to HDR dialog box, which lets you pick the source frames you'll merge into a final high dynamic range image.

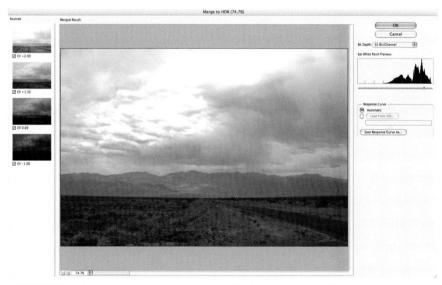

FIGURE 15.20   After merging, Photoshop will display this dialog, which allows you to remove images from the final merge.

An HDR image contains 32 bits of data per pixel, which allows for a *tremendous* amount of color. Far more color than any monitor can show. As such, there's no way for your monitor to show the true color contained in the image. The window Photoshop presents after merging shows you one small slice of the entire 32-bit scene. You can use the slider on the right side, just below the histogram, to select a different part of tonal range to view.

There's not a lot of point to looking around the image, except to examine shadow details. You may find that your shadows have picked up some noise from the very dark parts of some of your source images. If this is the case, try turning off some of the darker images by unchecking them in the filmstrip pane on the left. Your image will rerender, and you may find that the noise disappears.

If there are highlights that appear to be blown out (as in Figure 15.19), you don't necessarily have to worry about them. As you can see from the histogram, the highlights in our image are not actually clipped. We're simply viewing a slice of color that is beyond the range of our display.

When you're satisfied, click OK, and Photoshop will perform its final merge and present you with a final, 32-bit image that looks like the last slice you viewed in the Merge to HDR dialog box.

This image will not appear to be anything special because, again, we're only seeing a small part of its data. We now need to sample the image down to a regular 16-bit image. This will take select tones from the 32-bit image and push them together into a 16-bit space. To do this, select Image > Mode > 16 Bits/channel.

Photoshop will present its HDR Conversion dialog box, which provides several different algorithms for sampling a 32-bit image down to a 16-bit image. (See Figure 15.21.)

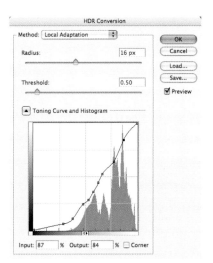

FIGURE 15.21   Photoshop's HDR Conversion dialog box, which allows you to control how the tones in your 32-bit merged image are converted down to a regular 16-bit image.

In Photoshop's online help, you can read about what each of these algorithms does. For most images, you'll probably find that Local Adaptation affords the most control.

Very often, your strategy when performing your HDR conversion is to simply get the image looking okay, with no clipped highlights or shadows. Just like when you're shooting, you're trying to produce an image that has a lot of data you can work with using Photoshop's normal controls. (See Figure 15.22.)

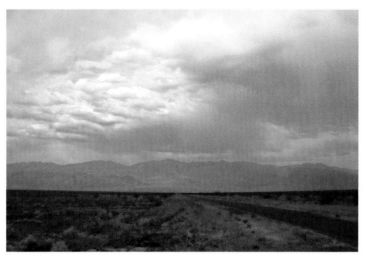

FIGURE 15.22   This rather flat image was produced by the Merge to HDR command. With some simple Levels adjustments and a little careful masking, we can produce the final image shown in Figure 9.38.

PhotoMatix for Easier Merges

HDRSoft's PhotoMatix (www.hdrsoft.com) provides an easier HDR merge solution that provides some extra benefits, such as more intelligent "tone mapping" as you sample down to 16 bits. Check out the HDRSoft Web site for samples.

16

OUTPUT

In This Chapter

- Resizing
- Sharpening
- Painting Sharpening
- Web and Email Output
- Outputting Electronic Files
- Choosing a Printer
- Printing
- Conclusion

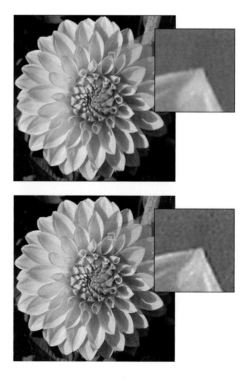

Y̲ou can perform a lot of tweaking, correcting, adjusting, and editing of your images, but none of it does any good if you can't get your results out into the world for other people to see. In general, output falls into two categories: printing to a desktop printer, or electronic output for posting on the web, emailing, giving to a client, or for sending to a photo printing service.

Earlier, we listed output as the last step in your workflow, but your output process will have its own workflow considerations. You'll need to get your image sized appropriately, possibly sharpened, and then output according to your specific output needs. Finally, you'll probably want to save your new resized, sharpened, output version so you can output it again later, and to preserve your original full-resolution version.

In Photoshop (and many other image editors), you'll need to perform these steps in the order just described. You'll resize first, because resizing can affect sharpness. Only after your image is your desired output size do you consider additional sharpening actions.

If you're using Lightroom, Aperture, or iPhoto, you won't necessarily need to perform separate resizing steps. These programs handle resizing on their own when you choose your chosen output method. However, both Lightroom and Aperture *do* provide sharpening that performs the same types of tricks we'll discuss here.

One advantage to nondestructive editors like Lightroom, Aperture, and Nikon Capture NX is that their resizing and sharpening operations are also nondestructive, so you can always undo, or change them later.

We're going to look at these operations in the typical order you'll perform them.

RESIZING

Your camera probably captures far more pixels than you need for typical output. If you're exporting for the web or email, or printing out a 4" × 6" print, you'll probably need to reduce the size of your image. If your camera yields images with a very high pixel count—8 megapixels or higher—you might even need to resize when printing out to 8" × 10". Similarly, if you're delivering images to a client for use in a publication, they may have specific size and resolution requirements.

If you're printing at very, very large sizes, you might need to *enlarge* your image. In either case, understanding the nature of image sizing is an important first step in your output workflow.

Resolution

Although your camera may capture millions of pixels, it doesn't necessarily create files that have a resolution that is appropriate for your intended output. In imaging terms, resolution is simply the measure of how many pixels fit into a given space. For example, if your image has a resolution of 72 *pixels per inch (ppi)*, the pixels in the image are sized and spaced so that 72 of them lined up alongside each other cover a distance of one inch.

The average computer screen has a resolution somewhere between 72 and 96 ppi, so almost all digital cameras output files at 72 pixels per inch. At 72 ppi, an image from a four- or five-megapixel camera will have an area of several square feet. When viewing on-screen, this huge size isn't a problem, because the computer can zoom in and out of the image to fit it onto your screen. For printing, though, this is far too large an area to fit on a typical printer, and 72 ppi is too low a resolution to yield good quality.

PPI versus DPI

Pixels (short for pixel elements) are the colored dots that appear on your computer screen. It's very important to understand that, when speaking of printing from your computer, there is a difference between the pixels on your screen—which are measured in pixels per inch—and the dots of ink your printer creates, which are measured in dots per inch. We'll be discussing this in more detail later. For now, take note that we're measuring our images in pixels per inch.

Resolution is a term that is usually misused these days. People speak of a camera having "6-megapixel resolution," but a camera doesn't actually *have* a specific resolution, unless you want to talk about the pixel density on the camera's sensor itself. A camera produces a certain number of pixels—we call this *pixel dimensions*. How you choose to space those pixels is up to you, and we refer to that amount as *resolution*.

The resolution of an image file is simply a tag that is stored in the header information of the file. So, you can create two copies of the exact same image file and set one to 72 ppi, and the other to 300 ppi. The size of the file *will not change!* Both files contain the same number of pixels; they are simply tagged so that the pixels are spaced closer together or farther apart.

Different programs will choose to use this resolution setting or not. For example, a presentation program like Microsoft PowerPoint® or Apple Keynote doesn't care about resolution, and so ignores the setting. These programs are only concerned with pixel dimensions, and they usually display one image pixel per screen pixel (unless you shrink the image within the application, so you can fit more image area on-screen).

When you resize an image, you will have to decide whether you want to change the number of pixels in the image (to change its pixel dimensions), and whether you want to change the resolution setting of the file.

Resizing an Image

Most image-editing applications let you resize an image in two ways: by squishing the dots in your image closer together, or by stretching them apart to achieve different sizes—in other words, by changing the resolution in your image—or by making up or discarding data to change the number of pixels in your image.

Let's say you have a 3-megapixel digital camera that outputs an image with dimensions of 2160 × 1440 pixels and a resolution of 72 ppi. That is, if you line up 72 of your image's pixels side by side, you will cover one inch of space. At this resolution, 2160 × 1440 pixels will take up 20" × 30". Obviously, this is too big to fit on a piece of paper.

If you want to print this image on an 8" × 10" piece of paper, you could tell your computer to throw out enough pixels so it only has 8" × 10" worth of pixels at 72 ppi. It would then discard every third pixel, or so, to reduce the pixel dimensions of the image from 1440 × 2160 pixels to 576 × 720 pixels. (See Figure 16.1.) This process of changing the amount of data in the image is called resampling (or, more specifically, downsampling), because you are taking a sample of pixels from your original image to create a new, smaller image. Resampling can also be used to scale up images, but, just as downsampling requires your computer to throw away data, upsampling requires your computer to make up data.

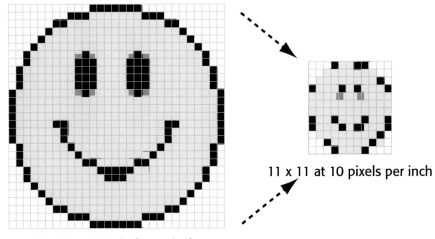

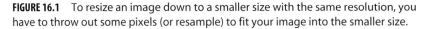

11 x 11 at 10 pixels per inch

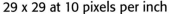

29 x 29 at 10 pixels per inch

FIGURE 16.1   To resize an image down to a smaller size with the same resolution, you have to throw out some pixels (or resample) to fit your image into the smaller size.

For example, if you have an image that is 4" × 6" at 200 ppi and you want to enlarge it to 8" × 10" at 200 ppi, you'll need to resample it upward, which will force the computer to interpolate new pixels. Most applications offer a variety of interpolation techniques. Photoshop, for example, offers five interpolation methods: nearest neighbor, bilinear, bicubic, bicubic smoother, and bicubic sharper. When sampling up, it's best to use bicubic smoother, while bicubic sharper is best for sampling down. If your image editor doesn't offer these choices, bicubic is fine.

The problem with our previous printing example is that 72 ppi is too low a resolution to get a good print. It should be obvious that, after you've spent all that money for all those millions of pixels, the last thing you want to do is to throw a bunch of them out. So, rather than resampling your image from 20" × 30" down to

8" × 10", it's better to change the resolution of your image so the dots are closer together, allowing you to cram more of them onto a page.

Imagine the same 20" × 30" image printed on a sheet of rubber graph paper. If you wanted to shrink this image to 8" × 10", you could simply squeeze down the sheet of paper. You would not throw out any pixels, but now your pixels would be much smaller and more of them would fit into the same space. That is, the resolution of your image—the number of pixels per inch—would have increased. This is what happens when you resize your image without resampling. (See Figure 16.2.)

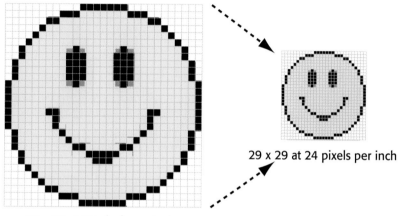

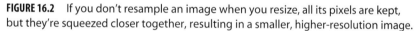
29 x 29 at 24 pixels per inch

29 x 29 at 10 pixels per inch

FIGURE 16.2   If you don't resample an image when you resize, all its pixels are kept, but they're squeezed closer together, resulting in a smaller, higher-resolution image.

Similarly, if you have a 4" × 6" image with a resolution of 200 dpi and you scale it up to 8" × 10" without resampling, you're effectively stretching the image. Its pixels get larger, and fewer of them fit into the same space—that is, the resolution goes down—as the image gets larger. This is what happens when you resize up without resampling.

Most of the time, when you scale up, you'll want to resize without resampling to prevent the computer from making up new data. However, if your camera did not produce a big enough image to start with, you might not be able to achieve the size you want with the resolution you need unless you resample.

TUTORIAL 16.1   UNDERSTANDING RESOLUTION

In addition to providing controls for resizing your images, Photoshop's Image Size dialog box provides a great tool for understanding the relationship between pixel dimensions, resolution, and image size. In this tutorial, we're going to take a quick look at this control, and hopefully arrive at a better understanding of resolution, size, and resampling.

Photoshop or Elements?

Both of the tutorials in this chapter work with either Photoshop or Photoshop Elements. You can download a time-limited trial version of either application from the Adobe web site. You'll need either installed for these tutorials. For the rest of this tutorial, when we refer to "Photoshop," we mean either Photoshop or Photoshop Elements.

Step 1: Open the Image

ON THE CD

In Photoshop, open the `flower.jpg` image, located in the Tutorials/Chapter 16 folder on the companion CD-ROM. This image was shot with a Canon G3, a 3-megapixel digital SLR.

Step 2: Open the Image Size Dialog Box

From the Image menu, select Image Size (or Image > Resize > Image Size if you're using Elements). (See Figure 16.3.) For the purpose of this step, make sure the Resample Image checkbox is unchecked. Take a moment to familiarize yourself with the contents of this dialog box. In the Pixel Dimensions section, you can see the actual pixel dimensions of the image—in this case, 2160 × 1440—and the total size of the image, 8.9 MB. Note that right now, these pixel values are *not* editable.

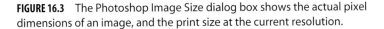

FIGURE 16.3   The Photoshop Image Size dialog box shows the actual pixel dimensions of an image, and the print size at the current resolution.

The Document Size section of the dialog box shows the resolution of the image in pixels per inch and the resulting print size in inches.

Step 3: Resize the Image without Resampling

Notice that width, height, and resolution are linked by a thick black line. This line is to indicate that you cannot change one of these values without changing the others.

For example, if we enter 10 in the Width field, and then press the Tab key to apply the entry, Photoshop will automatically calculate a new height of 6.667" at 216 pixels per inch. (See Figure 16.4.)

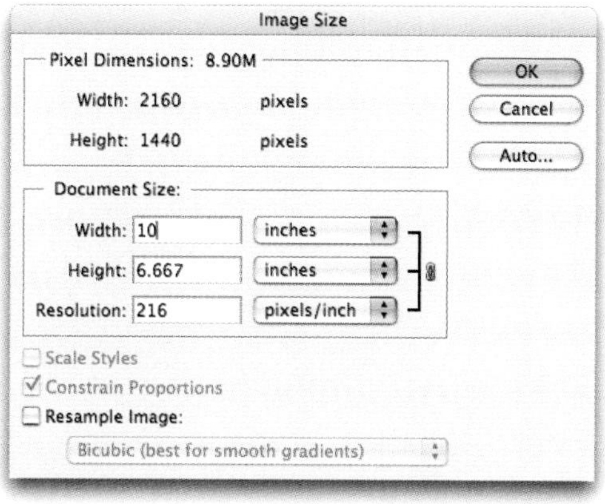

FIGURE 16.4   After entering 10 in the Width field, Photoshop automatically calculates a new height and resolution, as indicated by the linking bars next to the pop-up menus.

Photoshop has automatically adjusted the height to preserve the aspect ratio of the image and has calculated a new, higher resolution. Because Resample Image is *not* checked, Photoshop is not allowed to add or remove any data, so the only way it can fit the image into our requested size is to increase the resolution—that is, cram the pixels closer together.

When Resample Image is unchecked—when Photoshop is not allowed to add or remove data—it is as if your image is on a giant rubber sheet that can be stretched and compressed. As it gets compressed, resolution goes up because the pixels get pushed closer together. As it stretches, resolution goes down because the pixels get pulled farther apart.

Step 4: Resize with Resampling

As you'll learn later, the optimum image resolution for printing on many ink-jet printers is 240 pixels per inch. Enter 240 into the Resolution field and press Tab. At that resolution, Photoshop calculates an image size of 9" × 6" for our image. Suppose, though, that you want to print the image at 3" × 5". Enter 5 into the width field and press Tab. Photoshop calculates a new height of 3.3" and a resolution of 432.

This resolution is much too high for our printer, but if you enter 240 in the Resolution field, your print size will change back. This image simply has too much data to print 3" × 5" at 240 pixels per inch.

Click the Resample Image checkbox. Note that the Width and Height fields in the Pixel Dimensions area are now editable. With Resample Image checked, it is now possible to change the number of pixels in the image. Note, too, that Resolution is no longer linked to Width and Height. You're now allowed to change the resolution independently of the width and height, because it is now possible for Photoshop to throw out data if it needs to.

With your Document Size width still at 5" × 3.3", change your resolution to 240. (See Figure 16.5.)

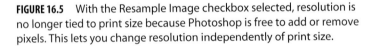

FIGURE 16.5   With the Resample Image checkbox selected, resolution is no longer tied to print size because Photoshop is free to add or remove pixels. This lets you change resolution independently of print size.

Note that several things have happened. First, the pixel dimensions dropped from 2160 × 1440 to 1200 × 800. Our file has gone from 8.9 MB to 2.75 MB. More important, our print size did not change. We now have the width, height, and resolution we want.

Note, too, that we changed the Resample Image pop-up menu to Bicubic Sharper, since this is the best mode to use when resampling down.

When using the Image Size dialog box, pay attention to which fields are editable and which are linked. This will give you a better understanding of how pixel dimensions, print size, and resolution are all interrelated.

When Should You Resample?

You should resample your image any time you have an image with more pixel data than you need for your intended output, (downsampling) or not enough pixel data for your intended output (upsampling).

Downsampling

If you're outputting for the web or email, you will definitely have to resample, unless you shot your images at a small size (640 × 480, for example). Similarly, if you're delivering electronic files for print, and your camera produces more pixel data than your printer needs, you'll need to downsample. If you're printing to your own desktop printer, you might also have to downsample if your image has more pixels than you need for your desired print size. If you're preparing images for use in a video, or for a DVD menu, or other electronic application, you'll almost certainly need to downsample.

Downsampling your image data is a fairly pain-free process. In fact, downsampling tends to improve sharpness and contrast in your image.

The Photoshop bicubic interpolation algorithm does a very good job of downsampling, and all versions of Photoshop back to version 1 offer the option. As mentioned earlier, more recent versions also offer Bicubic Sharper, which is a better choice for downsampling as it yields higher-quality images with better sharpness.

Upsampling

As you learned earlier, many digital cameras use interpolation to increase the resolution of their images. As explained, these interpolation schemes often degrade the quality of an image by introducing artifacts. Simply put, calculating new image data is a tricky, difficult thing to do. When it's done poorly, aliasing artifacts, loss of sharpness, and other image problems can appear. The same holds true when upsampling an image using an image editor.

The most basic rule of thumb for upsampling is that you want to do as little of it as possible. So, you'll want to think very carefully about the precise print size and resolution you need and upsample to exactly those pixel dimensions. Any more, and you'll run the risk of increased artifacts.

We'll discuss print size and resolution choice in the "Printing" section, later in this chapter.

As with downsampling, in more recent versions of Photoshop, you have several different algorithm choices you can use when upsampling. While bicubic interpolation can work very well, bicubic smoother will usually yield results with fewer artifacts.

When resampling with bicubic interpolation, it's best to not make any single re-sizing step greater than 10 percent. If you need to enlarge by *more* than 10 percent, use multiple 10 percent steps. This is not a concern when using bicubic smoother—with this algorithm, you can perform a single resizing step of any kind.

There are several products on the market designed specifically for enlarging images for print. Alien Skin's BlowUp and AltaMira's Genuine Fractals are two Photoshop plug-ins that use proprietary algorithms for making enlargements. While these products sound great in theory, in practice, you'll see little difference between them and Photoshop's bicubic smoother interpolation. In fact, in some instances, you'll find you get *better* results with Photoshop, even when performing very large enlargements.

SAVING A RESIZED VERSION

If you're resampling your image in Photoshop, either up or down, you'll want to perform a Save As to create a separate resized version. Since downsampling throws out data, and up-sampling creates new, possibly soft, pixels, it's important to preserve a copy of your original file. By doing a Save As, either before or after you perform your resizing, you'll create a second version of your document with your new sizing. You can, of course, return to your original full-size version at any time.

SHARPENING

With all your edits and corrections made, and with your image at its final output size, you're finally ready to apply any necessary sharpening. As with resizing, you don't want to sharpen too early because you'll run the risk of accentuating noise and other unwanted artifacts. Also, you won't know how much sharpening you need until you've adjusted the image's contrast—after all, an image with more contrast looks sharper—and until you've resized the image. If you shrink an image, it's going to get sharper; if you enlarge it, it will almost always get softer. Consequently, sharpening should be the last step you take before outputting the image.

Photoshop includes a number of sharpening filters. In addition to these, there are third-party sharpeners are procedural techniques you can use to sharpen your image. Unfortunately, Photoshop does not offer editable sharpening layers. Once you apply your sharpening effects, that's it. Consequently, it's a good idea to save a copy of your image before you sharpen, or to duplicate a layer before you sharpen it. By sharpening a duplicate, you can always throw it out and go back to your original if you change your mind.

In Aperture, Lightroom, and Capture NX, sharpening—like every other edit—is nondestructive. You can change or remove it at any time.

Your biggest concern when you sharpen, however, is to not sharpen too much. Oversharpening can create a number of undesirable artifacts.

How Sharpening Works

Photoshop, like most image editors, has several sharpening filters: Sharpen, Sharpen More, Sharpen Edges, and Unsharp Mask can all be found under the Filter > Sharpen menu. However, the Unsharp Mask (USM) filter is the only one you ever need to consider. If you're using Photoshop CS2 or CS3, you'll also have a Smart Sharpen option in the Sharpen menu. This is a variation of the standard Unsharp Mask filter, and we'll look at it in more detail later. Sharpen, Sharpen More, and Sharpen Edges are simply too uncontrollable and destructive for quality sharpening.

Unsharp Mask gets its name from a darkroom sharpening technique wherein a blurry copy of a negative (an "unsharp" copy) is sandwiched with the original negative, and a print is made using a doubled exposure time. The unsharp mask negative, and lengthened exposure time serve to darken the dark side of an edge and lighten the light side, causing the edge to exhibit a halo. This renders the edge more pronounced and the image appears sharper.

The USM filter works the same way. When you apply the filter, your image is examined 1 pixel at a time. Obviously, the filter can't really tell what counts as an edge in your image, so it looks for sudden changes in contrast. If there is a sudden change in value between two adjacent pixels, it's safe to assume that that represents an edge. The darker pixel will be darkened and the pixels around it will be ramped down, whereas the lighter pixel will be lightened and the pixels around it ramped up.

If you look at an edge in an image that has had a USM filter applied, such as the one in Figure 16.6, you'll see that one side of the edge is darker, and the other side is lighter. The result is a bit of a halo. As long as this halo isn't distractingly strong, the image will appear much sharper.

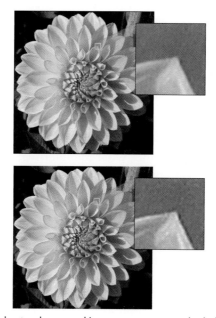

FIGURE 16.6   If you look closely at a sharpened image, you can see the halos the Unsharp Mask process creates along the edges of shapes to make them appear sharper. Notice that the sharpened version also has more noticeable noise and texture, as these elements have also been sharpened.

The key to good unsharp masking is to know when to quit. Too much sharpening, and your image will appear unrealistically sharp, and the edge halos will be bright enough to be distracting. Your final picture will have too much contrast, and the preponderance of halos will add a type of visual noise to your image.

The Photoshop Unsharp Mask tool provides three controls: amount, radius, and threshold. (See Figure 16.7.) This is typical of USM controls, so even if you're using a different image editor, its Unsharp Mask tool probably offers the same options.

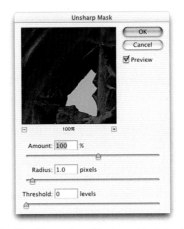

FIGURE 16.7 The Photoshop Unsharp Mask tool provides three simple controls for sharpening your images.

Amount: Controls how much the pixels along an edge will be darkened and lightened. The higher the number, the more the USM filter will change the pixels. Too much of a change and your edge will become unnaturally contrasty and will possibly posterize.

Radius: Determines the width of the halo that will be created. The wider the radius, the more pixels that will be altered around an edge to create a halo.

Threshold: Determines what the filter will consider an edge. A higher threshold value requires more contrast between two pixels before the filter will consider it a sharpenable edge. With a high threshold, USM will find fewer edges and perform less sharpening.

To learn what makes good sharpening, it's worth spending some time looking at some professional photos. Notice that even images that have lots of detail and contrast are not necessarily razor sharp. As you saw in Figure 4.6, your image editor can actually sharpen an image far beyond what looks realistic.

When you use a USM filter, start with a high Amount setting—300 to 400 percent—and a small Threshold. Then, try to find a Radius that produces minimal halos. (See Figure 16.8.) Sharpening is a subjective process, of course, so find a level of halo that suits you. However, be sure to consider your entire image.

Once you've found a Radius that is right, you can back off the Amount and increase the Threshold. Your goal is to use these two sliders to apply your desired radius to the appropriate amount of edge detail in your image.

Always Sharpen at 100 Percent

Be sure you're looking at your image at 100 percent, or 1:1, when sharpening. If you've zoomed out from your image, your image editor is already downsampling its screen image, which will serve to render the image sharper. Consequently, accurate sharpening may not be visible.

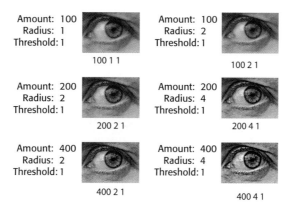

Amount: 100
Radius: 1
Threshold: 1

100 1 1

Amount: 100
Radius: 2
Threshold: 1

100 2 1

Amount: 200
Radius: 2
Threshold: 1

200 2 1

Amount: 200
Radius: 4
Threshold: 1

200 4 1

Amount: 400
Radius: 2
Threshold: 1

400 2 1

Amount: 400
Radius: 4
Threshold: 1

400 4 1

FIGURE 16.8   The right level of sharpening is a balance of all three Unsharp Mask parameters.

Not All Sharpness Is Created Equal

Note that some subjects can withstand more sharpening than others can. Foliage and small, very detailed background elements, for example, usually don't stand up to a good deal of sharpening, whereas simple shapes with well-defined edges do. If these types of objects are mixed together, you might be better served by selectively applying different amounts of sharpening to different parts of your image.

Based on the techniques you've learned so far, there are a number of ways you can selectively apply sharpening. You can, for example, create selections using selection tools. Or, because sharpening is an effect you want to apply to edges, you can use the luminance masking technique we learned earlier to build a mask from the image's edge detail, and then apply sharpening through that mask. For this tutorial, though, we're going to apply sharpening by painting, a technique discussed earlier in this chapter.

PAINTING SHARPENING

Figure 16.9 shows an original, unsharpened image that was pulled directly from a Canon EOS 10D. Like many higher-end digital SLRs, the 10D does not apply much sharpening to an image, leaving you in complete control of the sharpening process. After all, you can't remove sharpening once it's there, so it's often better for a camera to err on the side of too soft, because you can always sharpen later.

Because this image was shot with a shallow depth of field, there's really no reason to apply any sharpening to the background. Because there's no real edge detail there anyway, sharpening would only serve to exaggerate any noise or artifacts that might be lurking in the image. The woman's face, on the other hand, could definitely use some sharpening. However, even the face doesn't need equal sharpening all over.

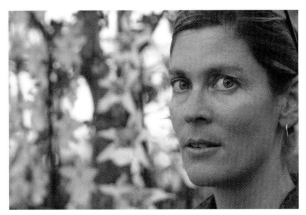

FIGURE 16.9   This image was taken with a Canon EOS 10D, a camera that, by default, performs very little sharpening. Here we want to sharpen some areas but not others.

Eyes are the most important part of any portrait, so we want to sharpen them up quite a bit. Skin tones, however, can suffer from sharpening, because it will intensify pores and wrinkles, so we'd like to apply less sharpening to those areas.

As already mentioned, sharpening is greatly affected by image size and printing technology. Consequently, it's hard to see the full impact of sharpening changes in the images in this book. In the next section, you'll learn how to selectively sharpen the portrait shown in Figure 16.9. As you work with the images on your screen, subtle sharpening differences will be easier to see and understand.

ON THE CD

TUTORIAL 16.2   SELECTIVE SHARPENING OF A PORTRAIT

Step 1: Open the Image

In Photoshop, open the image `Portrait.tif` from the Tutorial/Chapter 16 folder. Because all sharpening should be performed at a zoom ratio of 100 percent, you might want to zoom in to the image and look around to scope out the edge detail and begin to assess which areas could use more or less sharpening.

ON THE CD

Our intent with this image is to print it out as an 8" × 10" print on an Epson photo ink-jet printer. As such, it has already been resized to 8" × 10" at 240 dpi. (Note that because this image was shot in the 3:2 aspect ratio of 35 mm film, 10" wide results in a height of 6.6".)

Step 2: Prepare the Layers

In the Layers palette, duplicate the base layer by dragging it onto the Create a New Layer button at the bottom of the palette.

Add a Layer mask to the duplicate layer by selecting the layer and then clicking Layer > Add Layer Mask > Reveal All. In the next step, it will become clear why we selected Reveal All rather than Hide All.

Step 3: Determine Max Amount of Sharpening

As you've already seen, by painting into a Layer mask with gray, we can make that layer more or less visible. Our plan here is to sharpen the top layer and then paint into its Layer mask to control which layers are visible in which parts of our image. In other words, because of our Layer mask, the sharpened layer will be visible in some parts of the image, and the original softer image will be visible in other parts. This technique effectively lets us "paint" sharpening into our image.

Our next step, then, is to apply sharpening to the upper layer. To determine correct sharpening settings, we want to pick the area where we want the most sharpening and sharpen it accordingly. This level of sharpening will be applied to the entire image. We will then use our mask to paint in lesser amounts in areas where the max sharpening is too much.

In the Layers palette, click the image icon in the top layer to select it. Remember, when you have a Layer mask attached to a layer, you can switch between editing the image data and the Layer mask data by clicking the appropriate thumbnail in the Layers palette.

We know we want the most sharpness in the woman's eyes, so zoom in on her eyes and click Filter > Sharpen > Unsharp Mask. (See Figure 16.10.)

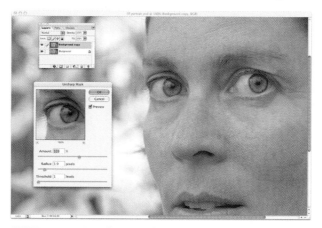

FIGURE 16.10   First, choose a sharpening level based on the area that needs the most sharpening. This maximum sharpen will be applied to a copy of the image, stored in a second layer.

As previously mentioned, digital SLRs often tend to produce soft images, so this picture can withstand rather aggressive sharpening. Feel free to sharpen to your personal taste. We chose an Amount setting of 120 percent, a Radius of 1.9, and a Threshold of 1.

Again, you need to be focusing only on the woman's eyes. Note, however, that the sharpening effect is making her skin more contrasty.

Once you've found the settings you like, click OK.

Step 4: Mask the Entire Image

We're ready to start painting our mask, so click the mask icon in the upper layer. Select black as the foreground color, select the Paint Bucket, and then click somewhere on the image. The image should go soft because the sharpened layer is now completely masked, revealing the original layer. (If your image turns black, you haven't properly selected the mask layer. Click Undo, and try again.)

Step 5: Sharpen the Eyes

You can now apply varying amounts of sharpening by simply painting into the mask. With the mask still selected, choose white as the foreground color and begin painting over the woman's eyes. This will reveal the fully sharpened layer. (See Figure 16.11.)

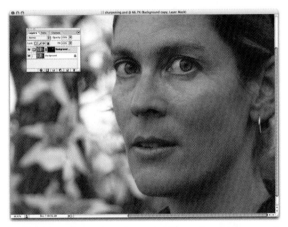

FIGURE 16.11   Here, the upper, sharpened layer has been completely masked. Next, a white brush was used to paint over the eye, knocking a hole in the mask to reveal the sharpened eye from the upper layer. With this technique, we can paint in sharpening only where we want it.

Step 6: Mask the Edges of Her Face

The edge of her face and nose can also withstand full sharpening, although you might need to use a very small brush to keep from sharpening the skin tones around the edge. Her ear is far enough in the distance that it's soft simply because of shallow depth of field. It needs no sharpening.

Step 7: Mask Hair and Skin Tones

Hair is a detail that looks nice when sharp, but the hair in this image does not need our full sharpening. Select a 50 percent white color (or, if you're more of a pessimist, select a 50 percent black color) and paint over the hair. This will effectively apply half the sharpening effect.

You might also want to experiment with applying a little sharpening to the skin tones, especially around the eyes. By selecting different gray tones, you can add more or less sharpening. What's more, if you don't like the effect, you can simply re-paint it with a different color, or you can paint with black to eliminate it. Figure 16.12 shows our final image and our final layer mask.

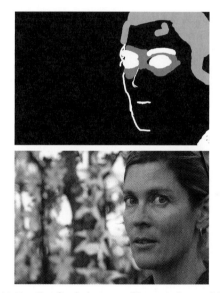

FIGURE 16.12   Our final, sharpened image, along with the mask that was painted to constrain the sharpening effect.

This same approach can be used to apply any type of filter or operation. You can use it to variably add noise, blur, sketch effects, or any other alteration that can be made to a layer. Want to change the color of one element in an image? Just dupli-cate your base layer, alter its color, and then use a layer mask to "paint in" only the altered areas you want.

Sharpness is a very subjective quality, and different people think different amounts of sharpness are "correct." What's more, some images might need more or less sharpening, depending on their content. Facial textures *very* rarely need a lot of sharpening, as most people don't appreciate it if you render every pore, hair, and line with terrific clarity. Some people also believe that foreground images don't need to be sharpened as much as more distant objects, since foreground objects are larger and easier to see. Others believe foreground elements need *more* sharpening *because* they're larger and easier to see.

If all this sounds confusing, remember to judge your final sharpening in your actual output. If your final output is a print, you need to judge your sharpening by looking at the print. Too much sharpening will make the image appear busier—sharp edges will have bright and dark lines around them.

As with any edit, bear in mind that it's the *content* of your image that matters. Some of the most famous photographers in the world shot images that were, by today's standards, very soft. But because they composed and exposed well, the images remain evocative and effective.

SMART SHARPENING IN PHOTOSHOP CS2/CS3

Photoshop CS2 and CS3 include a variant of the standard Unsharp Mask filter called Smart Sharpen. Smart Sharpen does the same thing Unsharp Mask does—find edges and lighten and darken the pixels on either side to make the edge more pronounced—but adds a few additional controls. (See Figure 16.13.)

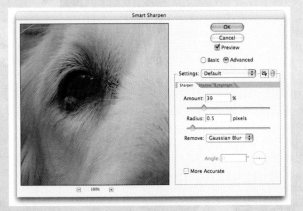

FIGURE 16.13 Photoshop CS2 and CS3 provide a Smart Sharpen filter, which performs an Unsharp Mask operation, but provides more control, and allows for more subtle, controlled effects.

Remove lets you define exactly which blurring algorithm is used to create the "unsharp" copy of your image that is used internally by the filter. Gaussian Blur yields the same type of sharpening as Unsharp Mask. Lens Blur will provide finer detail sharpening and possibly yield fewer halos. Motion Blur (and the accompanying Angle parameter) can yield better sharpening depending on the image. Experiment to determine which algorithm is best for your image.

In the Advanced section of the dialog box, you'll find some additional parameters.

$\rightarrow$

> **Fade Amount** lets you adjust the amount of sharpening that is applied to highlights and shadows.
>
> **Tonal Width** allows you to control the range of shadow and highlight tones that are affected by the filter.
>
> **Radius** lets you control the size of the area that is analyzed to determine if a pixel is a shadow or highlight.
>
> In general, when you use Smart Sharpen, you'll use the same methodology, and need to keep an eye out for the same types of artifacts, as when you use Unsharp Mask. You'll probably find that Smart Sharpen does a better job of constraining its sharpening effects to edges. This makes it especially useful for sharpening portraits.

Sharpening in Aperture

Aperture includes a standard Unsharp Mask adjustment, but in 1.5, an Edge Sharpen adjustment was added and does an excellent job of protecting areas that shouldn't be aggressively sharpened. This makes it ideal for sharpening portraits and other images that need a subtler form of sharpening.

WEB AND EMAIL OUTPUT

Web output is very simple. Unfortunately, this is because there are no color management controls for the web. Because there's nothing you can do but post your images and hope your viewers are using decent monitors, you don't need to spend time trying to tweak your final image to look good on a particular monitor or paper type.

Your main concern when you prepare an image for the web (or for email) is file size. You probably already know what it's like to wait for a large image to download, either from the web or from your mail server. Don't inflict the same data glut on other people by posting or emailing really large files. Obviously, if you and your recipient have high-speed connections, you can probably get away with creating larger files. Be aware, however, that the mail servers provided by many Internet service providers put a limit on the maximum size of an email attachment. If you absolutely *have* to email a large image to someone, consider segmenting it using a file-compression utility.

Fortunately, images for the web tend to be very small. Most users don't have screens that are wider than 1024 pixels, and most web images clock in around 300 or 400 pixels wide. Save a copy of your image (be careful not to recompress it), and resize it to an appropriate pixel size. Be sure to set the resolution to 72 dpi.

The two most common graphics file formats on the web are GIF and JPEG. For photos, JPEG is really the only format you need to use. Fortunately, Photoshop offers an excellent Save for Web option that lets you experiment with different JPEG compression ratios and compare the effects of different compression settings side by side. (See Figure 16.14.)

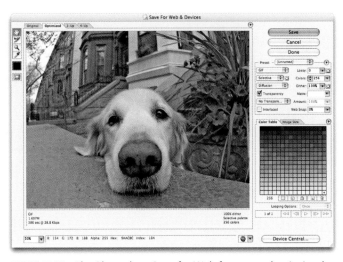

FIGURE 16.14   The Photoshop Save for Web feature makes it simple to try different JPEG settings to balance size and quality.

If you're sending your images to post on another person's website, consider sending an uncompressed image. That person may have his own size and compression requirements, and so will want to perform his own resizing and compression. If you send him an uncompressed file, he'll be able to compress it to his specifications without introducing further image degradation.

If you'd like to have your own photo website but don't have access to any web space, consider using a photo-sharing website, such as Flickr. Flickr is a clever combination of photo sharing and social networking, which means a greater number of people are likely to see your images. Many online printing services (which we'll look at in the "Printing" section) include photo-sharing features that allow you to post images for other people to use in a web browser. They can even order their own prints.

While there's no standard color management system for the web, there is a color space many web browser makers try to respect and optimize for. Before outputting, if you convert your images to sRGB, there's a good chance your results will be a little more predictable and consistent from browser to browser. In Photoshop, you can convert to sRGB by choosing Edit > Assign Profile, and then selecting the sRGB profile in the resulting dialog box.

If you already have a website, or if your Internet service provider includes web serving in your account, you can create your own online photo gallery using the Photoshop CS and Photoshop Elements web Photo Gallery feature. In Photoshop CS, click File > Automate > Web Photo Gallery. In Elements 2, click File > Create web Photo Gallery. (See Figure 16.15.)

Web Photo Gallery offers many options for gallery layout and image size. When you've configured it the way you want, it automatically resizes and recompresses your images according to your specifications and creates a single folder containing

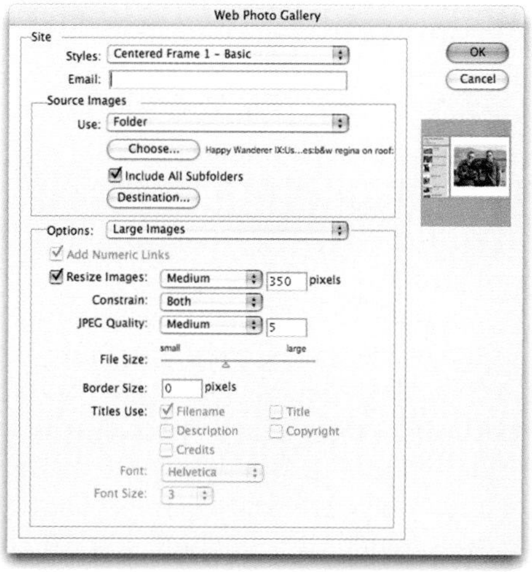

FIGURE 16.15   The Photoshop Web Photo Gallery feature can automatically create a Web-based photo album from a collection of images.

your new images and all relevant HTML files. You then upload this folder to your web server.

Aperture and Lightroom also provide automatic web gallery features that make it simple to output a selection of images as an easily navigable web album. Aperture also provides custom Export plug-ins for automatically outputting images to photo-sharing services such as Flickr. You can download these for free from *www.apple.com/ aperture/resources*. With a little Googling, you'll find similar plug-ins for Apple's iPhoto.

If you're using Aperture, Lightroom, or iPhoto and you simply need to output files for use on the web (without creating a full-blown web gallery), you'll simply use those programs' Export facilities to create JPEG images at a smaller size. All three apps allow you to choose an output size at the time of export. Aperture, Light-room, and iPhoto also provide special email functions that automatically create a small, email-ready image, and then automatically attach this to an email in your chosen email client.

Don't Forget Your Copyright

Before posting your images to the web, use your image editor to fill in the Copyright IPTC metadata field to include your name, and the copyright year. For example "Copyright © 2007, by Joe Kodak." This information will stay in the file even if people download a copy of it from your web gallery. Of course, they can change it using their own metadata editor, but willfully changing a piece of copyright metadata can be construed as copyright violation, so ensuring a good copyright tag can afford a good amount of protection.

Outputting Electronic Files

While web and email outputs are, technically, electronic files, there will be other times when you need to output full-res electronic files. Maybe you need to deliver images for printing to an electronic printing service, or simply create a file someone else can edit. In any case, there are a few things to consider.

Outputting for delivery to a printing service. If you plan to do your printing through an online service, camera store, or drug store, you'll need to output in a specific way. We'll discuss this in detail when we cover these services in the printing section, later in this chapter.

Outputting for delivery to a designer or printer. If you're producing images that will be used by a graphic designer or printer, you'll need to check with them to find out exactly what their specifications are. They will probably need an image sized to very specific pixel dimensions, and with a very specific resolution. They might also need an image that has been converted to CMYK, (something you cannot do in Photoshop Elements, Aperture, Lightroom, or iPhoto), and they'll probably have specific file format requirements. Finally, they might also have specific color space requirements. They should be able to provide you detailed instructions on exactly how to save the file, and can probably do any necessary CMYK conversions for you, although they may charge a fee for this service. You'll also want to find out what file format they expect for delivery. In many cases, a high-quality JPEG file will be fine, although some printers will insist on an uncompressed format such as TIFF, PSD, or possibly EPS.

Outputting for delivery to a retoucher or photographer. Many photographers prefer to work with a professional retoucher, rather than perform retouching and editing on their own. After all, if someone else is handling your retouching, you'll have more time for shooting. There might be other times when you simply need to deliver an editable file for someone else because he or she needs a copy for his or her own use. In these instances, you'll want to deliver a full-res file, possibly with any layers you've created, and usually at the highest possible bit depth. So, if you've been shooting raw, you'll want to deliver a 16-bit file, while JPEG images will have to be sent at 8 bits. If possible, you'll want to send it in an uncompressed format such as TIFF or PSD (obviously, if you were shooting in JPEG mode, you'll have to send JPEG).

Photoshop's Image Processor

Photoshop CS2 and CS3 include a handy feature that makes it easy to quickly convert batches of files from one format to another. If you choose File > Scripts > Image Processor, you'll be presented with the Image Processor dialog box, which lets you select a folder full of images, a destination location, and check boxes to select the file format of your output files. (See Figure 16.16.)

→

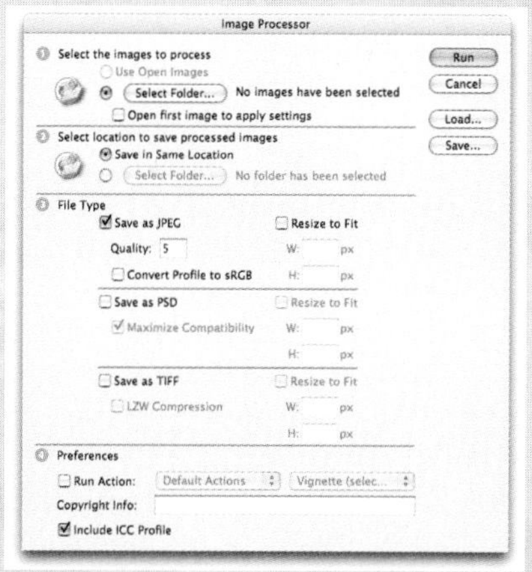

FIGURE 16.16   The Photoshop Image Processor lets you easily batch process entire folders full of images into different file formats.

In addition, you can opt to resize your files at the time of output, and you can even output in JPEG, PSD, and TIFF files simultaneously. Finally, using the Preferences section at the bottom of the window, you can choose an Action to run on the processed images (an action you've defined in the Actions palette), and a Copyright tag to embed in the file's IPTC info.

If you need to convert many images to TIFF or JPEG very quickly, the Image Processor is an easy way to do so.

CHOOSING A PRINTER

With pixel counts climbing ever higher and prices continuing to drop, it's not hard to see that digital camera technology is constantly improving by leaps and bounds. But desktop printing technology has been making equally impressive advancement as evidenced by the fact that you can now buy a printer that delivers photo-lab-quality prints for under $100. For years, longevity and durability of prints was the Achilles' heel of desktop printing, but over the last couple of years, new pigment ink formulations have addressed this problem, and desktop ink-jets are now capable of producing prints that are *more* durable than traditional film printing processes.

Many new users are quick to point out that although the printers are cheap, ink cartridges are very expensive, and therefore, digital printing is a rip-off. This may be true when compared to having your film processed at your local Wal-Mart, but you need to remember that you get what you pay for. Odds are, you'll get better-looking prints from your desktop printer than you'll ever get from a cheapo drugstore photo lab.

Here's another way of looking at it. If you're like most people, when you shoot a roll of 36 exposures, you probably get five or six prints you want to keep. If the film costs you $6, and processing costs you $15, you're effectively paying $3.50 each for those six prints you like. And those are 4" × 6" prints! You can print out 8" × 10" prints on a typical ink-jet printer at a cost of somewhere between $1.50 and $2.00.

If you tend to print most of the pictures you shoot, a desktop printer will be more expensive per print. If this sounds like you, you will want to use a less-expensive photo printing service, and think of your desktop printer as a replacement for a custom photo lab you would go to for those times when you want enlargements, special prints, or precise control over color. Or, you might think of it as a replacement for a color darkroom you'd normally have to keep in a closet or bathroom. When viewed this way, you'll see that desktop printing is much cheaper than using a custom lab, and definitely cheaper than the equipment and materials required for a wet darkroom.

What you may find is that the ideal printing solution is a combination of mail-order printing for your everyday prints, and a desktop printer for larger prints or for times when you want to tweak and adjust the color of a print.

We'll discuss both technologies in this chapter. Fortunately, all the work you've done in the preceding pages should leave you well prepared for a discussion of printing. Most of the color theory you learned when you were working with your camera will apply to your printer as well. This section begins with a discussion of the issues and questions you'll face when you buy a printer. Following that, you'll learn more about how to adjust and prepare your images for printing.

There are many different ways to print a color image on a piece of paper, so your first choice when you shop for a printer is to choose a printing technology.

Ink-Jet Printers

The best photo-printing solution is a color ink-jet printer. Ink-jets work by shooting tiny (*really* tiny—most ink-jets use a drop that is only a few picoliters) drops of ink out of a nozzle. As with any color-printing technology, different colored drops are combined to create full-color images.

Ink-jet printers have a number of advantages over other printing technologies. They have larger color gamuts, better sharpness, produce prints that are more durable, and provide much greater media flexibility than any other printing technology. With the right paper, a good ink-jet printer can create an image that's indistinguishable from a photographic print.

Ink-jet printers are typically far cheaper to buy than any other type of printer, although their cost per print can be expensive—up to $2 per page for a photo-quality 8" × 10" print. However, because of their capability to handle different media, you can also create lower-quality, less-expensive prints by using cheaper paper.

Ink-jet printers can currently be divided into two major categories: four-color printers and more than four-color printers. Four-color printers use the same cyan, magenta, yellow, and black colors an offset printing press uses. These printers are usually considered general-purpose color printers. They're suitable for printing text at reasonable speeds and will do a very capable job of printing color photos. (HP even makes a *three*-color printer that uses cyan, magenta, and yellow inks, and then mixes these together to create black.)

Photo printers also use cyan, magenta, yellow, and black colors, but augment them with additional colors. For example, six-color photo printers usually add extra light cyan and light magenta cartridges, which allow the printer to reduce the visible printer dots that can appear in highlight areas, and make it possible to create smoother color transitions and gradients. The extra colors also help improve fade resistance. Some primary colors fade faster than others, so by mixing colors from different, sturdier primaries, the printer can produce prints with better fade resistance.

Seven-color printers use those same six colors, but usually add an additional black cartridge specifically for printing on glossy paper. Several vendors make eight-color printers, but choose different mixes to achieve different results. For example, some printers use the same six colors as a six-color inkjet and add red and green ink to yield prints with better reds and greens. Other printers start with the usual six-color mix and add two lighter shades of gray to produce truly neutral gray tones.

There are even more complex ink systems, but they're all designed to do the same thing: expand the gamut and improve neutrality.

Additional inks are also employed to help reduce *metameric shift*, a property of some inks that can cause them to appear different in different types of light. A print that suffers from bad metameric shift might appear fine in bright daylight, but have a greenish cast under tungsten light. Metameric shift (sometimes referred to, incorrectly, as *metamerism*) is usually caused by a slight color cast in the black ink of a printer. To combat metameric shift, many printers mix a primary color with the black ink.

Ultimately, you don't need to concern yourself with the specifics of your printer's color mix. You simply want to find the printer that produces the best output. However, paying attention to the color mix in a printer can give you a good idea of what qualities to look for in a print.

With the jump from a three- or four-color printer to a six-color printer, you'll use almost twice as much ink per print. A printer that uses eight, nine, or more inks will suck up more ink per print than a six-color printer, but not substantially more.

Archivability

After you've perfected a print's color, the last thing you want is for the color to fade or alter once the print is hung on the wall. A printer's archival characteristics are a measure of how well the print will hold up over time in real-world display conditions. A print with good archival qualities will go for years without fading or changing color.

Some ink colors are more vulnerable to light than others. Yellow, for example, fades much faster than other primary ink colors. Because the color in a print is composed of a mix of primary inks, if the yellow begins to fade, the colors in an image are no longer mixed properly, and the hues begin to skew.

The interaction between inks and paper also affects the life of a print. For example, when ink sits in an emulsion on the paper's surface, the emulsion encapsulates the ink, giving it extra stability. In a less stable ink/paper duo, the ink seeps deep into the paper, where it's more prone to light, humidity, and acids in the paper itself.

There are two main categories of ink: pigment and dye. Until recently, pigment inks were the only way to get extreme longevity out of a print. However, pigment inks typically have a much narrower color gamut than dye inks, so pigment-based inks often yield images that lack bright reds and blues.

Over the last few years, this difference has, well, faded. The latest generation of pigment printers has a much wider gamut, while the latest generation of dye printers provides much better longevity. Consequently, you no longer have to make an immediate "dye or pigment" choice when considering printers. Instead, you can examine both image quality and longevity claims to decide which printer is right for you. Whether that printer turns out to use pigment or dye-based inks doesn't really matter.

Obviously, it's impossible to know the lifespan of a print from a printer that's only a year or so old. Wilhelm Imaging Research is a laboratory that specializes in evaluating and predicting the archival qualities of printed output. You can find stats for specific ink/paper combinations created by specific printers at *www.wilhelm-research.com*. These stats are the industry-accepted standard for longevity predictions.

A traditional silver-halide print (the type made in a darkroom) will last from 20 to 40 years. If your printer claims longevity of at least 30 years, you'll know that your prints will last at least as long as the photographic prints that have been made and sold for the last 100 years or so.

Note that some people take the Wilhelm Imaging Research numbers with a few grains of salt. The WIR numbers are based on subjecting a print to a particular stress condition for a certain amount of time. The procedure does not test a print for how it holds up under years' worth of variable light and climate conditions (seasonal changes, being moved around, etc.). As such, many people think it's wise to reduce the WIR numbers by 25 to 50 percent. Even after this reduction, many printers will still yield much better longevity than traditional wet darkroom prints. Also, note that if a paper/ink combination is rated for 50 years, that doesn't mean that on the first day of year 51, you'll be looking at a blank piece of paper. Rather, after 50 years or so, the print will begin to exhibit hue shift and fading, some of which might be barely perceptible. It could still be many more years before the print looks outright bad.

When considering archival quality, you should also think about durability. How waterproof is the output from a particular image? Does it scratch easily? Can it hold up to repeated handling? Depending on how careful you are (and what will be done with your prints), some of these issues may be more important than others.

Really Big Printing

If you need to print images with print sizes over 13" × 19", you'll need to go with a large-format printer. These giant ink-jet printers range in size from 24" wide to over 50" wide, offer dye-based or archival pigment inks, and typically accept sheets or rolls of paper, allowing you to create huge images. They also come with huge price tags. Don't expect to get a large-format printer for under $1,200.

Image Quality

In the end, you'll want to base your buying decision on overall output quality. The best way to judge final quality is to make prints on your candidate printers. Many printer vendors provide free samples, although these have often been crafted to show off the printers' strongest points. The ideal test is to print your own images on the printers you're considering. Some photo stores will let you do this, and you may find friendly people in online photography forums with your candidate printers who are willing to print a couple of sample pages for you.

You'll be best served by printing tests on both matte and glossy papers, as these yield very different results. You'll also want to pick an image, or images, with a broad range of colors (both in terms of hue and lightness), and light and dark areas, and areas of fine detail. Once your sample prints are in front of you, evaluate them for the following:

Color. How is the color overall? Don't consider color accuracy, since accuracy is dependent on how well you drive the printer, and right now, you're just doing simple tests. Instead, look at overall range of color. Can the printer produce bright reds, greens, and blues? How are the colors in between? Overall, do the colors look vibrant, or are they dull and flat?

Continuous tone. Can you see visible printer dots, or does the print appear to be continuous tone? Pay close attention to bright highlight areas (clouds, specular highlights on glass or metal), as these areas usually show visible dots when the printer is having troubles. Also, look at the transition zones (the gradients around these highlights) and ensure they're smooth.

Neutrality. If you intend to do a lot of black-and-white printing (more accurately called "grayscale"), you'll want to do some grayscale tests as well. Printing neutral gray tones is very difficult for a printer and, until recently, it wasn't possible to get a truly neutral gray print from an inkjet.

Even if you're not planning to print grayscale images, check the neutral tones in your image (clouds in skies, for example) to make sure they're neutral. True neutral can be a hard thing to spot because your eye does a pretty good job of correcting grays that aren't truly neutral. What you're trying to spot are color casts (usually green, but sometimes reddish or blue) in tones that should be gray. To ease your search, keep an actual black-and-white photographic print handy, as a reference to what true neutral really looks like.

DMax. The blackness of the black a printer can produce is measured as a property called DMax. Blackness is very important, because as your ability to produce a black black increases, so does the contrast range you can reproduce. Go for the blackest black possible. Because glossy papers usually yield blacker blacks than matte papers, test on both types.

Detail. How good is the detail in the image? Detail is also a function of how well you drive the printer (and how good your source image is), so don't lend too much weight to this parameter unless you're confident you know what you're doing.

Metameric shift. View the prints under different kinds of light—direct sunlight, shade, tungsten light, fluorescent, mixed lights—and look for shifts in overall color. If you see a shift, your print is suffering from metameric shift, which is most prevalent in pigment-based printers and most visible in gray tones. (Metameric shift is sometimes mistakenly referred to as *metamerism.*)

Bronzing. A print whose black tones appear reddish-brown is suffering from bronzing. To spot it, view prints from an angle, and pay particular attention to the shadow areas.

Gloss differential. When printing on glossy papers, some printers yield blacks that have more of a matte finish than do the other colors. In such a print, the overall image will appear glossy, but when viewed at an angle, the blacks will appear varnished with a matte finish. Some printers have a special "gloss optimizer" that's sprayed over the print to even out the gloss.

Overall quality. Finally, assess the overall quality of an image. Stand back, look at the prints, and decide whether you like one better than the others. It's OK if you're not sure why you like one print better. Sometimes, it's an unquantifiable combination of factors that combine to produce a superior print.

If you have special printing needs—the capability to print on watercolor paper or cloth, for example—examine output on those media as well. Just because a printer prints well on one kind of media doesn't mean it will perform as well on another.

The good news is that if you're looking for a fine-art quality photo printer, the latest generation of printers from Epson, HP, and Canon are all excellent. Epson and HP still have a slight lead over Canon, but when comparing competing models you'll probably find very little difference in image quality, which means you can make your decision based on printer features and media supply.

Features

Since current fine-art, archival photo printers (as of spring, 2007) are yielding prints of excellent, nearly indistinguishable quality, you can base the bulk of your buying decision on features. A number of features and options can make one printer a better choice than another, depending on your output needs, computer system, and what and how you like to print.

Output size. One of your most important decisions will be output size. Is letter size as big as you need, or might you like to go up to 13" × 19". A 13" × 19" printer offers more flexibility, but also takes up more space. If you want larger still, you can go for 24", 36" or larger. However, don't expect to get into a 24" printer for less than $1,200. It takes a lot of data to make a large print. If you're shooting with a 3-megapixel camera, a 13" × 19" print won't look too good. Basically, don't pay for more printer than you can use.

Borderless support. When considering image size, take note of whether the printer can create borderless prints, and at what sizes. Just because a printer can output 13" × 19" doesn't mean it can produce a borderless 13" × 19" print.

Connectivity. These days, all printers come with a speedy USB-2 interface, which is all you need to connect to most Macs and PCs. Some printers also offer FireWire ports, which can offer a degree of convenience, as they don't require you to tie up a USB port. Perhaps the most significant connectivity option is an Ethernet port, with built-in network support so you can easily share the same printer amongst different computers.

Paper handling. How easy is it to load and unload the printer? Does it provide a straight-through paper path that will allow you to feed thicker, heavier media? If not, what's the thickest media it will support?

Roll feeder. Some printers offer the option to print on rolls. Rolls can sometimes be cheaper per print than cut sheets, and offer the option to print odd aspect ratios, which make them ideal for printing panoramas and other less-common sizes.

Ink usage. Some printers are more economical with their inks than others, which equates to a lower cost per print, and makes for more hassle-free printing, as you won't be running to the ink store as often. Ink usage is not something you can evaluate on your own before buying, but many printer review sites will provide you with good information on ink consumption.

Ink swapping. At the time of writing, some Epson printers require you to swap out one black ink cartridge for a different type any time you want to switch between matte and glossy papers. In addition to being a hassle, it consumes a fair amount of ink. Due to the way the Epson print heads work, it must "recharge" the print head with new ink, which can use up a significant volume of ink if you regularly change from one paper type to another. Other printers switch, internally from one type of black to another, but don't consume extra ink. You'll want to do a little research and investigate this property before you settle on a particular model, as this will greatly affect your ink usage and printing flexibility.

Longevity. If selling fine art prints is your goal, you'll want to consider the longevity of the prints a particular printer can generate. Fortunately, most vendors are very good about publishing longevity claims, and the entire industry is pretty much in agreement that the data provided by Wilhelm Imaging is an acceptable standard for archival estimation. Be aware that longevity is not just a function of ink; the type of paper you print on also impacts whether an image will fade or discolor. Pay close attention to longevity claims to ensure the printer in question delivers the archival qualities you want on the type of paper you want to use.

Quality of the print driver. In general, most print drivers these days are very good; however, HP and Canon have taken the lead in ease of use and flexibility with some of their printers. For Photoshop users, both companies have developed special Photoshop plug-ins for some of their printers, which allow for much easier printing. As we'll see later in the chapter, Photoshop printing often involves multiple dialog boxes. With a custom plug-in, printing becomes a simple matter of using a single dialog box.

Portability. Epson and HP both make dedicated 4" × 6" printers that are very small, and easily moved about. In addition to allowing you to quickly and easily produce 4" × 6" images, some of these models offer the option of battery power, allowing you to take them anywhere to produce prints in the field. In a way, these printers turn your digital camera into a Polaroid—a small, portable device that can produce prints anywhere. Currently, these devices are all four-color printers, meaning they don't produce images with the quality you'll get from a more advanced photo printer.

Extra features. Depending on the price point you're shopping at, you may find additional features. For example, HP's large-format Z-series printers include built-in paper calibration devices that can automatically generate profiles for any type of paper. Other printers might include special software for printing PostScript files, or offer very high speed for high-volume printing. Obviously, these are specialized features, but can be very handy if you need them.

Finally, printers have a resolution property, just like cameras. You'll see printers that list resolutions of 1440 dots per inch, or 2880 dots per inch. When it comes to printer selection, this number is pretty much meaningless. Printer dots are very different from screen pixels, and dot size is as important as number of dots. So, don't worry about keeping track of this number when evaluating a printer. Just pay attention to final image quality and pick the printer that produces images you like.

STANDALONE INK-JET PRINTERS

One of the great advantages of digital photography is the ease with which you can edit and correct your image before printing. However, if you've been out shooting snapshots with a decent camera, you might not care so much about finicky correction—you might just want a decent print. For these situations, having to transfer your images to your computer can be a frustrating time-drain. To address this issue, many vendors now make ink-jet printers with built-in media slots and the capability to print without connection to a computer. The good news is that these printers use the same engines as printers you connect to a computer, meaning you don't have to compromise on image quality to get this ease of use. And, of course, you can still print from your computer for those times when you want to correct and fiddle with your images.

In addition to all the usual print quality and connectivity concerns, when shopping for a printer with standalone capabilities, you'll want to be sure it provides support for the type of media card your camera uses. If you're looking at a printer made by the same manufacturer as your camera, there's a good chance you'll be able to print to the printer directly from your camera, via your camera's serial cable. Some printers offer a built-in LCD so you can easily select the images you want to print.

→

If the printer doesn't offer a screen, it should at least offer the capability to print out a contact sheet showing thumbnails of all the images on the card. This will make is easy to select the images you'd like to print.

Some standalone printers allow you to print out a page of thumbnails, with check boxes for various print sizes. You can then check off the images you want—at specific print sizes—and feed that "order form" back into the printer. It will then print out the selected images according to your specs, all with no computer involvement.

Finally, some printers offer built-in image correction. These are usually simple tools such as Auto-Levels adjustments, or the capability to convert to black-and-white or sepia tone. Although no substitute for what you can do using your image-editing software, these features do provide a quick and easy way to punch up a simple snapshot.

Laser Printers

You're probably familiar with using a laser printer to print text or simple graphics. If you already have a laser printer, or if you use one at work or at a service bureau, you already know that, in addition to being very speedy, laser printers can produce very high-quality output. However, their prints don't come close to the quality provided by even the cheapest ink-jet printer, so if you're looking to get photo-quality output, a laser printer is going to be the wrong choice. In general, color laser printer quality is about on par with what you'd see in a magazine, rather than what you'd get from a photo lab.

Although a laser printer can cost more than an ink-jet, your cost per print will be much lower than ink-jet printing, and they're much speedier than ink-jets, so if mass-production is your goal, a laser printer might be the best choice. Your prints will also be waterproof and will look good even on regular copier paper. Laser printers can be good for outputting quick mockups and work prints, but they are not photographic quality.

Whether you are buying a color or a black-and-white laser printer, your main concern should be image quality. Look at lots of output samples, and pay attention to how well the printer reproduces color. Make sure it can reproduce all color ranges (reds, blues, purples, and so on) accurately. Also, keep an eye out for artifacts—dots and patterns—throughout the print, but especially in the highlights and shadows. Finally, you'll want to check compatibility with your operating system, hardware, and image-editing software. If you have any special networking concerns (for workgroup use, for example), you'll want to evaluate the printer's networking options.

Dye-Sublimation Printers

Sublimation is the process of converting a solid into a gas without passing it through a liquid stage. (For example, dry ice sublimes at room temperature, melting from a solid block into vapor without becoming liquid.) A dye-sublimation printer (also called a dye-sub) works by using special solid dyes that can be sublimed into a gas that adheres to special paper. As with any other printing technology, these primary-color dyes are combined during the sublimation process to create full-color images.

The advantage of a dye-sub printer is that it is truly continuous tone. That is, no dots or patterns will be visible in your final print because the ink hits the paper in a diffuse, gaseous form. Dye-sub paper also looks like real photo paper, giving your prints a true "photo finish."

The downside to dye-sub printers is that their prints can lack sharpness. The same soft, diffuse property that creates continuous tone also means that it's hard for a dye-sub printer to produce a very hard edge. Dye-sub printers are also a tad slow when you compare them to ink-jets or laser printers, and typically have a high cost per print because of their expensive, proprietary media. In addition, if you're looking for a printer that can be used for other tasks—printing text, for example—a dye-sub is definitely not for you. Finally, dye-sub printers work *only* with dye-sub media. You won't be able to generate prints with different finishes, or experiment with papers of different quality.

On the upside, dye-sub printers can be made very small, and their prints are very durable. Most of the dye-sub printers you'll see today are small units that create 4" × 6" prints. Most of these printers, such as those made by Olympus and HP, can be attached directly to a camera, providing you with a Polaroid-like facility for getting instant prints from your digital camera. Because the media is somewhat pricey, these can be expensive prints, and of course, you have no option to color-correct when you print directly from your camera. If you need a portable (some of these printers can run off batteries) 4" × 6" printing tool, a small dye-sub can be a good solution.

As with other printing technologies, when you shop for a dye-sub printer, image quality should be your highest concern. Try to look at a variety of samples that cover a full range of color and detail levels, and a full assortment of light and shadow. Dye-sub resolutions are typically lower than laser printer or ink-jet resolutions due to the nature of their printing method. Three hundred and 400 dpi printers are common and perfectly acceptable.

As with purchasing any printer, make certain the printer provides the necessary connections for your computer, and that its driver software is compatible with your operating system.

Media Selection

You can, of course, stick any old paper in your printer (as long as it's not a dye-sub printer), including the normal 20-pound copier paper one typically uses for office correspondence. However, paper choice can have a huge bearing on the appearance of your final image.

Glossy, or "luster" papers, for example, will yield blacker blacks than matte papers, but at the cost of overall contrast ratio and shadow detail. Matte papers, meanwhile, will be able to display a greater color range, but at the cost of deeply saturated colors. Which choice is right depends on the image you're printing, what type of look you're going for, and how you will display the image. So, if a particular image is dependent on supersaturated colors, you'll want to go with a glossier paper, while an image with a very broad tonal range and lots of fine detail will need a matte-finish paper. If an image is going to be displayed under glass, you may find that the paper finish is less relevant because the glass obscures a lot of gloss, and adds an apparent finish of its own.

Finally, you may make your decision purely on cost. Some papers are much cheaper than others are. If you simply need to get some sample images to someone, or want to print out some snapshots, you might be best served by an inexpensive matte-finish paper.

In general, you'll want to experiment with your paper selections to find out what works best for your intended output. Be *certain* to read your printer's manual before you shove an experimental piece of paper through your printer. Most printers have thickness limits, and many printers—particularly archival-quality printers—can be damaged if you use media that wasn't specifically designed for the printer. Some types of handmade papers can produce lots of dust and particulate matter that can be hard on a print head, resulting in clogs and frequent cleanings.

Ink Choice

In general, you should always buy ink manufactured and certified by your printer manufacturer. There are cheaper, third-party inks available for specialized printing applications, such as high-quality grayscale printing, and these sometimes work just fine. However, be aware that it is possible for your printer head to be damaged by noncertified inks. More important, though, to get accurate color, your printer driver needs to know that the ink formulations in your printer will mix and blend in a particular way. If you use a third-party ink, there's no guarantee that they will have mixed their ink correctly, and you'll rarely have any idea of the archival qualities of third-party inks.

If you do a lot of black-and-white printing, you might want to consider a set of quad-tone inks. Typically, the black ink included in a normal four-color or six-color printer doesn't allow for a full range of grayscale printing. Printer manufacturers get around this by trying to blend all four (or six) ink colors to create shades of gray. Unfortunately, this approach usually doesn't yield a full range of gray and often produces an image with a bad color cast.

High-quality black-and-white commercial printing—the kind used to print black-and-white photography books, for example—often uses combinations of multiple shades of black or gray ink. Such ink sets are also available for some desktop ink-jet printers. Typically, these quad-tone ink sets provide four shades of black ink and special drivers for printing black-and-white images. For more information on quad-tone inks, check out *www.completedigitalphotography.com/quadtone*.

However, now that many photo printers include multiple blacks within the printer, there's far less need for these specialized black-and-white ink systems, unless you're extremely picky, or have specific printing needs.

PRINTING

In an ideal world, once you'd finished correcting and adjusting your images, you would simply click the print button and out of your printer would pop a print that looked exactly like it did on-screen. In the real world, printing is a bit more involved than that.

Earlier, we discussed the processes of resizing and sharpening. What we *didn't* discuss, though, was how to determine an appropriate resolution when resizing. After making all those decisions about how many pixels you need in your camera, you want to be sure you're using all those pixels to your maximum advantage. Therefore, choosing a resolution is your first major decision when preparing to print.

Choosing a Resolution

Before you can resize an image (as discussed earlier), you need to know the resolution that is best for your printer. Different printing technologies have different resolution requirements, so calculating optimal resolution differs from printer type to printer type.

If you've ever looked at a black-and-white newspaper photo up close, you've seen how dot patterns of varying size can be used to represent different shades of gray. (See Figure 16.17.) This type of image is called a *halftone* and, traditionally, was created by rephotographing a picture through a mesh screen.

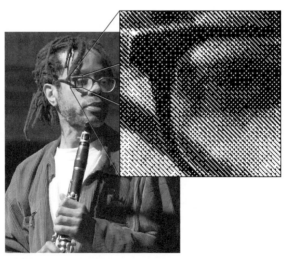

FIGURE 16.17   In a black-and-white halftone, patterns of differently sized black dots are combined to create the appearance of various shades of gray.

The color photos in this book are printed using a similar process. To create a color halftone, four halftones are created, one each for cyan, magenta, yellow, and black. When layered on top of each other, these four halftones yield a full-color image.

All color printing processes use variations on this practice of combining groups of primary colored dots to create other colors. Nowadays, of course, halftones are usually created digitally, by scanning an image into a computer (if it didn't start out as a digital image in the first place) and then letting the computer create a halftone.

Your computer monitor works differently, of course. Unlike a printer, your computer monitor can actually make a single dot that's any one of millions of colors. In other words, there is not a one-to-one correspondence between a pixel on your screen and a dot printed on paper. Although a single pixel on your screen might be defined as being dark purple, your printer might have to print a combination of 50 different cyan, magenta, yellow, and black dots to reproduce that one purple dot from your monitor.

So, although your printer may claim to have 1400 dots per inch of resolution, those are 1400 *printer dots,* not 1400 pixels. Choosing a resolution, then, is dependent on how much information your printer needs to do its job.

Choosing a Resolution for an Ink-Jet Printer

Rather than usual newspaper-like halftone patterns, ink-jet printers use special, seemingly random mezzogram patterns to create colors.

As you saw earlier when you worked with Photoshop's Image Size dialog box, there is a relationship between print size and resolution. As resolution increases, print size decreases (assuming you're not resampling your image), and vice versa. So, as you try to make your image larger, your resolution will go down. If you don't have enough resolution for your intended print size, your prints can come out lacking detail and sharpness.

Conversely, if you have *too much* resolution for your intended print size, your printing process will go much slower, as the printer will have to slog through all that extra data, sampling down on the fly to get just the information it needs. What's more, when it samples down, you have no idea how the image might be sharpening up. It's much better to get the image to the proper size yourself, so you can judge sharpness and true image quality. Consequently, choosing an appropriate resolution for your intended print size is an important step in preparing your image for print.

It is generally agreed that, at a normal reading distance of 10 inches, your eye cannot resolve much—if any—image detail past 300 pixels per inch. We say "generally" because this number is debated a little bit, with many detractors usually going *lower*, to say that you can't resolve better than 240 pixels per inch. Whatever the truth is, it's safe to say that if your image is sized at 300 dots per inch, you're going to get as much detail as it's possible to see (assuming that detail is there in your image).

However, note that we specify a specific viewing distance for that resolution claim. As you might expect, as you move farther from your image, the amount of detail you can see goes down. This is actually good news for your digital printing efforts, because it means that larger images—which are usually viewed from farther away—can be lower resolution. (The best examples of this are billboards, which typically have resolutions of two or three pixels per inch, because they're designed to be viewed from distances of hundreds of feet.)

Complex visual acuity formulas can be used to determine the precise optimum resolution for a given print size at a given distance, but in general, you can use the information shown in Figure 16.18 to select a resolution for your prints, whether you're printing on a four-color ink-jet or a photo ink-jet with six or more colors.

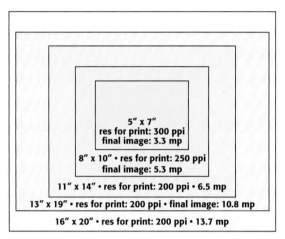

FIGURE 16.18   In general, you can follow this table when selecting a resolution for a given print size. Note that because larger images are usually viewed from farther away, you can usually manage just fine by selecting a lower resolution as print size increases.

These numbers are good news if you're using a camera with a lower resolution, because it means that you can still get a large-sized print. Obviously, there's nothing wrong with using higher resolutions (except for the potential slowdown in print time), and if your camera packs enough pixels, you might want to print your 8" × 10" prints at a full 300 dpi so they're razor-sharp even up close. However, you should do some tests of your own to decide if you can discern a difference in detail in sharpness between 200 and 300 dpi. Depending on your subject matter and the quality of your camera, there may be little perceptible difference.

Paper quality is also a contributing factor in resolution choice. If you're printing on coarse, highly textured paper, you can probably get away with going to a much lower resolution. The lack of resolution will often be hidden by the fact that the ink will bleed and smear when it hits the paper. Conversely, if you're using a higher-quality paper that does a better job of holding a dot, you'll need to stick with a higher-resolution image.

Choosing a Resolution for a Laser Printer

Laser printers generate different tones—both gray tones and color tones—using the same type of halftone patterns you see in offset presses. As discussed earlier, a halftone is a pattern of dots that, when viewed from far away, appear as a tone of gray or color.

How big the dots are (and hence, how far away you have to be to see tone instead of a dot pattern) is governed by the *line screen frequency* that is used to generate the halftone. In traditional halftoning, line screen frequency is controlled by selecting a particular screen to use when shooting the halftone. The line screen frequency of the screen—that is, how coarsely it is woven—is measured in lines per inch (lpi).

Digital halftoning doesn't involve a physical screen, of course, but the algorithms that create the halftone are still governed by a line screen frequency measured in lines per inch. For high-resolution printing (1200 dpi or higher), this screen frequency is typically 133 or 166 lines per inch. This is a very fine screen that produces a magazine-quality image. Lower-resolution printers (300 to 600 dpi) typically use a much coarser screen, usually around 85 to 100 lines per inch. Many laser printers (and most high-resolution image setters) let you specify a line screen.

Why does this matter? Because different line screens require images of different resolutions. Typically, the rule for resolution (as measured in ppi) is that your image should be 1 to 2 times your line screen. In other words, if your printer uses a 133-line screen, your image needs to have a resolution of 200 to 266 pixels per inch.

In practical terms, this means that if you have a laser printer that requires 200 ppi images (because it uses a 133 line screen) and you have a two-megapixel camera that produces 1,600 × 1,200 pixel images, you can print your image at 8" × 6" at 200 dots per inch—1600 ÷ 200 = 8" wide; 1200 ÷ 200 = 6" high.

Let's say, though, that you want to print an image that can be copied on a photocopier. Images for photocopying typically need to be printed with a much coarser line screen, usually around 85 lines per inch, which means your image needs to be only around 150 dpi. At this resolution, the same two-megapixel image could be printed at 10" × 8". (An 85-line screen is also appropriate for newspaper or phonebook printing.)

When you print to a laser printer, it's best to turn off any special graytone correction features the printer may have.

Printer Profiles

No matter what type of printer you're printing on, or what program you're printing from, to get the best output from your printer, you need to have a good printer profile. In Chapter 10, "Workflow," you learned about monitor profiles and went through the process of calibrating and profiling your monitor. Just as you need to have an ICC profile for your monitor, you also need to have an ICC profile for your printer. More specifically, for the particular type of paper you're going to print with in your particular type of printer.

Good profiles are essential for consistency from monitor to paper, and to ensure the best possible output from your printer. When you installed your printer software, a collection of profiles should have been installed for each paper type your printer company sells. There may even be several profiles for each paper: some profiles are for specific viewing conditions (daylight, tungsten, etc.) or printer settings.

Unfortunately, not all vendor-supplied printer profiles are reliable. One reason is that some printers are easier to control with profiles than are others. For example, some higher-end printers include sensors that carefully monitor ink flow through the print head to better determine exactly how much ink is being delivered to the paper. Some printers are carefully calibrated as soon as they leave the assembly line. On the flip side, less-expensive printers often vary significantly from one unit to the next, meaning a generic, vendor-supplied profile may be of little use.

When you use a paper sold by someone other than the company that makes your printer, you'll need to make or find a profile for it. Many third-party vendors provide free profiles for download. Crane has an extensive profile collection, as does Hahnemühle and Ilford. Finally, you can often find free profiles on the web simply by searching. I keep a collection of free profiles available for download at *www.completedigitalphotography.com.*

If you're not getting good output with vendor-supplied profiles, or if you're using a paper you can't find a profile for, it's time for a custom job. Several services, such as Inkjetart.com, make custom profiles for around $25. Simply download the supplied profile target, print it out on your printer, and mail it back. The company then sends you a standard color profile. When printing the target, be sure to set your printer settings to the ones you typically use, and turn off the printer's built-in correction.

While $25 is cheap, you may find that as you change ink cartridges, your profile becomes less accurate. Continually regenerating a profile can become expensive. If you regularly create paper profiles, you may want to invest in your own profiling hardware. A paper-profiling system consists of a hardware/software combination that measures a sample output by your printer and generates a profile. To create a profile, you first print test target images, which are color swatches that come with the paper profiling system. Then you measure these targets with the included hardware. The XRite Pulse Color Elite is one such system. It ships in various configurations that can include a monitor calibrator as well.

However, paper-profiling systems are not cheap. Expect to spend at least $600 for an entry-level system. Such a system can pay for itself in saved ink and paper costs if you regularly use third-party papers, but if you only occasionally need to make a profile, it's probably not worth it.

If you're having trouble getting good prints from your printer, the solution may be nothing more than upgrading to a better profile, so you'll want to look into profile options as a first attempt at a solution.

On the Mac OS, you install printer profiles in the Library > ColorSync > Profiles folder. On Windows, install your printer profiles in WINDOWS\system32\spool\drivers\color.

You might need to relaunch your image-editing application to see the new profiles.

Soft Proofing

Some image-editing programs such as Adobe Photoshop CS, CS2, CS3, Nikon Capture NX, and Apple's Aperture let you view a photo in a special soft-proofing mode, which uses a color-management system and installed profiles to simulate on-screen what a print will look like when output to a specified printer.

We'll be using Photoshop for these examples, but similar options exist in Aperture and Capture NX. If you're using a different editor that provides soft proofing, its controls and options should be similar to Photoshop.

To generate a printer profile, have your most recent monitor profile active. Your profiling package should have installed it for you. If it's been more than a month since you profiled the monitor, do it again. It's best to profile your monitor at least once a month—more often if it's an older monitor.

TUTORIAL 16.3   GENERATING A SOFT PROOF IN ADOBE PHOTOSHOP

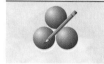

Before your editor can generate a soft proof, it must know what printer profile to use, and it needs a few other bits of configuration data to properly make use of that profile. This tutorial assumes you have an image you want to soft proof open in Photoshop, and you have a printer installed and connected.

Step 1: Open the Custom Proofing Dialog Box

In Photoshop, you configure your soft-proof settings by choosing View > Proof Setup > Custom. (See Figure 16.19.)

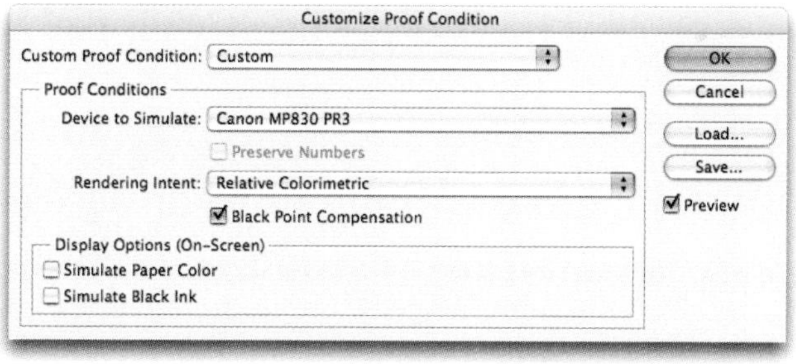

FIGURE 16.19   You'll use Photoshop's Custom Proof Condition dialog box to configure the program's soft-proofing feature.

Step 2: Choose a Printer Profile

The Custom Proof Condition dialog box is straightforward. From the Device to Simulate menu, select the paper profile that corresponds to the type of paper you'll print on. If your printer uses different types of ink for different paper types, select the appropriate profile. For example, the Epson R2400 can use one of two different kinds of black ink, Photo Black and Matte Black. When printing on Enhanced Matte paper, you can choose to use either the Enhanced Matte profile for Photo Black (labeled "PK") or Matte Black (labeled "MK").

Sometimes, paper profiles are intended for specific driver settings. For example, an HP printer driver might have an option called Maximum Detail. If the profile name includes "MaxDetail," the assumption is that you'll choose the Maximum Detail setting when you print. If you don't, your print may not match your screen as closely.

Step 3: Select a Rendering Intent

Your image most likely contains far more colors than your printer can print. There are several algorithms an image editor can use to cram all those colors into the small gamut of your printer. The Rendering Intent menu lets you specify which method to use. We'll look at rendering intents in more detail in the next section. For now, choose Relative Colorimetric. (If you're working with Aperture, you won't find a control for Rendering Intent. Aperture defaults to a Relative Colorimetric rendering intent.)

Step 4: Configure the Other Parameters

Don't check the Preserve Color Numbers checkbox. This tells Photoshop to use the color data in the image, but you want the color data altered according to the needs of your color-management system. This control is useful only for simulation of certain types of CMYK output.

Black Point Compensation remaps the black in your image so it matches the black point of your chosen paper. With Black Point Compensation set, you'll get better shadow detail and will use your printer's full dynamic range.

Step 5: Simulate Paper Color

Check Simulate Paper Color. While your monitor displays the whites of your image as true white, on a piece of paper white is actually the color of the paper. By activating Simulate Paper Color, you tell Photoshop to more accurately display the white (and lighter tones) in your image. More than any other setting, this will change the appearance of the on-screen image. What's more, it won't necessarily change it for the better. Simulate Paper Color often kills a lot of the contrast in your image, and makes it appear duller and dingy. Sometimes, it's a good idea to look away from the screen when you check the Simulate Paper Color box, so you don't actually see the change from your original image to a dingier image.

Step 6: Evaluate Your Proof

At this point, your onscreen image should look a bit different from before you began. Uncheck the Preview checkbox to see your unproofed image, and then recheck the box to see the soft proof. Leave Preview checked and click OK to dismiss the dialog box. You can use the Load and Save buttons to save proof conditions for specific papers and printers, making for easier activation of particular soft-proof setups.

You can now generate the proof using the parameters you just defined by pressing Command-Y or choosing View > Proof Colors.

You'll use this process when you want to have Photoshop generate a preview of what your final printed output will look like. Don't forget what you learned in Chapter 10, though: *your screen will* never *exactly match your final print.* Your goal with soft proofing and color management is to get *closer* to your final print, to reduce the number of test prints you need to make. To see how close we got, it's time to try printing.

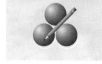

TUTORIAL 16.4   PRINTING FROM PHOTOSHOP

After you've soft proofed, you'll be ready to print your image. Soft proofing might also reveal tonal adjustments and color shifts that need to be made, and we'll discuss how to handle that shortly. First, though, let's see how a color-managed printing process works in Photoshop. This tutorial assumes you have an image you want to print open in Photoshop, and you have a printer installed and connected.

Step 1: Open the Print Dialog Box

If you're using Photoshop CS or CS2, choose File > Print with Preview. If you're using CS3, choose File > Print. In either case, Photoshop will show you a thumbnail view of your chosen paper size, with your image positioned as it will appear when printed. (See Figure 16.20.)

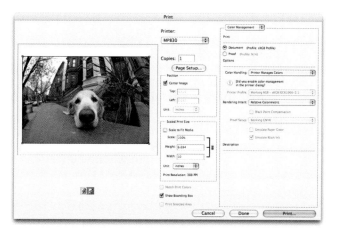

FIGURE 16.20   Photoshop CS3's Print dialog box provides all the controls you need to run a color-managed print process. In Photoshop CS and CS2, you'll get the same types of controls from the Print with Preview dialog box.

You can use the Page Setup button to change the current paper size and orientation, and then use the Position and Scaling controls to change how your image will be positioned and sized on the page. We're assuming you've already resized your image to your desired print size and resolution. If you haven't, you can use the Scaled Print Size controls to tell Photoshop to resize the image now. You'll have no control over interpolation method, whether the image is resampled, or final sharpening, so this is not the best resizing option.

Step 2: Tell Photoshop to Take Control of the Color

When you print, you can have Photoshop manage the color, or you can let the printer manage the color. We want Photoshop to manage the color so it can generate the same colors for our print that it came up with for our soft proof. If we let the printer manage the colors, there's no guarantee it will make the same color decisions.

In Photoshop CS3, change the Color Handling pop-up menu to Photoshop Manages Color.

In Photoshop CS and CS2, click the More Options button (if it's not already clicked), and then change the Color Handling pop-up menu to Let Photoshop Determine Colors.

Step 3: Set the Rendering Intent

As we learned when we generated our soft proof, rendering intent is simply the method Photoshop uses to cram the large color space your camera captures into the smaller space provided by your paper. You want to set the Print dialog to use the same rendering intent you chose when you soft proofed. In our soft proofing example, we used Relative Colorimetric, so set the Rendering Intent pop-up menu to Relative Colorimetric.

Step 4: Choose a Paper Profile

Now set the Printer Profile pop-up menu to the same profile you chose when you soft proofed. This will be the paper profile you selected in Step 2 of the previous tutorial.

Step 5: Black Point Compensation

If you chose Black Point Compensation when you configured Proof Setup, you need to check it now. As you'll recall, we chose to enable Black Point Compensation, so check it now. (See Figure 16.21.)

Step 6: Print

Now, click the Print button. Photoshop will display your operating system's normal Print dialog box. From here, you can select the printer you want to print to (if you have more than one) and configure the printer driver's controls.

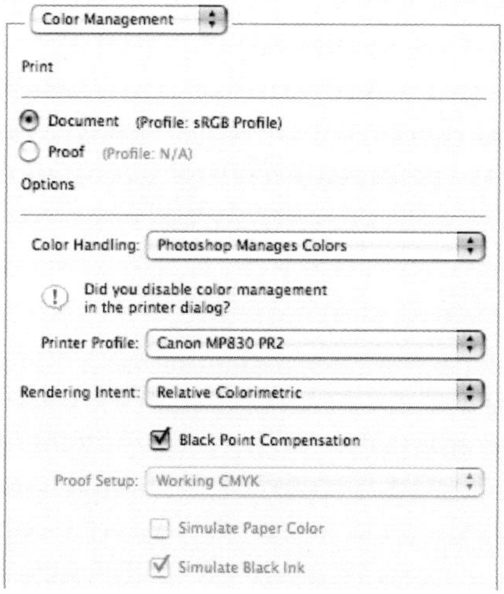

FIGURE 16.21   Photoshop's Print dialog should now look something like this.

You'll need to tell the printer what type of paper you're printing on. This allows the printer to position the print head an appropriate distance from the paper, depending on how thick the paper is.

Finally, find the control in the printer driver that turns *off* color management. This may sound counter-intuitive, but it's really quite simple. Most printer drivers have their own color-management routines that try to correct an image's color for printing. However, you're asking Photoshop to take care of managing color, so you don't want the printer driver to be involved as well. If both systems mess with the color in your image, things get very unpredictable.

The method for turning off color management varies from printer to printer. For example, in most Epson printers, you'll find a Color Management option in the Printer dialog, which looks something like the controls shown in Figure 16.22.

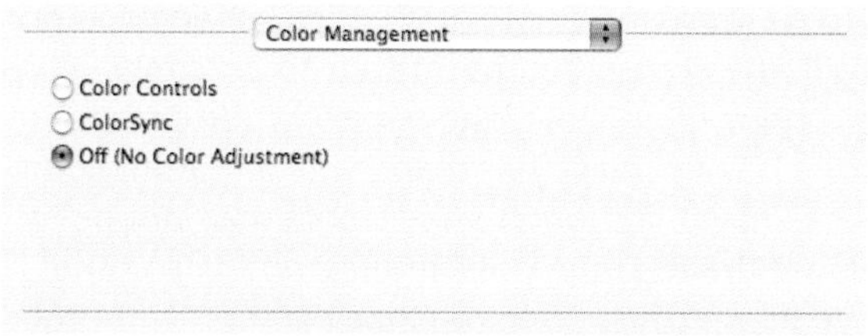

FIGURE 16.22   It is essential that you disable your printer's built-in color management, using the Printer Driver dialog.

Different printers will have different mechanisms for disabling printer color correction. This is an essential step when printing using Photoshop's color management. Consult your printer manual if you can't find the color management control.

Click the Print button, and your image should print. Compare the printed page to the soft proof on your screen. If you have a good-quality monitor, printer, and profiles, the print should match the screen fairly well. You'll probably see that the blacks and overall contrast range are a little different. The monitor image is probably a little more saturated because of the nature of a self-illuminated display, but the overall hues should be fairly close. ✄

Improving Your Print

In Chapter 10, we issued the disclaimer that color management is not a magic bullet. Your final print will never exactly match the image that appears on your screen, because your monitor is simply a very different technology from a printed page. However, soft proofing can allow you to get pretty close, and reduce the number of test prints required to get a good print.

If you're sorely disappointed with the results of your print, there are a few things you can do to improve your output quality.

Change Your Rendering Intent

As you just learned, when you soft proof and print, you must select a rendering intent; that is, you tell the printer how to map "illegal" (out-of-gamut) colors to the color space of your printer—and, more specifically, to the color space of your paper.

In the last two tutorials, you selected Relative Colorimetric as your rendering intent because it's a good, general-purpose intent. It maps the white in your image to the white of your paper profile, so the whites in the print are represented by the white of the paper, not by ink. The Relative Colorimetric rendering intent doesn't touch any other color that falls within the gamut of your ink and paper. Illegal colors are mapped to the nearest in-gamut color. If you're a stickler for color accuracy, you'll probably prefer Relative Colorimetric.

As you've learned, while your digital camera must be white-balanced to accurately reproduce color, your eyes have the amazing ability to automatically adjust so that white tones always look truly white (or nearly so). Your eyes are also far more sensitive to contrast and the relationships between colors than to absolute hues. With this in mind, the Perceptual intent tries to compress all the colors in your image to fit within the color gamut of your paper, while preserving the relationships between those colors. If your image has many out-of-gamut colors, Perceptual intent creates a nice-looking image, although your colors may not be especially accurate.

You'll use the Relative Colorimetric and Perceptual rendering intents the most. If your image doesn't have out-of-gamut colors, you probably won't find much difference between the two. On a few images, you may find that one intent yields more "pop" than another—your images will look brighter and punchier. You can usually see this difference when soft proofing, so let soft proofs be your guide to which rendering intent to use. In Photoshop's Customize Proof Condition dialog box, you can select the rendering intent you'll ultimately print with, and see on-screen how it will affect your image. When you find the intent you like best, take note of it and select that same intent when you print.

Photoshop has two more rendering intents. Saturation produces as much saturation as possible and is intended for illustrations and business graphics. Absolute Colorimetric is similar to Relative Colorimetric in that it clips illegal colors. However, it doesn't remap the whites in an image. If the whites in a picture have a slight cast, a printer will print the whites with that cast, rather than leave them as paper white. In other words, Absolute Colorimetric never alters any legal colors in your image.

Many people say you should never use Absolute Colorimetric for photo printing. However, on images with a large dynamic range, you might find that Absolute Colorimetric is actually the best choice. It sometimes provides a brightness that is missing from other intents. However, when Absolute Colorimetric is wrong for your image, it tends to be wrong in a very ugly way. You'll blow out an image's highlights or cause dark shadows to turn splotchy and weird. Pay close attention to these areas when soft proofing to determine if it's the right intent.

Perceptual and Relative Colorimetric also include the option of Black Point Compensation. In most cases, activating this feature is good, but again you should preview it in your soft proofs to be sure. Take note of your final choice, as you'll need to select this as your intent in the Print with Preview dialog.

Finally, there's another option for improving the quality of your prints, which is to ignore Photoshop's color management altogether and let your printer handle your color.

Soft Proofing in Other Programs

Both Apple Aperture and Nikon Capture NX provide soft-proofing tools that are very similar to Photoshop's, and you should be able to easily find your way through their controls based on what you've learned in the last two tutorials. Both programs have simpler interfaces to their soft-proofing and print features than does Photoshop. As noted earlier, Aperture only provides a single rendering intent, Relative Colorimetric. Both programs provide options for selecting a paper profile and black point compensation.

Printing with Driver Color

In our previous printing example, we let Photoshop calculate the color values sent to the printer. In the Photoshop Print dialog box, you chose Let Photoshop Determine Colors in the Options panel, and then turned off Printer Color Management in the printer's driver dialog box. This left Photoshop in charge of all color calculations.

Now we're going to look at another way to print: choose Let Printer Handle Colors from the Color Handling menu of the Photoshop Print dialog box (or the Print with Preview dialog box if you're using CS or CS2). Leave Color Management turned on in your printer's driver dialog, and all color calculations will be performed by your printer. It's helpful to try this alternate method because you may find that your printer's included driver yields better results than Photoshop-managed color.

If I had suggested such a notion a few years ago, angry mobs of color geeks and printing nerds would have pelted me with empty ink cartridges. However, nowadays, many printer vendors are engineering very good drivers that can outperform Photoshop's built-in color handling.

This is especially true for black-and-white output on some printers. Epson printers that use the K3 ink system, for example, yield substantially better black-and-white output if you use the driver's built-in Advanced Black and White mode, rather than letting Photoshop determine colors. This is also true for HP's Vivera pigment inks, and Canon's latest family of archival inks.

With color images, when you let the printer driver control color, you might notice improvements in everything from overall cast, highlight or shadow detail, certain color ranges, and even continuous tone.

Now the bad news: printer driver color has nothing to do with Photoshop's soft-proofing feature. In other words, there's no reason to bother with soft proofing in any soft-proof-enabled application if you're going to print with driver color. So, you may find that there's less of a match between your screen and printer when using driver color. On the other hand, on some images, you might find a *better* match.

This points out another weakness of driver color: you might find that some images print better with Photoshop-controlled color, while others print better with printer driver-controlled color.

So, does this mean you need to use even more ink and paper by printing every image using both methods? Probably not. You'll need to experiment a little, but what you'll likely find is that the differences between Photoshop and printer-generated color are very slight, and you can easily alter one to look like the other. With a little initial trial and error, you might also come to understand which types of images work better with one method than another.

Correcting Your Images

After enabling soft proofing, or printing a test print, you can now think about correcting your image to fix any tone or color problems you found in your initial test print.

In Photoshop, the easiest way to make corrections is via Adjustment Layers. Since your corrections will be specific to the type of paper you're printing on, you can create separate Adjustment Layers for each paper type and activate them as needed. In addition, with the masks built in to Photoshop's Adjustment Layers, you can easily constrain adjustments to particular areas in an image.

Many color problems will be the result of your image editor remapping out-of-gamut colors to fit them into the target color space. You can solve some color problems simply by bringing these colors back to legal. Choose View > Gamut Warning, and Photoshop will display out-of-gamut colors as gray pixels. (You can use this feature with Soft Proofing on or off.)

In most cases, you can bring illegal colors back into gamut by using a Hue/Saturation Adjustment Layer. Simply lower the Saturation level and the gray gamut warning pixels disappear.

If you're using an editing system that supports multiple versions—like Apple Aperture, Nikon Capture NX, or Adobe Lightroom—you can easily create multiple versions tailored for printing on different paper types

---

TWEAK YOUR VIEWING CONDITIONS

The quality of your monitor and printer profiles has a huge bearing on how well your printed page will match your screen. However, your viewing conditions can also have a pronounced impact on how you perceive color and contrast consistency from display to print.

When you build a monitor profile using a monitor calibrator, you tell the calibration software some of the details of the ambient lighting situation in your room. The ideal room has a fairly low level of ambient light, with no bright lights or colors in your field of view.

To make the most accurate assessment of your printer's output, view images under the ambient lighting conditions specified by your paper profile. For most paper profiles, this means daylight or artificial lighting that has the same color temperature as daylight. (Some vendors create multiple profiles for each paper, each tuned for different viewing conditions.)

If your print-viewing lighting is less than ideal, you'll want to consider getting some D50 lighting. D50 lights shine at 5000°K and so are good matches for daylight.

If you happen to have a lot of cash laying around, you might want to spend it on a viewing station, such as a GTI Graphic Technology Professional Desktop Viewer. GTI makes all types of well-constructed viewing stations, from large stand-up units to collapsible, portable stations and you can learn more about them at *www.graphiclite.com*.

A less-expensive option is the Ott-Lite, a 5300°K lamp that sits easily on your desk. You can order one for about $60 from Lumenet, and you can find details at *www.lumen-light.com*.

The cheapest D50 lighting option is to build your own. SoLux manufactures D50 lamps that start at $6.95 each. You'll need your own fixtures, which are easy to find at any hardware store. Check out *www.usalight.com* for a full assortment of SoLux lamps.

Web-based Printing

A number of web sites offer photo-printing services. After you upload your images to these sites, they will print the images and mail them back to you. These services typically use pictographic processes—traditional chemical-based printing processes that expose a piece of photographic paper using a laser or LED device.

The advantage to these services is that they're very simple to use. The downside is that you have to wait for your prints, and you don't know what sort of color and tonal corrections the service will make to your images. In other words, what you see on your screen may not be close to what you get in your prints. Typically, a particular printing service will be consistent about the type of adjustments they make to their images. So, once you've figured out a particular service's idiosyncrasies, you can adjust your images accordingly before you submit them.

Pay close attention to a service's cropping guidelines. Some services will blow up your image to fill an entire print. If your original was a different aspect ratio than the final print, your image will be cropped. Most services allow the option of blowing up to full print size or padding the image to preserve your original aspect ratio.

Most services also provide photo-sharing facilities, which allow you to create one or more online photo albums. You can send the address of these albums to other people who can view your images and, if they want, order prints. Posting images to a website is convenient because you only have to upload them and then send out a link. You'll have no concerns as to whether a particular recipient can receive large amounts of data through email. Photo sharing and printing can also save you the hassle of preparing prints for a bunch of people, because they can simply order their own.

Finally, some services offer much more than simple paper printing. Coffee mugs, T-shirts, banners, cakes, and cookies can all be adorned with your photographs.

In general, these services are expecting images in an sRGB color space. If you were shooting with your camera set to Adobe RGB (which you should be), you'll need to tag the images as sRGB before you upload them. In Photoshop, you use the Edit > Assign Profile command to assign a new color space.

These services also expect images to be delivered as JPEGs, and many will have specific size and resolution requirements. Consult each service's guidelines for more details.

CONCLUSION

Once you start using a digital camera, it becomes hard to imagine that film cameras have much of a future—not because film cameras produce inferior results, but simply because digital cameras provide such enormous creative flexibility. Hopefully, this book has helped you understand more about the specific issues and concerns you'll face when you shoot digital, and provided you with solutions for working around those concerns.

Your next step? Start shooting and editing! Your skill with both your camera and image editor will greatly improve as you practice. Take your camera with you wherever you go, and don't hesitate to fire away.

If you'd like to learn more, check out the *www.completedigitalphotography.com* website, where you'll find more articles, camera reviews, custom printer profiles—even free software!

GLOSSARY

1-bit image An image composed of pixels that are either black or white. Called 1-bit (or single-bit) because only one bit of information is required for each pixel.

8-bit image An image that uses 8 bits of data for each pixel. Because you can count from 0 to 255, a pixel can be any one of 256 different colors.

24-bit image An image that uses 24 bits of data for each pixel. Because you can count from 0 to roughly 16-and-a-half million, a pixel can be any one of 16.5 million colors.

32-bit image An image that uses 24 bits of data to store the color of each pixel and an additional eight 8 bits of data to store the opacity of each pixel. This transparency information is called an *alpha channel*.

35 mm equivalency What a lens would be equivalent to in terms of a standard 35 mm SLR camera. Used as a standard for discussing the field of view and magnification power of a lens. In 35 mm equivalency, lenses over 50 mm are telephoto, whereas lenses below 50 mm are wide-angle or fisheye.

aberrations Irregularities in a piece of glass that cause light to be focused incorrectly. Aberrations produce artifacts and anomalies in images.

acquire plug-in A special type of *plug-in* that allows for communication between your image-editing application and your digital camera.

action-safe area The area of a video image that will most likely be visible on any video monitor. Essential action should be kept within the action-safe area, because action that falls outside might be cropped by the viewer's screen. See *title safe*.

active autofocus An autofocus mechanism that achieves focus by transmitting something into the scene, usually infrared light or sonar.

adaptive editing control An adjustment that allows you to alter the shadow and highlight tones in your image. Adaptive editing adjustments analyze your image to determine exactly which tones are shadows and highlights, rather than simply altering all pixels that have a given color value.

additive Light mixes together in an *additive* process whereby, as colors are mixed, they get brighter; that is, light is added as the colors are mixed. Additive colors eventually produce white. Red, green, and blue are the primary additive colors that can be used to create all other colors.

adjustment layers Let you apply Levels, Curves, and many other image-correction functions as a layer, allowing you to remove or adjust the effect at any time.

aliasing The stair-stepping patterns that can appear along the edges of diagonal lines in an image.

alpha channel Extra information stored about the pixels in an image. Alpha channels are used to store transparency information. This information can serve as a mask for compositing or applying effects.

analog As regards photography, light in the real world travels in a continuous wave. To record those continuous analog waves, your digital camera must first convert them into a series of numbers, or digits.

aperture An opening that is used to control the amount of light passing through the lens of a camera. Typically constructed as an expanding and contracting *iris*.

aperture priority A shooting mode on a camera. Aperture priority lets you define the camera's aperture. The camera will then calculate a corresponding shutter speed based on its light metering.

APS Advanced Photography System. A fairly new format of film and cameras.

artifacts Image degradations caused by image-processing operations. Compressing an image, for example, often results in the creation of many image-compression artifacts. Different image-processing tasks create different types of artifacts.

ASA A measure of film speed. See also *ISO*.

aspect ratio The ratio of an image's length to its width. Most computer screens and digital cameras shoot images that have an aspect ratio of 4:3. 35 mm film and some digital cameras shoot in a 3:2 aspect ratio.

aspherical A lens that contains some elements that are not perfect hemispheres. These nonspherical elements are used to correct certain types of aberrations.

autobracketing Some cameras include special functions that cause them to automatically shoot a series of bracketed images when you press the shutter release.

autofocus-assist lamp See *focus-assist lamp*.

automatic exposure A feature that will automatically calculate the appropriate shutter speed, aperture, and sometimes ISO at the time you take a picture.

backs In a medium- or large-format camera, the film is held in the back of the camera. The back can be removed and replaced with other backs, including digital backs.

barrel distortion A type of distortion caused by a lens. Causes the edges of an image to bow outward. Most prevalent in wide-angle and fisheye lenses. See also *pincushion distortion*.

Bayer pattern The most common color filter array. A pattern of red, green, and blue filters that can be laid over the photosites of an image sensor and used to calculate the true color of every pixel in the sensor.

bicubic interpolation A method of interpolation used in a resampling process. Usually the best interpolation choice when you scale an image.

bilinear interpolation A method of interpolation used in a resampling process.

bit depth A measure of the number of bits stored for each pixel in an image. Images with higher bit depths contain greater numbers of colors. Also known as *color depth*.

black and white In the film world, "black and white" is used to refer to images that lack color; that is, images that are composed of only shades of gray. In the digital world, it's usually better to refer to such images as "grayscale" because your computer is also capable of creating images composed only of black and white pixels.

blending mode A setting that determines how the pixels in composited layers blend together. Also known as *transfer mode*.

blooming A flaring, smearing artifact in a digital photo caused by a photosite on the camera's CCD getting overcharged. The extra charge spills into the neighboring photosites and creates the artifact.

bokeh The quality of the defocused area in an image with shallow depth of field. A better lens will produce smoother, more diffuse bokeh.

boot time How quickly (or slowly, depending on the camera) the camera will be ready to shoot after powering up.

bracketing The process of shooting additional frames of an image, each over- or underexposed. By intelligently bracketing your shots, you stand a better chance of getting the image you want.

bulb mode A special shutter mode that opens the shutter for as long as you hold down the shutter release button.

burst See *drive*.

catchlight The white highlight that appears in people's eyes.

CCD Charge-coupled device, the image sensor used in most digital cameras.

center-weight metering A light-metering system similar to *matrix metering*, but that lends more analytical weight to the center of the image.

channel One component of a color image. Different channels of color are combined to produce a full-color image. For example, red, green, and blue channels are combined by your monitor or digital camera to create a full-color picture. Also known as *color channel*.

chromatic aberrations Color artifacts caused by the inability of a lens to evenly focus all frequencies of light. Usually appears as colored fringes around high-contrast areas in a scene. See also *purple fringing*.

chrominance Color information.

chrominance noise One of the two types of noise that can occur in a digital image. Luminance noise appears as brightly colored specks—usually red, green, purple, or blue—in an image. As with chrominance noise, luminance noise gets worse at higher ISOs, and you'll most often find it in the shadowy areas of your image.

clipping When highlights or shadows suddenly cut off to completely white or black in an image, rather than fading smoothly.

clone See *Rubber Stamp*.

CMOS Complementary Metal Oxide Semiconductor. A type of image sensor. Not yet widely used, but offers the promise of better image quality, lower cost, and lower power consumption than a CCD.

CMS See *color management system*.

CMYK Cyan, magenta, yellow, and black, the primary subtractive colors that are used by a printing process to create all other colors. Although cyan, magenta, and yellow are subtractive primaries, it is impossible to create perfectly pure pigments. Therefore, black ink must be added to create true blacks and darker colors.

coating Special chemicals applied to a lens that serve to reduce flares and reflection.

color calibration The process of calibrating your input and output devices, as well as your monitor, so that color is accurately displayed on each.

color channel See *channel*.

color depth See *bit depth*.

color filter array The colored filters that are placed over the photosites on an image sensor. Because image sensors can only "see" in grayscale, a color filter array is required for them to capture color information.

color gamut The range of colors that can be described by a particular color model. Also known as *gamut* or *color space*.

color management system (CMS) A set of software components that work together to compensate for the differences in your monitor, printer, and scanner so that your images appear as accurately as possible on your display.

color matching engine The software component of a color matching system that performs the translations from one color space to another.

color model A method of representing color. RGB, CMYK, and L*a*b are all color models, and each takes a different approach to representing color. See also *color gamut*.

color space See *color gamut*.

color temperature Different lights shine at different temperatures, measured in degrees Kelvin (°K). Each temperature has a different color quality.

CompactFlash A type of reusable, removable storage. The most common form of storage used in digital cameras.

compositing The process of layering images on top of each other to create composite images. Compositing is used for everything from creating simple collages to performing complex image correction and adjustment.

continuous mode See *drive*.

continuous autofocus An autofocus mechanism that constantly refocuses as new objects move into its focusing zone.

continuous tone A printed image that is made up of continuous areas of printed color. Photographic film prints are continuous tone. Ink-jet printers, laser printers, and offset presses use printing methods that don't print continuous tone. If you look closely at a print from one of these devices, you can see that it is made up of small patterns of dots.

contrast detection An autofocus mechanism that determines focus by measuring contrast in a scene. The mechanism assumes that maximum contrast means sharpest focus. Contrast detection is a method of *passive autofocus*.

contrast filters Filters that you can add to the end of a lens to increase contrast in an image.

contrast ratios The ratio of the darkest to lightest tones in an image. The higher the ratio, the more contrast there is in the image.

CRT Cathode ray tube.

dark frame subtraction A method of reducing noise in long-exposure digital photos.

demosaicing The interpolation process that a CCD uses to calculate color. The color of any individual pixel is determined by analyzing the color of the surrounding pixels.

depth of field A measure of the area of an image that is in focus. Measured as depth from the focal point of the image.

destructive effects Filters that actually modify the pixels in your image. Unlike nondestructive effects, there's no easy way to go back and change a destructive effect's settings, or undo its effects if you change your mind about it later.

device-dependent color space A color space that represents colors as combinations of other colors. RGB and CMYK are device-dependent color spaces, because accurate color representation in these spaces is dependent on the quality of your primary colors.

device-independent color space A color space (such as L*a*b color) that records what a color actually looks like, rather than how it is made.

device profile A description of the color qualities of a particular device, such as a printer, scanner, digital camera, or monitor. Also known as *profile* or *ICC profile*.

digital photography In this book, the term *digital photography* is used to refer to images shot with a digital camera.

digital zoom A feature on many digital cameras that creates a fake zoom by capturing the center of an image and blowing it up to full image size.

digitizing The process of converting something into numbers (digits). In a digital camera, an image sensor captures an image that is then converted into numbers, or digitized.

diopter An optical control that lets you adjust the viewfinder on a camera to compensate for nearsightedness.

downsample The process of reducing the size of an image by throwing out data.

DPI Dots per inch, a measure of resolution.

drive A special shooting mode for shooting a sequence of images in rapid succession. Also known as *burst* or *continuous*.

drybag A sealable, waterproof bag that will keep your camera dry, even if it gets submerged.

dual-axis focusing zone An autofocus mechanism that measures contrast along both horizontal and vertical axes.

dynamic range The range of colors that a device can represent. A digital camera with larger dynamic range can capture and store more colors, resulting in truer, smoother images.

effective pixel count The actual number of pixels that are used on an image sensor. In many digital cameras, some of the pixels on the camera's sensor are masked away or ignored.

electron gun The image on a CRT screen or television screen is created by three electron guns that paint the screen with three different streams of electrons. Separate guns are provided for the red, green, and blue components of a color image.

electronic TTL viewfinder An eyepiece viewfinder that uses a tiny LCD screen instead of normal optics, and looks through the lens. (This is the same mechanism you'll find on most video camcorders.)

element One individual lens. Most camera lenses are composed of many different elements.

emulsion The light-sensitive chemical coating on the surface of a piece of film.

EXIF Exchangeable Image File. A digital image file format used by most digital cameras. Notable because it includes special header information where all of an image's parameters (shutter speed, aperture, and so on) are stored.

exposure The combination of aperture, shutter speed, and ISO settings that determines how much light will be recorded at the focal plane.

exposure compensation A mechanism for adjusting the exposure on your camera that is independent of any particular exposure parameter. In other words, rather than specifically changing the aperture or shutter speed, you can simply use exposure compensation to over- or underexpose an image. The camera will calculate the best way to achieve the compensation.

exposure lock A mechanism that lets you lock the exposure on your camera independently of focus.

external flash sync connection Allows you to connect an external flash (usually a specific model) to the camera using a small cable.

falloff How quickly an effect changes. For example, a depth-of-field blur might have a quick falloff, meaning that the blur goes from sharp to blurry very quickly.

fast shutter mode Forces a large aperture to facilitate a fast shutter speed. Sometimes called *sports mode*.

feather The process of blurring the edge of a selection to create a smoother blend between an edit and the rest of an image.

fill flash Allows you to force the flash to fire to provide a slight fill light. Also known as *force flash*.

film A quaint nineteenth-century analog technology for recording images. Requires lots of-many hazardous chemicals, a lot of patience, and doesn't offer cool features such as Levels dialog boxes or Rubber Stamp tools. Not for the impatient. Does have the advantage that the recording and storage mediums are included in the same package.

filter factor Most lens filters are documented with a filter factor, which will inform you of the exposure compensation (in stops) required when you use that filter.

filters Either colored plastics or glass that you can attach to the end of your camera's lens to achieve certain effects, or special effects that you can apply to your image in your image-editing program. See also *plug-ins*.

FireWire A type of serial connection provided by many computers and digital cameras. Can be used for transferring images between camera and computer. Much faster than USB. Also called *IEEE-1394* or *i.Link*.

fisheye An extremely wide-angle lens that creates spherical views.

flash exposure compensation A control that allows you to increase or decrease the intensity of your camera's flash. Usually measured in stops.

flash memory A form of nonvolatile, erasable memory. Used in digital cameras in the form of special memory cards.

focal length The distance, usually measured in millimeters, between the lens and the focal plane in a camera.

focal length multiplier Many digital SLRs use an image sensor that is smaller than a piece of 35 mm film. If you attach a lens to one of these cameras, its 35 mm equivalency will be multiplied by the focal length multiplier. For example, if your digital SLR has a focal length multiplier of 1.6x, a 50 mm lens mounted on your camera will have an effective focal length of 80 mm.

focal plane The point onto which a camera focuses an image. In a film camera, there is a piece of film sitting on the focal plane. In a digital camera, a CCD sits on the focal plane.

focus-assist lamp A small lamp on the front of the camera that the camera can use to assist autofocusing. Also known as an *autofocus-assist lamp*.

focus ring The ring on a lens that allows you to manually focus the lens. Most smaller digital cameras lack focus rings, which can make them difficult to manually focus.

focus tracking An autofocus mode provided by some cameras that can track a moving object within the frame and keep it in focus. Sometimes called *servo focus*.

focusing spot See *focusing zone*.

focusing zone An area in the camera's field of view in which the camera can measure focus. Most cameras only have one focusing zone. The camera will focus on the object in this zone. Some cameras have multiple zones.

force flash See *fill flash*.

f-stop Sometimes synonymous with *stop*, more specifically a measure of the size of the aperture on a camera. F-stop values are the ratio of the focal length of the lens to diameter of the aperture.

gamma The midpoint (between black and white) in a tonal range.

gamma correction The process of correcting the midpoint in an image, without altering the black or white point.

gamut See *color gamut*.

gels Thin pieces of plastic that are usually placed in front of lights to create colored lighting effects.

gigapixel Dream on.

grayscale An image composed entirely of shades of gray, rather than color. (Basically, a fancy name for "black and white.")

group Multiple elements cemented together in a lens.

halftoning A process used for printing photos that begins by shooting a photo of an image through a special halftone screen. The resulting photo gets broken down by the screen into a pattern of dots that can be easily printed using a single ink. Your computer can generate halftone output from a laser printer, allowing you to skip the photographic halftoning step.

hardware calibration Special devices that measure the color of an output device. The data gathered by the device is then used to create a color profile of the device. This profile is, in turn, used by color management software to ensure accurate color output.

histogram A graph of the distribution of tones within an image.

hot shoe A mount for attaching an external flash to a camera.

ICC profiles See *device profile*.

i.Link Sony's name for *FireWire*.

IEEE-1394 The official name for *FireWire*.

image buffering The capability of a camera to temporarily store images in an internal memory buffer before writing them out to a memory card. A large image buffer facilitates the rapid shooting of multiple frames, because the camera doesn't have to stop shooting to offload images to storage.

image stabilization Some telephoto camera lenses offer special optics that can stabilize the tiny shakes and jitters that can be caused by your hand.

interpolation The process of calculating missing data in an image based on data that is already there.

iris A mechanism that can expand and contract to create circular apertures to control the amount of light passing through a lens.

ISO A measure of a film's "speed" or light sensitivity. The higher the ISO, the more sensitive the film. The sensitivity of digital camera sensors is also rated using the ISO scale.

JPEG Joint Photographic Experts Group. More commonly, the name of a popular lossy image compression scheme.

L*a*b color See *Lab color*.

Lab color A color model created by the Commission Internationale de l'Éclairage. Lab color describes colors as they actually appear, rather than by how they are made. As such, Lab color makes a great reference space for performing color management and calibration.

latitude How far colors in an image can be pushed or pulled.

LCD Liquid crystal display.

lens flares Bright color artifacts produced in a lens by reflections within the lens itself.

line screen frequency The density of the screen that is used in a halftoning process. A screen with more density yields an image with smoother tones and more detail.

L-Ion Lithium Ion. A type of rechargeable battery.

linear array A digital camera mechanism that uses a single row of sensors that makes three separate filtered passes over the imaging sensors to create a full-color image.

lossless Indicates that a particular process does not result in any loss of quality.

lossy Indicates that a particular process results in loss of quality.

luminance Brightness information.

luminance noise One of the two types of noise that can occur in a digital image. Luminance noise appears as brightly colored specks, usually without a color in an image. As with chrominance noise, luminance noise gets worse at higher ISOs, and you'll most often find it in the shadowy areas of your image. Of the two types of noise, luminance noise is the least annoying, because it can look a lot like grain.

macro A special type of lens used for photographing objects at extremely close distances.

manual mode A shooting mode on a camera that allows you to set both the aperture and shutter speed, giving you full control over the camera's exposure.

matrix meter A light meter that analyzes many different areas of your scene to determine proper exposure.

megapixel A million pixels. Usually used as a measure of the resolution of a digital camera's sensor.

Memory Stick A type of reusable, removable storage developed by Sony, not yet adopted by any other camera vendors.

metering The process of measuring light with a light meter (or by eye) so as to determine proper exposure for a shot.

metamerism A property of inks that can cause a print to exhibit color shift when viewed under different types of light. All inks have metameric properties. In desktop inkjet printers, it's usually just pigment-based inks that exhibit metameric shift.

MicroDrive A tiny hard drive that fits in a Type II CompactFlash slot on a camera. Note that a camera usually has to be approved for use with a MicroDrive.

mirror lockup The capability to lock a camera's mirror into the "up" position to reduce vibration when shooting long-exposure images. Some higher-end cameras also provide a lockup feature to aid in cleaning the camera's sensor.

multiple array A digital camera mechanism that uses three separate CCDs for capturing a color image, one each for red, green, and blue.

multisegment meter See *matrix meter*.

multispot focus An autofocus mechanism on a camera that can focus on one of several different places within an image.

nearest neighbor A method of interpolation used in a resampling process.

neutral density filter A filter that cuts down on the light entering your camera's lens, without altering the color of the light. Enables you to use wider apertures or faster shutter speeds in bright light.

NiCad Nickel Cadmium. A type of rechargeable battery. Not recommended for use in a digital camera.

NiMH Nickel Metal Hydride. A type of rechargeable battery.

nodal point The optical center of a camera's lens.

noise The bane of all digital photographers. Noise appears in an image as very fine-grained patterns of multicolored pixels in an area. Shadow areas are particularly susceptible to noise, as are images shot in low light. Noise is very different looking than the grain found in film photos. Unfortunately, it's also far less attractive.

nondestructive editing A piece of editing software that doesn't alter your original image data when you perform an edit. Nondestructive editing systems work by maintaining a list of edits that get applied to your original image data in real time, anytime the image needs to be displayed, printed, or output. Because the edits are kept separate from the image data, you can change or alter the edits at any time. Apple Aperture, Adobe Photoshop Lightroom, and Nikon Capture NX are all examples of nondestructive editors. In Photoshop, Smart Objects and Adjustment Layers provide nondestructive editing capabilities.

normal lens A lens that has a field of view that is equivalent to the field of view of the human eye. Roughly 50 mm.

overexposed An image that was exposed for too long. As an image becomes more overexposed, it gets brighter and brighter. Highlights and light-colored areas wash out to completely white.

parallax The easiest way to understand parallax is simply to hold your index finger in front of your face and close one eye. Now close the other eye and you'll perceive that your finger has jumped sideways. As you can see, at close distances, even a change of view as small as the distance between your eyes can create a very different perspective on your subject. A camera that uses one lens for framing and another for shooting faces the same problems. Parallax is not a problem at longer ranges, because the parallax shift is imperceptible.

passive autofocus An autofocus mechanism that achieves focus by analyzing the camera's view of the scene.

PC card adapter A special adapter that lets you insert a storage card from your camera into the PC card slot of your computer.

PC cards Small, credit–card–sized peripheral cards that can be inserted into a PC card slot on a laptop computer, or into a special PC card drive on a desktop computer. PC card adapters are available for most types of digital camera media, allowing you to insert media directly into your PC card slot.

PCMCIA See *PC cards*.

phase detection See *phase difference*.

phase difference An autofocus mechanism that uses measurements taken through different parts of the camera's lens to determine focus. Also known as *phase detection*.

photosite A tiny electrode that sits on the surface of an image sensor. There is one photosite for each pixel on a sensor.

picture elements The smallest area of color information that can be displayed on a computer monitor. Also, the smallest area of color information that can be detected by a digital imaging sensor. Also known as *pixels*.

pincushion distortion A type of distortion caused by a lens. Causes the edges of an image to bow inward. Most prevalent in telephoto lenses. See also *barrel distortion*.

pixel See *picture elements*.

pixel mapping A feature included on some digital cameras. When activated, the camera examines all of the pixels on the camera's image sensor and creates a map of which ones are bad. It then excludes these pixels from all color calculations. The pixel map is stored and used for all shots until you execute the pixel mapping again. Some cameras lose their pixel maps when you change the camera's batteries.

pixellate Sometimes, the individual pixels in an image can become visible, a process called *pixellation*.

plug-ins Special bits of code, usually effects or image-processing filters that can be added to your image-editing application. Most plug-ins conform to the Photoshop plug-in standard.

polarizers Special filters that can be fitted onto the end of a lens. Polarizers allow light that is polarized only in a particular direction to enter your lens. Polarizers can completely remove distracting reflections from water, glass, or other shiny surfaces. Polarizers can also be used to increase the contrast in skies and clouds.

posterization Reduction of the number of tones in an image. As a particular tonal range gets posterized, it will appear more "flat."

PPI Pixels per inch, a measure of resolution.

prefocus The process of autofocusing, metering, and white balancing that occurs when you press your camera's shutter-release button halfway.

prefocus time How long it takes a camera to perform its prefocus steps (autofocus, metering, and white balance).

prime lens A lens with a fixed focal length.

profile See *device profile*.

proportional zoom control A zoom control whose rate of zoom changes depending on how far you push or pull the control.

prosumer A marketing term for a camera that sits somewhere between the professional and consumer market.

purple fringing A color artifact specific to digital cameras with resolutions greater than 2 megapixels. Appears in an image around the edges of high-contrast objects, usually shot with wide-angle lenses. Usually confined to the edges of the screen. See also *chromatic aberrations*.

quantization In JPEG compression, the process of averaging the colors in one 64-pixel square area.

quantizing The process of assigning a numeric value to a sample. Part of the digitizing process.

rangefinder A viewfinder mechanism on a camera. A fixed-focus or zoom lens is used for imaging, whereas a separate optical viewfinder is used for framing your shot.

raw converter A program that can process raw files from a digital camera into a regular bit-mapped, full-color image. A raw converter must include special profile information to process the files from any given camera, as there is currently no accepted standard for raw images.

raw data Pixel data that comes directly from the CCD with no further processing. Processing is usually performed later using special software. Raw files offer quality equivalent to an un-compressed image, but require much less space.

read-out register The mechanism that reads the signals from each row of photosites on an image sensor. The read-out register amplifies the signals from the photosites and sends them to the camera's analog-to-digital converter.

reciprocity Exposure parameters have a reciprocal relationship so that different combinations of parameters produce the same exposure. For example, setting your camera to a shutter speed of $1/250^{th}$ of a second at f8 is the same as setting it to $1/125^{th}$ at f16.

rectilinear A type of wide-angle lens that includes corrective elements that prevent barrel distortion.

recycling The time it takes a camera to reset itself and prepare to shoot another shot.

red-eye reduction A special flash mode that attempts to prevent red-eye by firing a short initial flash to close down the pupils in your subject's eyes.

red-eye When the flash from a camera bounces off a subject's eyes and back into the camera's lens, the subject will appear to have bright red eyes. Most prevalent in cameras where the flash is very close to the lens.

registration When primary color channels are positioned over each other so that a full-color image is produced, the images are said to be "in registration."

refraction The process of slowing and bending light using a transparent substance such as air, water, glass, or plastic.

refresh rate How often the image on a camera's LCD viewfinder is redrawn. An LCD with a higher refresh rate will produce an image with smoother motion.

resampling The process of computing new pixel information when resizing a document in your image-editing application. If you are resizing upward, the resampling process will generate new pixels. If you are resizing downward, the resampling process will discard pixels.

resolution In a monitor or digital camera, the number of pixels that fit into a given space. Usually measured in pixels per inch (ppi) or dots per inch (dpi). In a printer, the number of printer dots that fit into a given space, usually measured in dots per inch (dpi).

RGB Red, green, and blue, the additive primary colors that are used by your computer monitor and digital camera to produce all other colors.

sampling The process of analyzing something to determine its content. A digital camera samples light to determine how much, and what color the light is, at any given point in a scene.

saturation A characteristic of color. Colors that are more saturated are typically "deeper" in hue and often darker. As saturation increases, hue shifts slightly.

SCSI Small Computer System Interface. An older, high-speed computer interface for attaching hard drives, scanners, and other peripherals.

servo focus See *focus tracking.*

sharpening The process of using software to increase sharpness in a digital image. Sharpening can happen inside a digital camera or through post-processing on your computer.

shutter A mechanism that sits in front of the focal plane in a camera and can open and close to expose the image sensor or film to light. Many digital cameras do not have physical shutters, but instead mimic shutter functionality by simply activating and deactivating their image sensors to record an image. Cameras that do have shutters typically use a two-curtain mechanism. The first curtain begins to slide across the focal plane to create a gap. It is followed usually very quickly by a second shutter that closes the gap. As the gap passes across, the entire CCD is exposed.

shutter lag A delay between the time you press the shutter release button on a camera and the time it actually shoots a picture.

shutter priority A shooting mode on a camera. Shutter priority lets you define the camera's shutter speed. The camera will then calculate a corresponding aperture based on its light metering.

shutter speed The length of time it takes for the shutter in a camera to completely expose the focal plane.

single array system A digital camera mechanism that uses a single image sensor for imaging. Sometimes called a "striped array."

single lens reflex A camera whose viewfinder looks through the same lens that your camera uses to make its exposure. Also known as *SLR.*

single-axis focusing zone An autofocus mechanism that measures contrast along a single axis only, usually horizontal.

slow-sync mode A special flash mode that combines a flash with a slow shutter speed to create images that contain both still and motion-blurred objects.

SLR See *single lens reflex.*

SmartMedia A type of reusable, removable storage.

soft proof An on-screen proof of a color document.

specular highlights The bright white glints and reflections that occur on very shiny surfaces and on the edges of objects.

spot meter A light meter that measures a very narrow circle of the scene.

sRGB An RGB color space defined by Microsoft and Hewlett-Packard. It is intended to represent the colors available on a typical color monitor. A little too small for digital photography work.

step-up ring An adapter that attaches to the end of a lens and allows for the addition of filters or other lens attachments. Serves to change the thread size of the lens.

stitching The process of joining and blending individual images to create a panoramic image.

stop A measure of the light that is passing through a camera's lens to the focal plane. Every doubling of light either through changes in aperture, shutter speed, or ISO is one stop. See also *f-stop*.

striped array See *single array system*.

subtractive Ink mixes together in a *subtractive* process whereby as colors are mixed together-together, they get darker; that is, light is subtracted as the colors are mixed. Subtractive colors eventually produce black. Cyan, magenta, and yellow are the primary subtractive colors that can be used to create all other colors.

telephoto A lens with a focal length that is longer than *normal*. As a lens gets more telephoto, its field of view decreases.

TFT See *Thin Film Transistor*.

Thin Film Transistor A technology used to create LCD screens. Typically used for the LCD viewfinder/monitors included on the backs of many digital cameras.

three-shot array A digital camera mechanism that uses three *single arrays*, one each for red, green, and blue.

through the lens See *TTL*.

title safe A guide similar to the *action-safe* area. The title-safe area is slightly smaller.

transfer mode See *blending mode*.

trilinear array A digital camera mechanism that uses three *linear arrays* stacked on top of each other to create a full-color image in a single pass over the image sensor.

TTL When a camera system, be it the viewfinder, white-balance system, light meter, or autofocus, views the scene through the same lens that exposes the sensor, that system is said to be a *through the lens* or *TTL* system. A viewfinder mechanism that looks through the same lens that is used to focus the image onto the focal plane. Short for *through the lens*.

underexposed An image that was not exposed enough. In an underexposed image, dark or shadow areas turn to completely black.

upsample The process of enlarging an image by calculating (interpolating) new data.

USB Universal Serial Bus. A type of serial connection provided by many computers and digital cameras. Can be used for transferring images between camera and computer.

VGA resolution 640×480 pixels.

Video LUT Animation A feature available in some versions of Photoshop that allows for real-time, on-screen viewing of color corrections and changes.

video RAM The memory in a computer that is used for displaying images on-screen. The more video RAM, the larger your images can be, and the greater the bit depth they can have. Also known as *VRAM*.

vignetting A darkening of the image around the edges.

virtual reality movie See *VR movie*.

VR movie A digital movie that lets you pan and tilt in real time to explore and navigate a virtual space.

wavelet compression A new fractal-based compression scheme. Converts your image from a series of raster dots into a collection of tiny fractal curves.

white balance A color calibration used by a camera. Once a camera knows how to accurately represent white, it can represent all other colors. Because white can look different under different types of light, a camera needs to be told what white is, a process called *white balancing*.

wide-angle A lens with a focal length that is shorter than *normal*. As a lens gets more wide-angled, its field of view increases.

XGA resolution 800 × 600 pixels.

zone system A method of calculating exposure.

zoom lens A lens with a variable focal length.

ABOUT THE CD-ROM

OVERALL SYSTEM REQUIREMENTS

Windows

- Intel Pentium processor
- Microsoft Windows XP Professional or Home Edition (Service Pack 1 or 2), Windows 2000 (Service Pack 2), Windows XP Tablet PC Edition, Windows Server 2003, or Windows NT (Service Pack 6 or 6a)
- 128MB of RAM (256MB recommended)
- Up to 90MB of available hard-disk space
- Microsoft Internet Explorer 5.5 (or higher), Netscape 7.1 (or 8.0), Firefox 1.0, or Mozilla 1.7

Macintosh

- PowerPC G3, G4, or G5 processor
- Mac OS X v10.2.8, 10.3, or 10.4
- 128MB of RAM (256MB recommended)
- Up to 110MB of available hard-disk space
- Safari 1.2.2 browser supported for Mac OS X 10.3 or higher

DISK CONTENTS

Tutorials: Contains all of the files needed to use the book's tutorial lessons, as well as additional tutorial movies (in QuickTime format) and additional tutorial articles (in PDF format, suitable for printing or viewing on-screen). All information is organized into sub-folders by chapters, and each piece of tutorial information is explicitly referenced in the book. So, if you follow along in the book, you'll be led through each tutorial in the proper order.

The QuickTime movies have all been compressed using an MPEG-4 CODEC, which should be playable by any current version of QuickTime.

QuickTime is available as a free download from *www.apple.com/quicktime*. QuickTime System Requirements:

Macintosh

- 400 MHz Power PC G3 or faster Macintosh computer
- At least 128MB of RAM
- Mac OS X v10.3.9, v10.4.9, or later

Windows

- Pentium processor-base PC or compatible computer
- At least 128MB of RAM
- Windows 2000 Service Pack 4 or XP

To view the included PDF files, you'll need a PDF viewer such as the Adobe Acrobat Reader, available for free download at *http://www.adobe.com/products/acrobat/readstep2.html*.

ACROBAT READER SYSTEM REQUIREMENTS:

Windows

- Intel Pentium processor
- Microsoft Windows XP Professional or Home Edition (Service Pack 1 or 2), Windows 2000 (Service Pack 2), Windows XP Tablet PC Edition, Windows Server 2003, or Windows NT (Service Pack 6 or 6a)
- 128MB of RAM (256MB recommended)
- Up to 90MB of available hard-disk space
- Microsoft Internet Explorer 5.5 (or higher), Netscape 7.1 (or 8.0), Firefox 1.0, or Mozilla 1.7

Macintosh

- PowerPC G3, G4, or G5 processor
- Mac OS X v10.2.8, 10.3, or 10.4
- 128MB of RAM (256MB recommended)
- Up to 110MB of available hard-disk space
- Safari 1.2.2 browser supported for Mac OS X 10.3 or higher

You'll need an image editor for many of the tutorials, and most of the tutorials in the book have been built around Photoshop, or Photoshop Elements. However, for many of the tutorials you'll do fine with Adobe Photoshop Lightroom, Apple Aperture, Nikon Capture NX, or other editors. Each tutorial in the book includes a description of which features it will require.

If you don't already have a copy of one of these programs, you can download free demo versions using the following web links. Many of the demos have a time limit on them, so you'll want to be careful to get through the tutorials that you want before your allotted time expires. Even if you already have an image editor, it can be interesting to download demos of other applications to see how you like their approach to workflow or editing.

Adobe Photoshop CS3 for Mac or Windows

At the time of this writing, Adobe had not yet posted a trial version of Photoshop CS3. However, their web site claims that they should have a trial version within "6 to 8 weeks" which means there should be a trial version available by the time you read this. Check out *www.adobe.com/downloads* to find a link.

Adobe Photoshop Lightroom for Mac or Windows

Go to *www.adobe.com/downloads* and choose Photoshop Lightroom from the Trial Versions pop-up menu.

Adobe Photoshop Elements 5 for Windows

Go to *www.adobe.com/downloads* and choose Photoshop Elements 5 for Windows from the Trial Versions pop-up menu.

Apple Aperture for Macintosh

Go to *www.apple.com/aperture* and click on the Free Trial link.

Nikon Capture NX for Mac or Windows

Go to *www.capturenx.com*.

INDEX